The Original Meaning of the Fourteenth Amendment

The Original Meaning *of the* Fourteenth Amendment

Its Letter and Spirit

RANDY E. BARNETT

EVAN D. BERNICK

Foreword by

JAMES OAKES

THE BELKNAP PRESS OF
HARVARD UNIVERSITY PRESS
Cambridge, Massachusetts
London, England
2021

Third printing

Library of Congress Cataloging-in-Publication Data

Names: Barnett, Randy E., author. | Bernick, Evan D., author. |
Oakes, James, writer of foreword.
Title: The original meaning of the Fourteenth Amendment : its letter
and spirit / Randy E Barnett, Evan D Bernick ; foreword by James Oakes.
Description: Cambridge, Massachusetts : The Belknap Press of Harvard University Press,
2021. | Includes bibliographical references and index.
Identifiers: LCCN 2021009361 | ISBN 9780674257764 (cloth)
Subjects: LCSH: United States. Constitution. 14th Amendment. | Privileges
and immunities—United States. | Due process of law—United States. |
Equality before the law—United States.
Classification: LCC KF4558 14th .B37 2021 | DDC 342.7308/5—dc23
LC record available at https://lccn.loc.gov/2021009361

CONTENTS

Part II: The Due Process of Law Clause

Part III: The Equal Protection of the Laws Clause

FOREWORD

THERE ARE FEW HISTORICAL clichés more hoary than this one: *The abolitionists were a tiny, beleaguered minority, widely despised all across the North.* The evidence compiled by Randy E. Barnett and Evan D. Bernick strongly suggests that this is a cliché badly in need of revision. Not because the abolitionists were in fact popular—they were not—but because they were influential. Profoundly influential, in fact. For it was the "constitutional abolitionists" who developed, as the title of this book says, "the original meaning of the Fourteenth Amendment."

Historians do not write books like this one, aimed as it is at getting the justices of the United States Supreme Court to change the way they interpret the Constitution. Written by two law professors, this book is explicitly, unabashedly designed to persuade the Court to reconsider some longstanding constitutional assumptions about the Fourteenth Amendment.

But to make their case, the lawyers have written a history book. The questions they raise are deeply historical. Where did the phrase "privileges and immunities" originate? What did the phrase originally mean, and how did that meaning change over time? What did it mean by the time the authors of the Fourteenth Amendment invoked it? So, too, with "due process of law" and "equal protection of the law." Where did those terms originate, and what did they mean in 1868, when Republican lawmakers inserted them into the amendment?

To be sure, Barnett and Bernick are "originalists." They would have the Constitution interpreted, even today, in accordance with the original *public* meaning of the text. At first glance this might raise eyebrows among my fellow historians. We are generally more comfortable with multiple or conflicting meanings, with meanings that change over time. We tend to be empiricists more than theorists. We are willing to consider original *intent* as well as original *public meaning*—and we don't usually distinguish between the two. Although we prefer contemporary evidence, we are often forced to rely on memory, fallible though memory undoubtedly is. And yet, "original public meaning," though terminologically alien, is conceptually familiar to historians. Think of it as reading ideas in context, not unlike what Quentin Skinner challenged historians to do several decades ago.

Nor should historians be too concerned that originalism necessarily freezes the Constitution in time. The Fourteenth Amendment, as Barnett and Bernick read it, authorizes the federal government to protect the civil rights of citizens in the states. This, they tell us, is its original and therefore unalterable meaning. What has changed over time, however, is what the political culture has deemed to count as a constitutionally protected "civil right."

In the early republic, for example, voting was considered a mere "political" right, a right that varied from state to state, a right that could be granted or withdrawn at the pleasure of a state legislature. Voting was still thought of that way when congressional Republicans drafted the Fourteenth Amendment. But by 1920, Barnett and Bernick argue, "the right of citizens who had reached the age of majority to vote was deemed fundamental. What was once a mere 'political' right to suffrage had *become* a fundamental civil right." Once that happened, the authors argue, the Fourteenth Amendment empowered the federal government to protect every citizen's right to vote.

Because a right that comes to be accepted as *fundamental* cannot, almost by definition, be taken away, the Fourteenth Amendment created a floor but not a ceiling for the privileges and immunities to which we are entitled. In this telling, then, the unchanging original meaning of the Constitution allowed for a Constitution that can adjust to changes in the political culture. The number of constitutionally protected civil rights could rise, but it could not fall—except by a formal constitutional amendment that changes the meaning of the text.

This is where the abolitionists come in, for they were instrumental in changing the way Americans came to think about the privileges and immunities of citizenship. According to Barnett and Bernick, the original public meaning of the Constitution—the Constitution of 1787—was that civil rights were protected as a matter of interstate comity. But states themselves could respect or disrespect rights as they chose, as long as every state citizen's rights were respected or disrespected in the same way. And not all states considered African Americans to be citizens of the United States.

As the debate over slavery intensified, abolitionists began to argue that some rights were *fundamental*, that free Blacks born in the United States were citizens, and that every US citizen was entitled to the same rights everywhere. In the abolitionist reading, for example, no state could deprive *any* citizen of the rights of due process.

The radicals who pioneered this way of thinking—Lysander Spooner, William Goodell, Gerrit Smith, and others—were dubbed "constitutional abolitionists" by the historian Richard Sewell, and more recently, Manisha Sinha has labeled their doctrine "abolitionist constitutionalism." By the 1850s the radical precepts of abolitionist constitutionalism had infiltrated American politics and became the baseline premises of the new, antislavery Republican Party.

Defenders of slavery responded in kind. They, too, began to argue for a fundamentalist understanding of rights, in this case a slaveholder's right to hold property in human beings. So fundamental was this right, Chief Justice Roger B. Taney would argue, that the Constitution obligated the federal government to protect slave property in the territories.

By the 1860s, then, there was wide agreement that the privileges and immunities of citizenship were fundamental and that the federal government was therefore obliged to protect citizens in the enjoyment of those rights.

The significant point the authors make is that the original meaning of the Fourteenth Amendment is to be found in the antislavery constitutionalism that was developed by abolitionists in the decades between the Revolution and the Civil War, particularly after the Missouri Crisis in 1820. By the time congressional Republicans proposed a Fourteenth Amendment, in the immediate aftermath of the Civil War, they understood their proposal to mean several things: Blacks born in the United States were citizens. All citizens were entitled to a number of rights, some of them enumerated in the Constitution, some spelled out in the first eight amendments, and some unenumerated. These rights were fundamental, not simply a matter of mere state comity. Consequently, the federal government was constitutionally obliged to protect those rights in the states.

This is a bracingly expansive reading of the original meaning of the Fourteenth Amendment. No doubt constitutional scholars will debate its merits or demerits as an originalist thesis. No doubt historians will similarly debate it as an interpretation of Reconstruction. But to this reader, Barnett and Bernick have made at least one point in this superb book that seems beyond doubt: the abolitionist movement bequeathed to all Americans, through the Fourteenth Amendment, a better Constitution, an egalitarian understanding of citizenship, and a more robust conception of our fundamental rights.

James Oakes

PREFACE: THE LETTER

On March 12, 1871, Supreme Court Justice Joseph Bradley penned a re-markable letter to a federal district judge in New Orleans who would one day join Bradley on the nation's highest court. Judge William Woods was mired in a case involving the constitutionality of the Enforcement Act of 1870—an ambitious piece of civil-rights legislation, crafted by a Republican-dominated Congress to enforce the recently adopted Fourteenth Amend-ment. Judge Woods sought Bradley's advice because the justice also served as the judge for the federal circuit in which Judge Woods's district was located.

At issue in *United States v. Hall* was whether Section 5 of the Fourteenth Amendment empowered Congress to criminalize private conspiracies against the First Amendment rights of free speech and peaceable assembly. The case arose from the indictment of two white men for violently breaking up a po-litical meeting of mostly Black Republicans, killing two and wounding more than fifty people. The defendants argued that because no federal rights were at issue, the charges should be dismissed. In *Barron v. Baltimore,* decided in 1833, the Court held that the first eight amendments constrained only the federal government; they did not restrict the exercise of state power. And they did not authorize the federal government to reach private individuals. Had the Fourteenth Amendment changed this? Woods wanted to know what Bradley thought.

In his four-page handwritten letter, Bradley succinctly described what he took to be the meaning of the text of the Fourteenth Amendment. To our knowledge, a transcript of Bradley's draft of this letter, which resides in the

New Jersey Historical Society, has never been published in its entirety. So we reproduce it here with its original underlining and crossed-out passages.

Washington, March 12, 1871

My dear Judge,

I am sorry I could not have answered your letter of 7th last sooner. But my duties here have been so arduous that it has been impracticable. I will now attend to do so.

The 6th section of the act, known as the Enforcement Act, makes it felony for <u>two or more persons to conspire together, or to go in disguise, with intent</u> to prevent a citizen of the U.S. from registering or voting, or to injure or intimidate him to prevent the free exercise and enjoyment of any right or privilege secured to him by the Constitution or laws of the U.S.

You ask whether the breaking up of a peaceable political meeting, by riot and murder, when committed simply for that purpose, without any defendant's intent to prevent the exercise of the right of suffrage, is a felony under this section, in view of the 1st Amendment of the Constitution, which says, that "Congress shall make no law abridging the right of the people peaceably to assemble and to petition the government for a redress of grievance"?

Supposing the 1st Amendment to embrace the right peaceably to assemble for the purpose of discussing political questions, (which I think it does) the case <u>is</u> within the <u>words</u> of the statute. The right is a right <u>secured</u> by the Constitution. True, it is <u>secured</u> only as against the action of Congress itself. But, still, it is a right that is secured. But where Congress is prohibited from <u>interfering with</u> a right by legislation, does that authorize Congress to <u>protect</u> that right by legislation? The same amendment prohibits Congress from passing any law respecting an establishment of religion, or prohibiting the free exercise thereof. Does this give to Congress the power to protect by law the people of a state in the free exercise of religion? Is not that subject left to the discretion of the States or the people? Until the passage of the XIVth amendment this was undoubtedly so.

Does the XIVth Amendment, in giving Congress power to enforce its provisions by appropriate legislation, make any alteration in this respect?

By that Amendment, Sect. 1, "No state shall make or enforce any law which shall abridge the privilege or immunities of citizens of the U. States; nor shall any state deprive of life, liberty, or property without due process of law, nor deny to any person within its jurisdiction the equal protection of the laws."

Now, the privileges and immunities of citizens of the United States here referred to, are undoubtedly those which may be demonstrated fundamental (See [*Corfield v. Coryell*] 4 Wash. C.C. Rep. 380): and among these I suppose we are safe in including those which in the constitution are expressly secured to the people, either as against the action of the federal government, or the state government.

If this is so, then, undoubtedly, Congress has a right, by appropriate legislation, to enforce and protect such fundamental rights, against unfriendly or insufficient state legislation. I say unfriendly or insufficient for the XIVth amendment not only prohibits the making or enforcing of laws which shall abridge the privileges of the citizen; but prohibits the states from denying to all persons within its jurisdiction the equal protection of the laws. Denying includes inaction as well as action. And denying the equal protection of the laws includes the omission to protect, as well as the omission to pass laws for protection. Our controversy with England at this moment is, not only that her neutrality laws were not sufficient but that she did not properly enforce those which she had. It is a poor consolation for me to be told, "Our laws are sufficient to protect you," if those laws are not enforced, and any rights are supinely permitted to be invaded. Therefore, to guard against the invasion of the citizen's fundamental rights, and to secure their adequate protection, as well against State legislation as state inaction or incompetence, the amendment gives Congress power to enforce the amendment by appropriate legislation. ~~The extent to which Congress should exercise that right will depend upon its discretion in view of the circumstances of each case.~~ And as it would be unseemly for Congress to interfere directly with state enactments, ~~or state officials,~~ and as it cannot compel the activity of state officials, the only appropriate legislation it can make is that which will operate directly on offenders and offenses and protect the rights which the amendment secures.

The extent to which Congress shall exercise this power must depend on its discretion in view of the circumstances of each case. If the exercise of it in any case should seem to interfere with the domestic affairs of a state, it must be remembered that it is for the purpose of protecting Federal rights; and these must be protected whether it interferes with domestic laws or domestic administration of laws.

In my judgment, therefore, the case you suppose is within the law, and the law is within the legislative power of Congress.

Yours truly,

Joseph P. Bradley

P.S. I expect when our court adjourns, about the 1st of May, to visit Savannah and Mobile in succession and spend, say a ~~fortnight~~ week or ten days in each place, perhaps longer. If you will make arrangements to have cases of special importance laid over till I can appear, I will cheerfully hear them. I would a little prefer not to be bothering with jury cases unless you decide it important. I shall probably visit Savannah first. I doubt whether I can get as far as New Orleans. Should you specially wish me to hear any cases there I might perhaps go there for a short time.

In this letter, Justice Bradley summarized, with just one omission, our thesis concerning the original meaning of the Fourteenth Amendment:

- The Privileges or Immunities Clause protects those substantive rights "which may be demonstrated fundamental" from being violated by state governments.
- These "fundamental" rights include the unenumerated rights discussed by Justice Bushrod Washington in the 1823 case of *Corfield v. Coryell,* which Bradley cites.
- They also include enumerated rights, such as those set forth in the First Amendment, which Bradley affirms were "expressly secured to the people."
- The Equal Protection of the Laws Clause is not limited to barring state action but also imposes an affirmative duty on states to act. As Bradley put it: "*Denying* includes inaction as well as action."
- A denial of "the equal protection of the laws" extends beyond a state's officials failing to protect the privileges or immunities of its citizens; it extends as well to failures of states to enact laws for their protection—

or, in Bradley's words, "the omission to protect, as well as the omission *to pass laws* for protection."

- Section 5 of the Fourteenth Amendment empowers Congress to remedy the failure of state governments to protect these rights by creating its own federal enforcement procedures: "[T]o guard against the invasion of the citizen's fundamental rights, and to secure their adequate protection, as well against State legislation as *state inaction or incompetence*, the amendment gives Congress power to enforce the amendment by appropriate legislation."

- Finally, laws enacted by Congress pursuant to its Section 5 powers "will operate directly on offenders and offenses." Indeed, given that Congress cannot commandeer or "*compel* the activity of state officials," this is "the only appropriate legislation it can make."

Justice Bradley packed a lot into a four-page letter. There is just one major component of our approach that is missing from his account of the original meaning of Sections 1 and 5: Bradley does not consider whether "the due process *of law*" requires a judicial assessment of whether the *substance* of state laws *arbitrarily* restricts the privileges or immunities of citizens of the United States. That issue was not implicated in *United States v. Hall*.

Each element of what Justice Bradley so clearly saw and expressed in 1871 would be purged from our constitutional law—denied by the Supreme Court, and repudiated by generations of scholars. Indeed, Justice Bradley's own jurisprudence tracked the rise and fall of the original meaning of the Fourteenth Amendment.

Bradley's decline began in April of 1873, when the Court handed down two pivotal decisions. In his dissenting opinion in the *Slaughter-House Cases*, Bradley reiterated the fundamental-rights theory of the privileges and immunities of citizenship that he conveyed to Judge Woods; and he determined that the privileges or immunities of US citizens included a right to pursue a lawful trade or occupation. But then, the very next day in *Bradwell v. Illinois*, Bradley published an infamous concurrence endorsing the constitutionality of the complete exclusion of women from the practice of law.

Three years later, Bradley joined the majority in *United States v. Cruikshank*, reversing the convictions (under the Force Bill) of the perpetrators of the Colfax Massacre. This was the horrific slaughter of dozens of Black Republicans and three white Republicans that Eric Foner rightly characterizes as "[t]he bloodiest single instance of racial carnage in the Reconstruction era."[1] Contrary to the interpretation expressed by Bradley in his letter, in *Cruikshank*, the Court held that the Privileges or Immunities Clause did not protect the rights enumerated in the Constitution from violation by private actors.

Finally, in the 1883 *Civil Rights Cases*, Bradley himself authored an opinion for the Court holding unconstitutional key provisions of the Civil Rights Act of 1875 that prohibited racial discrimination in public accommodations. Contrary to his letter, Bradley's majority opinion limited the operation of the Fourteenth Amendment to state action, as opposed to state inaction. It would be another eighty-two years before Congress would again enact major civil rights legislation. When it did so, due to the precedent of the *Civil Rights Cases*, Congress invoked its Commerce Clause power rather than its enforcement power in Section 5.

Whatever may have moved him to change his mind, the overwhelming weight of the evidence shows that Justice Bradley's first instincts were correct. In this book, we urge the Supreme Court to change course and restore the original meaning of the Fourteenth Amendment in full—the meaning described by Justice Bradley in his letter to Judge Woods. Doing so will surely require a change in some existing doctrine. But, as important, it will legitimate many current doctrines that have been called into question.

Just as one swallow does not a summer make, neither does one letter establish the original meaning of the Fourteenth Amendment. That requires the evidence we will present. But Justice Bradley's letter offers a succinct preview of all but one of our findings. And it shows that our thesis is no mere academic theory. It was once considered a nearly self-evident truth.

The Original Meaning of the Fourteenth Amendment

Introduction

The Letter and Spirit of the Fourteenth Amendment

NOTHING IN THE CONSTITUTION of the United States is more important to contemporary American law and politics than the Fourteenth Amendment. This book provides a comprehensive account of the original meaning and purposes of those components of the amendment that are most salient and controversial today. Those components are Sections 1 and 5. Here they are in full, unbundled to highlight their principal parts:

Section 1:

All persons born or naturalized in the United States and subject to the jurisdiction thereof, are citizens of the United States and of the State wherein they reside.

No State shall make or enforce any law which shall abridge the privileges or immunities of citizens of the United States;

[N]or shall any State deprive any person of life, liberty, or property, without due process of law;

[N]or deny to any person within its jurisdiction the equal protection of the laws.

Section 5:

The Congress shall have power to enforce, by appropriate legislation, the provisions of this article.

Sections 2, 3, and 4 of the Fourteenth Amendment are of great historical significance, and Section 2 in particular still carries practical weight. But the

Citizenship, Privileges or Immunities, Due Process of Law, and Equal Protection of the Laws Clauses in Section 1 and Congress's enforcement power in Section 5 are far more frequently litigated and politically contested.

And yet only relatively recently have scholars provided accounts of the original *public* meaning of Sections 1 and 5—the meaning conveyed by the text to the public when the Fourteenth Amendment was ratified into law in 1868. That shouldn't be as surprising as it probably is for many readers. The focus today on original public meaning is a product of a legal movement that is relatively young. Prior to the rise of originalism in the 1980s, "proto-originalists" focused their attention on "the original intentions of the framers" of the Constitution.[1] This approach characterized Raoul Berger's 1977 tome, *Government by Judiciary: The Transformation of the Fourteenth Amendment.*[2]

In a very real sense, modern originalism arose in response to Berger's book. Our book is the culmination of that response. It provides a theory of the Fourteenth Amendment's original public meaning that honors the text and history, including a history of constitutionalism outside the courts that is often overlooked. And it articulates a novel strategy for implementing today what Schuyler Colfax—Speaker of the House when the Fourteenth Amendment was framed and ratified—called "the gem of the Constitution"[3] in a way that is faithful to the goals of those who fought to make it law.

The Intellectual Origins of Modern Originalism

In 1980, Stanford law professor (and future dean) Paul Brest wrote a path-breaking article in which he coined the term "originalism." Brest's principal targets were Raoul Berger and Robert Bork. It was Brest who first dubbed Berger and Bork "originalists" and their approach "originalism." "By 'originalism,'" wrote Brest, "I mean the familiar approach to constitutional adjudication that accords binding authority to the text of the Constitution or the intentions of its adopters."[4] He contrasted originalism with "what I shall call 'nonoriginalism.'"[5] Brest's article may well have provided the most influential labeling scheme in the history of constitutional theory.[6]

Because Berger, Bork, and others who appealed to "the intentions of the framers" lacked an explicit formulation of their methodology, Brest constructed one. He conceded up front that "[a]t least since *Marbury,* in which Chief Justice John Marshall emphasized the significance of our Constitution's being a written document, originalism in one form or another has been a key theme in the American constitutional tradition."[7] Nevertheless, Brest took aim at what he called "strict originalism," which he said was characterized by its "strict intentionalism."[8] "For the strict intentionalist, 'the whole aim of construction, as applied to a provision of the Constitution, is . . . to ascertain and give effect to the intent of its Framers and the people who adopted it.'"[9]

Brest then identified the problem with strict intentionalism:

> Strict intentionalism requires the interpreter to determine how the adopters *would have applied a provision to a given situation,* and to *apply it* accordingly. The enterprise rests on the questionable assumption that the adopters of constitutional provisions intended them *to be applied* in this manner. But even if this were true, the interpreter confronts historiographic difficulties of such magnitude as to make the aim practicably unattainable.[10]

As we will see, Brest's focus on the "applic[ation] [of] a provision to a given situation" anticipated an important distinction that originalists would draw some twenty years later but that was unknown to constitutional theory at the time.

For Brest, the "historiographical difficulties" associated with application to a given situation result from having to aggregate the intentions of individual persons into a collective intention that is attributable to everyone responsible for the Constitution's adoption. Brest regarded this as a fool's errand.[11] This general line of objection has come to be called the "summing problem."[12]

Only after Brest invented the term "originalism" did originalists adopt and defend the label.[13] Perhaps the earliest, most visible embrace was that of Edwin Meese III, President Ronald Reagan's attorney general during Reagan's second term. In his address to the American Bar Association on July 9, 1985, Meese advocated for "a jurisprudence of original intention."[14]

Meese's address created quite a stir. At a conference at Georgetown University Law Center, Justice William Brennan replied to the attorney general. Echoing Brest, Brennan declared that it was "far from clear whose intention is relevant—that of the drafters, the congressional disputants, or the ratifiers in the states—or even whether the idea of an original intention is a coherent way of thinking about a jointly drafted document drawing its authority from a general assent of the states."[15]

The battle over originalism was fully joined. Still, originalism's only theoretical explication remained Paul Brest's critical reconstruction. For this reason, Larry Solum has dubbed early writers such as Berger and Bork "proto-originalists."[16] But a theory of originalism was in the offing.

Original Public Meaning, Not Framers' Intent

Early theoretical development of originalism was in part a political project, initiated by lawyers in the Meese Justice Department. As these lawyers met in seminars and produced blue books on the original meaning of various constitutional provisions, they were addressed by then–Circuit Court Judge Antonin Scalia. Scalia admonished the attorneys to abandon their quest to discover the original intentions of the Framers and to pursue instead the original public meaning of the text.[17]

The shift from Framers' intent to original public meaning was a response to Brest's critique of "strict intentionalism." Gone was the need to ascertain the collective intentions of multiple decision-making bodies (the Philadelphia Convention, state ratifying conventions, and so on). And the shift transformed what was, in practice, a counterfactual hypothesizing about how the Framers of the Constitution *might* have handled an issue facing us today into an empirical investigation of how a competent speaker *did* use language at the time the Constitution was ratified.

Ironically, to this day, many historians who choose to engage in constitutional interpretation employ "Framers' intent" proto-originalism despite its now well-recognized drawbacks among legal scholars—originalists and nonoriginalists alike.[18] So too did the Supreme Court invite proto-originalist intentionalist arguments in the landmark case of *Brown v. Board of Education*.[19] The Court did not decide the case after the first round of briefs and arguments; rather, it set the case down for reargument and asked the parties to brief the following questions:

1. What evidence is there that the Congress which submitted and the State legislatures and conventions which ratified the Fourteenth Amendment *contemplated or did not contemplate, understood or did not understand*, that it would abolish segregation in public schools?

2. If neither the Congress in submitting nor the States in ratifying the Fourteenth Amendment *understood* that compliance with it would require the immediate abolition of segregation in public schools, was it nevertheless the *understanding of the framers* of the Amendment

(a) that future Congresses might, in the exercise of their power under Section Five of the Amendment, abolish such segregation, or

(b) that it would be within the judicial power, in light of future conditions, to construe the Amendment as abolishing such segregation of its own force?[20]

The Court did not ask the parties to establish the likely meaning of the language of the amendment. Instead, it asked them to brief whether the Framers or ratifiers expected the application of the amendment to have a specific result: either the abolition of segregated schools by its own force or the empowerment of Congress to do so by statute. Its unanimous answer to its questions is well known to legal scholars:

> This discussion and our own investigation convince us that, although these sources cast some light, it is not enough to resolve the problem with which we are faced. At best, they are inconclusive. The most avid proponents of the post-War Amendments undoubtedly *intended* them to remove all legal distinctions among "all persons born or naturalized in the United States." Their opponents, just as certainly, were antagonistic to both the letter and the spirit of the Amendments and wished them to have the most limited effect. What others in Congress and the state legislatures *had in mind* cannot be determined with any degree of certainty.[21]

Most modern originalists now ask different questions. They ask, for example, what *publicly available* concepts a competent user of the English language would have associated with the phrase "privileges or immunities of citizens of the United States" when it became law.[22] Only then do they apply the result of this inquiry into public meaning to the facts of particular cases— with the assistance of intermediary doctrine.[23]

Of course, we can't determine what any given words or phrases meant to *every* member of the public in 1868—or, for that matter, what any given words or phrases mean to every member of the public today. All analysis of public meaning—whether original or contemporary—requires a certain measure of abstraction. The "competent" speaker or reader is a methodological device that is intended to capture the meaning that the constitutional text conveyed to *most* people when it was ratified. And that meaning is *objective,* in the sense that whether X is the original public meaning of a given provision turns on facts about *prevailing* linguistic practice that are independent of the contents of the minds of *individual* speakers or interpreters.

Originalists attribute to the competent reader (1) the ability and disposition to use and understand the English language in accordance with conventional rules governing public discourse at a given time; (2) familiarity with publicly accessible contemporary communications about particular constitutional words and phrases; and (3) an appreciation of basic features of the political, cultural, and legal context in which those words and phrases took shape. The assumption is that most members of the national community to which the text was addressed satisfied all three of these criteria. One should thus take "public meaning" to denote "the meaning that most actual people attributed to the text when it was ratified into law."[24]

Back to *Brown*. The Court did not ask the parties to brief, nor did it consider, the original meaning of "the privileges or immunities of citizens of the United States." So it did not investigate whether nondiscriminatory access to public or common schools qualified as a privilege of national citizenship under this meaning in 1868 or at some later time. We closely consider these questions in Part I, where we ultimately conclude that original meaning of the Privileges or Immunities Clause strongly supports the outcome in *Brown*.

The move from original Framers' intent to original public meaning was the first big step in formulating a defensible theory of originalism. The next big step was taken, not by a judge or a law professor, but by a political scientist.

The Interpretation–Construction Distinction

In two separate books both published in 1999, Keith Whittington introduced into modern originalism a distinction between two essential components of constitutional decision-making: first, the activity of identifying the original meaning of constitutional texts; second, the activity of making constitutional judgments when the meaning of the text is underdeterminate.[25] The first of these activities he called constitutional *interpretation*, and the second constitutional *construction*.[26]

Although unfamiliar to constitutional scholars when Whittington advanced it, an explicit distinction between interpretation and construction can be found in constitutional theory as early as the 1830s.[27] In an 1839 treatise entitled *Legal and Political Hermeneutics*, legal scholar Francis Lieber formally distinguished between interpretation and construction. Lieber defined "interpretation" as "[t]he art of finding out the true sense of any form of words: that is, the sense which their author intended to convey, and of enabling others to derive from them the very same idea." He defined "construction" as "the drawing of conclusions respecting subjects that lie beyond the direct expression of the text, from elements known from and given in the text—conclusions that are within the *spirit*, though not within the *letter* of the text."[28]

In 1868, Thomas McIntyre Cooley incorporated Lieber's distinction into a constitutional treatise that became highly influential in the late nineteenth century. Cooley was a professor at the University of Michigan Law School from 1859 to 1884 and served as its dean from 1871 to 1883. He was also the chief justice of the Michigan Supreme Court from 1864 to 1885. His *Treatise on the Constitutional Limitations Which Rest upon the Legislative Power of the States of the American Union* was published the same year that the Fourteenth Amendment was ratified.[29]

In a chapter on the construction of state constitutions, Cooley explained that interpretation differs from construction in that the former "is the act of finding out the true sense of any form of words, that is, the sense which their author intended to convey, and of enabling others to derive from them the same idea which the author intended to convey."[30] Construction, on the other hand, "is the drawing of conclusions respecting subjects that lie beyond the direct expressions of the text, from elements known from and given in the text; conclusions which are *in the spirit, though not in the letter* of the text."[31] In addition to Lieber, Cooley relied on *Bouvier's Law Dictionary:*

> Bouvier defines the two terms succinctly as follows: "*Interpretation*, the discovery and representation of the true meaning of any signs used to convey ideas." "*Construction*, in practice, determining the meaning and application as to the case in question of the provisions of a constitution, statute, will, or other instrument, or of an oral agreement."[32]

According to Cooley, the need for construction arises from a number of sources. The first is that the imprecision of human language itself "[is] such that if written instruments were always carefully drawn, and by persons skilled in the use of words, we should not be surprised to find their meaning often drawn in question, or at least to meet with difficulties in their practical application."[33] The second is "when draughtsmen are careless or incompetent."

A third arises when the text needs "to be applied, not only to the subjects directly within the contemplation of those who framed them, but also to a great variety of new circumstances which could not have been anticipated, but which must nevertheless be governed by the general rules which the instruments establish." Finally, construction is needed when their different opinions and interests "incline men to take different views of the instruments which affect those interests." Cooley concluded that "from all these considerations the subject of construction is always prominent in the practical administration of the law."[34]

The interpretation–construction distinction was subsequently refined by contracts scholars, including Arthur Corbin, Edwin Patterson, and E. Allan Farnsworth.[35] Corbin went beyond Lieber to maintain that any judicial activity that did not involve ascertaining the meaning of expressions or determining that a contract existed was not part of interpretation but rather was part of construction.[36] Thus refined, the interpretation–construction distinction eventually made its way into the *Restatement of Contracts* and continues to play a role in contracts scholarship and case law.[37]

In 2004, Whittington's scholarship was adopted by one of us in a book further developing the modern theory of originalism.[38] Soon thereafter, echoing Corbin, Larry Solum clarified that whereas constitutional interpretation was the activity of ascertaining the text's communicative content, constitutional construction was the activity of giving the text legal effect.[39] Even when the communicative content of the text is "thick" enough for a constitutional decision-maker to determine what is required in a particular setting, deciding actually to use that text to make a legally effective decision is an act of construction.

For example, Article I, Section 3's mandate that "[t]he Senate of the United States shall be composed of two Senators from each State" leaves little room for doubt about whether a state may have three senators. But the further decision to adhere to this clear meaning and give it legal effect is not itself an act of interpretation; it is an act of construction. Still, if the text is sufficiently "thick," conveying very detailed guidance about what a decision-maker must do, the decision-maker need not enter what Solum has termed the "construction zone" and develop a rule not specified in the text to resolve the matter at hand.[40]

The interpretation–construction distinction thus became the second component of a defensible theory of originalism. What was still needed, however, was an originalist theory of constitutional construction to go along with the public-meaning theory of interpretation.

The Letter and the Spirit of the Constitution

To understand how an originalist approach to constitutional construction can complement originalist interpretation, it is useful to distinguish—as did both Lieber and Cooley—between the letter of the Constitution and its spirit. The "letter" of the Constitution consists of the meaning that it originally conveyed to the public. The "spirit" of the Constitution consists of the ends, purposes, goals, or objects that the Constitution was adopted to accomplish—its design functions.

Public-meaning originalism seeks to identify the concepts that most members of the ratifying public associated with the words and phrases that constitute the Constitution. We hasten to add that original public meaning is not identical to—although it may be informed by—"original expected applications."[41] Although the criteria governing the meaning of concepts are a function of the conventional use of language in a linguistic community, those concepts are not identical to the things to which they are applied by people at a given time. Anyone who has "misspoken" or revised one's understanding of something in light of new factual information can so attest.

The meaning–application distinction is particularly important in two situations. First, it is important when a concept ("search") applies to an entity or activity (say, the use of thermal imaging technology to detect increased heat within a home caused by marijuana cultivation) that did not exist at the time a provision was enacted but satisfies the criteria conventionally associated with the concept nonetheless. Second, it is important when later inquiry reveals that a prior application of a concept to an existing thing was in error because of a mistake of fact or reasoning.

In ordinary life, we make such factual and reasoning mistakes all the time. We think a family member is watching a "movie" and discover that it is in fact a TV show; or we think we are seeing an "alligator," only to learn it is in fact a crocodile. We wouldn't conclude that the words "movie" or "alligator" no longer mean what they once did if someone pointed out our mistaken application.

As we will discuss in Chapter 6, we believe that eight justices were mistaken in how they applied the Privileges or Immunities Clause to sex discrimination in *Bradwell v. Illinois*. They were not mistaken because the framers of the Fourteenth Amendment believed that excluding women from the practice of law "abridg[ed] the privileges or immunities of citizens of the United States." Most of them likely did not so believe. Rather, five justices were mistaken about the original meaning of the Privileges or Immunities Clause. These five never reached the issue of application. Three justices got the meaning of the clause right, but were mistaken in their application of that meaning to the facts. In particular, they erred in their analysis of the factual justification for barring women from practicing law as a reasonable regulation of a profession.[42] One justice—the chief justice—got both answers right.

This is not the place to address the variety of linguistic, epistemological, and normative objections to originalism that have been offered by critics. But few nonoriginalists contend that original meaning—where it can be ascertained—should be entirely irrelevant to constitutional interpretation. Instead, they maintain either that the original meaning is indeterminate or that it should sometimes be trumped by competing considerations.[43] Therefore, even most of those who disagree that original meaning must *always* be given primacy should take an interest in where the evidence of original meaning leads so long as they think it is *sometimes* relevant.

But what about when original meaning "runs out," failing to provide a determinate, clearly best answer to a particular legal question? Here, we turn to the original, publicly accessible function of the constitutional text. At common law in eighteenth-century America, the distinction between the linguistic meaning of a provision of a legal instrument and that instrument's purpose(s) or function(s)—whether a contract or a constitution—was expressed through a Christian trope: the distinction between the "letter" and the "spirit."[44] Although the letter was ordinarily sufficient to resolve a given question, where the letter was obscure and judges confronted a need to choose, judges followed the spirit of the text.

An instructive example: When Edmund Pendleton, then president of the Virginia Court of Appeals, gave his opinion in the 1782 case of *Commonwealth v. Caton,* he said that because "[t]he language of the clause [of the Virginia Treason Act] . . . admits of both the constructions mentioned by the attorney general," the choice of constructions should be "decided according to the spirit."[45] Revealingly, Pendleton stated that he "prefer[red] the first, as most congenial to the spirit, and not inconsistent with the letter, of the constitution."[46] In this respect, Pendleton, like many American judges,[47] followed Sir William Blackstone, who wrote that "the most universal and effectual way of discovering the true meaning of a law, when the words are dubious, is by considering the *reason* and *spirit* of it."[48]

The distinction between letter and spirit captures an enduring truth. The Constitution's provisions, like the Constitution as a whole, are calculated to accomplish particular ends or goals that were deemed normatively desirable when they were ratified into law. Truly understanding the original meaning of the text may require an understanding of those original functions.[49] This is especially important for resolving textual ambiguities—where the text has more than one possible meaning.

The spirit also has a role to play in faithfully applying unambiguous original meaning to particular facts. Lacking certainty about how to resolve a given case on the basis of the Constitution's linguistic meaning alone, judges must make a decision on the basis of *some* reason. To formulate a rule with reference to the function—or functions—that a relevant provision was designed to perform is not a matter of making the law "the best it can be"[50] but of giving effect *to* the law as best one can.

We recognize that judges may have difficulty identifying even one among several functions of a given provision or determining whether one function rather than another is more contextually relevant and should be allotted priority, given scarce time and research capacity. Our point is normative, not epistemic: to be faithful to the letter of the text, judges should seek, identify, and use the original functions to guide their implementation of the original meaning of the text to the extent that it is possible to do so.

Viewing constitutional construction as a product of, and limited to, the original spirit of the Constitution strikes some of the same chords as appeals to the original intentions of the Framers—that is, it echoes proto-originalism. The appeal of proto-originalists' invocation of "original intent" has always been that it purports to put the "Framers' values" ahead of the judge's own and thereby constrains the judge's discretion. This is just what we advocate: putting the *original* functions of the text itself ahead of extralegal considerations.

It is often forgotten that even Paul Brest acknowledged that the "general purposes" of constitutional provisions are ascertainable and that it is "a perfectly sensible strategy of constitutional decisionmaking" to seek to adhere to them.[51] Judges, he observed, "are more concerned with the adopters' *general purposes* than with their intentions in a very precise sense."[52] Describing what he called "moderate intentionalism," he wrote, a "moderate intentionalist applies a provision consistent with the adopters' intent at a relatively high level of generality, consistent with what is sometimes called the '*purpose* of the provision.'"[53] The moderate intentionalist "attempts to understand what the adopters' *purposes* might plausibly have been, an aim far more readily achieved than a precise understanding of the adopters' intentions."[54]

Whether a law designed by a collective decision-making body was aimed at a particular goal turns on facts in the world that are independent of individual speaker / interpreter beliefs and must be answered through an empirical investigation. This investigation is not different in kind from the inquiry into whether a community's linguistic conventions operated so as to give a string of words and symbols a particular meaning at that same time.[55] The ascription of intentional attitudes to groups for explanatory and predictive purposes is common practice, not only in public and private law but across a variety of social sciences, including political science, social-choice theory, and economics.[56] Determining which attitudes best explain how and why a particular group output was designed to shape the world—be it a contract, a statute, or a constitutional provision—may require inquiry beyond the output itself. It may extend to the political conditions or context in which the output took shape; what was said about it by those who designed it and those who commented on it; and what use was made of it.

This isn't proto-originalism. When seeking to apply the text to modern circumstances, proto-originalists often went beyond identifying the original function of a provision to ask, "What would the Framers do?" One of us early on disparaged this as "channeling" the Framers. "One may think of this as a type of constitutional 'channeling' in which originalist clairvoyants ask: 'Oh Framers, tell us what would you think about the following law?'"[57] Unlike inquiring into the public meaning or function of constitutional text at the point of ratification, asking how the Framers *would have* applied the text to facts inconceivable to them—think thermal imaging or violent video games[58]—is not an empirical inquiry. It is a counterfactual thought experiment. We repudiate it as a means of conclusively determining original meaning.

The Framers as Designers

Because our approach to construction is distinctive even among originalists, it bears further explication. Like the inquiry into public meaning, what we have termed "good-faith construction" seeks to identify empirical facts: the original functions of the Constitution's provisions and structural design elements.

Why good-faith construction? Upon taking their Article VI oath to adhere to the Constitution, all constitutional actors receive a great deal of discretionary power.[59] With this power comes a corresponding normative obligation to implement the Constitution in good faith in a way that is analogous to the duty that private law imposes on "fiduciaries." Fiduciaries are power-exercising parties who have been delegated control over resources belonging to others (think attorneys, agents, and boards of directors).[60]

Similarly, to fulfill their duty, judges and legislators must act consistently with the letter of the instrument from which they draw their power. They also must not abuse their delegated powers by using whatever discretion that original meaning gives them to pursue their own extralegal ends, goals, purposes, or objects, rather than serving the interests of their principals. Where the letter of the Constitution is unclear, fidelity to the Constitution's design requires that judges, legislators, and other constitutional decision-makers turn to the law's original spirit.

Constitutions, statutes, and contracts are artifacts—they are products of human design. One need not read individual minds or posit shared neurological events to determine the meaning or purpose of artifacts.[61] The Constitution was the result of a careful, if often contentious, "design process." Each provision and structural design element was crafted to accomplish things in the world. We identify those things by examining how the Constitution's various components interact with one another, as well as by consulting what was said about them.[62]

Consider an old-fashioned mechanical analog watch. A watch has a primary function—to tell time. This function is discoverable by examining it and figuring out what the numbers around the circumference and the hands that point to them represent. Now open the watch and see the flywheel, gears, and springs, each of which has its own secondary function that facilitates the fulfillment of the watch's primary function. The functions of the constituent parts of the watch that were "intended" by its designer are different from the *motives* of the watch designer—the values or desires that explain why the primary and secondary functions were deemed worth designing. These motives may have been to earn a paycheck or even the esteem of fellow watch designers. None of these motives is the same as the purpose of the watch and the functions of its constituent parts.

One way to identify these functions would be to ask the watch designer, "Why did you do this the way you did?" Failing that, one could consult the written comments by the designer about what each part is supposed to do and why the watch was designed in a particular way rather than in another way. The watch designer's views are highly probative, not because they have some legal power over a watch user, but because of what they know about watch design in general and the choices they made when designing this particular watch.

As one of us has observed, the Framers of the Constitution can be viewed as "designers or architects of the lawmaking 'machine.'"[63] Accordingly, we "consult them when we want to know how the machine is supposed to work, not because they are a surrogate for the majority of the people who lived two hundred years ago, but because they might have special insight into the machine that they designed—especially its internal quality-control procedures." The designers, or Framers, "gave its purpose and design much thought—perhaps more thought than we have—and we benefit from their learning in interpreting their design."[64] Their beliefs about the functional construction of the Constitution play an evidentiary role.

This way of conceptualizing Framers' intent has two advantages. First, the "Framers-as-Designers" approach "explains why we remain so fascinated and influenced by the views of the small group of persons who framed—as opposed to ratified—the Constitution."[65] Indeed, "we generally confine our attention to just a handful of the Framers, such as James Madison or James Wilson" or Gouverneur Morris, who had the most direct role in actually drafting the text of the Constitution, "as opposed to the views of other members of the convention or of the reigning majority of the time."[66] We pay careful attention to these Framers in particular because we believe that they had unique insight into the functioning of the system they helped design. With regard to the Fourteenth Amendment, scholars have rightly focused attention on John Bingham, its principal drafter.[67]

Second, "according to the Framers-as-Designers approach, we consult the writings of the Framers to discern not their specific hypothetical intentions towards particular legislation, but the [design] *principles*" that explain the specific provisions and general structure of the Constitution.[68] "Among these [design] principles are federalism, separation of powers," and the duty to apply the Constitution as supreme law.[69]

The Constitution can be thought of as a device or mechanism like a watch. Like a watch, the Constitution as a whole has functions (described in the Preamble). Like the flywheel, gears, and springs of a watch, each of its clauses was designed to work harmoniously with the others to fulfill those functions. Like a watch, each of its constituent parts has its own secondary function as means to the more general ends.[70]

Like a watch, the Constitution was the product of deliberate human design rather than uncoordinated human action. Where the functions or purposes of a provision are not obvious, we can attempt to reverse engineer the design from close examination of its workings. But we can also seek out the explanations left behind by its designers.

Construction Should Be as Historically
Grounded as Interpretation

Some thoughtful critics of originalism have claimed that the recognition of the activity of constitutional construction renders originalism highly indeterminate. Reintroducing judicial and legislative discretion of this sort has been said to obviate the constraint that made the focus on the original public meaning of the text appealing in the first place. As Thomas Colby has put it, the original meaning of the Constitution is "sufficiently open-ended as to be incapable of resolving most concrete cases." Because there will be "multiple rules of decision that are each consistent with the original meaning of the vague or ambiguous constitutional command," judges engaged in construction might seem to be adrift in an ocean of discretion.[71] Eric Segall has written that because the "method of constitutional construction does not constrain judges in any meaningful sense," its "theoretical foundations are similar to those of living constitutionalism."[72]

Even some originalists have been skeptical about acknowledging a place for constitutional construction. This criticism by nonoriginalists and concern of originalists, however, predates anyone having advanced a *constraining* originalist theory of construction, such as good-faith construction, which is based on the original spirit of the text.

Not that invocations of the spirit of the text are free from difficulty. In the context of statutory interpretation, some textualists have noted that appeals to "the spirit" or purposes of the Constitution have been used to supersede, rather than implement, the requirements of the text. John Manning, for example, has worried that "efforts to augment or vary the text in the name of serving a genuine but unexpressed legislative intent risk displacing whatever bargain was actually reached."[73]

However, there is no objection to recourse to the original spirit that cannot be made against textualism more generally—whether it is focused on the public meaning of constitutional or statutory text. Yes, identifying original functions may be hard. Yes, implementing original functions is an enterprise that is fraught with peril. But so is ascertaining the linguistic meaning of decades-old statutes and centuries-old constitutional provisions. We claim only that recourse to the original spirit is the *best available* means of implementing the original Constitution when the text runs out, even if it may well fall short of some unattainable ideal.[74]

Having said this, we think it bears emphasizing that, although constitutional construction necessarily takes place every time constitutional text is given legal effect, judges need not—indeed, should not—create nontextual rules of construction in every constitutional case. Recall the two-senators-per-state provision of Article I. It can be applied without the need for any intermediary doctrine.

Much of the Constitution's text is thick enough to make recourse to nontextual rules unnecessary. Controversies tend to arise around a handful of provisions that are said to be more general or abstract—thereby allowing much more judicial discretion when implementing their meaning. Two of these provisions appear in Section 1 of the Fourteenth Amendment: the Due Process of Law and Equal Protection of the Laws Clauses.

The linguistic content of terms that appear to be thin and therefore require entrance into the construction zone may be considerably thicker after careful empirical work. Here are some other examples of provisions, the meaning of which has already been rendered more precise by scholarship: The original meaning of "recess" in the Recess Appointments Clause refers to the period between "sessions" of Congress, once context is taken into account.[75] "Commerce . . . among the several states" encompasses activity of particular kinds—namely, the trade, exchange, and transportation or movement of things.[76] The Eighth Amendment's ban on "cruel and unusual punishment" forbids cruel innovation in punishment—specifically, punishments that are unjustly harsh in light of longstanding common-law practice.[77]

Even where empirical inquiry into the context of constitutional communication does not yield answers to interpretive questions that are almost certainly correct, it may identify answers that are much more plausible than others.[78] When, and only when, no leading candidate can be ascertained through interpretation must judges enter the construction zone. A rule must be applied—either a previously formulated rule or a new one. We hold that any such rule must be informed by the Constitution's original spirit.

Judges do, however, need to take care to properly identify the level of abstraction at which the spirit of a provision or design element should be characterized, just as they must take care to properly identify the level of abstraction at which to understand particular words. And here there is no substitute for immersing oneself in the data of discourse; we cannot fall back on the hermeneutical cliché that words have no inherent meaning outside of discursive communities.

Jules Coleman and Brian Leiter have rebutted claims that legal language is radically indeterminate—claims that trade on the fact that all linguistic meaning is dependent on social conventions:

> All that follows is that there are no facts about meaning that are completely independent of how we are disposed to construe meanings. Meaning is not radically indeterminate; instead, meaning is public—fixed by public behavior, beliefs, and understandings. There is no reason to assume that such conventions cannot fix the meaning of terms determinately.[79]

The same can be said about original functions or purposes: that they are contingent on behavior and understandings at a given time does not make them illusory.

Judges should specify a construction—an implementing doctrine[80]—that resolves the case at hand in a manner that is consistent with the relevant original function and susceptible of application to future cases of a similar kind. Once derived and sufficiently explained, a construction can then stand on its own. In future cases, judges need only explain why and how a construction applies and then apply it.

The devising and application of such constructions make up much of what we call "constitutional law." Of course, as preexisting doctrines confront new and unanticipated circumstances, these implementing rules of constitutional law may have to be adjusted and refined to fit the functions that the textual provisions were adopted to perform. That, indeed, is just how the common law of contract was developed over the centuries.[81]

First Comes Interpretation; Only Then Comes Construction

If the Constitution's letter and spirit can both be ascertained empirically by investigating similar evidence, why persist in distinguishing between interpretation and construction? First, because identifying the linguistic meaning of a text is still a different activity than formulating implementing doctrines that are faithful to the text's intended function. Determining that the Second Amendment was designed to protect an individual right to possess and carry weapons does not tell us whether a machine gun is a protected "arm." Second, because the respective activities have a lexical order: consistency with the letter has priority. The spirit should not be used to override the letter; when the letter is clear, it controls. This priority is obscured or lost when these two activities are collapsed under a single rubric of "interpretation." Keeping the interpretation–construction distinction in view, and prioritizing the letter in cases of perceived conflict, are necessary to prevent the spirit from being used to undermine or supplant what interpretation yields about the meaning of the letter.

What we have called "good-faith" interpretation and construction thus consists of three separate steps:

1. Make a good-faith effort to determine the original public meaning of the text of the relevant provision and to resolve the case on the basis of the letter;
2. Failing this, identify the original, publicly accessible functions or spirit of the provision, and
3. Formulate a rule to be followed in the case at hand and in the future that is
   a. consistent with the letter and
   b. designed to implement the original public functions of
      i. the provision at issue or, failing that,
      ii. the structure in which the provision appears or, failing that,
      iii. the Constitution as a whole.

Each step must be performed candidly and carefully, explaining why the implementing rule is consistent with the spirit of the Constitution, setting forth the rule clearly and concisely, and modeling its proper application.

The attempt by originalists to dissolve the indeterminacy of the Constitution's text and uncover the more determinate, thicker meaning of these and other clauses is in its relative infancy. Work on rigorous originalist methodology and the development of best practices for originalist scholarship are recent. Important tools, such as corpus linguistics, have only just been introduced.[82]

In this book, we employ state-of-the-art originalist methodology to establish the original meaning of the letter of the Fourteenth Amendment and then to identify rules of construction that are true to the spirit of the text. To repeat, if we are correct, the original meaning of the Fourteenth Amendment is thicker than commonly assumed and thus requires less recourse to its original spirit to resolve particular cases. But the rules of construction we propose will further guide and constrain judicial discretion. And because our treatment of interpretation is separate from our treatment of construction, it is possible for readers to accept our conclusions about the former, while still disagreeing with our proposals for the latter.

Why Restore the Original Meaning of the
Fourteenth Amendment?

This book endeavors to assist conscientious constitutional decision-makers by adding specificity to the Fourteenth Amendment. We do so in two ways. First, we provide the context that shows that the meaning of the "letter" (or terms and phrases) of the Fourteenth Amendment is thicker than appearances might suggest. Part of this is accomplished by viewing as operative *all* the words of the text, not merely some. For example, in Part I, we contend that what is today called the "Due Process Clause," should be called the "Due Process *of Law* Clause"; in Part III, we adopt the neologism, "Equal Protection *of the Laws* Clause." We adopt these unconventional labels as a reminder to the reader that the text calls for more than "process"; it calls for the protection of "laws" that satisfy certain substantive criteria.

Second, we provide doctrines by which the original meaning of the text can be given legal effect. We construct these doctrines on the basis of the original functions of the provision that were publicly known at the time the Fourteenth Amendment was enacted in 1868. Doing this is going to upset some apple carts.

On the one hand, nearly everything that currently comprises the conventional wisdom about the meaning of the most salient clauses of the Fourteenth Amendment is wrong. This is not to say that individual scholars have not already identified a great many of these errors. We give full credit to those who have done so. But in most cases, these "revisionist" interpretations have not displaced the conventional wisdom among legal academics and, especially, among the judiciary.

On the other hand, we do not believe that adopting the original meaning of the Fourteenth Amendment as a whole would lead to *results* that differ radically from those that current doctrine would produce. Far from it. We are not the first to observe that misinterpretations of some of these clauses have led to misinterpretations of other clauses to compensate for the error. These compensating misinterpretations, in turn, lead to results that are often consistent with what the original meaning of the whole amendment would warrant. Given its compatibility with originalist results, we can call this "second-best" originalism.

Most notably, it has become conventional wisdom among scholars that the Supreme Court in the 1873 *Slaughter-House Cases* misinterpreted the Privileges or Immunities Clause to the point of effectively nullifying its original meaning. This led to a compensating expansion of the scope of the Due Process of Law and Equal Protection of the Laws Clauses in ways that are in conflict with their original meaning. In other words, despite being nonoriginalist in method, the Supreme Court's interpretations of the Due Process of Law and Equal Protection of the Laws Clauses have often converged on results that are consistent with the original meaning of Section 1 as a whole—just as if the Privileges or Immunities Clause were still operative.

Strict adherence to the original meaning of the Due Process of Law and Equal Protection of the Laws Clauses while disregarding the original meaning of the Privileges or Immunities Clause might well be worse from the standpoint of originalist results than is current nonoriginalist doctrine. From the standpoint of original meaning, it is better that a generally applicable nondiscrimination principle be implemented via the wrong clause of the Fourteenth Amendment—the Equal Protection of the Laws Clause rather than the Privileges or Immunities Clause—than that it not be implemented at all.

By the same token, however, if all of this is correct, then restoring the original meaning of the Due Process of Law and Equal Protection of the Laws Clause together with that of the Privileges or Immunities Clause would not lead to a radical departure from the results reached by existing doctrines that have compensated for its absence. But we will show why "first-best" originalism is better still.

Restoring the original meaning of these three clauses—together with that of Congress's Section 5 powers—would result in significant improvements in our constitutional practice. Two big departures from current doctrine would be (1) better judicial protection of economic liberties from arbitrary regulations by state legislatures; and (2) the judicial recognition of an affirmative duty on the part of states to provide protection against violence by "private" actors. We expect that the former of these departures would be welcome by some on the political Right; the latter would be welcome by some on the political Left.

Yet another effect of restoring the original meaning of these clauses would be to dispel the cloud of illegitimacy that currently enshrouds some important doctrines. This would include, for example, the application of the first eight amendments to the states via (the wrong clause of) the Fourteenth Amendment—the so-called incorporation doctrine—or the current protection of certain unenumerated personal liberties as fundamental rights. By itself, achieving this legitimation would be a very big deal for many on both the political Right and Left.

Finally, getting the original meaning of the Fourteenth Amendment right helps legitimate originalism itself. Nonoriginalists have trotted out a litany of entrenched constitutional doctrines that most Americans celebrate but are said to be contrary to the original meaning of the text. These critics then urge that this conflict between popular moral intuitions and originalism should be resolved against originalism. If, however, originalism not only fits but morally justifies popular doctrines,[83] there is no conflict to resolve.

Opening Statement: A Preview of Our Findings

Trial lawyers give opening statements to describe what they intend to prove so jurors can comprehend how the testimony of each witness fits into that broader narrative. What follows is a brief preview of the findings we reach and how they differ from the Supreme Court's current understanding of the Fourteenth Amendment.

The Citizenship Clause

All persons born or naturalized in the United States, and subject to the jurisdiction thereof, are citizens of the United States and of the State wherein they reside.

A late addition to Section 1, this language was meant to constitutionalize a similar declaration of natural-born citizenship in the Civil Rights Act of 1866. We do not devote a separate part of this book to examining the original meaning of the Citizenship Clause. But this meaning underscores our reading of the Privileges or Immunities Clause. In particular, we maintain that the original meaning of "the privileges or immunities of citizens of the United States" was deeply informed by a concept of *Republican citizenship* that was shaped by, although not identical to, abolitionist citizenship theory. So we will be referring to the Citizenship Clause as part of our discussion of the Privileges or Immunities Clause.

It will likely disappoint some readers that we do not investigate the original meaning of the phrase "and subject to the jurisdiction thereof." In recent years, some have contended that this language excluded from the status of natural-born citizenship the offspring of persons who are in the country illegally. This view has been fiercely criticized. Addressing this interpretative claim, however, would simply be too orthogonal to our goal of showing how the moving parts of Section 1 work with one another, and all work together with Congress's enforcement power in Section 5.

Putting that issue aside, the Fourteenth Amendment protects more than citizenship rights. It affords to all *persons* the "due process of law" before they can be deprived of their "life, liberty or property," and it entitles them to "the equal protection of the laws" as well. About the scope of these rights we will have much to offer.

The Privileges or Immunities Clause

No State shall make or enforce any law which shall abridge the privileges or immunities of citizens of the United States;

If a copy of the Privileges or Immunities Clause somehow found its way to another planet full of sentient beings much like us (a "Twin Earth," if you will[84]), it would no doubt be received as a momentous declaration. This alien civilization might then be surprised to learn that, since it was ratified in 1868, the Supreme Court has only once relied on it to decide a case involving fundamental rights.[85] We join the academic consensus that this is wrong, and so was the reasoning of Justice Miller in the *Slaughter-House Cases*, which in 1873 effectively redacted this clause from the Constitution.

THE LETTER   The consensus view that *Slaughter-House* misinterpreted the Privileges or Immunities Clause breaks down over exactly what are the privileges or immunities of citizens of the United States and how we should protect them. We conclude that "the privileges and immunities of citizens of the United States" referred to "civil rights," as opposed to either "political" or "social" rights. That's not exactly news. But we further conclude that civil rights were generally understood as the enforceable "positive-law" rights that are necessary to secure the fundamental rights of the people. (By "positive-law," we mean "produced by the legal institutions of the state, in conformity with the state's criteria for legal validity.") One set of these civil rights originates from natural, pre-political rights; the other, from post-political, state-created goods. We will discuss each in turn.

The first source of civil rights is natural rights, which are the "negative liberties"—or simply the "liberty"—that one would be morally entitled as a person to enjoy even absent a monopoly on legitimate force. (That is, in the "state of nature.") This is not the Hobbesian liberty to anything one wills or desires, but the liberty to do anything one wills or desires with what is properly one's own—consistent with the like liberty of everyone else. This is the bounded conception of liberty that John Locke and other influential natural-rights theorists articulated and that was centrally important to political theory in the United States at the (first) Founding and up through the ratification of the Fourteenth Amendment (the second Founding). A state that systemically failed to preserve this liberty was deemed morally illegitimate.

Per natural-rights theory, one leaves the state of nature for civil society to receive positive-law civil rights that better protect one's pre-political, "negative" liberties as compared with living outside the protection of civil society. As the Congress of the United States unanimously declared in 1776, "*to secure these rights,* governments are instituted among men."[86] The positive-law civil rights one gets on entering civil society include laws delimiting and securing one's life, liberty, and property rights, the impartial adjudication of disputes with others, and the equal enforcement of liberty-protecting laws. Moreover, the laws that are necessary to protect one's rights from others should not themselves infringe on the negative liberties of any person within a polity's jurisdiction. This postulated exchange of natural for civil rights is called the "social compact."

The second source of civil rights is the post-political goods one receives from the particular civil society in which one lives and to which one is entitled as a citizen of that polity, not by virtue of one's humanity. These goods are typically provided by institutions supported by general taxes. The connection between these goods and securing natural rights can be very attenuated, even nonexistent. Many post-political goods are designed only to promote the equal standing of citizens; to prevent the domination of some citizens by others in civic life; or to achieve some other legitimate end. When these goods become sufficiently entrenched—or as the Court would put it some centuries later, "deeply rooted in this Nation's history and traditions"[87]—we can say that they are *deemed* fundamental by the citizenry and thereby become civil rights of citizenship in addition to those that are necessary to secure the citizenry's natural rights.

At the core of this second category of post-political rights to a good or benefit is the right of similarly situated citizens to equality in the public sphere. As we will see, the public sphere circa 1868 included both governmental and nongovernmental actors in particular contexts. Most obviously, such rights resulted from the corresponding duty of government to provide its own services on an equal basis to all similarly situated members or citizens of the polity. In addition, these rights could be found in the preexisting common-law duties imposed on nongovernmental actors such as common carriers and innkeepers to provide their services on a nondiscriminatory basis and (more controversially) on those requiring a government license to operate. While the "public sphere" extended beyond state actors, there remained a "private sphere" to which such civil rights did not extend.

As we will explain, rather than think of binaries such as public/private or governmental/nongovernmental, it is useful to think of three categories: (1) public/governmental; (2) public/nongovernmental; and (3) private/nongovernmental. The first and third categories are familiar. The second is more unfamiliar—and slippery. But if the evidence shows that a right to nondiscrimination with respect to category 2 was widely included among the "privileges or immunities of citizens of the United States," then the continued existence of category 3 makes finding some limit to category 2 essential. By this we mean that category 2 should not be expanded so as to subsume and eliminate category 3.

The key to figuring out whether a particular post-political civil right has become a fundamental right that was among the privileges or immunities of US citizens is whether it has been demonstrably *accepted* as such by the polity. The Privileges or Immunities Clause protected post-political rights that were deemed fundamental by Republicans to citizenship at the time of its ratification; and it protects today those post-political rights that have since come to be accepted as fundamental.

To determine whether a post-political right is fundamental, we ask whether it was in 1868 or is today the object of a stable national consensus. That consensus can be established by showing that a right is enumerated in the text of the Constitution or is otherwise deeply rooted in the nation's history and traditions. Because civil rights are positive law rights, in addition to the positive law of the Constitution, one looks to the positive law of the states—both the common law and enacted statutes or ordinances—for evidence of deep-rootedness.

Perhaps the most prominent example of a post-political right that, at some point, came to be accepted as fundamental is the right of nondiscriminatory access to public schooling. We will show that this right is a corollary of a broader right—a right deemed fundamental in 1868—of nondiscriminatory access to public institutions intended to benefit the citizenry.

By definition, there are no governmentally provided public schools in a state of nature, so there is no natural right to public schooling that one re-

tains when one enters civil society. But a particular polity might choose to
create a system of common schools, which is paid for by the citizenry at large
through their taxes. This good is intended to benefit the individual citizen,
to be sure, but common schools were also provided to the citizenry at large
to promote the equal standing of citizens—indeed, to instill the values of
citizenship.

We maintain that, in 1868, the general principle of nondiscriminatory access to public institutions was a feature of the positive law of states—reflected
in common-law norms—although these norms were also selectively usurped
in practice. (Indeed, the doctrine of "separate *but equal*" pretended to honor
this norm even as it subverted it.) If this conclusion is correct, a citizen had
a civil right to participate in public schooling and other public institutions
even if a particular political establishment dominated by a majority or minority faction would rather not allow it.

To borrow a phrase, membership has its privileges—and corresponding
governmental obligations. In contrast with the positive-law civil rights that
secure pre-political natural rights to which all persons are entitled, all persons are not entitled to these post-political membership goods. Only citizens are so entitled. But, to reiterate, the civil rights of citizens of the United
States include *both* sets of entitlements. Or so we will argue.

The polity has no preexisting obligation to provide a particular good such
as common schools—or roads, sidewalks, or parks—in the first instance. Only
once a polity has chosen to create such a good does a fundamental right of
access to it preclude a polity from arbitrarily denying access to any of its members. In contrast, the duty of the polity to refrain from violating the civil
rights protecting one's pre-political natural rights is never optional. Such access must be afforded equally to every citizen, indeed to every person within
its jurisdiction.

As a result, while a state is free to deny to the citizenry as a whole a post-
political right not designed to protect natural rights, it may never arbitrarily
deprive any citizen, or the citizenry as a whole, of the civil rights that serve
to protect the natural rights of its members. The concept of "arbitrariness" is
crucial to making sense of all this, and we say much more about it in
Chapter 10.

Although we describe the institution of common schools as a post-political
"good," our argument does not depend on it being a good in some objective
sense. Common schools that indoctrinated the citizenry with propaganda
would actually be harmful. This source of civil rights arises because access

by citizens to public institutions—institutions that are usually funded by all citizens' tax revenues—is widely *deemed to be* a good and because public schools are such an institution. This is how access to public schools becomes a "privilege" of citizenship.

Two other post-political goods that became "privileges" of citizenship in this way are the rights of access to the jury and ballot boxes.[88] Neither juries nor the franchise exist in the state of nature. A right to serve on a jury or a right to vote was not expressly identified in the constitutional text; nor were they widely and deeply entrenched in the nation's history and traditions circa 1868. Indeed, the principal reason that Republicans distinguished between "civil" rights (which *were* privileges or immunities) and "political" rights (which were *not* privileges or immunities) was to exclude the right of suffrage from the scope of the Privileges or Immunities Clause. Jury service rights, too, were often categorized as political rights, and therefore also excluded.

However, it is also true that, in the years leading up to 1868, some thought that the rights of suffrage and jury service *ought to be* privileges of citizenship. For example, at the first convention of the Negro Republican Party, held in Louisville, Kentucky, in 1867, William F. Butler proclaimed: "First we had the cartridge box, now we want the ballot box, and soon we will get the jury box." [89] Frederick Douglass argued that Section 2 of the Fourteenth Amendment, which allowed states to exclude Blacks from suffrage (but penalized states that did so), contradicted Section 1 because voting was already among the privileges and immunities of citizenship. And the right of suffrage was categorized as such by Justice Bushrod Washington in a widely quoted opinion that we will discuss shortly.

This disagreement over the status of suffrage is revealing. It indicates that whether a right arising from the provision of a post-political good is a "political" right that can be granted or withdrawn at will, or a "civil" right or privilege of citizenship that states must recognize and protect, is contingent on an empirical fact: whether a right is *deemed to be* a privilege or immunity of citizenship by the polity. Under the law established by the Fourteenth Amendment, voting, jury rights, schooling rights, and so on may become privileges and immunities when they are so deemed.

The evidence we present supports a conclusion that, relatively early on, the rights to enjoy the benefit of attending a tax-supported common school and to participate in the jury were deemed fundamental because of their connection to fundamental rights to nondiscriminatory access to public institutions and to impartial adjudication by a jury of one's peers. The evidence will also show that somewhat later, by 1920, the right of citizens who had reached the age of majority to vote was deemed fundamental. What was once a mere "political" right to suffrage had *become* a fundamental civil right. We stress that the original meaning of the text of the Privileges or Immunities Clause didn't change; what changed were the social facts that the original meaning of the text made determinative of privilege-or-immunity status.

The fact the Privileges or Immunities Clause protects "citizens," while both the Due Process of Law and the Equal Protection of the Laws Clauses protect "persons," has led many to resist shifting current doctrine from the latter two clauses to the former. Appreciating the two different sources of civil rights helps ameliorate this concern (though perhaps not eliminating it altogether). The latter two clauses protect rights possessed by all "persons," and all persons have the natural right to be free from subjugation with respect to their lives, liberty, or property. In other words, all persons enjoy the civil rights that protect the pre-political natural rights of all persons.

The Privileges or Immunities Clause likewise bars laws abridging these civil rights enjoyed by citizens as persons. But, in addition, it *also* bars laws that deny to some citizens any entrenched post-political goods that a particular polity chooses to provide to its citizens. To reiterate, the privileges or immunities of citizens of the United States that are protected by the Privileges or Immunities Clause are drawn from *both* sources of civil rights.

In this way, the civil rights drawn from the first category—pre-political natural rights to which one is entitled as a person—provide a *floor* that is *fixed* and enforced *by all three clauses:* the Privileges or Immunities, Due Process of Law, and Equal Protection of the Laws Clauses. The civil rights drawn from the second category—additional post-political goods to which one is entitled as a citizen of a particular civil society—provide a *ceiling* that can *be raised* over time.

The polity is always free to raise this ceiling for both citizens and noncitizens alike. But, by its terms, the Privileges or Immunities Clause protects as a federally enforceable constitutional right only whatever this ceiling happens to be for citizens. We should stress, however, that under our approach, *judges* do not get to raise this ceiling; they must find that this ceiling has already been raised by the polity.

Further, as we show in Chapter 12, the Equal Protection of the Laws Clause affirms that state governments have an affirmative duty to enforce the civil rights in the first category from being violated by both private and public actors. The *protection* of this category of civil rights is not optional. All persons have a right to such protection. In contrast, governments have no affirmative duty to provide the privileges in the second category of civil rights. The *provision* of these privileges is optional. But *if* governments opt to do so, and such goods become perceived by the citizenry to be privileges of citizenship, they too become civil rights. And the Privileges or Immunities Clause bars the government from *arbitrarily* denying any citizen or group of citizens access to these government-provided goods.

We offer this conceptual scheme as the best way to accurately understand and interpret the great mass of evidence we present. Above all, this conceptual scheme is needed to make sense of the *text* of Section 1. That text distinguishes between the "privileges or immunities of *citizens* of the United States," on the one hand, and the fundamental guaranties of the "due process of law" and "the equal protection of the laws" that the text affords to all *"persons,"* on the other. Any interpretation of the Fourteenth Amendment that purports to be faithful to its text must somehow come to grips with the textual distinction between "citizens" and "persons." We believe ours is the first conceptual scheme to make sense of both the text and the available evidence of original meaning.

THE SPIRIT   Understanding the general concept of the civil rights that constitute the original meaning of "privileges or immunities of citizens of the United States" is one thing. Identifying them in practice is another. As we have already explained, while these members of the set of civil rights were *fixed* at the time of the amendment's adoption and cannot be repealed short of amending the Constitution, the set itself was not *closed.* Other rights can later become privileges of citizenship. The challenge is to identify when that occurs.

In Chapter 8, we invoke the original spirit of the Privileges or Immunities Clause to devise criteria by which particular rights can be identified as privileges or immunities of citizens of the United States. The object, end, or purpose of the clause was to protect what we call "Republican citizenship." By this we mean the distinctive theory of citizenship that was generally held by members of the Republican Party—from radicals to moderates to conservatives. We discuss the three criteria for identifying these civil rights, which were articulated by Justice Bushrod Washington in his crucially important 1823 circuit court opinion in *Corfield v. Coryell:*

We feel no hesitation in confining these expressions to those privileges and immunities [1] which are, *in their nature,* fundamental; [2] which *belong, of right, to the citizens* of all free governments; and [3] *which have,* at all times, *been enjoyed* by the citizens of the several States which compose this Union.[90]

We explain how, if very slightly adjusted (to eliminate "at all times"), Justice Washington's criteria of privileges and immunities well serve the spirit of the amendment.

Based on these criteria, we propose a four-part rule of construction by which judges and legislators can today identify privileges or immunities of Republican citizenship:

1. *Constitutional enumeration circa 1868.* If a right was enumerated in the text of the federal Constitution in 1868, and individual citizens were in 1868 entitled to enjoy that right, it is a privilege of US citizenship. Such rights were privileges or immunities at the time of ratification, were protected by the clause in 1868, and cannot be eroded by later history and tradition. In short, they were locked in by the original meaning of the text in 1868.

2. *Enumeration in the Civil Rights Act of 1866.* The rights listed in the Civil Rights Act of 1866 are also privileges of US citizenship. Such rights were privileges or immunities at the time of ratification, were protected by the clause in 1868, and cannot be eroded by later history and tradition. In short, they were locked in by the original meaning of the text in 1868.

3. *Later enumeration.* If an enumerated right was added to the federal Constitution after 1868, and individual citizens are today entitled to enjoy that right, it is presumptively a privilege of US citizenship. That presumption can be defeated by a showing that enforcing the right at issue would violate a right that falls within categories 1 or 2, unless the subsequent amendment expressly qualifies the Fourteenth.

4. *Unenumerated rights.* We adopt the standard laid down in *Washington v. Glucksberg* for the recognition of "fundamental" substantive-due-process rights: rights that are deeply rooted in the nation's history and traditions should be considered among the privileges and immunities of US citizenship. However, the Court has not specified rules for determining deep-rootedness. We suggest that if individual citizens have for at least a generation—that is, thirty years or more—been entitled to enjoy a right as a consequence of the positive constitutional, statutory,

or common law of a supermajority of the states, it ought to be presumptively a privilege of US citizenship. That presumption can be defeated if it is shown that enforcing the right at issue would necessarily violate a right that falls within categories 1, 2, or 3.

Why we propose these four categories will be fully explained in Chapter 8.

According to the first two categories, when the Fourteenth Amendment was enacted in 1868, the privileges or immunities of citizens of the United States included the specific personal rights that were enumerated in the Civil Rights Act of 1866 and in the Constitution itself. This was how the Senate sponsor of the amendment, Michigan Senator Jacob Howard, identified these privileges or immunities. By the early twentieth century, the right of suffrage had become a privilege of national citizenship under the third category.

Common schooling had not been pervasive for one generation by the early 1870s, when Republicans sought to bar discrimination in its provision when drafting what became the Civil Rights Act of 1875. But a more general right of nondiscriminatory access to institutions that were either (a) created and managed by the government for the benefit of the general public or (b) considered "affected with a public interest" by virtue of a natural or artificial monopoly *was* clearly widespread and entrenched in 1868. We think supporters of the 1875 act were correct in deeming the right of nondiscriminatory access to common schools to be a corollary of the latter right.

Whatever may have been the state of affairs in the 1870s, however, by the time *Brown v. Board of Education* was decided, a right to attend a public school clearly qualified as a privilege of citizenship under our fourth category. The existence of that right was not contested in *Brown*. Indeed, the doctrine of "separate but equal"—a constitutional construction—conceded the existence of a citizenship right to access common schools that were equal. At issue in that case was whether the doctrine of "*separate* but equal" was an unconstitutional abridgement of that privilege. We think the "separate but equal" doctrine was correctly held to be unconstitutional because it is a construction that was unfaithful to the concept of Republican citizenship comprising the original spirit of the clause.

Section 1: The Due Process of Law Clause

nor shall any State deprive any person of life, liberty, or property, without due process of law;

What is usually referred to as the "Due Process Clause" of the Fourteenth Amendment is among the most frequently litigated and controversial provisions in the US Constitution. The dominant originalist view has long been that "due process of law" is solely a procedural guarantee that does not constrain the substance or content of legislation.[91] "Substantive due process" has been long denounced as babble on par with "green pastel redness."[92] In recent years, however, originalist scholars have made fresh inquiries into the historical evidence and concluded that the case for some form of judicial review of the content of legislation under what we will henceforth refer to as the Due Process *of Law* Clause is weightier than initially supposed.

THE LETTER   We describe the evolution of the meaning of "due process of law" from British to pre-Revolution thought, from the adoption of the Fifth Amendment to the adoption of the Fourteenth. Like others, we take issue with the modern conception of "substantive due process," which authorizes judges to single out some liberties as fundamental and worthy of heightened protection and leave aside other mere "liberty interests," which are largely left to the discretion of legislators. Under this approach, Jamal Greene has observed, "unelected judges choose the rights we have and enforce them full-throttle against bad-faith bigots and good-faith legislatures alike, while allowing the government free rein over whatever rights judges happen to leave behind."[93]

We concur with the claim that the "due process of law" is a "procedural" guarantee. But we then show that this procedure is "substantive" insofar as it requires judges to examine the substance of legislation. When it comes to the legitimacy of statutes, the "due process of law" is not limited to whether a statute was duly enacted by the requisite legislative procedure.

The original meaning of "due process of law" in the Fourteenth Amendment guarantees some judicial process before any person can be deprived of life, liberty, or property. This judicial process includes a jury trial. The question then concerns the proper scope of this process. Such a judicial process potentially involves an inquiry into two questions: (1) Was an accused person actually guilty of violating a preexisting law—whether a statute or the common law, and (2) if a statute was being enforced, was it within the proper power of the relevant legislature to enact? The second of these questions requires an examination of the *substance* of the statute that is being enforced.

Both inquiries date back to the Founding. But both were largely within the province of the jury, which was said to be the trier of law as well as fact.[94]

Before the adoption of the Fourteenth Amendment, judges tended to limit themselves to policing the far outer boundaries of the legislative power by equitably construing statutes so that they were within the proper power of legislatures. After the ratification of the Fourteenth Amendment, as the role of the jury was curtailed, judges became increasingly "realistic" and skeptical about legislative assertions of powers.

This substantive procedure is not the same as the modern doctrine of substantive due process. Under modern substantive due process, judges identify those substantive "fundamental rights" that are entitled to heightened protection, leaving other mere "liberty interests" to little or no judicial protection. Thus, the modern critiques of this type of substantive due process do not apply to the substantive procedure that we maintain is required by the due process of law. That procedure is "substantive" in a different sense: because it sometimes requires an examination of the content or substance of legislation rather than deeming a statute to be "law" solely because it has been enacted through the appropriate procedures.

The relevant clauses in the Fifth and Fourteenth Amendments are today called the Due Process Clauses. However, to remind us that the "due process *of law*" requires that no person should be deprived of his or her life, liberty, or property, except according to a valid law, in Part II, we refer to them as the Due Process *of Law* Clauses. This is also a reminder that the original meaning of the so-called abstract or open-ended provisions of the Constitution is thicker than is commonly acknowledged. And this thicker original meaning, in turn, constrains the amount of discretion that is left to judges in the construction zone.

THE SPIRIT   We identify the original spirit of the due process of law as barring arbitrary power. In Britain, with its conception of parliamentary supremacy, this meant barring the arbitrary power of the Crown. In the United States, with its conception of popular sovereignty, this meant barring the arbitrary power of the government as a whole, which included the legislature.

Arbitrary power is power that is not grounded in a contextually legitimate reason for coercion. In Britain, it was not enough to justify execution or imprisonment that the monarch desired it. The Magna Carta affirmed, if it did not itself establish, that monarchs must have an adequate reason grounded in "the law of the land," which is external to their own will, for depriving people of customary rights. In the United States, this principle applies as well to legislatures. It is not enough that a majority of legislators will or desire to punish particular conduct. Before a person may be fined, imprisoned, or put to death, the legislature must have a reason that is within its proper power, or what was often called its "competence."

At the federal level, Congress must be acting within its delegated powers. At the state level, a statute that deprives any person of life, liberty, or property must take the form of a law and be within one of the reserved powers of a state legislature, such as its police power. The American conception of the police power is not unlimited; if it were, it would be arbitrary power. The "due process of law," therefore, requires a theory of that power and its limits.

As we chronicle, the concept of the police power long predates the Fourteenth Amendment, but the theory underlying the concept was much developed and refined thereafter. We identify this theory and further refine it for today's circumstances. We then propose doctrines to implement this theory in practice. In particular, we maintain that legislatures must ground their commands on fact-based analysis, the validity of which citizens may challenge before a neutral tribunal of justice—meaning the courts. Courts must adopt the appropriate burdens of production and proof to ensure that the legislature was invoking its police power in good faith. When legislation is not fact-based, it is not entitled to any deference. Neither are the commands of executive branch officials.

Section 1: The Equal Protection of the Laws Clause

nor deny to any person within its jurisdiction the equal protection of the laws.

Equality is a central theme in Section 1. The original meaning of both the Privileges or Immunities Clause and the Due Process of Law Clause guarantees equality between citizens and persons, respectively. As we will show in Part I, along with barring laws that deprive *all* citizens of their privileges or immunities, the Privileges or Immunities Clause also bars the making or enforcing of any law that abridges the privileges or immunities of only *some* citizens while protecting the privileges or immunities of others. Similarly, due process of law guarantees equality by providing *all* persons with a fair judicial proceeding before they may be deprived of their lives, liberty, or property. This entails that *some* may not be deprived of a fair judicial process that others enjoy.

What equality-related work is left for the Equal Protection Clause? Quite a bit, it turns out. And the clause today does both more and less work than its original meaning entails. We provide an account of how it can be given full effect.

THE LETTER   First, the original meaning of "the equal protection of the laws" requires the impartial enforcement of the laws by state executive branch officials. It is not enough that laws be nondiscriminatory on their face or that adjudications be fair; the executive branch of government must *take action* to enforce these laws and bring people who violate the rights of others to justice.

For example, there might be a perfectly good murder statute on the books, which when prosecuted is heard by impeccably neutral judges and juries. But were the local sheriff to refuse to enforce that law when certain people are the victims—as when Blacks were lynched by racist mobs for decades following Lee's surrender—this would be a denial of the equal *protection* of otherwise valid laws.

This example brings to the fore a fundamental difference between the Equal Protection of the Laws Clause and the Privileges or Immunities and Due Process of Law Clauses. Whereas the latter two clauses only bar a type of state action, the Equal Protection of the Laws Clause also imposes an affirmative *duty* on state governments to *act*. This, then, calls into question an important doctrine of modern constitutional law known as the "State Action Doctrine." This doctrine limits the scope of Section 1 to *actions* taken by state governments; inaction by a state is not a violation of any of its clauses. And actions by private actors are not restricted by Section 1.

As we explain in Part III, the original meaning of the Equal Protection of the Laws Clause requires the state to act to protect the rights of all persons from being violated by others—including by private actors. It is a deprivation of the equal protection of the laws for state actors to look the other way when private actors are violating the civil rights of others. In this regard, current constitutional doctrine conflicts with the original meaning of "the equal protection of the laws."

Some scholars have argued that the original scope of the Equal Protection of the Laws Clause was limited to the provision of protection by the executive branch of state governments. We explain why the "equal protection *of the laws*" also entitles people to equal access to security-protective state statutes and to any protection for life, liberty, and property afforded to people

INTRODUCTION   35

by federal statutes. That is to say, the duty of protection also includes the duty to provide people with equal access to the remedial processes of the courts and to refrain from enacting discriminatory laws that unreasonably leave the personal security of some people more uncertain than that of others. In serving both these functions, to some degree, the Equal Protection Clause overlaps the Privileges or Immunities and Due Process of Law Clauses. The three clauses are not hermetically sealed. Their overlap or redundancy is a feature, not a bug, of the Fourteenth Amendment.

THE SPIRIT   The affirmative duty to provide the "protection of the laws" can be traced back to the social contract theory of government associated with John Locke. People consent to leave the state of nature and enter civil society in return for better protection of their rights than they can achieve on their own. They cash in their power to enforce their natural rights for themselves in return for the "civil right" of government protection of their preexisting fundamental rights. A failure of protection is, therefore, a breach of that social contract.

The reciprocal relation of a person's allegiance in return for the protection of his or her government was a major theme of the abolitionist constitutionalism that informed the drafting, ratifying, and public meaning of the Fourteenth Amendment. Absent such protection, people are *subjugated*. Their lives, bodies, and possessions are left to the untrammeled will of others, over whom they lack control. Enslaved people, free Blacks, and their white allies knew this subjugation well.

With this anti-subjugation spirit in mind, we turn to how it may best be implemented. Modern doctrine limits the scope of Section 1 of the Fourteenth Amendment to state action. That is, Section 1 is said only to bar discrimination by state actors and to have nothing to say about the actions of private actors. As a result, modern doctrine denies that state governments have any affirmative "duty to act" to provide protection against private actors.

When it comes to the Privileges or Immunities and the Due Process of Law Clauses, we think this state action doctrine is correct. These clauses are rightly understood as limited to constraining state action. But it is wholly incompatible with the letter of the Equal Protection of the Laws Clause, which bars the *denial* of "protection." It is incompatible as well with the anti-subjugation spirit of the clause, which concerns the duty of government both to provide and enforce the civil rights that are necessary to protecting a person's natural rights. In sum, the State Action Doctrine should not be applied to limit the scope of the Equal Protection of the Laws Clause.

Having said this, we also acknowledge that the Supreme Court's concerns about judges enforcing such a duty on the states are not without merit. Rather than deny the existence of a *constitutional* duty of protection by the state, however, we urge the Court to acknowledge that it is "under-enforcing" this duty due to the inherent limitations of the judiciary. Such a recognition would then free Congress to use its Section 5 enforcement powers to establish statutory schemes by which parties who are denied protection by their states can seek remedies in federal court. Under current doctrine, Congress is largely barred from doing so. This brings us to the enumerated enforcement power of Congress under Section 5.

Section 5: The Enforcement Clause

The Congress shall have the power to enforce, by appropriate legislation, the provisions of this article.

Section 5 empowers Congress to enforce the rest of the Fourteenth Amendment. We will see in Part I that John Bingham's initial proposal for a constitutional amendment was limited to creating a power in Congress to enforce civil rights. This proposal was criticized as both over- and under-inclusive. It was over-inclusive insofar as it appeared to give to Congress a plenary police power that would supersede or supplant that of the states. It was under-inclusive because future Congresses might not be so protective of civil rights, in which case a constitutional amendment was required that itself imposed nonrepealable, judicially enforceable duties on states.

After Bingham revised his proposal to meet these challenges, the congressional empowerment aspect of Bingham's original proposal was preserved by the addition of Section 5. Section 5 created a new enumerated congressional power to enforce the rest of the Fourteenth Amendment. For our purposes, its most important aspect was the power to enforce the guarantees in Section 1.

Modern Supreme Court doctrine has limited Congress's remedial power to legislative measures that are "congruent and proportional" to the scope of the rights in Section 1. We concur that the scope of the clauses being enforced defines the limits of such a remedial power. But the Court's failure to recognize the full scope of the original meaning of Section 1—especially the scope of the Equal Protection of the Laws Clause—has had the effect of un-duly restricting Congress's power under Section 5.

Furthermore, the Supreme Court has sometimes restricted the scope of Section 1 out of concerns about the competence of the judiciary to impose affirmative duties on the states. By denying that the original scope of the clause is broader than what *the courts* can competently enforce, however, the Court also denies that *Congress* may constitutionally act where the courts justifiably fear to tread.

In *United States v. Morrison,* the Supreme Court held that Congress may not use its Section 5 power to establish a federal cause of action for gender-motivated violence committed by private parties. The law in question was the Violence Against Women Act. This act was supported by extensive leg-islative fact-finding showing that some states had neglected the equal pro-tection of women in their states. The act did not, however, command states to do what Congress thought was lacking. That would have raised constitu-tional concerns of its own. Instead, Congress addressed this unequal enforce-ment by providing federal remedies to be available in federal courts.

This was the very same tack taken by Congress when it enacted Section 3 of the Civil Rights Act of 1866. That section gave defendants a right to re-move a civil or criminal case from state to federal court when state court procedures failed to protect the civil rights protected by Section 1 of the act. *Strauder v. West Virginia* upheld this right of removal in 1880—an all-too-rare bright spot in the history of the Supreme Court's steady undermining of the original meaning of the Fourteenth Amendment, which began soon after its enactment.

Congress used the same means of protecting civil rights in the Civil Rights Act of 1875, which barred private discrimination with respect to public ac-commodations. Rather than mandate that states enforce these state common-law duties, Congress created a federal cause of action to enforce them in federal court. But this time, the Court invalidated the laws. In its 1883 deci-sion in *The Civil Rights Cases,* the Court did so by invoking the State Action Doctrine that it had previously articulated in *United States v. Cruikshank.*

It took ninety years for Congress to again bar discrimination in public ac-commodations in the Civil Rights Act of 1964. Due to the precedents of *The Civil Rights Cases* and *Cruikshank,* however, the Court upheld the act as an exercise of Congress's commerce power rather than its Section 5 powers under the Fourteenth Amendment. We think this shift of clauses unduly narrowed the scope of civil rights—while at the same time unduly expanding the scope of Congress's power to regulate commerce among the several states. This is yet another example of why it is important to base salutary constitutional doctrines on the right clauses.

In Chapter 13, we reconsider the constitutional merits of such congressionally created remedial schemes in light of the letter and the spirit of the Equal Protection of the Laws Clause. We conclude that such remedies are more properly warranted by Congress's Section 5 powers than by its power to regulate commerce among the several states.

* * *

These highlights of what will be covered in depth in this book reveal that a failure to appreciate the original meaning of the Fourteenth Amendment has led the Supreme Court into serious errors of omission and commission. Either the Court fails to enforce the requirements of the amendment itself, or it bars Congress from using its enumerated power of enforcement to do what the courts are not competent to do. Moreover, where the Court has eventually come to the right result on the basis of nonoriginalist reasoning, doing it this way has undermined the legitimacy of its doctrines and left them vulnerable.

Finally, where the Court relies on nonoriginalist reasoning to reach compelling results in cases such as *Brown v. Board of Education,* the perceived inability of originalism to justify these results is used to undermine the legitimacy of interpreting the Constitution according to its original meaning. And a failure to appreciate how originalism does support these results, in turn, has led to widespread academic criticisms of the Constitution itself.

For all these reasons, we must get our constitutional house in order. It is vital that we get the original meaning of the letter of the Constitution right. Then, when formulating doctrines to implement that meaning, it is vital that courts identify and faithfully adhere to the original spirit of the text. Assisting them in this endeavor is what we aim to accomplish with this book.

PART I

THE PRIVILEGES OR IMMUNITIES OF CITIZENSHIP CLAUSE

1

The Early Origins of Privileges
or Immunities

FEW, IF ANY, provisions in the Constitution of the United States have received both more attention from scholars and less attention from the nation's highest Court than the Privileges or Immunities Clause of the Fourteenth Amendment. What Justice Antonin Scalia disparaged as "the darling of the professoriate"[1] has been the subject of countless articles and books spanning thousands of pages.[2] But it contributes next to nothing to contemporary law.

The dominant view among scholars is that the Supreme Court erred disastrously in either the *Slaughter-House Cases*,[3] *United States v. Cruikshank*,[4] or both cases by holding that the clause protected only a handful of rights associated with citizens' interactions with the federal government and by denying that the clause "incorporated" the personal rights set forth in the first eight amendments against the states. Yet, until its 1999 decision in *Saenz v. Roe*,[5] the Court did not even once invoke the Privileges or Immunities Clause to hold state legislation unconstitutional.[6]

In 2010, a plurality of the Court in *McDonald v. City of Chicago*[7] declined an express invitation to revisit *Slaughter-House* or *Cruikshank*. Instead, it relied on the Fourteenth Amendment's Due Process of Law Clause in holding that the right to keep and bear arms was enforceable against the states. However, the fifth and deciding vote by Justice Clarence Thomas relied exclusively on the original meaning of the Privileges or Immunities Clause. His pivotal opinion is the clause's most significant appearance to date.

In *Timbs v. Indiana*,[8] the Court unanimously held that the Excessive Fines Clause of the Eighth Amendment was applicable to the states. Justice Ruth

Bader Ginsburg's opinion for the Court did not engage the question of whether the Privileges or Immunities Clause would be a more textually appropriate vehicle. Once again, Justice Thomas relied solely on the clause. While Justice Gorsuch expressed sympathy for that stance, he concurred in Justice Ginsburg's Due Process of Law Clause–based conclusion, as did Justice Brett Kavanaugh.

What accounts for this asymmetry of interest? Part of the problem appears to be that the Court is unsure about what the Privileges or Immunities Clause means. In his opinion for the Court in *McDonald*, Justice Samuel Alito highlighted the lack of "any consensus" concerning the clause's "full scope" among scholars "who agree that the *Slaughter-House Cases*' interpretation is flawed."[9] Another part of the problem may be that the justices are worried that its meaning will not lend itself to clear, predictable doctrine. Such worries were expressed by Justice Scalia at oral argument in *McDonald*.[10]

A third potential concern involves the legitimacy of judicially protecting unenumerated rights. It is feared that acknowledging the original meaning of the Privileges or Immunities Clause will legitimate the judicial protection of unenumerated rights in a way that the Court's reading of the Due Process of Law Clause does not. On this view, it is the illegitimacy of using the Due Process of Law Clause to judicially protect any unenumerated substantive rights that justifies limiting its scope. Once it is conceded that the Privileges or Immunities Clause legitimately protects unenumerated rights, these limits would be undermined. So it is best to let sleeping clauses lie.

Moreover, despite the consensus that the Supreme Court erred in *Slaughter-House*, scholars are divided concerning not only the details but the basic content of the Privileges or Immunities Clause. Among the leading theories of the clause are these:

- The clause requires only that every state give the same positive-law rights—of contract, property, and the like—to all of its citizens.[11]
- The clause protects only individual rights that are enumerated in the first eight amendments.[12]
- The clause protects all individual rights that are enumerated anywhere in the text of the Constitution, but no unenumerated individual rights.[13]
- The clause protects positive-law rights that are widely extended to citizens by states today; "outlier" states must be brought into line.[14]
- The clause forbids states from discriminating against out-of-state citizens because of their out-of-state citizenship—and nothing more.[15]

None of these theories can be dismissed out of hand. All of them, however, cannot be correct, and they can generate importantly different outcomes. The generally applicable Chicago handgun ban held unconstitutional in *McDonald*, for instance, would have been sustained had Justice Thomas adopted an anti-discrimination-only theory and sided with the four dissenters.

Uncertainty about the substance of privileges or immunities is nothing new. As Ohio Senator John Sherman observed in 1872, "There may be sometimes great dispute and doubt as to what is the right, immunity, or privilege conferred upon a citizen of the United States."[16] But the existence of dispute does not preclude the existence of right answers—or at least answers that are more likely to be right than others.

In Part I, we provide an account of the original meaning of the clause that is both novel and judicially administrable. We then offer a prescription for its implementation that is tailored to the unique doctrinal circumstances that the Court confronts today. We will contend that the clause can neither be fully understood nor be implemented without a firm grasp of a particular conception of United States citizenship—a conception that was part of the constitutional common sense on which Republicans in the Thirty-Ninth Congress, and those who ratified their handiwork into law, relied. We refer to this conception as *Republican citizenship.*

We argue that the original meaning—the "letter"—of the Privileges or Immunities Clause protects civil rights that are deemed fundamental to Republican citizenship. The category of "civil rights" includes (1) the fundamental rights found in the positive law, the legal enforcement of which is essential to securing a citizen's natural rights from abridgment by government and nongovernment actors, and (2) the rights to post-political goods that one is entitled to receive from a polity as a citizen of that polity. We contend that the original meaning of the clause "locked in" civil rights that were deemed fundamental to Republican citizenship in 1868. Among the civil rights in category 2 was the right of similarly situated citizens to equality in the public sphere.

Rights that are clearly "in" the category of civil rights when the Fourteenth Amendment was enacted include (a) the personal guarantees enumerated in the first eight amendments, (b) personal rights specified elsewhere in the Constitution, (c) personal rights specified in the Civil Rights Act of 1866, and (d) personal rights that were widespread and entrenched in state law in 1868. But, while all these rights were locked in by the original meaning of "the privileges or immunities of citizens of the United States," the set of privileges or immunities protected by this clause was not closed. The original meaning of the clause also empowered Congress and the federal courts to safeguard rights that might become a "privilege or immunity" of Republican citizenship in the future.

While the original meaning of "privileges or immunities" of US citizens included such later-developing rights, the precise identity of these rights is not fully specified by the constitutional text. In Chapter 8, we will turn to the original function, or "spirit," of the clause to provide criteria by which rights that have become privileges or immunities of national citizenship since 1868 can be identified. We will draw on the criteria provided by Justice Bushrod Washington in his landmark opinion in *Corfield v. Coryell*. One example of a right that later became a privilege of American citizenship is the right of suffrage. We then provide guidance to reviewing courts and legislators to aid with the clause's implementation in difficult cases. Our proposed construction of the Privileges or Immunities Clause closely resembles the historical approach taken by the Court in substantive due process cases such as *Washington v. Glucksburg*.

Our Sources

The terms "privileges" and "immunities" appear in countless documents over the course of centuries' worth of Anglo-American law. The original meaning of these particular words in the Privileges or Immunities Clause cannot be identified by considering their meaning in isolation. The clause speaks of privileges or immunities of a particular kind—privileges or immunities "of citizens of the United States." To bring in usages of privileges or immunities that were unconnected to *citizenship*, therefore, is to risk giving undue weight to irrelevant materials. We therefore limit our inquiry to usage of privileges and immunities in connection with citizenship.

Pre-Ratification Statements

Public meaning originalists who are skeptical of the reliability of legislative history when interpreting statutes have been taken to task for their focus on statements made during the Philadelphia Convention and the Thirty-Ninth Congress when interpreting the Constitution.[17] If legislators are capable of filling the record with self-serving statements concerning textual meaning designed to capture through later litigation what they could not get through the lawmaking process, surely so too were constitutional framers. Why have any more confidence in framing history than ordinary legislative history?

To begin with, not even the most ardent opponents of judicial recourse to legislative history deny that it might yield term usage that is probative of public meaning.[18] If the legislative record provides evidence that a particular term is being used by members of different political coalitions in much the same way, that is different from crediting a single legislator's potentially self-serving floor statement concerning his understanding of that term. It suggests—though it does not alone establish—the existence of a settled meaning that the term then carried. The same can be said concerning term usage by framers of a constitutional provision.

Further, in the context of the framing of the Fourteenth Amendment, many legislative statements were widely publicized. They thus may have shaped the public's understanding of its language, notwithstanding that those statements may have been self-serving. Even if Alexander Hamilton and James Madison were not entirely forthright when representing their understanding of the proposed, unamended Constitution, those who ratified it in reliance on Publius's commentary in *The Federalist Papers* may have effectively incorporated those representations into the law of the land.

To affect the public meaning of the text, however, those representations must have been widely disseminated. While this may or may not have been the actual case with *The Federalist Papers,* the speeches and debates about the Privileges or Immunities Clause we will discuss were widely disseminated. Thus, while we will not neglect the legislative history of the Privileges or Immunities Clause, our focus will be on widely publicized floor statements. When there is reason to believe that statements are not reliable, we will say so.

One thing we will not do is speculate about what the ratified text must have been understood to entail, or not entail, for it to be ratified into law. We have in mind here speculation about whether any text could have passed through the Article V process that, properly understood, required the desegregation of schools, or forbade states from excluding Blacks from juries, or required women to be admitted to their state bars. This type of reasoning pervaded Raoul Berger's 1977 book, *Government by Judiciary: The Transformation of the Fourteenth Amendment.*

Where advocates or opponents of the Fourteenth Amendment speak directly to what the text does or does not require concerning particularly controversial issues, we will consider the context, including the identity and reliability of the speaker, and consider any response or debate that it engendered.

We are cautious about the use of such evidence for several reasons. As we will see, the decision-making process that produced the Fourteenth Amendment was positively dizzying in its complexity. The range of possible outcomes of any complex collective decision-making process is extraordinarily difficult to specify.[19] That an amendment *clearly* requiring a profoundly controversial outcome would likely have been rejected does not justify the inference that an amendment which more *obscurely* required the same outcome would have met a similar fate.[20] Lastly, it is an undeniable fact that congressional Republicans were able to pass legislation and ratify amendments that were profoundly controversial during the course of Reconstruction.[21]

Because it is counterintuitive, the last of these points should be stressed. Southern states were absent from Congress, which resulted in the numerical dominance of the stridently antislavery Republican Party in both the House and Senate. This meant that civil rights laws could be enacted, and constitutional amendments proposed, with language and consequences that might be very unpopular with the general public. For example, the Fifteenth Amendment expressly prohibited racial discrimination with respect to the right (of males) to vote, even though African American suffrage was very unpopular. Therefore, the bare fact that a particular application of the far more abstract Privileges or Immunities, Due Process of Law, or Equal Protection of the Laws Clauses might have been unpopular with the public does not preclude a conclusion that the victors in a long and bloody civil war adopted text, the public meaning of which supported such an application.

Post-Ratification Statements

It is common methodological practice among originalists to prioritize pre-enactment over post-enactment usage of constitutional terms in ascertaining their original meaning. The reasons for this are threefold.

First, language undergoes diachronic change—its meaning changes over time.[22] (A good constitutional example is "domestic violence" in Article IV,[23] which obviously did not originally mean abuse in a household setting.) Even those present when words or phrases are ratified into law and who are acting in good faith may use those words or phrases at a later date in ways that they themselves would have previously regarded as out of bounds. It may become increasingly difficult to keep track of the contours of the original concept denoted by a word or phrase, particularly as political, social, legal, and economic environments change in dramatic ways and discourse changes as a consequence. Eventually, the original concept may be replaced by one that is subtly but importantly different.

Second, the costs to lawmakers of pushing linguistic boundaries are higher during the ratification process when a proposal can still be defeated than they are post-ratification after adoption is secured. As a result, it is easier for people to expand those boundaries post-ratification. It is true that those who push linguistic boundaries either pre- or post-ratification do so at the risk of objections or vetoes from those who recognize that they are breaking the rules of the existing language game. But it is easier to convince a majority of legislators or a court to accept an out-of-bounds interpretation than it is to convince a congressional supermajority *and* a supermajority of the states to do so.

Third, legislators can be carried away by the exigencies of the political moment. If the effect of the framing process is to encourage one to think about the long term and to take into account considerations of constitutional fidelity, the effect of the ordinary legislative process may be to focus on the short term and neglect the latter considerations.[24]

Nevertheless, we will consider post-ratification commentary and practice for two reasons. First, those who interpret and implement constitutional text shortly after its enactment can be presumed to be far more familiar with the discursive context than even the most informed students of the relevant history. When broad swaths of contemporaneous constitutional decision-makers endorse a constitutional proposition after thorough consideration, those who would deny that proposition ought to shoulder the burden of explaining why those decision-makers were wrong.

That is not to say that contemporaneous interpreters of constitutional language cannot be wrong. It is to say that, in the language of administrative law, their interpretations "constitute a body of experience and informed judgment to which [subsequent interpreters] may properly resort for guidance" and that the weight that any given interpretation should receive ought to "depend upon the thoroughness evident in its consideration, the validity of its reasoning, its consistency with earlier and later pronouncements, and all those factors which give it power to persuade, if lacking power to control."[25]

Second, there is *far* more, and far more precise, post-ratification than pre-ratification commentary concerning the meaning of the Privileges or Immunities Clause.[26] If this commentary were much less reliable than pre-ratification commentary, it might be better to ignore it. But a great deal of these statements appear to spring from a thorough consideration and are consistent with pre-ratification pronouncements.

Now that readers know how and why we consider evidence of original meaning the way we do, let us examine this evidence.

Privileges, Immunities, and Citizenship in the Early Republic

Before there were American citizens, there were British subjects, with rights that attached to subjectship. These "rights of Englishmen" were described in terms of natural and positive law. They were deemed to be both the fruit of inferences about human nature that were valid everywhere and always *and* the particular inheritance of British people that was embedded in British statutes and jurisprudence.

But the privileges and immunities that came to be associated with American citizenship in the early Republic weren't just the rights of Englishmen. Crucially, British authorities increasingly found it attractive to adopt a flexible approach to subjectship that enabled them to adjust subjects' rights as the perceived needs of empire required. By contrast, Americans reacted by affirming an unstratified citizenship that did not admit of adjustments. As we will show below, however, British and American lawyers shared common normative and methodological premises and reached similar conclusions about what the privileges and immunities of subjectship and citizenship were.

British Law

BLACKSTONE'S *COMMENTARIES*   The influence of Sir William Blackstone's *Commentaries on the Laws of England* on the Founding generation is well documented. It is uncontroversial that "most American lawyers began their legal education with Blackstone and the common law."[27] At the same time, it is also clear that Americans departed from Blackstone in certain important regards, particularly when it came to his conception of parliamentary supremacy[28] and the freedom of speech.[29] Blackstone's extensive discussion of the "civil privileges" and "private immunities" of British subjects thus merits extended but sensitive consideration.

As was common practice among jurists both on and off the bench, Blackstone's *Commentaries* began by laying political-philosophical foundations. Blackstone detailed how the law of England secures the "absolute rights of every Englishman."[30] He claimed that the rights are both "founded in nature and reason" *and* "coeval with our form of government," even if they are at times "subject to fluctuation and change."[31] What appear at first to be contradictory origin stories—nature and reason on the one hand, the British form of government on the other—are, on closer examination, compatible.

In a particularly relevant passage, Blackstone wrote that the rights of the people of England

> consist in a number of *private immunities;* which will appear, from what has been premised, to be indeed no other, than either that residuum of natural liberty, which is not required by the laws of society to be sacrificed to public convenience; or else those *civil privileges,* which society hath engaged to provide, in lieu of the natural liberties so given up by individuals.[32]

British subjects surrendered some, but not all, of their natural rights or "immunities" in return for certain civil rights or "privileges" that provide more effective security of their "natural inherent right[s]" than they could enjoy "in a state of nature."[33] This was a good deal because, on Blackstone's account, "most other countries in the world" were "debased and destroyed" and did not provide such security.

How did Blackstone define these natural rights? He "reduce[d]" these rights to "three principal or primary articles: the right of personal security, the right of personal liberty, and the right of private property."[34] The preservation of these through civil law, Blackstone explained, "may justly be said to include the preservation of our *civil immunities* in their largest and most extensive sense."[35]

We can appreciate now why the privileges thus secured by British law can be said to be *both* "strictly natural" *and* "in a peculiar and emphatical manner, the rights of the people of England."[36] Whether via the Magna Carta, other statutes, or the common law, British law "regards, asserts, and preserves" by tried-and-true positive-law guarantees, natural rights that are neglected by the positive law of "most other countries of the world."

Eric Claeys has shown that Blackstone used the terms "privileges" and "immunities" to "refer to positive laws that secure natural rights, especially rights that connect directly to the moral rights of life, liberty, or property," but that he did not use them to refer to those underlying moral rights themselves.[37] Thus, Blackstone cast privileges and immunities as civil rights, which are "rights-securing legal protections that may properly be reserved for the special enjoyment of citizens who pledge their allegiance to the republican political community."[38] That is not to say that non-subjects lacked any rights—only that it was not considered unreasonable to exclude them from certain positive-law protections that were afforded to subjects alone.

Claeys also elucidated the distinction Blackstone drew between privileges, on the one hand, and immunities, on the other. Claeys identified two sets of "civil immunities."[39] The first, called "civil privileges," were "entitlements that replicate in positive law the general substance of natural rights."[40] The second, called "private immunities," were "the domains of noninterference English subjects enjoy as residual rights to do that which is not prohibited by particular civil laws."[41] Both were in some sense the product of positive law. One set of rights consisted of affirmative positive-law protections for natural freedoms; the other set consisted of those natural freedoms that positive law did not take away and were thus retained by the people.

In sum, persons leave the state of nature and enter into civil society to receive the "civil privilege" of better positive-law protections of their "private immunities," such as their rights of personal security, personal liberty, and private property, than they can provide on their own. They are then entitled as citizens to the positive-law protections provided by their government of the natural rights they possess as persons. Whatever private immunities as are not necessary to be surrendered in return for the civil privilege of positive-law protections of their natural freedoms are retained by the citizenry.

We will be examining American usage of "privileges or immunities of citizens of the United States" in detail. For now, Blackstone provides us with helpful privileges and immunities heuristics—ready-to-hand concepts that help us understand what privileges and immunities meant in the early Republic.

THE RIGHTS OF BRITISH SUBJECTS   Of course, as is the case today, the term "privileges" did not always mean rights that belonged to private citizens. For example, Blackstone referred to the "privileges" of Parliament, including those enjoyed by members against royal oppression;[42] the "privileges" of the clergy, including the exemption from jury duty;[43] the "privileges" of the lords, including that of hunting in the king's forests;[44] the "privileges" of the commons, including that of framing taxes;[45] and the "privileges" of corporations, including that of establishing by-laws.[46]

When used to refer to the rights of British subjects, however, "privileges" and "immunities" consistently served as "placeholders for substantive positive law rights that Englishmen enjoy by virtue of being Englishmen."[47] That "privileges" and "immunities" of British subjects were positive-law rights protecting the natural liberties of the subject helps explain why they were thought to be *both* the peculiar rights of Englishmen *and* a protection of the natural rights of all persons. As we will see, a similar duality pertaining to citizenship was imported into the Privileges or Immunities Clause.

THE EQUAL RIGHTS OF ENGLISHMEN IN THE COLONIES   References to both privileges and immunities saturate American colonial charters that ensured that colonists carried the rights of Englishmen with them through territories under the dominion of the Crown. As American colonists came to see it, to be a British subject was thus to be entitled to be treated equally with respect to all other similarly situated subjects, including subjects in mainland England.[48] Inequality of treatment in respect of the privileges and immunities of subjectship was among the primary causes of Revolutionary-era complaints against the king and Parliament.

The American colonial experience encouraged the development of an understanding of equal subjectship that gradually diverged from that held in Whitehall. Aziz Rana has shown that, as the British Empire grew and became more culturally diverse, mainland authorities took an increasingly pragmatic, flexible view of the kinds of substantive rights to which subjects were entitled.[49]

For instance, the Quebec Act of 1774, which created a new, permanent government in Canada in the wake of the French and Indian War, retained French civil and property laws that did not—as did British law—include jury rights or exclude Catholics from public office.[50] Being that Quebec's Catholic population was neither trained in British law nor keen on being excluded from the new government, this was—in the eyes of mainland authorities—merely sensible management of an imperial order that needed to accommodate local customs and sensibilities if it did not want restive subjects.[51] It was not some conspiracy against the rights of *all* British subjects.

In contrast, American colonists had developed a conception of unstratified subjectship, the substantive contours of which they considered nonnegotiable and equally applicable to all subjects. They saw the absence of common-law procedural rights as an intolerable assault on basic principles of British freedom that portended a plan to enslave them.[52] What led colonists to thus diverge from mainland England?

Under the imperial policy of "salutary neglect," colonists had long enjoyed relative freedom from metropolitan oversight. They organized responsive representative legislative bodies and established justices of the peace who followed common-law norms.[53] Many of them had endured the difficulties of migration—often forced—and carved out a livelihood for themselves under extraordinarily arduous conditions. For this reason, they considered that they had "earned" their freedom the Lockean way—by mixing their labor with the land and by establishing representative institutions that were conducive to their economic and political independence.[54] Only a subset of property owners in mainland England enjoyed access to such institutions as the colonists had built.

Further, American colonists were surrounded by communities of Native Americans and enslaved Africans. Many colonists regarded members of these communities as unfit for economic and political independence. Those deemed unfit were dispossessed of their lands and denied some or any of the privileges of subjectship.[55] Colonists, therefore, did not need to strain their imagination to envision the condition of people who were dominated by an external will over which they had no effective control; and they were terrified of being reduced to that condition. Their persistent references to their own potential "servitude" or "slavery" at the hands of the Crown and Parliament are testimony to that awareness.

American Revolutionary Usage

The metropolitan policy of neglect ended with the defeat of France in the Seven Years' War when Parliament in 1765 imposed taxes on newspapers, playing cards, and legal documents. The Stamp Act required that legal documents and printed materials must bear a tax stamp provided by commissioned distributors who would collect the tax in exchange for the stamp. American colonists charged the Crown and Parliament with depriving them of their privileges and immunities as British subjects in two principal ways: first, by depriving them of lawmaking powers that were recognized in their colonial charters; second, by depriving them of individual rights.

An example of the first: In one of the earliest and most incisive critiques of the Stamp Act, Maryland lawyer Daniel Dulany wrote in 1767 that "[b]y their constitutions of government, the colonies are empowered to impose internal taxes" and described these "powers" as "privileges and immunities."[56] Although Dulany initially described these powers as having been "conferred," he quickly corrected himself and stated that they "necessarily belong[ed] to [the colonists] as British subjects" and were thus "solemnly declared and confirmed by their charters."[57]

An example of the second: Massachusetts lawyer and legislator James Otis, in the course of arguing against the legality of writs of assistance in 1761, described "the freedom of one's house" as a "privilege."[58] It was, Otis claimed, "one of the most essential branches of English liberty."[59]

In formal resolutions, Americans insisted on equality in respect of privileges and immunities with other British subjects. A 1765 Massachusetts resolution averred that Americans were "entitled to all the rights, liberties, and immunities of free and natural subjects of Great Britain."[60] A 1774 resolution from Georgia claimed that Americans were entitled to "the same rights, privileges, and immunities with their fellow subjects in Great Britain."[61] The resolves of the First Continental Congress demanded "all the rights, liberties, and immunities of free English subjects."[62]

Importantly, however, Americans did not necessarily conceive of their privileges and immunities in a legally conventional way. Michael Kent Curtis focuses attention on the Address of the Continental Congress to the Inhabitants of Quebec in 1774.[63] The address described the "inestimable advantages of a free English constitution of government, which it is the privilege of all English subjects to enjoy." It lamented that the king's ministers "would so audaciously and cruelly abuse the royal authority, as to withhold from you the fruition of the irrevocable rights, to which you were thus justly entitled."[64] Among the rights listed as secured by the British constitution was "the freedom of the press," which was said to encompass the "diffusion of liberal sentiments on the administration of Government."[65] Americans knew full well that the law of seditious libel had been used to suppress such sentiments; they did not care.

Historians have also documented the revolutionaries' transition from the rights of Englishmen to natural rights as English authorities rejected revolutionaries' appeals to "the principles of the English constitution."[66] That transition was not merely rhetorical. It reflected an ideological transformation that, as Eric Foner put it, "formed the essence of American nationalism."[67]

Revolutionaries came to regard their struggle as a universal rather than parochial one—a struggle against domination and for economic and political independence as such, for all people in all places.[68] This universalism had consequences. Almost immediately, it began to undermine the perceived legitimacy of existing institutions—such as chattel slavery—that were thought to subject people to arbitrary power.[69] It very soon led Northern states to adopt measures abolishing slavery at varying rates, and even to fledgling—though ultimately unsuccessful—antislavery movements in the South.[70]

The significance of the move from subjectship to citizenship should not, however, be overstated. The mingling of natural and customary rights–based claims was an eighteenth-century habit in England, Germany, and colonial North America.[71] The "rights of Englishmen" were never thought to be distinctively British—even by Blackstone—solely on account of their being protected by British political authority. Rather, they were thought to be distinctively British both because they were protected by British authorities *and* because the British experience had shown that they "worked" to secure natural rights.

Americans did not want to replace the privileges and immunities of subjectship with an entirely different set of privileges and immunities. Rather, as the Declaration of Independence affirmed, the natural individual rights of the people were unalienable, but allegiance to any particular government "to secure these rights" was subject to "the consent of the governed." Whenever "any Form of Government becomes destructive of these ends" of securing the natural rights of the people, "it is the Right of the People to alter or to abolish it, and to institute new Government."

Framing Privileges and Immunities at the Founding

Article IV of the 1781 Articles of Confederation contained a verbose precursor of what would become the Privileges and Immunities Clause in Article 4, Section 2, Clause 1 of the federal Constitution:

> The better to secure and perpetuate mutual friendship and intercourse among the people of the different states in this union, *the free inhabitants* of each of these states (paupers, vagabonds, and fugitives from justice, excepted) shall be entitled to all *privileges and immunities of free citizens in the several states;* and the people of each state shall have free ingress and regress to and from any other state, and shall enjoy therein all the privileges of trade and commerce, subject to the same duties, impositions, and restrictions, as the inhabitants thereof respectively. Provided that such restriction shall not extend so far as to prevent the removal of property imported into any state to any other state of which the owner is an inhabitant; provided also, that no imposition, duties, or restriction, shall be laid by any state on the property of the United States, or either of them.[72]

Article IV of the 1788 Constitution is not only more succinct than its precursor but differs from it in important respects:

> The Citizens of each State shall be entitled to all privileges and immunities of citizens in the several States.[73]

The preamble to Article IV of the Articles of Confederation announces its spirit or goal: to "better . . . secure and perpetuate mutual friendship and intercourse among the people of the different states in this union." The means by which Article IV was to achieve that end was by guaranteeing "all privileges and immunities of free citizens" and by barring parochial discrimination in respect of travel and trade. British "subjects" have now become "free citizens."

Whereas all "free *inhabitants*" could claim the "privileges and immunities of free citizens" under the Articles, they could not do so under the Constitution. The change was suggested by John Rutledge of South Carolina, the proslavery representative of the convention's most proslavery state delegation, during the work of the Committee of Detail.[74]

The committee, which deliberated from May 25 until July 23, 1787, assigned to Edmund Randolph of Virginia the task of making an initial outline of the Constitution. The outline did not include a privileges and immunities clause. Rutledge added the following language quite obviously cribbed from the Articles: "The free (inhabs) Citizens of each State shall be entitled to all Privileges & Immunities of free Citizens in the sevl States."[75]

Later, South Carolina delegates Pierce Butler and Charles Pinckney would move to add a clause that would "require fugitive slaves and servants to be delivered up like criminals."[76] As will be discussed at greater length below in the context of the Fugitive Slave Clause of Article IV, this proposal would have negated the principle established in England by the 1772 *Somerset* case.[77] This case held that slavery is contrary to natural right and, therefore, could only be established through positive law. Some derived from this the conclusion that slaves became emancipated if they made it to a free state.[78]

In another respect, however, Article IV of the Constitution was more egalitarian than its precursor. It removed the exclusion of "paupers" and "vagabonds," thus ensuring that the enjoyment of the privileges and immunities of citizenship was not tied to financial status. The Article's exclusion for fugitives from justice was also removed.

Finally, the specific guarantees of "free ingress and regress to and from any other State" and "all the privileges of trade and commerce, subject to the same duties, impositions, and restrictions as the inhabitants thereof respectively" were not retained. Given widespread agreement concerning the importance of commercial comity, it seems unlikely that this change sprang from a newfound tolerance of economic protectionism by the states.[79] More plausibly, it was driven by the conviction that Congress already had power over interstate commerce that it could use to thwart interstate protectionism and therefore only state discrimination in internal affairs needed to be addressed.[80]

Public discussion of the Privileges and Immunities Clause was limited. What discussion did take place evinced a concern with comity—with both guaranteeing the equal treatment of citizens and permitting the unequal treatment of noncitizens. In Federalist 42, James Madison disparaged the "confusion of language" in Article IV's precursor and confessed surprise that the confusion had not led to "serious embarrassments."[81] He pointed out that the precursor seemed to leave open the possibility that "those who come under the denomination of free inhabitants of a State, although not citizens of such State, are entitled, in every other State, to all the privileges of free citizens of the latter."[82]

Even if one understood "free inhabitants" to denote only "free citizens," problems could arise. One state could naturalize noncitizens in every state through permissive citizenship rules, thus generating conflict with objecting states. Alexander Hamilton in Federalist 80 characterized the clause as forming "the basis of the union" and as guaranteeing an "equality of privileges and immunities to which the citizens of the Union would be entitled."[83] Notably, he mistranscribed the clause thus: "[T]he citizens of each State shall be entitled to all . . . privileges and immunities of citizens *of* the several States."[84]

Textually, the "in" in the Privileges or Immunities Clause could be read to denote the location of citizens who were entitled to enjoy certain freestanding privileges and immunities—namely, in the several states. Or it could be read to denote the source of their citizenship—namely, the several states. Or it could be read to denote both location and source.

Under the first reading, the clause would protect citizens *of the United States* when they traveled throughout—or "in"—the several states: "[T]he citizens of each State shall be entitled to all . . . privileges and immunities of *[US] citizens* [when traveling] in the several States." Under the second reading, the clause would protect citizens *of particular states* when they traveled across state lines: "[T]he *citizens of each State* shall be entitled to all . . .

privileges and immunities of citizens [of] the several States [in which they are traveling]." On the first reading, US citizenship blessed one with a distinct set of privileges or immunities that US citizens took with them when sojourning in other states. On the second reading, when sojourning in other states, citizens of the United States were entitled to nondiscrimination with respect to whatever set of privileges or immunities were afforded by states to their own citizens.

Hamilton's discussion is ambiguous. On the one hand, he refers to "citizens of the several States"; on the other, he refers to "citizens of the Union." Under either reading, the clause could protect a set of privileges or immunities belonging to citizens of the United States that could not be denied by any state. Or it could ensure that, if states decided to extend certain privileges or immunities to their own citizens, they would have to extend those same privileges or immunities to the citizens of other states when those citizens visited. We do not know.

This subtle ambiguity in the wording of Article IV, Section 2 is difficult both to describe and to grasp, which may explain why it was not spotted during the framing and clarified. Having survived ratification, however, this ambiguity has pervaded discussions of "privileges" and/or "immunities" ever since.

Commentaries

Early commentators split concerning whether "in" denoted location or foundation. But they generally shared the belief that the Privileges and Immunities Clause of Article IV guaranteed the equal treatment of citizens by states and allowed the unequal treatment by states of noncitizens. It was not widely thought that the clause guaranteed the enjoyment of any particular bundle of substantive rights attaching to citizenship. That notion was to arise later.

In his annotated edition of Blackstone's *Commentaries*, first published in 1803, St. George Tucker interpreted the clause to affirm that states "retain the power of admitting aliens to become denizens of the states respectively" but that those denizens "would still be regarded as aliens in every state."[85] Thus, Tucker, like Madison, believed that the clause promoted comity by requiring the equal treatment of citizens and allowing the unequal treatment of noncitizens.

Writing in 1823, James Kent stated that the clause meant only that "if [citizens] remove from one state to another, they are entitled to the privileges that persons *of the same description* are entitled to in the state to which the removal is made, and to none other."[86] Kent offered the following illustration: "If . . . free persons of color are not entitled to vote in Carolina, free persons of color emigrating there from a Northern State would not be entitled to vote."[87] The converse implication is that if free persons of color were entitled to vote *in Carolina*, free persons of color who emigrated there *would* be entitled to vote.[88] The clause would bar such state discrimination among citizens therein.

Six years later, William Rawle characterized the Privileges and Immunities Clause as the "same rule . . . ambiguously laid down in the articles of confederation" and affirmed that "every person born within the United States, its territories or districts, whether the parents are citizens or aliens, is a natural born citizen in the sense of the Constitution, and entitled to all the rights and privileges appertaining to that capacity."[89] Although he did not elaborate on the content of those rights and privileges, he did say that citizens "alone can elect, and are capable of being elected to public offices." Citizens "alone can exercise authority within the community." They "possess an unqualified right to the enjoyment of property and personal immunity . . . [and] are bound to adhere to [the republic] in peace, to defend it in war, and to postpone the interests of all other countries to the affection which they ought to bear for their own."[90]

In his 1833 *Commentaries on American Law*, Joseph Story averred that "[e]very citizen of a state is ipso facto a citizen of the United States" and that the clause created a "general citizenship."[91] He understood that citizenship, however, to "communicate" to sojourners "all the privileges and immunities, which the citizens of the same state would be entitled to under the like circumstances."[92] He did not indicate that there was any "floor" of privileges and immunities that states could not fall below.

Treaties

Language from antebellum treaties and territorial acts has been said to have served as the inspiration for the text of the Fourteenth Amendment's Privileges or Immunities Clause. The first scholar to consider the relevance of treaty jurisprudence to the original meaning of the Fourteenth Amendment was Arnold Guminski. But it is Kurt Lash who has investigated this jurisprudence most thoroughly and whose work has proven most influential.[93]

Lash has argued that the language of "rights, privileges, and immunities"—variations of which permeate treaties and territorial acts—became understood by antislavery advocates during the antebellum period to denote all and only personal rights enumerated in the text of the federal Constitution.[94] An association of this language with enumerated personal rights was, on Lash's account, forged through debates over whether to condition the admission of Missouri into the Union upon the state's abolition of slavery.

Lash claims that free-state proponents, such as Senators Daniel Webster and David Morril, sharply distinguished between the "privileges and immunities of citizens of the several states" that are protected by Article IV of the Constitution, on the one hand, and the "rights, privileges, and immunities of citizens of the United States" that were protected by the Louisiana Cession Act, on the other. He further claims that free-state proponents insisted that the Cession Act, unlike Article IV, protected all and only enumerated rights, among which the right to hold property in people was not included. Lash concludes that the Cession Act did not prohibit Congress from conditioning the admission of Missouri upon its abolition of slavery.[95] In addition, he finds that even slavery proponents generally acknowledged the distinction between Article IV–protected comity rights and Cession Act–protected enumerated rights.[96]

In a lengthy article, we examined Lash's claims and found them to be unsubstantiated.[97] It is true that free-staters included a number of enumerated rights among the "privileges, advantages, and immunities" protected by the Cession Act. But the rights that they mentioned were what Lash refers to as "constitutionally express structural guarantees" related to participation in and access to institutions of the national government on equal footing with citizens of other states upon admission—not personal rights, such as the freedom of speech.[98] Morril listed rights relating to federal representation and to the jurisdiction of the federal courts.[99] Webster listed rights to federal representation and the right to a republican form of government.[100] Neither claimed that any of the personal rights listed in the first eight amendments were protected by the Cession Act.

Lash infers from the inclusion of *some* enumerated rights that Webster and Morril held a theory according to which *all and only* enumerated personal rights were among the "privileges, advantages, and immunities" of US citizenship. We find the inference untenable. The evidence adduced by Lash is consistent with an equal-footing reading of Article III of the Cession Act that finds support in early antebellum jurisprudence. In contrast, the all-and-only-enumerated-personal-rights theory articulated by Lash seems to have been unknown.[101] Further, David Upham has shown that later antebellum authorities associated treaty language with property rights, economic rights, and nondiscrimination rights that are difficult to distinguish from those that—as we will see—were associated with Article IV's Privileges and Immunities Clause.[102]

It is not impossible that understandings of treaty language made a distinctive contribution to the original meaning of the Privileges or Immunities Clause. But proponents of the argument that it did so have yet to provide a persuasive account of that contribution. Significantly, they have so far offered no direct evidence that anyone involved in the adoption of the clause actually made a connection between its language and treaty jurisprudence.[103]

When Republicans in the Thirty-Ninth Congress did invoke treaty jurisprudence in connection with the Fourteenth Amendment, they did so when discussing the Citizenship Clause and did not use the language of treaty jurisprudence to identify particular citizenship rights.[104] Of course, some ideas can be so basic that they need not be stated. But we lack evidence of a well-established association between treaty language and the privileges and immunities of US citizenship that would have been so obvious to participants in the framing and ratification of the Fourteenth Amendment as to preclude the need to expressly make the connection.

Accordingly, we will focus our attention on other evidentiary sources. In contrast with treaty jurisprudence, we join with those historians who have stressed the antislavery origins of the concepts contained in Section 1 of the Fourteenth Amendment. The development of antislavery constitutionalism is, perhaps, the single most important driver of the change between the original meaning of the Privileges and Immunities Clause of Article IV in 1788 and the original meaning of the Privileges or Immunities Clause of Section 1 in 1868. This popular constitutionalism is the subject of the next chapter.

2

The Antislavery Origins of "Privileges or Immunities"

THE ORIGINAL MEANING of the Privileges and Immunities Clause of Article IV most likely required only that citizens of any given state be treated the same as local citizens when they traveled—that is, the clause was a "Comity Clause," as it is often labeled by scholars today.[1] Scrutiny of antebellum law yields compelling evidence that this meaning remained dominant for decades.

This comity-only legal meaning was not, however, uncontested either inside or outside the courts, and the relative consensus over it fell apart entirely under the strain of ascendant antislavery and proslavery nationalism. By the eve of the Civil War, both Democratic proponents and Republican opponents of slavery agreed that Article IV, Section 2 established a floor of fundamental substantive rights that could not be abridged by states. They disagreed, of course, about the content of those rights.

Corfield v. Coryell

Far and away the leading antebellum judicial account of the meaning of the Privileges and Immunities Clause in Article IV was the 1823 circuit court opinion of Justice Bushrod Washington in *Corfield v. Coryell*. When explaining the meaning of the "privileges or immunities of citizens of the United States," several Republicans, including Senator Jacob Howard, who introduced the final version of the Privileges or Immunities Clause to the

Senate, quoted Washington's opinion in *Corfield* verbatim and at length. Here is the pertinent passage:

> The inquiry is, what are the privileges and immunities of citizens in the several states. We feel no hesitation in confining these expressions to those privileges and immunities which are, in their nature, fundamental; which belong, of right, to the citizens of all free governments; and which have, at all times, been enjoyed by citizens of the several states which compose this Union, from the time of their becoming free, independent, and sovereign.
>
> What these fundamental principles are, it would perhaps be more tedious than difficult to enumerate. They may, however, be all comprehended under the following general heads: Protection by the government; *the enjoyment of life and liberty, with the right to acquire and possess property of every kind, and to pursue happiness and safety;* subject nevertheless to such restraints as the government may justly prescribe for the general good of the whole. The right of a citizen of one state to pass through, or to reside in any other state, for the purposes of trade, agriculture, professional pursuits, or otherwise; to claim the benefit of the writ of habeas corpus; to institute and maintain actions of any kind in the courts of the state; to take, hold and dispose of property, either real or personal; and an exemption from higher taxes or impositions than are paid by the other citizens of the state; may be mentioned as some of the privileges and immunities of citizens, which are clearly embraced by the general description of privileges deemed to be fundamental: to which may be added, the elective franchise, as regulated and established by the laws or constitution of the state in which it is to be exercised. These, and many others which might be mentioned are, strictly speaking, privileges and immunities.[2]

Certain of the rights identified by Justice Washington in *Corfield* are clearly natural: "the enjoyment of life and liberty" and the right to "pursue happiness and safety" among them. Indeed, in the italicized passage, Justice Washington was merely paraphrasing the canonical statement of natural rights at the Founding: George Mason's draft for the Virginia Declaration of Rights, which began:

> THAT all men are born equally free and independent, and have certain *inherent natural rights,* of which they cannot, by any compact, deprive or divest their posterity; among which are, *the enjoyment of life and liberty, with the means of acquiring and possessing property, and pursuing and obtaining happiness and safety.*[3]

Variations on Mason's formulation had been adopted by four states in their constitutions. When Representative Madison proposed adding a portion of this wording to the Preamble, he characterized this language as "relat[ing] to what may be called a bill of rights." (Keep this reference to "a bill of rights" in mind, as it will assume significance in Chapter 4 when we consider what people meant by that label during the debates over the Fourteenth Amendment.)

Other rights listed by Washington are clearly post-political. One cannot claim "the benefit of the writ of habeas corpus" or "institute and maintain actions of any kind in the courts of the state" in the state of nature. Washington's criteria for fundamentality are tethered both to nature and to custom—rights must not only (1) be "in their nature, fundamental" but (2) "belong of right, to citizens in all free governments"; and (3) to "have at all times been enjoyed by citizens of the several states." Washington made no effort to demonstrate that the rights he listed met the letter of these demanding criteria; but we will return to his criteria in Chapter 8 when we formulate rules of construction for identifying the privileges or immunities of US citizens.

Comity's Early Dominance in the Courts

An intrastate equality–based understanding of the Privileges and Immunities Clause dominated early antebellum case law. Courts split concerning whether the clause required states to grant all visiting citizens (a) the same rights that they enjoyed in their home state; (b) some of the rights that the visited state extended to its own citizens; or (c) all of the rights that the state extended to its own citizens.[4] For the most part, however, courts did not hold that the clause secured the enjoyment of a set of fundamental rights associated with national citizenship that states simply could not deny to citizens coming from other states.[5]

The circuit court decision in *Corfield v. Coryell* does not appear to have been an exception to the comity-only consensus. Justice Washington seems to have viewed the clause solely as guaranteeing sojourning citizens equal privileges. After noting that the rights he listed, together with "many others which might be mentioned, are, strictly speaking, privileges and immunities," he stated that the "enjoyment of them by the citizens of each state, *in every other state* was manifestly calculated (to use the expressions of the preamble of the corresponding provision in the old articles of confederation) 'the better to secure and perpetuate mutual friendship and intercourse among the people of the different states of the Union.'"[6] Washington concluded that Article IV, then, guaranteed "the enjoyment of privileges and immunities by the citizens of each state, in every other state"—*not* only in their own states.

Further, Gerard Magliocca's examination[7] of Washington's notes has revealed that Washington relied on *Livingston v. Van Ingen*[8] for his privileges and immunities analysis. This was a case in which Chancellor James Kent wrote that the clause "mean[t] only that the citizens of other states shall have equal rights with our own citizens, and not that they shall have different or greater rights."[9] Washington noted that he was "inclined to the opinion" that the "meaning of this article is that the citizens of each state shall within every other state have equal privileges or rights as the citizens of such state have."[10]

Still, fundamental-rights theory was in the air as early as 1797. *Campbell v. Morris*,[11] sometimes cited as a comity-only case,[12] is best read as a fundamental-rights case. In his opinion for the court, Maryland Judge Jeremiah Chase—the cousin of US Supreme Court Justice Samuel Chase—referred to the "privileges and immunities of citizens of the several states" and explained that the clause

> means that *citizens of all the states shall have the peculiar advantage of acquiring and holding real as well as personal property,* and that such property shall be protected and secured by the laws of the state, in the same manner as the property of the citizens of the state is protected. It means, such property shall not be liable to any taxes or burdens which the property of the citizens is not subject to. It may also mean, that as creditors, they shall be on the same footing with the state creditor, in the payment of the debts of a deceased debtor.[13]

As David Upham has noted, Judge Chase identified not one but two distinct requirements that the Privileges and Immunities Clause imposes on the states, which correspond to two distinct kinds of privileges identified by Blackstone.[14] The first: "the peculiar advantage of acquiring and holding real as well as personal property"—a "private immunity." The second: "[S]uch property shall be protected and secured by the laws of the state, in the same manner as the property of the citizens of the state is protected"—a "civil privilege." Intrastate comity, then, can itself be viewed as just one of many fundamental rights that attach to citizenship.

More notable still, given its provenance, is an 1844 decision by Justice Nathaniel Reed of the Ohio Supreme Court.[15] In determining whether an

Ohio statute that authorized the arrest of nonresidents for debt violated the Privileges and Immunities Clause, Reed interpreted the clause to "mean[] that the residents of the several states, if they be citizens of the United States, shall be protected and defended . . . in the full enjoyment of all the rights to which they are entitled *as citizens of the United States*."[16] Those rights were "to be determined by a reference to the letter and spirit of our national constitution, and also to the general custom of other nations."[17]

Reed expressly rejected the comity-only theory of the Privileges and Immunities Clause, determining that "the spirit and intention of [the clause] is, not to secure to the non-resident the same rights and indulgence with the resident in every state, but simply to secure to the citizen of the United States . . . the full enjoyment of all the rights of citizenship, in every state of the Union."[18] We will see that prominent and influential Ohio Republicans, including Joshua Giddings, John Bingham, Samuel Shellabarger, William Lawrence, and John Sherman, would adopt the same view as this Ohio Supreme Court justice.

Corfield seems to have been well received. Kent cited it approvingly. Likewise, in *Tatem v. Wright*,[19] Judge Lucius Elmer cited *Corfield*'s "fundamental" dictum and followed Washington in including "exemption[s] from higher taxes or impositions than are paid by the other citizens of the state" among the privileges and immunities of citizens. In *Commonwealth v. Milton*,[20] Judge Marshall cited Washington's "comprehensive description" of privileges and immunities and averred that they included "the natural faculties and rights of individuals to the law of nature from which they are derived." We found no criticism of *Corfield* prior to the Civil War, a period when federal circuit court opinions carried great weight.[21]

The Rise of Fundamental Privileges and Immunities

The political economy of the antebellum period brought the decline of the comity-only view of the Privileges and Immunities Clause. Anti- and proslavery elements converged on a fundamental-rights view of the privileges and immunities of US citizens. According to this view, certain rights could be reasonably regulated but never denied outright, anywhere.

Antislavery advocates were bent on resisting and displacing a proslavery hegemonic bloc—dubbed the "Slave Power"[22]—that not only controlled Southern political life but all three branches of the federal government. They asserted a substantive rights reading against the Southern slave states. In a like fashion, albeit for very different reasons, those who sought to expand slavery into new territories and to secure the right of slaveholders to travel with their captives through free states to get there, found a comity-only Privileges and Immunities Clause inadequate to that objective.

Understanding the original public meaning of the Fourteenth Amendment requires an appreciation for how public debates over slavery altered the public meaning of constitutional terms. Ironically, just as the fundamental conflict between a proslavery hegemony and an antislavery counterhegemony produced assertions by both sides of what is today misleadingly called "substantive due process,"[23] this same conflict produced a convergence on fundamental privileges and immunities.

The Admission of Missouri

The first extended congressional discussion of the privileges and immunities of *national* citizenship took place in 1819. The discussion concerned both whether free Blacks were citizens and whether the right to hold property in people was among the privileges of US citizenship. The discussion was prompted by congressional efforts to condition Missouri's admission into the Union upon its abolition of slavery.

Free staters, led by Senators Daniel Webster, David Morril, and John Sergeant, among others, argued that Congress did indeed have the power to condition Missouri's admission upon its abolition of slavery. They further contended that free Blacks were citizens and that the right to hold property in people was not among the privileges of US citizenship.[24] Their opponents urged that conditioning Missouri's admission upon abolition would both deny the (white) citizens of Missouri "the rights, advantages, and immunities of citizens of the United States" recognized in Article III of the Louisiana Cession Act and violate the Privileges and Immunities Clause.[25]

Free staters sought to distinguish the "rights, advantages, and immunities" recognized in Article III of the Louisiana Cession Act from those protected by the Privileges and Immunities Clause. They argued that neither provision guaranteed to Missouri citizens the right to hold enslaved people.[26] Free staters contended that the Cession Act's reference to "rights, advantages and immunities of citizens of the United States" was limited to those "such as are recognized or communicated by the constitution of the United States; such as are common to all citizens, and are uniform throughout the United States."[27] Different free-staters produced different lists of these rights, advantages, and immunities. But they generally maintained that the right to hold property in enslaved people was neither "recognized or communicated by the Constitution of the United States" nor "common to all citizens, and . . . uniform throughout the United States."

What about the rights conferred to US citizens by the Privileges and Immunities Clause of Article IV? This clause, free-staters maintained, only "secur[ed] to . . . migrating citizen[s] all the privileges and immunities of citizens in the state to which he removes," whatever those privileges and immunities might happen to be under the latter state's constitution and laws.[28] Free-staters denied that a single state could, by recognizing the right of its citizens to hold enslaved people as a form of property, require the recognition of that property right by every other state to which—or through which—one of its citizens might travel. Were such a thing possible, they argued, it "would at once destroy all the fundamental limitations of the state constitutions upon the rights of their own citizens."[29]

Thus, free-staters argued that, whereas the Cession Act guaranteed a "floor" of fundamental rights, the Privileges and Immunities Clause protected only against parochial discrimination. If a state did not recognize property in people, then a citizen of a slave state could not assert such a right when sojourning to or through another state. And Congress had the power to condition statehood on a territory banning slavery in its new constitution.

Proslavery legislators responded by contending that the right of states to decide whether to recognize property in people was itself among the Cession Act's "rights, advantages, and immunities of citizens of the United States," as much as the right to freedom of religious opinion.[30] Because free Blacks were not citizens of the United States, they possessed no federal privileges and immunities under Article IV to be denied.[31]

Free-staters' efforts to condition Missouri's admittance upon abolition proved unsuccessful. But privileges and immunities were debated again when Missouri applied in 1820 for admission with a constitution that charged Missouri's legislature with "prevent[ing] free negroes and mulattoes from coming to, and settling in, this state, under any pretext whatever."[32] Free-staters reiterated their beliefs that free Blacks were citizens and interpreted the Privileges and Immunities Clause to secure free Blacks' rights to emigrate into other states.[33]

Proslavery advocates admitted that the Privileges and Immunities Clause did secure such emigration rights to people who were entitled to enjoy all the privileges and immunities of citizens in the states to which they were emigrating. But they denied that Blacks were so entitled, either under the proposed Missouri constitution or under the federal Constitution.[34]

There followed a series of votes.[35] First, the House voted against Missouri's admission with the provision excluding Blacks intact. Then, the House voted against admitting Missouri on the condition that the exclusion be removed. After this, the Senate passed a joint resolution admitting Missouri. Efforts to broker a compromise between free-state and proslavery advocates in the House proved unsuccessful. Finally, Representative Henry Clay proposed the creation of a joint committee that would resolve the issue.

The committee produced a remarkable document in which it acknowledged that "of all the articles in our constitution, there is probably not one more difficult to construe" than the Privileges and Immunities Clause. The committee then proposed requiring Missouri to pledge that the exclusion provision would not be construed to authorize any act which deprived "citizens of either of the states" of "the privileges and immunities to which they are entitled under the Constitution of the United States."[36]

The committee didn't take a definitive position concerning the provision's constitutionality. It pointed out that states did "discriminate between the white and black man" in respect of "the right of voting and of serving on juries," but expressed uncertainty as to "[h]ow far this discrimination may be carried."[37] It then "remitted to judicial cognizance" what it characterized as "a matter of nice and difficult inquiry."[38]

This resolution papered over a fundamental disagreement, the importance of which was laid bare in a debate between Representative Henry Storrs of New York and Representative Philip Barbour of Virginia. For Storrs, nothing less than "the whole structure of [the] National Government" depended on a firm grasp of, and adherence to, the Privileges and Immunities Clause.[39] Far from being obscure, Storrs argued, the clause was "capable of no construction which does not plainly denote the universality of its operation and its uniform application to individual right throughout every portion of the nation."[40]

Representative Barbour considered the matter at hand equally clear and argued for the opposite conclusion. On his account, nothing prevented Missouri or any other state from declaring that "certain persons shall not be her citizens," regardless of whether other states recognized those persons as citizens. States had the right to "say who shall be entitled to citizenship within their limits."[41] Just as, according to Storrs, the Union depended on equality between all whom states elevated to the rank of citizens, according to Barbour, survival of the Union depended on Black people *not* being treated like white men.

Predictably, Missouri legislators responded to the condition with thinly veiled contempt. They began by denying that Congress had the power to impose the condition at all. Then, in 1825, they enacted a law that conditioned free Blacks' entrance into the state upon possession of naturalization papers—an effective ban, since states could not naturalize native citizens. In 1847, Missouri formally prohibited all free Blacks from entering the state.[42]

The resolution of Missouri's admission was intended to avoid taking sides in the immediate constitutional controversy between free-staters and pro-slavery advocates—much less the conflicts concerning the nature of citizenship and of the republic that gave rise to that controversy. But its effect was to allow Missouri to act on an understanding of the Privileges and Immunities Clause that excluded free Blacks from the Clause's protection.

The Negro Seamen Acts

Whereas antislavery forces adopted a comity-only reading of the Privileges and Immunities Clause in the debate over admission of new states created from the territories, they used a fundamental-rights reading to contest the Negro Seamen Acts.

The acts were the immediate product of an unsuccessful rebellion. Antebellum Southerners lived in perpetual fear of an uprising—particularly in the lower South, where Blacks outnumbered whites by considerable margins. This fear inspired restrictions on civil and political liberties that free Blacks had enjoyed during the colonial years.[43] Denmark Vesey was a free Black carpenter who had purchased his liberty with lottery winnings. When his plans to raise a slave rebellion in Charleston were betrayed to Charleston authorities by two of Vesey's confederates, South Carolina's response was swift and brutal.[44] Thirty-five Blacks were hanged in connection with Vesey's plot, and thirty-seven Blacks were banished.[45]

It was widely believed that others stood ready to participate in a future uprising. The South Carolina legislature therefore enacted a law requiring the seizure and imprisonment of all Blacks—whether free or enslaved—upon their arrival in South Carolina ports. What became known as the "Negro Seamen Act" then provided for the release of imprisoned Blacks upon payment of their expenses by their ship's captain; and their sale into slavery if no payment was made.[46] Other Southern states subsequently enacted similar legislation.[47]

The Seamen Acts provoked sustained controversy. The British government complained of South Carolina's seizure of free Blacks from British ships, leading Secretary of State John Quincy Adams to admonish the state. Although the law was temporarily suspended, South Carolinians then created an organization of private citizens that called for the act's continued enforcement. Soon after, authorities resumed seizing and imprisoning free Blacks. Even after President James Monroe's attorney general, William Wirt, concluded that South Carolina's law violated the Commerce Clause, as well as an 1815 treaty with Great Britain, South Carolina continued to arrest free Black seamen.[48]

In 1842, John Quincy Adams, having since become a member of the House of Representatives, sponsored resolutions asking the president for the release of state department documents related to the Negro Seamen Acts.[49] Upon their release, Adams arranged for the publication of an opinion by Supreme Court Justice William Johnson, in which Johnson concluded that South Carolina's act was unconstitutional and violated the United States' treaty obligations. But Johnson also determined that the Judiciary Act did not authorize him to issue a writ of habeas corpus.[50]

Two years later, Massachusetts sent distinguished lawyer—and former representative—Samuel Hoar as an emissary to Charleston "for the purpose of instituting suits and bringing the question of the constitutionality of the acts before the Supreme Court."[51] Hoar was promptly driven out of Charleston by a flurry of official and unofficial threats. The South Carolina legislature sought his expulsion, on the ground that he was spreading sedition and that persons of color were not US citizens and therefore not protected by the Privileges and Immunities Clause. Before he could be formally expelled, however, Hoar was forced to flee by a hostile mob.[52]

The flight of such a prominent white man became a cause célèbre in the North and was not soon forgotten. Massachusetts immediately issued a series of resolutions condemning South Carolina and repeatedly called on Congress to enact legislation to protect sojourning Massachusetts citizens of any color.[53] The legislatures of Arkansas, Georgia, Mississippi, and Alabama, by contrast, all endorsed the actions of South Carolina and condemned those of Massachusetts. Northern representatives invoked Hoar's treatment throughout congressional debates as illustrations of Southern hostility to citizens' rights, as did antislavery advocates outside the halls of Congress.[54]

Both sides of the debate over the Negro Seamen Acts invoked the Privileges and Immunities Clause. Opponents of the acts claimed they violated the fundamental rights of citizens, both Black and white, who were protected by the clause. For its part, South Carolina justified its attempted expulsion of Hoar on the ground that free Blacks were not citizens—thus implicitly conceding that the state's actions would be unconstitutional if Blacks were citizens.[55]

The political salience of Hoar's treatment was due, in part, to the fact that Southern states were alleged to be denying the privileges and immunities of *white* citizens, not merely those of free Blacks. In particular, South Carolina denied the freedom of speech of a Massachusetts citizen—who was unquestionably protected by Article IV—notwithstanding the fact that South Carolina equally forbade its own citizens as well as out-of-staters from engaging in antislavery speech. Because South Carolina did not discriminate against Hoar, a comity-only reading of the Privileges and Immunities Clause was inadequate to explain why Hoar's treatment was unconstitutional.

Hoar's treatment galvanized opponents of slavery and inspired their use of the clause in other contexts. They invoked it during debates over slavery in the District of Columbia, over the admission of Kansas and Nebraska as free states, and, later, in the course of advocacy of the Thirteenth Amendment, the Civil Rights Act of 1866, and the 1871 Enforcement Act.[56]

In sum, constitutional discourse outside the courts started to put distance between the contemporary public meaning of the Privileges and Immunities Clause and the comity consensus that dominated antebellum law that was based on the likely original meaning of the clause. While proslavery South Carolina adopted a comity-only reading of the Privileges and Immunities Clause, the antislavery forces in the North asserted a core of fundamental rights that were protected when citizens of one state were traveling in another.

Commonwealth v. Aves

Beginning in the 1830s, Northern courts—starting with the Massachusetts Supreme Judicial Court—began to rule in favor of the freedom of enslaved people whom slaveholders voluntarily brought into free states. Judges invoked a rule laid down in the famous King's Bench case of *Somerset v. Stewart*.[57] Because *Somerset* provided an important background principle or assumption of these debates, it is worth reviewing.

In 1769, Charles Stewart, a British customs officer who lived in Virginia, traveled to England on business with an enslaved person named James

Somerset. Somerset escaped two years later but was captured and consigned to John Knowles, a ship captain who was instructed to take Somerset to Jamaica and sell him. Somerset's lawyers—who had the benefit of briefing from abolitionist Granville Sharp—convinced William Murray, the Earl of Mansfield and Lord Chief Justice of England and Wales, to issue a writ of habeas corpus. This proceeding ultimately required Lord Mansfield (as he is known) to confront the question whether enslaved people could be transported against their will from England.[58]

Mansfield held that Somerset was to be freed. He wrote that no enslaved person could be compelled to leave England both because "[t]he state of slavery is of such a nature that it is incapable of being introduced on any reasons, moral or political; but only by positive law," and because slavery was contrary to the positive law of England.[59] Mansfield's opinion dealt only with coerced transportation, and people remained enslaved in Britain until the institution was abolished by Parliament in 1833. Still, many antebellum lawyers and politicians believed that Mansfield had ended slavery in Britain.[60]

In the 1836 case of *Commonwealth v. Aves*,[61] Chief Justice Lemuel Shaw of the Massachusetts Supreme Judicial Court held in favor of the freedom of an enslaved six-year-old girl named Med, who had been brought into Massachusetts from Louisiana.[62] Shaw followed *Somerset*. He analogized the law of Massachusetts to the law of England and reasoned that because "slavery is considered as unlawful and inadmissible in both . . . because contrary to natural right and to laws designed for the security of personal liberty," enslaved people "bec[ame] entitled to the protection of [Massachusetts] laws" and could not be subjected to "forcible arrest and removal."[63]

Shaw acknowledged but did not address the question of whether enslaved people who were "voluntarily" brought into Massachusetts and returned with their "own consent" to slave states would be entitled to their freedom upon returning. Nor did he say what would happen when slaveholders passed through free states or were compelled to remain in free states temporarily "by accident or necessity."[64]

This question would continue to loom large among Northerners as events continued to escalate. Given the slow pace of travel, a reading of the Privileges and Immunities Clause that allowed citizens of Southern states to freely traverse Northern free states with their slaves threatened to spread slavery as they went. Or so Northerners came increasingly to believe.

Shaw also made clear that his holding did not apply to enslaved people who escaped into free states. This would implicate Article IV's clause governing the return of persons "held to Service or Labour in one State, under the Laws thereof, escaping into another" state where slavery was not protected by local laws.[65] Indeed, the so-called Fugitive Slave Clause is best read as negating the default rule established by the 1772 *Somerset* case, which would otherwise apply to enslaved people who made good their escape from a slave state and into a free state.

Although it avoided several tough questions, *Aves* immediately became a landmark for the one it resolved: slaves whom their masters had voluntarily brought into a free state could not be transported back to a slave state against their will. Participants in Massachusetts' vibrant and active abolitionist movement rejoiced at "little Med's" liberation.[66] Abolitionists elsewhere brought cases to extend *Aves* into their own jurisdictions and vetted candidates for office on the basis of whether they supported repeal of laws allowing the coerced transportation of enslaved people.[67] All Northern states at the time freed any slaves who were brought to live in their jurisdiction.[68] (This is an important background fact to the Supreme Court's 1857 decision in *Dred Scott v. Sandford*.)

But some of these states also accommodated visiting slaveholders by extending to them time-limited rights of transit. No court had yet addressed—as future Supreme Court Justice Benjamin Curtis put it in arguing for Thomas Aves—whether a "citizen of a slaveholding State, who comes to Massachusetts [or any other free state] for a temporary purpose of business and pleasure" with an enslaved person could "restrain the slave for the purpose of returning to the [slaveholder's] domicil [*sic*]."[69] Further, Shaw soon extended *Aves* by loosely construing the requirement that slaveholders "voluntarily" enter Massachusetts with their slaves to reach even cases in which slaveholders did not want their human property to enter the state.[70]

To be sure, Massachusetts was an exceptionally antislavery state. Its abolitionists were well organized, able, and influential. In 1851, the Free Soil Party garnered enough state legislators to compel a deal with Democrats to send the antislavery proponent Charles Sumner to the US Senate. In 1783, it became the first state to end slavery through court rulings by its highest court; and Chief Justice Shaw held powerful antislavery convictions.

Yet, between 1836 and 1860, *Aves* became generally accepted elsewhere in the North. The exceptions were states with Democratic strongholds and those that bordered slave states, including Indiana, Illinois, and New Jersey. By 1860, any enslaved person who was voluntarily brought into New England was immediately freed, whether by virtue of court decisions or of statutes that embodied *Aves*'s principle. All but four of eighteen Northern states freed enslaved people in transit by that time.[71]

Slaveholders found *Aves* and the cases following it frightening for two main reasons. First and most obviously, it rendered their "property" increasingly insecure in Northern states. Second, it stoked anxiety about hostile British abolitionism. By bringing *Somerset* into American law, Shaw and those who followed his lead effectively aligned themselves with an imperial power that was seen as threatening an increasingly nationalist proslavery agenda.[72]

Four years after *Aves*, proslavery's most influential exponent, South Carolina Senator John C. Calhoun, denounced Britain's attempt to bring the law of nations into line with its own municipal law. He averred that slavery followed slaveholders, not only across North America, but into foreign jurisdictions as well.[73]

Meanwhile, former Alabama slaveholder turned Ohio abolitionist James Birney, writing in the *New-York American* before departing to London for the inaugural World Antislavery Conference, denounced the attempt to "engraft the rights (!) of the slave-trader and slave-holder on the law of nations."[74] In two resolutions issued at the London conference, Birney affirmed what had become a guiding principle of British policy: slaves were artificial property *to which comity did not apply*. For proslavery advocates, localized legal resistance to slavery was bad enough. Even worse was the apparent agreement between Northern judges and a foreign power that seemed bent on liberating enslaved people across the Atlantic world.

It is a mistake to regard antebellum proslavery advocates as defending slavery only in the handful of states and territories where it had already been established. Matthew Karp has shown that proslavery advocates sought to transform the United States into the leader of a global slavery vanguard, even as they faced a surge of domestic antislavery reaction.[75] Indeed, it was the growth of the former that fed the growth of the latter, including among Northerners who were otherwise indifferent to slavery within the Southern states. The increasing political success of antislavery parties—from the Liberty, to the Free Soil, to the Republican Parties—was a product of increasingly widespread Northern fear of the nationalist ambitions of the Southern Slave Power.

Today, these imperial ambitions look absurd. But slaveholders who looked abroad and saw the ascendance of colonial empires that were predicated on strict racial hierarchies and bound laborers regarded themselves as being on the right side of history.[76] The reception of British antislavery principles into American law thus threatened not only slaveholders' immediate property interests but a proslavery worldview to which those interests gave rise—a worldview that exerted an autonomous influence on slaveholders' political goals.

The Compromise of 1850

Despite proslavery foreign policy, slavery's domestic prospects looked increasingly grim in the early decades of the nineteenth century. In *Prigg v. Pennsylvania*,[77] the Supreme Court upheld the constitutionality of the Fugitive Slave Act of 1793, which entitled slaveholders to seize runaways found in Northern states. But Justice Joseph Story's opinion for the Court also stated that slaveholders were not entitled to the assistance of Northern law enforcement. Northern states responded by prohibiting state officials from rendering such assistance, effectively rendering the act a dead letter.[78]

Slavery was also excluded from all territory covered by the Louisiana Purchase; Oregon country; all land north of the southern boundary of Missouri; and all land acquired from Mexico as a consequence of the Mexican War.[79] Abolitionists called on Congress to ban the interstate slave trade and abolish slavery in the District of Columbia and in Florida territory.[80]

Although these calls went unheeded, proslavery advocates found them profoundly alarming. Alabama Senator Jeremiah Clemens gave voice to their fears thus:

> We know well what we have to expect. Northern demands have assumed a form which it is impossible for us to misunderstand. First comes our exclusion from the territories. Next abolition in the District of Columbia. . . . Then the prohibition of the slave trade between the States; and, finally, total abolition. . . . Our duty and our obvious policy alike demand that we should meet the danger on the threshold, and fall or conquer there.[81]

The domestic state of play changed dramatically in the middle of the century, thanks to a series of laws that collectively became known as the Compromise of 1850. The compromise was presented to the Senate by Henry Clay in the form of eight resolutions. They included:

1. A new fugitive slave law that sent federal commissioners to every county in the nation to decide cases involving purported runaways

under minimal standards of proof and imposed heavy penalties on anyone who interfered with the operation of the law.

2. A plan for the reorganization of all new federal territories "without the adoption of any restriction or condition on the subject of slavery."

3. Federal assumption of the debts incurred by Texas—a slave state—prior to its entrance into the Union.

4. A guarantee that Congress would never end slavery in the District of Columbia without the support of the people of the district and state of Maryland.

5. An affirmation that Congress would never interfere with the interstate slave trade.

6. A provision for California to enter the Union as a free state.

7. A prohibition on the public sale of enslaved people in the District of Columbia.

8. A settlement of Texas's boundary dispute with New Mexico.[82]

All in all, this was a huge win for slaveholders. Five of these resolutions strongly favored slaveholders' interests, as did the bills that emerged from them. The reorganization of new territories without any restriction on slavery effectively opened the entire New Mexico territory to slavery.[83] Slavery went from being banned in almost all federal territories to being legal in all newly acquired lands in the Southwest—including what would later become Kansas, Montana, Nebraska, North Dakota, and South Dakota, as well as parts of Colorado, Idaho, and Wyoming.[84] The slave state of Texas gained more land and about $10 million.[85] To make matters still worse, the Fugitive Slave Act of 1850 created a national system of law enforcement that ran roughshod over due-process norms, threatened free Blacks with the loss of their liberty, and conscripted ordinary citizens as well as public officials in free states into slaveholders' service.[86]

The antislavery benefits of the "compromise" were insubstantial. California's admission as a free state was worth little; few thought California would become a slave slate to begin with.[87] A ban on open sales of slaves in the District of Columbia had symbolic value, but slaveholders needed only travel to nearby Virginia to make sales.[88] And the ban on open sales may have benefited slaveholders by reducing political pressure to categorically ban slavery in the district.[89]

The degree of Northern outrage at the Fugitive Slave Act cannot be overstated. The 1850 act's manifest goals of rendering ineffectual Northern laws that ensured due process of law for alleged runaways and facilitating the kidnapping of free Blacks who were not runaways created entirely new antislavery communities and new modes of resistance to a seemingly insatiable "Slave Power."

In response, Northern states enacted further laws withdrawing cooperation in the return of "runaways." Northern juries refused to convict people charged with interfering with the act. Free Blacks and their white allies organized self-defense groups and teamed up to rescue Blacks from federal custody by force of arms.[90]

Private violence was frequently urged as a legitimate response to public violence that was deemed both flagrantly unconstitutional and, like slavery itself, a relic of barbarism. Thus did Frederick Douglass tell a Free Soil Party convention that "the only way to make the Fugitive Slave Law a dead letter is to make a dozen or more dead kidnappers."[91] Few kidnappers were in fact killed, but the resistance was sufficient to embarrass President Millard Fillmore's steadfast efforts to enforce the law on a number of high-profile occasions.[92]

Proslavery advocates, in turn, were outraged by what they perceived as Northern lawlessness and intransigence in the face of slavery's global progress. Their success in securing passage of a sweeping, one-sided law that compelled Northerners to serve as kidnappers left them only more outraged when Northerners refused to help them vindicate what they regarded, not only as valid constitutional claims, but as moral rights that they believed ought to be secured everywhere on Earth.[93]

The Missouri "Compromise" thus settled nothing. It was a tremendous boon to proslavery activists that left both sides of the "debate" over slavery convinced that powerful political forces were bent on attacking sacred individual rights and impeding the march of modern civilization. It is not difficult to see how the next development, when combined with the compromise and all that led to it, fueled the collapse of the Whigs and the rise of a new expressly antislavery party dedicated to opposing the expansion of slavery beyond its existing borders.

Dred Scott

The judicial tide against slavery in state courts following *Aves* turned as slaveholders won victory after victory in the Supreme Court from the late 1840s through the 1850s. The Court held that Northerners could be held liable for aiding runaways even if they lacked "notice" of enslaved people's fugitive status;[94] that slave states could determine for themselves whether someone was enslaved or not;[95] and that citizens could be punished by states for harboring runaways.[96] None of these decisions, however, was as momentous as *Dred Scott v. Sandford*.[97]

In *Dred Scott*, the Court notoriously declared that free Blacks had never been, and could never become, citizens of the United States.[98] It also held that Congress lacked power to ban slavery in federal territories because slave "property" taken into the territories was protected by the Fifth Amendment's Due Process of Law Clause.[99] Ironically, despite its infamy—both then and now—Chief Justice Roger Taney's opinion contributed to the public meaning of the "privileges or immunities of citizens of the United States" because the decision colored much of the ensuing public discussion of that concept. Later actions by Congress designed to "reverse" the case did so by adopting two critical aspects of its reasoning. We cannot let the moral repugnance of the majority's handiwork obscure its relevance to the Fourteenth Amendment's salutary public meaning.

DUAL CITIZENSHIP   Taney's first crucial move was to distinguish between national and state citizenship. Doing so enabled him to deny that state citizenship conferred on free Blacks the status of US citizens. "[W]e must not confound the rights of citizenship which a State may confer within its own limits," he admonished, with "the rights of citizenship as a member of the Union. It does not by any means follow, because he has all the rights and privileges of a *citizen of a State*, that he must be a *citizen of the United States*."[100] It is not clear whether this concept of dual citizenship preceded *Dred Scott*, but it certainly affected legal analysis thereafter.

FUNDAMENTAL RIGHTS OF US CITIZENSHIP   Taney's second move was to deny that persons of African descent could ever be citizens of the United States. He reasoned that, were they to be citizens, they would be entitled to the fundamental rights protected by the Privileges and Immunities Clause of Article IV. In an effort to establish the absurdity of this conclusion, Taney provided a list of the fundamental rights he said were already guaranteed to US citizens by Article IV. It is worth quoting in its entirety:

> [I]f they were so received, and entitled to the privileges and immunities of citizens, it would exempt them from the operation of the special laws and

from the police regulations which they considered to be necessary for their own safety. It would give to persons of the negro race, who were recognised as citizens in any one State of the Union, the right to enter every other State whenever they pleased, singly or in companies, without pass or passport, and without obstruction, to sojourn there as long as they pleased, to go where they pleased at every hour of the day or night without molestation, unless they committed some violation of law for which a white man would be punished; and it would give them the full liberty of speech in public and in private upon all subjects upon which its own citizens might speak; to hold public meetings upon political affairs, and to keep and carry arms wherever they went. And all of this would be done in the face of the subject race of the same color, both free and slaves, and inevitably producing discontent and insubordination among them, and endangering the peace and safety of the State.[101]

Taney's discussion of the Privileges and Immunities Clause has been read as affirming a fundamental-rights theory of the clause by some scholars[102] and a comity-only theory by others.[103] It is hard to say. On the one hand, Taney identifies the fundamental rights "to hold public meetings upon political affairs, and to keep and carry arms" as privileges and immunities that Blacks would be entitled to enjoy without qualification.[104] On the other hand, white citizens generally enjoyed these rights in 1857, so it would be fair for Taney to assert that Blacks would have the same general rights as a matter of comity. Given that Taney's discussion of these rights was preceded by references to "the right to enter every other state" without "pass or passport, and without obstruction,"[105] perhaps he meant only that Blacks would be entitled to enter other states and claim whatever speech and gun rights white citizens enjoyed under state law.

But Taney's original intentions do not matter for our purposes. Both antislavery and proslavery advocates who focused on Taney's discussion of the Privileges and Immunities Clause appear to have understood him to be adopting a fundamental-rights theory. Indeed, Dred Scott's lawyer, Montgomery Blair, had relied on a fundamental-rights theory in arguing that the Privileges and Immunities Clause protected formerly enslaved people who had acquired their citizenship in free states from being re-enslaved upon their return to slave states. "[W]hatever may be the extent of the rights conferred by that clause," contended Blair, "it must at least exempt citizens from being made slaves."[106]

Antislavery advocates who repudiated Taney's conclusions concerning Black citizenship and the constitutional status of slaveholding did not take issue with this fundamental-rights reading of his opinion. Jurists William Larned and John Codman Hurd used Taney's interpretation to argue that the privileges of national citizenship included the right to speak one's mind on any subject, including slavery. The clause, they maintained, established a fundamental-rights floor, below which states could not fall.[107] The memory of Samuel Hoar's treatment by South Carolina lived on in infamy.

The Court did not address whether slaveholders' "property" was protected when taken into free states, as opposed to a federal territory. But antislavery Northerners feared that would be the second shoe to drop. After all, Dred Scott had been taken by his master to reside in the free state of Illinois; it was on this basis that Scott had been freed by the lower Missouri courts before the Missouri Supreme Court ruled against him by reversing its precedents on that question. In his "House Divided" speech, Abraham Lincoln famously predicted that "the next *Dred Scott* decision" would grant slaveholders a national right to travel with their captives.[108]

This wasn't paranoia. In a brief concurrence in *Dred Scott*, Justice Samuel Nelson stated that the question of "the right of the master with his slave of transit into or through a free state . . . being a citizen of the United States . . . is not before us."[109] He noted, however, that the question "turn[ed] upon the rights and privileges secured to a common citizen of the republic under the Constitution of the United States"—that is, on the Privileges and Immunities Clause of Article IV.

Taney's discussion of the rights and privileges of citizens of the United States made plain both that citizens enjoyed the right to travel with lawfully acquired property and that neither free nor enslaved Blacks were citizens. Following his lead, proslavery advocates combined the due process of law component of Taney's opinion together with a fundamental-rights reading of the Privileges and Immunities Clause to argue that every slaveholding citizen was entitled to migrate and settle in free states with their now con-stitutionally enshrined "property."[110]

Previous judicial renderings notwithstanding, supporters and opponents of slavery—working very much at cross-purposes—converged in elevating the fundamental-rights reading of the Privileges and Immunities Clause above the comity-only reading in constitutional law and public constitutional discourse. The contemporary public meaning of "privileges and immunities" evolved accordingly.

Censorship of Antislavery Speech

Throughout the antebellum period, antislavery voices were stifled by censorship by the executive branch of the federal government, by state legislatures, and by racist mobs. Such censorship was not limited to slave states. And avowed abolitionists—lonely radicals at the time—were not the only ones who suffered under it.

In 1835, Congress considered legislation aimed at suppressing antislavery publications, and President Andrew Jackson's postmaster general, Amos Kendall, opined that the Privileges and Immunities Clause posed no obstacle.[111] Jackson urged Congress to target "incendiary publications intended to instigate slaves to insurrection."[112] John Calhoun considered this insufficient and proposed prohibiting postmasters from circulating publications that "touch[ed] on the subject of slavery" and the circulation of which was prohibited in addressees' states.[113]

No federal legislation was enacted. But Southern states adopted their own laws forbidding members of "abolition" societies to enter their states. And they criminalized the circulation of antislavery books.[114] Southern states also issued resolutions calling on Northern states to take similar action.[115]

Northern states of course did not follow the South's legislative lead. But neither did they forcefully defend the freedoms of speech and the press. Indeed, some Northern governors expressed sympathy for the South's arguments. The governor of New York pointed out that local mobs made official suppression of abolitionist speech unnecessary.[116] Abolitionists were persecuted by mobs in New York, Ohio, Pennsylvania, Massachusetts, and elsewhere in the North.[117] They were tarred and feathered, hit in the head with rocks, and pushed from platforms.[118] Their homes were sacked, their churches were burned, and their meeting halls were vandalized.[119]

In an act of violence that exceeded the treatment of Samuel Hoar in its notoriety among antislavery forces, newspaper editor Elijah Lovejoy was murdered while defending his printing press from a mob in southern Illinois.[120] Abolitionists such as James Birney in nearby Cincinnati, Ohio, turned trauma into an opportunity to present the antislavery cause as the cause of all American citizens. Birney pointed to mobbings as proof that slavery threatened not only "freedom for the black" but "freedom for the white"—a potent political argument in the North.[121] In 1836, an attack on Birney and the destruction of his press by a Cincinnati mob first engaged the young Ohio attorney Salmon P. Chase publicly in the slavery issue.[122]

Similarly, the New York antislavery convention's platform described free discussion as a "high constitutional privilege."[123] It asserted that it was "the right of American citizens to discuss the subject of slavery as well as any subject" and lamented that "the privileges of the free are now doomed as a sacrifice on the altar of perpetual slavery."[124] Moderate antislavery politicians who were by no means abolitionists, but who could not campaign on antislavery platforms in the South, drew the same connection between slavery, censorship, and the violation of all citizens' constitutional privileges.

The Rise of the Republican Party

A comprehensive account of the emergence of the Republican Party is beyond the scope of this book.[125] In the following discussion, we will limit our focus to a variety of Republican commitments that took shape in the years preceding the Civil War and led toward a fundamental-rights conception of privileges and immunities. Neither a reading of the clause that was limited to comity nor a reading limited to racial discrimination fit their political or moral purposes.

Politically, white Southern Republicans generally found that they could not successfully campaign without the freedom to speak in opposition to slavery's continued expansion.[126] A legally orthodox comity reading of the Privileges and Immunities Clause might secure that freedom to Republicans who traveled to states of which they were not citizens, but it would not protect Republicans who campaigned in their home states. Complaints that both white and Black Republican citizens of both free and slave states were silenced by censorious legislation or mobs became increasingly frequent as Republican fortunes became dependent on their capacity to speak unimpeded.

Morally, Republicans believed that all citizens of the United States ought to enjoy civil rights that they considered essential to American citizenship. As we will detail in Chapter 3, Republicans' understanding of American citizenship was grounded in three fundamental commitments: (1) to natural rights; (2) to civic equality between similarly situated citizens; and (3) to governmental protection of 1 and 2, given in return for citizens' allegiance. Not all Republicans shared abolitionists' moral abhorrence of slavery, and some Republicans espoused profoundly racist views.[127] Yet, even the latter were generally prepared to encourage moral aversion to slavery among Northern voters and propagate Republican citizenship for the sake of white rights.[128]

Much has been written about the fact that Republicans did not, for the most part, insist on equal "political rights" for Blacks, among which the most frequently mentioned were the rights to vote, hold office, or sit on juries.[129] As we will see, however, Republicans at the time did not generally understand such political rights to be essential to *anyone*'s citizenship. Republicans may have held a narrow understanding of citizenship, but they were not inconsistent in this respect.

When it came to civil rights—rights that they did regard as essential to citizenship—Republicans insisted on all citizens' full equality. Republicans fought state-level efforts to abridge due process of law, travel, economic, and speech rights and boasted of their own states' solicitude for the same. Some of them, like Salmon Chase, defended the due process of law rights of runaways in court at the cost of their own political advancement.[130] Even though proslavery dominance of all three branches of the federal government made Republicans wary of federal intervention in state affairs during the antebellum period, Republicans consistently affirmed that US citizenship carried with it certain fundamental rights that needed to be secured against state abridgments—somehow.

Few Republicans were abolitionists. But one did not need to be an abolitionist to fear slavery's increasingly tight grip on the reins of federal policy, the increasingly oppressive state legislation that it inspired, or the bloody personal violence meted out by its proponents—even on the Senate floor to one of their own, Charles Sumner.[131] The spread of the Republican Party's antislavery nationalism popularized an interpretation of a fundamental-rights reading of the Privileges and Immunities Clause that might otherwise have remained marginal.

For purposes of understanding the original public meaning of the Fourteenth Amendment, it is highly significant that, in 1860, the Republican National Convention invoked an explicitly fundamental-rights reading of the Privileges and Immunities Clause in a supplemental resolution, authored by Ohio Representative Joshua Giddings:

> Resolved, That we deeply sympathize with those men who have been driven, some from their native States and others from the States of their adoption, and are now exiled from their homes on account of their opinions; and we hold the Democratic Party responsible for this gross violation of *that clause of the Constitution which declares that the citizens of each State shall be entitled to all the privileges and immunities of citizens in the several States.*[132]

The resolution of this soon-to-be-triumphant Republican Party clearly and publicly expressed an understanding of the Privileges and Immunities Clause that encompassed more than a comity-only protection against parochial discrimination against out-of-staters. Southern states were enforcing their bans on pro-slavery speech equally against their own citizens and out-of-staters alike.

As we have acknowledged, this understanding was both legally unorthodox and likely contrary to the original meaning of Article IV. But the premises on which legal orthodoxy rested had been eroding for decades. So it is unsurprising that the popular understanding and legal understanding of the Privileges and Immunities Clause began to diverge well before the enactment of the Fourteenth Amendment.

The Admission of Oregon

In 1854, the House considered an enabling act for authorizing the people of Oregon to frame a constitution and seek admission to the Union.[133] Although Oregon was composed largely of middle-class emigrants from slave states, Congress had prohibited slavery in 1848 when making it a territory.[134] Accordingly, Southerners generally opposed statehood, for fear of altering the now-favorable balance of power between free and slaveholding states.[135] After the House passed the enabling act, the act became mired in sectional debate in the Senate. In the meantime, Oregon framed a constitution in 1857 without waiting for Congress. The constitution forbade slavery, but it also contained a provision that forbade free Blacks from either entering the state or initiating lawsuits.[136]

A number of Republicans vigorously objected to the latter provision. John Bingham called it "odious" and opined that "a State which, in its fundamental law, denies to any person, or to a large class of persons, a hearing in her courts of justice, ought to be treated as an outlaw, unworthy of a place in the sisterhood of the Republic."[137] In this speech, Bingham made plain that he understood the clause to secure a floor of fundamental national rights:

> The citizens of each State, all the citizens of each State being citizens of the United States, shall be entitled to "all privileges and immunities of citizens in the several States." *Not to the rights and immunities of the several States;* not to those constitutional rights and immunities *which result exclusively from State authority or State legislation;* but to "all privileges and immunities" of citizens of the United States in the several States. There is an ellipsis in the

language employed in the Constitution but its meaning is self-evident that it is "the privileges and immunities of citizens of the United States in the several States" that it guarantees.[138]

Bingham's claim that the clause protected the "privileges and immunities of citizens *of the United States* in the several states" did not necessarily commit him to a fundamental-rights theory of the clause. Justice Story similarly claimed that the clause protected the privileges and immunities of US citizens in the several states but understood the clause only "to communicate all the privileges and immunities which citizens of the same state would be entitled to under the like circumstances."[139] It was the distinction Bingham drew between the "constitutional rights and immunities which result exclusively from State authority or State legislation" and those protected by the clause that signaled a fundamental-rights theory. Unlike Story, Bingham did not tie the privileges and immunities of sojourning US citizens to the positive law of the particular states in which they sojourned.

What were these privileges or immunities of US citizens? Bingham specifically identified "the rights of life and liberty and property, and the due protection in the enjoyment thereof by law" as "privileges and immunities of citizens of the United States" that no state could decline to secure to any class of citizens. Echoing the Declaration of Independence, he went still further, denying

that the majority of any republican state may, in any way, rightfully restrict the humblest citizen of the United States in the free exercise of any one of his natural rights; those rights common to all men, and to protect which . . . all good governments are instituted; and the failure to maintain which inviolate furnishes, at all times, a sufficient cause for the abrogation of such governments.[140]

In his view, Oregon's odious provision was "not only a violation . . . of the Constitution of the United States[]"—it was "a flagrant violation of the law of nature, as recognized by every civilized nation in the world." Striking a similar chord, James Wilson described the provision as "unconstitutional, inhuman and unchristian."[141]

Henry Dawes accused the Supreme Court in *Dred Scott* of having "struck more fatal blows at the rights of men than ever before, in the history of the Government." But he then contended that, even by Chief Justice Taney's reasoning, Oregon could not exclude free Blacks from its borders or its courts. Because Blacks had, since the adoption of Massachusetts' constitution, "stood forth clothed with all the rights, privileges, and immunities of the citizen," they could not be driven from other states or prevented from "holding property, making contracts, suing in [their] courts, or even eating the bread of life within [their] borders."[142]

Like Bingham, Dawes assumed the existence of citizenship privileges and immunities that were independent of state law rights. He focused on a provision of the proposed constitution stating that "[n]o Chinaman, not a resident of the state at the adoption of this constitution, shall ever hold any real estate, or mining claim, or work any mining claim therein."[143] Dawes contended that this provision would "build[] up two classes of foreign men in th[e] community; one with personal rights and privileges as citizens, and another disabled, with no rights to hold real estate or to exercise any of *the great immunities of citizens.*"[144]

Proslavery Southerners predictably responded by denying that free Blacks were citizens of the United States. They charged free-state "moralists" with ignorance of the "contaminating, vicious, depraved, unprincipled" character of the "great mass of the emancipated negroes." They expressed confidence that free states would eventually "find, whatever may be their theoretic or their abstract opinions; that their obligations to themselves and to their communities will compel them" to similarly exclude free Blacks, who would then return to the South and "ask as a boon to be admitted into slavery."[145] Of course, denying that free Blacks were citizens was not to deny that citizenship entailed privileges or immunities beyond the right to be free from parochial discrimination.

It is highly probative of the diachronic changes in Article IV's public meaning between 1788 and 1868 that neither antislavery nor proslavery legislators articulated a comity-only reading of the Privileges and Immunities Clause during this debate. To be clear, the fact that the public meaning of the Privileges and Immunities Clause was evolving from a comity-only to a fundamental-rights reading did not affect *its* original meaning. But this evolution does significantly affect the original public meaning of the Privileges or Immunities Clause of the Fourteenth Amendment at the time it was enacted in 1868, which is the subject of this study.

Discrimination against Free Blacks

Most free Blacks lived in the South and did not leave it.[146] Many were too poor and too attached to their families and friends to make their way North.

Some elite Blacks worked at trades that were monopolized by whites in the North and feared a loss of status.[147] Owing to the costs of travel, those who did migrate North tended to stop at the first free state, even though New England states allowed them more freedom.[148]

Those who made their way to New England still encountered discriminatory laws and social norms. Some such Northern laws required Blacks to leave if they could not post bonds of $500; allowed steam boat and stage companies to discriminate on the basis of race; imposed property qualifications for Black suffrage or denied Blacks suffrage entirely; excluded Blacks from public schools; forbade Blacks to testify in court; and precluded them from enrolling in the militia.[149]

Consequently, free Blacks and their white supporters had compelling reasons to complain about the abridgment of Black rights, regardless of whether they were traveling or staying put in the North or in the South. From the 1830s into the 1850s, Blacks assembled in conventions where they argued for their rights as citizens.[150] When they did, they emphasized the Constitution and—especially—the Declaration of Independence, both of which they generally read as abolitionist and racially egalitarian in spirit, if not maximally so in letter.[151]

In denouncing discriminatory state laws, Blacks repeatedly referred to the privileges and rights of citizenship and specifically cited the Privileges and Immunities Clause of Article IV.[152] They did so not only when complaining about the laws of other states to which they might travel, but when criticizing the laws of their own states. In some of the "freest" states in the North, they urged Republicans who had recently ascended to power to ensure that the privileges of Black citizens were no longer abridged.[153]

Unlike some white abolitionists, however, not a single Black participant in any of the conventions denied that citizenship entailed suffrage, and numerous Black participants insisted that it did.[154] We will return to this disagreement and its relevance to public meaning in due course.

★   ★   ★

We do not claim that the above factors were the only ones that contributed to the convergence by antislavery and proslavery forces on a fundamental-rights reading of the Privileges and Immunities Clause. That convergence was overdetermined by economic, political, and cultural factors that made the conflict over slavery national in scope. These factors made a fundamental-rights reading of the federal Constitution attractive to both sides as a means of securing rights that they deemed especially important across the expanding nation.

The proslavery side advocated for the fundamental rights of slaveholders to their "property" when a comity-only interpretation would not suffice. They also asserted a fundamental-rights reading as a reductio ad absurdum of claims that free Blacks could ever be citizens. The antislavery side, for its part, advocated for the fundamental rights of whites and free Blacks to such freedoms as those of speech and the press—both when sojourning and when at home—that a comity-only approach would leave at the mercy of local majorities.

Of course, antislavery and proslavery readings of the clause were not equally important to the original meaning of the Fourteenth Amendment. To the contrary, the Fourteenth Amendment was framed by antislavery legislators and ratified by an antislavery public. In the next chapter, we will discuss the theory of citizenship that informed antislavery advocates' distinctive understanding of the Privileges and Immunities Clause.

3

The Antislavery Origins of Republican Citizenship

IT IS WIDELY AGREED that Republican constitutional thought was deeply influenced by the constitutional thought of antislavery advocates who would today be classified as abolitionists—even if some of them resisted the label at the time.[1] It is also accepted that Republicans brought this constitutional thought to bear on the work of Reconstruction.[2] The precise nature of this influence is, however, hotly disputed.

Abolitionists were not all constitutionalists. Those who followed William Lloyd Garrison strenuously denied that the Constitution was morally legitimate.[3] Nor did abolitionist constitutionalists agree on every interpretive question. Further, we have no direct evidence that abolitionist constitutionalism influenced the framing of the Fourteenth Amendment, as congressional Republicans did not cite abolitionist authorities.

Still, Salmon P. Chase, who first made his name in the 1830s opposing the constitutionality of the Fugitive Slave Act of 1793, shared many of the constitutional positions of others whom Richard Sewell has usefully dubbed "political abolitionists."[4] Chase was instrumental in founding—and devising and drafting the constitution platforms of—the Liberty, Free Soil, and Republican Parties. He is credited with inventing the slogan "Free Soil, Free Labor, Free Speech, Free Men" for the Free Soil Party, which the Republicans in 1856 adopted as "Free Soil, Free Labor, Free Speech, Free Men and Fremont!"[5]

As one of the founders of the party—and its legal fountainhead—Chase had impeccable Republican credentials. After serving as US senator from

Ohio as a Free Soiler, Chase became the first Republican governor of Ohio—the first Republican elected governor of any state. He was a strong contender for the 1860 presidential nomination, treasury secretary in the Lincoln administration, and chief justice of the United States.[6] His views on the Constitution conformed with the mainstream of antislavery constitutionalism he was instrumental in developing.[7] That both he and John Bingham hailed from Ohio is also significant.

Whatever their differences, constitutional abolitionists and Republicans worked within a common political-philosophical framework and conceived of American citizenship in much the same way. We also have compelling circumstantial reasons to believe that influential Republicans were exposed to and influenced by constitutional abolitionist arguments. But the value of examining abolitionist thought about citizenship is not contingent on the truth of any particular causal story. The contours of abolitionist and Republican thought about citizenship are sufficiently similar for the former to be of use in understanding the latter regardless.

We will begin by disentangling two strands of abolitionist thought concerning the Constitution. The first rejected the Constitution on the ground that it was a proslavery document that was utterly incompatible with natural-rights principles. The second embraced the Constitution on the ground that its overarching function was to implement natural-rights principles that were utterly incompatible with slavery. We will then turn our attention to the latter view, which was the view that most closely resembles that of the Republican Party. Finally, we will sketch the conception of citizenship that Republicans articulated before and after the Civil War and compare it to the conception articulated by constitutional abolitionists.

Abolitionist Constitutional Thought

In 1833, William Lloyd Garrison articulated what was at the time a common abolitionist view of the relationship between first political-philosophical principles and the Constitution. *The Declaration of Sentiments of the American Anti-Slavery Convention* affirmed that "the right to enjoy liberty is inalienable"; that "every man has a right to his own body—to the products of his own labor—to the protection of law—and to the common advantages of society"; and that "all persons of color who possess the qualifications which are demanded of others, ought to be admitted forthwith to the enjoyment of the same privileges, and the exercise of the same prerogatives, as others;

and that the paths of preferment, of wealth, and of intelligence, should be opened as widely to them as to persons of a white complexion."[8] It condemned "all those laws which are now in force, admitting the right of slavery" as "before God, utterly null and void."[9]

Crucially, however, it acknowledged that "Congress, under the present national compact, has no right to interfere with any of the slave States in relation to this momentous subject" and urged "moral and political action" to remove "the Constitutions' [sic] protections for slavery."[10] Garrison and his followers disavowed the use of "carnal weapons"—in other words, violence—to achieve the end of abolition, and they largely eschewed electoral politics.[11]

Although slavery opponents of all stripes held to natural-rights principles throughout the antebellum period, they disagreed about the relationship between those principles and the Constitution. In the wake of proslavery's gains throughout the 1830s and the seizure of alleged freedom-seeker George Latimer under the 1793 Fugitive Slave Act in Boston, newspaperman Garrison and the Harvard-trained lawyer Wendell Phillips contended that the Constitution was a proslavery, racist document and could not be used to contest proslavery hegemony.[12]

This anticonstitutionalism may have been, as William Wiecek has put it, "a post-hoc rationalization for disunion," which Garrison and Phillips viewed as morally and strategically preferable.[13] Specifically, they considered that disunion would enable abolitionists to clear themselves of moral complicity with slavery and deprive slavery of the support that the constitutional system provided.[14]

Although they were ardent natural-rights adherents, Garrisonians were "exclusive" positivists who denied that consistency with natural-rights principles could ever be a criterion of constitutional validity. They also insisted that those who did not view the Constitution as thoroughly evil had the weight of "the concurrent, unbroken practice of every department of government . . . and the acquiescence of the people for fifty years" arrayed against them.[15] Their legal and constitutional philosophy served their ideological and tactical goals well. Had they set out to design a constitutional theory to convince the public that working within the constitutional system to attack slavery was impossible and that secession from the Union was the only moral and prudent path toward abolition, they could hardly have done better.

Phillips took full advantage of the publication in 1840 of James Madison's record of the 1787 debates. In 1844, Phillips published *The Constitution: A Pro-Slavery Compact; or Selections from the Madison Papers*, in which he mined

Madison's notes for evidence that the Framers consciously protected the interests of slaveholders. Garrison insisted that the words of the Constitution should be interpreted according to the intentions of its Framers—what today would be called "Framers' intent originalism."

But Garrison and Phillips did not go unanswered. In 1845, Lysander Spooner, a country lawyer from Athol, Massachusetts, responded with *The Unconstitutionality of Slavery*. In this work, he repudiated reliance on Framers' intent, asserting instead that it was the original public meaning of the text that courts were bound to follow.[16] Then Spooner went to great lengths to establish that the public meaning of the text—even that of the Fugitive Slave Clause—admitted of both a just and an unjust meaning.

When confronting ambiguity of this type, Spooner advocated a rule of construction favoring the just meaning. Spooner drew this constitutional construction from a principle of statutory construction articulated by Chief Justice John Marshall in the 1805 case of *United States v. Fisher:* "Where rights are infringed, where fundamental principles are overthrown, where the general system of the laws is departed from," wrote Marshall, "the legislative intention must be expressed with irresistible clearness, to induce a court of justice to suppose a design to effect such objects."[17]

In 1847, "goaded by charges that he was afraid to tackle the most famous antislavery analysis of the Constitution—Lysander Spooner's *The Unconstitutionality of Slavery*,"[18] Phillips self-published a ninety-page reply. Later that same year, Spooner responded with a "part second" of *The Unconstitutionality of Slavery*, in which he expanded on his interpretive methodology and offered additional evidence to support an innocent reading of the text. When combined, Spooner's book ran to nearly 300 pages, and that version was repeatedly reprinted.

In denying that the Constitution protected slavery anywhere in the Union, Spooner was joined by William Goodell, Gerrit Smith, Alvan Stewart, Joel Tiffany, and Theodore Dwight Weld. This group contended that the Constitution made enslaved people both free and citizens.[19]

Before Spooner wrote, Frederick Douglass had publicly defended the Garrison-Phillips reading of the Constitution. Then, in 1851, after "[a] careful study of the writings of Lysander Spooner, of Gerrit Smith, and of William Goodell,"[20] Douglass adopted the public-meaning approach. While Douglass never went so far as to claim that slavery was unconstitutional, he used the public-meaning approach to deny that the Constitution expressly sanctioned the concept of property in man. Instead, he claimed that the Founders tacitly allowed the practice to survive until it could be extirpated by the states.

Although Douglass adopted Spooner's interpretive approach, his conclusions about the Constitution's public meaning more closely resembled that of Salmon Chase and the soon-to-be-formed Republican Party in which he became thoroughly involved. The theories of constitutional abolitionists such as Douglass and Chase have the stronger claim to have contributed to the content of the Fourteenth Amendment because they most closely resemble the one embraced by Republicans.

But, to avoid any misunderstanding, we reiterate that both the Spooner-Goodell group and the Douglass-Chase group adopted a public-meaning approach, as opposed to the Garrisonians' Framers' intent approach. They principally disagreed with one another about the extent to which the alleged textual references to slavery in the Constitution were ambiguous. Consequently, they disagreed on the permissibility of resorting to Marshall's rule of construction in *Fisher* to resolve the alleged ambiguity. More importantly for present purposes, however, both groups shared a common approach to national citizenship.

Citizenship in Constitutional Abolitionism

As early as the 1830s, constitutional abolitionists deployed the concept of national citizenship to argue that Blacks were entitled to the liberty to speak, to organize their domestic affairs, and to pursue livelihoods, among other rights; to equal treatment under the law; and to protection by the government against coercion by other citizens. Initially, these demands were only loosely associated with any constitutional text, and abolitionists did not specifically refer to the rights of "citizens of the United States."

The first noteworthy abolitionist step toward a definition of "citizens of the United States" was taken by the prominent lawyers William Ellsworth, son of the second chief justice of the United States, and Calvin Goddard. In 1836, Ellsworth and Goddard advocated on behalf of Prudence Crandall before the Supreme Court of Connecticut.[21] Crandall was a Quaker who had in 1833 established a private boarding school for Black girls in Canterbury, Connecticut. Neighboring townspeople secured the passage of a measure that prohibited "the instruction or education of colored persons . . . not resident of this state," absent "the consent in writing of a majority of the civil authority and also of the selectmen of the town."[22] She was arrested, jailed, twice tried, and eventually convicted of "harboring" and "boarding" a seventeen-year old Rhode Island girl, Eliza Hammond.[23]

Ellsworth and Goddard's legal costs were paid by the New York abolitionist philanthropist Arthur Tappan.[24] So it is no accident that their arguments on Crandall's behalf were subsequently circulated widely as a tract.[25] These arguments included a discussion of the reciprocal relationship between the allegiance of citizens and protection by the government of a set of equal rights associated with citizenship:

> These pupils [are] human beings, born in these states, and owe the *same obligation* to the state ... as white citizens.... All writers agree that allegiance demands obedience from the citizen and protection by the government. If allegiance is due from our colored population, its correlative is due from the government, viz. protection and equal laws.[26]

In other words, the natural *duty of obedience* to government authority owed by a citizen entails a reciprocal *duty of protection* toward citizens that is owed by the government. These reciprocal duties attach both to free Blacks and to their state governments:

> Here the free man of color may take his position, and upon the immutable principles of justice and truth demand his political rights and aid from that government which he is bound to defend.... [H]e is not a *citizen* to obey and an *alien* to demand protection.... [H]is absolute and relative rights, his rights of person and to things, his acquisitions of property by contract and by inheritance—and even the soil, which no alien inherits—are the same.[27]

Of particular relevance here is that Ellsworth and Goddard then proceeded to derive a national entitlement of citizens to the above "fundamental rights" from the Privileges and Immunities Clause, arguing that the clause was designed

> to declare a citizen of one state to be a citizen of every state, and as such, to clothe him with the same *fundamental rights,* be he where he might, which he acquired by birth in a particular state ... to do away with the character and consequences of alienage among the citizens of these United States, to the extent of the reciprocity of the privileges and immunities secured, be they what they may.[28]

Finally, Ellsworth and Goddard made plain that the "fundamental rights" protected by the clause were ontologically national, in the sense of being derived from the nature of the national government:

If 4th art. sec. 2 means anything, [it secures] to *a citizen of New York,* a right to come here, and remain here, if he offends against no general law. . . . [H]e may present the shield of the constitution, and as Paul claimed the immunity of a Roman citizen, he may claim the immunity of *an American citizen.* Neither present nor future poverty can strike out of the constitution the word citizen, and *a citizen has a universal right, title, and immunity, to a residence, and other fundamental rights.*[29]

We have, then, in embryonic form, a concept of national citizenship that includes nonnegotiable fundamental rights, including property rights, rights of education, and rights of travel. It is embryonic because Ellsworth and Goddard do not clearly assert that these rights could not be denied equally by states to their own citizens *and* to visitors. Rather, they take as a given that states do in fact generally secure the citizens' property, education, and travel rights. Their arguments are thus consistent with the proposition that the rights that attach to national citizenship through the Privileges and Immunities Clause are a function of state law.

Where did all of this come from? As good nineteenth-century lawyers, Ellsworth and Goddard drew from a variety of sources, including Story, Kent, Blackstone, and Justice Washington's opinion in *Corfield.* They appealed to the Declaration of Independence, to the Articles of Confederation, to state constitutions, to prior Supreme Court decisions, and to "reason, justice, and policy."[30] They cited authorities on the law of nations, claiming that "all writers" agreed that "while the residence of the citizen continues, in the state of his birth, allegiance demands obedience from the citizen, and protection from the government."[31]

It is significant that they did not perceive any need to choose between natural law, constitutional law, or common law—all these sources of law pointed toward a concept of citizenship that entailed protection of certain rights in return for allegiance and was incompatible with racial discrimination. Ellsworth and Goddard pointed out that free Blacks' allegiance, like that of whites, could be presumed from their birth under the jurisdiction of US law. But they also emphasized that many free Blacks had proven their allegiance on the battlefield—that Blacks had served "in the army that achieved for us our liberty."[32]

Ellsworth and Goddard did not specify *which* "fundamental rights" attached to national citizenship. They were clear that the "right[s] of residing in Connecticut, and pursuing the acquisition of knowledge" were fundamental and insisted that "[m]ere birth in another state cannot be seized upon" to deny someone the ability to "be a lawyer, or doctor, or farmer."[33] (File this quotation away for our later discussion of *Bradwell v. Illinois* in Chapter 6.) At the same time, Ellsworth and Goddard expressed uncertainty about the right to vote, opining that the right was "valuable but perhaps . . . not a natural so much as an artificial right" and that the natural rights of persons "do not seem . . . to embrace the right of suffrage."[34] Although they drew from Justice Washington's opinion in *Corfield,* they omitted his reference to the right to vote.[35]

Ellsworth and Goddard also did not state any set of necessary-and-sufficient conditions for fundamentality. They cited Washington's all-states-since-independence language. But they did not rely on it when either affirming the fundamentality of residence, education, or economic rights or questioning the fundamentality of voting rights.

The Supreme Court of Errors reversed Crandall's convictions on the ground that the indictment was insufficient, without addressing Ellsworth and Goddard's constitutional arguments.[36] As we already noted, those arguments nonetheless were widely circulated within abolitionist circles in pamphlet form. They served as a frequent point of reference by constitutional abolitionists who would more fully develop the concept of national citizenship.

Both *Crandall v. State of Connecticut* and the arguments of Ellsworth and Goddard became famous among constitutional abolitionists.[37] Legal arguments such as these were circulated as pamphlets. Just three years later, in 1837, the constitutional arguments unsuccessfully made by Salmon Chase in seeking to thwart the seizure of a free Black household worker, Matilda Lawrence, under the Fugitive Slave Act appeared as a pamphlet.[38] As they circulated, these pamphlets also accumulated to form the building blocks of a distinctive theory of the Constitution's meaning.

At roughly the same time, dissident antislavery groups that had been driven out of the South into Ohio and the Northwest began to organize local abolitionist societies, preach sermons, and circulate tracts that Howard Jay Graham aptly characterized as a "fusion of the Bible and Blackstone."[39] These groups formed part of the constituencies that later sent Free Soiler Salmon Chase from Cleveland to the Senate, where he joined fellow Free Soiler Charles Sumner from Massachusetts. In both states, the Free Soil Party held the balance of power in the state legislature, and the Free Soilers agreed to throw their support to the Democrats in return for the Senate seat. In Ohio, they also demanded and received the abolition of its discriminatory Black codes.

Later, these antislavery groups would send Joshua Giddings, John Bingham, and William Lawrence, among other Ohio Republicans, to the House. Bingham and Lawrence were both students at Franklin College—an abolitionist stronghold—during the height of these abolitionists' campaigns.[40] Their discussions of citizenship were strikingly similar to Ellsworth and Goddard's.

Specifically, Ohio Republicans Henry Stanton, Charles Olcott, and James Duncan argued that slavery violated not only natural law but common law. They took the latter to guarantee—in Olcott's words—"to all human beings within its jurisdiction and under its protection the free use of all their natural rights, in the highest perfection."[41] Stanton characterized slavery as tantamount to "outlawry, with its concomitants, outrage and vice" and cast the abolitionist demand as one for "emancipation into law," specifically, "citizenship, with the dignities and immunities of manhood."[42]

Duncan claimed that "[a]ll men have a natural right to be citizens, and to enjoy civil protection." He lamented that enslaved people were "placed under the arbitrary power of their masters, and have no more protection from the laws than horses or cattle, except so far as it will serve the worldly interest of slaveholders."[43] All of these figures understood citizenship to come with a duty of allegiance and a reciprocal entitlement to governmental protection in respect of one's natural rights through law.[44]

In the 1840s, Lysander Spooner and Joel Tiffany fleshed out a sophisticated theory of national citizenship that was tethered to the Anglo-American legal tradition. As already noted, Spooner was a lawyer from rural Athol, Massachusetts. Tiffany was a lawyer who was born in Connecticut and went on to be a reporter for New York's highest court. But both spent time in Ohio.[45] Both relied on Blackstone, on the text of constitutional provisions, on state law, and on doctrines extracted from case law, as well as on social-contractual premises that they considered to be self-evidently true.

Jacobus tenBroek dubbed Spooner's and Tiffany's theory of national citizenship "paramount national citizenship." Their theory merits careful examination, both because of its sophistication and because of its close resemblance to the theory of national citizenship on which Republicans later converged. We will start with Spooner.

Spooner inferred the existence of a national citizenship from the words "the people" in the Preamble: "We, the people of the United States do ordain and establish this constitution."[46] He observed that the text drew no distinctions between people, whether racial or otherwise. He denied that "state governments have the right of determining who may, and who may not be citizens of the United States government." If states could do so, he reasoned, "then it follows that the state governments may at pleasure destroy the government of the United States, by enacting that none of their respective inhabitants shall be citizens of the United States."[47] That would be absurd.

Spooner pointed out that "the preamble itself . . . declares that 'the people' (and not the State governments) . . . ordain and establish it."[48] As any "arbitrary power" to make—or unmake—"citizens of the United States" was foreclosed to states, Spooner concluded that "all the native born inhabitants of the country are at least competent to become citizens of the United States, (if they are not already such,)" and, therefore, "[s]tate governments have no power, by slave laws or any other, to withhold the rights of citizenship from them."[49] What did national citizenship entail?

To affirm that state governments could not withhold the rights of citizenship from them is to imply that national citizenship comes with a set of rights. When analyzing the "three-fifths" clause of Article II, Section 1, Spooner argued that the clause did not sanction slavery but "purport[ed] only to prescribe the manner in which the population shall be counted, in making up the basis of representation and taxation."[50] He then decried those who had "transmuted, by unnecessary interpretation, [the three-fifths clause] into a provision denying all civil rights under the constitution to a part of the very 'people' who are declared by the constitution itself to have 'ordained and established' the instrument."[51]

Enslaved people, stated Spooner, "have equal rights in [the Constitution], *and in all the privileges and immunities* it secures."[52] Precisely what those "privileges and immunities" were or how one went about ascertaining them was left largely unexplored. Still, Spooner left no doubt that national citizenship entailed "the protection of the laws."[53] Protection was both a "right" and a means of preserving other rights—rights that Spooner did not discuss in detail.

Further, Spooner drew a distinction between the rights of citizens, who were "full members of the state" in virtue of being "parties to the [constitutional] compact," and those of noncitizens. The latter, Spooner explained, "could claim hardly anything as a right, (perhaps nothing, unless it were the privilege of the writ of habeas corpus)." Noncitizens were allowed "as a matter of favor and discretion, such protection and privileges as the general and State governments should see fit to accord to them."[54]

Believing, as he did, that all people possessed natural rights and that no government could legitimately be empowered to "destroy or take from men their natural rights," Spooner could hardly have meant that noncitizens were not entitled to claim their *natural* rights.[55] Rather, as the reference to the "privilege of the writ of habeas corpus" suggests, Spooner meant that noncitizens were not entitled to claim certain post-political, historically rooted civil rights that had long distinguished citizens from noncitizens.

Spooner also denied that suffrage was among the civil rights that citizens were entitled to enjoy, pointing out first that women and children did not vote on the Constitution's adoption.[56] And yet uncontroversially, women and children were citizens. Second, "[u]nder . . . most, probably under all, the State constitutions, there are persons who are denied the right of suffrage."[57] Again, persons who are undeniably citizens nonetheless cannot vote, per widespread positive law.

Finally, Spooner interpreted Article II, Section 1's provision that "[n]o person, except a natural born citizen, or a citizen of the United States at the time of the adoption of this constitution, shall be eligible to the office of President" as an "implied assertion" that "natural birth in the country gives the right of citizenship."[58] With citizenship came protection by the law and "freedom," meaning that "all born since the adoption of the constitution of the United States have been born free" and could not legally be enslaved.[59]

Joel Tiffany arrived at similar conclusions through similar reasoning. Like Spooner, he inferred from the Preamble's language that no race or class of people was excluded from US citizenship.[60] Like Spooner, Tiffany determined that the Constitution created a national citizenship that did not previously exist and that embraced "all . . . citizens and subjects of the National government who are born within its jurisdiction."[61] Finally, like Spooner, Tiffany distinguished between the rights of US citizens and the rights of noncitizens, as well as between the natural rights of all people and the privileges and immunities of citizenship.

Tiffany's discussion of the content of those privileges and immunities, however, was far more extensive than was Spooner's and more closely tethered to Anglo-American history and tradition. It also made more explicit the federal government's duty to secure the privileges and immunities of national citizenship.

Tiffany adopted Blackstone's premises concerning the ends of civil government, as well as Blackstone's account of "civil liberty." Tiffany asserted that civil governments were "institutions of society, established for the aid and protection of the members thereof."[62] He regarded natural rights—"man's right to use his faculties and powers to provide for his present and future well-being"—as "the basis of the authority with which civil governments are necessarily invested."[63] Tiffany then described the "civil liberty" that people enjoyed under well-functioning governments as "the right to seek after, and employ, every means essential to the perfection of the individual in every department of his being . . . without encroaching upon the equal liberty of others."[64]

But Tiffany was not content to rely on Blackstone when identifying the privileges and immunities of US citizenship. He argued that "citizens of the United States" are "as such, . . . entitled to the benefits of the standing guarantys [sic] of the constitution for personal security, personal liberty, and private property."[65] Their government, Tiffany maintained, afforded "nothing short" of the protection for the rights that "are inalienably ours"—rights that "the ancient Roman or the present British" governments extended to their citizens and subjects, respectively.

Tiffany listed a number of rights specified in the text of the antebellum Constitution that provided every man with

> the right of petition,—the right to keep and bear arms, the right to be secure from all unwarrantable seizures and searches,—the right to demand, and have a presentment or indictment found by a grand jury before he shall be held to answer to any criminal charge,—the right to be informed beforehand of the nature and cause of accusation against him, the right to a public and speedy trial by an impartial jury of his peers,—the right to confront those who testify against him,—the right to have compulsory process to bring in his witnesses,—the right to demand and have counsel for his defence,—the right to be exempt from excessive bail, or fines, &c., from cruel and unusual punishments, or from being twice jeopardized for the same offence; and the right to the privileges *of the great writ of Liberty, the Habeas Corpus.*[66]

Like Spooner, Tiffany regarded such textually specified privileges as time-tested traditional means of securing natural and inherent rights.

Consider Tiffany's discussion of the writ of habeas corpus and right to keep and bear arms. Drawing from both Blackstone and Story, Tiffany argued that "the writ itself is based upon the hypothesis that all men have a natural inherent right to liberty." Providing for its availability served "one of the professed objects of the constitution," namely, that of "secur[ing] the blessings of liberty to the people."[67] Similarly, Tiffany described the right to keep and bear arms as "subordinate" to the "great, absolute rights of man"—as an immunity "accorded to every subject for the purpose of *protecting and defending himself,* if need be, in the enjoyment of his absolute rights to life, liberty and property."[68]

Tiffany acknowledged that it remained "peculiarly the province of state governments" to secure historically rooted privileges that, in turn, specified and protected natural rights to life, liberty, and property.[69] But he then contended that the federal government was empowered to "pass all the laws necessary" to enforce those historically rooted privileges.[70] Taken together with his determination that all persons born in the United States were citizens of the United States, this position led to radical conclusions.

Not only were all people—including enslaved people—"entitled to all the privileges and immunities of citizenship, which are guaranteed in the Federal Constitution for personal security, personal liberty, and private property," but "the whole nation individually and collectively, st[ood] pledged to protect and defend [slaves] in the enjoyment of those rights."[71] This duty of protection followed directly from the citizen's allegiance—allegiance being presumed in the case of those born in the United States and expressly given by those naturalized.[72] Accordingly, the federal government was obliged, not merely to confine slavery, but to "abolish[] it with all convenient dispatch."[73]

More emphatically than Spooner, Tiffany insisted on unstratified national citizenship. Again and again, he reiterated that the "constitution knows no *class* among its citizens."[74] This did not, however, exclude states from distinguishing between different groups of citizens when extending or regulating "political rights" such as suffrage that were "not necessary incident[s] to citizenship."[75] Because these rights did not belong to individuals but to "society," they could be conferred "upon such classes of individuals as is consistent with public safety and welfare."[76]

Thus, we have in the writings of Spooner and Tiffany a theory of paramount national citizenship that

- was based on natural-rights premises;
- derived the privileges and immunities of citizenship from constitutional text and from customary practice in the states;
- insisted on equality with respect to those privileges and immunities—civil rights—but not with respect to political rights, over which state governments enjoyed absolute discretion; and

- regarded the federal government as duty-bound to protect those civil rights that are essential to national citizenship, in return for citizens' allegiance.

As we have seen, not all abolitionists categorized particular rights as Spooner and Tiffany did. But Spooner's and Tiffany's articulation of the general contours of national citizenship was not controversial among constitutional abolitionists. Such citizenship was grounded in natural rights, was discernible through federal constitutional text, state practice, and case law, and was unstratified when it came to fundamental rights that are essential to citizenship.

Republican Citizenship

Prior to the Civil War, most Republicans did not take the view that the Constitution prohibited slavery in the states, and many took pains to distance themselves from "abolitionists." This label was freighted with radicalism and tainted by the memory of abolitionist John Brown's ill-fated 1859 effort to catalyze a general uprising of enslaved people by raiding and distributing weapons from a federal armory at Harpers Ferry, Virginia.[77] At the same time, Republicans articulated a common understanding of a national citizenship that they claimed was created by the Constitution and insisted that states were obliged to respect civil rights that were essential to citizenship.

Most Republicans believed that the federal government had more limited power to intervene within the states to protect citizens' civil rights than did constitutional abolitionists such as Spooner and Tiffany. But constitutional abolitionists and Republicans agreed that the federal government was obliged to protect civil rights in federal territories. They maintained that slavery was illegal in federal territories absent express legislative sanction and that it could constitutionally be banned in the District of Columbia.[78]

Like constitutional abolitionists, Republicans drew on social-contract and natural-rights theory, as well as on legal theory and case law. In the course of opposing slavery and articulating their conception of US citizenship, Republicans, too, appealed to Locke, Blackstone, Story, Kent, and commentators on the law of nations, including Samuel Pufendorf, Emmerich de Vattel, and Jean-Jacques Burlamaqui.[79] Republicans, too, argued that the supreme law of the land and the citizenship it created rested on the social-contractual and natural-rights premises from which these political philosophers and jurists worked.[80]

Were Republicans' claims about the social-contractual and natural-rights premises of the Constitution and their claims about the text's toleration of slavery confused? Salmon Chase asserted that "[t]he provisions of the constitution . . . were mainly designed to establish as written law, certain great principles of natural right and justice, which exist independently of all such sanction" and "announce restrictions upon legislative power, imposed by the very nature of society and of government." If so, how could it be that the Constitution left states to maintain, if they chose, an institution as hostile to "natural right and justice" as slavery?[81] John Bingham contended that government's "primal object must be to protect each human being within its jurisdiction in the free and full enjoyment of his natural rights." If so, how could it be that the Constitution left those natural rights to be voted up or down?[82]

Chase's approach to the tension was representative of that of Republicans more generally. He argued that the Framers did what they could to "repress[], limit[], and discourag[e]" the institution of slavery that they found among them and did not believe that they could speedily destroy.[83] Together with other Republicans, Chase argued that the Framers viewed slavery as a violation of natural rights. The Framers took pains to give it no endorsement and to separate the federal government from it. And they "anticipated with confidence the auspicious result of universal freedom."[84] Modern scholarship lends more support to Chase's historiography than some today assume.[85]

Of course, that Founding-era "confidence" proved unwarranted, and Republicans acknowledged as much. But they nonetheless insisted that the Constitution, properly interpreted, was an antislavery document. They maintained that slaveholders who had captured control of the federal government went beyond both the letter and the spirit of the Constitution by using federal power to perpetuate and extend slavery.

Consider Chase's analysis of the Fugitive Slave Act of 1793, which he claimed was unjust and unconstitutional. Chase conceded—as constitutional abolitionists such as Spooner and Goodell did not—that Article IV, Section 2, did indeed refer to slaves who escaped their captors, despite the fact that the Framers studiously avoided using the term "slave."[86] But he also pointed out that the clause lacked any express provision for its federal enforcement; that Article IV, Section 1 (the Full Faith and Credit Clause) had such a provision; and that the Tenth Amendment reserved to the states or

to the people (respectively) all powers not delegated to the federal government nor prohibited to the states.[87]

"[I]f a special provision was necessary to enable congress to legislate in
regard to the authentication and effect of records," asked Chase rhetorically,
"why is not a special provision necessary to enable congress to legislate in
regard to fugitive servants?"[88] For Chase, it was obvious both (a) that such
power needed to be expressly granted by the Constitution if Congress was
to exercise it lawfully and (b) that the states would not have assented to an
express grant of such power because of the threat it would have posed to "personal right[s] conferred by God and guarantied by the state constitutions."[89]
To claim such power, therefore, was to effectively amend the Constitution—
and to do so in the service of a proslavery goal that the Framers would have
deemed odious.

By acknowledging that the Constitution did not prohibit slavery outright
while simultaneously claiming that it embodied a "freedom national, slavery
local" policy, Republicans were able to invoke the authority of Framers, deflect charges of radicalism, reaffirm federalism as distinguished from Democrats' "state sovereignty," and paint proslavery advocates as constitutional
subversives.

Republicans could invoke the authority of the Framers because the Framers
did, for the most part, abhor slavery; and they refused to enshrine it by name in
the Constitution due to that abhorrence—even if they did accede to Southern
demands for structural constitutional protection of slavery.[90] Moreover, Republicans could deflect charges of radicalism because they did not claim any
constitutional authority to displace slavery where the Framers reluctantly
accepted its existence (while hoping it would eventually wither away).

Republicans could paint proslavery advocates as constitutional subversives
by showing how different proslavery advocates' views of slavery and federal
power were from those of the Founding generation who continued to maintain a larger-than-life heroic status among the public.[91] They could also in-
dict proslavery advocates for their eagerness to override the enumerated
powers scheme and federalism to impose slavery on the nation by compelling Northerners to aid an institution that the Framers sought to divorce from
the federal government. This last charge was particularly potent among
the Northern electorate, who might otherwise have been indifferent to the
South maintaining its peculiar institution.[92]

However, because they admitted the constitutionality of slavery and acknowledged limits on federal power to protect individual rights, Republi-

cans prior to the Civil War articulated a less inclusive vision of citizenship than did constitutional abolitionists. And they tied citizens' allegiance to a more modest amount of federal protection. John Bingham's 1859 opposition to the Oregon Constitution's exclusion of free Blacks from the state's borders and its restrictions on the civil rights of those remaining illustrates Republican citizenship's more limited scope.

When addressing the question of who are the citizens of the United States, Bingham said what at first glance could well have been penned by Tiffany or Spooner:

> First, all free persons born and domiciled within the United States—not all free white persons, but all free persons. You will search in vain, in the Constitution of the United States, for that word white; it is not there. . . . The omission of this word—this phrase of caste—from our national charter, was not accidental, but intentional.[93]

While limited to "free persons" rather than all persons, this is orthodox antislavery constitutionalism. But Tiffany and Spooner also pointed out that the Constitution's Preamble did not refer to "we the free people" any more than it did "we the white people." In contrast, according to Bingham, free Blacks were part of We the People but slaves were not.

True, the Oregon Constitution banned slavery and the exclusion provision applied only to "free Negro[s] [and] mullatos." But there is no indication here or in any other of Bingham's pre–Civil War speeches or writings that he considered enslaved people to be citizens of the United States who were constitutionally entitled to enjoy the privileges and immunities of US citizenship. To conclude that slaves were so entitled would, of course, compel the further conclusion that slavery was everywhere unconstitutional. Most Republicans were unwilling to take such a position for reasons of both principle and politics.

As Republicans' less-inclusive view of citizenship confined the scope of the Constitution's promises of freedom, their less-robust view of the federal protection that came with citizens' allegiance might be thought to have rendered that freedom more elusive. Proslavery dominance of the national government, however, made federal intervention on behalf of the rights of free Blacks and abolitionists exceedingly unlikely during the antebellum period.

When Chase argued that the federal government lacked power to compel Northern states to return freedom-seekers on the ground that such power was not expressly delegated to Congress, he did so in a context in which one could be confident that federal power would not generally be exercised in a manner friendly to antislavery interests. Put differently, a modest view of federal protection may have been more operationally antislavery during the antebellum period than one that allowed—as constitutional abolitionists did—that "if the constitution guaranty [*sic*] a right, the natural inference certainly is, that the National Government is clothed with appropriate authority to enforce it."[94]

When it came to the specific privileges and immunities of national citizenship, Republicans distinguished between civil rights and political rights even more sharply than did constitutional abolitionists. Prior to the Civil War and for some time afterward, Republicans generally and emphatically denied that they supported Black suffrage or Black office-holding, to say nothing of believing that such political rights necessarily followed from national citizenship. To be sure, there were outliers—Representative Thaddeus Stevens and Charles Sumner being among the prominent ones. But most Republicans carefully distinguished political rights from civil rights and did not claim that the extension of the former to Blacks was constitutionally compelled.

Why was it that Republicans considered suffrage in particular to be inessential to citizenship? We must remember that the Republican Party was comprised of political exiles from the Whigs and Democratic parties who brought with them some of their prior political commitments. A number of Republican leaders and a significant part of their constituency were disaffected Jacksonian Democrats who resented what they considered to be undemocratic machinations by the Southern wing of the party and its efforts to make slavery an object of national policy.[95] Certainly Jacksonians believed suffrage to be important—Jacksonian populism inspired state constitutional reform that greatly expanded the franchise.[96] That expansion, however, embraced only white males.[97]

On the other hand, had Republicans taken the view that voting rights were among the privileges and immunities of citizenship, they would have had to explain why most states—especially Northern states—did not extend those rights to Blacks. Recall how Dred Scott's lawyer, Montgomery Blair, had insisted that "the essence of citizenship is the right of protection of life and liberty, to acquire and enjoy property, and equal taxation" and that "[s]uffrage is not an absolute right of citizenship."[98] This, however, did not stop Chief Justice Taney from attempting to reduce Blair's argument for Black citizenship to absurdity by claiming that Black citizenship would entail Black suffrage.

It is counterintuitive and somewhat speculative, to be sure, but it appears that denying that voting rights were among the privileges and immunities of citizenship may have aided Republican advocacy of Black citizenship. It made plain that Black citizenship would not yield conclusions that were widely regarded as politically unacceptable, even by opponents of slavery. Further, like constitutional abolitionists, Republicans did not reason directly from natural rights to the privileges and immunities of national citizenship but, rather, looked to federal and state constitutions and to case law.

None of the state constitutions in force in 1788 granted the vote to all citizens, and only New Jersey's permitted women to vote.[99] By the beginning of the Civil War, in significant part because of the efforts of Jackson and his followers to build an electoral base, the franchise had been greatly expanded, but unevenly. In a series of state constitutional conventions between 1832 and 1851, Jacksonian Democrats would abolish property and taxpaying requirements and extend the principle of universal white manhood suffrage in six states, half of them in the South.[100]

Still, some form of property requirement survived in three states. Taxpayer requirements existed in six others. Racial barriers to voting—which did not exist even in certain Southern states early in the nineteenth century—increased as socioeconomic barriers to voting disappeared.[101] And New Jersey's constitution was revised to exclude women from voting in 1807.[102]

As to case law, numerous antebellum opinions distinguished political rights—and the right to suffrage in particular—from civil rights. Even Justice Washington's opinion in *Corfield*—on which Republicans primarily relied when arguing from case law—expressed uncertainty concerning the status of the elective franchise. Washington emphasized that the latter was "regulated and established by the laws or constitution of the state in which it is to be exercised."[103]

Republicans did not often rely on case law when discussing either citizenship or its privileges and immunities. But they did so occasionally, and they also responded to case law–based arguments made by others. The few cases that saw judges treating political rights as essential to citizenship were, for the most part, decided by judges with Southern sympathies who held that Blacks were not citizens because they were denied suffrage rights.[104]

Precisely what Republicans said about civil rights will be examined in more detail in Chapters 5 and 6. For now, it suffices to say that, in the run up to the Civil War, Republican citizenship, like abolitionist citizenship, was

- grounded in social-contract and natural-rights theory;
- tethered to the positive law of federal and state constitutions and to prior case law; and
- posited a reciprocal relationship between allegiance to, and protection by, the federal government.

Unlike some abolitionist constitutionalism, Republican citizenship

- did not affirm the citizenship of enslaved people, but only that of free persons born in the United States or naturalized under US law;
- distinguished more sharply between political and civil rights; and
- had a more limited conception of the federal protection that came with allegiance.

In the next chapter, we focus on the further development of Republican national citizenship after the initiation of hostilities.

4

Reconstructing National Citizenship

THE ELECTION OF Abraham Lincoln in 1860 and the Union's victory in the Civil War did not bring civil or political equality to Black people. But it broke the federal proslavery hegemony in one fell swoop. By 1865, the executive and legislative branches were dominated by officials who understood slavery to be the primary cause of the Civil War. They viewed the institution as incompatible with the civil rights of Blacks and whites. And they understood the task before them as one of guaranteeing all American citizens the rights that, as Alexander Tsesis has put it, were "essential for the common good of citizens."[1]

Yet, hewing to their previous constitutional stances, few Republicans believed that the Constitution in its present form empowered them to accomplish that task. The Emancipation Proclamation was understood to rest on the president's wartime powers and thus was uncertain constitutional ground on which to base slavery's abolition.[2]

As we will see, Republicans hoped that a constitutional amendment abolishing slavery would be sufficient to secure not only previously enslaved people's freedom from institutionalized bondage but their full citizenship, with all its attendant civil rights. But Southern states soon dashed those hopes by a combination of both state action and inaction. They enacted state laws designed to ensure continued racial segregation and domination.[3] And local officials either tolerated or actively participated in violent attacks on Blacks, white Republicans, and Southerners who remained loyal to the Union.[4]

The Thirteenth, Fourteenth, and Fifteenth Amendments constituted an effort to reconstruct American citizenship in a manner that was both faithful to Republicans' constitutional ideals, sensitive to the nonideal conditions on the ground, and informed by the success—or lack thereof—of previous measures in achieving their ends. The framing and ratifying of each text generated discourse about the privileges and immunities of citizenship that bears careful study. For obvious reasons, we will devote the most time to the framing and ratification of the Fourteenth Amendment. But we begin by discussing an important opinion issued by Lincoln's attorney general, Edward Bates.

The Opinion of Attorney General Bates

In 1861, when President Lincoln took office and the Southern states seceded, Republicans found themselves in complete control of Congress. While continuing to insist that they had no authority under the Constitution to abolish slavery within the existing states, they swiftly abolished slavery in the District of Columbia. The admission of new states, such as West Virginia, was conditioned on their abolishing slavery within. As authorized by Congress, the Union army began "confiscating" slaves as contraband of war under the doctrine of military necessity.

In 1862, Congress barred the US military from enforcing the Fugitive Slave Clause. The Militia Act of 1862 "explicitly freed any slave who enlisted in the Union army and at the same time freed 'his mother and his wife and his children.'"[5] Congress authorized the president to emancipate any slave upon the president's determination that emancipation was necessary to advance the military objectives of the Union army. This authorization culminated in the Emancipation Proclamation, which declared that any enslaved person held in disloyal territory was hereafter and forever free. Less well known, however, is a lengthy written opinion by Attorney General Edward Bates, which stated that free Blacks were citizens of the United States. As such, they were entitled to all the "privileges and immunities" of citizens of the United States that were secured by the Privileges and Immunities Clause. Of course, this directly conflicted with Chief Justice Taney's opinion in *Dred Scott,* in which he denied that free Blacks could *ever* be citizens of the US.

Bates wrote his opinion at the behest of Treasury Secretary Salmon Chase. Chase was looking for a way to support Black participation in the creation of an antislavery, pro-Union constitution for Louisiana.[6] Michael Vorenberg relates the incident: "Knowing that free blacks might be excluded from the process of state reconstruction if they were categorized as noncitizens, Chase looked for a way to have their citizenship established by law." Chase "knew he could get what he needed straightaway with an opinion from Bates. To solicit an opinion, though, he needed a specific case."[7]

David M. Selsey was a free Black ship master operating small ships along the mid-Atlantic coast. His schooner, the *Elizabeth & Margaret*, was stopped off the southern New Jersey coast by a Treasury cutter.[8] "Ship masters had to be citizens to be licensed, a policy that excluded blacks. With Selsey's ship in custody, Chase had the perfect test case."[9] When Chase appealed in person to Bates to write an opinion, the attorney general initially balked, demanding that the request be in writing. On September 24, Chase wrote Bates an official letter soliciting an opinion on the question: "Are colored men Citizens of the United States, and therefore Competent to command American vessels?"[10]

Bates struggled with the opinion for two months. "He read treatises on international law, he studied ancient Greek and Roman texts and he sought the counsel of Francis Lieber,"[11] whom we credited in our Introduction for contributing the interpretation–construction distinction to legal theory in the 1830s. "American lawyers and judges, Bates complained to Lieber, had failed 'to give a precise definition of Citizen (which I admit is very hard, if not impossible, to do).'"[12]

On November 29, 1862, Bates issued his opinion in the form of a letter to Chase. Chase then "sent copies of the opinion to his agents in Louisiana, who used it to silence those who denied the right of free blacks to participate in conventions leading to a new state constitution."[13] In December, the opinion was published by the Government Printing Office as a pamphlet entitled *Opinion of Attorney General Bates on Citizenship*.

The Bates opinion "received extensive coverage in newspapers and was often portrayed as a direct rebuttal of *Dred Scott*."[14] For example, under the headline "The Dred Scott Decision Pronounced Void," the *New York Times* immediately heralded the opinion, while acknowledging that it did not affect Black suffrage. "African Americans could only vote or enjoy other political rights if allowed by state laws."[15] The *Times* found that the "primary benefit of Bates's opinion would be to remove the 'stigma brought upon American jurisprudence' by the Supreme Court's actions in Dred Scott's case."[16] The *Milwaukee Daily Sentinel* called the Bates opinion "another sign of progress."[17]

Four weeks after Bates issued his opinion, on January 1, 1863, Lincoln announced the Emancipation Proclamation. This timing led the proclamation and the Bates opinion "to become linked in the minds of many, even though neither document mentions the other."[18] For example, the *New York Tribune* "declared that the opinion 'properly precedes and ushers in that other great act which is to come from the president on the 1st of January.' Some outright abolitionist newspapers printed the opinion and the final proclamation side by side."[19] In 1863 "it was republished in Hartford, Connecticut, as *What Constitutes Citizenship?* It also appeared in 1863 in a French translation printed in New Orleans, *Opinion de l'Avocat-Général Bates sur le droit de citoyenneté.*"[20]

While the Bates opinion denied that citizenship entailed suffrage, Salmon Chase employed it in support of allowing Blacks to vote.

> Without some official statement on the subject . . . any effort to obtain suffrage for former slaves could be countered by the simple argument that blacks were not citizens and so could not participate in government. To promote universal suffrage in restored states such as Louisiana, Chase needed the Dred Scott decision out of the way, and for practical reasons at least as much as symbolic.[21]

The Bates opinion served this purpose, though Chase's efforts on behalf of Black suffrage in Louisiana ultimately failed and "Reconstruction based on near-universal suffrage did not develop as Chase had hoped it would."[22] Nevertheless, "[i]n the early stages of Reconstruction, . . . , before the Fourteenth Amendment, Bates's opinion on citizenship was an essential component of Chase's vision."[23]

So, what did Bates say about citizenship? "In my opinion," he wrote, "the Constitution uses the word citizen only to express the political quality of the individual in his relations to the nation; to declare that he is a member of the body politic, and bound to it by the reciprocal obligation of allegiance on the one side and protection on the other."[24] As in standard abolitionist constitutional theory, the duty of protection reciprocally followed from the demand for allegiance and obedience.

"Every citizen of the United States is a component member of the nation," Bates continued, "with rights and duties, under the Constitution and laws of the United States, which cannot be destroyed or abridged by the laws of any particular State."[25] If they conflict with the laws of the nation, the laws of a state are of no force. Over and above any special rights, privileges, or immunities he may hold as a citizen of a state, a citizen of the United States has those rights that "legally and naturally belong to him in his quality of citizen of the United States."[26]

Free Blacks were US citizens because they were born in the United States and "the Constitution says not one word, and furnishes not one hint, in relation to the color or to the ancestral race of the 'natural born citizen.'"[27] Obliquely referring to the Supreme Court's denial of this proposition in *Dred Scott,* Bates wrote that

> regardless of what may have been said, in the opinions of judges and lawyers, and in State statutes, about negroes, mulattoes, and persons of color, the Constitution is wholly silent upon that subject.
>
> The Constitution itself does not make the citizens, (it is, in fact, made by them.) It only intends and recognizes such of them as are natural—home-born—and provides for the naturalization of such of them as were alien—foreign-born—making the latter, as far as nature will allow, like the former.[28]

In this way, the Republican reading of the Constitution enabled Blacks freed by the Emancipation Proclamation to be US citizens. And the Militia Act of 1862, in turn, emancipated their families, even if they resided in a slave state that was not then in rebellion and not subject to the other provisions of the Emancipation Proclamation. Thus, when combined with the Militia Act of 1862 and Attorney General Bates's opinion on Black citizenship, the Emancipation Proclamation's legal effect on January 1, 1863, extended beyond the slaves who were behind Confederate lines.

The theory of citizenship expressed in Bates's opinion also contributed to the content of the Thirteenth Amendment.

The Thirteenth Amendment

The language of Section 1 of the Thirteenth Amendment was taken in part from Article 6 of the Northwest Ordinance of 1787: "There shall be neither slavery nor involuntary servitude in the said territory, other than in the punishment of crimes, whereof the party shall have been duly convicted."[29] Congress's choice of this language was borne of experience. In 1862, similar language had been used to end slavery, first in the District of Columbia and then in all federal territories.

When Charles Sumner proposed that Congress integrate language from the French Declaration of Rights of 1791 and provide in part that "[a]ll persons are equal before the law, so that no person can hold another as a slave," this proposal was rejected.[30] One might at first be tempted to infer from the rejection of Sumner's proposal that Congress did not mean to secure equality before the law in general. But none of the opposition to Sumner's proposal stemmed from concerns that the proposal was overly broad.

Indeed, Republicans generally claimed that the abolition of slavery would be sufficient to make enslaved people citizens and to secure equality under the law with respect to all citizens' civil rights. Representative James Ashley, who introduced the amendment, went so far as to suggest that it would secure the right to vote.[31] Other Republicans agreed that it would "make every race free and equal before the law" and "recogni[ze] . . . natural rights."[32] But they demurred on suffrage. One Republican, Representative John McBride, responded to the objection that emancipation entailed enfranchisement by distinguishing between "natural rights" and "political franchises" and arguing that Blacks would have to "prove themselves worthy" of the latter.[33]

Ashley's response to Democrats' claim that the amendment would violate state sovereignty, however, contained a discussion of citizenship that did not trigger any Republicans objections. Ashley flatly denied that states enjoyed any "sovereignty" that would enable them to devalue what he described as the "universal franchise" that "belongs to citizens of the Republic."[34] He drew attention to "that provision of the Constitution which secures nationality of citizenship"—that is, the Privileges and Immunities Clause of Article IV.[35]

For Ashley, this clause was an expression of a "unity of the people of the United States" that "antedate[d] the Revolution."[36] The "men who carried us through the revolutionary struggle never intended . . . to destroy that unity or lose their national citizenship."[37] Ashley also stated that the "allegiance . . . due from the citizen to the national government" gave rise to a duty on the part of the federal government to protect all citizens, including formerly enslaved people[38] (the allegiance-protection reciprocal relationship again).

To abolish slavery was thus to enable the federal government to enshrine in positive law an understanding of national citizenship that had been lost for generations. And Section 2 of the amendment gave Congress a new enumerated power "to enforce this article by appropriate legislation." Therefore, pursuant to Section 2, Congress would now be empowered to protect the privileges and immunities of national citizenship.

If the claim that the Thirteenth Amendment carried with it the congressional power to protect the privileges and immunities of national citizenship still seems farfetched, think of it this way. Prior to the amendment, the

Constitution was thought by Republicans to recognize three categories of "persons":

1. Natural born "citizens" of the United States—including women and children—with their natural rights and immunities plus the additional privileges of citizenship (see *Dred Scott* and the Bates opinion);
2. Resident aliens with their natural rights (see the Due Process of Law Clause's protection of any "person" and the Bates opinion); and
3. Enslaved "persons held to service" possessing neither type of rights.

While Congress had the naturalization power to move persons from category 2 to 1, in *Dred Scott* the Supreme Court had held that neither Congress nor the states had the power to move "persons held to service" from category 3 to 1. (Chief Justice Taney made the same claim about *free* Blacks or "denizens" of African descent—but this was sharply contested by the dissenting justices and later rejected by Republicans in general and the Lincoln Administration in particular in the Bates opinion.)

The power to move persons from category 3 to 1 required a constitutional amendment: the Thirteenth Amendment. Because all enslaved people were, by constitutional amendment, now moved from 3 to 1, they thereby acquired all the privileges and immunities of citizens of the United States. Then Section 2 gave Congress a *new enumerated power* that had previously been lacking under Article IV to protect these "privileges and immunities" by appropriate legislation.

That Republicans continued to understand the Privileges and Immunities Clause to protect US citizens within their home states after the Civil War is clear from the observations and commentary of John Kasson, James Wilson, Isaac Arnold, Ebon Ingersoll, and others during the Thirteenth Amendment debates. Senator Kasson described the Thirteenth Amendment as a means of "carry[ing] into effect one clause of the United States which has been disobeyed in nearly every slave State of the Union," namely, the Privileges and Immunities Clause, and declared:

You cannot go into a State of the North in which you do not find refugees from Southern states who have been driven from the States in the south where they had a right to live as citizens, because of the tyranny which this institution exercised over public feeling, and even over the laws of those States.

In my own State there are numbers of men who have been driven from their farms, not for any offense against any of the laws which usually constitute crime, but because in opinion they did not agree with those who adhere to the institution of slavery.[39]

Kasson was clearly not employing a comity-only reading of the Privileges and Immunities Clause. To the contrary, he was complaining that citizens' were being deprived of their rights by their own states.

Similarly, James Wilson recited the Privileges and Immunities Clause and asked rhetorically, "To what extent has this been regarded as the supreme law of the land in States when slavery controlled legislatures, presided in the courts, directed the Executives and commanded the mob?"[40] He identified the clause as "the peerage title of our people" and proceeded to detail the "great rights" that had been "disregarded and practically destroyed by slavery."[41] Among them: free exercise of religion, freedom of speech, freedom to petition the government for redress of grievances, freedom of peaceable assembly, and "many other constitutional rights."[42] With the abolition of slavery, Wilson argued, would come "[a]n equal and exact observance of the constitutional rights of each and every citizen."[43]

Isaac Arnold spoke in sweeping terms about the "new nation" that would be "born" with the ratification of the amendment, proclaiming that "[l]iberty [and] equality before the law would be [the nation's] cornerstone."[44] Ebon Ingersoll stated that the amendment would secure for a previously enslaved man "the freedom of speech," as well as "a right to till the soil, to earn his bread by the sweat of his brow, and enjoy the rewards of his own labor" and "a right to the endearment and enjoyment of family ties."[45] He added that abolition would have the effect of restoring "the blessings of manhood" to "seven millions of poor white people" who were "kept in ignorance, in poverty, and in degradation" by a "thrice-accursed institution."[46] With the destruction of a stagnant plantation economy and the construction of a thriving industrial economy in which free laborers could pursue noble callings, he predicted, "school-houses will rise upon the ruins of the slave mart, intelligence will take the place of ignorance, wealth of poverty, and honor of degradation."[47]

During the ratification process, Republicans assured Northern Democrats whose votes they needed that the abolition of slavery would not require the recognition of Black political rights. They acknowledged, however, that abolition meant legally protected natural rights—that is, some important civil rights. During a prolonged debate over the meaning of the proposed Thirteenth Amendment, one frustrated Indiana senator, A. C. Downey, complained that "[s]ome cannot, or will not, distinguish between the right to live, to be free and enjoy the fruits of one's labor, and the right to vote, to sit on a jury or to hold an office."[48] The former he referred to as "absolute rights" and as "natural rights" that "belong to men in a state of nature," the latter, as "relative rights" that "have their origin in the regulations of human society."[49]

Downey went on to say that "[i]t does not follow that if you recognize and secure to the colored man his natural rights, you must confer upon him all those relative rights which you have conferred upon the white man, and make him his equal."[50] Abolishing slavery would require the government to protect only the former. When Democratic legislators objected to "mak[ing] white and black equal before the law,"[51] Republicans responded, not by denying that the amendment would do so, but by distinguishing legal equality from political and social equality and expressing "no fear" of the former.[52]

We need not take a position here on whether Section 1 of the Thirteenth Amendment was indeed sufficient to prohibit the states from abridging the privileges and immunities of national citizenship, or whether Section 2 was sufficient to empower Congress to secure them. We highlight Republican discussions of the rights of citizenship in connection with the Thirteenth Amendment's framing and ratification because they evince an understanding of what those rights consisted in, and what was later made manifest by the Privileges or Immunities Clause. Those discussions would continue as Republicans confronted a hostile Southern response to abolition.

The Civil Rights Act of 1866

Shortly after Appomattox, planters who faced the collapse of their personal authority over Blacks sought to subjugate Black people and to maintain as nearly as possible a system of coerced economic production. To that end, they pressed for the enactment of what came to be called the "Black Codes."

On the one hand, these codes authorized Blacks to acquire and own property, make contracts, and testify in court in cases involving persons of their own color.[53] But on the other, they punished Blacks who refused to contract, forbade Blacks to rent land in urban areas, imposed fines and involuntary plantation labor for "vagrancy" and "insulting" gestures, required Blacks to carry written evidence of employment for the coming year, and otherwise limited their economic opportunities and reinforced their social subordination.[54]

Blacks were even denied certain freedoms that they had once enjoyed prior to the Thirteenth Amendment. For instance, several states made it illegal for Blacks to own weapons and imposed taxes on their dogs and guns, owing to both planter fears of insurrection and planter resentment of hunting as a means through which Blacks could avoid dependence on plantation labor.[55]

These Black Codes were enforced by urban police forces and state militias from which Blacks were excluded and which were often composed of former Confederates who wore their old uniforms. Justice was not forthcoming in the courts, owing to Black exclusion from jury service, official reluctance to prosecute whites accused of crimes against Blacks, and penalties that were imposed on Blacks who "falsely and maliciously" brought charges against whites.[56] Although Blacks could no longer be held in involuntary servitude on the initiative of individual whites, courts could force Black convicts to labor without compensation on public projects.[57] They could also bind them out to white employers who would pay their fines, via a convict lease system that was greatly expanded in order to ensure a steady supply of cheap forced labor.[58] The Thirteenth Amendment's exception for "punishment for crime whereof the party shall have been duly convicted" was interpreted in bad faith as a license for these practices, over vociferous Republican objections.[59] As Dorothy Roberts summarizes, the amendment thus ultimately "provided insufficient protection to black citizens from being exploited, tortured, and killed."[60] The Supreme Court would not address this abuse of the amendment until 1911, when it held unconstitutional a statute that criminalized the breach of a contract.[61]

The lengths to which Southern officials were prepared to go to subordinate Blacks were illustrated by officials' willingness not only to exclude Blacks from poor relief, schools, and other public institutions, but to dismantle those institutions altogether to prevent Blacks from participating in them on equal terms. Governor Jonathan Worth of North Carolina had once secured the enactment of a bill establishing public education in North Carolina. Now he convinced the legislature to abolish the state's education system and authorized localities to establish private academies to which only relatively well-to-do whites would have access.[62] Better, he considered, that poor whites be denied education than that the state "be required to educate the negroes"— as he feared the state would be, if white children were educated at public expense.[63]

On the opening day of the Thirty-Ninth Congress, Senator Lyman Trumbull reported two bills to the Senate. The first bill would extend the operations of the Freedmen's Bureau. Created in 1865, the bureau provided clothing, food, fuel, and abandoned and confiscated land for rent and eventual sale to freed Blacks and Southern white refugees.[64] It was given broad discretionary powers to oversee "all subjects" related to the condition of free Blacks and white refugees.[65] The new bill further empowered the bureau both to take jurisdiction of cases involving Blacks and to punish state officials who denied Blacks the "civil rights belonging to white persons."[66]

The Freedmen's Bureau was not established as a "permanent institution." Nor did Trumbull propose that it be turned into one. But the bureau did institutionalize a federal commitment to assisting freed people in improving their conditions, rather than simply leaving them to their own devices. Trumbull's bill added a declaration of civil rights to the act and empowered bureau officials to protect those rights. They included:

> [T]he right to make and enforce contracts, to sue, be parties, and give evidence, to inherit, purchase, lease, sell, hold, and convey real and personal property, and to have full and equal benefit of all laws and proceedings concerning personal liberty, personal security, and the acquisition, enjoyment, and disposition of estate, real and personal, including the constitutional right to bear arms.[67]

The second bill he reported would become known as the Civil Rights Act of 1866. It was positioned as a direct response to the Black Codes.[68] Following the reasoning of Attorney General Bates's opinion, Section 1 of the proposed bill defined all persons born in the United States—with the exceptions of those who were "subject to any foreign power" and of Native Americans—as citizens of the United States.[69] Echoing both the Thirteenth Amendment and the Freedmen's Bureau Act, Section 2 of the proposal initially provided that

> [t]here shall be no discrimination *in civil rights or immunities* among the inhabitants of any State or Territory of the United States on account of race, color, or previous condition of servitude. And such citizens of every race or color, without regard to any previous condition of slavery or involuntary servitude except as a punishment for crime whereof the party shall have been duly convicted, shall have the same right to make and enforce contracts, to sue, be parties, and give evidence, to inherit, purchase, lease, sell, hold, and

convey real and personal property, and to full and equal benefit of all laws and proceedings for the security of person and property, and shall be subject to like punishment, pains, and penalties, and to none other, any law, statute, ordinance, regulation, or custom, to the contract, notwithstanding.[70]

The protection of "civil rights and immunities" in the first sentence led to a floor debate on the meaning of "civil rights." When pressed, Trumbull said the term embraced "fundamental rights belonging to every man as a free man, and which under the Constitution as it now exists we have a right to protect every man in" but not "political rights."[71] He emphasized that it had "nothing to do with the right of suffrage."[72]

Democratic Senator Andrew Davis denied that Congress had any constitutional authority to pass the act. He identified the Privileges and Immunities Clause as the most plausible constitutional hook for the act. But he argued for a comity-only understanding of the clause that would not empower Congress "to go into Kentucky, and to regulate the free negro of that State who has lived there always, whose business and interest are entirely local to that State."[73] To that end, he relied on case law, including *Corfield v. Coryell*, which he read as a comity-only decision.[74]

In response, Trumbull conceded that Davis had accurately interpreted the case law. But he insisted that *Corfield*'s description of "the rights of a citizen of the United States" were "the same rights" that "appertain[ed] to all persons who were clothed with American citizenship" after "the Constitution was amended and slavery abolished."[75] Thus, Trumbull affirmed that the Thirteenth Amendment provided Congress with all the authority it needed to protect the privileges and immunities of all US citizens covered by Article IV, whether those privileges and immunities were abridged by their home states or by states that they were visiting.[76]

Democratic senators relentlessly questioned whether "civil rights" would in practice have so narrow a reach as Trumbull claimed. Senator Willard Saulsbury Sr. charged that Trumbull's definition of civil rights "cannot control the operation or the effect of this law." He predicted that "your judges in most of the States will determine that under these words the power of voting is given."[77]

Trumbull stood his ground. Drawing on Blackstone's definition of "civil liberty," Trumbull identified "that . . . liberty" with "the liberty which was intended to be secured by the Declaration of Independence, by the Constitution of the United States originally, and more especially by the amendment which has been recently adopted."[78] Trumbull insisted that "at all events [a citizen] is entitled to the great fundamental rights of life, liberty and the pursuit of happiness, and the right to travel, to go where he pleases."[79] Certain fundamental rights would be protected by the bill "as appertaining to every freeman."[80] He specified these as "the right to acquire property, the right to go and come at pleasure, the right to enforce rights in the courts, to make contracts, and to inherit and dispose of property."[81]

In the House, controversy over "civil rights" was even more heated. When introducing the act, Representative James Wilson began by defending its definition of citizenship. He argued that, just as Blackstone identified two paths to subjectship—birth and naturalization—the Constitution recognized two paths to citizenship, and that neither the Constitution nor British law "made [any] distinction on account of race and color."[82] After marshaling additional authorities for racially unstratified national citizenship and repudiating *Dred Scott*, Wilson turned to "civil rights," rightly anticipating that this language would "excite more opposition and elicit more discussion than any other."[83]

Wilson began by denying that it meant "that in all things, civil, social, political, all citizens, without distinction of race or color, shall be equal." He stated that suffrage, the right to sit on juries, and the right to send one's children to the same schools as other citizens were "not civil rights or immunities."[84] (We will address the significance of these abbreviated statements in greater detail in Chapter 6.)

To affirmatively define civil rights, he relied on Kent's *Commentaries*, on Attorney General Bates's opinion, and on Bouvier's *Law Dictionary*. From these sources, he "gather[ed] an understanding that civil rights are the natural rights of man" and that "immunities" were "right[s] of exemption" from "duties which the law generally requires other citizens to perform."[85] To illustrate, he indicated that, pursuant to the act, "[a] colored citizen shall not, because he is colored, be subjected to obligations, duties, pains, and penalties from which other citizens are exempted."[86]

Even more explicitly than did Trumbull, Wilson identified the act as a means of enforcing the Privileges and Immunities Clause of Article IV. After citing *Corfield*—conspicuously omitting Washington's reference to the elective franchise—Wilson opined that "'general citizenship' . . . under this clause entitles every citizen to security and protection of personal rights."[87] If all states followed the clause, he continued, "we might well refrain from the enactment of this bill into law."[88] Like Trumbull, however, Wilson said that the Thirteenth Amendment supplied Congress with a new authority to "insure to each and every citizen these things which belong to him as a constituent member of the great national family."[89]

Adopting the rule articulated by Chief Justice John Marshall in *McCulloch v. Maryland*, Wilson identified "the end" of the act as "the maintenance of freedom to the citizen."[90] This end was "legitimate, because it is defined by the Constitution itself."[91] It was then "appropriate" to "punish[] a man through the ordinary channels of the law and the courts for depriving the citizen of the rights which, while he enjoys them, are his sure defense against efforts to reduce him to slavery."[92]

Even if the Thirteenth Amendment did not supply the requisite authority for the act, Wilson maintained that Congress was nevertheless empowered to protect citizens' civil rights. Wilson drew on Blackstone's three categories of absolute rights and stated that "English and American doctrine" harmonized concerning them. He added, however, that he would "not admit that the British constitution excels the American Constitution in the amplitude of its provisions for the protection of these rights."[93]

Wilson observed, "[T]here is no right enumerated in [the American Constitution] by general terms which is not definitely embodied in one of the rights I have mentioned, *or results as an incident necessary to complete defense and enjoyment of* the specific right."[94] That is, every right enumerated in the Constitution either specifies *or serves to protect* the absolute rights to life, liberty, and property—the civil rights of citizens. Wilson concluded that the "mere possession of these rights by the citizen raised[] by necessary implication the power to protect them."[95]

Although this might strike a modern audience as an extravagant claim, the Supreme Court had already so ruled in *Prigg v. Pennsylvania*. In that 1842 case, Justice Story held that if "the Constitution guaranties the right, . . . the natural inference certainly is that the National Government is clothed with the appropriate authority and functions to enforce it."[96] While constitutional abolitionists abhorred *Prigg*'s outcome, some (such as Joel Tiffany) were prepared to employ its reasoning concerning the breadth of federal power to enforce guaranteed rights. So too were some Republicans.

Wilson's definition of civil rights and his claim that Congress did not need to rely on an enumerated power to protect those rights were both challenged not only by Democrats but by a prominent fellow Republican. John Bingham submitted that "civil rights" included "political rights," which "*by general ac-*

ceptation signifies that class of civil rights which are more directly exercised by the citizen in connection with the government of his country."[97]

Bingham bolstered this interpretive claim by meeting Blackstone with Blackstone. Blackstone, he said, "uses in that classic of the law [the *Commentaries*] the terms 'civil liberty' and 'political liberty' everywhere as synonymous."[98] Accordingly, Wilson's assurances concerning political rights were worth little. Bingham predicted that the act would "make it a misdemeanor . . . for the Governor of Ohio to obey the requirements of the constitution of the state, which requires that none shall be elected, and therefore none commissioned, to office in that State save white citizens of the United States."[99]

Even if the act prohibited states only from violating rights that it specifically listed, Bingham continued, he could still not support it. First, by protecting only citizens, it implicitly allowed states to engage in "discrimination in the administration of justice for the protection of life against the stranger irrespective of race or color"—and this despite the fact that the Fifth Amendment's Due Process of Law Clause protects all "person[s]."[100]

Bingham also made an argument reminiscent of his fellow Ohioan Salmon Chase's enumerated-powers objection to the Fugitive Slave Act—an argument that was rejected by the Court in *Prigg*. Bingham claimed that Congress lacked constitutional authority to take "care of the property, the liberty, and the life of the citizen."[101] Bingham called instead for "an amendment which would arm Congress with the power to compel" state officials to abide by their oaths to the federal Constitution.[102]

Bingham interpreted that oath to require state officials to abide by the "bill of rights." Unlike others, Bingham was aware that the Court in *Barron v. Baltimore*[103] had held that the first ten amendments did not "limit the powers of the states."[104] What Bingham meant by "bill of rights" has been disputed.[105] But it is clear that he did not agree with Wilson that the mere guarantee of constitutional rights implied the federal power to protect them. For that another amendment would be needed.

Concerns about the scope of the phrase "civil rights and immunities" led to the act's amendment. Wilson deleted the general prohibition against "discrimination in civil rights and immunities," which Bingham claimed would proscribe race-based restrictions on suffrage. This left only a list of particular rights that all citizens would be entitled to enjoy. The final version read, in pertinent part:

[A]ll persons born in the United States and not subject to any foreign power, excluding Indians not taxed, are hereby declared to be citizens of the United States; and . . . shall have the same right, in every State and Territory in the United States, to make and enforce contracts, to sue, be parties, and give evidence, to inherit, purchase, lease, sell, hold, and convey real and personal property, and to full and equal benefit of all laws and proceedings for the security of person and property, as is enjoyed by white citizens, and shall be subject to like punishment, pains, and penalties, and to none other, any law, statute, ordinance, regulation, or custom, to the contrary notwithstanding.[106]

The deletion of "discrimination in civil rights and immunities" from the bill suggests a less-than-perfect consensus about what was generally accepted to be in the set of privileges or immunities of national citizenship at this time. Enough people seemed to think suffrage was such a privilege as to make so general a prohibition seem risky to those who thought it was not (or those who did not want it to be protected whether it was or was not). Yet the fact that "civil rights" remained in the title of the act suggests a deep consensus that *these particular* civil rights—as opposed to all and every purported civil right—were privileges or immunities of citizenship. This consensus will become important to identifying the rights protected by the Privileges or Immunities Clause.

So revised, the act passed both Houses. On February 2, 1866, the Senate passed the bill by a vote of 33 to 12, with 5 not voting. A month later on March 13, the House, by a vote of 111 to 38, passed the bill with 34 not voting.[107] Most Republicans did not agree with Bingham's constitutional objections, and the act's supporters fully expected that President Andrew Johnson would sign it into law. When, on March 27, he did not, his veto opened up a schism that would never be healed. Shocked and outraged Republicans overrode the veto in April, with only one initial supporter bowing to presidential pressure.[108]

Republicans' widely publicized speeches in response to the veto merit careful attention. Johnson founded his veto on constitutional objections to the authority of Congress to pass the act. Supporters of the act responded by reiterating and elaborating on the constitutional arguments they had deployed prior to its enactment.

In the House, Representative William Lawrence spoke at greatest length. Like Trumbull, he relied on Blackstone's definition of "absolute" rights, claiming that they belonged to "every citizen" and were "natural, inherent, and inalienable."[109] As "necessary incidents" of these "rights of citizenship," Lawrence explained, "there are other[] [rights] such as the right to make and enforce contracts, to purchase, hold, and enjoy property, and to share the benefit of laws for the security of person and property."[110]

The act, Lawrence stated, merely declared "what is already the constitutional rights of every citizen in every state" in virtue of "the provisions of the Constitution, Article IV, Section 2, and the equal civil rights which it recognizes or by implication affirms to exist among citizens of the same state."[111] Again echoing Trumbull, he stated that Congress had "incidental power to enforce and protect the equal enjoyment in the States of civil rights *which are inherent in national citizenship.*" By implication, Congress did not need to rely on any affirmative delegation of power, as Bingham claimed.[112] Lawrence "conced[ed], as the courts have held, that the privileges referred to in the Constitution are such as are fundamental rights, not political rights nor those dependent on local law"; but he insisted that the Privileges and Immunities Clause guaranteed "equal fundamental civil rights for all citizens."[113] That Lawrence considered "civil rights" to be synonymous with "fundamental" rights—hence, "fundamental civil rights"—is telling.

In the Senate, Trumbull responded to Johnson's veto message point by point. Johnson had claimed that "[i]f it be granted that Congress can repeal all State laws discriminating between whites and blacks in the subjects covered by this bill," it could "repeal . . . all state Laws discriminating between the two races on the subjects of suffrage and office" and prevent states from excluding Blacks from juries.[114] To this, Trumbull responded that "the granting of civil rights does not, and never did . . . carry with it rights, or more properly speaking, political privileges."[115]

What civil rights, then, *did* US citizens have? Trumbull answered that "[t]hey are those inherent, fundamental rights which belong to free citizens or free men in all countries . . . and they belong to them in all the States of the Union."[116] As he did before the veto, he invoked Blackstone, adopting Blackstone's definition of "civil liberty" and stating that the rights of personal security, personal liberty, and property "belong[ed] to every citizen of the United States, as such, no matter where he may be."[117]

Turning next to Kent's *Commentaries,* Trumbull cited Kent's favorable summary of Washington's opinion in *Corfield:*

> The privileges and immunities conceded by the Constitution of the United States were to be confined to those which were, in their nature, fundamental, and belonged of right to the citizens of all free Governments. Such are the rights of protection of life and liberty, and to acquire and enjoy property.[118]

With American citizenship, Trumbull reasoned, came federal "protection" of these rights at home and abroad in return for "allegiance"—the burdens of which had lately been imposed on "the father whose son was starved at Andersonville . . . the widow whose husband was slain at Mission Ridge . . . [and] the little boy who leads his sightless father through the streets."[119] It could not be that the federal government had the right to conscript citizens "to its defense, but ha[d] no right to protect the survivors or their friends in any right, whatever, in any of the states."[120]

Trumbull also reiterated his belief that the Thirteenth Amendment conferred power on Congress "to protect the freedman in his rights that he should have authority to go into the Federal courts in all cases where a custom prevails in a State, or where there is a statute-law of the State discriminating against him."[121] Trumbull interpreted the Thirteenth Amendment to "authorize Congress to do whatever is necessary to protect the freedman in his liberty."[122]

Overall, Republicans were remarkably consistent in defining civil rights and distinguishing them from political rights. They identified civil rights with the privileges and immunities of US citizenship and located their authority to protect civil rights in the Privileges and Immunities Clause, as well as in the Thirteenth Amendment. There was also no substantial disagreement that the rights listed in the Civil Rights Act or in the Freedmen's Bureau Bill—a bill that Bingham had supported—were among the fundamental rights of citizens of the United States. The dispute was solely about the power of Congress to enforce these rights. Nor did any Republicans object to the identification of these fundamental rights with the "privileges and immunities" protected by Article IV.

Finally, when prominent Republicans invoked the Privileges and Immunities Clause as authority for the act, members of their party did not object on the ground that the former protected only sojourning citizens, whereas the act protected *all* citizens. In other words, no Republican—including John Bingham—invoked the "comity-only" conception of Article IV as a reason why Congress lacked power under the clause to protect the privileges and immunities of US citizens from being violated by their own state governments.

Bingham's other constitutional objections were not widely shared and thus did not dissuade Republicans from enacting the Civil Rights Act of 1866. Nor did President Johnson's constitutional argument dissuade Republicans from overriding his veto. Yet, these objections were enough to raise questions about whether the act—and subsequent civil rights legislation like it—would be sustained against inevitable legal challenges. Johnson's opposition also raised concerns over whether the act would survive even modest changes in the political composition of Congress.

Democrats, of course, could be counted on to try to do away with the Civil Rights Act at the first opportunity. And moderate Republicans such as Bingham and Cowan could not be counted on to resist them. By the time that Congress overrode Johnson's veto, Bingham had presented two drafts of an amendment that was designed to supply the federal power that he found lacking in the existing Constitution. Bingham's proposal would empower Congress and the federal courts to enforce what he called "the bill of rights." Johnson's veto of the act a month later set the stage for extended consideration of what would become the Fourteenth Amendment.

5

The Letter

Writing and Ratifying the Privileges
or Immunities Clause

IF ANY ONE PERSON could be identified as the prime congressional mover behind what would become the Privileges or Immunities Clause, it would be Ohio Representative John Bingham—an extraordinary figure on whom scholars of the Fourteenth Amendment have rightly focused their attention. It was Bingham who first proposed what would become the Fourteenth Amendment, and the influence he exerted on its ultimate form is discernible in the midst of what was often a chaotic framing process.

In this chapter, we will track Bingham's successive drafts of the clause. While this narrative is uncontroversial among Fourteenth Amendment scholars, readers may be unaware of it. It is commonly said that the Fourteenth Amendment was meant to constitutionalize the Civil Rights Act of 1866, and so it was—in part. But Bingham began pursuing a constitutional amendment well before the Civil Rights Act was enacted.

Framing and Explaining the Clause

Bingham's First Draft

On December 4, 1865, President Andrew Johnson, having succeeded the slain Abraham Lincoln as president in April of that year, delivered his first annual message to Congress. While stressing the importance of states' rights, he also invoked the authority of the Declaration of Independence to affirm the "equal right of every man to life, liberty, and the pursuit of happiness

[and] to freedom of conscience."[1] Johnson insisted that, because of these pre-existing rights, the powers of both the federal government and the states were limited: "With us this idea of limitation spreads through every form of administration—general, State, and municipal—and rests on the great distinguishing principle of the recognition of the rights of man."[2]

Two days later, on December 6, Bingham used the occasion of Johnson's message to propose a constitutional amendment:

> Mr. Bingham . . . introduced a joint resolution to amend the Constitution of the United States so as to empower Congress to pass all necessary and proper laws to secure to all persons in every state of the Union equal protection in their rights [of] life, liberty, and property.[3]

On December 8, 1866, Bingham explained the need for his proposed amendment. He praised the president's message, stating that "[t]he spirit, the intent, the purpose of our Constitution is to secure equal and exact justice to all men."[4] But he lamented that "in respect of white men as well as black men," equal and exact justice had "failed."[5]

Bingham denied that the Constitution itself was responsible for this failure. He urged legislators to read the Privileges and Immunities Clause of Article IV and explained that although "this guarantee of your Constitution applies to every citizen of every State of the Union," it had been "disregarded" by Southern states that had expelled critics of slavery, notoriously including Samuel Hoar.[6] After detailing systematic violations of "the absolute guarantees of the Constitution" by predominantly Southern states in preceding years, Bingham provided the following interpretation of the meaning of the Article IV clause:

> "The citizens of each state (*being ipso facto citizens of the United States*) shall be entitled to all the privileges and immunities of citizens (applying the ellipsis 'of the United States') in the several States." This guarantee is of the privileges and immunities of citizens of the United States *in, not of,* the several states. This guarantee of your Constitution applies to every citizen of every State of the Union; there is not a guarantee more sacred, and more vital in that great instrument.[7]

Raoul Berger and Charles Fairman belittled Bingham for his so-called "ellipsis theory" of the Privileges and Immunities Clause of Article IV.[8] In Chapter 2, however, we saw that this same theory informed an 1844 decision by Ohio Supreme Court Justice Nathaniel Reed.[9] To reiterate, Reed interpreted the clause to "mean[] that the residents of the several states, if they be citizens of the United States, shall be protected and defended . . . in the full enjoyment of all the rights to which they are entitled *as citizens of the United States*."[10] Those rights were "to be determined by a reference to the letter and spirit of our national constitution, and also to the general custom of other nations."[11] Rejecting the comity-only theory of the Privileges and Immunities Clause, Justice Reed reasoned that "the spirit and intention of [the clause] is, not to secure to the non-resident the same rights and indulgence with the resident in every state, but simply to secure to the citizen of the United States . . . the full enjoyment of all the rights of citizenship, in every state of the Union."[12]

Reed and Bingham's "ellipsis theory" of the Privileges and Immunities Clause read its text as consistent with the concept of national, as distinct from state, citizenship. This reading stressed the fact that the text referred to US citizens *in* the states, rather than citizens *of* the states. Although the text does not explicitly refer to citizens "of the United States," Bingham maintained that this content was implied. On his rendition, therefore, the clause should be read as follows: "The Citizens of each State shall be entitled to all Privileges and Immunities of Citizens [of the United States while] in the several States." Thus read, the clause protects a set of fundamental "privileges and immunities of citizens of the United States" from infringement.

It is worth noting a few things about the wording of Bingham's resolution. His "necessary and proper" language was evidently drawn from the Necessary and Proper Clause of Article I. We have seen that some Republicans agreed with Justice Story in *Prigg v. Pennsylvania* that the Necessary and Proper Clause empowered Congress to protect any of the rights included in the Constitution.

Furthermore, Bingham framed his resolution as a means of enforcing an existing constitutional guarantee that had lately been ignored. But the public meaning of his resolution's language differed from what was eventually included in the Privileges or Immunities Clause in three respects. First, the resolution would have protected all "persons," not merely citizens. In the actually enacted Fourteenth Amendment, all persons are guaranteed the due process of law and the equal protection of the laws, but the Privileges or Immunities Clause protects only citizens.

Second, the language of "equal protection" did not appear either in Article IV or anywhere else in the antebellum Constitution. In the actually enacted Fourteenth Amendment, it would become a provision (protecting all persons) distinct from the Privileges or Immunities Clause (which protected citizens). Third and finally, Bingham's resolution referred not to "privileges and immunities" but to "rights."[13] The actually enacted Fourteenth Amendment also protects more than the privileges and immunities of US citizens—it protects as well the rights of all persons to the due process of law and the equal protection of the laws.

In sum, Section 1 of the actually enacted Fourteenth Amendment would expressly unpack many of the ideas compressed within Bingham's first single-sentence resolution and separate them into distinct clauses. Moreover, as we will soon see, Section 1 as a whole would provide a more limited federal power than what Bingham initially proposed.

Bingham characterized his proposed amendment as a means of ensuring that "hereafter there shall not be any disregard of *that essential guarantee* of your Constitution in any state of the Union."[14] Being that the Privileges and Immunities Clause was the only "guarantee" to which Bingham had referred, it seems clear that Bingham presented his amendment as being tailored to enforce the rights secured by *that clause*. At the very least, then, he maintained that the Privileges and Immunities Clause of Article IV guaranteed to all US citizens the "equal protection in their rights to life, liberty, and property."

Every one of Bingham's examples of previous breaches of the Privileges and Immunities Clause is consistent with both a comity-only and a fundamental-rights reading of the clause. At one point, however, he seems clearly to go beyond comity to imply that states were barred from violating the fundamental rights of any US citizen. Besides alluding to Hoar's expulsion, Bingham pointed out more generally that "[t]ime was . . . when it was entirely unsafe for a citizen of Massachusetts or Ohio . . . [who was] the avowed advocate of the foundation principle of the Constitution—*absolute equality* of all men before the law—to be found anywhere in the streets of Charleston or in the streets of Richmond."[15] His amendment, he said, would empower the federal courts to take cognizance of cases in which "the tribunals of South Carolina [do] not respect the rights of citizens of Massachusetts under the Constitution of their common country."[16]

We need not settle on a comprehensive understanding of Bingham's pregnant proposal, as it would soon give birth to other formulations.

Bingham's Second Draft

The Joint Committee on Reconstruction revised Bingham's first draft several times. The committee ultimately reported the following language on February 10:

> The Congress shall have power to make all laws which shall be necessary and proper to secure to the citizens of each state all privileges and immunities of citizens in the several states; and to all persons in the several States equal protection in the rights of life, liberty, and property.[17]

This language was suggested by Bingham, who had moved successfully to substitute it for a different draft that would have "secure[d] to all persons in every State full protection in the enjoyment of life, liberty, and property" and "to citizens of the United States in every State the same immunities, and equal political rights and privileges."[18]

Bingham's new language clearly covered more than did the Privileges and Immunities Clause of Article IV. Bingham's motion included parenthetical references to the two provisions in the existing Constitution that he sought to empower Congress to enforce by adopting this language:

> The Congress shall have power to make all laws which shall be necessary and proper to secure to the citizens of each state all privileges and immunities of citizens in the several states (Art. 4, Sec. 2); and to all persons in the several States equal protection in the rights of life, liberty, and property (5th amendment).[19]

In his introductory speech, Bingham stated that this proposal would "arm the Congress with the power to enforce the bill of rights as it stands in the Constitution today." This sentence has generated a great deal of controversy concerning both Bingham's thinking and the meaning of the Fourteenth Amendment. This controversy centers on whether the label "the bill of rights" did not mean then what it means today.

In separate works, historian Pauline Maier, political scientist Michael Douma, and legal scholar Gerard Magliocca have contended that it was not until sometime in the twentieth century that it became conventional to refer to the first eight or ten amendments as "the Bill of Rights."[20] According to their research, before then, the first eight or ten amendments to the Constitution were usually referred to simply as "amendments." The label "the bill of rights" had no standard usage and could be used in a variety of ways. Even as late as 1880, Webster's *Dictionary of the English Language* defined "bill of rights" as follows:

> [A] summary of rights and privileges claimed by a people. Such was the declaration presented by the Lords and Commons of England to the prince and princess of Orange in 1688. In America, a bill or declaration of rights is prefixed to most of the constitutions of the several states.[21]

The first eight amendments are conspicuously absent from this definition. Debate on the public meaning of "bill of rights" circa the framing of the Fourteenth Amendment is ongoing. Kurt Lash has argued that "bill of rights" did carry a settled, ten-amendments-only meaning by 1868.[22] Nothing about our thesis is affected by the outcome of this debate. We raise it only to stress that when that label appears in nineteenth-century sources, care must be taken to contextualize it. In this context, it is particularly relevant to how we interpret statements by John Bingham, which some scholars have disparaged as reflecting his confusion.[23]

With this debate in mind, we can see from the following passage of his explanatory speech that Bingham at this stage was not using the phrase "the bill of rights" the way we would today. Referring to critics of his proposal, he continued:

> Gentlemen admit the force of the provisions in the bill of rights, that the citizens of the United States shall be entitled to all the privileges and immunities of citizens in the several States, and that no person shall be deprived of life, liberty, or property without due process of law; but they say, 'We are opposed to its enforcement by an act of Congress under an amended Constitution, as proposed.' . . . Why are gentlemen opposed to the enforcement of the bill of rights, as proposed?[24]

Bingham clearly claimed that the label "the bill of rights" encompassed both the Fifth Amendment's Due Process of Law Clause *and* the Privileges and Immunities Clause. Later, in the course of discussing this language, he repeated that he sought only to arm Congress to enforce "the bill of rights"— that his proposal "hath that extent—no more."

Likewise, Bingham emphasized that his language was taken directly from the existing Constitution and thus did not impose any new limits on state power—it only gave Congress more power to ensure that state officials adhered to their constitutional oaths:

> Every word of the proposed amendment is to-day in the Constitution of our country, save the words conferring the express grant of power upon the Congress of the United States. *The residue of the resolution*, as the House will see by a reference to the Constitution, *is the language of the second section of the fourth article, and of a portion of the fifth amendment* adopted by the First Congress in 1789 and made part of the Constitution of the country. . . . [I]t has been the want of the Republic that there was not an express grant of

power in the Constitution to enable the whole people of every state, by congressional enactment, to enforce obedience to *these requirements* of the Constitution. . . . The House knows, sir, the country knows, the civilized world knows, that the legislative, executive, and judicial officers of eleven States within this Union within the last five years, in utter disregard of these injunctions . . . have violated in every sense of the word *these provisions* of the Constitution of the United States, the enforcement of which are absolutely essential to American nationality.[25]

At issue here is not how others may have used the phrase "the bill of rights," but what John Bingham meant when *he* used the phrase. This portion of Bingham's speech further underscores that by "the bill of rights" he was not referring to the first eight or ten amendments, but to "these provisions of the Constitution": the Privileges and Immunities Clause of Article IV and the Due Process of Law Clause.

Despite the assurance that the scope of Bingham's second proposal was limited to enforcing existing constitutional guarantees, Democrats nonetheless denounced what they described as an intrusion on states' reserved rights. Republicans, too, were skeptical, for diverse reasons. Conservative Republicans complained that Bingham's second draft granted Congress too much power.

Robert Hale of New York described the proposed amendment as a "grant of power in general terms . . . to legislate for the protection of life, liberty, and property, simply qualified with the condition that it shall be equal legislation."[26] That is, Hale thought Congress would be empowered by the language of equal protection to take over states' reserved police powers. Because Hale apparently thought the states were already forbidden to violate "the bill of rights,"[27] Bingham's second draft was unnecessary as well as dangerous to federalism.

Bingham responded to Hale by citing *Barron* for the proposition that "the power of the Federal Government to enforce in the United States courts the bill of rights under the articles of amendment to the Constitution had been denied," so that his amendment was indeed necessary.[28] Bingham here specified that the bill of rights to which Hale was referring was "the bill of rights *under the articles of amendment.*" But that is not the same "bill of rights" to which Bingham was earlier referring.[29] (By the way, Chief Justice Marshall's opinion for the Court in *Barron* does not refer to the first ten amendments, which he held applied only to the federal government, as "the bill of rights.")

Bingham also dismissed Hale's concerns about federalism. Bingham denied that "any state . . . reserved to itself the right . . . to withhold from any citizen of the United States within its limits . . . any of the privileges of a citizen of the United States." And he questioned how "the right of a State [could] be impaired" by empowering Congress to enforce the clause that recognized those privileges.[30]

While Radical Republicans shared Hale's concern that Bingham's second draft granted Congress too much power, at the same time they also worried that it did not do *enough* to limit state power. Giles Hotchkiss of New York emphasized his "desire to secure every privilege and every right to every citizen in the United States that [Bingham] desires to secure."[31] But, he worried that Bingham's language was ill-suited to achieve them:

> As I understand it, [Bingham's] object in offering this resolution and proposing this amendment is to provide that no state shall discriminate between its citizens and give one class of citizens greater rights than it confers upon another. If this amendment secured that, I should vote very cheerfully for it today, but as I do not regard it as permanently securing those rights, I shall vote to postpone its consideration until there can be a further conference between the friends of the motion, and we can devise some means whereby we shall secure those rights beyond a question.[32]

To Hotchkiss, Bingham responded that his amendment would not empower Congress to, as Hotchkiss put it, enable "rebel laws to govern and be uniform throughout this Union" but merely provided for the enforcement of existing constitutional guarantees.[33] This did not satisfy Hotchkiss, who insisted on the need for an amendment that would "secure beyond question what [Bingham] desired to secure," lest a future "rebel" Congress deprive both "the black man [and] the white man" of "equal rights."[34]

Bingham had some supporters. Among them was Representative Frederick Woodbridge, who stated that "four million separate chattels . . . have become in an hour living, thinking, responsible beings, and citizens of the United States" and called on Congress to discharge its duty to "provide for those people."[35] Bingham's amendment, he claimed, "merely gives the power to Congress to enact those laws which will give to a citizen of the United States the natural rights which necessarily pertain to citizenship."[36]

Woodbridge stated that Congress would be empowered to protect "a citizen of the United States, in whatever state he may be."[37] This would not "destroy the sovereignty of a State, if such a thing exists" but only "keep[]

whatever sovereignty it may have in harmony with a republican form of government and the Constitution of the country."[38] Woodridge read Bingham's language as empowering Congress to secure citizens' fundamental rights and to protect them against parochial discrimination—to "enable Congress to give all citizens the inalienable rights of life and liberty, and to every citizen in whatever State he may be that protection to his property which is extended to other citizens of the State."[39]

Another supporter, Representative William Kelley, took the view that "all the power this amendment will give is already in the Constitution" but stated that he was "persuaded that it will yet be quickened and called into action" by the amendment, which would "more explicitly empower Congress."[40] He noted that "there are those, and some of them on this side of the House, who doubt that the powers to be imparted by it are already to be found in the Constitution."[41] Significantly, Kelley opined that the "right of franchise" was "property" that would be protected by the amendment—indeed, "to the American citizen, the dearest property he owns."[42] He seems to have been the only supporter who identified the latter as being among the rights of citizenship at this time.

Almost without exception, Republicans who discussed the amendment at length either did not clearly take either a fundamental-rights or a comity-only view or they interpreted it to protect the fundamental rights of all US citizens, both in their home states and in states that they were visiting. The sole exception was Hiram Price, who clearly took a comity-only view. According to Price, Bingham's amendment "mean[t] simply this: if a citizen of Iowa or a citizen of Pennsylvania has any business, or if curiosity has induced him to visit the State of South Carolina or Georgia, he shall have the same protection of the laws there that he would have had had he lived there ten years."[43]

But Price conceded three times that he was "not a constitutional lawyer." He said that he "came to [his] conclusion" because "for the last thirty years a citizen of a free State dared not express his opinion on the subject of slavery in a slave state."[44] That he was the only Republican to express such a view underscores the degree to which Republicans had moved on from the comity-only interpretation that had been adopted by antebellum courts.

Bingham's second draft thus faced opposition in committee not only from Democrats but from conservative Republicans. To avoid defeat, he postponed its consideration. In the meantime, the Joint Committee began work on yet another draft.

Bingham's Third Draft

On March 13, 1866, Congress enacted the Civil Rights Act. Shockingly, President Andrew Johnson vetoed both the act and the Freedmen's Bureau Bill, thus making plain his determined opposition to Reconstruction. Although Republicans swiftly overrode the veto, it became clear that Congress now needed to do more than pass a statute that could later be invalidated by a court or repealed by a future Congress when the Southerners returned. This development paved the way for Bingham's third draft of the Fourteenth Amendment.

The Joint Committee on Reconstruction revisited the Fourteenth Amendment on April 10. The first text to be considered emerged from a proposal by former Indiana Congressman Robert Dale Owen. Section 1 of this proposal provided that

> [n]o discrimination shall be made by any state, nor by the United States, as to the civil rights of persons because of race, color, or previous condition of servitude.[45]

Bingham quickly suggested the following amendment:

> Nor shall any State deny to any person within its jurisdiction the equal protection of the laws, nor take property for public use without just compensation.[46]

After his amendment was defeated—possibly because of concerns about whether it would limit the confiscation of Confederate property—Bingham voted in support of Owen's proposed language.[47]

Later that day, however, he proposed language that would not amend but instead replace Owen's Section 1. It should look familiar:

> No State shall make or enforce any law which shall abridge the privileges or immunities of citizens of the United States; nor shall any State deprive any person of life, liberty, or property without due process of law, nor deny to any person within its jurisdiction the equal protection of the laws.[48]

Thus, John Bingham was the framer of the language that was actually adopted.

For a short time, Bingham's language was put at the end of the draft amendment in addition to Owen's nondiscrimination proposal. Apparently at least some members of the committee saw these proposals as distinct. One weak inference that might be drawn from this is that it is a mistake to limit the provisions of Bingham's language, now in Section 1, to discrimination based on race—a limitation that is not in the text itself. (We will return to the significance of this drafting sequence in Part III, when we discuss the original meaning of the "equal protection of the laws.") For whatever reason, eventually, Bingham's proposal would replace Owen's as Section 1. It is possible that his provision came to be thought to subsume rather than supplement Owen's. We do not know.

It was this Section 1 that would emerge from committee. Except for the Citizenship Clause that would be added later on the motion of Jacob Howard, it is otherwise identical to the Section 1 that was ratified into law on July 28, 1868. Although Republicans were able to override Johnson's veto of the Civil Rights Act, they were unable to muster the two-thirds majority required to override his veto of the Freedmen's Bureau Bill. Because constitutional amendments also require a two-thirds majority, it was clear that no such amendment would be sent to the states for ratification without moderate and conservative Republican support.[49]

Bingham's third draft differed in two major ways from his second. First, it is phrased as a restriction on the states rather than a grant of power to Congress. Second, it departed from the language of the Privileges and Immunities Clause of Article IV so as to express Bingham's ellipsis theory. It referred to the "privileges or immunities of citizens *of the United States*," rather than the "privileges and immunities of citizens *in the several states*." After a flurry of votes in which it was adopted, rejected, and readopted, in that order, Bingham's language cleared the committee.

The precise significance of the differences between the public meanings of the second and third versions warrants further exploration. In presenting his amendment to the House on May 10, Bingham emphasized that it took "from no State any right that ever pertained to it" and stated that it would "not give . . . the power to Congress of regulating suffrage in the several States."[50] What it *would* do was "supply" a "want . . . in the Constitution of our country" for "the power in the people, the whole people of the United States . . . to do that by congressional enactment which hitherto they have not had the power to do."[51] Bingham said that the amendment would empower the federal government to "protect by national law the privileges and immunities of all the citizens of the Republic and the inborn rights of every person within its jurisdiction whenever the same shall be abridged or denied by the unconstitutional acts of any State."[52]

Bingham enumerated a handful of specific rights that he claimed were "privileges of a citizen of the United States." The first two were "[t]he franchise of a federal elected office" and "the elective franchise for choosing Representatives in Congress or presidential electors."[53] Shortly after so identifying them, however, Bingham stated that his amendment "d[id] not give, as the second section shows, the power to Congress of regulating suffrage in the several states."[54] Perhaps Bingham was simply reaffirming his belief that suffrage was a privilege of citizenship, while reassuring listeners that Section 2 expressly exempted this privilege from being protected by the amendment, so not to worry. It is otherwise difficult to reconcile these seemingly conflicting claims, and we do not claim to have succeeded in the attempt.

Bingham also identified (1) the right to "be protected in life, liberty, and property"; (2) the right to be free from "cruel and unusual punishments"; and (3) the right to "bear true allegiance to the Constitution and laws of the United States" as "privileges and immunities of citizens in the several States."[55] He did not articulate any criteria for identifying them as such. Bingham stated that the imposition of cruel and unusual punishments was "contrary to the express letter of [the] Constitution."[56] But, of course, neither a generalized right to protection in life, liberty, and property—as distinct from a right to due process of law prior to the deprivation of one's life, liberty, or property—nor a right to bear true allegiance is part of the semantic content of the constitutional text. Bingham did not pretend to derive either right from the text.

Another explanation of Section 1's public meaning was provided to the House by Representative Thaddeus Stevens. Stevens lamented that Section 1 "f[ell] short of [his] wishes"—which included voting rights—but stated that "it is all that can be obtained in the present state of public opinion."[57] He said that Section 1 "allow[ed] Congress to correct the unjust legislation of the States, so far that the law which operates upon one man shall operate equally upon all."[58] He provided several examples of the ways in which Section 1 would do so: guaranteeing equality in access to legal redress, equality in respect of testimonial rights, and equality in respect of criminal punishment for the same offenses.[59]

Stevens conceded that it was "partly true" that the Civil Rights Act of 1866 already guaranteed such equality. But he then pointed out that "a law is repealable by a majority" and predicted that the Civil Rights Act *would* be repealed "the first time the South with their copperhead allies obtain the command of Congress."[60] In brief, according to Stevens, Section 1 answered

Hotchkiss's objections to Bingham's second draft by providing a more permanent security to these rights.

Unfortunately, Stevens did not clearly distinguish between Section 1's various components. Therefore, it is uncertain whether he thought the Privileges or Immunities Clause, the Due Process of Law Clause, or the Equal Protection of the Laws Clause, or all three together guaranteed the equality of which he spoke, or that anyone who listened to or read his statement would have understood him to be taking a position on the subject.

Jacob Howard's Explanation of Privileges or Immunities

Jacob Howard's presentation in the Senate was far more extensive and spoke more directly to the public meaning and purposes of particular provisions. Moreover, Howard was speaking as the Senate sponsor of the amendment, and his remarks were widely disseminated in newspapers—some of which dubbed it the "Howard Amendment." For all these reasons, we consider Howard's speech more probative of the ratified amendment's public meaning than any other congressional speech concerning Section 1 and will discuss it separately and at some length.

According to Howard, the "privileges or immunities" of US citizens consisted of two categories of "fundamental guarantees."[61] In the first category were "the privileges and immunities spoken of in the second section of the fourth article of the Constitution."[62] To identify these, Howard read from Justice Bushrod Washington's opinion in *Corfield*[63]—including the passage about voting rights.

Howard then located a second category of fundamental rights: "To these privileges and immunities, whatever they may be—for they are not and cannot be fully defined in their extent and precise nature—to these should be *added* the personal rights guarantied [sic] and secured by the first eight amendments of the Constitution."[64] After providing a nonexhaustive list[65] of those enumerated personal rights, Howard summarized his understanding of the two categories of "privileges or immunities": "Now, sir, here is a mass of privileges, immunities, and rights, *some of them secured by the second section of the fourth article of the Constitution,* which I have recited, *some by the first eight amendments of the Constitution.*"[66] (Notice that in neither reference to "the first eight amendments" does Howard call them "the bill of rights.")

Howard then explained that an amendment was necessary to protect both sets of fundamental rights because, at present, "[t]hey d[id] not operate in the slightest degree as a restraint or prohibition on state legislation."[67] So, "[t]he great object of the first section of this amendment is . . . to restrain the power of the States and compel them at all times to respect these fundamental guaranties."[68]

Christopher Green has examined Howard's handwritten notes for this speech for some additional context of his published remarks. Howard's reference to "the first eight amendments" was apparently inserted into his speech as an additional passage—suggesting he originally was going to refer *only* to *Corfield* rights. Then, after the inserted pages 2a and 2b, page 3 of Howard's notes continues: "By the first clause, each state is prohibited from restricting these fundamental civil rights of citizens, whatever may be their nature and extent."[69]

Assuming page 3 was originally written to follow page 2, on which *Corfield* is discussed, Howard was referring to the rights in *Corfield* as "these fundamental civil rights of citizens." This inference is strengthened by his qualifying phrase, "whatever maybe their nature and extent," which in the published version of the speech is explicitly a reference to *Corfield* rights. Indeed, at least one newspaper reported on Howard's speech as if his discussion concerned only *Corfield* rights.[70]

With respect to this "mass," Howard lamented in his floor speech that "the course of decision of our courts is . . . that all these immunities, privileges, rights, thus guarantied by the Constitution or recognized by it" did not "operate in the slightest degree upon State legislation."[71] He further explained that no such power had yet been "granted to Congress" to enforce these guarantees and that it was "necessary, if they are to be effectuated and enforced . . . that additional power should be given to Congress to that end."[72]

Howard then recited the language of what would become Section 5 of the Fourteenth Amendment: "The Congress shall have the power to enforce by appropriate legislation the provisions of this article."[73] He described this as "a direct affirmative delegation of power to Congress to carry out the principles of all these guarantees."[74] Section 1 "d[id] not, of itself, confer any power on Congress."[75] By enacting Section 5, Republicans declined to rely on the capacious reading of the Necessary and Proper Clause adopted by the Court in *Prigg v. Pennsylvania.*

In sum, Howard claimed that the Privileges or Immunities Clause would protect the "civil rights" enumerated in the Civil Rights Act in two ways: (1) by empowering Congress to protect them under Section 5 and (2) by protecting these rights judicially in the event that the act was repealed by a future Congress.

Howard took care to emphasize that Section 1 did *not* give voting rights to anyone. As we have repeatedly noted, in *Corfield,* Justice Washington *had* identified "the elective franchise" as among the privileges and immunities of citizens in the several states. Lest his heavy reliance on Washington's opinion be taken to imply that Section 1 would confer the right to vote, Howard canceled that implication in the very same speech.

The right of suffrage, Howard stated, was not "in law, one of the privileges or immunities thus secured by the Constitution."[76] Why not? Because it "is merely the creature of law" and had never been "regarded as one of those fundamental rights lying at the basis of all society and without which a people cannot exist except as slaves, subject to a despotism."[77] That is, suffrage was not a privilege or immunity of national citizenship because it was neither a natural right, nor was it deemed essential to securing one's natural rights when in civil society.

The two Republicans who spoke most specifically about the Privileges or Immunities Clause were Bingham in the House and Howard in the Senate. They agreed that it did not confer a general, personal right to suffrage. Howard did so by omitting the right to suffrage from his summary of privileges and immunities, as did the vast majority of Republicans. As a dissenter from this consensus, Bingham did so, perhaps, by pointing to Section 2's qualification of the scope of protection afforded to this privilege—although he also seemed to allow that particularly extreme instances of disenfranchisement might trigger the clause. They also agreed that at least some rights that were enumerated in the constitutional text would be protected by the clause.

Howard added the "personal rights" contained in the first eight amendments to his "mass" of "privileges, immunities, [and] rights."[78] He specifically listed:

> the freedom of speech and of the press; the right of the people peaceably to assemble and petition the Government for a redress of grievances, a right appertaining to each and all the people; the right to keep and bear arms; the right to be exempted from the quartering of soldiers in a house without the consent of the owner; the right to be exempt from unreasonable searches and seizures, and from any search or seizure except by virtue of a warrant issued upon a formal oath or affidavit; the right of an accused person to be informed of the nature of the accusation against him, and his right to be tried by an impartial jury of the vicinage; and also the right to be secure against excessive bail and against cruel and unusual punishments.[79]

The preceding "such as" indicated that this list of enumerated personal rights was illustrative, not exhaustive. For his part, as we have seen, Bingham mentioned the due process of law and the right to be free from cruel and unusual punishments.

Finally, Bingham and Howard agreed that at least some unenumerated rights would be protected by the clause. Howard's recitation of Justice Washington's *Corfield* opinion committed him to the proposition that rights of that "character"—with the exception of the franchise, which Howard specifically disclaimed—would "probably" be covered, including such unenumerated rights as the right to be free from discriminatory taxation. Bingham, for his part, mentioned a right to bear true allegiance to the federal government. Without question, neither man denied that the Privileges or Immunities Clause would protect unenumerated rights.

By referring several times to "the bill of rights," Bingham effectively put his colleagues on notice that any rights that he associated with "the bill of rights" would be covered. He would not express an understanding that "the bill of rights" encompassed *only* the first eight amendments, however, until five years later—a subject to which we will return.[80]

Ratifying the Fourteenth Amendment

The constitutional text was sent to the states for ratification on January 30, 1867. Most subsequent discussion of the amendment was focused on Section 3, which disqualified former Confederates and those who gave aid and comfort to rebels from holding civil or military office.[81] But Section 1 did receive a good deal of attention, as did the Privileges or Immunities Clause in particular. The discussion of the public meaning of the clause largely took place at a high level of generality, with supporters claiming that the Privileges or Immunities Clause merely guaranteed "equal civil rights" and opponents claiming that it gave the federal government authority to grant anything that Republicans deemed valuable to Blacks.

Examples and Criteria of Privileges or Immunities

Christopher Green has usefully divided ratification evidence into two general categories: (1) *examples* of the privileges and immunities of citizenship and (2) *criteria* used to identify the privileges and immunities of citizenship.[82] We would, however, classify the available evidence slightly differently. We have identified six prominent kinds of examples of privileges or immunities of US citizenship:

1. civil rights protected by the Civil Rights Act of 1866;
2. rights protected by the first eight amendments, including First Amendment rights to the free exercise of religion, freedom of speech, freedom of the press, and freedom of assembly; Second Amendment rights to bear arms; and Fifth Amendment rights to due process of law;
3. rights protected by other constitutional provisions, including the right to habeas corpus;
4. rights specifically mentioned in *Corfield*;
5. political rights, especially the right to vote, but also including the right to sit on juries and to hold office; and
6. rights to be free from various kinds of racial discrimination, including exclusion from quasi-monopolistic institutions and services such as common schools and street cars.

We have identified seven different criteria for identifying privileges or immunities of US citizenship:

1. rights to equal treatment in respect of civil rights;
2. natural rights;
3. civil rights as distinguished from "political" or "social" rights;
4. whatever civil and political rights are at a given time enjoyed by white men;
5. whatever rights are extended by a particular state to its own citizens;
6. any rights that the federal government deems fit to confer on US citizens; and
7. all rights that are commonly extended to citizens by the states generally.

Some of these examples and criteria were put forward in obvious bad faith. For instance, Democrats frequently claimed that Section 1 would compel Black suffrage. We have seen that Howard specifically denied this in presenting Section 1 to the Senate.[83] And during the ratification process, even the most radical of Republicans publicly insisted that voting rights were not among the privileges of citizenship secured by Section 1. This included Thaddeus Stevens, who deemed voting rights as essential to citizenship, if not more so, than any uncontroversial civil rights and who continued to demand their extension to Blacks.[84] Claims that the Privileges or Immunities Clause would give the federal government a blank check to extend rights to citizens also represented patent distortions of the Republican project.

A substantial minority of Republicans in the Thirty-Ninth Congress did believe that the right to vote was among the privileges of national citizenship and, more generally, believed that civil rights and political rights were both essential to national citizenship. Their views are significant to the public meaning of the clause because they bemoaned that meaning for its failure to include political rights. These members included Thaddeus Stevens, James Garfield, Thomas Eliot, and William Stewart.[85]

Outside of Congress, supporters of the Fourteenth Amendment frequently pointed out that neither women nor children could vote, despite uncontroversially being citizens.[86] In contrast, Frederick Douglass campaigned against the proposed amendment on the ground that Section 2 denied what Section 1 appeared to declare—namely, that Blacks were entitled to all of the privileges and immunities of national citizenship, which included the right to vote.[87] While Bingham was prepared to support the amendment despite this lack of protection for what he too considered to be a privilege of citizenship, Douglass was not. Yet, Douglass nevertheless shared the bottom line that the original meaning of the Fourteenth Amendment did not protect the right of suffrage.

The debate over the elective franchise is revealing in another way. Against the claim by some scholars that privileges or immunities were limited to rights enumerated in the text, there is a very large dog that did not bark. When responding to Democratic claims that the Fourteenth Amendment would secure voting rights, Republicans *never* argued that only rights enumerated in the Constitution were privileges of citizenship. Such a response, if generally thought to be true, would have disposed of the objection.

Nor, indeed, did *any* Republicans unambiguously use enumeration as a criterion for identifying the privileges of citizenship prior to the amendment's ratification. This is why we include enumerated rights on our list of *examples* of privileges or immunities, but not on our list of *criteria* for identifying such rights. "All and only enumerated rights" was never a criterion anyone employed for identifying the privileges and immunities of citizens of the United States.

True, Republicans produced numerous lists of rights they believed would be covered by the proposed amendment. And certain of those rights were textually enumerated. But these lists often enumerated different rights and either (a) did not purport to be exhaustive; (b) did purport to be exhaustive, but conspicuously omitted other enumerated rights; or (c) used criteria other than textual enumeration to explain why the listed rights qualified as privileges of citizenship.

Consider, for example, a March 1867 report of the majority of the Massachusetts Committee on Federal Relations. The report voiced disapproval of Section 1 on the ground that it was "difficult to see how [its] provisions differ from those now existing in the Constitution."[88] After quoting the Privileges and Immunities Clause, the Guarantee Clause, and the First, Second, Fifth, Sixth, and Seventh Amendments verbatim, the report stated that it was "difficult to conceive how *the provisions above quoted,* taken in connection with the whole tenor of the instrument, could have been put into clearer language" and asserted that "*these* provisions cover the whole ground of section first of the proposed amendment."[89] "The provisions quoted above" included rights not enumerated in the first eight amendments and excluded other rights that were enumerated there.

By contrast, Republicans often claimed that the Privileges or Immunities Clause would secure a broader set of rights than those enumerated in the first eight amendments: namely, civil rights that were associated with national citizenship. Rights enumerated in the text of the Constitution, rights enumerated in the text of the Civil Rights Act, rights enumerated in the text of *Corfield, and* rights that were *not* enumerated in *Corfield* might all meet this criterion.

Protecting Civil Rights Substantively or Solely against Discrimination?

Republicans, however, also often spoke of equal civil rights or equality before the law. It is therefore necessary to consider the possibility that they did not understand the Privileges or Immunities Clause to substantively secure the fundamental civil rights they identified as associated with citizenship; that the clause ensured only that whatever rights were secured for some citizens would be secured for all other similarly situated citizens. Republican claims that the Privileges or Immunities Clause secured rights listed in the Civil Rights Act of 1866 can help here.

By overriding President Johnson's veto, a supermajority of Republicans in the Thirty-Ninth Congress expressed their belief that the Civil Rights Act of 1866 was constitutional. But the consistency with which Republicans publicly stated that the Privileges or Immunities Clause would place the 1866 act beyond constitutional doubt is striking.[90] Therefore, the following proposition is worth highlighting: *Any account of the clause's public meaning must be able to explain why Republicans believed that the language of "privileges or immunities of citizens of the United States" would remove any constitutional doubt about the 1866 Act.*

The Civil Rights Act is conventionally read as solely prohibiting discrimination with respect to the civil rights specified in the act.[91] This reading relies on the act's requirement that all citizens enjoy the "same right[s]" to make and enforce contracts, to sue, be parties, and give evidence, and so on, "as [are] enjoyed by white citizens."[92] This requirement might seem to allow for the possibility that it would be constitutional for a state to prevent white citizens from enjoying one or all of the specified rights and thereby relieve itself of any obligation to ensure that Blacks enjoyed those rights. Under these circumstances, all would "enjoy[]" the "same right[s]."

But was the Civil Rights Act limited to barring nondiscrimination in this way? The possibility that a state would thus deny any of the rights specified in the Civil Rights Act to all of their citizens (so as not to deny them only to the freedmen or Republicans) does not appear to have been actively considered by anyone during discussions of the act. Perhaps such state action was deemed so unlikely that legislators did not consider it worth their time to safeguard citizens against it. Perhaps legislators were content that an equality-only Civil Rights Act would indirectly secure fundamental rights because they were confident that no state would deny the specified rights to white citizens.

On the other hand, "as is enjoyed by white citizens" might have expressed in 1868 only the social fact that white citizens were enjoying the specified rights. Going forward, states might be forbidden to deny those rights currently "enjoyed by white citizens" to anyone. On this reading, "as is enjoyed by white citizens" was a means of identifying fundamental rights in the positive law of states that were discriminating against Blacks.

Suppose Republicans had said, "Let's write a bill protecting the fundamental rights of Blacks" and someone responded, "What are those fundamental rights?" Their reply was: "Well, they are just the fundamental rights now enjoyed by white citizens!" In other words, "as is enjoyed by white persons" may well have provided a discernable *criterion* by which fundamental rights, privileges, or immunities of citizenship could be identified in the positive law of 1866—most pertinently, the law of the Southern states at which the Civil Rights Act was primarily aimed. But how do we know which reading is the correct one?

Consider that the language "as is enjoyed by white citizens" was not part of Wilson's original proposal. It was added via amendment later. Comparing the original to the amended language enables us to appreciate its potential public meaning and purpose:

> shall have the same right to make and enforce contracts, to sue, be parties, and give evidence, to inherit, purchase, lease, sell, hold, and convey real and personal property, and shall be subject to like punishment, pains, penalties, taxes, licenses, and exactions of every kind, and to no other.

> shall have the same right to make and enforce contracts, to sue, be parties, and give evidence, to inherit, purchase, lease, sell, hold, and convey real and personal property *as is enjoyed by white citizens,* and shall be subject to like punishment, pains, penalties, taxes, licenses, and exactions of every kind, and to no other.[93]

The original language declares that all citizens are to "have" certain rights; that everyone's rights are to be "the same"; and that everyone is to be subject to "like" impositions "and to no other." The amended language introduces what might appear to be a contingency: the enjoyment of the listed rights by a subset of the citizenry. *If* "white citizens" did not enjoy the specified rights in a given state, perhaps *no one* in that state would be entitled to enjoy them. This was not, however, the explanation offered by Wilson for the amendment.

In response to a query by Representative Columbus Delano, Wilson explained that concerns had been expressed that the unqualified language would "confer[] the right of being jurors" on all citizens:

> [T]he reason for offering [the amendment] was this: it was thought by some persons that unless these qualifying words were incorporated in the bill, those rights might be extended to all citizens, *whether male or female,* majors or minors.[94]

That is, Wilson sought to clarify that, by providing that all citizens would have the "same right" to make and enforce contracts, and so on, the act would not obliterate distinctions between citizens that were not related to race and that were still accepted as reasonable. "White citizens" had "enjoyed" those rights subject to reasonable regulation, and these regulations would not change.

In particular, under existing law, white women could not sit on juries. And, as Justice Joseph Bradley took pains to explain five years later in his now infamous concurring opinion in the 8-1 decision in *Bradwell v. Illinois,* (nearly) every man then thought the laws of coverture were "reasonable." Representative Delano responded that he had "no doubt" that the amendment was introduced for the reason stated by Wilson.[95]

Wilson's apparent assumption that it would be reasonable to regulate access to the jury box by excluding women from juries entirely is repugnant, and we will soon consider its relevance to *Bradwell*. But it does suggest that "as is enjoyed by white citizens" provided a positive-law criterion to identify the *substantive scope* of the fundamental rights protected; it was not imposing a "discrimination-only" limitation on the act. After all, we today accept the fact that minors cannot sit on juries, and Wilson explained that the language "as is enjoyed by white citizens" was similarly aimed at preserving what he considered a reasonable regulation of the privilege of jury service.

Consistent with this reading, neither Wilson nor anyone else in the House claimed that the additional words would give states latitude to deny civil rights to white citizens and thereby to justify denying them to all citizens—a tactic recalcitrant Southerners would later employ. In the Senate, Trumbull stated that he "d[id] not think they alter[ed] the bill" and that "the bill would be better without them."[96] Moreover, Republicans did not seek to ensure that Blacks enjoyed a lowest common denominator of white rights. We have already seen that the states they sought most to constrain had been hostile to *white* citizens who opposed slavery before the Civil War and who opposed revanchist white supremacy after Appomattox. For example, all whites were equally forbidden to speak against slavery. Republicans sought to ensure that *all* citizens—white and black—enjoyed fundamental civil rights.[97] The fundamental-rights reading of the Civil Rights Act is consistent with the text and fits this original purpose better than the discrimination-only alternative.

John Harrison has focused attention on Representative Samuel Shellabarger's statement that the act "neither confers nor defines nor regulates any right whatever" but, rather, "require[s] that whatever of these enumerated rights and obligations are imposed by State laws shall be for and upon all citizens alike without distinctions based on race or former condition in slavery."[98] Harrison reads Shellabarger as affirming that "the states would remain free to create *whatever rights they pleased,* as long as they gave them to all citizens."[99]

But Shellabarger delivered that statement during a speech in which he stated that "the right of petition and the right of protection in such property as is lawful for that particular citizen to own" were among the "indispensable rights of American citizenship." He identified the rights listed in the Civil Rights Act as rights that the federal government "must" protect in return for the "service and allegiance" it demands from citizens.[100]

The examples Shellabarger gives of rights that the federal government could not guarantee without "invad[ing] the rights of the states" were testimonial and contractual rights, which he apparently believed could reasonably be denied to married women and minors.[101] Like Wilson, Shellabarger is best read as stressing that the Civil Rights Act would not displace what he deemed reasonable distinctions that were not tied to race. He was not representing that states were free to confer—or deny—whatever civil rights they please, so long as they conferred or denied them on all.

Does this mean that all states are required to protect property, contract, and evidentiary rights in precisely the same way? If so, it would seem that federalism had not merely been revised but obliterated; the most minute details of state regulation of individual rights would be nationalized. But to insist that states secure the same rights is not to require them to do so through the same means. No one seriously contends that every state must regulate speech in the same way because the Fourteenth Amendment guarantees the freedom of speech everywhere.

To be sure, however, we must take care in specifying the balance struck between ensuring a national commitment to fundamental rights of citizenship and accommodating local variation in rights regulation. In Chapter 7, we will present the evidence showing that there were two sources of civil rights protected by the Privileges or Immunities Clause. The first are those civil rights that protect, both directly and indirectly, the natural rights one has in the state of nature. The second are civil rights to equal access to the post-political goods that the state need not, but may still choose to, provide its citizenry.

The first set of rights is not optional. These rights must be provided (equally) to everyone. The latter set of rights is optional. But while these rights may be denied to all, they may not be given to some and denied to others. Harrison's interpretation of the Privileges or Immunities Clause is accurate with respect to the second of these categories of civil rights but not the first. The failure to acknowledge these two distinct sources of civil rights has thus led to much confusion in interpreting the evidence.

Claims that the Privileges or Immunities Clause secured to Blacks the "same rights" as white citizens or "equal privileges" to those enjoyed by white citizens or that it secured "equal rights" for all citizens should be scored in favor of an equality-only understanding of the clause only after careful investigation of the specific context in which those claims were advanced. Here's what we mean.

The author of a July 23, 1868, editorial in the West Virginia *Wheeling Daily Intelligencer* stated that the Privileges or Immunities Clause would ensure that "[c]itizens . . . have the same rights everywhere, and they are placed beyond the reach of sectional fanaticism."[102] At first blush, the "same rights" language might seem to express an equality-only view of the clause's coverage. Yet the editorial also describes the clause as a "complete guarantee of civil rights everywhere," which "renders null and void any local law infringing the freedom of speech, or of the press, forbidding the settlement of any race or color, & c."[103] We have, then, not an equality-only view but a fundamental-rights view, according to which *all* citizens are *equally* entitled to enjoy the *same* fundamental rights.

Still, a few editorialists do appear to have understood the clause to guarantee only equal enjoyment of the rights extended to citizens under state law at any given time—whatever those rights might be. A particularly colorful expression of this view appeared in North Carolina's *Daily Standard* on October 6, 1866. One "Moscow" criticized a candidate for the North Carolina Senate for claiming that Section 1, "per se, established Negro suffrage." Speaking with reference to the Privileges or Immunities Clause, Moscow wrote:

> What does it say?—that none of the privileges or immunities which [Blacks] now possess[] shall be abridged. Does the negro possess the privilege of suffrage in North-Carolina or even Connecticut? How then can you abridge a privilege which he does not possess? He can vote in Massachusetts under certain qualifications; and perhaps, if this amendment be adopted by three-fourths of the States, his privilege in that respect in that State could never be abridged. But as he has never been granted such a privilege in this State, how can you pass or enforce a law to abridge him in it?
>
> But what privileges or immunities does the negro now possess? In times of slavery he had none—his life, liberty and property belonged to a master. Now he has the privilege to bear arms, to speak his sentiments freely, to assemble and petition for a redress of grievances, to give testimony, to sue and be sued and to hold property, and to make wills; and no man can deprive him of life, liberty or property without due process of law. These are the privileges which he now possesses in this State, and which this amendment says shall not be abridged . . .

Should the privilege of suffrage be extended the negro by North-Carolina that would alter the case. Perhaps she could never abridge it. . . . [104]

But Moscow's view was unusual. Supporters of Section 1 generally denied that suffrage was a privilege or immunity of citizenship even in those states that did extend suffrage to Black citizens. These supporters did not claim that the Privileges or Immunities Clause would secure only whatever privileges states chose to extend to Blacks.[105] Overwhelmingly, they represented that the clause would secure to all citizens equal enjoyment of civil rights that inhered in national citizenship. When they were more specific, they claimed that those rights included those specified in the Civil Rights Act,[106] those embodied in the text of the federal Constitution,[107] or those long recognized in the law of the states, whether in constitutional or common law.[108]

There is a wealth of evidence of a fundamental-rights-*plus*-equality meaning that forbade states from unreasonably discriminating *when regulating the exercise of civil rights*. Such discrimination was barred whether it was between white and Black citizens or between their own citizens and citizens of other states. Republicans consistently stated that all citizens who were similarly situated would be entitled under the clause to similar treatment under the law.

An editorial in the *Chicago Tribune* claimed that states would be obliged by the Fourteenth Amendment not only to provide all citizens with the rights to purchase, lease, and hold real estate and to maintain actions against their fellow citizens, but to provide those rights to all citizens "on an equality with the old first-class people."[109] The editorial was careful to stress that national citizenship "carrie[d] with it no political rights" but insisted that, when it came to "legal or civil status," national citizenship was to be unstratified, "uniform."[110]

Can a prohibition against unreasonable discrimination between citizens be incorporated into a pure fundamental-rights framework, and, if so, how? Does the Privileges or Immunities Clause require that fundamental rights be extended to all similarly situated citizens, but permit unreasonable discrimination between citizens that is unrelated to fundamental rights? Should freedom from unreasonable discrimination vis-à-vis other citizens *itself* be conceived as a fundamental right that cannot be abridged? Or, should we regard the clause as imposing two distinct requirements: (1) an extension of certain fundamental rights to all citizens; and (2) equality—or no unreasonable distinctions among citizens—in the regulation of these rights? (The latter of these interpretations is our view.)

The newspaper materials do not provide much help in choosing between these characterizations. To identify the public meaning of the Privileges or Immunities Clause, we must rely primarily on publicly accessible records of debates concerning legislation that was designed to implement it. During those debates, some Republicans denied that particular rights—including rights of access to schools, common carriers, and theaters and rights to sit on juries—were privileges or immunities of citizenship at all. Other Republicans responded by claiming either that they were indeed privileges of citizenship or that, even if they were not, discrimination with respect to them nonetheless triggered the Privileges or Immunities Clause. We will focus on these debates in Chapter 6, when we investigate post-ratification materials.

Overall, the views of the Privileges or Immunities Clause that the Fourteenth Amendment's supporters expressed in the newspaper literature are consistent with these representations that Republicans made during the framing process:

- The clause would secure civil rights as distinct from political or social rights.
- Examples of those rights were listed in the Civil Rights Act or in the text of the federal Constitution, or were widely recognized and entrenched in the law of the states.
- States were barred from adopting unreasonable distinctions when regulating the rights of US citizens.

This was the common ground. Different editorialists produced different lists of privileges and immunities that they believed would be protected. So too did different legislators, governors, activists, and influencers. But all the privileges and immunities they mentioned were widespread and entrenched means of securing citizens' natural rights and civic equality.

An increasingly influential interpretation of the Privileges or Immunities Clause holds that the clause solely prohibits states from depriving citizens of rights enumerated in the federal Constitution.[111] True, various enumerated rights were frequently mentioned, which generally supports something like what is today called "incorporation." But the newspaper literature provides scant support for any claim that the clause protected *only* enumerated rights. Moreover, as we noted above, if the original meaning of "privileges or immunities" was limited to enumerated rights, why didn't supporters of the amendment just say that when they tried to dispel the claim that the clause protected unenumerated voting rights?

We have also seen that partial lists of enumerated rights do not support any such enumerated-rights-only theory. Although Jacob Howard's introduction to the Senate discussing the rights specified in the "first eight amendments" was published in several widely circulated papers, we have no record of anyone drawing on his introduction to argue that *only* enumerated rights would be secured by the Fourteenth Amendment. We therefore did not include the enumeration of certain rights among our seven criteria for privileges or immunities that were mentioned at the time.

What about those seven that do appear? To reiterate, those criteria are:

1. rights to equal treatment in respect of civil rights;
2. natural rights;
3. civil rights as distinguished from "political" or "social" rights;
4. whatever civil and political rights are at a given time enjoyed by white men;
5. whatever rights are extended by a *particular* state to its own citizens;
6. any rights that the federal government deems fit to confer on US citizens; and
7. all rights that are commonly extended to citizens by the states *generally*.

Republicans consistently and publicly denied that the Fourteenth Amendment would secure voting rights, so we can exclude the fourth and fifth criteria from consideration. Many white men, after all, did enjoy the right to vote, and many states extended the right to vote to their own citizens. Another reason to exclude the fifth criterion is the scarcity of claims that states could confer whatever rights they chose on citizens, so long as they did so impartially. We can also exclude the sixth criterion. Claims that the Privileges or Immunities Clause amounted to a congressional blank check were advanced exclusively by the Fourteenth Amendment's Democratic opponents.

That leaves us with four criteria that *might* have been incorporated into the Privileges or Immunities Clause. The clause might secure:

1. rights to equal treatment in respect of civil rights;
2. natural rights;
3. civil rights, as distinguished from "political" or "social" rights; and
4. all rights that are commonly extended to citizens by the states generally.

The application of some of these criteria may yield the same constitutional conclusions. The set of civil rights that was distinguished from political or social rights might be identical to the set of rights that was commonly extended to citizens by the states generally in 1868. Other criteria may overlap; a right to equal treatment vis-à-vis other citizens might itself be one among citizens' other civil rights.

With respect to natural rights, we have seen that congressional Republicans did not always cleanly separate civil rights from natural rights. They sometimes referred to natural-rights-protective positive rights, such as the rights to due process of law and habeas corpus, as natural rights. And they spoke both of absolute rights and equality between citizens. Members of the public do not appear to have been exposed to ideas about civil rights or natural rights that were cleaner than those of congressional Republicans who discussed the privileges and immunities of US citizenship in connection with either the Civil Rights Act or the Fourteenth Amendment.

For present purposes, the key takeaway is that the partial lists of rights generated during the framing and ratification process do not point decisively in the direction of any of these four remaining criteria. We perceive in these lists a "network of similarities overlapping and crisscrossing" similar to that which Wittgenstein perceived in the various activities that are conventionally called "games."[112] It may be that no single criterion can be used to separate the privileges and immunities of citizenship from other kinds of rights. Before we reach that conclusion, however, we need to examine evidence from the post-ratification period.

6

Enforcing Citizenship

Discussion of privileges and immunities did not cease upon the ratification of the Fourteenth Amendment. The imperative of implementing the amendment's promises by legislation led to extensive, often vitriolic, congressional debates, not only between Republicans and Democrats but between moderate and radical Republicans. When it came time to remedy state failures to protect citizens against racial and political terrorism, as well as racial exclusion from important public institutions, Republicans who shared an abstract commitment to securing citizens' civil rights disagreed about both the necessity and the propriety of specific congressional interventions.

As we have noted, the epistemic value of post-ratification interpretations of the meaning of constitutional text diminishes over time as memories fade and political incentives change, and it becomes harder for us to distinguish between innocent interpretive errors and bad-faith misrepresentations of original meaning. Fortunately, Republicans who were present at the framing were willing to call out their peers for perceived departures from original meaning. And Republicans appear to have operated within the same basic constitutional-theoretical framework both pre- and post-ratification.

Scholars seeking the original meaning of terms in the 1788 constitution often consult debates in the first Congress. For example, when considering the meaning of "necessary and proper," they focus on the constitutional arguments advanced in the debate over the first Bank of the United States. It is thought that how those who were familiar with the public meaning of the

Constitution applied that meaning soon after it was enacted is probative, though not dispositive, evidence of that meaning.

Likewise, Republicans' deliberations about proposed legislation, their responses to citizens' calls for action on civil rights, and their responses to judicial interpretations of the Privileges or Immunities Clause are worth canvassing.[1] When there is reason to doubt their epistemic value, owing to inconsistency or contestation by fellow Republicans, we will say so.

The Fifteenth Amendment

In 1870, the Fifteenth Amendment was adopted by the Fortieth Congress to extend constitutional protection to the right of suffrage of Blacks, which had been omitted from the scope of the Fourteenth. During the legislative debate on the necessity of the amendment, a number of Republicans advanced claims about the meaning of the Privileges or Immunities Clause that Republicans had generally repudiated when campaigning for the Fourteenth Amendment's ratification. For example, Richard Yates, George Boutwell, George Edmunds, and Charles Sumner, among others, contended that voting was among the rights of citizenship already protected by the Privileges or Immunities Clause. There was, they maintained, no need for a new amendment; a statute to secure voting rights enacted under Section 5 of the Fourteenth Amendment would suffice.[2]

This claim did not go uncontested. Because of his role in introducing and expounding the Fourteenth Amendment to the Senate, Jacob Howard's rejection of these claims is particularly significant. Howard felt "constrained" by what he described as his "duty" to "say here now that this is the first time it ever occurred to me that the right to vote was to be derived" from the amendment.[3] In his view, Section 2 amounted to a "plain, indubitable recognition" that the amendment left voting regulations to the states.[4]

In the course of arguing that voting rights were not among the privileges and immunities of national citizenship, Howard elaborated on the meaning of the Privileges or Immunities Clause thus:

> The occasion of introducing the first section of the fourteenth article of amendment into that amendment grew out of the fact that there was nothing in the whole Constitution to secure absolutely the citizens of the United States in the various States against an infringement of their rights and privileges under the [Privileges and Immunities Clause of Article IV]. . . .

[U]nless the Senator from Vermont and the Senator from Massachusetts can derive the right of voting from this ... upon the ground that the citizens of the United States are entitled to all the privileges and immunities of citizens of the several states, they must give up the argument.

The commentators upon the Constitution apply it simply to the right of purchasing, owing, holding, and enjoying property by the citizen of one State, lying and being situate in another State, of receiving property by descent, &c; relating to those personal rights and privileges connected with property which it was intended by the Convention which framed the Constitution to make common and uniform among the citizens of the United States; but never applying it to political rights of any description, either of voting or of holding office. . . .

The immediate object of [the Privileges or Immunities Clause] was to prohibit for the future all hostile legislation on the part of the recently rebel States in reference to the colored citizens of the United States who had become emancipated, and who finally were declared to be citizens by the civil rights bill passed by Congress.[5]

Four features of Howard's response are worth highlighting. First, he identified the "rights and privileges" protected by the Privileges or Immunities Clause with those that were insufficiently protected by Article IV. "[T]here was nothing in the whole Constitution to secure absolutely the citizens of the United States in the various States against an infringement of their rights and privileges" under the Privileges and Immunities Clause. As we have seen, this identification traces back to the earliest proposals by John Bingham.

Second, Howard denied that the rights of national citizenship were the same as the rights of state citizenship. Unless those who claimed that voting rights were included "can derive the right of voting from" the Privileges or Immunities Clause "upon the ground that the citizens of the United States are entitled to *all* the privileges and immunities of citizens *of* the several states, they must give up the argument." Howard implied here that voting rights could not be so derived because the set of national citizenship rights did not embrace every right afforded to citizens by their state.

Third, Howard distinguished rights of state citizenship that were protected by Article IV from rights that were not by invoking a distinction between "personal rights and privileges connected with property" and "political rights." The "common and uniform" treatment of these property rights, he said, was "intended by the Convention which framed the Constitution." As we have seen, the protection of "the right to acquire and possess property of every kind" was at the core of Justice Washington's list of privileges and immunities in *Corfield*. And the rights "to inherit, purchase, lease, sell, hold, and convey real and personal property" were expressly protected by the Civil Rights Act of 1866.

Fourth, Howard then associated the Privileges or Immunities Clause with "the civil rights bill passed by Congress." His statement conflicts with any claim that it was some other clause in Section 1 that constitutionalized the Civil Rights Act of 1866. Further, Howard emphasized that the clause was designed to prohibit hostile legislation targeting emancipated Blacks—an unmistakable reference to the Black Codes. By so doing, Howard also made clear that the clause was not a comity-only source of protection and, once again, that it was the Privileges or Immunities Clause, not some other, that was aimed at the Black Codes.

Why give any epistemic weight to Howard's claims about original meaning several years after the fact? It was entirely consistent with his introduction of the Fourteenth Amendment to the Senate and the pre-ratification claims of other Republicans. As we have seen, Republican supporters of the Fourteenth Amendment did not generally distinguish between Article IV rights and rights protected by the Privileges or Immunities Clause; the distinction between civil rights and political rights was widely accepted by the amendment's supporters; and the Black Codes were an agreed-upon target of the Privileges or Immunities Clause.

Republican Senator Aaron Cragin lent further support to Howard's recollection, remembering that "it was announced upon this floor by more than one gentleman, and contradicted and denied by no one so far as I can recollect, that that amendment did not seek to confer any right to vote."[6] Senator Richard Yates recalled that he had been one of only a few Republicans who had during the framing process taken the view that "the badge of an American citizen is the right to deposit his ballot in the ballot-box."[7]

It is worth stressing that Yates claimed in 1866, as he did in 1869, that "to say that the African should only have his civil rights without his political rights would be worse than slavery," as Blacks would be at the mercy of their enemies without the latter.[8] So his interpretive stance toward the meaning of the clause ran against his normative commitments. Nevertheless, he remembered that his colleagues had in 1866 "read authority after authority to show that to be a citizen was to be invested merely with civil and not with political rights" and that they had claimed that "the African had the right to acquire property, to testify in the courts of justice, to sue and be sued, to plead and be impleaded, but . . . no right to vote."[9] Although Yates affirmed that his "faith remain[ed] unchanged," he acknowledged that the Senate had "decided upon [the latter] interpretation."[10]

The Force Bill

By the time that the Fourteenth Amendment was ratified into law on July 28, 1868, the need for vigorous implementing legislation was apparent. More than a year earlier, in April 1867, the Ku Klux Klan had met in Nashville, Tennessee, to plan a response to Reconstruction policy. What resulted was its transformation from a loosely organized group of marauders into an instrument of organized terror.[11] The Klan promoted white supremacy through whippings, rapes, and murders; and it effectively disabled law enforcement in several Southern states.[12] Governors cried out for federal assistance from the Republican now in the White House. President Ulysses Grant responded by calling on Congress to act to enforce the Fourteenth and Fifteenth Amendments, the latter of which was ratified in 1870.[13]

The Enforcement Acts of 1870 and 1871 both targeted conduct that threatened civil rights and inspired vigorous debates among legislators concerning the meaning of the Privileges or Immunities Clause. The 1870 act—the "Force Bill"—focused on voting rights. It declared that citizens otherwise qualified to vote could do so without regard to race, color, or previous condition of servitude and outlawed private interference with the right to vote.[14] More generally, it made it a felony to conspire or to ride the public highways to deprive any citizen of "any right or privilege granted or secured to him by the Constitution or laws of the United States."[15]

The Force Bill also reenacted the 1866 Civil Rights Act's provisions for the protection of all the rights of "citizens" listed in the original act and extended a smaller set of rights to all "persons."[16] As introduced in the Forty-First Congress, the bill would have reenacted the Civil Rights Act of 1866 without addressing the rights of noncitizens. When an amendment was proposed to extend to "all *persons* within the jurisdictions of the United States" the rights listed in the Civil Rights Act, the amendment excluded the right "to inherit, purchase, lease, sell, hold, and convey real and personal property." Bingham supported it.

It seems likely that Bingham—like Senator William Stewart, who proposed the amendment[17]—distinguished between the civil rights or privileges of *citizens* and the protection of the laws that he believed all *persons* were constitutionally entitled to enjoy. With respect to the latter, because immigrants were "persons within the express words of the fourteenth article of amendment," Bingham maintained that they were "entitled to the equal protection of the laws."[18] In contrast, certain landownership rights were privileges of citizenship.

That citizens were constitutionally entitled to enjoy more landownership rights than noncitizens was not controversial either when the Fourteenth Amendment was ratified or in the years following ratification. Indeed, Polly Price has shown that the rights of noncitizens to hold land were restricted throughout the nineteenth century. This was pursuant to common-law norms that held fast against political and economic forces that supported land liberalization.[19] Even when fee tails, coverture, and other features of English property law were being discarded as feudal relics, state courts resisted alteration of noncitizen property disabilities.[20]

The conjunction within the Force Bill of the reenactment of the Civil Rights Act of 1866 and the extension of a smaller set of rights to noncitizens suggests that Republicans in 1870 continued to believe that citizenship came with certain constitutional benefits to which noncitizens were not entitled. Further, this distinction between the rights of citizens and persons has another important interpretive implication.

It suggests that the protections afforded "persons" by the Due Process of Law and the Equal Protection of the Laws Clauses do not reach every right specified in the Civil Rights Act of 1866. The original meaning of these clauses in 1868, therefore, could not have constitutionalized the act, as some scholars have claimed. In particular, these clauses did not protect certain landownership rights. As we have maintained, virtually all evidence points to the Privileges or Immunities Clause as the relevant provision that locked the Civil Rights Act into constitutional law. And the fact that the Privileges or Immunities Clause was what constitutionalized the act provides important information about its original meaning.

The Woodhull Report

The Fifteenth Amendment barred discrimination with respect to voting rights on account of race, not sex. Several months after its ratification in 1870, women's rights advocate Victoria Woodhull submitted a memorial to both houses of Congress in which she argued that denying the right to vote to women violated the Privileges or Immunities Clause.[21] When Woodhull presented her memorial before the House Committee on the Judiciary on January 11, 1871, Albert Riddle, a DC lawyer and suffragist who spoke in support of the memorial, drew on Justice Washington's opinion in *Corfield*.[22]

The House Judiciary Committee responded that, because the Privileges or Immunities Clause did not secure the right of *any* citizens to vote, it did not secure the right of women to vote. Its report was submitted by John Bingham, who chaired the committee—although his precise involvement is contested. Importantly, the Woodhull Report stated that the clause "does not, in the opinion of the committee, refer to privileges and immunities of citizens of the United States *other than those privileges and immunities embraced in the original text of the Constitution, article 4, section 2*."[23] This language is consistent with everything we have heard from John Bingham about privileges and immunities to this point.

Although the Woodhall Report cited Justice Bushrod Washington's opinion in *Corfield*, it also drew from Daniel Webster's arguments as counsel for the Bank of the United States in *Bank of Augusta v. Earle*.[24] Webster stated that the Privileges and Immunities Clause "d[id] not confer on the citizens of each State political rights in every other state." Accordingly, Pennsylvania citizens were not entitled to exercise voting rights in Virginia until they met the qualifications set forth in Virginia's constitution.[25] The report proclaimed it "obvious" that Webster "did not include the privilege of the elective franchise" among the privileges and immunities of citizens.[26]

Responding to the report at a February 16, 1871 lecture, Woodhull singled out Bingham for harsh criticism: it was "almost impossible to conceive that the author of this report was the same person who drew the XIVth Amendment" and the 1870 Force Bill. "[W]e find Mr. Bingham," she explained,

> in the XIVth Amendment, declaring that all persons are citizens . . . making it a penal offence for any officer of election in any State to refuse to all citizens the same and equal opportunities . . . to become qualified to vote; less than a year afterwards informing us that women are not citizens . . . and adding that Congress has no power to enforce their rights as citizens in the States. . . . What he may think tomorrow or next month it would be quite impossible to predict.[27]

For reasons that will soon become apparent, we sympathize with the last of her complaints.

Woodhull made clear that she did not believe that the Fourteenth Amendment "confer[red] rights not possessed."[28] Instead, in her opinion, it "declare[d] positively" that "[a]ll persons born or naturalized in the United States are citizens of the United States." Woodhull then contended that such citizenship entailed voting rights for all "who [were] responsible, taxed, and who contributed to the maintenance of an organized government."[29]

Women had demonstrated that they were no longer "an unassuming, acquiescing part of society." Rather, women were "so much individualized as to demand the full and unrestrained exercise of all the rights which can be predicated of a people constructing a government based on individual sovereignty."[30] As authority for the proposition that citizenship entailed both civil and political rights, she cited Chief Justice Taney's opinion in *Dred Scott*.[31]

Recall Jacob Howard's denial that the right to vote was among the rights without which a people would be subject to despotism. Woodhull argued otherwise, contending that "the right to self-government [was] possessed equally by all" and that without it, women were subjected to "arbitrary rule," indeed, "tyranny" no less grievous than that exercised "over our fathers" by George III.[32] Freedom, in her view, "consiste[d] in having an actual share in appointing those who frame the laws," and those who lacked such a share were "in absolute bondage."[33]

Woodhull's account of the "tyranny" to which women were subject is worth quoting at length. For she powerfully articulated a conception of citizenship that was in the process of expanding to encompass this paradigmatic political right:

> I am taxed in every conceivable way. For publishing a paper I must pay; for engaging in the banking and brokerage business I must pay; of what it is my fortune to acquire each year I must turn over a certain per cent; I must pay high prices for tea, coffee, and sugar. To all these must I submit, that men's government may be maintained, a government in the administration of which I am denied a voice, and from its edicts there is no appeal. I must submit to a heavy advance upon the first cost of nearly everything I wear in order that industries in which I have no interest may exist at my expense. I am compelled to pay extravagant rates of fare wherever I travel, because the franchises, extended to gigantic corporations, enable them to sap the vitality of the country, to make their managers money kings, by means of which they boast of being able to control not only legislators but even a State judiciary.

> To be compelled to submit to these extortions that such ends may be gained, upon any pretext or under any circumstances, is bad enough; but to be compelled to submit to them, and also denied the right to cast my vote against them, is a tyranny more odious than that which, being rebelled against, gave this country independence.[34]

For Woodhull, to be denied the right to vote was to be compelled to endure oppression that was either initiated or facilitated by a state that did not pursue her interests, whether because of indifference or because the state was captured by corporate interests. If she considered the right to vote to be an inherent right of citizenship, she also regarded it as an instrumentally important one that protected other rights that were more traditionally associated with citizenship, such as property and travel rights.

Woodhull's views were echoed by a few Republicans. A minority on the House Judiciary Committee agreed with Woodhull that the privileges and immunities of US citizenship "attach[ed] to the female citizen equally with the male" and that "the right of suffrage is a fundamental right of citizenship."[35] The minority noted that Justice Washington in *Corfield* had mentioned the elective franchise, observed that Washington's opinion was "cited approvingly by Chancellor Kent," and took the majority to task for citing *Corfield* "as sustaining their view of the law" even though "[i]t is for them an exceedingly unfortunate opinion."[36]

More generally, the minority affirmed that the Fourteenth Amendment "abolishe[d] the theory of different grades of citizenship" and that, under the Constitution, "all citizens are sovereigns . . . and therefore it must necessarily be that the right to a voice in the government is the right and privilege of a citizen as such."[37] Like Woodhull, the minority also emphasized the instrumental value of the right to vote, describing it as a "means of asserting and protecting rights that existed before any civil governments were formed—the right of life, liberty, and property." They cited Thomas Paine, who claimed that to take away the right to vote "[wa]s to reduce man to a state of slavery, for slavery consists in being subject to the will of another."[38] Like Woodhull, the minority drew support for the proposition that citizenship entailed voting rights from Chief Justice Taney's opinion in *Dred Scott*.[39]

The minority also anticipated the original-Framers'-intent counterargument that women were in all states denied the right to vote in 1788; that no one claimed that the Constitution would change their status; and that "such a construction of [the Constitution] is against what must have been *the in-*

tention of the framers."⁴⁰ They answered this with the original public-meaning methodology pioneered by Lysander Spooner, William Goodell, Frederick Douglass, and other abolitionist constitutionalists: "We are to judge of the intention of those who established the Constitution *by what they say,* guided by *what they declare on the face of the instrument* to be their object."⁴¹

Applying this approach, they remarked that "[g]eneral understanding and acquiescence is [an] unsafe rule by which to try questions of constitutional law, and precedents are not infallible guides towards liberty and the rights of man."⁴² Turning to the Fourteenth Amendment, the minority denied that Section 2 implicitly acknowledged that states could deny the right to vote. They declared that "the fundamental rights of citizens are not to be taken away by implication, and a constitutional provision for the protection of one class can certainly not be used to destroy or impair the same rights in another class."⁴³

All of these are perfectly appropriate original-meaning interpretive moves, and it is good to see them being employed. In addition, the minority also based its argument on what we call the spirit of the text: that every stated object in the Preamble was contravened by the denial of the right to vote to women. Such an argument is particularly germane to interpretive claims based on implication. Nevertheless, in our view, the majority who issued the Woodhull Report had the better of the argument.

The majority's distinction between political and civil rights and its denial that the former were protected by the Privileges or Immunities Clause are more consistent with what Republicans—radical, moderate, and conservative—had said publicly about the Privileges or Immunities Clause pre-ratification. Absent this pre-ratification evidence, this post-ratification argument might well be persuasive. As it stands, the report provides better evidence of the clause's original meaning.

To be clear, we deny that the original expected application of the amendment comprises its meaning. We reject the argument that the Privileges or Immunities Clause did not protect the right of women to vote because the Framers of the original Constitution or of the Fourteenth Amendment would not have expected or desired that it have that effect. Our claim is that the widespread and repeatedly stated meaning of the phrase "privileges or immunities of citizens of the United States" became its public meaning. And we think that the weight of the evidence establishes that the public meaning of these words did not embrace the political rights of anyone—male or female, minor or major, Black or white. This distinction between original expected application and original public meaning will become important later on in this chapter when we consider *Bradwell v. Illinois,* which held that women could be denied the privilege of practicing law by a state.

Moreover, if the privileges or immunities of citizenship refer to those fundamental rights that are deemed to be fundamental in the positive law, it is simply false that citizens generally enjoyed the privilege of the franchise when the amendment was adopted. Woodbridge and the minority's claim about "privileges or immunities" is a plausible, indeed a persuasive, moral reading of the text. But this reading was not the law adopted in 1868. That was to come later by means of formal amendments.

There is, however, common ground to be found between supporters and opponents of Woodhull's constitutional claims. First, both sides appealed to *Corfield,* which some scholars, such as Kurt Lash, have claimed was abandoned as interpretive evidence of the meaning of the Privileges or Immunities Clause during the debate over its adoption.[44] Second, both sides failed to express any awareness of the view that the only rights secured absolutely to citizens were those enumerated in the Constitution—the enumerated-rights-only thesis that has been defended by Kurt Lash.[45] Certainly they did not endorse it.

Victoria Woodhull's constitutional arguments and those of the minority of the committee merit close study for another reason. They illustrate the difference between the *criteria* for finding a right to be a privilege or immunity of citizenship that were established by the original meaning of the text and an *example* of a right that was thought to meet those criteria or fail to do so. Woodhall contended that the right to vote was essential to preserving the fundamental rights of citizenship. Because the majority was not yet willing to accept this claim and enshrine it in positive law, the right of suffrage had not *yet* become a privilege of American citizenship. But it might one day meet that criterion. And, as arguments like Woodhull's were increasingly advanced and accepted as persuasive, eventually it would.

The Ku Klux Klan Act of 1871

Like the Force Bill, the 1871 act—also called the Ku Klux Klan Act—targeted not only state action but conspiracies by private individuals who prevented any "persons" from "exercising any right or privilege of a citizen of the United States" because of racial or political prejudice.[46] Defenders of the constitutionality of the Ku Klux Klan Act spoke at great length of the need to ensure the equal protection of the laws, but they also discussed privileges and immunities. Once again, Justice Washington's opinion in *Corfield* had not been forgotten, either for its criteria or for its examples of privileges and immunities of citizenship.

Paraphrasing Washington's criteria, Representative Samuel Shellabarger claimed that the Privileges or Immunities Clause, together with Section 5, empowered Congress to protect "those privileges and immunities which are in their nature fundamental," which "inhere and belong of right to the citizenship of all free governments," and which were denoted in Article IV of "the old Constitution." Shellabarger then recited examples of such privileges or immunities identified in Justice Washington's opinion, stressing the following passage: "protection by the Government; the enjoyment of life and liberty, with the right to acquire and possess property of every kind, and to pursue and obtain happiness and safety, subject nevertheless to such restraints as the Government may justly prescribe for the general good of the whole."[47] *Corfield* still lived!

Representative Austin Blair stated that the act "has for its object the securing to the people of the several States the rights, privileges, and immunities which pertain to them as citizens of the United States under its Constitution and laws." These rights he described as "recited in" but not "created by" Section 1 of the Fourteenth Amendment. This was because they were "fundamental in all just, free government."[48]

On March 30, Representative Horace Maynard had declared that the "rights, privileges, and immunities" to be protected by the Ku Klux Klan Act included "all privileges and immunities of citizens of the several states" *and* "also the right of voting secured by the fifteenth amendment" and "every personal right enumerated in the Constitution." He did not specifically refer to the first eight amendments.[49]

The next day, on March 31, 1871, Bingham defended the constitutionality of the Klan Act and provided a retrospective account of his goals in framing the Fourteenth Amendment and his understanding of the Privileges or Immunities Clause. For the first time, Bingham now espoused a comity-only understanding of the Privileges and Immunities Clause of Article IV. He stated that the Privileges or Immunities Clause was designed, not to enforce Article IV, Section 2, but to secure the rights that were "chiefly defined" in the first eight amendments, which Chief Justice Marshall had in *Barron v. Baltimore*—correctly, in Bingham's view—held not to be limitations on the states.

Bingham's account flatly contradicted not only Shellabarger's interpretation of the clause but the interpretation that Bingham himself signed off on in response to Victoria Woodhull's petition. Compare these two statements:

Woodhull Report, January 1871:

The clause of the fourteenth amendment, "No State shall make or enforce any law which shall abridge the privileges or immunities of citizens of the United States," does not, in the opinion of the committee, refer to privileges or immunities of citizens of the United States *other than those* privileges embraced in the original text of the Constitution, article 4, section 2 . . . [50]

Bingham, March 1871:

Is it not clear that other and different privileges than those to which a citizen of a State was entitled are secured by the provision of the fourteenth article, that no State shall abridge the privileges and immunities of citizens of the United States, which are defined in the eight articles of amendment . . . ? [51]

To appreciate the magnitude of this shift, it helps to rearrange and add ellipses to Bingham's March statement: the "privileges" that "are secured by the provision . . . that no State shall abridge the privileges and immunities of citizens of the United States . . . are defined in the eight articles of amendment." This is a far cry from the Woodhull Report's citation in January of "those privileges embraced in the original text of the Constitution, article 4, section 2," which Justice Washington had authoritatively interpreted in *Corfield*.

Bingham's speech was unusual in another respect. No Republican had previously repudiated *Corfield* as a guide to the rights protected by the Privileges or Immunities Clause. No Republican had previously claimed that only the rights secured by the first eight amendments constituted the privileges and immunities of US citizens. Yet, whereas Bingham had, in January, joined a report that cited *Corfield* favorably, in March he criticized Shellabarger for relying on the case.

We should take care not to over-read a single speech—even a single speech by John Bingham, who deserves our respect and appreciation for his efforts to give us the Fourteenth Amendment. This speech was delivered three years after ratification. It contradicted a statement that Bingham submitted as chairman of his committee only three months previously. And Bingham's colleagues did not express similar views. Indeed, their views were the same as those Bingham had previously expressed.

Furthermore, this was not the only reference Bingham made to "the first eight amendments" in this speech. He also said "the privileges and immunities of citizens of the United States, as contradistinguished from citizens of a State, are *chiefly* defined in the first eight amendments to the Constitution of the United States."[52] As we have noted elsewhere,[53] to say that privileges or immunities are "chiefly defined" in the first eight amendments is to imply that they are not *entirely* defined in the first eight amendments.

After emphasizing his goal of securing the rights protected by the first eight amendments against the states, Bingham stated that he had "referred only incidentally to the provisions of the Constitution guarantying [*sic*] rights, privileges, and immunities to the citizens of the United States."[54] Bingham then asked "the House, when they come to deliberate upon this question, not to forget the imperishable words of our great Declaration [of Independence], 'All men are created equal and endowed by their Creator with the rights of life and liberty.'"[55] He also asked "gentlemen not to forget those other words of the Declaration, that 'to protect [*sic*] these rights' (not to confer them) 'governments are instituted among men.'"[56]

After thus affirming natural rights, Bingham valorized the unenumerated "liberty . . . to work in an honest calling and contribute by your toil in some sort to the support of yourself, to the support of your fellow men, and to be secure in the enjoyment of the fruits of your toil."[57] Bingham was not here referring to some comity-only protected natural rights—or rights protected only by the due process of law. That is made clear from Bingham's equation of these rights to "the right 'to know, to argue, and to utter freely according to conscience.'"[58] In sum, this speech by Bingham is a muddle.

Moving on, and as we noted above, other Republicans continued to treat *Corfield* as salient to original meaning. For example, three days after Bingham spoke, Vermont Representative Charles Willard invoked *Corfield* to identify the rights protected by Article IV *and* by the Fourteenth Amendment. He pointed out that *Corfield* had "already been several times quoted in this debate" but contended that it was "frequently used" in error—"as though it was a declaration of certain absolute rights" rather than an entitlement to "an equality of privileges and immunities with the citizens of the State in which he may happen to be."[59]

Although it initially appears as if Willard was adopting a comity-only understanding of both Article IV and the Fourteenth Amendment, Willard went on to state that *Corfield* declared "the right to which a citizen is entitled wherever he may go."[60] Willard was concerned to emphasize that "rights are always held in subordination to the laws" of states. By this we think he meant that states may differ in how they reasonably regulate the exercise of the rights of national citizenship, so long as they regulate the exercise of all citizens' rights impartially.[61] Thus, a citizen of one state "may take and hold and convey property, but this must also be under and in pursuance of the laws of the State in which that property is situate."[62] Nowhere does Willard intimate that states could broadly *deny* "rights to which a citizen is entitled."[63]

On April 13, Republican Representative John Boreman of West Virginia characterized Justice Washington's opinion in *Corfield* as the "most extended and satisfactory" account of the privileges and immunities secured by both Article IV and by the Privileges or Immunities Clause.[64] He stressed the protections afforded by both provisions to sojourning citizens and recounted how, in Southern states, "men have been subjected to the infliction of great wrongs . . . simply because they had emigrated from other states."[65] If he understood either provision to protect citizens against their *own* states, however, he did not expressly say so.

The next day, Senator George Edmunds opined that the Privileges or Immunities Clause did not merely protect the rights of "the citizens of one state going to another" but the rights of all citizens "whether they are citizens of one state or another—absolute and complete."[66] He further argued that the clause did not only constrain legislatures but also "the judicial and executive departments of State governments" insofar as the clause prohibited the "enforce[ment] of any law" that abridged citizens' privileges or immunities and "the enforcement of the law belong[s] to the judiciary and the executive combined."[67]

Earlier, in an exchange with Senator Lyman Trumbull, Edmunds had claimed that the Privileges or Immunities Clause *alone* provided absolute security to the privileges and immunities of citizens, and he interpreted Article IV as protecting only comity rights.[68] But he went on to say "that every person born in the United States" is "first and always . . . a citizen of the nation" who is entitled to enjoy "the right to life, the right to liberty, the right to property, the right to freedom from all interference without due process of law." Such a citizen is secured "against invasion of [their rights] by any State or any person in a State with or without the authority of its laws."[69]

Overall, these discussions shed only dim light on the original meaning of the Privileges or Immunities Clause. The most specific commentary on its meaning—Bingham's March 1871 commentary—bears indicia of unreliability. The disagreement between Bingham and Shellabarger notwithstanding, the brunt of the controversy between Republicans about the Ku Klux Klan Act concerned not what the privileges and immunities of citizenship were, but whether congressional action to protect people against violence by nonstate actors was necessary.

That debate, moreover, centered primarily on the Equal Protection of the Laws Clause rather than the Privileges or Immunities Clause. As Christopher Green has shown—and we will further document in Part III—Republicans agreed that the Equal Protection of the Laws Clause extended to every person a *positive right* of protection from the government, which, being "deni[ed]," could support federal intervention.[70] Republicans disagreed about whether Southern failure to protect citizens from the Klan was pervasive enough to deny the equal protection of the laws.

In the end, thirty-one of thirty-six Republicans present at the framing of the Fourteenth Amendment endorsed the act, and none ultimately voted against it. This was true even of those who expressed misgivings about whether the act was necessary to secure the constitutionality of civil-rights legislation.

Case Law and Legal Commentary

During the five years between the ratification of the Fourteenth Amendment and the Supreme Court's pivotal 1873 decision in the *Slaughter-House Cases*, state and federal courts issued a number of decisions in which the Privileges or Immunities Clause was discussed. And learned commentators weighed in concerning its meaning. In none of the cases decided before *Slaughter-House* did a court distinguish between the rights protected by Article IV and those protected by the Privileges or Immunities Clause. Only two courts made what could be construed as a reference to federally enumerated rights.

One is *Garnes v. McCann*,[71] in which the Ohio Supreme Court rejected a claim that the Privileges or Immunities Clause forbade segregated schools, reasoning that "[t]he language of the clause . . . taken in connection with other provisions of the amendment, and the constitution of which it forms a part, affords strong reasons for believing that it includes only such privileges or immunities as are derived from, or recognized by, the constitution of the United States."[72]

The other is *United States v. Hall*,[73] in which then-Judge (and future Supreme Court Justice) William Woods included those rights "which are in the constitution expressly secured to the people" among those "which may be denominated fundamental; which belong of right to the citizens of all free states and which have at all times been enjoyed by the citizens of the several states which compose this Union from the time of their becoming free, independent, and sovereign."[74] (These are, of course, the now-familiar criteria provided by Bushrod Washington in *Corfield*.)

As we saw in the preface to this book, in deciding *Hall*, Woods had consulted Justice Joseph Bradley, who was also the judge of the circuit. Woods asked Bradley for his advice on the constitutionality of the Enforcement Act. In his letter, Bradley replied:

> Now, the privileges and immunities of citizens of the United States have referred to, are undoubtedly those which may be demonstrated fundamental (See [*Corfield*] 4 Wash. C.C. Rep. 380): and *among these* I suppose we are safe in including those which in the constitution are expressly secured to the people, either as against the action of the federal government, or the state government.
>
> If this is so, then, undoubtedly, Congress has a right, by appropriate legislation, to enforce and protect such fundamental rights, against unfriendly or insufficient state legislation.[75]

In this 1871 letter, we see Bradley relying on *Corfield*. And he does not limit the "fundamental" rights protected by the clause to those that are "expressly secured to the people." (In Part III, we return to Justice Bradley's letter because his initial interpretation of the Equal Protection of the Laws Clause in 1871 comported with ours—before he changed his mind in the *Civil Rights Cases*.)

On the other hand, five courts expressly endorsed the proposition that the Privileges or Immunities Clause protected unenumerated rights. These rights included the unenumerated right to make and enforce contracts, the rights to enjoy life and liberty, the right to acquire and possess property, the right to demand and receive the protection of one's rights from the government, and the right to be exempt from discriminatory taxation. Some, but not all, of these rights were enumerated in the Civil Rights Act of 1866.

Most significant was the circuit court decision in the *Live-Stock Dealers Case*,[76] holding unconstitutional the Louisiana slaughterhouse monopoly that would later be upheld in the *Slaughter-House Cases*. In his opinion, Justice Bradley equated the rights protected by Article IV with those protected by the Privileges or Immunities Clause. He then identified the unenumerated "privilege . . . of every American citizen to adopt and follow . . . lawful industrial pursuit[s]" alongside the enumerated rights to due process of law and equal protection of the laws as privileges.[77] Bradley stated that those privileges, which "cannot be invaded without sapping the very foundations of republican government," were "essential" and therefore protected by the Privileges or Immunities Clause.[78]

Bradley also expressly adopted a fundamental-rights reading of these privileges or immunities. Whereas Article IV had "secured by the original Constitution . . . only such [rights] as each state gave its own citizens," Bradley held that the Fourteenth Amendment "demands that privileges and immunities of all citizens shall be absolutely unabridged, unimpaired."[79] Bradley's opinion was cited favorably by Senator Frederick Frelinghuysen when he called for federal legislation to protect the "free speech, free thought, and free action" of formerly enslaved people and Northerners who made their way South in search of employment and land.[80]

Pre-*Slaughter-House* commentators on the Privileges or Immunities Clause included Thomas Cooley, Timothy Farrar, John Norton Pomeroy, and George Paschal. In the second edition of his *Constitutional Limitations*, published in 1871, Cooley took a narrow view of Section 1. Although it "very properly put[] an end to any question of the title of the freedman and others of their race to the rights of citizenship," he doubted whether it "surround[ed] the citizen with any protections additional to those before possessed under the State constitutions."[81]

Some of Cooley's language suggests that he viewed the Privileges or Immunities Clause as securing only comity rights. The clause "secures in each State to the citizens of all other states" the right to earn a living, acquire property, and to be exempt from discriminatory taxation, among other *Corfield* rights.[82] At the same time, Cooley affirmed that the Fourteenth Amendment was adopted to ensure that "the same securities which one citizen may demand, all others are now entitled to"—a formulation that could capture instate discrimination as well as discrimination against out-of-staters.[83]

Pomeroy and Paschal both interpreted Section 1 as overturning *Barron v. Baltimore* and applying at least the personal rights enumerated in the first eight amendments to the states.[84] Farrar claimed that the Privileges *or* Immunities Clause and the Privileges *and* Immunities Clause protected the same rights, including the unenumerated rights specified in the Civil Rights Act of 1866.[85] Article IV rights, explained Farrar, "whether originally natural, personal, or common-law rights, or civil and political rights" were now "legal rights secured by the Constitution to every citizen of the United States," citing "Am. 14, § 1."[86]

Paschal appears to have taken an enumerated-rights-only view of the Privileges or Immunities Clause and a comity-only view of Article IV's Privileges and Immunities Clause. He interpreted Section 1 of the Fourteenth Amendment as "impose[ing] upon the States" those "general principles, which had been construed to apply only to the national government." He then identified those principles as embodied in the "guarant[ees]" of both the Privileges and Immunities Clause and "the thirteen amendments."[87]

The lack of consensus among these commentators does not make this easy for us. But we must reach a judgment based on the weight of the evidence. We think that this evidence, which we have strived fairly to present here, when combined with the previous pre- and post-ratification evidence we have surveyed, strongly favors reading the clause to protect from state abridgment of a set of fundamental rights that are possessed by citizens of the United States.

The Supreme Court Redacts the Clause

The Slaughter-House Cases

The Supreme Court first considered the meaning of the Privileges or Immunities Clause in the *Slaughter-House Cases. Slaughter-House* arose from a challenge to a provision of a Louisiana statute that granted a monopoly on slaughtering animals in New Orleans to a single corporation—the Crescent City Livestock Company—which charged fixed fees for slaughtering on the corporation's premises.[88] The plaintiffs argued that there existed a common-law right to labor in a legal trade without arbitrary interference, and that this common-law right was protected by the Thirteenth and Fourteenth Amendments—including the Privileges or Immunities Clause.[89]

Although the Court as a body had not evaluated the monopoly, one justice—Justice Joseph Bradley—had done so while riding circuit. Along with District Judge William Woods, Bradley had concluded that the right to free labor was indeed protected by the Privileges or Immunities Clause, and that Crescent City's state-sanctioned monopoly violated that right.[90] In contrast, the Supreme Court upheld the monopoly grant by a vote of five to four, with Justice Bradley in the minority.

In an opinion that has traditionally been regarded as taking an extremely narrow view of the Privileges or Immunities Clause,[91] Justice Samuel Miller claimed that the Reconstruction Amendments had "one pervading purpose." That purpose was to establish the "freedom of the slave race, the security and firm establishment of that freedom, and the protection of the newly-made freeman and citizens from the oppression of those who had formerly exercised dominion over him."[92] In this regard, despite his passing caveat that the amendments were not only limited to the protection of former slaves, Justice Miller employed a purposivist methodology to limit what the minority claimed to be the original meaning of the text. From the attention that he devoted to the Reconstruction Amendments' "pervading purpose," it is apparent that Justice Miller viewed the Privileges or Immunities Clause through the lens of emancipation.

To this narrowing frame, Justice Miller added concerns about the implications for federalism of taking a broader view of the amendments' coverage for federalism. Thus, Miller contended that interpreting the Privileges or Immunities Clause to transform the comity rights listed in *Corfield* into fundamentally protected national rights would "radically chang[e] the whole theory of the relations of the State and Federal governments to each other and of both of these governments to the people."[93] He contended that such an interpretation ought to be avoided "in the absence of language which expresses such a purpose too clearly to admit of doubt."[94]

Given his stress on the "one pervading purpose of the Amendment" as "freedom of the slave race, the security and firm establishment of that freedom, and the protection of the newly-made freeman and citizens from the oppression of those who had formerly exercised dominion over him," the list of privileges or immunities provided by Justice Miller was, well, bizarre. These included:

- the rights to come to the seat of government to assert any claim he may have upon that government, to transact any business he may have with it, to seek its protection, to share its offices, to engage in administering its functions;
- the right of free access to its seaports, through which operations of foreign commerce are conducted, to the sub-treasuries, land offices, and courts of justice in the several States;
- the rights to demand the care and protection of the Federal government over his life, liberty, and property when on the high seas or within the jurisdiction of a foreign government;

- the right to peaceably assemble and petition for redress of grievances, the privilege of the writ of habeas corpus, are rights of the citizen guaranteed by the Federal Constitution;
- the right to use the navigable waters of the United States, however they may penetrate the territory of the several States, all rights secured to our citizens by treaties with foreign nations;
- the right of a citizen of the United States to become a citizen of any State of the Union by a bona fide residence therein, with the same rights as other citizens of that State.
- Finally, "to these may be added the rights secured by the thirteenth and fifteenth articles of amendment, and by the other clause of the fourteenth, next to be considered."[95]

These rights of citizens *of the United States,* wrote Miller, were absolutely protected. *Corfield* rights, by contrast, were rights of citizens *of a state* and protected only against parochial discrimination.[96]

The handful of rights specified by Justice Miller, for the most part, appeared to have little to do with what he insisted was the "one pervading purpose" of protecting the freedom of enslaved people from states. For example, the rights to demand the care and protection of the federal government over one's life, liberty, and property *when on the high seas or within the jurisdiction of a foreign government* were hardly being violated by the state governments to which the clause applied.

Most scholars who have devoted attention to the *Slaughter-House Cases* read Justice Miller as implicitly denying that the personal rights enumerated in the first eight amendments were protected by the Privileges or Immunities Clause.[97] This reading draws support, not only from Miller's mention of only one enumerated personal right—the right to assemble and petition for redress of grievances—but from Miller's failure to respond to Justice Bradley's dissent.

In that dissent, Justice Bradley unequivocally affirmed that rights "specified in the original Constitution, or in the early amendments of it" were "among the privileges and immunities" of US citizens.[98] If Miller was in partial agreement with Bradley concerning enumerated rights and disagreed only about unenumerated rights—such as the right to free labor—it is surprising that he did not use this partial agreement to rebut Bradley's charge that his interpretation was unduly narrow.

In his dissent, Bradley reiterated the views that he had expressed while riding circuit: that the right to "choose a lawful calling" was among the privileges of *national* citizenship, being "an essential part of that liberty which it is the object of government to protect"; that "[t]he keeping of a slaughter-house is part of, and incidental to, the trade of a butcher"; and that "[t]o compel a butcher . . . to slaughter their cattle in another person's slaughter-house and pay a toll therefore" is "onerous, unreasonable, arbitrary, and unjust."[99]

Bradley emphasized that he had no objection to other regulatory provisions of the Louisiana act which contained the monopoly grant. For example, he found provisions that "require[d] all slaughter-houses to be located below the city, and to be subject to the inspection"[100] to be an unproblematic exercise of the police power. In contrast, the monopoly grant had "none of the qualities of a police regulation" and was evidently "made in the interest of a few scheming individuals."[101]

For Bradley, the "mischief to be remedied" by Section 1—that is, its spirit—was not, as Justice Miller claimed, "merely slavery and its incidents and consequences."[102] It was "that spirit of insubordination and disloyalty to the National government which had troubled the country for so many years and some of the States, and that intolerance of free speech and free discussion which often rendered life and property insecure, and led to much unequal legislation."[103] Readers will recall that this was a major theme of antislavery advocates in general and constitutional abolitionists in particular.

The goal of ensuring that "American citizenship should be a sure guaranty of safety" was given expression in language that was "general, embracing all citizens."[104] This language secured all rights derived from three sources: (1) what Blackstone identified as the rights of Englishmen; (2) what Justice Washington identified as the privileges and immunities protected by Article IV; and (3) the rights enumerated in the federal Constitution. Bradley regarded "equality under the law" as "one of the privileges and immunities of every citizen" and laid stress on the inequality of the Louisiana monopoly. But he left no doubt that he understood the Privileges or Immunities Clause to be a fundamental-rights provision—the right to equality under the law was but one of those fundamental rights.[105]

Also dissenting was Justice Stephen Field, whose defense of the right to free labor would eventually be vindicated in the Court's Due Process of Law Clause jurisprudence, in which he was a moving force.[106] Like Bradley, Field stressed that he had no objection to any feature of the Louisiana statute at issue beyond the grant of monopoly privileges.[107] He further acknowledged that "the police power of the State . . . undoubtedly extends to all regulations affecting the health, good order, morals, peace, and safety of society." Such regulations "cannot be successfully assailed in a judicial tribunal" if they are "not in conflict with any constitutional prohibitions *or fundamental principles.*"[108] But, he went on, "under the pretence of prescribing a police regulation[,] the State cannot be permitted to encroach on any of the just rights of the citizen."[109] (In Part II, we will return to the role that "pretence" or pretext plays in the due process *of law.*)

Field argued that the Fourteenth Amendment "was adopted to obviate objections which had been raised and pressed with great force to the validity of the Civil Rights Act." It did so by "remov[ing] . . . from the region of discussion and doubt" that "[t]he fundamental rights, privileges and immunities which belong to [a person] as a free man and free citizen, now belong to him as a citizen of the United States, and are not dependent upon his citizenship of any State."[110] The amendment did not "confer any new privileges or immunities upon citizens." Rather, it "assume[d] that there are such privileges and immunities which belong of right to citizens as such, and ordain[ed] that they shall not be abridged by State legislation."[111]

Field noted that Senator Trumbull in introducing the 1866 Act "cit[ed] the definition of civil liberty given by Blackstone"; that the Thirty-Ninth Congress had by enumerating certain rights in the 1866 act "stated some of the rights which, in its judgment" were among the privileges and immunities of citizenship; and that "repeated reference was made" to *Corfield,* which was taken to set forth "the very rights belonging to a citizen of the United States."[112] In light of the common law's hostility to monopolies and the United States' reception of the common law, Field considered it obvious that the right to pursue a lawful employment was among these rights.[113]

Whatever one may conclude about a "right to pursue a lawful employment," and whether a slaughterhouse monopoly abridged it, the evidence presented in the previous chapters supports the dissenters' historiography over that of Justice Miller.

Bradwell v. Illinois

The day after holding in *Slaughter-House* that the right to pursue a lawful occupation was not a right of national citizenship, the Court rejected a challenge to an Illinois rule denying Myra Bradwell the right to practice law on the ground of her sex. Justice Miller again wrote for the Court and made plain that the outcome was determined by the Court's reasoning in *Slaughter-House*. As Miller put it:

> The opinion just delivered in the *Slaughter-House Cases* renders elaborate argument in the present case unnecessary, for, unless we are radically mistaken in the principles on which those cases are decided, the right to control and regulate the granting of license to practice law in the courts of a state is one of those powers which are not transferred for its protection to the federal government, and its exercise is in no manner governed or controlled by citizenship of the United States in the party seeking such license.[114]

Of course, the statute in *Slaughter-House* did not involve "a license to practice law." For that case to control this one, Miller must have read the right denied in *Slaughter-House* at a higher level of generality than a right to butcher meat. He must have viewed it as a right (in Justice Bradley's words) to "choose a lawful calling." Because Miller had concluded in *Slaughter-House* that no citizen enjoyed such a federally protected right, he did not need to consider whether the Illinois rule was tailored to a legitimate end of government.

Unlike Miller, however, Justice Bradley did not deny that American citizens enjoy a federally protected right to pursue lawful occupations. Instead, he argued that the Illinois rule was a reasonable regulation of that right or—more specifically—that the sex-based distinction adopted by Illinois was not arbitrary. Bradley's reasoning in *Slaughter-House* required him to explain why not. Because Miller's reasoning in *Slaughter-House* allowed him to dismiss Bradwell's claim without addressing this issue, he has escaped the opprobrium that has justly been heaped on Bradley's now-infamous concurrence.

In that concurrence, Bradley stated that "the civil law, as well as nature herself, has always recognized a wide difference in the respective spheres and destinies of man and woman." Further, the "[t]he harmony, not to say identity, of interests and views which belong, or should belong, to the family institution is repugnant to the idea of a woman adopting a distinct and independent career from that of her husband."[115] Bradley made plain his belief that women *ought* to be subordinate to their husbands and excluded from "many of the occupations of civil life" because of self-evident and fixed empirical truths about female fragility—"[t]he natural and proper timidity and delicacy which belongs to the female sex."[116]

In view of his perception of the relevant facts, Bradley did not deny that the right to pursue a lawful occupation existed but concluded instead that excluding women from the legal profession was a reasonable means of regulating it. The law was not arbitrary because it was fully within the "prerogative of the legislator to prescribe regulations founded on nature, reason, and experience for the due admission of qualified persons to professions and callings demanding special skill and confidence." Most women, lacking "that decision and firmness which are presumed to predominate in the sterner sex[,]" did not meet those demands.[117]

In this assessment, Bradley was joined by Justices Field and Noah Swayne. Because both had also dissented in *Slaughter-House*, they presumably agreed with Bradley that the Illinois law implicated a privilege of national citizenship and so had to be shown to be a nonarbitrary exercise of the state's police power.

And yet it is sometimes forgotten that there was a dissenter: Chief Justice Salmon P. Chase—the former antislavery lawyer and author of the constitutional platforms of the Liberty, Free Soil, and Republican Parties. As we saw in Chapter 4, it was Chase who, as treasury secretary, prevailed upon Attorney General Bates to write his momentous opinion affirming the national citizenship of free Blacks. In *Slaughter-House*, Chase joined Justice Field's dissenting opinion.

In *Bradwell*, Chase was the sole dissenter. Wracked by a series of strokes, he was too weak to pen his own dissent. He was to die three weeks after the decisions were announced. No doubt, the lack of a written dissent has led to Chase's stance for women being largely forgotten. Yet, a remarkable notation appears in the Supreme Court reports: "THE CHIEF JUSTICE dissented from the judgment of the Court and from *all* the opinions."[118] In other words, Chase dissented not only from Justice Miller's majority opinion but also from Justice Bradley's opinion for Justices Field and Swayne. We know of no other dissent from a concurring opinion.

Chase's one sentence dissent is nonetheless significant for what it implies about his interpretation of the original meaning of the Privileges or Immunities Clause. The chief justice clearly believed not only that an unenumerated right to pursue a lawful occupation was a privilege or immunity of citizens of the United States—a view he shared with Bradley, Field, and Swayne. He also believed that this right had been violated in both the *Slaughter-House Cases* and *Bradwell*.

Unlike the majority, the chief justice concluded that, in addition to those who had recently been freed from bondage, the clause also protected both white male butchers and white female attorneys. All enjoyed the same rights of national citizenship, which entitled them to federal judicial relief from a state's arbitrary abridgement of their unenumerated fundamental rights. And, unlike Bradley, Field, and Swayne, Chase must have concluded that the Illinois law was arbitrary and that Bradley's effort to justify it as reasonable was unpersuasive.

Of course, the fact that Chase thought that the meaning of the Privileges or Immunities Clause barred both forms of legislation does not automatically make it so. After all, he alone reached that conclusion in both cases. But the other eight justices were also split among themselves. What Chase's dissent in both cases demonstrates is that such a reading and application of the Privileges or Immunities Clause to protect the rights of women was available when both cases were decided and that at least one person thought it was the most reasonable reading and application. That one person just happened to be the aged chief justice of the United States, who had been so instrumental in developing the abolitionist constitutionalism that informed the Fourteenth Amendment.

Chief Justice Chase's votes in these two cases bring to mind Justice John Marshall Harlan's solo dissents in the *Civil Rights Cases* and in *Plessy v. Ferguson*. Most now think Harlan was right about the meaning of the Fourteenth Amendment, notwithstanding that eight then thought otherwise. We submit that the lone stance of the chief justice in the *Slaughter-House Cases* and *Bradwell v. Illinois* should be remembered alongside those of Harlan's as more faithful to original meaning than that of his eight colleagues.

United States v. Cruikshank

If Judge Miller's reasoning in *Slaughter-House* left open the door for including among the privileges and immunities of citizenship the rights enumerated in the first eight amendments, the Court's decision in *United States v. Cruikshank*[119] slammed that door shut. *Cruikshank* involved the prosecution under the Force Bill of 1870 of the perpetrators of the single bloodiest act in the history of Reconstruction—the Colfax Massacre.[120]

The massacre marked the end of a conflict that arose after a hotly disputed governor's election in 1872. Republican candidate William Pitt Kellogg and Conservative candidate John McEnery both claimed victory.[121] Each candidate held inaugural ceremonies and assumed the title of Louisiana governor.[122]

Each had commissioned members of his party to serve in Grant Parish as judge and sheriff.[123]

In late March, Grant Parish's Republican officeholders seized the courthouse.[124] Democrat planter and reputed Klan leader James Hadnot responded by mustering men with the intention of attacking Colfax, taking possession of the courthouse, and hanging prominent Republicans.[125] After finding Colfax well defended, Hadnot was forced to abandon his plans, but tensions remained high.[126]

Efforts to defuse the crisis collapsed after the murder of a Black man, Jesse McKinney, outside of his home in the town of Colfax by whites.[127] On April 13, a paramilitary force led by former Confederate captain and deputy sheriff Columbus Nash commenced an assault to take the town. Black militiamen built trenches around and gathered inside of the Grant Parish courthouse. They were surrounded by as many as three hundred whites—nearly four times the number of armed Blacks present in Colfax.[128]

Militia leader Levin Allen refused to surrender, declaring that he would not share Jesse McKinney's fate. After allowing Allen thirty minutes to remove any women and children from the courthouse, Nash then attacked. By the time the smoke cleared, three whites and between sixty-four and four hundred Black people lay dead. At least thirty-seven Black prisoners were mercilessly shot several long hours after the fighting had ceased.[129]

On April 21, federal troops arrived. Armed with orders from the United States marshal in New Orleans, they arrested suspected participants in the massacre. Although ninety-seven men were indicted, only nine were eventually tried under the 1871 Enforcement Act. The defendants were tried twice.[130]

The first trial ended in a mistrial for eight defendants and the acquittal of one. The second trial acquitted five defendants but found the other five guilty of conspiracy against the victims' rights to peaceably assemble to petition the government and to bear arms for lawful purposes. The trial also found that the defendants deprived the victims of their lives and liberty without due process of law and denied them the equal protection of the laws. The convictions on these charges were reviewed—and reversed—by the Supreme Court in *Cruikshank*.[131]

Chief Justice Morrison Waite's reasoning in *Cruikshank* is difficult to follow. He distinguished between (1) rights that existed "long before the adoption of the Constitution of the United States," (2) rights that are "attributes of citizenship under a free government," and (3) rights that are either created by the federal Constitution or dependent on the federal government for their existence.[132] The first set of rights, he claimed, falls within the jurisdiction of the states. The second, he claimed, falls "within the scope of the sovereignty of the United States."[133] He identified only the third set of rights as privileges or immunities of *United States* citizenship.

Thus, Waite concluded that the right to peaceably assemble "for lawful purposes"[134]—a right that preceded the Constitution—was *not* a privilege or immunity of national citizenship. In contrast, the right to peaceably assemble "for the purpose of petitioning Congress"[135] *was* protected by the Fourteenth Amendment. He then determined that the right to bear arms was secured against interference *by Congress*, but not against interference by the states, nor against interference by private citizens.[136]

It is hard to make sense of Waite's reasoning without assuming the correctness of *Slaughter-House*'s constitutional conclusions. Waite in *Cruikshank*, like Miller in *Slaughter-House*, sharply distinguished between the rights of state citizenship and the rights of national citizenship.[137] Waite, like Miller, treated the distribution of power between the federal government and the states as being essentially unmodified by the Reconstruction Amendments. Waite cited *Barron v. Baltimore* for the proposition that the rights enumerated in the first eight amendments—"the Bill of Rights" again goes unmentioned—constrained only the federal government without considering the possibility that the Reconstruction Amendments might have changed the antebellum status quo.[138] The Court's failure even to engage the framing and ratification history of the Fourteenth Amendment suggests that this question was believed to have been resolved by *Slaughter-House* in the negative. In *Cruikshank*, Justice Bradley, who had dissented from *Slaughter-House*'s narrow reading of the Privileges or Immunities Clause, now joined the majority.

What did Republicans have to say about these two decisions? Two Republican legislators—Frederick Frelinghuysen and George Hoar—favorably cited Justice Bradley's circuit court opinion holding the Louisiana slaughtering monopoly unconstitutional.[139] They thus aligned themselves with the fundamental-rights theory that Bradley deployed in his circuit court opinion, in his *Slaughter-House* dissent, and in his letter to Judge Woods. To the extent that they did comment on *Slaughter-House*, Republican legislators for the most part either criticized it[140] or argued that it posed no impediment to civil-rights legislation that was unrelated to occupational freedom. After all, theirs was legislation clearly aimed at preventing racial discrimination, which Miller had identified as the primary purpose of the amendment.[141]

Democratic legislators, by contrast, praised Justice Miller's opinion and invoked his distinction between the rights of state and national citizenship to criticize civil-rights legislation on the ground that it protected rights of state citizenship that were beyond Congress's reach.[142]

The response to *Cruikshank* was still more sharply divided. Democrats trumpeted *Cruikshank* and deployed it against civil-rights legislation.[143] Republicans scarcely acknowledged *Cruikshank* and, when they did, either struggled to work their way around it or—as did Senator Oliver Morton— "repudiate[d] it utterly."[144]

The key framers of the Fourteenth Amendment had left Congress by the time that *Slaughter-House* and *Cruikshank* were decided.[145] Thaddeus Stevens and Jacob Howard were deceased, and John Bingham—having been denied renomination for Congress—was about to serve as ambassador to Japan.[146] But the fact that Frederick Frelinghuysen,[147] Morton,[148] George Boutwell,[149] George Edmunds,[150] and Timothy Howe[151]—all of whom were present at the framing—criticized the Court's decisions suggests that it had departed from the amendment's original meaning.

By contrast, *Bradwell* does not appear to have divided Republicans and Democrats. Myra Bradwell was represented by Republican Senator Matthew Carpenter, who had successfully defended the monopoly provision of the Louisiana statute in the *Slaughter-House Cases*. After *Bradwell* came down, however, neither Carpenter nor any other Republican in Congress criticized Justice Miller for denying women the privileges and immunities of citizenship. Because the outcome in *Bradwell* was widely understood to be compelled by the Court's holding in *Slaughter-House* and because Republicans did criticize the latter, however, this silence is not probative of original meaning. Why not?

It is reasonable to speculate that at least some of the Republicans who remained silent shared Justice Bradley's opinion that the sex-based distinction made by Illinois was not an arbitrary one. This speculation is supported by the drafting of the Civil Rights Act of 1866, which we surveyed in Chapter 5. As we reported, the qualifier, "as [are] enjoyed by white citizens," was likely added to support existing sex-based distinctions in state law. In other words, the outcome of *Bradwell* might well have been consistent with the original expected application of the framers of the Privileges or Immunities Clause. So, most did not object. But original expected application is not the same as the original public meaning, which Chief Justice Chase may have more faithfully followed.

The Civil Rights Act of 1875

In 1870, Senator Charles Sumner proposed to amend legislation that allowed former Confederates to serve in office.[152] As explained by Sumner, his amendment would "secure equal rights in railroads, steamboats, public conveyances, hotels, licensed theaters, houses of public entertainment, common schools, and institutions of learning authorized by law, church institutions, and cemetery associations incorporated by national or State authority; also on juries in courts, national and State."[153] Over the course of four years, this amendment would evolve into a standalone bill that did not address discrimination in public schooling or churches but did guarantee equal access to common carriers, inns, theaters, and places of public amusement and forbade racial discrimination in jury selection.[154]

The Civil Rights Act of 1875 was enacted by a lame-duck Congress after Sumner's death as a tribute to his lifelong commitment to racial equality.[155] It was never actively enforced, and all of its provisions save the jury provision were held unconstitutional by the Supreme Court in the *Civil Rights Cases*.[156] Still, examining the controversy over its constitutional basis sheds a great deal of light on Republicans' understanding of the privileges of US citizenship and Congress's power to enforce those privileges.

Republican supporters of what would become the Civil Rights Act of 1875 contended that the act was not designed to create new rights. Instead, it was designed to ensure the equal enforcement of long-established civil rights that were deeply rooted in the nation's history and traditions—specifically, in the common law. They argued that common carriers and places of public accommodation had "franchises" from the government and thus were obliged to serve all persons equally in return for enjoying a public monopoly or quasi-monopoly.[157]

Republicans accused Southern states of passing laws that prevented Blacks from taking trains or staying at inns, as well as failing to enforce common-law rules in actions for damages brought for refusal of service.[158] Democrats and some more conservative Republicans responded by either denying that Southern legislators or judges discriminated in these ways or by denying that the covered businesses were monopolistic or quasi-monopolistic.[159]

Republicans repeatedly tried to include a protection from discrimination with respect to public schools, which Sumner contended were "kindred to inns and public conveyances" in respect of the equal-access duties that attached to them.[160] The constitutional debate generated by this proposal was sufficiently detailed and consistent with pre-ratification constitutional discourse to be worthy of consideration in connection with the Fourteenth Amendment's original public meaning, even if we give it less weight because of its distance from ratification.

Sumner most thoroughly elaborated the case for including schools in the bill. He argued that public schools were created through public taxation and ought to prepare children to become republican citizens.[161] Taxing Blacks to support a segregated school system, he contended, transformed an institution that derived its justification from its service to the general welfare into a means of perpetuating caste.[162]

Sumner did not defend the inclusion of schools alongside inns and common carriers in the act on the ground that there existed a common-law heritage of nondiscriminatory access to public schools. Rather, he moved up a level of generality to claim that there existed a common-law heritage of nondiscriminatory access to taxpayer-funded institutions that were organized by law and oriented to the benefit of the community. Because public schools were taxpayer-funded, organized by law, and oriented to the benefit of the community, they satisfied these criteria.[163]

It is significant that the schools provision was repeatedly supported by majorities in both House and Senate. Ultimately, it was deleted from the act because it failed to get the supermajorities required in both the House and Senate under rules akin to what is known as the filibuster today.[164] Democrats, of course, were unanimously opposed. Some Republicans expressed fears that Southern states would respond to a mandate of integration by abolishing public schools altogether.[165] Of course, they may also have been motivated by fears of a backlash from their own electorates.

Neither of the latter considerations was of a constitutional nature. Therefore, any opposition to the schools provision based on them sheds no light on the public meaning of the Fourteenth Amendment. In the Senate, Lyman Trumbull did raise constitutional objections—but his was a lonely voice among Republicans who had supported the Fourteenth Amendment

When it came to the rest of the bill, not all Republicans supported either Sumner's initial proposal or the final 1875 act. Trumbull, along with Senators Orris Ferry and Lot Morrill, conceded the principle that rights of nondiscriminatory access to common carriers and public accommodations were civil rights. But they either contended that federal intervention was unnecessary to protect them, or questioned whether inns, theaters, and places of public amusement were really places of public accommodation.[166]

In one form or another, the Civil Rights Act of 1875 was under consideration in Congress for five years. During its pendency, *Slaughter-House* was decided in 1873. The length of deliberations over the act allowed some to change their views on either the wisdom or constitutionality of the scope of its coverage.

In 1872, Matthew Carpenter supported a version of the act that was slightly narrower than Sumner's initial proposal in that it did not prohibit discrimination by churches. Carpenter articulated a theory of the privileges of US citizenship that was broad enough to cover "the privilege of practicing law . . . the right of preaching the gospel . . . [and] the right of giving instruction in the public schools."[167]

Carpenter opined that the "best definition" of the privileges and immunities of US citizenship was provided by Justice Field in his opinion for the Court in *Cummings v. Missouri*.[168] Specifically, Justice Field stated in *Cummings* that "[t]he theory upon which our political institutions rest is, that all men have certain unalienable rights; that among these are life, liberty, and the pursuit of happiness; and that in the pursuit of happiness all avocations, all honors, all positions, are alike open to every one, and that in the protection of these rights all are equal before the law."[169]

Carpenter's successful defense in the Supreme Court of the Louisiana slaughtering monopoly in *Slaughter-House*, however, was based on a much narrower conception of the clause; and his unsuccessful defense of Myra Bradwell failed to broaden it. In the wake of this litigation, which ended in 1873, Carpenter now adopted that narrower view.[170] Eventually, he voted against the 1875 act, even though it was narrower than the bill he had supported in 1872. While he agreed that nondiscriminatory access to public schools was a civil right, he insisted that the right to sit on a jury was a political right, not a civil right, and he opposed the act on that ground.[171]

Other Republicans after *Slaughter-House* did not budge from their initial positions. Some argued that the decision did not affect the constitutionality of the act. Some argued that the case was wrongly decided. Others turned instead to the Equal Protection of the Laws Clause as a source of constitutional authority. Senator Frelinghuysen took the first approach, arguing that freedom from discrimination remained a right of national citizenship.[172] Senators Morton and Edmunds took the second.

Responding to Democratic Senator Thurman's claim that *Slaughter-House* rendered the act unconstitutional, Morton and Edmunds maintained that the Privileges or Immunities Clause absolutely secured *Corfield* rights and refused to "admit" that the Court had finally determined "what is the law and Constitution of this land."[173] In the House, Representative Robert Elliot took the third approach, admitting that the Supreme Court had "clearly pointed out th[e] distinction" between state and national citizenship but arguing that "whether his rights are held under the United States or under his particular State, [a person] is equally protected" by the Equal Protection of the Laws Clause.[174]

Significantly, neither before nor after the *Slaughter-House Cases* did any Republican assert an enumerated-rights-only view of privileges or immunities of the sort today advocated by Kurt Lash and others. None denied that the Privileges or Immunities Clause included at least *some* unenumerated rights that were associated with citizenship. Trumbull claimed that the "civil rights" belonging to citizens included the "right to come and go; the right to enforce contracts; the right to convey his property; the right to buy property" and other "common law right[s], regarded as a right appertaining to the individual as a citizen."[175] Morrill conceded that not only the rights specified in the Civil Rights Act of 1866, but rights of access to common carriers were among the privileges and immunities of citizenship. He then drew the line at rights of access to theaters and inns.[176]

Of course, the *Slaughter-House Cases* cast doubt on whether the act would survive a constitutional challenge if it rested on substantive fundamental rights. And, to defend the 1875 act, Republicans *needed* only to assert equality rights. So it is unsurprising that certain legislators—as James Fox has put it—"danced around the question of whether states could simply withdraw . . . state based privileges altogether."[177] Post-*Slaughter-House*, these lawmakers shifted their emphasis to equality rather than continuing to base their constitutional arguments solely on the ground that such rights as education were fundamental national privileges that states could not fail to recognize.[178]

Yet, some Republicans continued to claim that the Privileges or Immunities Clause protected rights that were not constitutionally enumerated and that those rights were protected outside of the context of comity. How was it that these Republicans were able to defend with a straight face the constitutionality of mandating racial equality in jury selection and nondiscriminatory access to public schools in the 1870s?

The right to sit on a jury was once a paradigmatic example of a political right. As we have seen, Republican supporters of the Civil Rights Act of 1866 and the Fourteenth Amendment for the most part disclaimed any intention of securing political rights. Although schooling came up less often during the Thirty-Ninth Congress, James Wilson denied that an early draft of the 1866 act would require that "[white] children shall attend the same schools [as Black children]." He stated that neither the right of all citizens to sit on juries nor the right to attend the same schools "are . . . civil rights or immunities."[179]

The apparent inconsistency between Wilson's 1866 statements and Sumner's 1875 insistence that racially exclusive juries and segregated schools violated the civil rights of Blacks requires some explanation. Did Sumner, together with the Republicans who agreed with his constitutional arguments, use different criteria for identifying civil rights than did those who framed the Fourteenth Amendment? If so, the views that they expressed later about the privileges and immunities of citizenship might reveal very little of epistemic value about the original public meaning of the Privileges or Immunities Clause in 1868.

We have already discussed Wilson's understanding of civil rights—an understanding shaped in significant part by Blackstone's *Commentaries*. Christopher Green has noted that after asserting that schooling rights were not civil rights, Wilson stated that "it is not the object of this bill to establish new rights, but to protect and enforce those which already belong to every citizen."[180] He thereby implied that civil rights were those rights that already belonged to every citizen. We don't know *why* he did not believe that schooling rights "already" belonged to every citizen, however, because he did not explain himself further.

We do know, however, why Sumner believed that the Fourteenth Amendment empowered Congress to prohibit racial discrimination in public education and in other public settings. That's because Sumner articulated those beliefs at great length on a number of occasions. Sumner read the Privileges or Immunities Clause as requiring that all citizens be admitted "without any discrimination to the equal enjoyment of all institutions, privileges, advantages, and conveniences *created or regulated by law*. . . ."[181] Sumner considered admission to such institutions on an equal footing with other citizens to be a right of citizenship.

On this view, neither governmental entities such as legislatures and courts, nor monopolistic or quasi-monopolistic entities that were obliged under the common law to serve all patrons, could discriminate on the basis of race.[182] All citizens enjoyed a fundamental right not to be branded as inferior to other citizens by being arbitrarily denied access to rights that were generally extended to other similarly situated citizens. The seemingly novel right to nondiscriminatory public schooling was in fact a corollary of a deeply rooted, traditional right of access to public institutions.

For this reason, states could not excuse their failure to secure a particular right of access to Black citizens by arguing that that right was not a preexisting natural one. Rather, the constitutional sin was the denial of equal access to a good that the state had, in its discretion, decided to provide to citizens, as citizens. On this theory, fellow Republicans who disagreed with Sumner over whether states were constitutionally obliged to provide public education nevertheless agreed that states that chose to provide for public education could not arbitrarily exclude Black citizens from the schoolhouse.[183]

We can only speculate about how Wilson might have responded to these arguments because we do not have any record of him doing so. Shortly after denying that "civil rights and immunities" covered jury rights and schooling rights, Wilson invoked Kent's *Commentaries* to define the absolute rights of citizens. Yet Sumner also relied on Kent to support a common-law right of access. Sumner then compared public schools to inns, conveyances, and other public institutions to which there was a common-law right of access.

Wilson, for his part, did not respond to this line of argument. Without such an explanation, the bare fact that they disagreed is not enough to justify discounting what Sumner or others who supported Sumner's bill said about the original meaning of the Privileges or Immunities Clause and privileging Wilson's view. Contrast this silence with the pushback John Bingham had received over the Ku Klux Klan Act when his fellow representatives accused him of having changed his interpretative stance.

Lyman Trumbull's persistent opposition to the 1875 act seems more significant than Wilson's lone assertion that the 1866 act did not implicate schooling rights. We have seen that Trumbull and Wilson articulated a common understanding of civil rights in 1866. Afterward, Trumbull not only regarded certain of the rights sought to be secured by Sumner as political or social rights rather than civil rights but was exercised enough about the differences between himself and Sumner to work to delay any consideration of Sumner's bill. Is this evidence that at least some Republicans in the 1870s used the term "civil rights" to refer to very different kinds of rights than did Republicans in the late 1860s?

To answer this, as with Wilson, we must ask why Trumbull believed that education was not a civil right. As he had during the 1866 debates, Trumbull looked to both nature and custom to identify civil rights. At one point he described civil rights as "rights pertaining to the citizen as such,"[184] at another as "common law right[s]," and at another as "general rights that belong to mankind everywhere."[185] When denying that education was a civil right, Trumbull stressed that "schools are regulated all over the land, and must be, for the advancement of education."[186]

In a key move, he emphasized that "[t]here may be no schools at all in the State of Indiana or the District of Columbia" and suggested that there could therefore be "no right appertaining to the individual as a citizen to go to school" in those states.[187] Given that it was uncontroversial that states could decline to provide for *any* public schooling, Trumbull evidently believed it was absurd to think a right that can be generally denied to all is a genuine civil right rather than a political or social right.

Sumner and like-minded Republicans responded to Trumbull's arguments by attempting to demonstrate that any differences between the civil rights secured by the 1866 act—which Trumbull insisted was constitutional—and the rights specified in the emerging bill were insubstantial. They also turned Trumbull's appeals to the common law against him.

Thus, Senator George Edmunds responded to Trumbull's argument that no right to equal participation in schools could "be a civil right in any sense" because "schools do not exist naturally" by pointing out that railroads did not exist naturally, either.[188] Trumbull implicitly granted the premise of the objection by protesting that Edmunds "kn[ew] very well" that the right "to be conveyed over the general lines of travel" was "a common law right, regarded as a right appertaining to the individual as a citizen."[189] Clearly, then, Trumbull did not think that civil rights only secured pre-political, natural rights.

Shortly afterward, John Sherman made reference to Trumbull's authorship of the 1866 Act and argued that there was "not one word in the bill" currently being considered "that is inconsistent with the civil rights bill [of 1866]."[190] Sherman then drew on his understanding of "the common law of England, which is part of the immunity of every citizen of the United States" for rights of access to "steamboats and railroads, and all modes of travel, including hotels," as well as "an equal and fair share in the enjoyment of that which is collected by public taxation"—including public schools.[191]

Republican supporters of Sumner's bill also reframed schooling rights and jury rights in ways that made their status as civil rights much more difficult to deny. For instance, Senator Morton accused those who, like Trumbull, denied that schooling was a civil right of "evad[ing] or dodg[ing]" the point of Sumner's bill. The point of the bill was "not to say that schools should be kept at all" but to say "where there are free schools kept at public expense . . . there should be an equal right to participate in the benefit of those schools."[192]

Under pressure from Matthew Carpenter concerning jury rights—which Carpenter insisted were political rights—John Sherman argued that the right to impartial adjudication was uncontroversially a civil right.[193] That is, he reframed the disputed jury right from the right of a citizen to serve on a jury to the right of an accused citizen to receive a fair trial.

The record of Southern justice during Reconstruction made it particularly evident how racial exclusions could undermine impartial adjudication. As the Supreme Court would later put it in *Strauder v. West Virginia*, holding unconstitutional a Virginia law that excluded Blacks from juries, "it is well known that prejudices often exist against particular classes in the community, which sway the judgment of jurors, and which, therefore, operate in some cases to deny persons of those classes the full enjoyment of that protection which others enjoy."[194] Like Sherman, the Court in *Strauder* did not claim that Blacks had a civil right to sit on juries, but that Black defendants were denied a fair trial from such systematic exclusion.[195]

These exchanges do not suggest that Republican supporters and opponents of Sumner's bill had any conceptual disagreements concerning what a civil right was—that is, what distinguished civil rights from other entities. True, legislators were seeking to secure rights that most Republicans would not have categorized as civil several years earlier. But they contended that, properly understood, these apparently novel rights were necessary corollaries of deeply rooted, traditional civil rights or that, as a contingent matter, they contributed to the enjoyment of such civil rights under particular circumstances. Although Sumner was especially fond of arguing directly from natural-rights principles—as chiefly embodied in the Declaration of Independence—he also drew on constitutional text, common law, and state practice to justify his identification of civil rights.[196] So too did both Republican supporters and opponents of his bill.

Constitutional disagreement over the Civil Rights Act centered on the sources of civil rights and the level of generality at which those rights should be identified. When an opponent of the bill such as Trumbull insisted that the only civil rights were those that protected pre-political natural rights, supporters of the bill reminded him that civil rights also included equal access to post-political goods that governments chose to provide. Their counter went uncontradicted. When opponents of the bill said that schooling had not heretofore been accepted as a civil right, supporters of the bill said equal access to schooling was entailed by a deeply rooted, traditional right of equal access to government-provided goods.

As in the late 1860s, so in the early-to-mid 1870s Republicans understood citizenship to entail civil rights that derived their normative *justification* from their connection to natural rights, but could best be *identified* through deeply rooted, widespread rights in the positive law. Republicans during both periods also understood citizenship to entail civil rights that had been, as a consequence of widespread and entrenched legal practice, extended to citizens regardless of whether they were connected to natural rights.

Those who tried, like Trumbull, to distinguish "novel" access rights on the ground that the underlying institutions were not natural struggled because everyone acknowledged some civil rights with an attenuated-at-best connection to natural rights. The differing conclusions that these Republicans reached concerning Sumner's bill do not diminish the epistemic value of the general consensus about civil rights. Those differing conclusions illustrate, rather, that identifying the referents of any concept with fuzzy edges is a tricky business in general and can generate heated controversy when the stakes are high.

When it came to identifying a civil right, how deeply rooted did a right have to be to qualify as a privilege or immunity of citizenship? Was there an "original method" of identifying civil rights that resolved this uncertainty back then, which we could employ today? Here is one reason to be skeptical.

Opponents of the 1875 act were clearly unaware of any method that was fine-grained enough to make obvious the distinction between the civil rights secured by the 1866 act, of which they approved, and rights sought to be secured through the 1875 act, of which they disapproved. Had they possessed such a method, it is difficult to imagine that they would not have deployed it to explain why the latter rights did not qualify as civil rights.

Instead, Lyman Trumbull, Lot Morrill, Matthew Carpenter, and others made general statements concerning rights inherent in citizenship, common-law rights, and a distinction between civil and political rights. But they did not draw these criteria with sufficient precision to resolve the controversies at hand, which suggests that no such finer-grained criterion or original method was available.

Taking Stock: What Are the Privileges
or Immunities of US Citizens?

Before turning our attention in the next chapter to competing interpretations of the Privileges or Immunities Clause advanced by other scholars, we will summarize the conclusions we think are warranted by the evidence of original meaning we have presented in Chapters 1 through 6. In particular, we ask: what does this evidence tell us about whether the "privileges or immunities of citizens of the United States" embraced rights enumerated in the text of the Constitution, rights that remained unenumerated, and specifically natural rights?

Enumerated Rights?

The evidence that the original public meaning of the Privileges or Immunities Clause protects at least some rights enumerated in the text of the antebellum Constitution is compelling. We have surveyed Jacob Howard's introduction to the Senate; newspaper editorials and speeches by the amendment's supporters prior to ratification; and post-ratification debates. Wherever one looks, one finds a broad consensus that the clause protected rights to freedom of speech, the free exercise of religion, and the right to habeas corpus. Other enumerated rights, such as the right to be free from unreasonable searches and seizures, turned up less frequently but did not inspire controversy.

We have also seen that different speakers either focused on or listed different enumerated rights and did not often articulate the criteria that they used to distinguish rights protected by the clause from other rights. But unless we find controversy between supporters over a particular enumerated right, we are justified in assuming that a right was "in" if it (a) was widely considered in 1868 to be personal; (b) was widely accepted in the states; and (c) had a reasonably tight connection to natural rights or the equal treatment of citizens by public institutions.

We must stress, however, that we have not found persuasive evidence that enumeration per se is either necessary or sufficient to categorize a right as a privilege or immunity of citizenship. When speakers did articulate criteria of what qualified a right as one inhering in citizenship, these did not map neatly onto the increasingly popular academic theory of the clause—the enumerated-rights-only theory.

In sum, the evidence is scant that rights were deemed to be privileges or immunities of citizenship *because* of their enumeration in the text. Rather, the fact that a personal right was enumerated in the text was dispositive *evidence* that the right was generally accepted as fundamental enough to attach to citizenship. The idea that enumerated rights were somehow "incorporated" into the Fourteenth Amendment is a modern post–New Deal notion.

Bingham's frequent claims that his proposed amendment sought to do "no more" than to apply the "bill of rights" to the states don't help us much. As articulated during the framing process, Bingham's conception of the "bill of rights" was broad enough to encompass the Privileges and Immunities Clause of Article IV, which Republicans generally had come to associate with a set of fundamental, unenumerated civil rights. No Republican unambiguously articulated an enumerated-rights-only understanding of the Privileges or Immunities Clause until Bingham's problematic 1871 speech—a speech given mere months after he submitted a report to Congress identifying such privileges or immunties with *Corfield v. Coryell*.

Unenumerated Rights?

We could rest our case for the inclusion of unenumerated rights among the privileges and immunities of citizenship entirely on the widely shared understanding that the Fourteenth Amendment would provide constitutional authority for the Civil Rights Act of 1866. The only way to escape this conclusion is to claim that the act solely barred nondiscrimination.

As we have explained, however, we think the act is best read as fundamental-rights legislation, not as a mere equality guarantee. To supply the requisite authority, Republicans needed a clause that empowered Congress to secure the unenumerated fundamental civil rights specified in the 1866 act absolutely. Everyone who addressed the questions asserted or assumed that this empowering clause was the Privileges or Immunities Clause. This is enough to prove that the privileges or immunities of US citizenship include at least these unenumerated rights.

But there is much more evidence that the clause protected these and other unenumerated civil rights that were deemed fundamental to republican citizenship. We have presented a great deal of pre-ratification evidence that Republicans—and supporters of the Fourteenth Amendment more generally—understood the Privileges or Immunities Clause to secure the fundamental rights they had come to associate with the Privileges and Immunities Clause of Article IV; and that they associated the Privileges and Immunities Clause with the rights listed by Justice Washington in *Corfield v. Coryell*—with the exception of the elective franchise. In contrast, we have found no evidence to support Kurt Lash's distinctive enumerated-rights-only theory of the privileges and immunities of US citizenship.[197]

Turning to post-ratification evidence, Bingham's March 1871 speech is not reliable. And its most salient constitutional claim—that Article IV protected "other and different rights" than did the Privileges or Immunities Clause—was immediately contradicted by a number of his peers. That single speech simply cannot outweigh the mass of contrary evidence that congressional Republicans—and supporters of the Fourteenth Amendment more generally—regarded the "privileges and immunities of citizens of the United States" and "civil rights" as synonymous. This evidence shows that they claimed that the Privileges or Immunities Clause secured rights deemed fundamental—whether enumerated or unenumerated—if these rights were deeply rooted in the nation's history and traditions. And it shows that such rights were deemed to be fundamental if they had been widely accepted in the positive law of the states and had a reasonably tight connection either to natural rights or to the equal treatment of citizens by public institutions.

Other Republicans did not make enumerated-rights-based arguments. Republicans who engaged in the debates over Sumner's emerging civil-rights bill broadly agreed that unenumerated civil rights were among the privileges and immunities of citizenship, even as they disagreed about whether particular rights qualified as privileges and immunities of citizenship under the prevailing criteria. And this was true whether those Republicans were present at the framing of the Fourteenth Amendment or not.

Natural Rights?

The opening case for including natural rights among the privileges or immunities of US citizens is *Corfield*. There, Justice Washington included the following among the core of privileges and immunities:

> Protection by the government; *the enjoyment of life and liberty, with the right to acquire and possess property of every kind, and to pursue happiness and safety;* subject nevertheless to such restraints as the government may justly prescribe for the general good of the whole.[198]

As we noted in Chapter 2, Justice Washington was quoting here the canonical statement of natural rights at the Founding: George Mason's draft for the Virginia Declaration of Rights, which began:

> THAT all men are born equally free and independent, and have certain *inherent natural rights,* of which they cannot, by any compact, deprive or divest their posterity; among which are, *the enjoyment of life and liberty, with the means of acquiring and possessing property, and pursuing and obtaining happiness and safety.*[199]

Countless speakers quoted all of *Corfield.* None whom we have found excepted these rights from the others identified by Justice Washington. We find it hard to imagine that anyone would have denied that citizens of the United States were entitled to enjoy the protection of these rights. So, if *Corfield* rights are in, so too it would seem are natural rights.

But not so fast. Justice Washington did not say that natural rights per se are privileges and immunities of citizenship. He said that *these* natural rights were privileges and immunities: "the enjoyment of life and liberty, with the means of acquiring and possessing property, and pursuing and obtaining happiness and safety." In other words, he did not say that citizens have a privilege or immunity to the protection of any or all of the rights they would enjoy in a state of nature. He said, they have a right to these rights in particular. Why these?

Consistent with our lengthy discussion of Blackstone, our answer would be that these natural rights are protected because (1) they are inalienable— that is, they cannot justly be demanded by a general government as a condition of entering into civil society; and (2) they are civil rights that the civil society protects in exchange for the allegiance it demands of citizens. This bifurcation reminds us of James Madison's justifications for amending the Constitution by including certain rights in its text.

The first of Madison's proposals was to add the language later found in *Corfield* to the Preamble of the Constitution: "That Government is instituted and ought to be exercised for the benefit of the people; which consists in *the enjoyment of life and liberty, with the right of acquiring and using property, and generally of pursuing and obtaining happiness and safety.*" Referring to this language, and in contrast with his many other proposals, Madison said that "[t]he first of these amendments relates to what may be called a bill of rights."[200] Moments later, however, Madison explained his proposed right to a jury trial this way: "Trial by jury cannot be considered as a natural right, but a right resulting from a social compact which regulates the action of the community, but is as essential to secure the liberty of the people as any one of the pre-existent rights of nature."[201]

We think that is a fitting description of a civil right that is a privilege or immunity of citizenship: a right the protection of which is "essential to secure the liberty of the people." Such rights include both "pre-existent rights of nature"—such as the rights of property and contract—and other positive rights or privileges by which a person's liberty is secured—such as the right to trial by jury or the writ of habeas corpus.

But identifying the *type* of rights that are privileges or immunities is not the same as identifying the particular rights themselves. After all, people could claim lots of rights as natural rights, and lots more rights as essential to protecting their liberties. How can we tell? We think the evidence we have canvassed provides important clues.

First, numerous rights specified in the various iterations of Sumner's bill were obviously not natural rights, there being no common carriers, juries, or schools in the state of nature. Lyman Trumbull claimed that Congress was not empowered to protect rights of access to these institutions because these were not "natural" rights, but his claim was swiftly rebutted. Were it *necessary* for a right to be natural in order for it to qualify as a privilege or immunity of citizenship, it is difficult to imagine why Trumbull and others would not hammer their opponents on this point. Instead, they fought over whether the rights at issue were deeply rooted in common law and state practice.

Might it be enough for a right to be natural in order for it to be a privilege or immunity of citizenship? We have encountered no unambiguous assertion that a particular, concededly natural right was *not* among the privileges and immunities of citizenship. No one said, "Ah yes, that is indeed a natural right of all persons, but it is not a privilege or immunity of American citizens." But Republican recourse to federal constitutional text, the common law, and state constitutional law for—as John Sherman put it—the "great fountain head, the great reservoir of the rights of an American citizen" was far more common than unadorned Republican appeals to the law of nature.[202]

In this respect, Republicans followed abolitionist constitutionalists such as Joel Tiffany, who hewed close to constitutional text and legal practice, even as he affirmed that those civil rights that were deemed fundamental to American citizenship were best understood as a *means* of implementing natural rights. On this account, civil rights—such as the right of trial by jury—are the essential means of implementing the natural rights that Madison proposed be added to the Preamble as a bill of rights. In this category we would include, in the words of "the civil rights bill," the rights

> to make and enforce contracts, to sue, be parties, and give evidence, to inherit, purchase, lease, sell, hold, and convey real and personal property, and to have full and equal benefit of all laws and proceedings concerning personal liberty, personal security, and the acquisition, enjoyment, and disposition of estate, real and personal.

Another way to think of this is that certain natural rights—such as the right of freedom of speech or the right to own property and enter into contracts—are "privileges or immunities of citizens of the United States" insofar as they became civil rights. That is, natural rights are subsumed by the category of civil rights when they are given positive law protections. But so too are other positive law protections—such as the right of trial by jury—that are not themselves natural rights, but are, in Madison's formulation, "essential to secure the liberty of the people."[203]

Natural rights are justified moral claims that preexist the creation of government, and by which the moral legitimacy of any government can be evaluated. The moral legitimacy of a particular government that is "instituted among men" is therefore dependent on a finding that the civil rights it protects in its positive law adequately secures the inalienable preexisting rights of the people. To the extent that a government effectively secures these rights, it is morally legitimate and capable of issuing commands that bind individuals in conscience to obey. To the extent that it does not, its commands are not so binding, and the people have the right to alter or abolish that government. Part of determining whether a government is legitimate, therefore, is to ask whether its civil rights adequately protect the natural rights of its people. But identifying the content of these civil rights in its positive law is a separate inquiry from identifying the content of natural rights.

As was repeatedly stated by its proponents, the Privileges or Immunities Clause created no new rights—neither natural nor civil. Instead, it sought to scale up the protection of the civil rights that were already recognized by state and federal positive law. It did so by adding a new federal protection from their being abridged by states. The failure to provide for the protection of these civil rights was the very deficiency in the original constitutional design that led to the Civil War.

To the disappointment of Republicans, this deficiency was inadequately remedied by the Thirteenth Amendment and the enforcement power it granted to Congress. They thought they had fixed the problem of civil rights, only to discover they had not. So they tried again, this time expressly protecting all "the privileges or immunities of citizens of the United States."

The positive-law civil rights that comprised these privileges or immunities included, but were not limited to, such natural rights as the enjoyment of life and liberty, with the right to acquire and possess property of every kind, and to pursue happiness and safety, as well as the right to make and enforce contracts, and the right to inherit, purchase, lease, sell, hold, and convey real and personal property. These civil rights, privileges, or immunities also included rights that were not natural but were as essential to the protection of liberty as any right to be found in the state of nature.

If positive-law civil rights identified in this way subsume natural rights, natural rights per se drop off the list of candidate criteria by which to evaluate claimed privileges or immunities of citizenship, leaving us with three:

- rights to equal treatment vis-à-vis other citizens;
- civil rights, as distinguished from "political" or "social" rights;
- all and only those rights that were in 1868 commonly extended to citizens by the states generally.

We noted above that these criteria might not be mutually exclusive. Post-ratification Republican representations that impartial treatment of similarly situated citizens was itself a civil right suggest the utility of treating the second criterion as subsuming the first. And the second criterion explains better than the third the following examples of privileges or immunities that appear to have been put forward in good faith during the framing and ratification process, as well as the reasoning that was used to justify their inclusion:

- rights protected by the Civil Rights Act of 1866;
- personal rights protected by the first eight amendments, including First Amendment rights to the free exercise of religion, freedom of speech, freedom of the press, and freedom of assembly, Second Amendment rights to bear arms, and Fifth Amendment rights to due process of law;
- personal rights protected by other constitutional provisions, including the right to habeas corpus;
- rights specifically mentioned in *Corfield*.

Treating the distinction between civil rights, on the one hand, and political and social rights, on the other, as *the* criterion that ought to be used to distinguish between the privileges and immunities of US citizenship and other kinds of rights and interests has two advantages. First, the distinction between civil rights, on the one hand, and political and social rights, on the other, can explain why the examples on this list of rights were prominent. Second, this criterion can also be used to identify other members of the privileges-or-immunities family. Better than any other theory put forward to date, this criterion fits the data.

To be clear, just because natural rights do not provide a criterion for identifying privileges or immunities does not make them wholly irrelevant to the enterprise. The most prominent examples of privileges and immunities generated during the framing and ratification of the Fourteenth Amendment can be accurately described as either the means of specifying and protecting natural rights or ensuring impartial treatment of citizens. Rights deemed to be privileges or immunities of citizens either (1) appear in constitutional text; (2) have deep roots in the common law; (3) were widespread and entrenched in the law of the states; or all of the above. As late as the debate over the Civil Rights Act of 1875, Republicans were describing civil rights in similar terms and drawing on similar authorities to either affirm or deny the federal government's constitutional power to secure rights of access to public institutions such as inns, schools, and juries.

The distinction between civil rights, on the one hand, and political and social rights, on the other, was not drawn by participants in Reconstruction-era debates as sharply as those who seek a clear rule of law for constitutional decision-makers to apply today might desire. For instance, as often as they invoked *Corfield* to explain what civil rights were, Republicans did not make any great effort to determine whether particular rights had been recognized by all states since independence, and *Corfield* itself expressed uncertainty about the status of voting rights. While Republicans accepted a core set of rights as civil rights, the fact that they disagreed among themselves about others—such as schooling or jury service—shows that their criteria could not mechanically be applied.

A clear, widely accepted method of distinguishing civil rights from political rights and social rights would have greatly aided those engaged in these debates. We have found that no such original method or rule was articulated. Instead, Republicans relied on common normative assumptions about natural rights and citizenship, analogies and disanalogies between controversial and uncontroversial rights, and both positive and common law to make their cases.

Those seeking clear decision rules will have to go beyond the original methods employed by the adopters of the amendment. To develop decision rules that are not found in the text itself but that can be used to implement the original meaning of the clause, we need to enter the "construction zone." Before we do so in Chapter 8, we need briefly to evaluate the competing originalist interpretation of the clause that has been offered by others. This we will do in Chapter 7. But first, we address one last vexatious question involving what is sometimes called "reverse incorporation."

May Congress Abridge the Privileges or Immunities of US Citizens?

The question of how, if at all, the Fourteenth Amendment's individual rights guarantees apply to the federal government has long been a source of embarrassment for both originalists and nonoriginalists alike. Does the original public meaning of the Privileges or Immunities Clause have anything to say about the powers of the federal government? Does it provide any persuasive legal justification for the Supreme Court's conclusion in *Bolling v. Sharpe* that school segregation in the District of Columbia was barred (it said by the Fifth Amendment's Due Process of Law Clause, which was said to incorporate equal-protection principles against the federal government)? Or must the decision be defended on extra-textualist moral grounds? Like "substantive due process," anything that can be called "reverse incorporation" seems automatically suspect—both phrases sound somewhat silly.

Yet there is more support for *Bolling* than one might imagine. In separate articles, Jack Balkin and Ryan Williams have contended that the Citizenship Clause's declaration that "[a]ll persons born or naturalized in the United States and subject to the jurisdiction thereof, are citizens of the United States and of the State wherein they reside" is enough to secure citizens' privileges and immunities against federal infringement as a matter of original meaning.[204]

Like them, we have found no examples of Republicans representing that any citizen could be deprived of rights of national citizenship by *any* governmental entity, whether state or federal, consistent with the Fourteenth Amendment. We have canvassed abundant evidence of categorical insistence on substantive citizenship rights—including rights to be free from unjustified discrimination—as well as Republican wariness of future retrenchment by a Democratic Congress. It is conceivable that Republicans neglected to secure citizenship rights against the federal government, but there is a more plausible explanation for the relative lack of Republican discussion of the issue. The cleanest explanation is also the simplest. The Citizenship Clause added an explicit textual recognition of the category of US citizenship, while the Privileges or Immunities Clause added an explicit textual affirmation that there is a set of "privileges or immunities" enjoyed by these same US citizens. The Supreme Court affirmed these two propositions in *Dred Scott*, but before the amendment was adopted, they were contested. In the process of "reversing" *Dred Scott*, Republicans adopted them both.

The *rest* of the Fourteenth Amendment was needed to empower the federal government—both the courts and Congress—to protect these privileges of national citizenship from abridgement by states. It was this need that led to its adoption. An amendment was obviously not required to empower Congress to protect these fundamental rights, which the Republicans had set about doing with remarkable unity of purpose on coming to power.[205]

Less obviously, an amendment was also not required to empower federal courts to find that a federal statute that violated these fundamental rights of national citizenship was not a "proper" law under the Necessary and Proper Clause. And, as we will explain in Part II, the Fifth Amendment barred any person from being deprived of life, liberty or property except by a valid law that was within the competence of Congress to enact. Propositions that state courts had used to limit the "plenary" legislative power of states were equally available to limit Congress's plenary police power to regulate the District of Columbia and the territories.

This explanation is supported by the fact that constitutional abolitionists had maintained at least since the 1830s that the Due Process of the Law Clause barred slavery in the District of Columbia and the territories.[206] Likewise, numerous Republicans maintained that the federal government lacked power under the antebellum Constitution to deny the privileges and immunities of national citizenship—in particular, by discriminating on the basis of race. Such a lack of power would make any specific prohibition to that effect unnecessary.[207] General agreement that national citizenship—borrowing again from Trumbull—everywhere "mean[t] something" substantive had already been hashed out over the course of prior debates by the time that Howard proposed to add the Citizenship Clause at a very late date.

All that was constitutionally disputed among Republicans involved the status of national privileges and immunities *in the states*. Republicans were focused primarily on state abridgments of citizenship rights because at the time the Fourteenth Amendment was drafted and ratified, it was states that were primarily responsible for rights-abridgment.[208] And under Republicans' interpretation of the Constitution, the federal government lacked the power to protect the rights of US citizens from being violated by their own states.

Having said this, we think there is now less at stake in this interpretive debate than is commonly assumed. Today, it is school segregation by Congress that is "unthinkable." The principal use of *Bolling* by courts today is to bar federal affirmative action and set-aside programs that use racial and other classifications to benefit certain categories of citizens. A majority of justices consistently (and uncritically) invoke the Warren Court's decision in *Bolling* as their primary constitutional objection to such classifications.[209]

We say more in Chapter 8 about the concept of paramount national citizenship that was developed by constitutional abolitionists and eventually adopted by Republicans, which we are calling Republican citizenship. A full and fair treatment of the issue of how this concept applies to the federal government would, however, require more space than we can afford it here. Suffice it to say that, when the original meaning of the text of the Citizenship and Privileges or Immunities Clause is properly identified, there is more originalist support for *Bolling* than one might imagine.

7

Competing Originalist Interpretations

WHILE THE ORIGINAL MEANING of any provision of the Constitution can be contested, there are usually a limited set of rival interpretations from which to choose the best. In this chapter, we examine five kinds of theories of the original meaning of the Privileges or Immunities Clause that judges and scholars have articulated and that differ from our own. By explaining why each does not fit the evidence we have canvassed in the previous chapters, we make more likely the conclusion that ours is the best reading of the clause. (Readers who are already persuaded as to the correctness of our reading can skip ahead to Chapter 8, in which we identify the doctrines by which the clause should be implemented.)

Theory 1: Rights "Associated with the National Government"

It has long been generally accepted that—rightly or wrongly—Justice Miller in *Slaughter-House* limited the rights protected by the Privileges or Immunities Clause to those that are associated with citizens' interactions with the national government. In recent years, however, a few intrepid revisionist scholars have sought to rehabilitate Justice Miller's once nearly universally derided opinion as leaving room for incorporating all enumerated rights.[1] They claim *Slaughter-House* as precedent for their enumerated-rights-only theory of "privileges or immunities."

For reasons previously noted, we are not persuaded by the revisionist view. Moreover, in letting Justice Miller and the *Slaughter-House* majority off the hook, the revisionists still concede that the Court in *Cruikshank* did adopt the rights-associated-with-federal-government view. From the perspective of original meaning, it matters not whether one attributes this view to *Slaughter-House*, to *Cruikshank*, or to both. The only pertinent issue here is whether this is a correct reading of the clause. But the evidence surveyed thus far offers no support for this view.

It is true that in his March 31, 1871, speech Bingham endorsed a notion of dual citizenship, with some rights attaching to national citizenship and some rights attaching to state citizenship. But in that speech Bingham articulated a first-eight-amendments-only conception of national citizenship and set forth a very different list of protected rights than did Miller. So that speech offers no support for the narrow holding commonly attributed both to *Slaughter-House* and to *Cruikshank*.

The rights-associated-with-federal-government view is also contradicted by a mass of evidence before and after the ratification of the Fourteenth Amendment. During both periods Republicans associated privileges and immunities with *Corfield* and with fundamental civil rights that had no essential connection to the federal government. Criticism of Miller's opinion was leveled both by congressional Republicans who were present at the framing of the Fourteenth Amendment and by legal commentators who sympathized with what they believed to be Miller's federalist goals.

These criticisms, together with the absence of any pre-*Slaughter-House* exposition of the Privileges or Immunities Clause that tracked Miller's, further suggest that his opinion for the Court deserves the derision that has been heaped on it. It did not adopt the broader (and more defensible) enumerated-rights-only view, and the view it did adopt was plainly wrong on the day it was decided.

Theory 2: Enumerated Rights Only

There are two variants of enumerated-rights-only theories: The first limits privileges or immunities to those enumerated in the first eight amendments. The second limits them to any right enumerated in the text of the Constitution.

First Eight Amendments Only

To begin, we need to distinguish a first-eight-amendment-*inclusive* view of the Privileges or Immunities Clause, which we hold, from a first-eight-amendments-*only* view, which we reject. The latter view can be dated to the 1947 case of *Adamson v. California.* In that case, the Supreme Court followed *Slaughter-House* in denying that a right enumerated in what was by then called "the Bill of Rights" was protected from state infringement by the Privileges or Immunities Clause. "It is settled law," wrote Justice Reed, that the Fifth Amendment's right against self-incrimination "is not made effective by the Fourteenth Amendment as a protection against state action on the ground that [it] is a right of national citizenship, or because it is a personal privilege or immunity secured by the Federal Constitution as one of the rights of man that are listed in the Bill of Rights."[2]

In reaching this conclusion, the Court cited *Barron v. Baltimore* for "the unquestioned premise that the Bill of Rights, when adopted, was for the protection of the individual against the federal government, and its provisions were inapplicable to similar actions done by the states."[3] It then rejected the suggestion that the adoption of the Privileges or Immunities Clause had affected the applicability of *Barron*. "*The Slaughter-House Cases* decided . . . that these rights, as privileges and immunities of state citizenship, remained under the sole protection of the state governments."[4]

In his voluminous and influential dissent in *Adamson*,[5] Justice Hugo Black reported the results of his study of the framing of the Fourteenth Amendment. Black concluded that at least one of the aims of Section 1 was to make the first eight amendments of the Bill of Rights applicable to the states. He criticized the *Adamson* majority for relying on a "natural law" formula to decide which rights to enforce against the states and argued that it should rely on "the language of the Bill of Right as its point of departure" rather than "substituting its own concepts of decency and fundamental justice."[6]

Previous cases limiting state power from violating substantive rights had avoided the precedent of *Slaughter-House* by relying on the Due Process of Law Clause.[7] Black made plain that he considered the Privileges or Immunities Clause to be the proper textual hook for the protection of such rights when he disparaged the Court's refusal to consider a number of enumerated rights to be "privileges or immunities" in prior cases.

Although Black referred to the "first ten amendments" as "the Bill of Rights," he made no mention of the Ninth or Tenth in his analysis. Instead, he spoke only of "personal liberties" that were set forth in the "first eight amendments."[8] He did not provide an explanation for omitting the Ninth and Tenth Amendments. Perhaps he regarded them as mere federalism provisions that did not protect individual rights.

Justice Black's dissent in *Adamson* marked the intellectual beginning of the modern "incorporation" doctrine of the Fourteenth Amendment. Modern incorporation doctrine limits the scope of the Fourteenth Amendment to the protection of rights that are enumerated in the text of the first eight amendments of "the Bill of Rights." Such rights are said to be "incorporated" into the Due Process of Law Clause. Although initially lonely, Black's first-eight-amendments-only incorporation approach would later receive support from William Winslow Crosskey in the 1950s, Alfred Avins in the 1960s, Michael Kent Curtis in 1980, Richard Aynes and Earl Maltz, among others in the 1990s, and Bryan Wildenthal and Kevin Newsom in the 2000s.[9]

The strongest evidence for the first-eight-amendments-only interpretation of the clause comes from Jacob Howard's introduction to the Senate and John Bingham's March 1871 speech. If one reads the portion of Howard's speech in which he cites *Corfield* through the lens of comity (which we do not), the personal rights enumerated in the first eight amendments are the only other fundamental rights in sight. Bingham's later speech clearly reads *Corfield* through the lens of comity and specifically lists only the first eight amendments as sources of fundamental rights. Howard (read this way) plus Bingham (in 1871) equals first-eight-amendments only.

Even if we were convinced that Howard's introduction and Bingham's March 1871 speech endorsed a first-eight-amendments-only interpretation of the Privileges or Immunities Clause, however, we would not embrace it. There is simply too much pre- and post-ratification evidence of Republicans representing the clause as encompassing rights that cannot fairly be described as "enumerated," such as those specified in the Civil Rights Act. And, as we have reported, there are far too many contests over the content of the Privileges or Immunities Clause in which Republicans did not deploy a first-eight-amendments-only interpretation, even though it would have served their interests to do so had it been available.

But, as discussed above, neither Howard's introduction nor Bingham's March 1871 speech is best read as endorsing a first-eight-amendments-only interpretation. We won't reiterate those reasons here except to say that Howard gave no inkling that the Article IV rights, which he said were included among the "mass" of privileges or immunities, were comity-only. That reading has been unnaturally imposed on his speech by scholars who favor that view. Unless you buy this, Howard's speech is exhibit #1 against the first-eight-amendments theory—indeed, against any enumerated-rights-only theory.

In contrast, the evidence in favor of the personal rights contained in the first eight amendments being *among* the privileges and immunities of US citizenship is compelling. Howard's introduction is perhaps the clearest example of a first-eight-amendments-inclusive understanding of the Privileges or Immunities Clause. We can add as well Bingham's 1867 description of the "pending constitutional amendment" as providing for "all the limitations for personal protection of every article and section of the Constitution," along with his specific mention of both the Fifth Amendment and "the other amendments for the protection of personal rights."[10]

Justice Joseph Bradley's enumerated-rights-inclusive theory of the privileges and immunities of citizenship—articulated in his *Slaughter-House* dissent and in his letter to Judge Woods about *United States v. Hall*—is also entitled to some weight, owing to its endorsement by Republicans who were present at the framing. So, too, are the enumerated-rights-inclusive theories of George Paschal, Timothy Farrar, and John Norton Pomeroy. As Bryan Wildenthal has noted, these were the "only three nationally known legal scholars who published treatises actually discussing the Fourteenth Amendment during 1867–69."[11]

That leaves us with the question of which provisions of the first eight amendments specify personal rights. According to Akhil Amar, some of the first eight amendments were federalism provisions at the Founding, which only came later to be understood as personal rights, whereas others remained federalism provisions. Amar gives the right to keep and bear arms as an example of the former having moved, he says, from a collective right of states to a personal right of individuals.[12]

Amar also claims that the Establishment Clause was understood in both 1788 and 1868 as a bulwark against both the establishment of a national religion and any federal interference with state establishments. It did not, he contends, become understood as a personal right to be free from state establishments.[13] Kurt Lash has challenged Amar's view, arguing that "[i]n the years following the adoption of the Bill of Rights . . . the idea evolved that citizens ought to be free from government imposed religious establishments."[14] By 1868, "the (Non)establishment Clause was understood to be a liberty as fully capable of incorporation as any other provision in the first eight amendments."[15]

In making the case that the framers of the Fourteenth Amendment so understood it, Lash points to Republican complaints about Southern states "silenc[ing] every free pulpit"; Bingham's March 1871 speech reciting the first eight amendments verbatim; and an 1864 speech by Senator Henry Wilson in which Wilson recited the entire First Amendment and then paraphrased the amendment as protecting "freedom of religious opinion, freedom of speech and press, and the right of assemblage for the purpose of petition."[16]

Lash also draws support for a broadly accepted principle of nonestablishment from Thomas Cooley's *Constitutional Limitations,* in which Cooley wrote that it was "not lawful under any of the American constitutions" to enact "any law respecting an establishment of religion."[17] Moreover, Steven Calabresi and Sarah Agudo have documented that, in 1868, twenty-seven of thirty-seven states had establishment clauses in their state constitutions, which individual citizens could invoke against their own governments.[18] That's just one state short of the three-quarters consensus required for an Article V amendment.[19]

On the other hand, as we noted in Chapter 6, in his speech, Senator Howard omitted the Establishment Clause from his list of "the personal rights guarantied and secured by the first eight amendments of the Constitution."[20] Also, as we noted in Chapter 4, after quoting the language of the First Amendment—including the Establishment Clause—Congressman James Wilson summarized "the great rights here enumerated" as: "Freedom of religious opinion, freedom of speech and press, and the right of assemblage for the purpose of petition." [21] Nothing here about state establishments.

These omissions are suggestive, but we haven't done the research needed to definitively decide whether the public meaning of the bar on "the establishment of religion" had or had not transformed into a personal privilege or immunity of national citizenship by 1868. However, no matter who has the better of this Establishment Clause debate, we can articulate the following rule: *all* enumerated personal rights are part of the privileges-or-immunities family. Regardless of how it was viewed at the Founding, if the Establishment Clause was in 1868 deeply rooted as a personal right, it is in; if not, then not.

Enumerated Rights Only

We now move from the theory that the set of privileges or immunities of US citizens is limited to rights enumerated in the text of the first eight amendments to the theory that the set is limited to rights enumerated *anywhere* in the text of the Constitution. In a series of articles that culminated in a book, Kurt Lash articulated a theory of the Privileges or Immunities Clause that resembles but is importantly different from Justice Black's incorporation theory. Like Black, Lash contended that the Privileges or Immunities Clause applied the first eight amendments to the states. Unlike Black, Lash claimed that *all* enumerated rights were protected by the Privileges or Immunities Clause wherever in the Constitution they may appear. These included not only those secured by the first eight amendments, but also the right to habeas corpus in Article I, Section 9, and the right to be free from discrimination with respect to one's fundamental civil rights when traveling in another state in Article IV, Section 2.[22] According to Lash, "privileges or immunities of citizens of the United States" was an antebellum term of art, familiar from treaty jurisprudence and congressional debates over the admission of Missouri, which (Lash claims) was widely understood by the legally educated to denote only enumerated rights.[23]

We have elsewhere dealt with Lash's theory at great length and can testify that the evaluation of evidence soon gets quite complicated.[24] But we have found no evidence that *any* Republican articulated an enumerated-rights-only theory prior to the ratification of the Fourteenth Amendment. This is so whether the theory is limited to the enumerated rights in the first eight amendments or includes as well rights that are enumerated elsewhere in the Constitution.

The omission is significant, given that such a theory would have been very helpful, if not imperative, for Republicans to rebut Democratic claims that the amendment would secure voting rights, rights to sit on juries, rights to interracial marriage, and other rights that were especially controversial but that were not enumerated.[25] Had the dominant public meaning of this concept been limited to rights enumerated in the first eight or ten amendments, this would been an easy rebuttal to make. It never was.

Lash has emphasized Bingham's March 1871 speech. As we have seen, this speech is unreliable. And even this speech does not unambiguously support a first-eight-amendments-only theory of the Privileges or Immunities Clause, much less Lash's more capacious one. In it, Bingham states that the substantive rights protected by the clause are "*chiefly* defined" in the first eight amendments. It certainly does not support Lash's distinctive enumerated-rights-only theory, as Bingham does not clearly identify any other enumerated right that, in addition to those enumerated in the first eight amendments, is substantively secured by the Privileges or Immunities Clause.

Finally, and we believe tellingly, Lash has had difficulty explaining exactly how, on his theory, Section 1 of the Fourteenth Amendment constitutionalized the Civil Rights Act of 1866. As we have seen, proponents of Section 1 frequently referred to the Civil Rights Act and claimed that it would be constitutionalized by Section 1—sometimes identifying the Privileges or Immunities Clause as having accomplished this.[26]

On Lash's account, it is hard to see how the Privileges or Immunities Clause would have done so. Recall that the act guaranteed the rights "to make and enforce contracts, to sue, be parties, and give evidence, . . . and to the full and equal benefit of all laws and proceedings for the security of persons and property." None of these rights is enumerated as such in the first eight amendments or elsewhere in the text.

Moreover, the act did not merely protect those unenumerated rights listed in the act's text against parochial discrimination. It also guaranteed that all citizens would have "the same right . . . [to contract, property, security] as is enjoyed by white citizens," *regardless of state citizenship*.[27] On Lash's account, then, the Privileges or Immunities Clause was not understood in a way that would give this legislation constitutional safe harbor.

And yet, not only did members of Congress widely assert that Section 1 was meant to so empower Congress, but Congress reenacted the Civil Rights Act in 1870 pursuant to the Fourteenth Amendment to ensure its constitutionality.[28] As we noted above, in his notes for his speech, Jacob Howard appears to have referred to the rights identified in *Corfield* as "fundamental civil rights."

Lash has questioned the connection between the Civil Rights Act of 1866 and Section 1, noting in particular that John Bingham opposed the former despite his central role in framing the latter.[29] But he has never denied that Section 1 *did* constitutionalize the Civil Rights Act. Indeed, in reviewing his various writings, we were surprised to discover that Lash has put forward no less than four theories of *how* Section 1 constitutionalized the Civil Rights Act. At one time or another, he has proposed that the rights it specified were protected by the Citizenship Clause, the Privileges or Immunities Clause, the Due Process of Law Clause, and the Equal Protection of the Laws Clause—that is, by each of the operative clauses of Section 1.[30]

Elsewhere we discuss these theories, focusing especially on his latest that it was the Due Process of Law Clause, which protected a dubious "natural right of due process," that constitutionalized the act. We urge those who are tempted by Lash's theory to read our lengthy critique of his whole body of work, his reply, and our response.[31] We are confident that a fair-minded reader will conclude that none of his theories adequately explains the available evidence.

Theory 3: Equality Only

Among scholars who reject incorporation, the dominant position is that the Privileges or Immunities Clause guarantees only equality with respect to certain rights. The identity of those rights is a matter of dispute. Put another way, on this account, the Privileges or Immunities Clause protects only whatever rights it protects from discrimination by states. Under this reading, a state remains free to deny *all* its citizens *equally* any privilege or immunity of US citizenship. Perhaps the most persistent advocate of a version of the equality-only position was Raoul Berger.

Raoul Berger

On Berger's account, the Privileges or Immunities Clause was designed to constitutionalize the Civil Rights Act of 1866—and nothing else. And because he read that act as protecting only against discrimination by states, that is the only protection afforded by the clause. It does not empower Congress, much less the federal courts, to do more than ensure that all US citizens "shall have *the same rights,* in every State and Territory in the United States . . . *as is enjoyed by white citizens,* and shall be subject to *like punishment,* pains, and penalties. . . ."[32] It protects only against discrimination and does not forbid states from generally curtailing the exercise of these rights.

Berger's argument rested on the premise that the Civil Rights Act of 1866 secured only equality rights, a not uncommon reading. To the contrary, however, in Chapter 5, we explained why the act is best read as a fundamental-rights statute. If we are right about the Civil Rights Act, then Berger is wrong about the Fourteenth Amendment.

Further, as Michael Kent Curtis, Bryan Wildenthal, and others have shown, Berger inexcusably neglected and diminished the significance of affirmative evidence that the clause was widely understood to substantively protect enumerated constitutional rights.[33] We have discussed this evidence at length and will not reiterate it here. Berger's research is also shot through with errors. His repetition, in the introduction of a 1997 edition of his *Government by Judiciary,* of an erroneous claim that Howard's introduction received no newspaper coverage—a claim that Curtis debunked in an exchange with Berger sixteen years earlier—is perhaps the most striking example.[34]

John Harrison and Ilan Wurman

John Harrison and Ilan Wurman have in separate work articulated equality-only theories of the Privileges or Immunities Clause that can accommodate evidence that Republicans did not take "privileges or immunities of citizens of the United States" to denote only the rights specified in the Civil Rights Act of 1866. These theories can also accommodate evidence that Republicans were determined to eradicate the Black Codes, which were designed to perpetuate inequality between Black and white citizens.

Both scholars, however, neglect the possibility that the 1866 act established a floor of fundamental civil rights: those enjoyed by white citizens because of their connection to natural rights and equality. To constitutionalize legislation that established such a floor, Republicans would need a theory of the privileges and immunities of citizenship with substantive content. In such a theory, state positive law might be relevant to the determination of which rights US citizens were entitled to enjoy by virtue of their citizenship—as we will propose in the next chapter—but would still not be dispositive.

Harrison's concern is that empowering the federal government to secure Republican citizenship by protecting the rights essential to it, wherever US citizens may be, would "abolish the doctrine of enumerated powers and with it American federalism."[35] We disagree. On Harrison's account, the privileges and immunities of citizenship are bounded; states are obliged to extend only certain kinds of rights equally to their citizens. But so, too, are privileges and immunities bounded under our theory of Republican citizenship; Congress and the courts are empowered to protect only certain kinds of fundamental rights against state infringement.

Harrison notes that the "rhetoric of privileges and immunities of citizens in the nineteenth century was heavily Lockean" and that abolitionists and Republicans claimed "that the individual, who had surrendered the natural right of self-protection by giving allegiance to the state, was entitled in return to be protected by the government."[36] He proposes that privileges and immunities be distinguished from mere government benefits by ascertaining whether "the government [is] undertak[ing] to provide something that individuals have a natural right to acquire, and either monopoliz[ing] its provision or forc[ing] citizens who obtain the benefit privately to pay for it a second time by taxing them for its public provision."[37] Harrison observes that "[t]his means that most government benefits with which we are familiar will be privileges of citizenship because most of them are supported by general taxation."[38]

We would say instead that a fundamental right to nondiscriminatory access to goods supported by general taxation is itself a privilege of citizenship and that a fundamental right to be free from unreasonably discriminatory tax burdens is an immunity of citizenship. Both are instances of the fundamental privilege to impartial treatment by public institutions. But, as we have shown, the Privileges or Immunities Clause secures other fundamental rights that were deemed fundamental in 1868, as well as leaving room for additional widely recognized and entrenched privileges to be elevated to fundamental status at a later date.

Harrison is right that Republicans were concerned with federalism as well as natural rights and equal citizenship. But he underestimates Republicans' commitment to establishing a federal floor of fundamental rights protected from state abridgment. Our federalism was preserved but significantly modified—and consciously so—by the authors and adopters of the Fourteenth Amendment.

Wurman largely agrees with Harrison but makes a distinctive claim about the language of the Privileges or Immunities Clause *as a whole* that is worth examining separately. Wurman contends that "privileges or immunities of citizens of the United States," "due process of law," and "the equal protection of the laws" are all legal terms of art. By this is meant that they carry a specialized meaning available firsthand only to members of a subcommunity of the general public—namely, the legally educated.[39]

As Larry Solum has explained, constitutional communication via terms of art depends on the operation of a linguistic division of labor whereby the specialists convey the meaning of relevant language to others.[40] We have argued that that division of labor can only operate if (a) there is a widely accepted specialized meaning to convey, and (b) the latter meaning is either communicated to the public or the public defers to those who are legally trained.[41] Otherwise, there will be a divergence between the meaning conveyed to most people and the specialized meaning conveyed to a select few—and the specialized meaning *will not* become the public meaning. Wurman does not establish either (a) or (b).

The evidence canvassed above discloses a divergence that developed over the course of the antebellum period between a dominant comity-only "legal-term-of-art" meaning of privileges and immunities in the courts and a fundamental-rights public meaning on which all sides in the battle over slavery eventually converged, even as they disagreed about the nature of fundamental rights. Another way of expressing this divergence is that the original public meaning of Article IV, Section 2 as a "comity-only" protection *came to be* a "term of art" as the contemporary public meaning of the clause evolved into a fundamental rights reading. The original public meaning of the Privileges or Immunities Clause of the Fourteenth Amendment was the then-prevailing public meaning of Article IV as protecting a floor of fundamental rights, rather than its term-of-art comity-only meaning in the courts.

Wurman reads several salient constitutional disputes—for instance, the expulsion of Samuel Hoar—as one over equality of rights rather than fundamental rights. We do not agree, but even if he were correct, there is no term-of-art case to be made on the basis of such evidence. These were very public arguments that strayed far from the legal-term-of-art comity consensus within the courts.

Moreover, as we have argued, the courts, too, eventually became more receptive to a more-than-comity view of the clause. But for any legal-term-of-art meaning to become public meaning, Wurman must offer more than Howard's statement that senators "may gather some intimations of what probably will be the opinion of the judiciary" and his reference to *Corfield*—a case that, as we have seen, Republicans had long read in a legally unorthodox way.[42] Because Wurman does not offer more than this, we should proceed on the assumption that the clause's language carries a public meaning that was enriched by decades of antebellum constitutionalism outside the courts. It was not written in the language of the law.

In the end, Wurman's case for equality-only is no stronger than Harrison's. Although Wurman correctly claims that the Privileges or Immunities Clause was enacted to constitutionalize the Civil Rights Act of 1866, he does not consider in any depth the possibility that the latter is not a mere antidiscrimination guarantee. If the act was more than this, then we have shown that an equality-only Privileges or Immunities Clause would not succeed in accomplishing what we and he agree is a minimal requirement for any viable account of the clause.

We share Wurman's skepticism of using "stray statements from legislative history"[43] to bolster a fundamental-rights theory—or any theory for that matter. We agree with Wurman that Bingham's 1871 eight-amendments-and-nothing-but speech is unreliable. But, as we have shown, far "more than a single statement by Senator Howard" and "a few stray and ambiguous statements" by Bingham support the inclusion of enumerated personal rights among the privileges and immunities of US citizenship.[44] In fairness to Wurman, he wrote his book before he had access to the evidence presented in ours.

Wurman urges that "no advocate on either side made explicit mention of incorporating the Bill of Rights."[45] True, but unsurprising given that "the bill of rights" had not yet been embedded in popular discourse. And we have seen that many advocates represented that particular enumerated personal rights would indeed be protected, without any suggestion that they would be secured only against discrimination. An equality-only Privileges or Immunities Clause simply would not have gotten the job done for the Republicans who devised, enacted, and sought to enforce it.

Philip Hamburger

Philip Hamburger has provided the sparest account of the clause's content. He reads it as empowering Congress to enforce the Privileges and Immunities Clause of Article IV, Section 2, understood as prohibiting discrimination on the basis of out-of-state citizenship.[46] Period. Thus, the Privileges or Immunities Clause does not protect citizens even from unequal treatment by their home state. For Hamburger, the interpretive key to the clause is a bill proposed by Samuel Shellabarger, which referred to the privileges and immunities "of U.S. citizens" and protected only comity rights.[47] This bill, Hamburger claims, inspired the language of Bingham's third draft, and that language carried the same meaning.[48]

Shellabarger's comity bill cannot bear the weight of Hamburger's theory. Hamburger adduces no direct evidence that Bingham borrowed the bill's language. We have seen that Shellabarger himself held an expansive fundamental-rights understanding of the Privileges and Immunities Clause. Responding to Hamburger, Lash has pointed out that Shellabarger amended his bill to clarify that "the enumeration of the privileges and immunities of citizenship in this act contained shall not be deemed a denial or abridgment of *any other* rights, privileges, or immunities which appertain to citizenship under the Constitution." This implied that Article IV did not protect merely comity rights.[49]

Hamburger takes pains to incorporate Black voices into Fourteenth Amendment scholarship. He criticizes other scholars for "treating the blacks like invisible men" and canvasses newspaper evidence to document the concerns of free Blacks about the security of their rights when traveling to other states.[50] These efforts are laudable, but the picture Hamburger paints of Black thought about the privileges and immunities of citizenship is incomplete and sometimes misleading.

It is certainly true that Southerners perceived free Blacks who traveled South as a threat to white supremacy, and that free Blacks who sought to enter Southern ports found it increasingly difficult to do so in the years preceding the Civil War.[51] But free Blacks were also profoundly concerned about their fundamental rights to the freedom of speech, the free exercise of religion, nondiscriminatory access to public institutions, and other rights that they associated with citizenship. These rights were either insecure or denied altogether, whether in the South or in the North.

The urgency of protecting Blacks' substantive rights in their home states became only more pressing in the wake of the Black Codes and reached its zenith in the summer of 1866 after Congress submitted the Fourteenth Amendment for ratification. On July 30, local law enforcement officials stood by as a white mob organized by the New Orleans mayor massacred scores of mostly Black marchers outside of a reconvened Louisiana Constitutional Convention. As Lash has pointed out, many of the murdered had fought in the Civil War.[52] Blacks' vulnerability to state-sanctioned violence in response to their exercise of rights to free speech and free assembly was made painfully clear. Hamburger's claim that Blacks "had little need for assurances of any particular substantive federal right" is untenable.[53]

Hamburger focuses attention on a memorial that Black abolitionist William Cooper Nell and other activists submitted to the Massachusetts legislature in 1858. He accurately describes the memorial as a "complain[t] that the *Dred Scott* decision had left [Blacks] more vulnerable than ever in Southern states." He then notes that Nell charged Chief Justice Roger Taney with effectively nullifying the Privileges and Immunities Clause.[54] Hamburger does not mention, however, that five years earlier Nell deployed the Privileges and Immunities Clause against his own state, arguing in a petition to the Massachusetts Constitutional Convention that, consistent with Article IV, Section 2, Black citizens could not be disabled from holding military commissions and serving in the volunteer militia.[55]

Finally, Hamburger lacks a convincing account of how the Fourteenth Amendment provided constitutional authority for the Civil Rights Act of 1866. He states that "[i]t is well-known that the Fourteenth Amendment's clauses on equal protection and due process gave constitutional force to positions Congress had earlier taken in the Civil Rights Act."[56] To the contrary. These are controversial and highly problematic claims that need to be defended.

Those who would claim that the Equal Protection of the Laws Clause constitutionalized the Civil Rights Act must confront the evidence presented by Christopher Green. Green shows that the clause guarantees "protection" against violence and access to the processes of "the laws"—including the courts—but does not serve as a general nondiscrimination guarantee.[57] We will return to the original meaning of the Equal Protection of the Laws Clause in Part III, where we will take a somewhat broader view of "the equal protection of the laws" than does Green. But even that broader view is not broad enough to provide all the protections afforded by the Civil Rights Act.

Theory 4: A Closed Set of Enumerated and Unenumerated Rights

Several scholars have contended that the Privileges or Immunities Clause "locks in" rights that were generally possessed by citizens at a particular date. Neither Congress nor the courts can add to them, and states cannot subtract from them. Earl Maltz and Douglas Smith are two such scholars.

On Maltz's account, the Thirty-Ninth Congress sought to "secure a fixed set of rights" and the set of protected rights was "fixed for all time in 1866."[58] Maltz describes the protected set as "relatively small" and as "clearly" including "the rights enumerated in the Civil Rights Act [of 1866]." To these he adds "some of the Bill of Rights," like the "basic guarantees of the First Amendment," "the Fifth Amendment's just-compensation and due process provisions," the right to keep and bear arms, the right to be free from cruel and unusual punishments, and the right to be free from unreasonable searches and seizures.[59] Maltz regards it as probable that Republicans "viewed the first eight amendments as incorporated in their entirety" but does not believe that rights must be enumerated to be "privileges or immunities."[60]

Douglas Smith has found that the social contract theories of John Locke, Samuel Pufendorf, Jean-Jacques Burlamaqui, and Emmerich de Vattel exerted an influence on antebellum legal thought. From this he concludes that the privileges and immunities of citizenship encompassed "more and less than those rights enumerated in the Bill of Rights."[61] Specifically, they included "fundamental" rights that "exist[ed] anterior to the establishment of the government, whether because they are inherent, belonging to all persons as natural rights, or because they flow from the social compact among the members of the political community, its citizens."[62] Among them, Smith argued, were the rights identified in the Civil Rights Act of 1866, such as "the capacity to enter into contracts, testify in court, and pass property through inheritance."[63]

We generally agree that the rights identified by Maltz and Smith were locked into the Constitution in 1868 as privileges or immunities of citizens. These rights cannot be repealed by ordinary legislation or by judicial interpretation. But while these rights were fixed, we do not believe that the set of privileges and immunities was closed in 1866, 1868, or at any other time. More rights could later qualify. At the same time, this set has boundaries that constrain such expansion.

While we disagree with Lyman Trumbull's stance on the Civil Rights Act of 1875, we do share his view that the original meaning of "privileges or immunities of citizens of the United States" covers *only* civil rights. It does not extend to "political rights"—that is, to rights widely recognized as falling within the absolute discretion of the political branches to extend or withdraw. Nor did it extend to "social rights" to the association, friendship, or favorable opinion of others, which even the most radical of Republicans disavowed any intention to secure during the relevant time period.[64]

It is true that—as Maltz and Smith emphasize—Republicans insisted that the Privileges or Immunities Clause did not protect political rights and explained that voting rights in particular were not protected because they were not essential to citizenship. It is also true that Republicans were concerned about delegating too broadly to future Congresses that might prove hostile to civil rights.

There is a difference, however, between locking in a closed set of civil rights and locking in a conceptual boundary between civil rights and other kinds of rights. Doing the latter would empower Congress and the courts to take measures that were necessary to protect deeply rooted civil rights to life, liberty, property, and the like, from new threats unimaginable in 1868. More controversially, it would also empower Congress and the courts to protect rights that later came to be understood as fundamental to Republican citizenship. Rights such as voting and jury service, which had previously qualified as "political rights" and were unprotected, could later become "civil rights" that could not be abridged by the states.

But we hasten to stress that this approach would not leave the federal government—and especially its judges—with unbounded discretion in designating rights as civil rights. As we will explain in Chapter 8, such rights must be *found* or *discovered* by the same backward-looking inquiry that was used by those who wrote and ratified the Fourteenth Amendment. Most importantly, it would require a finding that a particular right has become widespread and entrenched in the positive law of the states. An outlier state that declines to recognize a widespread, entrenched right can be brought into alignment with the national consensus. But such rights should not be *made* by judges absent such a consensus just because the judges consider them to be fundamental.

In the next chapter, we hope to mollify some of the understandable concerns about this approach by identifying the implementing rules to give legal effect to the original meaning of the clause. These rules closely resemble the Court's current, more "conservative," approach to substantive due process. Because they focus on the positive law, if anything, these rules are more determinate than the Court's current approach.

Theory 5: An Open Set of Widely Recognized Common-Law Rights

Finally, Christopher Green has argued that the Privileges or Immunities Clause guarantees some fundamental rights to all citizens and thereby prevents the stratification of citizenship. He has created a hierarchy of fundamentality, placing at the bottom those rights "guaranteed to citizens and aliens alike" and "political" rights and "social rights."[65] Although Green describes his examples of rights at each level of the hierarchy as merely "illustrative," the illustrations make plain the unique character of Green's theory.[66] Those at the top include both enumerated and unenumerated rights, such as "[a]nti-slavery rights, due process of law, protection from violence, making contracts, suing for injuries, [and] testifying in court."[67] For Green, then, enumeration in the constitutional text is neither necessary nor sufficient to make a right fundamental.

Green's account differs importantly from ours by contending that no "floor" of fundamental rights was fixed in 1868 or at any other time. In his view, fundamental rights are those that have long been generally enjoyed by citizens in the several states. Such enjoyment can wax and wane over time. "[T]here simply isn't [a] temporal qualifier like 'current' on the privileges or immunities of American citizens mentioned in the text," he notes, even though "[o]ther provisions in the Constitution do have explicit time stamps."[68]

How long, then, does it take for a right to become a privilege or immunity of citizenship? Although he expresses some uncertainty about this,

Green opines that "even a very young tradition, if it genuinely has spread through the bulk of the United States, should count."[69] Although he does not expressly say so, because there is no floor to his conception of privileges or immunities, this would seem to include a widespread practice of restricting liberty along with protecting it. In other words, a retreat from a tradition of rights-protection that has genuinely spread through the bulk of the United States—however rapidly—could reduce a right to nonfundamental and therefore unprotected status.

Consider that he finds it "quite plausible" that "laissez-faire economic rights" no longer qualify as fundamental because "the tradition of unregulated labor markets that existed at the time of *Lochner v. New York* or *Adkins v. Children's Hospital* has gone by the wayside."[70] On the other hand, he also notes that "[t]he right to contract was . . . in the Civil Rights Act of 1866, and *seen as a paradigm privilege of citizens of the United States.*"[71] That's a problem for his theory.

We agree with Green that Republicans understood the privileges and immunities of citizenship to be the product of induction from experience rather than deduction from natural-rights axioms. This is the method we too advocate and will elaborate in the next chapter. But he underestimates the degree to which Republicans believed that certain rights had proven so essential to citizenship that they ought to be locked into the positive law of the land.

We detect no uncertainty among Republicans in the Thirty-Ninth Congress about whether what they considered to be civil rights ought to be placed beyond the reach of ordinary politics. Republicans repeatedly claimed that they sought to permanently secure particular civil rights. We find no Republican endorsing the notion that a civil right ought no longer to qualify for constitutional protection if enough states neglected to secure it for a long enough period of time.

Consider that the freedom of speech—perhaps the most frequently mentioned of civil rights—could, on Green's view, cease to be protected by the Privileges or Immunities Clause if a very young tradition of censorship emerged. This is not a far-fetched hypothetical. The recently developed concept of unprotected "hate speech" is spreading through the legal and political culture like wildfire.[72] Green's theory provides no fire brake.

Republicans would not have needed to strain their imagination to contemplate such a development. They had seen the freedom of speech neglected or outright attacked by Southern states throughout the antebellum period. Absent any evidence that Republicans did believe that the rights they considered fundamental could lose their fundamentality through widespread state neglect, we should not interpret the clause to allow for this possibility. We are aware of no such evidence. We also agree with Green that there is no fundamental rights ceiling. And we agree that a right need not be enumerated to be deemed fundamental. Republican claims that the Privileges or Immunities Clause would secure *Corfield* rights and rights specified in the Civil Rights Act of 1866 are incoherent absent the assumption that rights can come to be deemed fundamental through means other than federal enumeration. Further, when Republicans contended for the recognition of "new" privileges and immunities in the 1870s, they looked not only to federal constitutional text. They looked as well to the constitutional and common law of the states—such as the nondiscrimination duty of common carriers.

We hasten to add that, by stating that there is no fundamental rights ceiling, we do not mean that state convergence on a right's importance is sufficient to make it a privilege or immunity of US citizens. To be deemed fundamental *to Republican citizenship*, a right must also have a tight connection *to* Republican citizenship. That is, it must have a tight connection either (1) to the protection of natural rights or (2) to the equal treatment—or the civic equality—of citizens by public institutions.

The development of a framework that judges and legislators can use to assess whether such a connection exists in a given case is a task that falls within the domain of constitutional construction. It is a task we will perform in the next chapter.

*   *   *

Before moving on to considering how the letter of the Privileges or Immunities Clause should be implemented in a manner that is faithful to its spirit, we offer some concluding observations about the task of identifying the original public meaning of the clause.

The privileges and immunities of American citizenship do not admit of a concise definition that sets forth their essence and cleanly distinguishes them from other interests. Their history is one of contestation within fuzzy conceptual boundaries. While these boundaries are ultimately grounded on empirical claims about human nature and the requirements of human flourishing in civil society, they are identified through past practice, not armchair philosophizing. If there was an "original method" of identifying privileges or immunities, this was it.

Such practice consisted in the working out, by people who were assumed to share common normative commitments, of how to realize those commitments institutionally—through constitutions, through legislation, through the courts. To put it crudely, a right came to be deemed a "civil right" if lots of people who thought about citizenship in roughly the same way deemed it to be important to citizenship for a long enough time. Determining whether a right is deemed important to citizenship for a sufficiently long period of time requires an empirical inquiry into our shared tradition and history, as opposed to a purely normative inquiry by judges.

The Privileges or Immunities Clause can be understood as an expression of Republicans' conviction that there existed an understanding of citizenship that had long been assumed to be common and a set of rights that had been deemed essential over time to securing this citizenship. Following the lead of constitutional abolitionists, Republicans traced this understanding to the Founding. Their historical claim stressed the Declaration of Independence, but they amassed other evidence, too.

As a result of the rise of the Slave Power after the Founding, however, this understanding of citizenship came to be rejected by some, and, consequently, the rights it required were no longer secure. The defeat of the Confederacy on the battlefield ended proslavery's dominance of the federal government. But Republicans then discovered that their victory failed to translate into a restoration of this understanding of citizenship or to an equal respect for its associated civil rights. Nor, to their surprise and dismay, did the abolition of slavery by constitutional amendment accomplish those goals. Another amendment was needed because future Congresses simply could not be counted on to respect the civil rights that Republicans took for granted as essential to American citizenship.

Yet, as we know, *all these laudable Republican efforts ultimately proved insufficient to the task.* Witness the defeat of Reconstruction and the rise of the legally ensconced system of white supremacy known as Jim Crow, both of which were aided and abetted by the Supreme Court. We hasten to add that the assistance provided by the Court included ignoring or distorting the original meaning of the Privileges or Immunities Clause from 1873 to this very day.

In the preceding chapters, we have identified the original meaning of "the privileges or immunities of citizens of the United States" as civil rights, as distinguished from "political" or "social" rights, *including the civil right to equal treatment by public institutions.* But how do we identify precisely these civil rights?

For better or worse, Republicans did not supply future constitutional decision-makers with fine-grained criteria or an original method for distinguishing civil rights from other interests that they considered valuable. It does not follow, however, that the quest for *the* original meaning of the Privileges or Immunities Clause has been so much wasted time and scholarly energy. We know a great deal more about the clause than we used to. There is much about the content of "privileges or immunities" in which constitutional actors can today be highly confident:

- Enumerated personal rights are clearly in;
- Rights specified in the Civil Rights Act of 1866 are clearly in;
- Rights specified in *Corfield*, with the exception of suffrage—to which we will return—are clearly in.

If it was clear that the set of privileges or immunities of citizenship was closed in 1868, this would end our inquiry into original meaning. These would be the privileges or immunities of US citizens and nothing more. Adopting this meaning would be a huge improvement over its current neglect by the courts.

But the evidence that persuasively shows that these three categories of rights were fixed as civil rights by the original meaning of the text in 1868 also shows that other rights could *later* become privileges or immunities of American citizens. Because of this, constitutional actors will need to devise rules of their own to settle the status of other rights. In doing so, they need to operate within the admittedly fuzzy boundaries set by those who ratified the text of the Fourteenth Amendment into law.

In the next chapter, we present the evidence showing that the set of privileges or immunities of US citizens was not closed in 1868. We then introduce criteria by which legislators and judges can identify additional rights that have since become privileges or immunities of American citizenship. These criteria will allow for the development of privileges and immunities that the Fourteenth Amendment's framers may not have contemplated but are faithful to the text they proposed. Recognizing these rights as fundamental will be faithful to *their* theory that privileges and immunities emerge from convergent practice and experience that demonstrates the centrality of certain rights to the flourishing of the citizenry.

After this, we propose decision rules by which all these privileges or immunities—whether old or new—can be implemented and enforced. To borrow from Bingham, those decision rules will be structured around the "spirit, the intent, the purpose" of the Privileges or Immunities Clause. This spirit includes a commitment to natural rights, to civic equality, and to a revised understanding of federalism in which the federal government actively responds both to state action and to culpable omission that puts citizens' rights at hazard.

It is unrealistic to demand 100 percent certainty from any text. It is particularly unrealistic to demand certainty from a constitutional text that was forged in the wake of war and in the midst of efforts by those who lost it to fight on through other means. Disputes and doubts about its full scope are inevitable. But we must do better than the Supreme Court of the United States has done to deliver on its promise. And we can.

8

The Spirit

Implementing the Privileges or Immunities Clause

IN THE PREVIOUS seven chapters we identified the original meaning of the phrase "privileges or immunities of citizens of the United States" by examining evidence from the Founding, from the antebellum period, from the drafting and ratification of the clause, and from post-ratification interpretations in Congress and by courts and academic commentators. This mass of evidence shows that "privileges or immunities" encompassed civil rights, as distinguished from "political" or "social" rights, and included the civil right to impartial treatment by public institutions. In this chapter, we address the question of how constitutional decision-makers in all three branches of government can identify the particular civil rights that are the privileges or immunities of Republican citizenship.

In previous work, we have articulated and defended a framework that constitutional decision-makers can use to implement constitutional text.[1] We have termed this framework *good-faith construction*. As we summarized this approach in the introduction, good-faith construction distinguishes between the "letter" and "spirit" of the text of the Constitution. When the original meaning or letter of the text is not sufficient to resolve a constitutional controversy, one must supplement that meaning with its original spirit. The spirit of the text is its original function(s), purpose(s), object(s), end(s), aim(s), or goal(s)—which for convenience we call simply the "original function" of the text.

Identifying this original function or spirit of the text requires the same sort of empirical inquiry as that required to interpret its letter.[2] Decision-makers must investigate not only the immediate context of communication but antecedent legal, political, and social history that might shed light on what kinds of normative goods the text was designed to capture. Then, they must formulate rules for decision-making that make it more likely that those goods will be captured in a given setting—rules that are well adapted to that setting.

Their aim should be to implement the original meaning of the text in a way that is faithful to the reason why the text was adopted. Being faithful also means that whatever rules decision-makers adopt to accomplish its aims must not contradict the original meaning of the text. Above all, they should not use any underdeterminacy in the text as an excuse or pretext for avoiding what the text *does* say—perhaps because the decision-maker does not like or approve of the original meaning of the text.

We believe that the key to understanding the spirit of the phrase "privileges or immunities of citizens of the United States" is the concept of *Republican citizenship*. In this chapter, we propose a modified version of the concept of paramount national citizenship first elucidated by scholar Jacobus tenBroek in his pioneering work on antislavery constitutionalism.[3] After summarizing Republican citizenship, we provide decision rules that judges and legislators can use to promote Republican citizenship today.

The Spirit of the Privileges or Immunities Clause

It would be tedious to enumerate all the occasions on which supporters of the Fourteenth Amendment represented that the Privileges or Immunities Clause was designed to establish a national citizenship. Instead, we will try to nail down the clause's spirit by identifying the *kind* of national citizenship the clause was designed to establish.

We think the evidence shows that the clause was designed to establish the kind of citizenship that was developed by radical antislavery scholars and activists—Joel Tiffany and Lysander Spooner being among the most prominent—and later embraced by thought-leaders within the Republican Party.[4] This *paramount national citizenship* held that (1) those born or naturalized in the United States were citizens of the United States first and of their own states second;[5] (2) a bundle of civil rights—both substantive rights and equality rights—attached to that shared national citizenship;[6] and (3) the federal government had a constitutional responsibility to ensure that those rights were secured.[7]

Those who supported paramount national citizenship associated it with a number of clauses in the antebellum Constitution. In particular, they focused on the Preamble,[8] the Guarantee Clause,[9] the Privileges and Immunities Clause,[10] and the Fifth Amendment's Due Process of Law Clause.[11] This group maintained that all or some of these clauses empowered the federal government under the antebellum Constitution to secure the natural and civil rights of enslaved Blacks and their abolitionist supporters, as well as the rights of free Blacks who risked imprisonment merely traveling to Southern states.

But the proposition that, even before 1868, the federal government had the power to act against slavery and Southern efforts to entrench it within the original states (as distinct from the territories and the District of Columbia) was not widely accepted by Republicans.[12] Nevertheless, many Republicans did believe that federal citizenship entailed the equal enjoyment of natural rights and civic equality. And they believed as well that federal power ought to be enlarged if necessary to secure civil rights that either protected or gave substance to these natural and equality rights.[13]

The disagreement between these two groups about the scope of federal power should not obscure the consensus that existed about the substance of paramount national citizenship. Although one group claimed that the federal government already had the power to protect citizens of the United States from their own state governments, the other group believed that the Constitution should be amended to give the federal government this power.

For both groups, then, the commitment to paramount national citizenship was common ground. And this commitment provided the spirit of the amendments that were added to the Constitution expressly to empower the federal government. We call this conception of citizenship "Republican citizenship" after the party that adopted and implemented it by revising the text of the Constitution and enacting legislation to enforce it. This nineteenth-century constitutional theory is distinct from the Renaissance concept of "classical republicanism" associated with such figures as Niccolò Machiavelli.[14]

Unlike some abolitionists, most Republicans did not understand Republican citizenship to entail a plenary federal power to legislate with respect to rights that were traditionally left in the charge of the states.[15] But they did understand Republican citizenship to be incompatible with the concept of "state sovereignty." That is, Republicans rejected the claims that states were the primary source of citizenship and that states enjoyed the same "supreme, irresistible, absolute, uncontrolled authority"[16] over their citizens that Sir William Blackstone had attributed to Parliament.[17] After Appomattox, both by statute and by written amendments to the Constitution, Republicans sought to realize a federalism-sensitive paramount national citizenship by equipping federal courts and Congress to ensure that states no longer acted as if they were sovereign in this sense.

We have described how Republican citizenship rested on political-philosophical premises that were drawn from eighteenth-century natural-rights thought. To be a citizen of the United States was to be a citizen of a government that defined itself by its commitments to natural rights—commitments that Republicans found in the writings of John Locke, Samuel Pufendorf, Emmerich de Vattel, Jean-Jacques Burlamaqui, the Framers of the 1788 Constitution, and, especially, the Declaration of Independence.[18]

There was more to Republican citizenship, however, than natural rights. There was also civic equality. Civic equality was understood as equality between citizens in respect of their treatment by, and access to, public institutions. The concept of public institutions included what we would today consider to be nonstate institutions that served the general public, such as railroads, theaters, inns, and the like. This is a key point.

Republican complaints about the discriminatory treatment of Black citizens by such public institutions, whether or not they were actually owned and operated by a state, culminated in the enactment of the Civil Rights Act of 1875. It would take considerable imagination to justify such legislation on the basis of a concept of citizenship that embraced *only* natural rights. And yet Republicans did contend that citizenship entailed the enjoyment of freedom from discrimination by the above actors.

We need to be careful here. It is anachronistic to project backward our understanding of what qualifies as a state actor into the late nineteenth century. A central premise on which Republican arguments for the Civil Rights Act of 1875 rested was that the listed institutions were, in an important sense, state actors. Some of these institutions were chartered by states and exercised powers that had traditionally been exercised by states—such as the power of eminent domain.[19] Others were licensed by states to serve the general public.[20] Still, the connection between discrimination by such institutions and violations of natural rights seems very attenuated. Something else appears to have been going on in Republican thought.

In his dissent in the *Civil Rights Cases,* Justice John Marshall Harlan articulated "the *substance and spirit* of the recent amendments of the Constitution," which is akin to the distinction we have drawn between the letter and spirit of the text.[21] For Harlan, that spirit included a civic-equality component of Republican citizenship that is critical to understanding the concept. Justice Harlan contended that the right to nondiscrimination with respect to public accommodations was a civil right that was entrenched in the common law. As Harlan put it, it was among "those [rights] which are fundamental to citizenship in a free government."[22]

What made this right so fundamental? And what made these government and nongovernment institutions "public"? Justice Harlan explained that institutions providing public accommodations owe their existence to the public and are given special privileges by the public. As a result, these institutions are charged with certain duties and responsibilities to the public. The next step in his argument, then, was crucial: "[T]he colored race is part of that public."[23] Therefore, to arbitrarily deny Black citizens access to public accommodations was effectively to diminish their citizenship by "brand[ing] [them] as . . . inferior and infected."[24]

To be sure, Republican citizenship maintains the distinction between civil rights and what were called "social rights." In a speech criticizing the majority opinion in the *Civil Rights Cases* and praising Harlan's dissent, Frederick Douglass asserted that to deny "social equality"—a reciprocal recognition of equal status between individuals—was not to deny "civil equality."[25] By "civil equality," he meant equality between citizens under the laws through which public institutions were established and maintained.

Neither Douglass nor Harlan contended that the Fourteenth Amendment empowered Congress to enact laws requiring that individual citizens perceive other individual citizens as their moral or intellectual equals or welcome them into their social circles. For example, while prohibiting discrimination by inns, the Civil Rights Act of 1875 exempted boarding houses,[26] where citizens boarded others in their own homes. But Republican citizenship required equal treatment under the law—including the law governing access to institutions that were considered to be public in nature.

This can be confusing if one is operating with two categories in mind: public and private, which correspond to state and nonstate, or governmental and nongovernmental. One way to dispel the confusion is to acknowledge that there are not just these two categories or realms but three: call them (1) public/governmental; (2) public/nongovernmental; and (3) private/nongovernmental. Only in the latter sphere are people constitutionally free to arbitrarily discriminate.

Even after the "civil-rights revolution," we today acknowledge that a legislature cannot tell you whom to date, whom to marry, whom to invite to dinner, or with whom to watch the game in your living room. In this realm, morally objectionable and hurtful discrimination is legally permissible—even constitutionally protected. It is this conception of "private," not the right of freedom of speech, that lies behind such "privacy" cases as *Stanley v. Georgia*[27] or the concept of "freedom of intimate association."[28]

This is not to say that these three categories carve social reality at the joints or that borderline cases pose no challenge. Nor are we claiming that Republicans in 1868 explicated these categories as we have. This is merely our attempt at clarifying that, for Republicans, the public–private distinction may not have mapped neatly on a binary distinction between state and nonstate actors.

Further, it may be that nonstate or "private" actors in the middle category who own and operate public facilities retain some discretion to discriminate that state institutions lack. "No shirt, no shoes, no service" is an acceptable policy, while "no dogs or Jews allowed" is not. Barring "arbitrary" discrimination is not the same as barring any and all discrimination.

This middle category shares attributes of both state and purely private institutions. Treating such privately owned and operated public institutions as though they were state institutions might be as mistaken as treating them as purely private. After all, the point of acknowledging three categories rather than two is to recognize that the middle one is not the same as the other two and may be subject to different obligations. At any rate, in trying to capture the concept of Republican citizenship that animated the Privileges or Immunities Clause, descriptive accuracy requires the recognition that equal citizenship included the privilege of reasonable access to privately owned and operated institutions serving the general public.

In addition, Republican citizenship did not entail equality in all respects between citizens and noncitizens. To be sure, Republicans believed that every *person* was a bearer of natural rights and equally entitled to a baseline of legal protection by the government of those natural rights. But citizenship had its constitutional privileges. Republicans saw no contradiction in reserving to citizens an additional bundle of state-created goods—goods that were not required to secure anyone's natural rights.[29]

This is the best way to explain the distinction drawn in Section 1 between the beneficiaries of the Privileges or Immunities Clause, on the one hand, and those of the Due Process of Law and Equal Protection of the Laws

Clauses, on the other. The latter two clauses provide a baseline of legal protection to all natural-rights-bearing "person[s]." In addition to these protections of negative liberties—freedoms *from* the state—the former clause also secures citizens of a natural-rights-centered republic in the enjoyment of state-*created* goods, the precise content of which is a function of a stable national consensus. Once a good becomes closely enough associated with US citizenship in virtue of such a national consensus, it becomes a privilege or immunity of US citizenship.

How broad, how entrenched must a consensus be before a right becomes a privilege or immunity? How do we determine whether such a consensus exists? Viewing the text through the lens of Republican citizenship provides decision-makers with the tools to discern whether states have denied people the kinds of goods that the clause was designed to secure. By the same token, Congress might—under the pretext of counteracting abridgments of citizenship rights—take actions that have no connection to the kind of citizenship that the clause was designed to constitute. Such a law would not be "appropriate" under Section 5 of the amendment.

A sound understanding of Republican citizenship can equip decision-makers to implement the Privileges or Immunities Clause in good faith themselves and ensure that those actors—whether state or nonstate—whom they are charged with monitoring do so as well.

Implementing Republican Citizenship

Unlike scholars, time-pressed, boundedly rational public officials cannot afford to engage in extensive historical and linguistic inquiries. Even if they could, they would still confront constitutional text that does not compel them to take one, and only one, course of action. Underdeterminacy is part of constitutional reality. Accordingly, they need a set of doctrinal tools that economize on time and cognitive effort and simplify constitutional decision-making. Such constitutional heuristics are the stuff of which constitutional doctrine is made. What doctrines best enable decision-makers to implement the Privileges or Immunities Clause in a manner that is faithful to its letter and spirit?

As we will explain in Part II, we reject the view of those who, like Justice Clarence Thomas, contend that the Due Process of Law Clause imposes no limits on the content or substance of legislation.[30] But we share with Justice Thomas the view that the business of identifying "fundamental" or substantive rights of citizens that states are obliged to respect should be performed under the Privileges or Immunities Clause. This can be confusing. Carefully distinguishing between the work done by the Privileges or Immunities Clause and the Due Process of Law Clause can help, which requires us to preview what is forthcoming.

As we will show in Part II, the "due process of law" includes a guarantee of a judicial *process* in which the *substance* of legislation is evaluated to ensure that it is within the proper power of the legislature to enact. As we have shown in Part I, a legislative act is improper if it abridges the substantive rights to which the Privileges or Immunities Clause refers. Put another way, the Privileges or Immunities Clause provides a restriction on state legislative power—"no state shall make or enforce any law"—based on the *substantive rights*, "privileges or immunities" enjoyed by all citizens. In contrast, the Due Process of Law Clause provides a procedure in which the *substance of legislation* is evaluated by the judiciary to ensure that a statute has not violated these privileges or immunities.[31]

The modern concept of "substantive due process" confusingly collapses these two substantive inquiries: (a) the judicial identification of substantive rights and (b) the judicial evaluation of the substance of legislation. We think that the original meaning of the Privileges or Immunities Clause authorizes and constrains the former and that the original meaning of the Due Process of Law Clause authorizes and constrains the latter.

At present, however, the Supreme Court identifies substantive rights under the rubric of the Due Process of Law Clause. To identify these fundamental rights, the Court generally—although not exclusively—relies on a two-pronged heuristic described in the "right to die" case of *Washington v. Glucksberg*[32]: a substantive right will be deemed fundamental only if it is found by the Court to be "deeply rooted in this Nation's history and tradition"[33] and given a "careful description."[34]

Considering how harshly one of us has criticized this "*Glucksberg* two-step,"[35] it may surprise some to learn that our proposed approach to identifying the unenumerated privileges and immunities of US citizenship closely resembles *Glucksberg*. Like *Glucksberg*, it is tethered to history and tradition. Like *Glucksberg*, it seeks to avoid abuses of the judicial power by constraining judicial discretion when identifying fundamental rights.

But our approach differs in important details. In the balance of this chapter we offer guidance to the judiciary and to legislatures in how to identify the "privileges or immunities" of US citizens that "no state shall abridge." The type of judicial process that is needed to protect these rights from being abridged will then be covered in Part II, when we consider the original meaning of "the due process of law."

Judicial Construction of Privileges or Immunities in Section 1

In the 2006 case of *Heller v. District of Columbia,* the Supreme Court held that the Second Amendment protected an individual right, including the individual right to own a handgun. Because the Second Amendment applies directly to the federal government and its creature, the capital district, the *Heller* decision rested on the original meaning of that amendment.

In the 2008 case of *McDonald v. City of Chicago,* Otis McDonald, a citizen of Chicago, challenged the city's ban on the private possession of handguns. Because the city of Chicago is a state entity, the Second Amendment does not directly apply to it. Accordingly, McDonald based his challenge on the Fourteenth Amendment, which restricts the powers of states.

McDonald claimed that the Chicago gun ban was unconstitutional under both modern substantive due process doctrine and the original meaning of the Privileges or Immunities Clause. Oral argument centered primarily on the latter theory, however, with every justice except Justice Thomas expressing skepticism about the feasibility of such an approach. In particular, they were concerned about how to identify the privileges or immunities of citizens.

At one point during oral argument in *McDonald,* Justice Antonin Scalia pressed McDonald's attorney, Alan Gura, to provide a test to identify fundamental rights under the Privileges or Immunities Clause. Justice Scalia playfully but revealingly queried: "Well, what about rights rooted in the traditions and conscience of our people? Would—would that do the job?" Here Justice Scalia was invoking the approach he previously described in his plurality opinion in *Michael H. v. Gerald D.*[36]—the approach that was then adopted by Chief Justice William Rehnquist in his majority opinion in *Glucksberg.*[37]

The *Glucksberg* two-step has been criticized—including by one of us—as too malleable and coarse-grained. As to malleability, in a highly influential critique of Justice Scalia's plurality opinion in *Michael H. v. Gerald D.,*[38] Professors Michael Dorf and Laurence Tribe observed that "historical traditions, like rights themselves, exist at various levels of generality."[39] For example, did the Establishment Clause embody the "deeply rooted tradition of separation of church and state," and how would one tell?[40]

To decide *Glucksberg*'s first step, does one look to the positive law of the states, some of which provided for religious establishments as late as 1833?[41] Or does one look instead to the Enlightenment ideals expressed in, say, Virginia's Bill for Religious Freedom, supported by James Madison and Thomas Jefferson and considered by both men to be among their greatest accomplishments?[42] Does one discount the latter ideals because "the primary political impetus behind the act's passage was a spirit of religious fervor, not enlightened ecumenicalism"?[43] Or does one discount the former because positive law may reflect patterns of unconstitutional behavior that have become entrenched owing to factional influences or lack of reflection?

There appears to be room for judges to conclude, in good faith, either in favor of or against the existence of such a tradition. And this difficulty is compounded by the need to ask whether the history and tradition between the Founding and 1868 had changed the public meaning of the concepts employed in the first eight amendments.

As to coarseness, what, specifically, does it take to make a tradition "deeply rooted"? Suppose that we look to positive law to define the relevant tradition about the right to use marijuana for medicinal purposes. Does one look to the positive law from the Founding until the mid-twentieth century, during which time marijuana use was entirely unregulated?[44] Or does one consult the positive law between Congress's enactment of the Comprehensive Drug Abuse Prevention and Control Act of 1970 and California's enactment of the Compassionate Use Act of 1996, during which time marijuana use was generally proscribed?[45]

Glucksberg's second step presents similar problems. In her challenge to the Controlled Substances Act, Angel Raich contended that the federal government had violated the Fifth Amendment's Due Process of Law Clause by infringing her fundamental right to preserve her life. Using marijuana ameliorated the life-threatening wasting syndrome from which she suffered as no other medication could. Surely the right to preserve one's life is deeply rooted in our history and tradition. Yet the Circuit Court of Appeals for the Ninth Circuit rejected her formulation of the right. The proper definition, it said, was a right to preserve one's life *by using medical marijuana*. This right, they then held, was not yet deeply rooted in our tradition and history.

Or consider what might appear to be an "easy" case for proponents of *Glucksberg* who regard it as a way to prevent "judicial activism" via substantive due process: abortion. Does "carefully describing" the right at issue entail describing it at a low level of generality—the right to choose to terminate a pregnancy within the first trimester? Or does it entail describing it at a high level of generality—the right to bodily integrity, which includes the right to prevent an unwanted physical invasion? The deep-rootedness of the latter right is easy to establish;[46] the deep-rootedness of the former right is considerably more difficult, particularly if one assigns weight to the positive law of the states circa 1868.[47]

Finally, and perhaps surprisingly, the *Glucksberg* approach does not treat *any* set of rights as having been locked in at the point of the Fourteenth Amendment's ratification. There remain individual-rights guarantees that are specified in the text of the Constitution and the text of the Civil Rights Act of 1866 that have yet to be held enforceable against the states. That result is not consistent with the evidence that we have canvassed above, which shows that the public meaning of the amendment provided a floor of rights protection below which states could not go. In this respect, the *Glucksberg* approach runs afoul of the letter of the Constitution and is, for this reason, an inadmissible construction.

Critiques of *Glucksberg* as too malleable and coarse-grained have force but could be addressed by giving more specificity to its two prongs. The breadth of the requisite consensus; the length of time it must be maintained; the evidentiary sources to be sifted in search of consensus—all of these could be detailed. "Carefully" could be considered synonymous with "accurately." A plaintiff could be made responsible for articulating the claimed right, the court for accurately determining the right's properties on the basis of the parties' arguments and investigating whether a right with those properties is sufficiently deeply rooted.

Glucksberg's treatment of enumeration as insufficient to find a right to be fundamental is, however, beyond saving. It goes so far as to empower judges to disregard rights considered fundamental enough to include in the text of the Constitution. And it is inconsistent with the evidence of original meaning of the letter of the clause that we have canvassed.

The approach we recommend is based on the premise that "the privileges or immunities of citizens of the United States" is a set of rights that preexists the interpretation and application of the clause by a judge. We maintain that, in 1868, a preexisting set of privileges or immunities was locked into the Constitution by the original meaning of the Fourteenth Amendment. These rights are beyond the power of the judiciary to repeal. The challenge confronting judges is to discover these rights, not to rely on their own normative commitments to create them.

But additional fundamental rights may also have become privileges or immunities of citizens since then. Although such a right may have become a privilege of citizenship after 1868, it must still preexist the decision of a court that *finds* it to be fundamental. So, to identify what "privileges or immunities" are today, a judge must have a way to identify these preexisting fundamental rights as well. It is here that something like *Glucksburg* has a role to play.

With this in mind, we find four distinct sources on which judges and other decision-makers can draw to identify or "find" those preexisting rights that are fundamental and, therefore, privileges or immunities of US citizenship. Each of these sources is similar to those invoked by Republicans when identifying privileges or immunities.

Our goal in identifying these sources resembles that of the Court in *Glucksberg:* to identify a judicially administrable method for identifying preexisting fundamental rights that the Fourteenth Amendment rendered enforceable against the states in a way that does not unduly empower judges to interfere with state legislative powers. Once identified, how exactly these rights are to be protected by judges is a separate subject that we will cover in Part II, when considering the requirement of "the due process of law."

To avoid confusion and mistake, it is vitally important to resist collapsing the issue of judicial *identification* into the issue of judicial *enforcement*. The former is a Privileges or Immunities Clause question; the latter is a Due Process of Law Clause question. Accordingly, in this chapter, we consider only the former.

The four sources for judges to consult when identifying fundamental rights are:

1. *Constitutional enumeration circa 1868.* If a right was enumerated in the text of the federal Constitution in 1868, and individual citizens were in 1868 entitled to enjoy that right, it is a privilege of US citizenship. Such rights were privileges or immunities at the time of ratification, were protected by the clause in 1868, and cannot be eroded by later history and tradition. In short, they were locked in by the original meaning of the text in 1868.

2. *Enumeration in the Civil Rights Act of 1866.* The rights listed in the Civil Rights Act of 1866 are also privileges of US citizenship. Such rights were privileges or immunities at the time of ratification, were protected by the clause in 1868, and cannot be eroded by later

history and tradition. In short, they were locked in by the original meaning of the text in 1868.

3. *Later enumeration.* If an enumerated right was added to the federal Constitution after 1868, and individual citizens are today entitled to enjoy that right, it is presumptively a privilege of US citizenship. That presumption can be defeated by a showing that enforcing the right at issue would violate a right that falls within categories 1 or 2, unless the subsequent amendment expressly qualified the Fourteenth.

4. *Other unenumerated rights.* The privileges or immunities of national citizenship include those unenumerated rights that, when accurately described, are found to be deeply rooted in the nation's history and traditions. Provisionally, we suggest that if individual citizens have for at least a generation—that is, thirty years or more—been entitled to enjoy a right as a consequence of the constitutional, statutory, or common law of a supermajority of the states, it is presumptively a privilege of US citizenship. That presumption can be defeated if it is shown that enforcing the right at issue would necessarily violate a right that falls within category 1, 2, or 3. But this generational approach is a matter of construction and is not compelled by original meaning. If it proves unworkable, we are prepared to discard it.

Let us now consider each of these sources in greater depth to see why exactly judges are warranted in consulting them.

Categories 1 and 2 follow directly from the original meaning of the Privileges or Immunities Clause. These categories enjoy the virtue of straightforwardness. Rights that fall within them were "locked in" as a matter of positive law in 1868, whether current constitutional actors like it or not. They were and remain privileges or immunities of citizens of the United States, until repealed by a subsequent amendment.

Category 1 corresponds to the modern doctrine by which the rights of the first eight amendments are "incorporated" through the Due Process of Law Clause. We think that is the wrong clause to rely on for the identification of fundamental rights; but textually enumerated rights are a proper source of privileges or immunities of citizens. Such rights are not enforceable as fundamental because they were enumerated; such rights were enumerated because they were fundamental. Put another way, enumeration in the text of the Constitution is compelling evidence of fundamentality that judges can treat as dispositive.

What about category 2? Just as category 1 is as determinate as the constitutional amendments that courts have felt comfortable enforcing for well over a century, so category 2 is as determinate as statutes that courts have been enforcing forever. Therefore, if judges are competent to enforce express constitutional and statutory rights, then they are competent to enforce these categories of privileges or immunities of US citizens against the states.

Categories 3 and 4 require some further explanation. Like *Glucksberg*, categories 3 and 4 are fodder for the construction zone. Unlike categories 1 and 2 they do not refer to rights that were "locked in" at the time the Privileges or Immunities Clause was enacted. But unless that set was considered at the time to be closed, the recognition of rights that have become fundamental since 1868 is not inconsistent with the original meaning of the text. We believe that consulting both sources of rights is faithful to the vision of Republican citizenship, which recognizes that the fundamental guarantees of citizenship can develop through law.

The text of the Privileges or Immunities Clause was clearly designed to "lock in" or fix some set of fundamental rights. Even Justice Samuel Miller in *Slaughter-House* conceded as much. But the enacted text does not expressly affirm the privileges or immunities it protects to be a closed set. Nor does the text specifically list freedom of speech, freedom from unreasonable searches and seizures, and so on, which might support an inference that unlisted rights are excluded.

We think the method of identifying privileges and immunities employed by Justice Bushrod Washington in *Corfield v. Coryell* reflects the fact that this set of privileges is not closed. Recall that Washington's method has three criteria of "privileges and immunities":

> We feel no hesitation in confining these expressions to those privileges and immunities [1] which are, in their nature, fundamental; [2] which belong, of right, to the citizens of all free governments; and [3] which have, at all times, been enjoyed by the citizens of the several States which compose this Union.[48]

As is to be expected and desired, these three criteria overlap and reinforce each other.

PRIVILEGES AND IMMUNITIES WHICH ARE, IN THEIR NATURE, FUNDAMENTAL   This criterion calls for a normative assessment that a right is, by its nature, fundamental. This criterion would include natural rights. Take, for example, the natural right of a parent to raise her own child.[49] But such rights need not be natural to be "in their nature" fundamental. A right is also in its nature fundamental if, as Madison described some of the rights he proposed be added by amendment, it "is as essential to secure the liberty of the people as any one of the pre-existent rights of nature."[50] In this category, Madison included the right to a jury trial.[51]

PRIVILEGES AND IMMUNITIES WHICH BELONG, OF RIGHT, TO THE CITIZENS OF ALL FREE GOVERNMENTS   This criterion calls for a normative assessment that such a right is a civil right to which a citizen is entitled from his or her government. There are two ways that this criterion can be satisfied. First, a civil right may be one that citizens are entitled to enjoy under all free governments because of the right's tight, time-tested connection to natural rights. In this category of civil rights, we would include all the rights identified in the Civil Rights Act of 1866, such as

> the right to make and enforce contracts, to sue, be parties, and give evidence, to inherit, purchase, lease, sell, hold, and convey real and personal property, and to full and equal benefit of all laws and proceedings for the security of person and property, and shall be subject to like punishment, pains, and penalties, and to none other, any law, statute, ordinance, regulation, or custom, to the contract, notwithstanding.[52]

Of these rights, those that might appear to be purely natural rights also have civil components. There is a natural right to acquire property, but also an enforceable civil right to "to inherit, purchase, lease, sell, hold, and convey" that property in a government-supplied legal system. Some of these rights, such as the right "to sue, be parties, and give evidence," are not rights one possesses in the state of nature at all. But, again to use Madison's felicitous formulation, each of these is "a right resulting from a social compact which regulates the action of the community" and "is as essential to secure the liberty of the people as any one of the pre-existent rights of nature."[53]

Second, a civil right may be one that citizens are believed entitled to enjoy in virtue of their citizenship, irrespective of any connection to natural rights. A paradigmatic example of this kind of civil right is the right to access public accommodations, about which Republicans expressed no doubt even as they differed concerning its scope. Absent a monopoly, it cannot be said that a denial of access to, say, a hotel or restaurant, would deprive someone of life, liberty, or property, understood in natural-rights terms. And yet Republicans agreed that such a civil right to access such institutions did exist because it had long been entrenched in the law of the states.

PRIVILEGES AND IMMUNITIES WHICH HAVE, AT ALL TIMES, BEEN EN-JOYED BY THE CITIZENS OF THE SEVERAL STATES WHICH COMPOSE THIS UNION   This criterion operates as a positive-law constraint on the normative assessments of the previous two: such a right shall "have, at all times, *been enjoyed* by the citizens of the several States which compose this Union." This is a requirement that such a fundamental right must not only be a good idea (in the opinion, say, of a judge or of Congress) or only be the object of a current consensus; it must also have become legally *entrenched*. Justice Washington here is articulating the traditional approach to the common law that was later ridiculed by realists and ultimately neglected and forgotten by generations of lawyers and judges: that a judge is to discover and not make law.

A right is not a privilege or immunity of citizenship just because the Supreme Court says so. In the famous and often misunderstood words of John Marshall in *Marbury v. Madison*, "It is emphatically the province and duty of the Judicial Department to say what the law *is*." Whereas modern readers reflexively take this to mean that judicial decisions are constitutive of the law, Marshall is here merely saying judges can declare what the preexisting law is already.

Likewise, Marshall's injunction in *McCulloch v. Maryland* that "should Congress, under the pretext of executing its powers, pass laws for the accomplishment of objects not intrusted to the Government, it would become the painful duty of this tribunal . . . to say that such an act *was not* the law of the land" is also an appeal to preexisting law.[54] As we will stress when discussing the "due process of law" in Part II, Marshall here draws a distinction between a mere *act* of a legislature and a binding *law*.

The reason why a court is empowered to say that a legislative act is not "the law of the land" is because such an act may conflict with the prior and higher law of the Constitution. As Marshall explained in *Marbury*, "If courts are to regard the constitution, and the constitution is superior to any ordinary *act* of the legislature, the constitution, and not such ordinary *act*, must govern the case to which they both apply."[55]

We rehearse all this here because it illuminates the positive-law constraint imposed on the judiciary by Justice Washington's third criterion in *Corfield:* that to be a privilege and immunity of citizenship, such a right must "have, at all times, *been enjoyed* by the citizens of the several States which compose this Union." "At all times" ought not be taken literally, however. We have not encountered any antebellum commentators or leading Republicans who made a concerted effort to determine whether a purported privilege or immunity had always, universally been enjoyed by American citizens.

What is clear is that a judicially cognizable "privilege or immunity" must have been longstanding and widespread, enjoyed by citizens of the United States as a matter of the positive law of the states or of the nation. Neither judges, nor Congress for that matter, are empowered to decide that a particular right is "of its nature fundamental" and "belong[s], of right, to the citizens of all free governments," and then impose their opinion on the people. Judges may only enforce as fundamental those rights that have already been recognized as fundamental by prior positive law.

The Fourteenth Amendment was designed to protect those privileges or immunities of citizens that were widespread and entrenched in 1868, and also those that might later come to be widespread and entrenched. It provides a floor but not a ceiling on the protection of entrenched rights. We read Justice Washington's third criterion as imposing a constraint on judges to enforce only those rights that they deem to be in their nature fundamental if such rights have previously been widely recognized in law over an extended period of time. A judicial finding that a particular right is already entrenched as a privilege of national citizenship does not require it to have always been so entrenched. A criterion of widespread entrenchment in the preexisting law does not require that they *always, universally* have been recognized in law.

With all this in mind, let us now consider sources 3 and 4 from which to identify a fundamental right meriting judicial protection.

> 3. *Later enumeration.* If an enumerated right was added to the federal Constitution after 1868, and individual citizens are today entitled to enjoy that right, it is *presumptively* a privilege of US citizenship. That presumption can be defeated if it can be shown that enforcing the right at issue would necessarily violate a right that falls within category 1 or 2, unless the subsequent amendment *expressly* qualified the Fourteenth.

This is the first of two ways by which a right can become an enforceable privilege or immunity of citizenship even if it was not so regarded in 1868. If such a right is expressly recognized by a later constitutional amendment—having survived the onerous super-majoritarian amendment process—it will presumptively be considered a privilege or immunity of citizenship. As such, it would be enforceable by the courts and by Congress against the states under the Fourteenth Amendment.

Like the Thirteenth and Fourteenth Amendments, later amendments have long contained an express clause giving Congress the power of enforcement. Such a clause is useful to show that the enumerated powers of Congress have been enlarged. But the rights that are subsequently added to the Constitution are, without any enforcement clause, available to the courts to enforce via the Privileges or Immunities Clause combined with the Due Process of Law Clause of the Fourteenth Amendment.

A right that falls into this category is the right to vote. While more than a few dissenters existed, we have seen that the overwhelming consensus, both before and immediately after the adoption of the Fourteenth Amendment, was that the right to vote was *not* a privilege of citizenship. But this does not mean that it could never become one. That process was begun with the enactment of Section 2 of the Fourteenth Amendment, which penalized states for failing to protect the equal rights of males to vote. It was then further entrenched by the Fifteenth Amendment, which extended the protection of this right to male citizens.

Because both Section 2 of the Fourteenth Amendment and the Fifteenth Amendment expressly limited the protection of the right to vote to male citizens, we do not believe these two amendments established it as a fundamental right of all citizens. These were, however, important steps along the way. We think it was the Nineteenth Amendment that finally accomplished this. Since 1920, the right to vote has been a fundamental privilege or immunity "enjoyed" by all major citizens of the United States who have not been dispossessed of their right by a judicial adjudication of either wrongdoing or mental incapacity. We know this because we can read the text of the Constitution.

The privilege was bolstered by the Twenty-Fourth Amendment barring poll taxes. It was then further expanded by the Twenty-Sixth Amendment even to some Americans citizens who are deemed to be minors by their states. But, consistent with the Privileges or Immunities Clause, all these amendments limited the privilege of the franchise to citizens. They did not extend the right to everyone.

This source of privileges or immunities also informs us how to handle the evidence that the right to vote was not, in 1868, considered among the privileges or immunities of citizens. For a variety of reasons already mentioned, we think this is indeed a limitation on the original meaning of Section 1 in 1868. Section 1 did not, and still does not, protect "political rights," which can be thought of as a catch-all category embracing all state-created goods that are not understood to belong, of right, to the citizens of all free governments.

But our third source acknowledges that a particular right can move from the set of political rights to the set of civil rights. The categories remain. But this source tells us that the right to vote later came to be understood as a civil right of paramount national citizenship, which no state shall abridge; it was no longer a political right that could be supplied or denied at a state's discretion. That understanding was embodied in the Nineteenth Amendment—and was further reinforced by the Twenty-Fourth and Twenty-Sixth Amendments. Other rights can be added in the same manner.

What about our qualification that such a newly enumerated right is presumptive and that the "presumption can be defeated if it is shown that enforcing the right at issue would necessarily violate a right that falls within category 1 or 2, unless the subsequent amendment expressly qualified the Fourteenth"? This qualification is intended merely as a bar on a claim that a right that was protected by the Fourteenth Amendment in 1868 was *implicitly* qualified or repealed by later amendment. We do not deny that such a right can be qualified or even repealed by later constitutional amendment. We claim only that such a repeal must be expressed by a "clear statement" putting everyone on notice that repeal is to be the effect of subsequent enumeration. Such repeal should not happen on the sly.

We do not see how a subsequently enumerated right to vote has any effect whatsoever on the other privileges or immunities of citizens that existed in 1868. So we do not think that the Nineteenth Amendment needed to expressly qualify the Fourteenth to add a new privilege of national citizenship enforceable against the states. Suppose, however, that the states had ratified the Equal Rights Amendment (ERA), which stated that "[e]quality of rights under the law shall not be denied or abridged by the United States or by any State on account of sex."[56]

As with the right to vote, we do not think that this amendment necessarily conflicts in any way with the rights that are identified as fundamental via routes 1 and 2. Still, had it been ratified, we can imagine some people subsequently contending that a later-adopted "equality" right of this sort implicitly qualified or overrode the protection of the rights, say, "to make and enforce contracts, . . . to inherit, purchase, lease, sell, hold, and convey real and personal property." Because the ERA lacked any express repeal of, or limitation on, the Fourteenth Amendment, however, our qualification of route 3 requires that such an Equal Rights Amendment be equitably construed or applied in a manner that is consistent with the rights that were locked in by the Privileges or Immunities Clause.

Of course, Article V does not specify any limitations on the content or substance of constitutional amendments that make their way through the requisite super-majoritarian veto-gates. Does this mean that judges implementing the Privileges or Immunities Clause should automatically accept that a subsequent amendment extending an individual right to citizens adds a privilege of national citizenship rather than merely presuming it?

This suggestion conflates two different issues: whether the amendment is a part of the Constitution, and how it should interact with other amendments that might be designed to serve very different functions. We do not doubt that the letter of the Privileges or Immunities Clause can be repealed entirely by a subsequent amendment tailored to that end; so too can any construction aimed at implementing it. But a subsequently enacted amendment should not affect the construction of a previously enacted amendment absent affirmative evidence that it was designed to have that effect.

Finally, these three categories of privileges or immunities are clearly not subject to the "levels of generality" issue that plagues the identification of unenumerated fundamental rights under *Glucksberg*. All of these rights have been expressly stated. They are to be protected at the level of generality in which they were expressed. To the degree that identifying the level of generality of a fundamental right is a problem, the first three categories of our construction avoid it. So too, we think, does the fourth.

4. *Other unenumerated rights.* The privileges or immunities of national citizenship include those unenumerated rights that, when accurately described, are found to be deeply rooted in the nation's history and traditions. Provisionally, we suggest that if individual citizens have for at least a generation—that is, thirty years or more—been entitled to enjoy a right as a consequence of the constitutional, statutory, or common law of a supermajority of the

states, it is presumptively a privilege of US citizenship. That presumption can be defeated if it is shown that enforcing the right at issue would necessarily violate a right that falls within category 1, 2, or 3. But this generational approach is a matter of construction and is not compelled by original meaning. If it proves unworkable, we are prepared to discard it.

Our approach would allow for the recognition of unenumerated fundamental rights unheard of in 1868—but it would not make that recognition cheap. First, and foremost, such a right must be recognized in preexisting law, but not only that. We also insist on a broad state consensus. A broad state consensus will ensure respect for federalism, lest the idiosyncrasies of one state be constitutionalized. The waiting period will yield valuable information about whether these rights will work in practice to promote Republican citizenship.

We are not the first to endorse the recognition of preexisting unenumerated rights by identifying a stable national consensus. Shortly after *Glucksberg* was decided, Michael McConnell endorsed its deeply rooted reasoning on similar grounds. His succinct account is worth quoting at length.

[The Privileges or Immunities and Due Process of Law] [C]lauses . . . have two common features. First, they take their bearings from the long established rights and procedures of the American states. They are, accordingly, preservative rather than transformative. They are guarantees against unwarranted and unwise innovation; they are not invitations to judicially-mandated social change. This does not mean that the rights protected by these clauses are frozen in time. They may change as society changes. But before a claim may be accepted as a Fourteenth Amendment right, and imposed on the people of all the states, it must have attained widespread support, and been confirmed by experience. The Fourteenth Amendment is not a license for judicial social experimentation. . . .

Prior to the Fourteenth Amendment, the states were the principal locus of rights protection. Accordingly, the privileges and immunities of Americans were described in Article IV as "Privileges and Immunities of Citizens in the several States." In the Fourteenth Amendment, these rights became known as "privileges or immunities of citizens of the United States." They had become national in character. Moreover, under the new Amendment the power of the United States was deployed to prevent any state from abridging these rights, even as to its own citizens. . . .

The traditionalist interpretation, embraced by the Court in *Glucksberg*, is consistent with this understanding because it allows diversity among state law rights when there exists no stable national consensus, and requires uniformity with respect to rights after a national consensus has emerged and persisted. . . . [57]

So far as we know, we *are* the first to endorse a thirty-year threshold as a rule for identifying deeply rooted fundamental rights. And whereas *Glucksberg* applies to all purported citizenship rights, we insist on deep roots only in considering purported citizenship rights that have not been textually unenumerated. Contrary to current "substantive due process" doctrine,[58] the criterion of "deeply rooted in our nation's tradition and history" does not apply to the rights enumerated in category 1, 2, or 3.

Finally, we think the level-of-generality problem is mitigated by specifying that courts must look to thirty years of positive state law to identify an unenumerated fundamental right that is deeply rooted. This body of law should define the level of generality at which an existing right has been recognized. Whatever uncertainty about levels of generality remains, however, is confined to this category. It does not extend to category 1, 2, or 3.

We urge those who regard the thirty-year threshold in category 4 as too arbitrary—why not thirty-five years, or sixty years?—not to consider it a deal breaker; we certainly do not. Even without this category, all the enumerated rights in the first three categories are "in" as a matter of original meaning, irrespective of deep-rootedness. If the courts choose only to go that far and no farther, it would be a huge improvement in our constitutional law from the perspective of original meaning.

Equally important, this fourth category should not be identified solely with "new" rights that have become privileges or immunities of citizenship since 1868. It also includes fundamental unenumerated rights that have existed for as long as the memory of men runneth. For example, we would locate in this category the fundamental right of parents to raise their children, a near universally acknowledged though unenumerated right that a majority of the Supreme Court (including Justice Thomas) recognized in *Troxel v. Granville* (over the dissent of Justice Scalia).[59]

The fundamental natural right of parents to raise their own children is a hard case for those who limit judicial protection to rights that are enumerated in the text of the Constitution—or who would limit courts to recognizing our first three categories of fundamental rights. To this we can add many more ancient fundamental natural rights, such as the right to self-defense, or the right to work to provide oneself and one's family with food, clothing, and shelter. Any theory that refuses to recognize unenumerated rights this fundamental as *constitutional* rights solely because they are not enumerated is problematic. After all, the Ninth Amendment commands that "[t]he enumeration in the Constitution of certain rights, *shall* not be construed to deny or disparage others retained by the people."[60]

It is fair to say that all these age-old unenumerated rights were simply *too* fundamental to warrant enumeration in the Constitution. It was on that basis that Representative Theodore Sedgwick objected to including the right of assembly in what became the First Amendment. Representative Egbert Benson defended the proposal on the ground that the "committee who framed this report proceeded on the principle that these rights belonged to the people; they conceived them to be inherent." To this, Sedgwick retorted that

> if the committee were governed by that general principle, they might have gone into a very lengthy enumeration of rights; they might have declared that a man should have a right to wear his hat if he pleased; that he might get up when he pleased, and go to bed when he thought proper.[61]

Category 4 acknowledges that rights such as these are privileges or immunities of citizens because they "are, in their nature, fundamental," they "belong, of right, to the citizens of all free governments," *and* they have long "been enjoyed by the citizens of the several States which compose this Union."

Category 4 is not limited to unenumerated natural rights, however. It also vindicates Justice Harlan's assertion of a common-law duty of nondiscrimination by inns and common carriers. Such a duty was deeply rooted in the common law of the states though denied in the case of African Americans. Implicit in the concept of Republican citizenship is the unenumerated right not to be unfairly treated by public institutions, which are there to protect and serve everyone.

Again, the primary issue from an originalist standpoint is epistemic. How is a judge to know that a particular right that he or she deems especially important is in fact deemed fundamental across the states and across time? That it is a right of US citizenship that may not be abridged by a state? Such a right must be *found*, not created. To make such a finding, that judge must look to preexisting law and find it to be widespread for a lengthy period. Only if it fits that description can a judge "find" it to be a privilege or immunity of US citizenship.

The *Glucksberg* approach, refined as we propose, also makes good practical sense as a decision rule. As McConnell points out, it takes time to determine whether an experiment in rights-creation is misguided.[62] If an outlier state decides to recognize a right, other state legislatures can observe the consequences and debate the costs and benefits of extending it to citizens within their jurisdiction. At the same time, we should not romanticize the kind of deliberation that takes place in state legislatures in connection with rights-experiments.

Furthermore, while there are costs associated with declining to adopt a net-beneficial rights innovation, there are also costs associated with compelling the adoption of a net-detrimental rights innovation. These costs are not symmetrical. The costs of federal judicial error in declining to nationalize a net-beneficial rights innovation are limited to those states that have not independently adopted that beneficial innovation on their own. Any state remains free to adopt it. In contrast, the costs of federal error in compelling a net-detrimental rights innovation will necessarily impose that detriment on every state across the nation. That is, the costs of false privilege-positives at the federal level—erroneous decisions to extend a right to all citizens—are much higher than the cost of false privilege-negatives—erroneous decisions not to extend a right to all citizens, who may still be protected by their states.

Moreover, an erroneous decision by the Supreme Court to compel a net-detrimental right on the entire nation can be rectified only by a change of heart in the justices that overcomes any felt commitment by them to stare decisis. In contrast, a failure of the Supreme Court to impose a net-beneficial right on the nation can be rectified state by state—by the legislature or the courts of each state who decide to join others in protecting the right. If that process proceeds long enough—again, we suggest thirty years—and is entrenched widely enough—again, we suggest in the common law, constitutional law, or statutory law of a supermajority of states—at that point, the Supreme Court or Congress can step in to bring outliers into line. Such a right will have become a privilege of citizens of the United States.

Congressional Construction of Privileges or Immunities under Section 5

Courts are not the only branch of government that must apply or implement the original meaning of the Privileges or Immunities Clause when exercising its powers. Congress too takes an oath to uphold the Constitution. Section 5 of the Fourteenth Amendment expressly empowers Congress "to enforce, by appropriate legislation, the provisions of this article."[63] It follows that Congress cannot enforce rights that are *not* within the letter or the spirit of Section 1 of the Fourteenth Amendment. Suppose that Congress enacts legislation that is purportedly designed to secure a privilege of US citizenship. How should the judiciary treat such a law?

Numerous scholars have observed[64] that the choice of the word "appropriate" appears to have been deliberately made to track Chief Justice John Marshall's language in *McCulloch v. Maryland.*[65] We believe that this argument is basically correct—albeit as a matter of construction, rather than interpretation. *McCulloch* was mentioned several times over the course of the Thirty-Ninth Congress's debate. It was not discussed in any great depth, but legislators did claim that *McCulloch* emphasized congressional discretion in adopting means to legitimate constitutional ends. For instance, Congressman James Wilson invoked *McCulloch* for the proposition that "of the necessity of the measure Congress is the sole judge."[66] And William Lawrence opined that "the degree of necessity is a question of legislative discretion, not of judicial cognizance."[67]

Wilson and Lawrence held an unusually capacious understanding of congressional power, so there is not enough here to support a widely shared understanding that Congress would enjoy plenary power to regulate civil rights in the states. But a presumption of congressional good faith is consistent with Republicans' choice of language and the modified understanding of federalism that appears to have informed that choice.

Matters get tricky when Congress disagrees with the Court about the precise scope of a privilege or immunity protected by Section 1. That's what happened in the wake of *Employment Division v. Smith.*[68] In *Smith*, the Court held that generally applicable laws that were neutral concerning religion did not prohibit the free exercise of religion. Congress responded by enacting the Religious Freedom Restoration Act (RFRA). The text of the act expressed the goal of restoring the pre-*Smith* baseline of applying strict judicial scrutiny to federal and state actions burdening religious exercise.[69]

In *City of Boerne v. Flores*, the Court held that RFRA was unconstitutional as applied to the states. The Court stated that Section 5 does not empower Congress to "attempt a substantive change in constitutional protections" against state action, only to remedy or prevent unconstitutional state behavior.[70] Writing for the majority, Justice Kennedy inferred from the lack of fit between "the means adopted and the legitimate end to be achieved" that

Congress had acted in bad faith—inconsistently with the preventive/remedial function of Section 5.[71]

We agree that, in principle, it is unconstitutional for Congress to redefine the substance of constitutional protections against state action on the pretext of fulfilling a preventive/remedial end. But the Court's claim that the Fourteenth Amendment was designed to leave the judiciary with "primary authority to interpret" the meaning of Section 1 and foreclose "Congress, and not the courts," from "judg[ing] whether or not any of the privileges or immunities were not secured to citizens in the several States" is not sustainable. In 1868, among even moderate Republicans, confidence in the courts was at a low ebb and remained so for some years. John Bingham went so far as to advocate limiting the Court's power to void legislation by requiring a two-thirds majority of the Court to hold an act of Congress unconstitutional. Oliver Morton explained that the "remedy for the violation of the fourteenth and fifteenth amendments was expressly not left to the courts."[72]

To our mind, the Supreme Court's later landmark decisions in the *Slaughter-House Cases, Bradwell v. Illinois,* the *Civil Rights Cases, U.S. v. Cruikshank,* and *Plessy v. Ferguson*—along with cases of lesser visibility—vindicated this Republican skepticism. More generally, congressional debates over civil rights legislation between 1866 and 1875 were sensitive to perceived limits on congressional power. But they were informed by legislators' own understanding of those limits. Such debates often proceeded without reference to decisions of the courts.

How to strike the balance between congressional discretion over privileges-or-immunities enforcement and the Court's duty to say what the law is, is an institutional question that falls squarely within the construction zone. The answer is not dictated by the constitutional text. But it is an institutional question quite familiar to the federal courts. In the context of administrative law, courts have developed doctrine to divide institutional labor between courts and other constitutional decision-makers—namely, executive-branch agencies—so as to enable both sets of institutions to capitalize on their comparative advantages.

Chevron deference to "reasonable" agency decisions about how to implement "ambiguous" statutes is controversial, to say the least.[73] On the one hand, it has been criticized for requiring judges to abdicate their constitutional duty to *independently* interpret the law.[74] On the other hand, it has been defended on the ground that, where it applies, interpretation has "run out"—and, with it, a judge's interpretive duty is exhausted.[75] In such a case, *Chevron*'s defenders contend that, if an agency to which power to implement a statute is delegated via statutory ambiguity convinces a court that it has made use of its institutional resources by showing its work, and its work does not contradict the statutory text, then a judge should defer to the agency.

Michael McConnell and Jack Balkin have both drawn a useful analogy between *Chevron* deference and the appropriate division of labor between courts and Congress in enforcing the Fourteenth Amendment.[76] Just as agencies have institutional advantages over courts to implement underdeterminate federal statutes, Congress has institutional advantages to implement the underdeterminate Privileges or Immunities Clause. Such advantages counsel in favor of deference to the good-faith exercise of Congress's Section 5 enforcement power. In contrast with an ambiguous congressional statute that may or may not have evinced a congressional intent to delegate power to an agency, Section 5 explicitly delegates to Congress a power to implement the Fourteenth Amendment.

As we have stressed, implementation involves construction, rather than interpretation. When it comes to implementation, Congress is generally acknowledged to have fact-finding capabilities that make it better positioned than courts to identify systemic social problems, even if it does not often make effective use of those capabilities. Of greater importance, Congress can and does draft remedial legislation that is broader in scope and more nuanced than judicially created doctrines can be. Such legislation can include penalties and enforcement mechanisms that are well beyond the judicial power. And it can include qualifications and exceptions that courts are simply not empowered to create. We need not confine ourselves here to hypotheticals.

Like the Republicans' Civil Rights Act of 1875, the Civil Rights Act of 1964 barred racial discrimination in public accommodations, among other forms of discrimination. The act was the product of almost a year of legislative debate, in the course of which participants disputed fundamental constitutional values related to citizenship.[77] The act's supporters framed the emerging statute as a means of filling what Democratic Senator Hubert Humphrey called the "citizenship gap"—the gap between the civil rights of white and Black citizens that existed in spite of the Fourteenth Amendment.[78] In his final speech before the Senate vote on the bill, Republican Senate minority leader Everett Dirksen declared, "There is involved here the citizenship of people under the Constitution who, by the Fourteenth Amendment, are . . . citizens of the United States of America."[79]

Some in Congress were wary of relying on their Section 5 enforcement power to remedy "private" discrimination because of the *Civil Rights Cases*.[80]

But others, such as Republican Senator John Sherman Cooper of Kentucky, argued that "[i]f there is a right to the equal use of accommodations held out to the public, it is a right of citizenship and a constitutional right under the Fourteenth Amendment."[81] The resulting legislation accomplished what *Brown v. Board of Education* and subsequent desegregation rulings could not in the face of massive resistance. It brought an end to the Jim Crow South.

The piecemeal, retail relief ordered by the courts desegregated some state-operated facilities.[82] The 1964 act's wholesale sweeping prohibitions on racial discrimination by recipients of federal funds, backed by threats of termination of funding for noncompliance, precipitated a jump in the percentage of Black children in desegregated schools from 1.18 percent in 1964 to 6.1 percent in 1966 to roughly 90 percent in 1973.[83] This is not to deny that courts can retrospectively vindicate the civil rights of citizens when other branches of government violate them. It is to illustrate that Congress has a comparative advantage in prospectively securing those rights against infringement on a national scale.

While the 1964 act was upheld under Congress's commerce power, some, including Justice William O. Douglas, agreed with Senator Cooper that it was better upheld as an exercise of Congress's power under Section 5. As Douglas wrote in the 1964 case of *Heart of Atlanta Motel v. U.S.*, "[T]he result reached by the Court is, for me, much more obvious as a protective measure under the Fourteenth Amendment than under the Commerce Clause. For the former deals with the constitutional status of the individual, not with the impact on commerce of local activities or vice versa."[84]

We agree. The obvious barrier to such a holding was the state action doctrine associated with *Cruikshank* and the *Civil Rights Cases*. Less obvious, perhaps, was the failure to recognize that, under the original concept of Republican citizenship, some nonstate actors may nevertheless properly be considered "public" for purposes of barring unreasonable discrimination among citizens of the United States. Given these barriers, the commerce power, as already expanded by the New Deal Court, was the doctrinal path of least resistance for a Congress on the cusp of enacting urgently needed civil-rights legislation.

We should not be understood as offering any moral criticism of this choice between Congress's powers under the Commerce Clause and Section 5. We are merely noting that this choice was not constitutionally required. And, because of our reading of the Commerce Clause[85] (which is beyond the scope of this book), we think Section 5 was the better constitutional path.

As in the *Chevron* context, deference by courts to Congress is not warranted if the comparative institutional advantages that Section 5 presupposes are not present or have not been harnessed. With administrative agencies, such is the case when an agency that is not empowered to enforce a particular statute weighs in on how it ought to be implemented. Such is also the case when an agency has not done anything to show that its choice of means is calculated to achieve a legitimate statutory end.

But, if (a) Congress has engaged in considered, fact-sensitive constitutional deliberation, and (b) it has not contradicted clear constitutional text or clearly gone beyond the bounds of unclear constitutional text, a Section 5 enforcement decision is at least as entitled to deference as an agency decision about how to implement an ambiguous statute. In passing RFRA, both of these conditions were satisfied by the congressional hearings and floor debates about the Free Exercise Clause and the extent of its Section 5 enforcement powers. Deference to such actual, as opposed to hypothetical, deliberation is consistent with the Congress-empowering spirit of Section 5.

It might be argued that the Court in *Boerne did* find that Congress clearly went beyond the bounds of constitutional text—and so the Court was duty-bound not to defer. This argument founders on the Court's silence in *Smith* itself concerning the original meaning of the First and Fourteenth Amendments. Justice Scalia's opinion for the *Smith* majority lacked any substantive discussion of the Free Exercise Clause's original public meaning. When the Court does not itself engage original meaning interpretation in case A, it should be estopped in case B from accusing Congress of exceeding the textual bounds delineated in case A.

As was not unusual for Justice Scalia, his analysis in *Smith* was primarily concerned, not with constitutional meaning, but with the institutional difficulties that *courts* face in "weigh[ing] the social importance of all laws against the centrality of all religious beliefs."[86] Yet, such "weighing" is exactly what Congress is better at doing. And it is what Congress did when it passed RFRA. In sum, RFRA was invalidated by the Court in *Boerne* on the ground that it conflicted with *Smith;* but *Smith* primarily concerned the limits of judicial, not legislative, competence.

In Chapter 12, we will return to the remedies that Congress can adopt pursuant to its enforcement power under Section 5, remedies that are beyond the competency of the judiciary. We will do so in the context of Congress's power to remedy a failure of states to perform their affirmative duty to provide "the equal protection of the laws."

* * *

During his confirmation hearing, Robert Bork famously analogized the Ninth Amendment to an impenetrable "inkblot" on the Constitution:

> I do not think you can use the Ninth Amendment unless you know something of what it means. For example, if you had an amendment that says "Congress shall make no" and then there is an ink blot and you cannot read the rest of it and that is the only copy you have, I do not think the court can make up what might be under the ink blot if you cannot read it.[87]

That analogy was met with protests.

By the time he wrote *The Tempting of America*, Bork had become aware of an article on the Ninth Amendment by Russell Caplan that purported to show that the original meaning of the Ninth Amendment was limited to a reinforcement of states' rights.[88] So Bork then switched his inkblot metaphor to the Privileges or Immunities Clause:

> No judge is entitled to interpret an inkblot on the ground that there must be something under it. So it has been with the clause of the fourteenth amendment prohibiting any state from denying citizens the privileges and [sic] immunities of citizens of the United States. The clause has been a mystery since its adoption and in consequence has, quite properly, remained a dead letter.[89]

But the Privileges or Immunities Clause is not an impenetrable inkblot. If it ever was a mystery, it is a mystery no more. We can state with confidence that the original public meaning of the Privileges or Immunities Clause does "lock in" certain identifiable rights; that it does not lock in others; and that it does not delegate to Congress or to the federal courts unbounded discretion to specify the rights that states cannot abridge.

True, we cannot hope to find in the mists of history an algorithm that will generate a complete and pristine set of rights of paramount national citizenship to which constitutional decision-makers cannot add without once again amending the Constitution. Nevertheless, the original meaning of the clause provides us with some fixed points that are not merely provisional but absolute.

For Congress or the courts to decline to enforce constitutionally enumerated rights, or the civil rights specified in the Civil Rights Act of 1866, would be an act of *de*struction, not *con*struction. Moreover, the clause also leaves space for institutional judgment—by state and federal legislators and by state and federal judges—concerning what measures are necessary to support Republican citizenship today. Time and experience will disclose the strengths and weaknesses of such measures.

New privileges should not be locked in without proving their worth across the states and across time, as had the "original" privileges. But to decline to permit the recognition and enforcement of privileges that have, for decades and across the nation, served the same republican end as those privileges listed by Jacob Howard would be a mistake. That result is neither compelled by the clause's letter nor consistent with the clause's spirit.

We sympathize with those who—like the late Justice Scalia—worry that reviving the Privileges or Immunities Clause and permitting the recognition of unenumerated privileges will lead to judicial mischief. But no set of decision rules will prevent willful judges from making things up. Shifting the protection of unenumerated rights to the Due Process of Law Clauses due to fear of the Privileges or Immunities Clause has been a cure that is worse than the disease. And our proposed approach to the Privileges or Immunities Clause closely resembles and is in fact *more* determinate and constraining than was Justice Scalia's own substantive-due-process approach.

Originalists have a duty to work with what the Constitution gives us. If its original meaning gives us some enumerated rights, some unenumerated rights, and some discretion, we cannot pretend that it does something else. As Justice Thomas observed in his concurring opinion in *McDonald*, which provided the fifth vote to apply the right to keep and bear arms to the state:

> To be sure, interpreting the Privileges or Immunities Clause may produce hard questions. But they will have the advantage of being questions the Constitution asks us to answer. I believe those questions are more worthy of this Court's attention—and far more likely to yield discernable answers— than the substantive due process questions the Court has for years created on its own, with neither textual nor historical support.[90]

As for those who would limit the Privileges or Immunities Clause to protecting enumerated rights only, there are far too many—and far too significant—anomalies in the historical record that such a paradigm cannot explain. These anomalies include the Civil Rights Act of 1866, the prominence of *Corfield*, post-ratification Republican discourse that assumed that at least some unenumerated rights were among the privileges of citizenship, and the enactment of the Civil Rights Act of 1875. Our theory of the original "letter" explains those anomalies. And our theory of the original "spirit" is tailored to discourage judicial mischief.

From a distance, our approach to privilege recognition may look quite a bit like *Glucksberg*—a resemblance that, hopefully, will give it traction with some skeptical jurists. But it differs from *Glucksberg* in that it (1) applies only to unenumerated rights; (2) has a fixed-rights floor; (3) suggests specific criteria for determining what it means for a right to be sufficiently deeply rooted; and (4) does not insist on a manipulable "narrowing" inquiry. What matters is accuracy, what the (common law, constitutional, and statutory) sources have said about the entrenchment of the claimed right over a defined period of time.

Our rules for identifying "privileges or immunities" to implement the spirit of the clause are sensitive to federalism. They prevent the clause from being abridged through construction. And they limit judicial discretion by compelling judges to find these privileges or immunities in concrete, discoverable, positive law, rather than rely solely on abstract moral principles. Finally, our rules for Section 5 enforcement recognize Congress's institutional advantages over the courts in respect of remedying civil-rights violations—without either giving Congress plenary power over civil rights or requiring judicial abdication.

But we are not done—far from it. In this part, we have focused on the need for judges accurately to *identify* the privileges or immunities of citizens of the United States. In Part II, we turn our attention to the judicial duty to *enforce* or protect these privileges as part of the Due Process of Law Clause. Is the due process of law—as many originalists have argued—simply a procedural guarantee? Or does it impose limits on the *substance* or content of legislation? Does what is called "substantive due process"—sometimes disparagingly—find any footing in the original meaning of the Fourteenth Amendment? We will also revisit the fact that the Privileges or Immunities Clause is textually limited to "citizens," while the Due Process of Law Clause protects all "persons." What rights to "life, liberty, and property" are states forbidden to deprive *any person* of without "due process of law"?

Read on.

PART II

THE DUE PROCESS OF LAW CLAUSE

9

The Letter

The Original Meaning of "Due Process of Law"

THE DOMINANT ORIGINALIST view has long been that due process of law is solely a procedural guarantee that does not constrain the content of legislation.[1] The proposition that the Due Process of Law Clauses of the Fifth and Fourteenth Amendments impose limits on the content or *substance* of federal and state statutes rather than merely guaranteeing a particular legal *process* prior to the deprivation of life, liberty, or property[2] is called "substantive due process."[3] The label "substantive due process" was originally coined to illustrate the supposed absurdity of the concept. And yet, despite continuing contestation over its legitimacy and its boundaries, substantive due process is today an entrenched doctrine of constitutional law.

In recent years, scholars have made fresh inquiries into the historical evidence and concluded that the case for some form of judicial review of the content of legislation under the Due Process of Law Clauses is weightier than initially supposed. Among the most notable examples are Frederick Gedicks's work undertaking to demonstrate that the original meaning of the Fifth Amendment's Due Process of Law Clause protects natural and customary rights against legislative deprivations;[4] Ryan Williams's investigation of the Fifth and Fourteenth Amendments, which concludes that the latter but not the former constrains the content of legislation in certain ways;[5] and Timothy Sandefur's argument that *both* clauses forbid legislation that has "no connection to a larger purpose or goal."[6]

Even scholars who continue to defend something resembling the once-dominant originalist interpretation of substantive due process have made important modifications of that view. For example, Nathan Chapman and Michael McConnell have argued that the due process of law requires judges to determine whether a legislative enactment is in fact legislation rather than an attempt to exercise judicial power.[7] On this "separation of powers" account, the due process of law guarantees a measure of judicial review of the content of legislation—if only to ensure that an enactment is general and prospective and does not abrogate common-law procedural rights.[8]

In this chapter, we revisit the original meaning of the text—the "letter"—of the Due Process of Law Clauses. We contend that the original letter and spirit of "due process of law" in both the Fifth and Fourteenth Amendments require legislatures to exercise their powers over the life, liberty, and property of individuals in good faith by enacting legislation that is actually calculated to achieve constitutionally proper ends. Further, the original letter and spirit of "due process of law" impose a duty on both state and federal judges to make good-faith determinations of whether legislation is calculated to achieve constitutionally proper ends.

In this way, the "process" in "due *process* of law" requires a judicial inquiry into the "substance" of a statute to assess whether a legislative act is a "law." A legislative act that deprives any person of "life, liberty, or property"[9] is a law only if it is within what Alexander Hamilton referred to as the "just and constitutional powers" of a legislature to enact.[10]

At the federal level, legislation must be within one of the delegated powers of Congress (including the incidental powers to which the Necessary and Proper Clause expressly refers).[11] At the state level, legislation is a proper law if it is within the so-called "police powers" of a state; such powers are not delegated by the text of the federal Constitution.[12] Our approach therefore provides guidance to state court judges enforcing their own state constitutions as well as to federal judges.

To avoid confusion, we should stress up front that our approach differs significantly from the modern doctrine of substantive due process. Under the modern doctrine, judges identify *substantive rights* or liberties they deem to be fundamental. They then give legislation that restricts the exercise of these rights heightened scrutiny. Legislation restricting other nonfundamental liberties gets little or no scrutiny.[13]

Our approach is purely procedural insofar as it concerns solely the judicial *process* that is required before someone may be deprived of his or her life, liberty, or property. But the scope of this judicial inquiry necessarily includes an examination of the *substance of a statute* to ensure that it is a product of a proper exercise of legislative power. So, while both conceptions of "the due process of law" have a "substantive" component, *identifying* substantive *rights* deserving of heightened judicial protection is a very different enterprise than *examining* the substance *of statutes* to see whether they were enacted pursuant to the just powers of a legislature.

In this chapter, we consider the original meaning of the "letter" of "due process of law." In Chapter 10, we consider its "spirit" or function of protecting against arbitrary power. Finally, we conclude our discussion of the due process of law in Chapter 11 by identifying the just and constitutional powers of Congress, as well as those of state legislatures.

The Letter

The British Origins of the Phrase "Due Process of Law"

There is not much dispute about the origin of the phrase "due process of law." Scholars with profound disagreements about the original meaning of the Due Process of Law Clauses trace the phrase to Magna Carta, which was a series of concessions extracted at sword point from King John at Runnymede in 1215.[14] The crucial language is found in chapter 39, which provides: "No free man shall be arrested or imprisoned, or disseised or outlawed or exiled or in any way victimised . . . except by the lawful judgment of his peers or *by the law of the land.*"[15] This language was directed against King John's notorious efforts to impose his will by avoiding the regular processes of the common-law courts, and his reliance instead on prerogative courts that lacked either independent, presumptively impartial judges or traditional procedures designed to protect traditional individual rights.[16]

In the fourteenth century, King Edward III disregarded the promises made by King John, summarily punishing subjects outside the common-law courts. Parliament responded by codifying a series of statutes that more particularly described what chapter 39 entailed.[17] A 1354 statute linked "due process of law" to access to common-law courts with judges and traditional proceedings: "No man of what Estate or Condition that he be, shall be put out of Land or Tenement, nor taken, nor imprisoned, nor disinherited, nor put to Death, without being brought in Answer by *due Process* of the Law."[18] In 1368, when Edward III failed to adhere to this prohibition, Parliament enacted yet another statute that specifically indicted the king for bringing subjects before his council and provided that "no man be put to answer without presentment before justices, or matter of record, or by due process and writ original, according to the old *law of the land*."[19]

King James I, the first Stuart king, sought to formalize the royal powers that had accreted to the Crown under his Tudor predecessors by maintaining that law consisted solely in his royal will. In particular, he claimed the authority to adjudicate cases outside of the courts of law, explaining that "[t]he King being the author of the Lawe is the interpreter of the Lawe."[20] That claim prompted a series of dramatic confrontations with Edward Coke, who was then Lord Chief Justice of the Court of Common Pleas. Coke invoked the Magna Carta's constraints on royal power to combat the king's absolutist claims.[21] Thanks in significant part to Coke's commentaries, the phrases "law of the land" and "due process of law" became synonymous.

Coke affirmed that Magna Carta recognized the existence of a law that was higher than the actions of the king and denied that "[t]he King in his own person [could] adjudge any case."[22] For such resistance, James I eventually dismissed Coke—but James I could not refute Coke.[23] English judges held acts of the king unlawful and refused to defer to mere executive will; instead, they exercised independent judgment in accordance with the law of the land, even if it meant holding royal acts void.[24]

By the eighteenth century, the proposition that the law of the land bound the king had become entrenched in England.[25] The more complicated question concerned Parliament. Philip Hamburger has detailed how the content of the unwritten English constitution and the status of Parliament as the highest court in the land created impediments to any judicial invalidation of acts of Parliament on the grounds that those acts were inconsistent with the law of the land.[26] Because England's constitution was developed in part through custom, and Parliament was the court in which customs were declared or altered, Parliament's "enactments amounted to decisions upholding their constitutionality."[27] That is to say, "the common law itself stood in the way of decisions holding acts of Parliament unlawful."[28]

Coke's report of *Dr. Bonham's Case*[29] has been interpreted by some as a declaration that judges may hold acts of Parliament void because they are contrary to even higher law—perhaps customary law, perhaps natural law.[30] The case itself concerned one Dr. Thomas Bonham, who had been sentenced to pay a fine and to be incarcerated for practicing medicine in London without permission from the Royal College of Physicians.[31] Bonham brought an action for wrongful imprisonment.[32] A majority of the Court of Common Pleas held that the college had no authority to imprison Bonham.[33]

In his report of the case, Coke explained the judges' reasoning thus:

> The censors cannot be [] judges, ministers, and parties. . . . And it appears in our books, that in many cases, the common law will [] controul Acts of Parliament, and sometimes adjudge them to be utterly void: for when an Act of Parliament is against common right and reason, or repugnant, or impossible to be performed, the common law will controul it, and adjudge such Act to be void.[34]

As Hamburger explains, Coke's words must be considered in the context of a long-standing common law tradition of equitable interpretation—interpretation that, where the letter of the law was unclear, avoided a conclusion that was contrary to natural right and thus void in *conscience*.[35] Thus, Hamburger argues that Coke was laying a "moral foundation for [an] equitable interpretation," not claiming the power to invalidate parliamentary statutes.[36]

And yet, regardless of what Coke originally meant, Hamburger finds that the notion that some kind of higher law bound even Parliament was expressed in the early eighteenth century, in the wake of the imprisonment of five petitioners from Kent by a Tory-dominated House of Commons in 1701.[37] Daniel Defoe and the Whigs drew on increasingly influential natural-rights theory to criticize not only the imprisonments but the idea of parliamentary supremacy.[38]

Perhaps the most sophisticated judicial effort to grapple with the tension between parliamentary supremacy and natural-rights theory was Chief Justice John Holt's opinion in the 1701 case of *City of London v. Wood*.[39] Therein, Holt declared both that Parliament was bound by natural right and that no judicial remedy was available for a parliamentary act that contradicted natural right—specifically, by making a person a judge in his own cause.[40]

Holt affirmed that the result of such an act would be to return individuals to the "state of nature"[41]—a condition in which rights were, as Locke put it, "very unsafe, very insecure," and the defects of which legitimate governments were designed to cure.[42] Such an act would be "a void Act of Parliament"[43]—that is, void in conscience. If it could not be construed otherwise, "government would be dissolved."[44] Judges would be bound to give effect to it. But the people might "appeal to heaven"—that is, exercise their natural right of revolution.[45] Fortunately, Holt found that the act at issue could be construed to avoid that unhappy outcome.[46]

The "Due Process of Law" in the United States in 1791

THE LAW OF THE LAND   In the wake of Americans' own successful "appeal to heaven," American judges did not face the impediments that constrained Coke and Holt from holding acts of Parliament unlawful. American corporations and colonies had written constitutions that could not be altered by ordinary legislation, as did most states after independence.[47] Ten of the newly independent state constitutions included law-of-the-land provisions that tracked the language of chapter 39.[48] Scrutiny of Founding Era interpretations of these provisions yields persuasive evidence that "law of the land" and "due process of law" were understood during the time period when the Fifth Amendment was ratified to guarantee *both* judicial process in courts of law *and* the application of law the content or substance of which conformed to written constitutions.

The landmark 1787 case of *Bayard v. Singleton*[49] is an instructive example. *Bayard* arose from North Carolina's confiscation of Tory property.[50] The Bayards, who were victims of this confiscation, sued Singleton, the subsequent buyer of the property, seeking to recover it.[51] In 1785, the legislature effectively acted as a judge in Singleton's case, enacting a statute that required courts to dismiss suits against purchasers of forfeited Tory estates "upon the motion or affidavit of the defendant."[52] Several dissenting legislators had raised constitutional objections to the act, claiming that it would violate the state's law-of-the-land-clause by "deny[ing] . . . the known and established rules of justice, which protect the property of all citizens equally" and by "plac[ing] [citizens] under the adjudication of the General Assembly, whose desire to redress the grievance may be fluctuating, uncertain and ineffectual."[53]

Although these arguments failed to win the day in the legislature, the Bayards' claims would be vindicated in court.[54] The court rejected Singleton's lawyers' contention that "all acts of Assembly were laws, and their execution could not be prevented."[55] It held that "the [C]onstitution (which the judicial power was bound to take notice of as much as of any other law whatever,) st[ood] in full force as the fundamental law of the land"; and that the legislature had deprived the Bayards of a right guaranteed by the law of the land—"a right to a decision of [their] property by a trial by jury."[56] Indeed, the court declared that "no act [legislators] could pass[] could by any means repeal or alter the [C]onstitution, because if they could do this, they would at the same instant of time destroy their own existence as a Legislature and dissolve the government thereby established."[57] Thus, a judicial process requiring an act of a legislature to be in accordance with the law of the land set forth in a written constitution that constrained the legislature—and was therefore a "law" that was binding on the parties[58]—eliminated the need for an appeal to heaven.

In 1784, Alexander Hamilton denounced a bill passed by the New York legislature that stripped Tories of their citizenship.[59] His reasons echoed those made by the dissenting legislators to the act that was ultimately held unlawful in *Bayard*. Hamilton argued that the bill was "contrary to the law of the land," specifically, the thirteenth article of the New York Constitution.[60] This article provided that "no member of this state shall be disenfranchised[] or deprived of any of the rights or privileges secured to the subjects of this state by the constitution, unless by the law of the land[] or the judgment of his peers."[61]

Hamilton adopted Coke's definition of the law of the land: "[D]ue process of law . . . [means] by indictment or presentment of good and lawful men, and trial and conviction in consequence."[62] Hamilton contended that "the legislature . . . cannot, without tyranny, disfranchise or punish whole classes of citizens by general discriptions [*sic*], without trial and conviction of offences known by laws previously established declaring the offence and prescribing the penalty."[63] Such acts of "tyranny," he contended, did not become part of the law of the land simply in virtue of their enactment.[64]

In 1787, Hamilton argued before the New York General Assembly that a proposed Senate amendment to an act regulating elections violated both the state's law-of-the-land clause and a recently passed statutory provision guaranteeing due process of law. The act disqualified the owners of British privateers of vessels of war that had attacked the "vessels, property or persons" of the United States from holding any state office of trust.[65] Hamilton denied that "the law of the land" would "include *an act* of the legislature"—denied that is, that legislative acts *necessarily* became part of the law of the land.[66]

Again, Hamilton drew on Coke, stating that Coke "interpret[ed] the law of the land to mean presentment and indictment, and process of outlawry, as contradistinguished from trial by jury."[67] Hamilton found confirmation of his position in the terminology of "due process" adopted by the legislature, which connoted "the process and proceedings of the courts of justice"—process and proceedings that the legislature was institutionally incapable of providing.[68] As before, he rejected the idea that legislative enactments necessarily became part of the law of the land, without appropriate scrutiny by "the courts of justice."[69]

Hamilton's reliance on Coke in explaining the meaning of "due process of law" and "law of the land" was not unique. Prominent and widely cited American jurists relied on Coke in interpreting both phrases. These jurists affirmed the connection between the concept of due process of law and the proceedings of the courts. St. George Tucker, a Virginia judge who taught constitutional law at the College of William & Mary in the 1790s, wrote that "[d]ue process of law must then be had before a judicial court, or a judicial magistrate."[70]

In his highly regarded *Commentaries on American Law*, one of the most influential legal minds of the Founding period, Chancellor James Kent of New York, defined due process of law as "law[] in its regular course of administration, through courts of justice."[71] In his *Commentaries on the Constitution*, Supreme Court Justice Joseph Story stated that due process of law entailed "due presentment or indictment, and being brought in to answer thereto by due process of the common law," and that it "affirms the right of trial according to the process and proceedings of the common law."[72] For these jurists, due process of law required individualized deprivations of life, liberty, or property to take place through the courts with their judges and juries—thus forbidding legislatures from denying access to the courts.[73]

The history of the drafting and ratification of the Fifth Amendment is sparse. It is not clear why Madison chose to use "due process of law" rather than "law of the land," despite his own state's support for the latter phrase.[74] It is plausible that Madison sought to avoid conflation of the phrase with the reference to "the supreme law of the land" in the Supremacy Clause of Article VI.[75] Such conflation might have given rise to the belief that the Fifth Amendment did not incorporate any independent procedural requirements that were unspecified in the Constitution's text and derived from the common law. The enactments identified as "the law of the land" in the Supremacy Clause are all examples of written law.[76]

Yet, it is significant that the proposal that ultimately became the Fifth Amendment was, according to Madison's original design, to be inserted into "article 1st, section 9, between clauses 3 and 4" alongside other limits on congressional power.[77] It would have followed the clause prohibiting Congress from enacting bills of attainder and ex post facto laws[78]—strongly suggesting that it, too, was designed to limit congressional action.[79]

Moreover, as Chapman and McConnell have observed, Madison emphasized the need for a federal bill of rights by pointing to the fact that Britain's declaration of rights had "gone no farther than to raise a barrier against the power of the Crown," and that "the power of the Legislature is left altogether indefinite."[80] "[T]he people of America are most alarmed," Madison explained, that "the trial by jury, freedom of the press, or liberty of conscience" are unsecured by "Magna Charta" or "the British Constitution."[81]

The First Amendment expressly begins with "Congress shall make no law . . ." When the first Congress included Madison's proposed amendments as separate articles appended to the end of the text, there is no reason to think that the Fifth Amendment was rendered any less applicable to Congress than were the other subject-less guarantees of the first eight amendments—such as the guarantees against quartering troops or cruel and unusual punishments.[82]

At first blush, many of the early state cases interpreting "law of the land" and "due process of law" appear to be concerned solely with access to courts and the personnel and procedures associated with the courts at common law rather than the substance or content of the law being applied. A number focus on legislative interference with the right to trial by jury and other procedural protections traceable to the common law.[83] Others focus on the statutory deprivation of "vested" property rights of specific persons who had acquired that property consistently with the positive law then in effect. Such deprivations were understood as adjudicative rather than legislative acts because they were neither generally applicable nor prospective in their operation.[84]

This appearance is deceptive. In the first place, viewing certain common-law rights that attached during judicial proceedings as merely procedural is anachronistic. Consider the right to trial by jury. During the Founding Era, juries could judge both law and fact. That is, juries could determine whether the substance of an act was constitutional before applying it in a civil or criminal case to deprive a defendant of his or her life, liberty, or property.[85] The "procedural" right to trial by jury, then, was a means of ensuring judicial branch review of the *substance* of governmental enactments.[86]

Second, determining whether statutory deprivations of vested rights were adjudicative rather than properly legislative acts required examination of the content or substance of legislative enactments to determine whether they were more like judicial decrees or sentences than general, prospective laws.[87] Finally, significant authority held that "due process *of law*" and "law of the land" required a legislative *act* to be consistent with applicable superior law to qualify as *law* at all. Let us now consider this last distinction in greater depth.

DISTINGUISHING A "LAW" FROM A MERE LEGISLATIVE "ACT." Numerous Founding Era cases distinguish between a mere legislative "act" and a "law." To be a law, and therefore part of "the law" of the land or the due process "of law," a legislative act had to be consistent with any higher laws, such as those found in federal or state constitutions or in the nature of the "social compact."

The proposition that only such acts consistent with the federal Constitution became part of the law of the land can be found in diverse Founding Era sources, both Republican and Federalist. In the 1798 Kentucky Resolutions, Republican Thomas Jefferson declared that the Alien and Sedition Acts were "*not law*, but . . . altogether void, and of no force" because they violated the First, Fifth, and Tenth Amendments.[88]

In his seminal opinion for the Court in the 1803 case of *Marbury v. Madison*, Federalist Chief Justice John Marshall asked whether "an *act*[] repugnant to the constitution[] can become the law of the land." He answered that "a legislative *act* contrary to the constitution is *not law*."[89] In the 1819 case of *McCulloch v. Maryland*, Marshall stated that "the laws" of Congress "*when made in pursuance of the constitution*, form the supreme law of the land,"[90] the implication being that when "the laws" of Congress are *not* made in pursuance of the Constitution, they are mere acts that do *not* become part of the "law of the land."[91]

State courts, too, affirmed this understanding in measuring legislation against state constitutions. Justice Francis Locke, in a highly influential opinion in *Trustees of the University of North Carolina v. Foy*, stated that North Carolina's law-of-the-land provision forbade "depriv[ations] of . . . liberties or properties, unless by a trial by jury in a court of justice, according to the known and established rules of decision derived from the common law and *such acts* of the Legislature *as are consistent with the Constitution*."[92] Another North Carolina case explicitly distinguished between a mere legislative "act" and "the law of the land": "[W]hat is the law of the land? Such *acts* of the Legislature *only* as violate none of the rules laid down in the constitution."[93]

Likewise, some judges did not consider a legislative act inconsistent with the nature of the social compact to be a "law." The most famous such opinion is probably Justice Samuel Chase's in *Calder v. Bull*. In this 1798 case, the Supreme Court considered the constitutionality of a resolution of the Connecticut General Court that granted a new trial in a probate proceeding.[94] Lawyers for Calder and his wife contended that the resolution violated the Ex Post Facto Clause of the federal Constitution, and that the legislature could not, consistent with the Connecticut constitution, "act as a court."[95] At the time, Connecticut had an unwritten, customary constitution.[96] The Court ultimately determined that the legislature's actions did not violate the federal Ex Post Facto Clause because that clause forbade only retroactive *criminal* punishments.[97] But Justice Chase also discussed the limits of legislative power under the Connecticut constitution.[98] Chase wrote that because "[t]he purposes for which men enter into society . . . determine the nature and terms of the social compact;" and even without an express constitution, "[t]he nature, and ends of legislative power will limit the exercise of it."[99] Chase then distinguished between a legislative "act" and a "law":

> There are acts which the Federal, or State, Legislature cannot do, without exceeding their authority. There are certain vital principles in our free Republican governments, which will determine and over-rule an apparent and flagrant abuse of legislative power; as to authorize manifest injustice by positive law; or to take away that security for personal liberty, or private property, for the protection whereof of the government was established. *An ACT* of the Legislature (for I cannot call it *a law*) contrary to the great first principles of the social compact, cannot be considered a rightful exercise of legislative authority.[100]

Chase offered several examples of exercises of legislative power that were sufficiently contrary to those ends that "it [could not] be presumed" that people had authorized such power; such power had to be expressly given, in terms that did not admit of doubt.[101] Among them:

> A law that punished a citizen for an innocent action, or, in other words, for an act, which, when done, was in violation of no existing law; a law that destroys, or impairs, the lawful private contracts of citizens; a law that makes a man a Judge in his own cause; or a law that takes property from A. and gives it to B.[102]

In a now equally famous opinion of his own in *Calder*, Justice James Iredell rejected the notion that legislative power was inherently limited.[103] He asserted that if "a government, composed of Legislative, Executive and Judicial departments, were established, by a Constitution, which imposed no limits on the legislative power, the consequence would inevitably be, that whatever the legislative power chose to enact, would be *lawfully* enacted, and the judicial power could never interpose to pronounce it void."[104] As authority for his position, Iredell cited Sir William Blackstone (who was, of course, describing the powers of Parliament).[105]

However persuasive it has seemed to some modern ears,[106] Iredell's view of legislative power seems to have been an outlier at the Founding.[107] For example, in 1795, Supreme Court Justice William Paterson, while riding circuit, stated in *Vanhorne's Lessee v. Dorrance* that "[t]he legislature . . . had no authority to make *an act* divesting one citizen of his freehold[] and vesting it in another, without a just compensation." Such an act was "contrary to the principles of social alliance[,] in every free government," as well as "contrary . . . to the letter and spirit of the Constitution."[108] Similarly, in his opinion for the Court in *Fletcher v. Peck*, Marshall acknowledged that "[t]o the legislature all legislative power is granted" but questioned whether "*the act* of transferring the property of an individual to the public, be in the nature of the *legislative* power."[109]

In the 1792 case of *Bowman v. Middleton*, the South Carolina Supreme Court evaluated a legislative act that transferred a freehold from the heir-at-law to another person, and also from the eldest son of an intestate, and vested it in a second son.[110] Those challenging the act allowed that "there might be great and urgent occasions wherein it might be justifiable for the state to take private property from individuals, (upon a full indemnification) for the purposes of fortifications or public works." But the legislature could not simply take property from A and give it to B absent either compensation or a jury trial.[111] The court agreed, determining that the act was "ipso facto[] void" because it was contrary to natural law and "common right."[112]

Textually, the Due Process of Law Clauses use four words, not two: the "due process *of law*," requires that no person could "be deprived of life, liberty, or property," except by the common law or by an act of a legislature that constitutes a "law." And the "*due process* of law" entitles every person to a judicial examination of, inter alia, the substance of a legislative act to ensure it was a "law." The criteria for "law" are less than perfectly clear. But it is demonstrable that Founding Era courts and commentators did insist on some such distinction and were prepared to hold legislation void because it was not law.

The "Due Process of Law" in the United States in 1868

The original meaning of the "due process of law" in the Fifth Amendment is not the principal subject of our inquiry, except insofar as it informed the original meaning of the Due Process of Law Clause in the Fourteenth Amendment. Whatever that phrase meant in 1791,[113] the distinction between a legislative act or enactment and a law continued to develop in the nineteenth century. A frequently cited use of the distinction was Daniel Webster's oral argument before the Supreme Court in *Trustees of Dartmouth College v. Woodward:*

> By the law of the land is most clearly intended the general law; a law[] which hears before it condemns; which proceeds upon inquiry, and renders judgment only after trial. The meaning is, that every citizen shall hold his life, liberty, property, and immunities[] under the protection of the general rules which govern society. Every thing which may pass under the form of an *enactment*[] is not, therefore, to be considered the law of the land. If this were so, *acts* of attainder, bills of pains and penalties, *acts* of confiscation, *acts* reversing judgments, and *acts* directly transferring one man's estate to another, legislative judgments, decrees, and forfeitures in all possible forms, would be *the law* of the land.[114]

Chapman and McConnell argue that Webster was only articulating a familiar distinction between legislation and adjudication.[115] But the idea that legislative power was inherently limited came to be understood as forbidding not only enactments that were not generally applicable or prospective but enactments that were not good-faith efforts to promote constitutionally proper governmental ends.

In two Tennessee cases, Judge (and future Justice) John Catron interpreted the state's law-of-the-land clause to require "general public law[s]" as distinct from "partial or private law[s]" that treated similarly situated individuals differently.[116] Judge Nathan Green of the Tennessee Supreme Court explained the perceived vice of the latter in a decision voiding an act that created a special court to handle all lawsuits brought against the Bank of the State of Tennessee. Such partial legislation was, he wrote, "the same in principle as if a law had been passed *in favor of* some one [individual or corporate body]."[117] Obviously, if it were deemed a constitutionally proper end for the legislature to seek to advance the interests of "favor[ed]" individuals or groups, such enactments would have been considered unproblematic.

Put another way, judges inferred from the differential treatment of similarly situated persons that legislation was designed to achieve constitutionally improper goals. By 1868, "due process of law" was a sufficiently familiar phrase that Representative John Bingham, the principal author of the Fourteenth Amendment, thought it unnecessary to elaborate in any great detail when questioned on the floor of the Thirty-Ninth Congress about its meaning.[118] "[T]he courts have settled that long ago," said Bingham, "and the gentleman can go and read their decisions."[119]

Which decisions? Although Bingham did not say, leading Republican Representative William Lawrence mentioned *Wilkinson v. Leland*,[120] *Terrett v. Taylor*,[121] *People v. Morris*,[122] and *Taylor v. Porter & Ford*[123] while on the floor.[124] Lawrence quoted a passage from Justice Joseph Story's opinion in *Wilkinson*.[125] In *Wilkinson*, Justice Story concluded: "That government can scarcely be deemed to be free, where the rights of property are left solely dependent upon the will of a legislative body, without restraint."[126] Whatever concept of government may have legitimized the "uncontrolled and arbitrary exercise" of legislative power "before the revolution," that "great event," wrote Story, amounted to a national rejection of that concept.[127]

In *Terrett v. Taylor*, the Court held that a legislative land grant made to the Anglican Church by the British Crown could not be rescinded—that the title to the property had been "indefeasibly vested."[128] Writing again for the Court, Story grounded this conclusion in "the principles of natural justice, upon the fundamental laws of every free government, upon the spirit and the letter of the constitution of the United States."[129]

Finally, in *People v. Morris*, a case interpreting the New York Constitution (which at the time had no bill of rights), Judge Nelson wrote that "[the] vested rights of the citizen," included "that private property cannot be taken for strictly private purposes at all, nor for public without a just compensation" and that the "obligation of contracts cannot be abrogated or essentially impaired." These rights are to be held "sacred and inviolable, even against the plenitude of power of the legislative department."[130] In each of these three cases, judges invoked inherent constitutional limits on legislative means and ends.

The fourth case, *Taylor v. Porter & Ford*, contains an extensive discussion of both "law of the land" and "due process of law," both phrases having been incorporated into New York's constitution by 1843.[131] Yet, before discussing these phrases, Judge Greene Bronson, echoing Locke, grounded one of the "ends" of state legislative power granted by the constitution in the "social compact"—namely, the protection of the individual rights of life, liberty, and property: "The security of life, liberty and property, lies at the foundation of the social compact," wrote Bronson, "and to say that this grant of 'legislative power' includes the right to attack private property, is equivalent to saying that the people have delegated to their servants the power of defeating one of the great ends for which the government was established."[132] Not only was legislative power subject to certain inherent limits, but those limits also constrained the purposes for which legislatures could act.

According to Bronson, then, even absent any law-of-the-land clause, the legislature could not "take the property of A, either with or without compensation, and give it to B."[133] But, Bronson expanded, "The people have added negative words, which should put the matter at rest," specifically in providing that "[n]o member of this state shall be disfranchised, or deprived of any of the rights or privileges secured to any citizen thereof, unless by the law of the land, or the judgment of his peers,"[134] and "[n]o person shall be deprived of life, liberty, or property, without due process of law."[135]

Relying on Coke, Bronson declared that the "law of the land" did not encompass "statute[s] passed for the purpose of working the wrong[]"—that is, of "tak[ing] the property of A, either with or without compensation, and giv[ing] it to B."[136] He stated that it "must be ascertained judicially that [someone] has forfeited his privileges, or that some one else has a superior title to the property he possesses, before either of them can be taken from him."[137] Similarly, he explained that "due process of law" connoted "a prosecution or suit instituted and conducted according to the prescribed forms and solemnities for ascertaining guilt, or determining the title to property."[138] "Mere legislation" could not serve as a basis for taking someone's property without permission and giving it to someone else.[139]

To sum up, the decisions cited by Lawrence involve themes that were echoed in numerous decisions by state courts as well as in leading treatises on constitutional law during the Founding Era. A legislative act—or "mere legislation"—was deemed not to be part of the law of the land and was therefore insusceptible of being applied to individuals consistently with "due process of law" (1) if it deprived individuals of certain procedural rights traceable to the common law; (2) if it was either retrospective or insufficiently general, and thus usurped judicial power; or (3) if more generally, it violated a written constitution.

A fourth category of enactments that came to be understood as contrary to the law of the land developed toward the middle of the nineteenth century. As was earlier stressed by Justice Chase in *Calder* and reiterated by Judge Bronson in *Taylor*, implicit in the invalidation of legislative acts that were neither prospective nor general was a conception of legislative power that was inherently limited by the nature of the social compact.[140] And the nature of the social compact barred any presumption that the people had consented to be governed by a legislature with arbitrary power.

All of this talk of the "social compact" may appear to be very abstract and therefore unhelpful to contemporary legislators and judges who must resolve hard questions about whether particular acts are constitutionally proper. But originalists must first go where evidence of original meaning leads, and only then consider how best to implement that meaning. As we will see, allowing persons to be deprived of their lives, liberty, or property by arbitrary legislation is not consistent with the original meaning of the Fourteenth Amendment.

The (False) Dichotomy between "Substantive" and "Procedural" Due Process

Current thought identifies substantive due process with the judicial recognition of particular individual rights—say, to marry, to decide whether to have children, or to associate with others for lawful purposes; and procedural due process with a set of judicial procedures that ensure that (a) a person is actually guilty of violating (b) a statute that was enacted according to the proper procedures. Under this dichotomy, procedural due process neither identifies nor enforces substantive rights; nor does it examine the substance of legislation to ensure it was within the power of the legislature to enact. So long as the proper legislative procedures were followed, procedural due process is satisfied.

The evidence surveyed in this chapter reveals this dichotomy of procedural and substantive due process to be unhelpful and potentially misleading. It overlooks an intermediate option: "due process of law" is a guaranty of a judicial *process* to ensure that (a) a person is actually guilty of violating (b) a statute that was enacted according to the proper procedures and (c) was within the ends of government that the legislature was constitutionally empowered to pursue.

This option resolves the alleged contradiction within "*substantive* due *process.*" Once it is acknowledged that due process of law guarantees an opportunity to challenge the *content* or "substance" of a statute for its conformity with the Constitution's limits on legislative power, and that a statute that does not conform with the Constitution is not a constitutionally proper law, the utility of the distinction between substantive and procedural due process vanishes.

Consider the First Amendment. We commonly speak of "First Amendment challenges" to the substance of legislation. Yet the right to a judicial determination of whether a legislative enactment prohibits "the free exercise of religion" is part of the "due process of law."[141] The due *process* of law guarantees a judicial forum in which people can contest whether the *substance* of a statute prohibits the free exercise of religion.[142] A statute that *does* prohibit the free exercise of religion cannot be used to deprive someone of life, liberty, or property, consistently with the due process *of law*, because it is not a constitutionally proper law.

Despite the role they are playing in guaranteeing a judicial forum, the Due Process of Law Clauses are rarely noticed in such cases, and we speak only of the First Amendment.[143] This is analogous to how we now commonly speak of "First Amendment challenges" to state laws when such challenges are, strictly speaking, Fourteenth Amendment challenges.[144] Indeed, according to the post–New Deal "incorporation doctrine,"[145] they are technically Due Process of Law Clause challenges![146]

So too with a "Commerce Clause challenge" to a federal law, which ineluctably connects the substance of the Commerce Clause with a judicial evaluation of the substance of an act of Congress.[147] Any challenge to a legislative act on the ground that the substance of the act exceeds the proper constitutional powers of Congress or a state legislature is, at the same time, a "Due Process of Law Clause challenge."[148] It is the latter clause that guarantees a judicial *process* in which the *substance* of the act will be evaluated before a person is deprived of life, liberty, or property.[149] Further, using an act that is beyond Congress's constitutional powers to deprive an individual of life, liberty, or property violates the Fifth Amendment's Due Process of Law Clause as well as the Commerce Clause.

The core question in every case involving a purported deprivation of life, liberty, or property without due process of law is whether that deprivation is consistent with the law of the land. As we have seen, there are several types of defects that may cause legislation to fail to become the law of the land. It is a mistake to reduce the due process of law to one of these defects or another. And nothing analytically useful is gained by dubbing one or more of those defects "procedural" or "substantive."

Worse, to separate procedure from substance is to risk failing to appreciate substantive aspects of what seem at first to be solely procedural guarantees—and vice versa. The right to trial by jury, which historically included a power of the jury to pass on the constitutionality of a statute, as we noted above, is only a particularly vivid example. Better to think of due process of law as requiring a "substantive procedure"—that is, a judicial *procedure* designed to ensure that the *substance* of a statute conforms with the higher law of the land before any person can be deprived of his or her life, liberty, or property.

While the Fifth and Fourteenth Amendments' Due Process of Law Clauses both guarantee a substantive procedure, there is an important distinction between the referents of "due process of law" in each amendment. Under the Fifth Amendment, before any person can justly be deprived of "life, liberty, or property" by operation of a congressional statute, the due process of law requires a judicial determination that the *substance* of such a legislative "act" is consistent with the higher law of the land provided by the *substance* of the written federal Constitution. Specifically, a legislative act must be an exercise of, or calculated to carry into effect, a delegated power.

As John Marshall explained in *McCulloch v. Maryland*, this judicial process includes a means–ends analysis, in the form of an assessment of whether a legislative act was taken in good faith:

> [S]hould Congress, under the *pretext* of executing its powers, pass laws for the accomplishment of objects not entrusted to the government; it would become the painful *duty of this tribunal*, should a case requiring such a decision come before it, to say that such an *act* was not *the law* of the land.[150]

By 1868, the concept of due process of law was understood to impose limits on the ends which state legislatures could pursue as well. And courts constructed a doctrine—the police power doctrine—to implement that understanding. Like the principle identified in *McCulloch*, this doctrine required that exercises of state police powers be in good faith.

As we will discuss in Chapters 10 and 11, the result of this distinction is that, although the Fifth and Fourteenth Amendments both place limitations on the ends that legislators may pursue, the substance of those limitations is different. The former limitations are specified by the letter of the Constitution;[151] the latter are not specified by the letter and therefore require constitutional construction.[152] This difference has implications for the implementation of the respective clauses.

The Meaning of "Life, Liberty, and Property"

A word about the original meaning of "life, liberty, [and] property" seems appropriate before we proceed to consider some alternative originalist interpretations of "due process of law" that have been offered by scholars. We have not devoted much attention to it notwithstanding the fact that whether a personal interest qualifies as "liberty" is perhaps the most litigated interpretive issue under modern substantive due process. Why not?

We believe that less turns on the original meaning of "liberty" than might be thought. Justice Antonin Scalia and Justice Clarence Thomas criticized substantive due process doctrine for recognizing various substantive rights—particularly rights relating to sexual and reproductive autonomy—as instances of "liberty." They have insisted that "liberty" meant only what Blackstone meant by "freedom of locomotion": individual freedom from bodily restraint.[153] Suppose that's right. What follows?

Not enough to decide many hard cases, we think. Suppose that "liberty" in the Due Process of Law Clauses does not extend to the right to earn a living in the lawful occupation of one's choice. Even so, Joseph Lochner faced fines (depriving him of property) and imprisonment (depriving him of liberty) for his failure to comply with a maximum-hours law. So even if the original meaning of "liberty" is as narrow as Justices Scalia and Thomas contend, this would not tell us whether *Lochner v. New York* was correctly decided.

Suppose that "liberty" does not encompass the right to consensual same-sex intimacy. Even so, John Lawrence faced fines (depriving him of property) and spent a night in jail (depriving him of liberty) for violating a statute criminalizing such activity. Blackstonian "liberty" would not resolve *Lawrence v. Texas*. (And had violation of these statutes been punishable by death, the defendants would have faced a deprivation of life.)

In our view, these and other substantive-due-process cases turn in the final analysis, not on whether interests at stake are in fact constitutional liberties, but on whether "due process of law" imposes any limits on the *ends* for which constitutional liberties can be restricted. We are glad to stipulate that "freedom of locomotion" is the most plausible interpretation of the original meaning of "liberty." If so, then any statute enforced by imprisonment threatens to deprive a violator of that liberty. We would then still need to confront the question of whether the original meaning of "due process of law" limits the ends that governments can constitutionally pursue before it may "lawfully" send you to prison.

Competing Originalist Interpretations of "the Due Process of Law"

We have now shown that the due process of law is, as originalists have long maintained, a procedural guarantee involving the judiciary. However, the judicial procedure it guarantees includes an opportunity for someone who stands to be deprived of life, liberty, or property to challenge the *substance* of legislation for its consistency with the law of the land. Such challenges in turn require a judicial inquiry into whether enactments (a) abrogate common-law procedural protections; (b) are adjudicative rather than legislative because retrospective or insufficiently general; (c) violate express constitutional guarantees; or (d) deprive people of life, liberty, or property in the service of no constitutionally proper end and are therefore arbitrary. The last of these categories of unlawful legislation—arbitrary legislation—is the most controversial among originalists, and we now respond to some criticisms of adding it to the list.

Nathan Chapman and Michael McConnell

While acknowledging its existence, Chapman and McConnell contend that judicial employment of a means–ends analysis to evaluate whether legislation is arbitrary represents a late, controversial, rare, and ultimately improper departure from a well-settled traditional understanding of due process of law.[154] They find "two principal instances of antebellum courts' applying due process to invalidate a general and prospective law."[155]

The first is Chief Justice Roger Taney's suggestion in *Dred Scott* that

> an *act* of Congress which deprives a citizen of the United States of his liberty or property, merely because he came himself or brought his property into a particular Territory of the United States, and who had committed no offence against the laws, could hardly be dignified with the name of due process of *law*.[156]

The second is *Wynehamer v. People*, an 1856 decision in which the New York Court of Appeals invalidated a statute prohibiting the sale of liquor.[157] The Court of Appeals reasoned that "[w]hen a law annihilates the value of property . . . the owner is deprived of it according to the plainest interpretation, and certainly within the spirit of a constitutional provision intended expressly to shield private rights from the exercise of arbitrary power."[158]

These "radical" decisions, Chapman and McConnell argue, are "faulty exceptions that prove the rule."[159] Because *Dred Scott* was universally rejected by Republicans when they proposed and adopted the Fourteenth Amendment, Chapman and McConnell maintain that "it would be perverse to think that the public . . . understood it to perpetuate Chief Justice Taney's approach to due process."[160] They claim that *Wynehamer* was "immediately controversial" and that there is "no evidence" that it had "any bearing on the meaning of the Fourteenth Amendment Due Process Clause."[161] According to Chapman and McConnell, these two cases were outliers and both misinterpreted the due process of law.[162]

But as Ryan Williams points out, while *Dred Scott* was despised by Republicans, "there is virtually no evidence to suggest that such controversy stemmed from Taney's use of the Due Process Clause to protect vested property rights."[163] Justice Benjamin Curtis's dissent, lauded by Republicans, did not take issue with Taney's suggestion that Congress could not generally obliterate vested property rights through legislation.

Instead, Curtis focused on the unique character of slave property, stating that "[s]lavery, being contrary to natural right, is created only by municipal law."[164] That principle is traceable to *Somerset v. Stewart*, which we encountered in Chapter 2. In *Somerset*, Lord Mansfield declared that slavery was "so odious, that nothing can be suffered to support it, but positive law."[165] As applied to the facts of *Dred Scott*, the *Somerset* principle compelled the conclusion that slaveholders' property in their slaves ceased to exist as soon as they voluntarily brought their slaves into federal territory where slavery was legally recognized "for the purpose of being absolutely prohibited, and declared incapable of existing."[166]

Dred Scott's rejection by Republicans tells us nothing interesting about the meaning of "due process of law." And Taney's use of this concept in dicta does not seem to have stirred any specific criticism or exerted any influence.[167] As distasteful as the case is, Taney's opinion in *Dred Scott* supports our claim about the original meaning of the "due process of law"—just as it supported our claim about the original meaning of the "privileges or immunities of citizens of the United States."

So too does *Wynehamer,* which was approvingly cited by multiple courts and treatise-writers around the time of the Fourteenth Amendment's enactment.[168] Those courts that did not follow *Wynehamer* determined that statutes prohibiting sales of alcohol fell within the scope of the police power. They did not hold that, to be consistent with the due process of law, statutes need only be general and prospective and not abrogate common-law procedural rights.[169]

Indeed, none of the cases that Chapman and McConnell cite held that the due process of law was limited in scope in the manner they propose. Theirs is an argument from silence.[170] As we will see, there was more noise than they acknowledge. Hesitance to invalidate is not the same as refusal to evaluate.

McConnell and Chapman note that the Supreme Court in *Mugler v. Kansas* later upheld similar legislation.[171] But they neglect the fact that the Court did so only after determining that the legislation was "enacted in good faith, and had appropriate and direct connection with that protection to life, health, and property which each State owes to her citizens."[172] Writing for the Court, Justice John Marshall Harlan noted that the Court would not uphold legislation if it was "apparent that its *real object* is not to protect the community, or to promote the general well-being, but, under the guise of police regulation, to deprive the owner of his liberty and property."[173]

Harlan's reasoning in *Mugler* is reminiscent of Marshall's "pretext" formulation in *McCulloch*.[174] No justice in *Mugler* doubted that purported exercises of the police power—whether they took the form of municipal by-laws or ordinances or statutes—needed to be evaluated for pretext if they deprived people of life, liberty, or property.

Thus, even if Chapman and McConnell are correct that none of the cases they discuss saw courts "applying due process to invalidate a general and prospective law,"[175] they have overstated the significance of this finding. Any contemporary criticisms of *Dred Scott* and *Wynehamer* were not of these cases' holdings that due process of law forbids general and prospective laws that deprive people of vested rights without furthering a constitutionally proper end. As Ryan Williams shows, the vested-rights interpretation implicit in both decisions was endorsed by state courts throughout the 1860s.[176]

Ilan Wurman

Ilan Wurman's account of due process of law closely resembles that of Chapman and McConnell, so we will not analyze it separately. His distinctive contribution to the "substantive" debate is an argument that means–ends analysis of legislation more or less snuck in, without warrant, in antebellum law from judicial review of means–ends analysis of municipal by-laws.[177] Antebellum law, he maintains, did not require state legislatures to pursue the public good; that requirement applied only to municipal corporations, which exercised delegated, and therefore limited, powers.[178] We are unconvinced, for two reasons.

First, both by-laws and statutes were evaluated by antebellum courts to determine whether they were reasonably calculated to serve proper ends, before and after the ratification of the Fourteenth Amendment. Wurman acknowledges this, but insists that they did so in limited settings—interference with contracts, dormant commerce-clause cases—and his arguments on this score are strong.[179] But when judges determined—as Wurman concedes that they did—whether an exercise of state power was a legitimate exercise of the police power or was an interference with Congress's power to regulate commerce, they presupposed that the police power was constitutionally limited. In short order, a theory of this limitation on state power was adopted by the legal community following ratification of the Fourteenth Amendment. This theory was then applied outside the limited domains Wurman identifies.

The question is whether this expansion of the scope of police-power analysis *violates clear* original meaning or *implements unclear* original meaning. We take the latter view. Wurman lacks a persuasive explanation of how the review of municipal by-laws and that of legislation came to be conflated without anyone noticing at the time. *Mugler* and *Barbier v. Connelly*,[180] which he identifies as responsible for the conflation, engendered no significant debate on the Court or in critical commentary.

In Wurman's telling, the "due process of law" was yet another legal term of art, like "privileges or immunities." Then somehow this settled legal meaning was discarded without objection within the relevant interpretive community.[181] This seems unlikely.

We think the more plausible reading of this history is that the meaning of "due process of law" for state laws was not so settled as to foreclose what Wurman considers a misunderstanding. Judges tasked with implementing the text of the Fourteenth Amendment in the face of novel progressive legislation, adopted novel constructions to identify the outer boundaries of the state police power. The constructions they developed were more faithful to the purpose of "due process of law" than a more deferential approach that left legislators with arbitrary power over everyone within their jurisdiction.

Ryan Williams

Like Williams, we find that "due process of law" took on a different meaning over the course of the nineteenth century. But we agree with Chapman and McConnell that Williams overstates the difference, and we think that Williams does not completely capture the meaning of either the Fifth or Fourteenth Amendment's Due Process of Law Clause.[182]

Williams contends that the Fifth Amendment's Due Process of Law Clause did not originally cover legislative acts.[183] To the contrary, we have shown how the language of "due process of law," like that of "law of the land," was used by key Framers, influential treatise-writers, and courts during the Founding Era to forbid legislatures from depriving persons of common-law procedural rights, engaging in what was in substance adjudication rather than legislation, or otherwise violating a source of superior law, such as a written constitution.

Concerning the Fourteenth Amendment, we share more common ground with Williams than with Chapman and McConnell. Williams finds that, by 1868, "due process of law" was used to prohibit legislative interference with vested rights and to guarantee "general and impartial laws rather than 'special' or 'class' legislation that imposed particular burdens upon, or accorded special benefits to, particular persons or particular segments of society."[184]

On the other hand, Williams denies that due process of law was used to require that legislation be necessary to achieve constitutionally proper ends and thus to authorize judicial inquiry into "both the ends that the legislature sought to achieve and the means employed to achieve such ends."[185] The latter use, he argues, did not develop until the 1890s—the beginning of the so-called *Lochner* era.[186]

We agree that the police-power doctrine that developed in state courts— and later in the Supreme Court—in the wake of the ratification of the Fourteenth Amendment is distinguishable from antebellum police-power doctrine in certain respects. Specifically, courts became more willing to look beyond the face of enactments to discern and evaluate the propriety of legislative ends. But there was continuity as well.

Long before the *Lochner* era, antebellum courts repeatedly affirmed that legislative power was inherently limited by the ends for which legitimate governments are established. And they affirmed further that legislatures could neither deprive people of vested property rights nor constrain them in their life, liberty, or property more generally, except—as Justice Harlan put it in *Mugler*—to "protect the community, or to promote the general well-being."[187]

Prior to the ratification of the Fourteenth Amendment, state courts upheld a variety of enactments as valid exercises of the police power. These ranged from prohibitions of dirt-removal from privately owned beaches,[188] to regulations specifying the hours during which cattle could be driven through the city streets,[189] to statutes authorizing cities to make by-laws governing the interment of the dead.[190] But the scope of the police power was understood to be limited by its functions: the protection of health, safety, and morals of the public.[191]

For example, in the 1834 case of *Austin v. Murray,* the Massachusetts Supreme Judicial Court sustained a challenge to a by-law prohibiting the bringing of the dead into Charlestown for purposes of burial. This prohibition affected only Catholic parishioners.[192] The court found that it was "manifest" that "the object and purpose" of a measure was not "made in good faith" and directed at the "public good."[193] The court refused to uphold the by-law simply because it was passed "under the guise of a police regulation."[194]

To be clear, we do not think that the letter of the Fourteenth Amendment compels judges to implement the precise police-power doctrine that was developed in either the early or late nineteenth century. But implementing the Fourteenth Amendment does require a conception of the legitimate ends of government that is consistent with the original function—the spirit—of the Due Process of Law Clause in the Fourteenth Amendment. And it requires a doctrinal approach to give the text legal effect today. Providing both will be our mission in Chapter 11.

John Harrison

Like others, we have argued that "due process of law" is synonymous with "law of the land." Therefore, because "law of the land" entails the opportunity to challenge the necessity and propriety of government actions in judicial proceedings, so, too, does "due process of law."[195] John Harrison disagrees. He contends that the case against substantive review of government actions under the Fifth Amendment would be much *stronger* if "law of the land" had been used instead of "due process of law," because "a substantive reading [of 'law of the land'] would be textually absurd."[196]

Specifically, Harrison claims that the Supremacy Clause provides that "[a]cts of Congress and treaties, the non-constitutional sources of federal law, are not just the law of the land, but 'the supreme Law of the Land.'"[197] Thus, a reference to "law of the land" in the Fifth Amendment would leave no room for substantive review of duly enacted federal statutes. And so neither does "due process of law," if indeed the terms are synonymous.

Harrison's critique rests on a false premise. The Supremacy Clause does not provide that *all* congressional acts become "the supreme law of the land"— but only those acts which are "made *in pursuance of*" the Constitution.[198] We have already seen in *Marbury* and *McCulloch* John Marshall's denial that an "act" of Congress *not* made in pursuance of the Constitution becomes part of the law of the land. Furthermore, Marshall maintained that determining whether a given act of Congress was made in pursuance of the Constitution requires inquiry into whether it was necessary to achieve constitutionally proper ends.

Marshall's understanding is consistent with Alexander Hamilton's exposition of the Supremacy Clause in *Federalist 33*, in which Hamilton expressly denied that unconstitutional statutes became part of the supreme law of the land.[199] Wrote Hamilton: "[T]he clause which declares the supremacy of the laws of the Union . . . *expressly* confines this supremacy to laws made *pursuant to the Constitution*."[200]

Thus, a law authorized by the Constitution—for example, one "laying a tax for the use of the United States"—"would be supreme in its nature." But a law not authorized by the Constitution—for example, one "for abrogating or preventing the collection of a tax laid by the authority of the State, (unless upon imports and exports)"—"would not be the supreme law of the land, but an usurpation of power not granted by the Constitution."[201]

Suppose that the "due process of law" is indeed synonymous with "law of the land," as we and others maintain. There is nothing textually absurd about the claim that due process *of law* entails substantive review of federal or state statutes and that "the supreme *law* of the land" likewise constrains the substance of legislation, not merely the procedures by which a statute is enacted. *Both* the Supremacy Clause and the Due Process of Law Clauses establish criteria that legislation must meet in order to be considered law.

Harrison also argues that the Due Process of Law Clause would be redundant if it included limits on legislative power that were already imposed by other constitutional provisions.[202] This is wrong. The Due Process of Law Clause is *always* operating in conjunction with other clauses, as we saw above with respect to the First Amendment and the Commerce Clause. These clauses provide the substantive limits on legislative power that the judicial process, which is guaranteed by the Due Process of Law Clauses, is to apply to a statute before depriving any person of life, liberty, or property. These Due Process of Law clauses are an express textual recognition of what was theretofore merely implicit.

Be this as it may, as Chapman and McConnell observe, redundancy is a weak objection, here and elsewhere, for "[t]he Constitution and Bill of Rights are shot through with prohibitions that some Founders thought to be redundant with enumerated powers or prohibitions."[203] Even on a procedural reading of the Fifth Amendment that does not incorporate substantive review, the due process of law would be redundant if it is understood—as it should be—to guarantee jury trials in civil and criminal cases, given that such trials are also guaranteed by other constitutional provisions.[204]

Christopher Green

Finally, Christopher Green has accumulated a body of evidence that "due process of law" in the Fourteenth Amendment and "duly convicted" in the Thirteenth Amendment are synonymous, and that neither phrase authorizes means–ends analysis.[205] Green argues that the term "duly convicted" was the product of "a tradition stemming from the Northwest Ordinance of 1787." This tradition "fully acknowledged the great evil of slavery . . . and fugitive re-enslavement in particular, while conceding that a slave could be 'lawfully' claimed and reclaimed."[206]

According to Green, if "due process of law" and "duly convicted" mean the same—or nearly the same—thing, "due process of law" cannot possibly impose "substantive constraints on statutes' propriety." This is because a "substantive" understanding of due process of law would exclude the possibility of "lawfully" enslaving anyone, slavery being widely thought by Republicans to be contrary to natural right.[207] For this reason, Green concludes that "due process of law" serves only as a guarantee of access to regular judicial proceedings in which general, prospective statutes are applied prior to criminal punishment.[208]

The evidence Green marshals for synonymy consists of several states' prohibitions on slavery, a letter from Abraham Lincoln to Major General Frederick Steele concerning Arkansas's prohibition, and explanations of the Thirteenth Amendment's language by several commentators.[209] Adopted on January 19, 1864, Arkansas's prohibition provided that "[n]either slavery nor involuntary servitude shall hereafter exist in this State, otherwise than for the punishment of crime, whereof the party shall [be] convicted *by due process of law.*"[210]

In his letter, Lincoln described the Arkansas slavery prohibition as follows: "There shall be neither slavery nor involuntary servitude, except in the punishment of crime whereof the party shall [be] duly convicted."[211] Lincoln here apparently translated the phrase "due process of law" into "duly convicted."[212] Finally, commenting on the Thirteenth Amendment, John

Burgess noted in 1893 that "[a]ccording to the terms of [the crime exception] it is only necessary that the person shall have been duly convicted; that is, shall have been convicted by due process of law."[213]

This evidence, while probative, is insufficient to establish synonymy. It is entirely consistent with the proposition that "due process of law" was understood to guarantee certain judicial proceedings prior to criminal punishment but was *also* understood to guarantee considerably more than that. If "duly convicted" is not synonymous with "due process of law" but instead captures a subset of what the latter requires, there is no tension between the authorization of judicial review of the content of legislation under the Fourteenth Amendment's Due Process of Law Clause and the Thirteenth Amendment.

Green could well be right that Charles Sumner's view that "injustice cannot be 'law'"[214] was not incorporated into the Thirteenth or Fourteenth Amendments.[215] But we do not claim that the Due Process of Law Clauses guarantee a judicial evaluation of whether deprivations of life, liberty, or property conform with ideas of justice that are unmoored from the original meaning of the letter and the original spirit of the Constitution. We claim only (1) that these clauses guarantee proceedings in Article III courts in which legislative deprivations of life, liberty, and property may be challenged for their conformity with the Constitution; and (2) that the Constitution limits the means and ends by which such deprivations can be justified.

In the next chapter, we identify the type of judicial evaluation of the relationship between legislative means and ends that is required by the due process of law.

10

The Spirit

Implementing the Due Process of Law Clause

Barring Arbitrary Power

Having identified the original meaning of the "due process of law" in both the Fifth and Fourteenth Amendments, we turn in this chapter to how it may be implemented in a way that is faithful both to its letter and to its original spirit. As we have explained, the "spirit" of the text is its original functions, purposes, ends, or objects. What was the original function (or functions) of the Due Process of Law Clause?

In Chapter 9, we chronicled how the concept of due process of law has been refined and even redefined over the course of centuries of Anglo-American jurisprudence. But throughout its development, the end or "spirit" of the concept remained the same: barring "arbitrary" power over life, liberty, and property. In England, the "due process of law" was designed to prevent innocent persons who had committed no breach of the law from being wrongfully deprived of their life, liberty, or property by the Crown.[1] But, while the English conception of "the law of the land" was understood as a guarantee against arbitrary executive power,[2] in the United States the due process of law came to be understood as a guarantee against *all* arbitrary government action.[3] So the "due process of law" not only protected people from arbitrary power by providing a judicial process by which a person could be accurately adjudicated as guilty or innocent, but also protected people from arbitrary power by denying that an arbitrary act of a legislature qualified as "a law."[4]

In whoever hands the legislative power resided, the power was inherently limited to enacting nonarbitrary laws. As John Locke explained:

> A man . . . cannot subject himself to the arbitrary power of another; and having in the state of nature no *arbitrary power* over the life, liberty, or possession of another, but only so much as the law of nature gave him for the preservation of himself, and the rest of mankind; this is all he doth, or can give up to the commonwealth, and by it to the legislative power, so that *the legislative* can have no more than this.[5]

Whether in England or the United States, however, "the due process of law" was understood to denote a concept of rule by principles that are distinguishable from the mere will of the holders of power. Ensuring impartial adjudication in neutral courts of law was thought essential to achieving this end.[6] This is what the right to "due process of law" guarantees in our Constitution.

"Arbitrary" is a difficult term to define or apply with precision. R. George Wright explains why context is critical in determining whether something is arbitrary—just as it is in determining whether something is "flat."[7] An airport runway and a glass table might both be identified as "flat," even though the regularity of their surfaces is quite different.[8] Why? As Wright points out, "different purposes and interests are at stake, themselves largely creating the crucial differences in context."[9] Whether a decision is "arbitrary" similarly depends on what purposes and interests are at stake. Reasons that might count as reasonable grounds for one's decision to see a particular movie— one's mood on a given day, and one's desire to be entertained—would be rightly regarded as arbitrary if used to ground a decision about whether to throw someone in jail.[10]

The context with which we are concerned here is the exercise of lawmaking power under "this Constitution"—what distinguishes a mere "act" of a legislature from "a law" that people have an obligation to follow.[11] We thus define arbitrariness with reference to *the ends* for which legitimate governments are established, according to the political-philosophical premises on which this Constitution rests, and also with reference to *the means* that the Constitution authorizes to effectuate those ends. Appropriate means must be in service of (or necessary to) a proper end. Legislation that lacks this fit is arbitrary—and therefore contrary to the original spirit of the Due Process of Law Clauses.

As we saw in Chapter 9, the letter of the Due Process of Law Clauses requires a *judicial* proceeding or "process" of *some* kind prior to any deprivations of life, liberty, or property. On this, everyone who has studied the original meaning of the Due Process of Law Clauses agrees. The disagreement concerns the *scope* of that judicial proceeding. The term "of law" clarifies this. It connotes that a statute purporting to justify a deprivation of "life, liberty, or property" be a valid "law," rather than an arbitrary legislative act. An arbitrary statute is one that is not within what Alexander Hamilton referred to as the "just and constitutional" powers of the legislature to enact.[12]

At the federal level, due process of law requires a judicial inquiry as to whether the end of the legislation falls within one of the delegated powers of Congress or is prohibited by the Constitution.[13] It also requires that the incidental means employed pursuant to the Necessary and Proper Clause be in service of a proper end or object, and not be one that is barred by the Constitution.

At the state level, identifying arbitrary legislation requires a two-fold judicial inquiry into whether (1) it is within the scope of power that is delegated to state legislatures by their own constitutions; and whether (2) it is prohibited by the federal Constitution's limits on state power, including Section 1 of the Fourteenth Amendment.[14] For a state statute to be a law rather than a mere act of power, it is necessary, but not sufficient, that a state constitution authorizes it.[15] The statute must also not deprive people of the due process of law or "abridge the privileges or immunities of citizens of the United States."[16]

In Part I, we presented a theory of the original letter and spirit of the Privileges or Immunities Clause. It is enough to say that, on any of the competing originalist interpretations—other than the discredited view of the clause as an indecipherable "ink blot"[17]—judicial enforcement of the clause clearly calls for judicial evaluation of a state law even if the law is authorized by a state's own constitution.[18] That evaluation will require the identification of the outer boundaries of state legislative authority. Unlike those of Congress, the outer boundaries of state legislative power are not expressly provided in the US Constitution, however. They must therefore be provided by originalist construction, rather than identified by originalist interpretation. The text of the Privileges or Immunities Clause—"no state shall make or enforce any law"—demands no less.

Having now identified the original spirit of the Due Process of Law Clauses—the prohibition of arbitrary power—we can begin to specify an approach that equips legislators and judges to implement faithfully the original meaning of the text.

Identifying Good-Faith Exercises of Legislative Discretion

Judges already routinely seek to determine whether legislative enactments that restrict individuals are law rather than exercises of arbitrary power by a legislature, even if they do not use this precise language.[19] They do not, however, do so in all contexts in which life, liberty, or property is at stake. Instead, since the late 1930s, judges have followed the Supreme Court's lead in distinguishing between "fundamental" rights and mere "liberty" interests. Burdens on the former "preferred freedoms" receive exacting judicial scrutiny; burdens on the latter receive more deferential review.[20] While the doctrines governing tiers of heightened scrutiny may slowly be eroding, the lack of judicial protection of economic liberty remains entrenched.[21]

The emergence of the tiers of scrutiny was anticipated in a famous footnote in *United States v. Carolene Products*.[22] It was later given an elaborate theoretical defense by John Hart Ely in his 1980 book, *Democracy and Distrust*.[23] The story of its development has been told repeatedly, and we will not recount it again here.[24]

One of us has argued that both the original "Footnote Four" framework and its present incarnation contradict the rule of construction provided by the original meaning of the Ninth Amendment by relegating rights not textually "enumerated in the Constitution" to a less-demanding standard of judicial review *because* they are not enumerated.[25] Some form of tiered scrutiny might be defended, however, not on the textually prohibited ground that some rights are enumerated in the text and others are not, but on the basis of concerns about institutional competence.

Specifically, the judiciary is institutionally incapable of thwarting all legislative opportunism—understood as the pursuit of constitutionally improper ends—and will inevitably err in identifying instances of opportunism. So perhaps it makes sense for judges to allocate scarce resources toward thwarting malign legislative behavior that the judiciary is better equipped to identify and away from legislative behavior that it is more likely to err in identifying. For instance, if judges are more likely to err in identifying arbitrary burdens on economic liberty than they are in identifying arbitrary burdens on political speech, it might make sense for judges to concentrate on the latter. As Neil Komesar has observed:

> The resource costs of judicial review . . . depend on the ease with which courts can distinguish valid from invalid governmental activity, and their

ability to formulate and articulate a corresponding clear test. Clear tests mean fewer cases brought, litigated, and appealed, and therefore a smaller burden on the judiciary. Such clarity, however, involves a degree of arbitrariness or, more gently, generalization, which risks invalidating good legislation or accepting bad. . . .

As the complexity of governmental regulation increased in the 1930s, the costs of court involvement also increased. Although many factors may have contributed to the retreat from economic due process which occurred, the sizable and increasing price tag for judicial involvement and the failure of judicial strategies to control these rising costs pushed relentlessly in that direction.[26]

In sum, in designing a mechanism to identify and screen arbitrary legislative power, we should avoid enabling arbitrary judicial power.

We agree with Komesar that the emergence of tiered scrutiny can be understood, in part, as a response to a perceived need to economize on scarce judicial resources in an increasingly complex policy environment.[27] We also agree that the courts need to be able to "distinguish valid from invalid governmental activity" with some degree of dispatch, given their heavy dockets and scarce judicial time and energy.[28] But Komesar's analysis overlooks the differences between the tiers of scrutiny assumed by *Carolene Products* in 1938 and those applied by courts today. Even if the Court in *Carolene Products* was right to distinguish between economic liberty and other rights because judicial error rates increase dramatically in the context of evaluating burdens on economic liberty,[29] it does not follow that the current allocation of judicial resources is correct.

This is because current rational-basis review has departed from the "due process of law" inquiry into rationality actually described by Justice Harlan Fiske Stone in the body of his *Carolene Products* opinion.[30] That type of inquiry reigned in the twenty-four years between 1931, when the Supreme Court adopted the presumption of constitutionality (in *O'Gorman & Young, Inc. v. Hartford Fire Ins. Co.*[31]), and 1955, when the Court embraced what can be called "conceivable-basis review"[32] (in *Williamson v. Lee Optical*).

Would replacing "conceivable-basis review" with a standard that more closely resembles the rationality review described in *Carolene Products* strain the judiciary to a breaking point? The *Carolene Products* Court did not think it would, and neither do we.[33] The rationality review described in *Carolene Products* would give legislatures the space that they need to exercise their constitutional powers for the benefit of the public while safeguarding the public against opportunism. To see why, we turn to Justice Stone's opinion for the Court in *Carolene Products* and the lower court decision that was reversed in *Lee Optical*.

Rationality Review: Means–Ends Fit

Constitutional scholars all remember Justice Stone's affirmation that "regulatory legislation affecting ordinary commercial transactions" would henceforth be presumed constitutional.[34] Few, however, seem to have noticed the length to which he went in his opinion for the Court to make plain that this presumption was rebuttable on the basis of facts presented to a court.[35]

Justice Stone explained that "no pronouncement of a legislature can forestall attack upon the constitutionality of the prohibition which it enacts"; that "the constitutionality of a statute predicated upon the existence of a particular *state of facts* may be challenged by *showing to the court* that those facts have ceased to exist"; and that "the constitutionality of a statute, valid on its face, may be assailed by *proof of facts* tending to show that the statute as applied to a particular article is *without support in reason*."[36] He also assumed that "a statute would *deny due process* which precluded the *disproof . . . of all facts* which would show or tend to show that a statute depriving the suitor of life, liberty or property had a rational basis."[37] "[W]ithout support in reason" is the very definition of "arbitrary."

Stone's formulation of rationality review indicates that litigants would be able to test legislation "by proof of facts" that the legislation is arbitrary.[38] Thus, legislation is not to be pronounced unconstitutional "unless in the light of the facts made known or generally assumed it is of such a character as to preclude the assumption that it rests upon some rational basis within the knowledge and experience of the legislators."[39] If "facts made known or generally assumed" preclude that assumption, legislation *would be* pronounced unconstitutional.[40] And in *Carolene Products* the Court did consider record evidence—however spurious[41]—about the alleged essential health benefits of milk fat that had been presented to Congress. While it is true that the Supreme Court did not find any economic regulation to be arbitrary after *Carolene Products*, the lower courts persisted in following its reasoning by engaging in genuine fact finding.

We find it intriguing that, from 1910[42] to 1976,[43] only a three-judge panel consisting of two federal district court judges and one circuit court judge, selected by the chief judge of the district, could declare a state or federal statute unconstitutional.[44] As Michael Morley has detailed, "Throughout much of the twentieth century, Congress prohibited individual federal judges from enjoining federal laws; only three-judge panels were permitted to adjudicate claims for injunctive relief against allegedly unconstitutional federal statutes."[45] The decisions of these panels would then be taken directly to the Supreme Court on a writ of certiorari.

Such a procedure guards against the error costs of relying on individual district court judges to make the first assessment of legislative arbitrariness. It eliminates one intermediary step in the review process: circuit courts of appeals. And it contemplates meaningful review of legislation. You do not need three judges to apply "conceivable basis review."

In 1954, a three-judge panel of the Western District of Oklahoma took the Court in *Carolene Products* at its word. The lower court dutifully stated that "all legislative enactments are accompanied by a presumption of constitutionality" and that "[a] court only can annul legislative action where it appears certain that the attempted exercise of police power is arbitrary, unreasonable or discriminatory."[46] The panel then realistically evaluated the record evidence and argument presented to the court by the parties at trial.

The Oklahoma statute in question forbade, among other things, anyone but a licensed optometrist or ophthalmologist to "[f]it, adjust, adapt, or to in any manner apply lenses, frames, prisms, or any other optical appliances to the face of a person" or to replace any lenses without a written prescription from an Oklahoma licensed ophthalmologist or optometrist.[47] Writing for the panel, District Judge Wallace noted that written prescriptions contain no instructions on how to fit glasses to the face, indicating that the fitting "can skillfully and accurately be performed" without specialized training.[48] He highlighted the fact that the device used to "measure[] the power of the existing lense [*sic*] and reduce[] it to prescriptive terms"—the "lensometer"—was "not operated by the physician but by a clerk in the office."[49]

On the basis of these findings and other record evidence, the court concluded that "[t]he means chosen by the legislature does not bear 'real and substantial relation' to the end sought, that is, better vision."[50] Those means served only "to place within the exclusive control of optometrists . . . the power to choose just what individual opticians will be permitted to pursue their calling"—an end to which the legislature was not competent.[51] The court did not directly accuse the legislature of protectionism, nor did it need to. It needed only to determine that the discrimination against opticians was not rationally justified as a health measure on the basis of the facts in the record and was therefore unconstitutional.[52]

The Supreme Court, of course, reversed,[53] applying a standard of review that is difficult to imagine any legislation failing to satisfy. Writing for the Court, Justice William O. Douglas made plain that, henceforth, legislation reviewed under the Court's constitutional default standard of review would be upheld if the Court could *conceive* of any hypothetical reason why the legislature *might* have enacted that legislation—even if that reason found no support in the record.[54]

In the instant case, despite acknowledging that it "appears that in many cases the optician can easily supply the new frames or new lenses without reference to the old written prescription," Douglas speculated that the "legislature might have concluded that the frequency of occasions when a prescription is necessary was sufficient to justify this regulation of the fitting of eyeglasses."[55] It did not matter that there was no evidence in the record that the legislature had so concluded. The move from a realistic evidence-based inquiry into whether legislatures were actually trying to achieve proper ends to a formalist hypothetical inquiry into whether the legislature might have had proper ends in sight was significant.

The new, formalist standard would be carefully and precisely articulated by Justice Clarence Thomas in an otherwise obscure case: *FCC v. Beach Communications.*[56] Writing for the Court, Thomas stated that judges applying rational-basis review must uphold legislation "if there is any reasonably conceivable state of facts that could provide a rational basis for [it]"; that those challenging legislation must negate "every conceivable basis which might support it"; and that the government need not justify legislation with "evidence or empirical data."[57] As Justice John Paul Stevens ruefully observed in concurrence, "conceivable" basis review is "tantamount to no review at all."[58]

The *Carolene Products* Court was on solid ground in assuming that it would deny due process of law to allow the government to forestall constitutional challenges by simply asserting the legitimacy of its ends and to deny litigants the ability to demonstrate that legislation was arbitrary.[59] Yet, that is effectively what is enabled by conceivable-basis review.[60]

Good-Faith Exercises of Legislative Discretion: Smoking Out Pretext

We have seen how, in *McCulloch*, Chief Justice John Marshall imposed a judicially administrable limiting principle on the discretion of Congress to enact laws that are necessary and proper for carrying into execution its discretionary powers.[61] His principle is worth repeating:

> [S]hould Congress, under the *pretext* of executing its powers, pass laws for the accomplishment of objects not entrusted to the government; it would become the painful duty of this tribunal, should a case requiring such a decision come before it, to say that such an act was not the law of the land.[62]

In other words, the due process of law *requires* a judicial examination of whether Congress's discretionary power to enact laws that are "necessary and proper"[63] has been exercised in good faith. Or, as Hamilton explained in his defense of the constitutionality of a national bank, Congress "has only a right to pass such laws as are necessary and proper to accomplish the objects intrusted [*sic*] to it," and "[t]he relation between the measure and the end . . . must be the criterion of constitutionality."[64] We might call this the "Hamilton Test."

The arbitrariness review employed by the lower court in *Lee Optical* to evaluate the "relation between the measure and the end" can be understood as an effort to determine whether the statute in question was a good-faith exercise of the legislative power. In contrast, conceivable-basis review is a formalist shell— it preserves only the appearance of a requirement to show that a law is necessary and proper to accomplish an end entrusted to state governments.

The due process of law to which a person is entitled before being deprived of his or her life, liberty, or property requires a realistic evaluation of a contested statute, not a formalistic one. We propose that such an inquiry ought to operate as follows: Once a party has made a threshold showing that he or she stands to be deprived of his or her life, liberty, or property, the government should be made to offer a reason for its actions and to bear the burden of producing evidence in support of its actions. Judges should then determine whether the government has demonstrated that its actions are calculated to achieve a constitutionally proper end or ends—whether the end sought is one to which the legislature is competent.

Allocating to Congress or a state legislature the burden of producing evidence that its actions are calculated to achieve a constitutionally legitimate end comports with the spirit of the Due Process of Law Clauses. Government officials are in control of the evidence concerning the ends that legislation is designed to achieve.[65] Placing the burden of producing evidence on the government is likely to yield more evidence than would otherwise be available.[66] This in turn allows judges to better determine whether an action is necessary to achieve a constitutionally proper end.

We have elsewhere argued that, because all judges, legislators, and executive-branch officials receive their powers over resources belonging to others after having made a voluntary promise to abide by the terms of "this Constitution," they ought to be understood to be fiduciaries.[67] Accordingly, like other fiduciaries, they ought to exercise their delegated powers in good faith, consistently with the ends that they have been empowered to pursue, rather than in pursuit of other ends.

Fiduciary law recognizes that policing of fiduciaries by generalist judges can sometimes harm beneficiaries more than help them.[68] Such monitoring can discourage competent would-be fiduciaries from entering into fiduciary relationships in the first place. Such second-guessing may also defeat the purposes for which beneficiaries grant their fiduciaries discretion.[69] One important reason that fiduciaries are delegated discretionary power is that they have specialized knowledge and judgment. Judges, by contrast, are generalists who are jacks of many trades but masters of none. The more that judges veto fiduciary decisions, the less scope is given to fiduciary expertise, and the less valuable fiduciary relationships predicated on expertise are to beneficiaries.

Yet, the risk of opportunistic behavior is too great, and the costs that it imposes on beneficiaries too high for judicial review to be toothless, whether the fiduciary be private or public.[70] Indeed, the need for such review is even greater when protecting the rights, privileges, and immunities of the people from legislation. Unlike beneficiaries of private fiduciaries, the people cannot divest themselves of the burdens of legislation the way shareholders may divest themselves of stock, or choose a new advisor.[71]

We have elsewhere described a theory of group agency that makes the concept of a legislative end ontologically coherent, notwithstanding the reality that different legislators may have different motivations and expectations, and we will not reiterate it here. We stress, however, that such ends can be inferred from the text, structure, and likely effects of legislation, and thus need not entail any direct judicial inquiry into the motivations or expectations of any particular individuals.[72]

Requiring the government to offer a reason for its actions and bear realistic review of whether a law is an appropriate or good-faith effort to pursue a proper end entails that courts distinguish between ends that are proper and ends that are beyond the competence of legislatures. As we will detail in the next chapter, these ends vary depending on whether the legislature is Congress or that of a state.

11

The Proper Ends of Legislative Power

To constitute a law, a legislative act must be "necessary and proper" to achieve a constitutionally proper end.[1] In considering the scope of the Due Process of Law Clauses, we need not present a theory of the full scope of federal or state legislative power. Instead, we need only consider the propriety of that subset of enactments that deprive a person of his or her life, liberty, or property. We have shown that such laws must be consistent with constitutionally proper ends. In this chapter, we identify these proper ends.

The Ends of Congressional Power: Few and Defined

That the Constitution limits the ends—or what were referred to as "objects"[2]—of the federal government is readily apparent. Article I vests "[a]ll legislative Powers *herein granted*" in "a Congress . . . which shall consist of a Senate and a House of Representatives."[3] Article I, Section 8, and Article IV, Sections 1 and 3, list the permissible ends of federal statutes.[4] Among the powers delegated to Congress is the incidental power to pass legislation that is "necessary and proper for carrying into Execution" the ends that are provided in Article I and elsewhere in the Constitution. To this list other ends have been added in a number of amendments.[5] The Tenth Amendment then reaffirms that all powers that have not been so "delegated to the United States by the Constitution . . . are reserved to the States . . . or to the people."[6]

The claim that there was widespread agreement concerning the scope of Congress's powers during the Founding Era might be questioned in light of the constitutional debates that immediately broke out after ratification. When then–Secretary of the Treasury Alexander Hamilton proposed the incorporation of a national bank to a Federalist-dominated first Congress in 1791, a flurry of opinions on the subject were issued by Attorney General Edmund Randolph, Secretary of State Thomas Jefferson, and Hamilton himself.[7] James Madison, then serving as a member of the first Congress, delivered a lengthy speech concerning the constitutionality of the bank bill. In this speech, he supplied a list of interpretive principles that he believed ought to guide consideration of whether assertions of government power were authorized by the Constitution.[8] Applying these principles, Madison concluded that it was "not possible to discover in [the Constitution] the power to incorporate a Bank."[9]

We won't dwell on their disagreements, most of which, we submit, concerned the particulars of a national bank rather than constitutional first principles. Instead, we wish to stress the commonality between Madison's and Hamilton's views on unenumerated incidental powers. Madison concluded that the Necessary and Proper Clause must be "limited to means necessary to the end, and incident to the nature of the specified powers."[10] He rejected any interpretation that would "give an unlimited discretion to Congress" and thus "destroy[]" the "essential characteristic of the Government, as composed of limited and enumerated powers."[11] But Madison did not deny that the national government had unenumerated, incidental powers or means to carry the enumerated powers or ends into execution. Indeed, he acknowledged that "some discretionary power, and reasonable latitude must be left to the judgment of the legislature" in pursuing the "great ends of government" set forth in the Constitution.[12]

Likewise, in defending the constitutionality of his bank proposal, Hamilton did not argue that Congress enjoyed unlimited discretion. To the contrary, he affirmed that government power was inherently limited, writing that "no government has a right to do merely what it pleases"[13]—which is a succinct description of an arbitrary power. As we've noted, like Madison, Hamilton maintained that the national government created by the Constitution "has only a right to pass such laws as are necessary and proper *to accomplish the objects intrusted [sic] to it.*" He provided what, in Chapter 10, we called the Hamilton Test: "*the relation between the measure and the end* . . . must be the criterion of constitutionality."[14]

Nearly thirty years later, Chief Justice John Marshall would reach the same conclusion as Hamilton. In *McCulloch*, Marshall set forth his own now canonical construction of the Necessary and Proper Clause: "Let the end be legitimate, let it be within the scope of the constitution, and all means which are appropriate, which are plainly adapted to that end, which are not prohibited, but consist with the letter and spirit of the constitution, are constitutional."[15] Apart from some loose talk about "convenien[ce],"[16] the actual construction adopted by Marshall in *McCulloch* was largely consistent with both Madison's and Hamilton's insistence that some means–ends scrutiny— "the relation between the measure and the end"—was required to set the boundaries of incidental powers.[17]

In addition, we have seen that Marshall expanded on the Hamilton Test by advocating a judicial inquiry into whether legislative claims to be pursuing proper objects or ends are asserted in good faith or are instead pretextual. Here it is (for a third time):

> [S]hould Congress, under the *pretext* of executing its powers, pass laws for the accomplishment of objects not entrusted to the government; it would become the painful duty of this tribunal, should a case requiring such a decision come before it, to say that such an act was not the law of the land.[18]

Here, Marshall stressed that the Court would be bound to invalidate legislative acts that, although cast as measures calculated to achieve legitimate ends, were in fact efforts to usurp powers not delegated to Congress.

In short, Marshall favored judicial scrutiny of the good faith of congressional assertions of its power "to make. . . . laws"—the basic approach we are proposing here. Identifying pretextual legislation in particular cases could entail assessing the fit between the government's purported ends and its choice of means, as both Hamilton and Madison had favored. On Marshall's account, Congress may not act pretextually to accomplish ends that it is not constitutionally empowered to pursue. And it is "the painful duty" of the judiciary to keep Congress honest.[19] Otherwise, Congress could in practice do what it pleased, so long as it pointed to a proper power and claimed that it was seeking to accomplish an object "intrusted to [the government]."[20]

Our claim can be summarized thus: (1) Congress has a constitutional duty to act in ways that are necessary to carry into effect proper delegated powers; (2) legislative enactments that are not necessary or proper are not made "pursuant to" the Constitution and, therefore, do not become part of the supreme law of the land; (3) the Fifth Amendment's Due Process of Law Clause forbids the federal government from depriving individuals of life, liberty, or property without a judicial process to ensure that such a deprivation is pursuant to the law of the land; (4) this judicial process includes ascertaining whether the government's actions are a necessary and proper means of carrying into execution a power delegated to Congress, rather than a power that has been delegated to another branch of government, or not delegated at all.

It bears emphasizing that we are not claiming that particular substantive limitations on congressional power are contained in the original meaning of the text of the Fifth Amendment. Rather, we are claiming that the Fifth Amendment recognizes the fundamental right to a *judicial process* to ensure that someone's life, liberty, or property is not being deprived, except by a constitutionally valid exercise of congressional power. The proper ends of Congress's legislative powers are specified elsewhere in the Constitution—in the limited objects or powers that the Constitution empowers Congress to pursue. Likewise, in the case of states, it is to be found in the texts of state constitutions.[21]

But both Congress and state legislatures are also constrained by the inherent limits on *all* legislative power, whether or not such limits are expressly acknowledged in a written constitution. As Justice Samuel Chase put it: "There are acts which the Federal, or State, Legislature cannot do, without exceeding their authority."[22] These inherent limits on legislative power apply to state legislatures. They also apply to Congress when it exercises its plenary power over the District of Columbia and the territories, as well as when it "carries into execution" its enumerated regulatory powers.[23]

For example, in the 1903 case of *Champion v. Ames,* the Court can be understood as splitting 5–4 over whether Congress has a police power with respect to interstate commerce. In his opinion for the majority. Justice John Marshall Harlan put the matter this way:

> As a state may, for the purpose of guarding the morals of its own people, forbid all sales of lottery tickets within its limits, so Congress, for the purpose of guarding the people of the United States against the "widespread pestilence of lotteries" and to protect the commerce which concerns all the states, may prohibit the carrying of lottery tickets from one state to another.[24]

While Harlan conceded "that the power of Congress to regulate commerce among the states, although plenary, cannot be deemed *arbitrary,*" he confined the limitations on this power to those that "are prescribed by the Constitution"—in particular, to the "rights secured or protected by that instrument."[25]

The dissenters' denial "that Congress has [a] general police power"[26] missed Harlan's point. Harlan was claiming that Article I, Section 8 gave Congress the same type of "plenary" police power to regulate interstate commerce that the states had to regulate intrastate commerce. Therefore, once it was assumed that the police power of states included the power to ban lotteries within their borders, the power of Congress to ban lotteries within its more limited domain over interstate commerce was all but conceded.

By the same token, if a state's general police power has inherent limits, then so too would Congress's more specific regulatory powers. Whether regulating the District of Columbia, the territories, or interstate commerce, a congressional act that exceeded these inherent limits would not be a law that is "proper for carrying into execution" its delegated powers. In the next section, we focus on the police power of states. But we can now see how, under certain circumstances, the inherent limits on this power will apply as well to Congress.

We turn now to these limits.

The Ends of State Legislative Power: General but Not Unlimited

The powers of state governments are not defined by the federal Constitution. Madison described these powers as "numerous and indefinite."[27] And the Tenth Amendment refers to "powers . . . reserved to the States respectively, or to the people," without specifying *which* remaining powers are reserved to states and which are reserved to the people.[28]

For this reason, following the ratification of the Fourteenth Amendment, state courts, and eventually the Supreme Court, needed to develop a construction of the scope of state power to give effect to the text of both the Fourteenth Amendment's Due Process of Law Clause and its Privileges or Immunities Clause. Then, once the latter had effectively been redacted by the Court in the *Slaughter-House Cases* and *United States v. Cruikshank,* the Due Process of Law Clause was made to do most of the work of protecting individual rights against state legislation.

As we have seen, the concepts of the "law of the land" and "due process of law" originally forbade deprivations of vested rights and arbitrary distinctions between persons and groups, as well as other deprivations of life, liberty, or property that served no proper governmental end. The text of the Constitution specifies the ends or objects of congressional power by which the constitutionality of federal legislation can be assessed. Not so for the states. But the substantive protection from arbitrary power provided by the text of the Fourteenth Amendment's Due Process of Law Clause would be empty without an implementing construction of the appropriate ends of state power, against which an act of the legislature can be evaluated.

After 1868, federal courts took this responsibility seriously. They adopted and refined the "police power" doctrine that state courts had begun to develop during the antebellum period.[29] We now trace the development of this judicial construction.

The Origins of the "Police Power"

At the time of the Framing, the phrase "internal police" or "police" was used to refer generally to the reserved powers of the states. For example, writing for the Court in *Gibbons v. Ogden,* Chief Justice Marshall distinguished between "regulations of [interstate] commerce" and police power regulations.[30] The latter encompassed "[i]nspection laws, quarantine laws, health laws of every description as well as laws for regulating the internal commerce of a State."[31]

The police power was not a new concept—it could be traced back centuries.[32] As Markus Dubber has explained, the historical police power authorized a powerful few to rule over their supposed inferiors.[33] It was rooted in a conception of state government as household governance: the householder's absolute power to arrange the household for the common good of the whole family served as a model for absolute continental monarchies.

Dubber's genealogy makes us cautious about endorsing the existence of *any* "police powers" within a republican form of government. But in the nineteenth-century, US courts sought to give the police power a more limited meaning. While space constraints prevent us from examining the origins and doctrinal development of the police power in detail, we can sketch its general contours.

Judges and legal commentators evaluating exercises of state power under state constitutions frequently noted the difficulty of identifying the limits of the police power.[34] They nonetheless sought to confine the police power to certain objects and to determine whether government officials were actually pursuing those objects when they invoked the police power.[35]

The police power was sometimes conceptualized as a means of enforcing a common law maxim governing the law of nuisance: *sic utere tuo, ut alienum non lædas*—use your own property in such a way that you do not injure other people.[36] An influential 1843 opinion, written by Judge Lemuel Shaw,[37] distilled it thus:

> We think it a settled principle, growing out of the nature of well ordered
> civil society, that every holder of property, however absolute and unqualified
> may be his title, holds it under the implied liability that his use of it
> may be so regulated, that it shall not be injurious to the equal enjoyment of
> others having an equal right to the enjoyment of their property, nor injurious
> to the rights of the community.[38]

In the early nineteenth century, judicial scrutiny of legislative ends was not particularly rigorous. Caleb Nelson observes that judges limited themselves almost exclusively to the text of statutes in evaluating them.[39] Consider the 1833 case of *Hoke v. Henderson*, which saw the North Carolina Supreme Court maintaining that a legislature could not validly use its admitted power over other aspects of the clerks' offices *for the purpose of* expelling clerks from office.[40] Chief Justice Thomas Ruffin's opinion noted that "if the law [were] couched in general terms, so that the Court, which cannot inquire into motives not avowed, could not see that the act had its origin in any other consideration but public expediency," the court would "be obliged to execute it as a law."[41] (Notice too how Ruffin employs the distinction between an "act" and "a law.")

Crucially, Ruffin added, such a general enactment, if designed only to expel the clerks, would be given effect by judges "not because it was constitutional, but because the Court could not see its real character, and therefore could not see that it was unconstitutional."[42] The implication was that such an enactment would indeed *be* unconstitutional but that judges could not invalidate it. In declining to inquire into legislative ends, judges sometimes advanced arguments based on the separation of powers, emphasizing the respect owed to members of a coordinate branch and that branch's unique province and duty to legislate.[43]

We stress that this judicial deference is wholly separate from identifying the substantive scope of a state's police power. It is informed by an understanding of the judicial role—a vision that is itself a constitutional construction, not part of the original meaning of the text of the Fourteenth Amendment.

We maintain that the original meaning of the Due Process of Law Clauses of the Fifth and Fourteenth Amendments forbids legislative enactments that arbitrarily deprive persons of their lives, liberty, or property. If so, then there is no textual bar against judges holding legislatures to this stricture by realistically evaluating "the relation between the measure and the end"[44] when those ends are cleverly disguised. After the Fourteenth Amendment was enacted, this is just what happened.

Police Power Doctrine after 1868

Nineteenth-century judges and commentators never quite confronted—let alone resolved—the tension between the absolutist origins of the police power and the Constitution's premise of limited government. But after the Fourteenth Amendment imposed new federal constraints on state power, judges made efforts to render the police power safe for a constitutional republic.[45] They did so in a manner that echoed the Declaration of Independence.

After affirming that "all men are created equal," and "that they are endowed by their Creator with certain unalienable Rights, that among these are Life, Liberty and the pursuit of Happiness," the Declaration offered the following concise summary of the purpose of all legitimate government: "That *to secure these rights,* Governments are instituted among Men, deriving their *just powers* from the consent of the governed."[46] According to this vision of the social compact, "just powers" are those that are delegated by "the governed" in order to secure the individual rights of "Life, Liberty and the pursuit of Happiness."[47]

Thomas M. Cooley was the elected chief justice of the Michigan Supreme Court from 1864 to 1884, while serving concurrently as a professor at the University of Michigan, as well as its dean from 1871 to 1883.[48] In 1868, Cooley wrote that, in any case involving a purported exercise of the police power, judges needed to ask "whether the State exceed[ed] its *just powers* in dealing with the property and restraining the actions of individuals."[49] What were those "just powers"?

Cooley articulated a construction of the police power that is consistent with the premises of the Declaration:

> The police of a State . . . embraces its system of internal regulation, by which it is sought not only to preserve the public order and to prevent offenses against the State, but also to establish for the intercourse of citizen with citizen those rules of good manners and good neighborhood which are calculated to prevent a conflict of rights, and to insure to each the uninterrupted enjoyment of his own, so far as is reasonably consistent with a like enjoyment of the rights by others.[50]

Cooley made no effort to create a comprehensive list of proper state powers, believing that one could not enumerate all of "the various cases in which the exercise by one individual of his rights may conflict with a similar exercise by others."[51] Instead, he focused on whether the state's actions were calculated to safeguard the rights of individuals.

Distinguishing a constitutionally proper law from pretended legislation would be impossible without some means of distinguishing proper from improper legislative ends. Giving effect to the letter of the Fourteenth Amendment's Due Process of Law Clause (together with the Privileges or Immunities Clause) thus requires a conception of the limits of legislative power. What distinguishes a genuine law from what the Supreme Court would describe as "mere will exerted as an act of power"?[52] What could legislatures do, consistent with nineteenth-century police power doctrine?

Legitimate exercises of the police power may be grouped under two headings: regulations and prohibitions. Legislatures were understood to have the just power to make *rightful* activities—activities that do not inherently injure other people—*regular.* That is, legislatures may specify the ways in which these activities are conducted so as to prevent rights violations before they happen (rather than relying solely on lawsuits for damages after the fact).[53] Thus, both the specification of what is required to make contracts legally binding and the specification of speed limits reduce the risk of accidental injury. In addition to this power of regulation, legislatures were also understood to have the just power to *prohibit* wrongful activities that inherently injure others, such as theft, murder, or fraud.[54] By securing the individual rights retained by the people in either of these ways, legislatures promote the public good.[55]

Yet, if police power doctrine was not in fact as incoherent as it was later made out to be by its legal-realist critics,[56] neither was it ever as entirely coherent as this conceptual grouping might suggest. And it became less coherent over time.[57] In the wake of an evangelical movement to simply obliterate certain categories of property (namely, liquor and lottery tickets), the malleability of the "public morals" prong of police power doctrine became apparent.[58]

John Compton has detailed how traditional "morals regulations" were justified in terms of "the maintenance of *public* order," rather than "the eradication of [*private*] vice."[59] Nevertheless, judges at first resisted *novel* morals regulations that were advanced by evangelical reformers, which the judges deemed incompatible with traditional limits on government power.[60] For example, while upholding traditional liquor licensing laws, judges struck down key components of temperance legislation that banned the manufacture and sale of intoxicating liquors altogether.[61]

This resistance did not last. Compton describes how state judges eventually upheld liquor and lottery prohibitions by sweeping them within the malleable "morals" prong of the police power.[62] The Supreme Court in *Mugler v. Kansas* upheld these laws as well, sanctioning the constitutionality of a state prohibition on manufacturing liquor against a due process of law challenge. The plaintiffs unsuccessfully alleged that the law did not fall within the scope of the police powers.[63]

Writing for the Court, Justice John Marshall Harlan insisted that the Court had a solemn duty to invalidate purported police measures with "no real or substantial relation" to the ends of "protect[ing] the public health, the public morals, or the public safety."[64] But, he wrote, "we cannot shut out of view the fact, within the knowledge of all, that the public health, the public morals, and the public safety, may be endangered by the general use of intoxicating drinks."[65]

As J. I. Clark Hare observed in an 1889 treatise, *American Constitutional Law*, the *Mugler* majority treated liquor as an inherently noxious category of property comparable to poisons or infected merchandise, without any concerted effort to demonstrate that liquor was "hurtful . . . when used in moderation."[66] The Court thereby allowed the police power to escape its traditional bounds without establishing an objective standard for evaluating future claims that a given measure was within the scope of the police power.[67]

Judicial scrutiny of statutes to identify pretended legislation was often painfully inadequate when the stakes were highest. Though typically not recognized as such, perhaps the most appalling failure of the old police power doctrine to limit arbitrary power is *Plessy v. Ferguson*. In *Plessy*, the Court upheld Louisiana legislation forbidding private street-car operators to provide service to both Blacks and whites.[68]

Writing for the Court, Justice Henry Brown spent all of a single paragraph analyzing "whether the statute of Louisiana is a reasonable regulation."[69] Brown emphasized that "there must necessarily be a large discretion on the part of the legislature." He then affirmed that legislatures are "at liberty to act with reference to the established usages, customs, and traditions of the people, and with a view to the promotion of their comfort and the preservation of the public peace and good order."[70]

In deferring to "established usages, customs, and traditions," the Court in *Plessy* neither required any proof of a threat to "the public peace and good order" posed by integrated trollies, nor inquired into the true ends of the challenged legislation (as it had in *Yick Wo v. Hopkins*[71]). This judicial failure was symptomatic of a doctrine that all too often took the government's representations concerning its ends at face value.[72] Indeed, *Plessy* was decided just three years after James Bradley Thayer published his paean to judicial restraint in the *Harvard Law Review*.[73]

As Justice Harlan pointed out in his now-canonical dissent, "Every one knows that the statute . . . had its origin in the purpose, not so much to exclude white persons from railroad cars occupied by blacks, as to exclude colored people from coaches occupied by or assigned to white persons"[74]—not to promote "public peace"[75] but to stamp Blacks with a "badge of servitude."[76] He agreed with the majority that "[i]f the power exists to enact a statute, that ends the matter so far as the courts are concerned." But he then denied that the government was constitutionally empowered to pursue the end of establishing a "superior, dominant, ruling class of citizens."[77] The end being sought was not one "to which the legislature was competent."[78] In short, under the pretext of exercising legitimate police power, the legislature had instead exercised arbitrary power.[79] As such, the measure was enacted in bad faith.

Harlan's *Plessy* dissent could have served as a blueprint for consistent and effective review of the state's exercise of their regulatory and prohibitory police powers over life, liberty, and property.[80] But as the eight-justice majority's opinion made plain, no such blueprint was consistently followed.[81] For every case in which the Court did smoke out improper goals after context-sensitive analysis of the government's means and ends during the late nineteenth century, one can point to another in which it fell short.[82] We need an approach that can better effectuate both the letter and the original spirit of the Fourteenth Amendment.

Protecting the Health, Safety, and Morals of the Public

We have generalized that the police power allows for the *prohibition* of acts that necessarily violate the rights of others—such as laws prohibiting murder, rape, robbery, fraud, and the like. No one disputes that state legislative power can be used to punish rights violations after they have occurred.[83]

We have also maintained that, to prevent the violations from occurring, the police power allows for the *regulation* of behavior that *risks* violating the rights of others. This type of regulation falls under the traditional rubric of regulations to protect the health and safety of the public.[84] Again, there is universal consensus on the propriety of this state legislative power—even as some may contest whether particular health and safety restrictions accomplish the end they purport to seek.[85]

What about the protection of public morals—the power at issue in *Champion v. Ames*?[86] A subset of such laws would clearly be warranted under the rights-protective conception of the police power: laws that regulate conduct in the "public sphere," by which is meant areas under the control of government to which the general public has access. These areas include streets, sidewalks, alleyways, and public parks.[87]

The scope of the police power most certainly did not include the taking of property from one person or class of people to give to another solely on the grounds that the latter would benefit from the taking.[88] But there was no constitutional barrier to legislatures using their general tax power to establish assistance programs for the poor or otherwise providing goods that would go undersupplied by the market—absent government intervention.[89] Whereas the tax power can sometimes be used in a regulatory fashion, in which case it would be subject to the same limitations as other police power regulations, the use of the tax power by a state to raise revenues to promote the public welfare is a power distinct from the police power to regulate rightful exercises of liberty and prohibit wrongful acts.[90]

The proper scope of the state tax power is beyond the scope of this chapter, and we take no position on its proper limit. But for those who think our construction of the state police power is overly narrow, we stress that the tax power stands available to states to pursue a variety of public policy objectives that are not limited to the protection of Lockean liberty. The existence of this power is also uncontroversial.

All of these exercises of the state police and tax powers were generally accepted in 1868 and remain so today.[91] To determine whether a deprivation of life, liberty, or property is arbitrary requires courts to assess whether there is a sufficient relationship between the means adopted and these undisputed ends to warrant a conclusion that the measure was adopted in good faith. The measure need not be shown to increase aggregate welfare or some such. Again, none of this is in dispute.

With all this consensus in mind, we are left with one last question about police power ends: whether states may prohibit conduct performed in private and outside the view of the general public—conduct that has no external social costs associated with it that would justify categorizing it as a nuisance—on the *sole* ground that the legislature deems such conduct to be immoral.[92] Addressing this question at length would take us too far afield.[93] But, to provide a sense of our answer, we offer three observations.

First, regardless of what view one takes on this issue, people of diverse constitutional views can agree that it is proper to protect public health and safety and regulate public conduct so as to minimize rights-conflicts.[94] So, nothing prevents courts from using these ends to engage in a means–ends analysis to prevent arbitrary legislative acts.[95] This is the consensus we just stressed.

Second, a power to regulate or prohibit private conduct outside of spaces controlled by the government on behalf of the general public *solely* on the basis that it is immoral is not contained anywhere in the text of the Constitution—either expressly or by implication.[96] If such a power exists, it is because judges say it exists.

Consequently, third, because no private morals power is textually specified, whether or not there exists such a power is a matter of constitutional construction.[97] For us, that is no deal breaker. But whether such a power is the best construction of the letter of the text of the Constitution will depend on whether it can fairly be within its original spirit.[98] We have demonstrated that the Due Process of Law Clauses were designed to bar arbitrary exercises of legislative power.[99] We doubt that the regulation of purely private acts based *solely* on claims about morality can be nonarbitrary in actual operation.

How would a legislature justify such a measure? Would it engage in philosophical or religious analysis of morality? Would it hold hearings on these moral claims? How could a citizen contest it? Would she be permitted to introduce "expert" testimony of moral philosophers or religious authorities? How could a court evaluate such moral claims when advanced by parties to a constitutional challenge? Would a judge reach a "finding" on whose moral stance was more justified?

Any purported governmental end, the scope of which cannot be objectively assessed by a citizen or independent judiciary, poses an intolerable risk of arbitrariness. In operation, how far legislators may go in depriving a person of life, liberty, or property on the sole ground that the legislature deems her act to be immoral will depend solely on their own will. In the parlance of present-day constitutional practice, such a power lacks a judicially administrable limiting principle.[100] And such a limiting principle is necessary to implement the original meaning of the Fourteenth Amendment's text.[101]

This stance is less radical than it may first appear. In practice, such legislative debates are typically waged in terms of risks of empirically ascertainable harms to the general public.[102] Bare moral disapproval is rarely considered sufficient to justify such measures in the absence of sometimes dubious empirical claims of harm to others that would fit within the health and safety rationales about which a consensus exists.[103]

Even in the early republic, one finds a stark contrast between strict adultery, anti-sodomy, and obscenity laws (in those places where such measures existed) and lax enforcement.[104] Most surviving morals laws trace not to the Founding, but to the Progressive Era. As Lawrence Friedman has documented, "[A] surge of interest in victimless crime, in vice, in sexual behavior"[105] took place during the late nineteenth century, when moralistic Progressivism driven by a marriage of evangelical religious fervor and quack science became influential.[106]

Still, the existence of the earlier laws has been offered as evidence that the police power of states includes the power to prohibit purely immoral activities—regardless of whether they pose any risk of injury to anyone.[107] We think the better view is that these laws were regarded as means of protecting members of the public from injury—but the connection between means and ends was very attenuated.

For example, Thomas West has detailed the lengths to which Americans went in the early republic to promote marriage in the belief that it was "indispensably necessary for the securing of natural rights."[108] He also showed how morals regulations—in particular, prohibitions on various kinds of sex outside of marriage—rested on that belief, rather than the belief that states enjoyed plenary power to shape and mold a virtuous citizenry.[109] Above all, by reinforcing the institution of marriage as the sole legitimate realm of sexual activity, these morals laws were thought necessary to protect the welfare of children.

The original public meaning of the constitutional text, however, does not address this issue. We think the rationality review deployed by the three-judge panel in *Lee Optical* is well tailored to implement the anti-arbitrariness spirit of the Due Process of Law Clauses. Under such rationality review, some strict morals laws might have been found unconstitutional in the early republic as well as now.[110] Had they been widely enforced, the issue of their unconstitutionality would then have been joined in earnest.[111] But they were not enforced, so it was not joined in earnest.[112]

Having offered these preliminary remarks on the propriety of regulating activities conducted in private solely on the ground that they are immoral, we close by reiterating that very few laws purport to be justified in this way.[113]

Instead, most deprivations of an individual's life, liberty, and property purport to be justified as reasonable means to safeguard the health and safety of the general public or to regulate conduct in the public sphere.[114]

In short, the overwhelming preponderance of laws are claimed to serve ends that nearly everyone agrees are within the just powers of state governments.[115] If so, what matters is whether the means adopted are so remotely connected to these well-accepted ends as to indicate that they were adopted to serve other forbidden ends that lie outside the original scope of the legislative power.[116]

Beyond Securing the Rights Retained by the People?

We have argued that the scope of the powers of state governments be defined with reference to the original function of the police power in 1868, which was grounded in a natural rights-based theory of the nature and limits of government.[117] Some will object that this conception is too narrow—that the scope of government power in general, and state power in particular, was not understood to be so limited in either 1791 or 1868. They may also contend that the amended Constitution is the product of "many minds" and resists any unified theory.[118]

As Jack Balkin has summarized, prominent historians (among them, Bernard Bailyn, J. G. A. Pocock, and Gordon Wood) have documented the influence of a "civic republican" tradition on Founding Era thought.[119] This tradition was characterized by opposition to monarchy, aristocracy, and oligarchy no less than to direct popular rule; belief in the priority of the public good; commitment to civic equality; opposition to "domination" either in civil society or in politics; commitment to self-rule, understood as representative government; and opposition to corruption.[120] Bailyn, Pocock, Wood, and others have contended that Founding Era thought "owed as much to the ideas of James Harrington, Baron de Montesquieu and 'Country Party' ideology, as [it] did to the work of John Locke and the liberal tradition of natural rights."[121]

We do not dispute that those who drafted and ratified the 1788 Constitution, those who amended it in 1791, and those who amended it in 1868 were influenced by a variety of political-philosophical sources. But, we think the purported tension between civic republican and Lockean liberal traditions has been exaggerated. The appearance of a tension may stem, in part, from a failure to appreciate how the concept of the "public good" was understood within classical liberalism.[122]

In an illuminating study of the concept of the public good within classical liberalism, generally, George H. Smith has shown that neither Locke nor his followers denied that government had an obligation to promote the public good or that the government might regulate—or even prohibit actions—that individuals would otherwise take in order to so promote it.[123] Rather, they were convinced that the public good was best promoted through the protection of natural rights, as well as such civil rights as had proven necessary to secure natural rights.[124]

Founding Era affirmations—of which there are many—that natural rights could be constrained by legislatures to promote the public good rested on the premise that such constraints were necessary "to secure and to enlarge . . . the natural rights" of members of the public.[125] Some people during the Founding Era undoubtedly spoke of the necessity of giving up or surrendering their natural liberty for the sake of the public good. But we should not assume they meant by this that the government could define the public good however the "felt necessities of the time"[126] may seem to demand. Nor did they think that government could invoke the "public good" to deprive people of their rightful liberty.

Rather, any necessary relinquishment of freedom was understood to be a tradeoff.[127] It was thought that all individuals would enjoy more freedom as a consequence than they would otherwise.[128] For example, by surrendering the right to personally execute the law of nature and receiving in return the civil right to the protection of the laws by an impartial enforcer, one gains more overall security for one's natural rights.[129]

Because the Founders did not simply identify the public good with whatever values were presently held by the general public, the purported conflict between the public good and individual rights did not take the form that some historians have posited.[130] True, the exercise of individual rights could, in certain contexts, be contrary to the public good and regulated accordingly. That is what the police power was for. Nevertheless, the public good was tethered to increased security and enlargement of the rights of all.[131] The core of this concept of the public good held throughout the Founding Era.[132] That the relationship between the public good and individual rights is complex does not make either concept an empty vessel or present us with a contradiction between two irreconcilable values.

The case for deploying natural-rights theory to implement the Fourteenth Amendment's Due Process of Law Clause is strengthened by investigation of the publicly available context in which it was enacted.[133] The influence of natural rights-infused abolitionist constitutionalism on Republicans in the Thirty-Ninth Congress has been well-documented, as have the premises on which that constitutionalism rested.[134] As Michael Kent Curtis has summarized in his pioneering study of the Fourteenth Amendment, "[B]y 1866 leading Republicans in Congress and in the country at large shared a libertarian reading of the Constitution,"[135] according to which "[g]overnment existed, as the Declaration of Independence asserted, to protect natural rights."[136]

As we saw in previous chapters, those who shaped the Fourteenth Amendment repeatedly and publicly articulated a theory of government according to which, as John Bingham put it, government's "primal object must be to protect each human being within its jurisdiction in the free and full enjoyment of his natural rights."[137] This is not to say that the Fourteenth Amendment enacted Locke's *Second Treatise*, much less Herbert Spencer's *Social Statics*.[138] Nor is it to say that government may *only* protect natural rights. Our claim is that, under this conception of the police power, government must do *at least* this much.

After enactment of the Fourteenth Amendment, the Constitution's newly expressed restriction on the power of states "to make or enforce any law which shall abridge the privileges or immunities of citizens of the United States," as well as the judicial duty to provide the "due process of law," required a theory of the state's police power to implement its constitutional mandate. And the Fifth Amendment's Due Process of Law Clause requires the same of judges when Congress is exercising its Necessary and Proper Clause power.

Insofar as constitutional decision-makers *must* construct a framework for implementing the Constitution's guarantees of due process of law, that framework *must* be informed by a theory of the nature and limits of government, period. It was just such a theory that informed the original design of those guarantees, thereby infusing its spirit.[139]

✴ ✴ ✴

Legislating is a decidedly complex activity. But it is not irreducibly complex, and we do not need to start from scratch in developing a theory of the nature or limits of government power. We have a written Constitution that was informed by a rich theory of the "just powers" of government and was carefully designed to implement that theory. We discard its letter and spirit at our peril. Accurately identifying the original meaning of the letter of the Due Process of Law Clauses, along with their original function or spirit, is the key to ensuring that we enjoy the substance of the Constitution's promises.

PART III

THE EQUAL PROTECTION OF THE LAWS CLAUSE

12

The Letter

The "Equal Protection of the Laws"

IT IS BLACK-LETTER LAW that the Fourteenth Amendment's guarantee of "the equal protection of the laws" generally prohibits discriminatory state action and does not ordinarily constrain nonstate, private actors. The Supreme Court has affirmed that the "[t]he State may not, of course, selectively deny its protective services to certain disfavored minorities without violating the Equal Protection Clause," but it has greatly hindered Congress in addressing systemic civil rights violations to which states are either unwilling or unable to adequately respond.[1]

Scholars have long doubted whether the Court's equal protection doctrine can be squared with the Fourteenth Amendment's original meaning. Some scholars have questioned whether the Court's interpretation of "equal protection of the laws" is too broad. They contend that the word "protection" denotes only security against physical violence and access to the remedial processes of the courts.[2] Other scholars have questioned whether the Court's interpretation of the clause is too narrow. They maintain that the state-action doctrine lacks any historical basis and contend that the Fourteenth Amendment forbids certain kinds of state *in*action—in particular, state failure to offer adequate protective services.[3]

Emphasizing that the Equal Protection Clause speaks not of "equality" but of "equal protection," proponents of the protection-only view have devoted a great deal of attention to the history of the governmental duty to protect not only citizens but noncitizens against violence. Most recently, Christopher Green has amassed evidence that protection was understood in

Anglo-American political theory to attach to a minimal allegiance, in the form of subjection to a state's laws.[4]

Green and others have also highlighted systematic failures of protection in the South during the antebellum period and in the wake of the Civil War. Enslaved people, free Blacks, antislavery whites, and Southern supporters of the Union (among others) could not count on protection by local law enforcement against violence or access to the legal system that would have enabled them to vindicate their natural rights to life, liberty, and property.[5]

Unlike the language of the other provisions of Section 1, there is vanishingly little pre-ratification exposition of the "equal protection of the laws." But what was said lends some support to the duty-to-protect interpretation. And what was said *after* ratification in connection with civil-rights legislation that was designed to enforce the Equal Protection Clause leaves little doubt that "protection" entailed at least state protection against violence; that state failure to protect against violence by nonstate actors was a paramount concern; and that Republicans believed state inaction in the face of such violence, whether the product of discriminatory intent, incompetence, or incapacity, to be sufficient to justify federal intervention.

We will show that the Fourteenth Amendment does indeed impose an affirmative duty on states to protect against violence by nonstate actors. But, just as the Court's present interpretation of the Fourteenth Amendment fails to sufficiently account for the word "protection," we will also show that supporters of the duty-to-protect understanding have failed to attend to the last two words of the clause: "the laws."

True, we do not have an "Equality Clause," but we do not have an "Equal Protection Clause" either. Instead, we have an "Equal Protection of *the Laws*" Clause, which is what we will call it hereafter. This clause entitles people not only to equal *enforcement* of whatever state laws are on the books to protect their personal security, but also to equal security-protective state *laws*, and any protection for life, liberty, and property afforded to people by federal *law*. That is to say, under the clause, state governments are

1. required to impartially execute nondiscriminatory state laws that are designed to protect people's life, liberty, and property;
2. required to provide people with equal access to the remedial processes of the courts;

3. prohibited from enacting discriminatory laws that unreasonably leave the personal security of some people more uncertain than that of others;

4. prohibited from denying to people security-related benefits derived from constitutionally proper federal statutes.

Notice that, while the last two of these bars particular "state actions," the first two impose on state governments affirmative duties to act. In other words, they bar a certain form of state inaction: the failure to protect. States have an affirmative duty to provide executive branch enforcement of laws protecting life, liberty, and property, as well as an affirmative duty to enact laws to provide access to the remedial processes of the judicial branch. This is important.

We begin by tracing the duty of protection back through Anglo-American legal history and disentangling the protection afforded to subjects (and later, citizens) from that afforded to other people who live under the laws. We will describe how the notion of a baseline guarantee of life, liberty, and property protection for all people became widely accepted during the antebellum period. We will also note the presence of a more radical strand of thought, according to which equal protection forbade *all* arbitrary discrimination, including especially racial discrimination—not only discrimination that involved the failure to protect natural rights.

We will investigate both the framing and ratification of the Fourteenth Amendment and the post-ratification period, documenting the prevalence of the duty-to-protect concept. We then trace the emergence of a distinctive general-antidiscrimination understanding of the equal protection of the laws that first arose in the wake of the *Slaughter-House Cases*. We explain why the latter is probably incorrect as a matter of original meaning, though understandable given the political context.

The Right to Protection in Anglo-American History

We have already detailed a tradition within Anglo-American political thought that posited reciprocal duties of allegiance on the part of subjects / citizens and a right to protection by the government of subjects / citizens. We have emphasized that subjects / citizens were understood to be entitled to enjoy certain civil rights because of their allegiance, whereas other people subject to governmental authority enjoyed those rights only by way of government grace. Yet, there was also a tradition of extending some measure of legal protection to nonsubjects and noncitizens who were bound by the government's laws.

The leading legal expression of the idea that nonsubjects were entitled to the protection of British law was Sir Edward Coke's 1608 opinion in *Calvin's Case*. Coke wrote that "when an alien that is in amity cometh into England . . . as long as he is within England, he is within the King's protection; therefore so long as he is here, he oweth unto the King a local obedience or ligeance, for that the one (as it hath been said) draweth the other."[6] This "local obedience or ligeance" Coke distinguished from obedience "due by nature and birth-right" from full-fledged subjects and indicated that to be in the king's protection was not necessarily to be a full-fledged British subject.[7]

Nonetheless, it was worth something. To begin with, the children of aliens in amity could acquire birthright subjectship. As Coke put it, "[I]f [an alien in amity] have issue here, that issue is a natural born subject."[8] Further, aliens in amity were entitled to due process of law and, more generally, to benefit from laws that were designed to secure a baseline level of protection for their natural rights to life, liberty, and property.

A dramatic illustration of the continued salience of this baseline protection during the Founding Era was provided in 1784, when a Frenchman named Charles Julian de Longchamps arrived in Philadelphia and promptly started a brawl with the French consul.[9] When the French government demanded that Longchamps be returned to France for trial under the law of nations, Americans united in defense of Longchamps's right to the protection of Pennsylvania law.[10] Ultimately, Longchamps was sentenced by a Pennsylvania court for violating the law of nations as incorporated by the state. But he enjoyed the full measure of Pennsylvanian legal process prior to his sentence.[11]

Americans believed that a government abdicated its fundamental duty if it denied to anyone over whom it exercised coercive power the benefits of life-, liberty-, and property-protective laws. This abdication risked dissolving any reciprocal obligation of allegiance on the part of the unprotected to the government. Indeed, it could give grounds for revolution. The Declaration of Independence charged George III with "abdicat[ing] government here, withdrawing his governors, and declaring us *out of his Protection* and waging War against us."[12] Numerous revolutionary state constitutions affirmed the right to refuse allegiance upon the withdrawal of protection.[13]

What, concretely, did protection entail? In his 1826 *Commentaries on American Law*, Chancellor James Kent affirmed that "[t]he personal security of every citizen is protected from lawless violence by the arm of the government and the . . . penal code."[14] He described "[the] duty of protecting every man's property by means of just laws, promptly, uniformly, and impartially administered," as "one of the strongest and most interesting of obligations on the part of government."[15] Besides protection against violence by non-state actors, Kent indicated that the right to protection included some protection against government. Specifically, it included the right to be free from "unequal and undue assessments" and to obtain just compensation for property seized for public use.[16]

The right-to-protection tradition persisted from the antebellum period through the framing and ratification of the Fourteenth Amendment. Throughout the early- to mid-eighteenth century, abolitionists and Republicans demanded the protection of the laws. They asserted that governments had a duty to secure all people under their authority against deprivation of their natural rights by providing nondiscriminatory laws and nondiscriminatory enforcement of those laws. This protection included enforcement by the courts.

As early as 1837, Henry Stanton denounced slavery in the District of Columbia as "denying to [the enslaved person] all of the protection of the law as a man."[17] In 1855, William Lloyd Garrison included "equal protection of the laws" among his demands for Blacks, together with his demand for their personal liberty, the right of locomotion, mental and moral culture, voluntary and remunerated labor, freedom of conscience, and freedom of speech."[18]

Numerous conventions of free Blacks complained of the denial of the protection of the laws. A resolution adopted by one convention invoked the reciprocal relationship between protection and allegiance. It asserted that, if the Supreme Court had held correctly in *Dred Scott* that Blacks "have fewer rights in our own native country than aliens," it followed that "colored men [we]re absolved from all allegiance to a government which withdraws all protection."[19]

From Anglo-American political and legal thought in the years preceding the framing and ratification of the Fourteenth Amendment, we can glean the concept of a baseline level of protection. This protection encompassed at least security against physical violence and equal access to redress in the courts. Ascertaining whether and how that concept was used by those who enacted the Fourteenth Amendment into law requires inquiry into not only what was publicly said about the protection of the laws during the framing and ratification process. It also requires an appreciation of the concrete evils that the framers and ratifiers understood themselves to be prohibiting, as well as the kind of protective legislation that they understood themselves to be authorizing.

Antebellum Usage of "Equal Protection of the Laws"

Prior to the Civil War, antislavery activists spoke often and eloquently about how slavery denied Blacks the protection of the laws. Henry Stanton's denunciation of slavery in the District of Columbia serves as a particularly illustrative example:

> His labor is coerced by laws of Congress; no bargain is made, no wage is given. His provender and covering are at the will of the owner. His domestic and social rights are as entirely disregarded in the eye of the law as if the Deity had never instituted the enduring relations of husband and wife, parent and child, brother and sister. There is not the shadow of legal protection for the family state among the slaves of the district . . . neither is there any real protection for the lives and limbs of the slaves. . . . No slave can be a party before a judicial tribunal . . . in any species of action against any person, no matter how atrocious may have been the injury received. He is not known to the law as a person: much less, a person having civil rights. The master may murder by system, with complete legal impunity, if he perpetrates his deeds only in the presence of colored persons. . . . [T]he slave should be legally protected in life and limb, in his earnings, his family and social relations, and his conscience.[20]

To be denied the protection of the laws, according to Stanton, was not merely to lack protection against violence and access to the courts. It was to be "[un]known to the law as a person." This included being denied the "domestic and social rights" that typically attach in the context of family relationships, the ability to make "bargain[s]" and earn "wage[s]" with which one can purchase "covering" and, more generally, the freedom to act in accordance with one's own "conscience." The lack of protection against physical subjugation—protection of "lives and limbs"—and lack of access to "judicial tribunal[s]" feature prominently in the list of evils recited by Stanton.

In conventions of free Blacks prior to the Civil War, protection against violence and access to the courts were repeatedly described as entailments of the protection of the laws. In an 1856 convention at Sacramento, Blacks complained that "the law, relating to our testimony . . . is but a shadow. It affords no protection to our families or property. I may see the assassin plunge his dagger to the vitals of my neighbor, yet, in the eyes of the law, I see it not."[21]

That same year an Illinois convention began with a call to oppose laws that "denied the right to testify against a white man before a Court of Justice, thereby denying us all means of access to law to protect ourselves against designing men to impose upon colored men at their will, because we are deprived of the key by which we gain access to the law in the absence of all white men."[22] In 1865, Blacks in Alexandria described themselves as being "without protection, so far as the laws of the State are concerned . . . that protection which is essential for the safety of our persons [and] our property" and related how they had been "left to the assaults of the vile and vicious to do with us as they please and . . . without redress."[23]

White abolitionists, too, called for these most basic of protections. Shortly before he was murdered by a mob, Elijah Lovejoy called for the protection of laws in an address delivered in Alton, Illinois:

Have I, sir, been guilty of any infraction of the laws? Whose good name have I injured? When and where have I published anything injurious to the reputation of Alton? . . . What, sir, I ask has been my offense? Put your finger upon it—define it—and I can stand ready to answer for it. If I have committed any crime, you can easily convict me. You have public sentiment in your favor. You have your juries, and you have your attorney. . . . If I have been guilty of no violation of law, why am I hunted up and down continually like a partridge upon the mountains? Why am I threatened with the tar barrel?

Why am I waylaid every day, and from night to night, and my life in jeopardy every hour? . . . I plant myself, sir, down on my unquestionable rights, and the question to be decided is, *whether I shall be protected* in the exercise and enjoyment of those rights . . . whether my property *shall be protected*, whether I shall be suffered to go home to my family at night without being assailed, and threatened with tar and feathers, and assasination [sic]; whether my afflicted wife, whose life has been in jeopardy, from continued alarm and excitement, shall night after night be driven from a sick bed into the garret to save her life from the brickbats and violence of the mobs.[24]

More capacious understandings of protection were also articulated. In 1857, a convention of free Blacks in Columbus, Ohio, declared that Blacks could not "defend and protect life, liberty, and property . . . by another than violent means" without access to the ballot. It called for the Ohio legislature to "strike or cause to be stricken from the Constitution the word white wherever it occurs." It denounced Blacks' exclusions from "the benefit of the Poor Fund," "all public institutions of the State for the benefit of the insane, blind, deaf and dumb," from juries, and from political office. Finally, it averred that "if you have the right to tax us for the benefit of the state . . . we have a right to demand of you protection."[25]

In 1865, Blacks in Sacramento claimed that the rights listed in the Declaration of Independence—"the great charter or bill of rights of our government"[26]—would "become a nullity" without "the protection of the laws" and affirmed the "necessity of the recognition of the right of suffrage for our own protection."[27] Indeed, the connection between protection and the ballot was a constant refrain in Black conventions. The view that ensuring Blacks would be protected by the laws required removing the word "white" from the laws was expressed on numerous occasions.[28]

It is worth noting that this reference to the "bill of rights" is consistent with our discussion, in Chapter 5, of the fact that this phrase did not commonly mean the first ten amendments until sometime in the twentieth century. Instead, it typically referred to express declarations of rights that prefaced constitutions—such as the Virginia Declaration of Rights. Since the Constitution lacked this sort of declaration in its preface, even after the first ten amendments were added to the end, people often characterized the rights affirmed by the previously enacted Declaration of Independence as a "bill of rights."[29]

Usage of "Equal Protection of the Laws" during the Framing

The words "equal protection" first became a focal point during the framing process when John Bingham introduced his second draft of Section 1. That draft provided:

> The Congress shall have power to make all laws which shall be necessary and proper to secure to the citizens of each State all privileges and immunities of citizens in the several States; and to all persons in the several States *equal protection* in the rights of life, liberty, and property.[30]

It is tempting to treat the second provision of this draft as a precursor of the Equal Protection of the Laws Clause and thus to read the latter solely as a guarantee of equal protection of life, liberty, and property. But "the laws" is absent from this formulation, and the words "life, liberty, and property" appear in the Due Process of Law Clause of the final amendment, not the Equal Protection of the Laws Clause. We cannot, therefore, safely assume that "equal protection in the rights of life, liberty, and property" carries precisely the same meaning as "equal protection of the laws."

Unfortunately, we have no record of any extended discussion of the significance of the move to "equal protection of the laws," which took place as the Joint Committee on Reconstruction was deliberating over the Owen Plan, which provided:

> No discrimination shall be made by any state, nor by the United States, as to the civil rights of persons because of race, color, or previous condition of servitude.[31]

To Owen's general prohibition against discrimination in respect of civil rights, Bingham then moved that the following language be added:

> Nor shall any state deny to any person within its jurisdiction the equal protection of the laws, nor take private property for public use without just compensation.[32]

Had Bingham's amendment carried, we might have ended up with the following constitutional text:

> No discrimination shall be made by any state, nor by the United States, as to the civil rights of persons because of race, color, or previous condition of servitude, nor shall any state deny to any person within its jurisdiction the equal protection of the laws, nor take private property for public use without just compensation.

One potential inference from this drafting sequence is that Bingham could not have understood his proposed equal protection language to be a general antidiscrimination guarantee, because it would have been redundant when added to the Owen Plan's general prohibition on discrimination. On the other hand, Owen's initial language targeted only discrimination against Blacks. And it might have been read to target only state activity—that is, the affirmative "ma[king]" of discrimination rather than malign neglect of some subset of the population or outright inability to protect that population. Perhaps Bingham wanted to ensure not only that all people would be protected in their civil rights against discrimination, but that they would be protected against both state action and state omission. We simply do not know.

In any event, Bingham's initial proposal failed. After a series of votes, he proposed the following language as a replacement for, rather than an amendment to, the initial anti-racial-discrimination language of the Owen Plan:

> No State shall make or enforce any law which shall abridge the privileges or immunities of citizens of the United States; nor shall any State deprive any person of life, liberty, or property, without due process of law, nor deny to any person within its jurisdiction the equal protection of the laws.

This time, Bingham succeeded. He secured not only the votes of radicals such as Thaddeus Stevens and George Boutwell but all three Democrats on the Joint Committee, including Reverdy Johnson, Andrew Rogers, and Henry Grider.[33] From May 8 to May 10 of 1866 this proposal by Bingham was discussed by the House. The equal protection of the laws received comparatively little attention. But, Bingham and Thaddeus Stevens both commented on it.

Bingham's May 10 comments were brief. He focused primarily on the Privileges or Immunities Clause in expounding Section 1:

> The necessity for the first section [is that] [t]here was a want hitherto . . . [of] express authority of the Constitution to do that by Congressional enactment which hitherto they have not had the power to do and had never even attempted to do; that is, to protect by national law the privileges and immunities of *all the citizens* of the Republic and inborn rights of *every person* within its jurisdiction whenever the same shall be abridged or denied by the unconstitutional acts of any State. . . .
>
> [T]his amendment takes from no State any right that ever pertained to it. No State ever had the right, under the forms of law or otherwise, to deny to *any free man* the equal protection of the laws or to abridge the privileges or immunities of *any citizens* of the Republic.[34]

Thus, Bingham distinguished between the protection of the "privileges and immunities of all . . . citizens" and the protection of the "inborn rights of every person"; between "deny[ing] to . . . free m[en] the equal protection of the laws" and "abridg[ing] the privileges or immunities of . . . citizens." All persons were entitled to the equal protection of the laws; only citizens were entitled to the protection of the privileges and immunities of citizenship.

Bingham did not speak with any precision here about what baseline protections all persons enjoyed. He made plain that he considered this protection to be guaranteed by the Constitution as it stood. But he also said that the federal government lacked the power to ensure that those constitutional entitlements were actually enjoyed.

Importantly, Bingham went on to assure the House that "[t]he second section [of the proposed fourteenth amendment] excludes the conclusion that by the first section, suffrage is subjected to congressional law. . . ."[35] Bingham did then immediately suggest an exception to this: "save, indeed, with this exception, that as the right in the people of each State to a Republican government and to choose their Representatives in Congress is of the guarantees of the Constitution."[36] This guarantee would apply, for example, "where treason might change a State government from a Republican to a despotic government and thereby deny suffrage to the people."[37] Bingham did not elaborate on how Section 1 provided for the enforcement of the Guarantee Clause, and we do not have a theory as to what he may have had in mind here.

We do know, however, that Bingham did not understand the equal protection of the laws or any other feature of Section 1 to guarantee Black suffrage, else he would not have been able to give such an assurance. In Chapter 5, we speculated that Bingham might have thought that the Privileges or Immunities Clause would have protected the right of suffrage but for the qualification of voting rights in Section 2. Because it protected "persons" and not "citizens," however, it is highly unlikely that Bingham thought the Equal Protection of the Laws Clause protected the right of suffrage—even absent the qualification in Section 2.

On May 8, Thaddeus Stevens spoke at greater length about the equal protection of the laws. Stevens stated that the Constitution at present "limit[ed] only the action of Congress, and is not a limitation on the States." He then averred that the proposed amendment would "allow[] Congress to correct the unjust legislation of the States, so far that *the law* which operates upon one man shall operate *equally* upon all."[38] The latter appears to be a reference to the Equal Protection of the Laws Clause, both because Stevens referred to equality in the operation of the law and because he referred to "m[en]" rather than to citizens. What followed tends to confirm this supposition:

Whatever law punishes a white man for a crime shall punish a black man precisely in the same way and to the same degree. Whatever law protects the white man shall afford "equal" protection to the black man. Whatever means of redress is afforded to one shall be afforded to all. Whatever law allows the white man to testify in court shall allow the man of color to do the same. These are great advantages over [the South's] present [legal] codes.[39]

It is probably a mistake to read Stevens's statement that the Equal Protection of the Laws Clause required the law to operate equally on all as an endorsement of a general antidiscrimination principle. If it had been so intended or received, it would have implicated suffrage rights. Stevens was himself an ardent proponent of suffrage rights and may have personally believed—as he claimed post-ratification—that equal protection of the laws did entail suffrage rights. But on the ratification campaign trail he expressly denied that voting rights would be guaranteed by Section 1.

We should instead use Stevens's specific claims about what the equal protection of the laws entailed as contextually enriching his statement concerning the equal operation of the laws. Its entailments included equal punishments, equal testimonial rights, and equal access to the courts in general. That is, we should read him as claiming only that laws governing criminal punishment, testimony, and access to the courts in general should operate equally on all people.

Finally, there is Jacob Howard's introduction of the Fourteenth Amendment to the Senate, which we previously discussed at length in the context of the Privileges or Immunities Clause to which he devoted most of his floor time. Like Stevens's, Howard's comments about the Due Process of Law and Equal Protection of the Laws Clause were brief, and did not clearly differentiate between different clauses:

> The last two clauses of the first section of the amendment disable a State from depriving not merely a citizen of the United States, but any person, whoever he may be, of life, liberty, or property without due process of law or from denying to him the equal protection of the laws of the State. This abolishes all class legislation in the States and does away with the injustice of subjecting one caste of persons to a code not applicable to another. It prohibits the hanging of a black man for a crime for which the white man is not to be hanged. It protects the black man in his fundamental rights as a citizen with the same shield which it throws over the white man. Is it not time, Mr. President, that we extend to the black man, I had almost called it the poor privilege of the equal protection of the law? Ought not the time to be now passed when one measure of justice is to be meted out to the member

of another caste, both castes being like citizens of the United States, both bound to obey the same laws, to sustain the burdens of the same Government, and both equally responsible to justice and to God for the deeds?[40]

What abolishes "all class legislation in the States"? The Due Process of Law Clause? The Equal Protection of the Laws Clause? Both together? Does prohibiting states from "met[ing] out" different "measure[s] of justice" to different "caste[s]" prevent them only from imposing discriminatory punishments, or does it prohibit them also from discriminating in providing access to the courts, as Stevens seemed to say? Might it encompass all arbitrary state discrimination, whether racial or otherwise, whether or not the discrimination implicates natural rights to life, liberty, and property?

Because Howard, like Bingham, went on to state that "[t]he first section of the proposed amendment does not give . . . the right of voting,"[41] we cannot attribute to him the view that anything in Section 1 generally forbade all arbitrary discrimination. It is true that Howard stated only that the right to suffrage "was not, in law, one of the privileges or immunities thus secured by the Constitution."[42] But, had it even been plausible that the right to suffrage was guaranteed by either the Due Process of Law or the Equal Protection of the Laws Clause, he could have been expected to explain why those clauses did not do so.

Howard's May 28 proposal to add what would become the Citizenship Clause to Section 1 touched off a discussion that indirectly sheds light on the meaning of the "equal protection of the laws." Senator Edward Cowan pressed Howard on the "length and breadth" of Howard's proposal.[43] After questioning what rights the children of Chinese immigrants and "Gypsies" would have under Howard's definition of citizenship, Cowan stated his understanding that

[i]f a traveler comes here from Ethiopia, from Australia, or from Great Britain, he is entitled, to a certain extent, to the protection of the laws. You cannot murder him with impunity. It is murder to kill him, the same as it is to kill another man. You cannot commit an assault and battery on him, I apprehend. He has a right to the protection of the laws; but he is not a citizen in the ordinary acceptation of the word. . . . So far as the courts and the administration of the laws are concerned, I have supposed that every human being within their jurisdiction was in one sense of the word a citizen, that is, a person entitled to protection; but in so far as the right to hold property, particularly the right to acquire title to real estate, was concerned, that was a subject entirely within the control of the States.[44]

Cowan was not speaking of the Equal Protection of the Laws Clause. Nevertheless, he drew a distinction between (1) the protection of the laws—enjoyed as of right by "every human being" within the "jurisdiction" of "the courts and the administration of the laws"—and (2) such civil rights as "the right to hold property, particularly the right to acquire title to real estate"—enjoyed as of right only by citizens. This division of protections into two categories, as well as Cowan's focus on court access in discussing protection, is consistent with Bingham's distinction between the privileges and immunities of citizens and the rights of all persons. It is consistent as well as with other Republicans' focus on equality of court access. Cowan was not contradicted by any of his colleagues concerning the distinction between the rights of all persons to protection of the laws, on the one hand, and the privileges and immunities of citizens, on the other.

Usage of "Equal Protection of the Laws" during Ratification

During the push for ratification, the Fourteenth Amendment's proponents expounded the clause in greater detail. Speaking to a crowd in Martinsville, Ohio, on September 5, 1866, Bingham described "the abuse of powers hitherto exercised by States, in which they denied the equal protection of the laws, or any protection of the laws whatever, to some of the most noble men of the Republic."[45] By this he meant Southerners who had fought on the side of the Union and whose "life and liberty and property" had been attacked for "the crime of fidelity to the flag and fidelity to the Constitution."[46]

Bingham then described the New Orleans massacre. He emphasized that it was organized by the mayor of New Orleans and carried out by Louisiana police.[47] He urged his audience "to put a fetter forever on the power of the state to do that thing" by placing the Equal Protection of the Laws Clause in the Constitution.[48] He stressed that every person—"no matter whence he comes, whether citizen or stranger, so long as he abides by the law, and comports himself well towards all other persons"—would be entitled to the "same protection as the most distinguished member of the commonwealth."[49]

Similarly, Indiana Governor (and eventual Senator) Oliver Morton stated in a July 18, 1866, message that the Equal Protection of the Laws Clause would secure "every person who may be within the jurisdiction of any State, whether citizen or alien, and without regard to condition or residence, not only as to life and liberty, but as to property."[50] He added that "[i]t has happened in times past that several of the Southern States discriminated against citizens of the other States by withholding the protection of laws for life and liberty, and denying to them the ordinary remedies in the courts for the vindication of their civil rights."[51] Morton proceeded to ridicule Democrats' arguments that Section 1 conferred suffrage rights, describing it as "one of the most flagrant and impudent attempts to practice a fraud on the public mind of which I have any knowledge."[52] On September 27, Representative Schuyler Colfax spoke of the "equal protection of just laws" and "equal laws" that could be "invoked by the poor as well as the rich." Like Morton, Colfax denied that Section 1 implicated suffrage.[53]

Even when not directly connected with the ratification debate, the equal protection of the laws was part of public discourse. Antislavery activist Daniel Goodloe inveighed against those who "jump to the conclusion that because men are not . . . equally blessed by nature and by circumstances, therefore they should not have equal rights before human tribunals."[54] Goodloe called for "a government that shall secure to every citizen of North Carolina equal rights before the law, and especially equal protection before the courts."[55]

Among the most detailed accounts of the equal protection of the laws was that provided by Representative John Mann of Pennsylvania during his state's ratification debate in 1867:

> I do not see how it is possible for human wisdom to frame a more perfect amendment to the Constitution of the United States than this section. It supplies a deficiency which every man has felt; it makes every person equal before the law; it aims to make every court in the United States what justice is represented to be, blind to the personal standing of those who come before it. Its adoption will prohibit any judge in any State from looking at the wealth or poverty, the intelligence or ignorance, the condition and surroundings, or even the color of the skin, of any person coming before him. It will require the court to look solely at the merits of the claim which he presents, or the details of the crime with which he is charged; and that I submit, is a duty that ought to be required of every judicial tribunal. The "equal protection of the law" is the talismanic charm which is to raise this Government to a position which it has never yet been able to occupy.[56]

Although Mann begins as if speaking generally of Section 1, his references to "person[s]," the theme of equality, and the invocation of the Equal Protection of the Laws Clause at the end, gradually make clear that he is speaking only of Section 1's final provision. Mann does not say that the clause's guarantee is limited to impartial adjudication, but it is clear that he does understand the clause to impose a duty of impartiality on "every judicial tribunal." It is also clear that he understands this duty of impartiality to extend beyond the context of race and to require equal treatment regardless of socioeconomic status or intellectual capacity.

Summing up, we have a wealth of evidence in support of an understanding of the equal protection of the laws that encompassed (a) executive protection of one's life, liberty, and property and (b) equal enjoyment of the remedial processes of the courts. While a broader nondiscrimination understanding was in the air, it was not widely shared by the ratifying public. Prominent speakers consistently linked equal protection to life, liberty, and property rights, and they denied that Section 1 implicated suffrage. An understanding of equal protection that forbade all arbitrary classifications could easily implicate suffrage rights and would not need to be tethered to life, liberty, or property rights.

But pre-ratification commentary on the Equal Protection of the Laws Clause does not shed much light on whether and how the duty of protection bound legislatures. Stevens and Howard talked of "codes" and "class legislation" that would be abolished, and Colfax spoke of "equal laws." Other discussions, however, seem concerned only with the executive and judicial branches.

With the unresolved question of the Equal Protection of the Laws Clause's application to legislatures in mind, we turn to the post-ratification period. As with the Privileges or Immunities Clause, this period contains far more, and more detailed, commentary on the Equal Protection of the Laws Clause than the pre-ratification period. We have previously explained why the epistemic value of this commentary drops off precipitously after the Supreme Court's decision in the *Slaughter-House Cases*. Consequently, we will focus our attention on commentary that preceded it.

Pre-*Slaughter-House*, Post-Ratification Usage of the "Equal Protection of the Laws"

As we have seen when discussing the original meaning of the Privileges or Immunities and Due Process of Law Clauses, shortly after the ratification of the Fourteenth Amendment, Republicans undertook to implement its guarantees through a series of ambitious civil-rights statutes. Republicans described key components of Reconstruction policy as means of enforcing the Equal Protection of the Laws Clause.

By the time that the Fourteenth Amendment was ratified on July 28, 1868, there existed a desperate need for its vigorous enforcement. For over a year before the amendment was adopted, the Ku Klux Klan had been promoting white supremacy through whippings, rapes, and murders, effectively disabling law enforcement in several Southern states.[57] Racist mob violence was rampant.

For example, in its final report on the Fourteenth Amendment, the Joint Committee on Reconstruction described the dire circumstances that Blacks faced in Memphis. There, on May 1, 1866, an altercation between police and Black soldiers precipitated a three-day massacre in which whites killed scores of Blacks and destroyed hundreds of homes, churches, and schools:

> [Blacks] have had no protection from the law whatever. All the testimony [taken by the Joint Committee] shows that it was impossible for a colored man in Memphis to get justice against a white man. Such is the prejudice against the negro that it is almost impossible to punish a white man by the civil courts for any injury inflicted upon a negro.[58]

Governors cried out for federal assistance. President Ulysses S. Grant responded, calling on Congress to act to enforce the Fourteenth and Fifteenth Amendments (the latter of which was ratified in 1870).[59] Republicans formed a united front against Democrats who insisted that Congress could not use its Section 5 powers to enforce the Equal Protection of the Laws Clause to impose criminal penalties on nonstate actors. Republicans also agreed that protection was denied not only by states that themselves deliberately discriminated against particular classes when enforcing the laws, but by states that simply lacked the resources to effectively enforce the laws.

To the extent that they addressed the issue, Republicans agreed that equal protection of the laws imposed duties on all three branches of government, not just the executive and judicial branches. The clause compelled state legislatures to enact general laws that protected life, liberty, and property and forbade legislative discrimination in the protection of people's life, liberty, and property.

Finally, numerous Republicans—including prominent framers—claimed that equal protection of "the laws" did not merely guarantee nondiscriminatory state statutes, state execution of those statutes, and state adjudication of violations of those statutes. It required as well that states comply with federal law—including the law of the Constitution. That is, equal protection of the laws required both proper protective laws and effective enforcement.

The most extended early discussion of the Equal Protection of the Laws Clause took place during the framing of the Enforcement Act of 1871. Also known as the "Ku Klux Klan Act," this law was a direct response to Klan terrorism. The text of the act targeted conspiracies "with intent to deny to any citizen of the United States the due and equal protection of the laws."[60] It also provided that if violence (1) obstructed the execution of either state or federal laws so as to (2) deprive people of any of the rights "named in the constitution and secured by this act" and (3) deprive states "from any cause" either "fail[ed]" or "refuse[d]" to protect them from that violence, "such facts shall be deemed a denial by such State of the equal protection of the laws to which they are entitled under the Constitution of the United States."[61] The violence to which the statute referred included violence by nonstate actors.

This text clearly expressed a concept of equal protection of the laws according to which state *inaction* could constitute a denial of protection, and Republicans consistently expressed this understanding. Here are but a few examples:

> Rep. Garfield: The chief complaint is not that the laws of the state are unequal, but that even when the laws are just and equal on their face, yet, by a systematic maladministration of them, or *a neglect or refusal to enforce* their provisions, a portion of the people are denied equal protection under them.[62]
>
> Rep. Pool: By the first section of the fourteenth amendment a new right, so far as it depends on express constitutional provision, is conferred upon every citizen: it is the right to the protection of the laws. This is the most valuable of all rights, without which all others are worthless and all right and all liberty but an empty name. To deny this greatest of all rights is expressly prohibited to the States as a breach of that primary duty upon them by the national Constitution. Where any State, by commission *or omission*, denies this right to the protection of the laws, Congress may, by appropriate legislation, enforce and maintain it.[63]
>
> Rep. Perry: It is argued that if infringements can be made by others than the State, and if the State merely permits but without giving active help in depriving of rights, Congress can do nothing. This argument defeats itself. . . . When a State is forbidden to "deny to any person within its jurisdiction the equal protection of the laws," the command is that no state shall *fail to afford* or *withhold* the equal protection of the laws.[64]
>
> Rep. Stevenson: Unexecuted laws are no "protection." And this brings us to this very case: the States have laws providing for equal protection, but they do not, because either they will not or cannot, enforce them

equally; and hence a class of citizens have not "the protection of the laws."[65]

Rep. Beatty: [C]ertain States have denied to persons within their jurisdiction the equal protection of the laws. The proof on this point is voluminous and unquestionable. It consists of the sworn testimony of ministers of the Gospel who have been scourged because of their political opinions, of humble citizens who have been whipped and wounded for the same reason, of learned judges within whose circuits men were murdered, houses were burned, women were outraged, men were scourged, and officers of the law shot down; and the State *made no successful effort* to bring the guilty to punishment or afford protection or redress to the outraged and innocent.[66]

Rep. Bingham: Admitting that the states have concurrent power to enforce the Constitution of the United States within their respective limits, must we wait for their action? Are not laws preventive, as well as remedial and punitive? . . . Why not in advance provide against the denial of rights by States, whether the denial be acts of commission *or omission*, as well as against the unlawful acts of combinations and conspiracies against the rights of the people?[67]

Democrats contended that the federal government could intervene only if state legislatures facially discriminated against particular classes of people. Republicans responded by emphasizing that—unlike the Privileges or Immunities Clause—the text of the Equal Protection of the Laws Clause did not mention legislation at all. Senator George Edmunds, one of the framers of the Fourteenth Amendment, pointed out that the Privileges or Immunities Clause specifically forbade states from "mak[ing] or enforc[ing] any law" that abridged citizens' rights. It was absurd to maintain, he continued, that

a great constitutional amendment, carefully prepared, discussed in both branches of Congress, passed by two thirds of each House, ratified by three fourths of the States, committed the awkward blunder of stating over again, in obscure language, what it had stated in its second provision only four lines above in clear language: that it had said that no State (which can only act through its Legislature) shall make any law which shall do this thing, and when it had, then, coming in the last clause, had restated the same thing in vaguer language, that they should not deny to any person the equal protection of the law.[68]

Indeed, Edmunds went on to say that "[a] Legislature acting directly does not afford to any person the protection of the law; it makes the law under which and through which, being executed by the functionaries appointed by the State for that purpose, citizens receive the protection of the law."[69]

Other Republicans, too, at points seemed to suggest that legislatures were not the primary focus of the Equal Protection of the Laws Clause. Senator John Pool stated that the clause "relates more particularly to the executive branch of the State governments."[70] Others averred that the duty of protection constrained courts and connected the equal protection of the laws with chapter 40 of the Magna Charta, which declared: "To no one will we sell, to no one deny or delay, right or justice."[71]

It does not follow from these statements, however, that the Equal Protection of the Laws Clause does not constrain legislatures. It is unsurprising that Republicans did not discuss this issue at any great length. Democrats did not deny that the clause constrained legislatures—indeed, they contended that it constrained *only* legislatures! Yet, Republicans did discuss the issue and expressed the belief that the clause did apply to legislatures—albeit not as a general prohibition against arbitrary legislative classifications but as a guarantor of natural-rights-adjacent civil rights.

For instance, Representative Horatio Burchard described the Equal Protection of the Laws Clause as "wide and general in its application" and claimed that it imposed a duty that "must be performed through the legislative, executive, and judicial departments of the government."[72] He neatly detailed the ways in which each of these departments might "den[y] the enjoyment of the right."

State legislatures would breach this duty "[i]f the law-making power neglects to provide the necessary statute, or if the State Legislature pass a law discriminating against any portion of its citizens. . . ." State courts would breach this duty if "the judicial authorities wrongfully enforce the law so as to neutralize its beneficial provisions." Lastly, state executive branch officials would breach this duty if "the executive allows it to be defied and disregarded. . . ."[73] Burchard then elaborated:

> If the State *Legislature* pass a law discriminating against any portion of its citizens, or if it fails to enact provisions equally applicable to every class for the protection of their person and property, it will be admitted that the State does not afford the equal protection. But if the statutes show no discrimination, yet in its *judicial* tribunals one class is unable to secure that enforcement of their rights and punishment for their infraction which is accorded to another, or if secret combinations of men are allowed by *the Executive* to

band together to deprive one class of citizens of their legal rights without a proper effort to discover, detect, and punish the violations of law and order, the State has not afforded to all its citizens the equal protection of the laws.[74]

According to Burchard, then, the clause imposed duties on all three branches of state governments. He indicated that this was uncontroversial—hence, "it will be admitted." He went on to specify that legislatures were both *forbidden* by the Equal Protection of the Laws Clause to pass discriminatory laws and *obligated* to enact equal laws that protected life, liberty, and property. Judges were obligated by the clause to impartially adjudicate and punish violations of protective laws. Executive officials were obligated to prevent private actors from conspiring to violate life, liberty, and property rights. By "obligated," we mean each of these government actors had an affirmative *duty* to do these things.

Similarly, Senator Henry Wilson took all parties to the debate to have "conceded" that a "refusal to legislate equally for the protection of all would unquestionably be a denial [of the equal protection of the laws]."[75] The "State" in the Equal Protection of the Laws Clause, Wilson argued, "is a trinity; the legislative, the judicial, and the executive[,]" and protection requires "the combination and cooperation of these three coordinate branches."[76] Should "one or the other of the coordinate branches of the State government" fail to afford equal protection, "it is not only within the power, but it is the solemn duty of Congress to enforce the protection which the State withholds."[77] (Notice the invocation of congressional power here; we return to this in Chapter 13.)

One might assume from Burchard's and Wilson's commentary that "the laws" by which people are entitled to be protected are solely state laws, as Burchard and Wilson do not mention any other laws. Other Republicans, however, did mention other laws, including federal laws.

Back in 1870, John Bingham made a speech proposing an amendment to a bill for removing political disabilities from former Confederates. He cast his proposal as an "echo of the People's voice" expressed through the Equal Protection of the Laws Clause.[78] After reciting the clause, Bingham interpreted it to embrace not only state laws, but "all laws, and above all other laws, of the law of the Republic, the Constitution itself, which is the supreme law of the land."[79] Bingham then repeated that the equal protection of the laws included "especially [the laws] of the Constitution and of all laws made in pursuance of it."[80]

When discussing the 1871 act, Bingham again claimed that the Equal Protection of the Laws Clause guaranteed protection by "the supreme law of the land." He interpreted the clause to "mean[] that no State shall deny to any person within its jurisdiction the equal protection of the Constitution of the United States, as that Constitution is the supreme law of the land."[81] He added "that no State should deny to any such person any right secured to him either by the laws and treaties of the United States or of such State."[82]

That same year, Bingham defended provisions of the Force Bill of 1870 that were designed to protect Chinese immigrants from discrimination. On his account, these provisions were justified by the Equal Protection of the Laws Clause. He pointed out that "immigrants" were "persons within the express words of the fourteenth article of the constitutional amendments."[83] They were therefore "entitled to the equal protection of the laws."[84] He emphasized that the equal protection of the laws did not merely guarantee protection of the laws "of the state itself, but of the Constitution of the United States as well."[85]

Bingham was not alone in advocating a "substantive" reading of the equal protection of the laws. Representative John Mann, responding to Democratic arguments that equal protection entailed only protection against discriminatory legislation, provided the following account of conditions in the South:

> [T]he fact remains ... that Union people, particularly of the colored race, do not have the equal protection of the laws in North Carolina and most of the other States engaged in the rebellion. . . . *Though the laws do not in terms discriminate* against them, still the fact is that they invoke their protection in vain. . . . There is either such a condition of public sentiment that they cannot be executed, or there is a complicity with their oppressors on the part of the officers who should, but do not, execute them.[86]

He then posed a series of rhetorical questions:

> Now, sir, is not this state of things a practical denial of the equal protection of the laws? One of the definitions of the verb "deny" is "not to afford; to withhold." Now, can it with fairness be said this equal protection is not denied, when it is withheld, when it is not afforded? Is there not a *positive duty* on the States by this language to see to it—not only that the laws are equal, affording protection to all alike, but that they are executed, enforced?[87]

Note that, on Mann's account, protection required both equal laws and equal enforcement. It constrained legislation as well as execution. Mann then proceeded to give examples of failures to protect through execution:

Suppose the legislature of North Carolina provided a proper law and proper courts but the Governor commissioned no judges or sheriffs; or suppose, having commissioned them, they should all resign or refuse to act.... [C]ould it be maintained that the State had not denied protection? No, sir; the Constitution fairly interpreted means this protection is to be exerted by a law, interpreted, applied, and executed in conformity with the constitution and laws of the state.[88]

In context, Mann's reference to "proper law[s]" seems to be a reference to laws that are at a minimum "equal, affording protection to all alike"—not just *any* laws that the state happened to generate. It would be incoherent for him to affirm that the Equal Protection of the Laws Clause required the even-handed execution of discriminatory laws, given that he had previously stated that the clause imposed "a positive duty on the States" not to enact such legislation.

In 1870, the *New Era*, a weekly newspaper established in Washington, DC, to serve freed people and edited by Frederick Douglass, published an article that invoked the equal protection of the laws in the context of public education. The article disclaimed any intent to seek "social or conventional advantages which we cannot fairly win." But it then declared that Blacks would "submit to no legal disabilities in public places or institutions, merely to gratify the wealth and intelligence of the minority."[89] The article included a "demand" for all children to receive the "equal advantages in all the public institutions, and equal protection under all the laws of the state."[90]

The latter article was not the only pre-*Slaughter-House* instance in which equal protection of the laws was discussed in connection with generally available advantages or in the context of public education. Mississippi's application for readmission to the Union was considered by Congress in 1870. Republicans debated whether to condition its readmission upon its pledge never to amend its constitution to deprive any citizen or class of citizen from "school rights and privileges" secured by that constitution.

In an exchange with Senator George Edmunds, Senator William Stewart contended that the condition was unnecessary because Mississippi had already made "ample provision for common schools."[91] But, he said, "[I]f the State of Mississippi should pass a law which would deprive the colored man of the same rights and privileges or schools that the white man has, or make any other discrimination which would deny him *the equal protection and benefit of the laws*, we have direct constitutional power to interfere."[92]

In 1873, Senator Oliver Morton provided the most extensive pre-*Slaughter-House* articulation of a general antidiscrimination theory of the Equal

Protection of the Laws Clause. In the course of a discussion of what would eventually become the Civil Rights Act of 1875, Morton argued that provisions forbidding states from excluding Blacks from juries were justified by the Equal Protection of the Laws Clause. He contended that "the word 'protection[]' . . . means not simply the protection of the person from violence, the protection of his property from destruction, but it is in the sense of the equal benefit of the law."[93] He repeated the phrase "equal benefit of the law" and urged that the Equal Protection of the Laws Clause was "intended to promote equality in the States, and to take from the States the power to make class legislation and to create inequality among their people."[94]

Such statements notwithstanding, there remain deep difficulties with taking the original meaning of the Equal Protection of the Laws Clause to encode a general antidiscrimination principle. First, a general antidiscrimination theory is unsupported by the duty-to-protect tradition that conceptualized protection of the laws in terms of the protection of basic life, liberty, and property rights. Second, as we will see, none of Morton's fellow Republicans endorsed a general antidiscrimination theory until after the *Slaughter-House Cases* made the Privileges or Immunities Clause a weak constitutional foundation—at least where the courts were concerned—for antidiscrimination legislation. And, even then, they did not do so unambiguously.

Third, Morton himself, when pressed by Democrats, drew a connection between the exclusion of Blacks from jury boxes and the denial of life, liberty, and property rights. He did not rely on the proposition that equal protection of the laws generally forbade discrimination. Thus, he asked "whether the colored men of North Carolina have the equal protection of the laws when the control of their right to life, liberty, and property is placed exclusively in the hands of another race of men, hostile to them."[95] Relying on Section 2 of the Fourteenth Amendment and invoking the distinction between civil and political rights, Morton acknowledged as well that equal protection of the laws did not require voting rights.[96] Had he understood the equal protection of the laws to require equality in respect of all legal advantages, he could not have conceded this much.

Fourth—although it is less probative of *public* meaning—pre-*Slaughter-House* case law tended toward a duty of protection that prohibits discrimination with respect to life, liberty, and property but did not prohibit all discrimination. In three challenges to segregated schools canvassed by Green—one successful, two unsuccessful—the Equal Protection of the Laws Clause is not even mentioned.[97] By contrast, equal protection of the laws arguments were made by counsel and engaged by the California Supreme Court in the 1870 case of *People v. Brady*.[98] In *Brady*, a divided court upheld a California law that prevented people of Chinese ancestry from testifying in trials of white people. The majority rejected the government's argument that "[e]quality of protection, demanding equality in the means of conviction . . . demands that whether a Chinaman or a white man be concerned, the modes of judicial investigation shall be the same."[99]

Justice Jackson Temple acknowledged that the Equal Protection of the Laws Clause was designed to prevent inequality in criminal punishments that did not serve any legitimate state end. But he then speculated that the exclusion of Chinese people might have reflected the legislature's "good faith" judgment that "Chinese testimony could never have any weight, or that it would be more likely to cause the escape of the guilty than their punishment, and as likely to cause the conviction of the innocent as the guilty."[100]

Senator Matthew Carpenter's 1873 argument on behalf of his client, Myra Bradwell, in favor of a woman's right to practice law did not mention the Equal Protection Clause.[101] Christopher Green highlights this omission, which would be an inexplicable error on the part of one of the Senate's leading constitutional lawyers if the clause was taken to generally forbid unjustified discrimination.[102] Indeed, Carpenter asserted:

> [T]he only provision in the Constitution of the United States which secures to colored male citizens the privilege or admission to the bar, or the pursuit of the other ordinary avocations of life, is the provision that "no State shall make or enforce any law which shall abridge the privileges or immunities of a citizen." And if this provision does protect the colored citizen, then it protects every citizen, black or white, male or female.[103]

Had Carpenter thought it plausible that the Equal Protection of the Laws Clause might generally forbid discrimination, it is difficult to imagine why he would not have argued that the clause protects every person and that Illinois's exclusion of women from the practice of law denied women the equal protection of the laws. Clearly, he believed that the exclusion was unjustified discrimination. That was the thrust of his privileges-or-immunities argument. Clearly, he supported not only economic rights but suffrage rights for women—he said so.[104] Apparently, therefore, he did not think that the Equal Protection of the Laws Clause generally forbade unjustified discrimination.

There was little pre-*Slaughter-House* scholarly commentary on the equal protection of the laws. The most extensive commentary is also the most puzzling. In 1873, Thomas Cooley affirmed that the "sole office" of the clause was "to ensure impartial legal protection to such as under the laws may exist."[105] Cooley drew from Chief Justice Lemuel Shaw's opinion in *Roberts v. Boston*.[106]

In *Roberts*, Shaw interpreted the Massachusetts Constitution's declaration that "[a]ll men are born free and equal" to mean "only that the rights of all, as they are settled and regulated by law, are equally entitled to the paternal consideration and protection of the law for their maintenance and security." Consequently, Shaw rejected Charles Sumner's argument for the plaintiff that the Massachusetts declaration forbade school segregation.[107]

But Cooley then went on to explain that "though there may be discriminations between classes of persons where reasons exist which make them necessary or advisable, there can be none based upon grounds purely arbitrary."[108] He even expressed "doubt if any distinction whatever, in right or privilege, which has color or race for its sole basis, can be established in the law or enforced where it had been previously established."[109] Cooley then cited Charles Sumner's unsuccessful brief for the plaintiff in *Roberts*, which Sumner had republished in 1870 as part of his campaign for antidiscrimination laws.[110]

Alas, Cooley did not discuss the respective merits of Shaw's and Sumner's conflicting analysis of segregated public education. His "doubt" concerning the constitutionality of any racial discrimination was expressed without further elaboration. If he believed that Sumner's understanding of the Massachusetts Constitution was embodied in the Equal Protection of the Laws Clause, and that segregation in public education or in other areas of civic and political life violated the federal Constitution, he neither said so nor explained how he came to that belief.

Post-*Slaughter-House* Usage of "the Equal Protection of the Laws"

Scholars have documented a shift in Republican constitutional discourse after the Supreme Court's decision in the *Slaughter-House Cases*.[111] Forerunners of the Civil Rights Act of 1875 targeted race-based exclusion from inns, places of public amusement, common carriers, tax-supported cemeteries, benevolent institutions, public schools, and juries. Democrats who opposed all this made immediate use of Justice Samuel Miller's opinion. They argued that the rights to be protected by the proposed legislation were all rights of state citizenship rather than national citizenship.

In response, as we have seen, Republicans sometimes repudiated *Slaughter-House* outright and sometimes attempted to argue that *Slaughter-House* did not address racial discrimination. A few Republicans, however, now invoked the Equal Protection of the Laws Clause to defend civil-rights legislation. When they did, they occasionally mixed together the Equal Protection of the Laws Clause and the Privileges or Immunities Clause in ways that suggest that the latter rather than the former was still anchoring their constitutional reasoning.

Thus, Representative William Lawrence affirmed that "the word 'protection' must not be understood in any restricted sense, but must include every benefit to be derived from laws." This affirmation might initially be taken as endorsing a general antidiscrimination principle.[112] But Lawrence went on to say that Section 1 "deals with 'the privileges' and the 'immunities of citizens'—not some privileges, but 'the privileges'—all privileges, and for all *these* the 'equal protection,' the equal benefit, of all laws is to be extended to all *citizens.*"[113]

In this way, Lawrence effectively substituted the Equal Protection of the Laws Clause for the now-inoperative Privileges or Immunities Clause. This is underscored by the fact that he confined the antidiscrimination principle he articulated to the rights of citizens. And he cast what became the Civil Rights Act of 1875 as a measure that protected the rights of citizens.

Similarly, Senator Frederick Frelinghuysen described the Equal Protection of the Laws Clause as "a provision against all discrimination and in favor of perfect equality before the law."[114] But he then paraphrased Justice Stephen Field's dissent in *Slaughter-House* thus: "[A]s no State under the old Constitution could discriminate in law against a citizen of another State *as to fundamental rights* to any greater degree than it did against a citizen of its own State, of the same class, so now no State must discriminate against a citizen of the United States merely on account of his race."[115] Again, the Equal Protection of the Laws Clause was doing the intended work of the Privileges or Immunities Clause.

Finally, Representative Robert Elliott argued that the clause forbade "all discrimination," suggesting a generalized antidiscrimination principle. But he then specified that "[i]f a State denies to me rights which are common to all her other citizens, she violates this amendment."[116] This focus on rights "common to all her other citizens" suggests something less than generalized antidiscrimination. In the minds of these men, the original meaning of the Privileges or Immunities Clause died hard.

Melissa Saunders points out that, before and after *Slaughter-House*, Oliver Morton articulated an equal-benefits understanding of the Equal Protection of the Laws Clause.[117] We cannot therefore say that he shifted to the clause merely because of Justice Miller's opinion, as his colleagues appear to have done. But, as we noted above, when pressed, Morton drew a connection between the equal protection of the laws and life, liberty, and property. And he disclaimed any understanding of the Fourteenth Amendment that would implicate voting rights. On the basis of this evidence, we are simply not justified in attributing to him an understanding according to which all similarly situated people were entitled to be treated equally under all laws.

Michael McConnell has documented how the language of the 1875 act was revised in ways that suggest an effort to avoid conflict with the *Slaughter-House Cases* and to rely on the Equal Protection of the Laws Clause rather than the Privileges or Immunities Clause.[118] Sumner's initial bill—introduced pre-*Slaughter-House*—borrowed language from the Privileges or Immunities Clause. It provided that "no *citizen* of the United States shall, by reason of race, color, or previous condition of servitude, be excepted or excluded from the full and equal enjoyment" of specified rights.[119] But as reported by the Senate Judiciary Committee shortly after Sumner's death in 1874, the bill provided that "all *persons* within the jurisdiction of the United States shall be entitled to the full and equal enjoyment" of specified rights.[120]

It is possible that the Republicans discussed above had always believed that *both* the Privileges or Immunities Clause *and* the Equal Protection of the Laws Clause provided constitutional authority for the Civil Rights Act of 1875. The epistemic value of claims about the meaning of constitutional provisions should not be discounted simply because those claims are novel. We do not dismiss the probative value of Republicans' post-*Slaughter-House* discussions of the equal protection of the laws for identifying the original meaning of the clause because they were novel. Rather, we do so because it is not clear that they were discussing the original meaning of the clause at all.

Republicans appear instead to have been incorporating their understanding of the original meaning of a different clause—the Privileges or Immunities Clause—into the Equal Protection of the Laws Clause. By this device, they hoped to increase the likelihood that the Supreme Court would allow Congress to protect citizens' privileges and immunities. By so doing, they may have contributed to the public understanding of the clause *at the time that they spoke* and thereafter. But it is doubtful that they are revealing anything interesting about the meaning communicated by the clause to the public in 1868.

Post-*Slaughter-House* jurisprudence is of even less epistemic value where the original meaning of the Equal Protection of the Laws Clause is concerned. In *Strauder v. West Virginia*[121] the Court upheld provisions of the 1875 act that provided removal to federal courts by defendants in states that excluded jurors on account of race. In its opinion, the Court spoke of citizenship, civil rights, and "legal discriminations, implying inferiority in civil society," not of persons and the duty of protection. Indeed, the court emphasized the fact that West Virginia excluded Blacks "as jurors, because of their color, though they are *citizens*."[122]

It is true that the Court expressed its difficulty in "comprehend[ing] how it can be said that while every white man is entitled to a trial by a jury selected from persons of his own race or color, or, rather, selected without discrimination against his color, and a negro is not, the latter is equally protected by the law with the former."[123] The Court, however, did not locate the source of this difficulty in any specific theory of the meaning of the equal protection of the laws.

In *Ex Parte Virginia*,[124] the Court characterized *Strauder* as holding that "*the Fourteenth Amendment* secures, among other civil rights, to colored men, when charged with criminal offences against a State, an impartial jury trial, by jurors indifferently selected or chosen without discrimination against such jurors because of their color."[125] Again, the Court did not cleanly distinguish the provisions of the Fourteenth Amendment or expound the Equal Protection of the Laws Clause at any length. It merely stated that "immunity from any such discrimination is one of the equal rights of all persons, and that any withholding it by a State is a denial of the equal protection of the laws, within the meaning of the amendment."[126] Nor did the Court respond to Justice Field's arguments in dissent that "[t]he equality of the protection secured extends only to civil rights as distinguished from those which are political, or arise from the form of the government and its mode of administration" and that "the privilege or duty of acting as a juror in a State court" was not among those rights.[127]

To be clear, we are persuaded that *Strauder* and *Ex Parte Virginia* were correctly decided as a matter of original meaning—that *both* the Privileges or Immunities Clause and the Equal Protection of the Laws Clause forbid racial discrimination in jury selection. Our point is only that *Strauder* and *Ex Parte Virginia* did not say enough about why either clause forbade racial discrimination in jury selection to count Justice William Strong's majority opinions as evidence of original meaning.

Finally, Justice Bradley's opinion for the Court in the *Civil Rights Cases*[128] tells us next to nothing about original meaning. In this landmark—and tragic—case, the Court held unconstitutional the Civil Rights Act of 1875's provisions forbidding discrimination in places of public accommodation. In his opinion, Bradley asserted that the Fourteenth Amendment prohibited "[s]tate action of a particular character" and was "intended to provide against . . . State laws, or State action of some kind, adverse to the rights of the citizen secured by the amendment."

But Bradley failed to support this claim by engaging with the duty-to-protect tradition.[129] Nor does he provide any analysis of the context in which the Fourteenth Amendment was framed and ratified. Nor does he investigate post-ratification implementation, when—as we've seen—Republicans united around the proposition that state *in*action could constitute the denial of the equal protection of the laws. All this stands in sharp contrast with his originalist dissenting opinion in *Slaughter-House*.

Indeed, Bradley's state-action language is difficult to reconcile with his own 1874 circuit court opinion in *U.S. v. Cruikshank*,[130] a case involving violence against Blacks by nonstate actors. In his circuit court opinion, Bradley stated that he was "inclined to the opinion that congress has the power to secure [the right of Black witnesses to testify] not only against the unfriendly operation of state laws, but against outrage, violence, and combinations on the part of individuals, irrespective of state laws."[131]

Furthermore, Bradley's opinion on the *Civil Rights Cases* is impossible to reconcile with his letter to Judge Woods with which we began this book. There he expressly stated:

> [T]he XIVth amendment . . . prohibits the states from <u>denying</u> to all persons within its jurisdiction the equal protection of the laws. <u>Denying</u> includes inaction as well as action. And denying the equal protection of the laws includes the omission to protect, as well as the omission to pass laws for protection.[132]

The evidence shows that Justice Bradley was right the first time.

Pamela Brandwein has challenged the standard reading of the *Civil Rights Cases* as a state-action case and sought to vindicate Bradley from the charge of inconsistency.[133] She argues that Bradley developed in his circuit-court opinion a "state neglect" doctrine that enabled the federal government to punish racially motivated private acts of violence if states neglected to supply protection.[134] She contends that the *Civil Rights Cases* turned on Bradley's belief that public-accommodation rights were not fundamental rights of citizenship—not on his belief in any state-action doctrine.[135] The Court, she maintains, did not definitely abandon Black rights through these decisions.

It is important to emphasize the modesty of Brandwein's claims and their limited relevance to ours. She does not dispute that Blacks were definitely abandoned to the Jim Crow South by the federal government, including the federal judiciary, by the turn of the twentieth century.[136] And she concedes that Bradley's state-neglect doctrine required racial motivations that lack any mooring in the Fourteenth Amendment's text or the history of the Enforcement Acts.[137] Finally, she acknowledges that there exists a state-action doctrine today and that that doctrine is associated—wrongly, she insists—with the *Civil Rights Cases*.[138] Even if she is right about all of this, our original-meaning based argument against the state-action doctrine is unaffected.

For what it is worth, however, we agree with Michael Kent Curtis that Brandwein overstates the political possibilities left open to a civil rights–minded Congress by Bradley's state-neglect doctrine.[139] Requiring proof of racial motivation made it more difficult for Congress to protect the rights of Blacks than it would otherwise have been, and made it impossible to protect white Republicans who were subjected to violence, not because of their race but because of their politics.[140] As Black-white Republican coalitions were essential to Blacks' security from state subjugation, political violence against Republicans contributed to that subjugation by boosting the electoral prospects of racists. State-neglect doctrine may not have been the product of a conscious design by Bradley to thwart Reconstruction, but it threw up procedural hurdles that, however well-intended, strike us as an important part of the story of the federal abandonment of Blacks.

We think Bradley's 1871 letter to William Woods is evidence of two things. First, that the original meaning of "the equal protection of the laws" barred, in Bradley's words, state "inaction as well as action."[141] Second, that Bradley changed his mind about the merits of the Fourteenth Amendment and abandoned its original meaning. Since he did not admit the change, we can only speculate on its motivation.

It is possible that Bradley changed his mind about the wisdom or feasibility of the Republicans' reconstruction program. Many Americans eventually came to have such doubts. It is also possible that Bradley's views of federalism came to dominate his judicial rulings as the Civil War receded into the rear view mirror and he changed his stance on the Fourteenth Amendment accordingly. Again, he would not have been alone among Republicans in having second thoughts about national power. Still, Brandwein may well be correct that Bradley's departure from original meaning was less extreme than is commonly thought.

⋆ ⋆ ⋆

In a panel opinion that would later be affirmed by the Supreme Court in *DeShaney v. Winnebago County Department of Social Services*,[142] Seventh Circuit Judge Richard Posner wrote that the "Constitution is a charter of negative rather than positive liberties" and that "[t]he men who framed the original Constitution and the Fourteenth Amendment were worried about government's oppressing the citizenry rather than about its failing to provide adequate social services."[143] The history we have surveyed is to the contrary.

The Equal Protection of the Laws Clause requires that states provide services that secure natural rights to life, liberty, and property that all people possess in virtue of their humanity. That is, the clause recognizes a *positive* right to have one's *negative* liberties secured by the state. Action or inaction on the part of any branch of the government that results in systemic failure to secure those rights can deny people the equal protection of the laws.

As we concluded following our investigation of the original meaning of the Privileges or Immunities and Due Process of Law Clauses, so we conclude here: to implement this language, constitutional decision-makers have to enter the construction zone. The letter of the Equal Protection of the Laws Clause requires judges to identify state failures of protection and evaluate federal legislation that is claimed to be remedying such failures of protection. Performing these judicial tasks properly will require recourse to the spirit of the clause.

13

The Spirit

Implementing the Equal Protection of the Laws

DID THE EQUAL PROTECTION of the Laws Clause protect against *any* denial by a state of the protection of its laws? Or did it protect only against *discrimination* in providing the protection of its laws? While the bare semantic meaning of the text can support either proposition, we think the contextual evidence we presented in the previous chapter more strongly favors the former over the latter as a matter of original public meaning. But this issue need not concern us too much.

Most real-world failures by states to provide protection can be characterized as involving discrimination in the provision of protection. That is, some are being denied protection that is afforded to others. So whether or not the clause was limited to discrimination matters little in practice. Regardless of which meaning is adopted, however, we must still decide how to implement the right, so conceived. In this chapter, we tackle the issue by appealing to the spirit of the clause. Our rule of construction would apply to either formulation.

Identifying that spirit requires us once again to confront the level-of-generality problem that bedevils inquiry into the function or end of any law. We have seen that Republicans described the clause as a means of

1. protecting formerly enslaved people against Ku Klux Klan violence;
2. guaranteeing particular protective services and procedural rights;
3. protecting people against subjugation of their life, liberty, and property, whether by state or nonstate actors;
4. securing equality, full stop.

As these formulations become more general, each subsumes the previous ones. How do we decide *which* formulation most accurately describes *the* spirit of the clause?

After answering this question, implementing the spirit of the clause then presents us with institutional problems. In particular, we need to address the controversial landmark case of *DeShaney*. In this tragic case, four-year-old Joshua DeShaney became comatose and then profoundly intellectually disabled due to traumatic head injuries inflicted by his father, who physically beat him over a long period of time.[1] Though it took various steps to protect the child after receiving numerous complaints of the abuse, the Winnebago County Department of Social Services did not act to remove Joshua from his father's custody.[2]

Joshua's mother sued the department alleging he had been deprived of his "liberty interest in bodily integrity, in violation of his rights under the substantive component of the Fourteenth Amendment's Due Process Clause, by failing to intervene to protect him against his father's violence."[3] The Supreme Court denied the claim for reasons we need to confront when considering the "protection" afforded to all persons by the "equal protection of the laws."

In his circuit court opinion, Judge Posner acknowledged that Joshua DeShaney was the victim of both his father's physical abuse and the "reckless failure" of local authorities to protect him from it.[4] But the state cannot provide anyone with *absolute* security. How much is it constitutionally obliged to provide? How bad must things get before Congress can intervene to protect people? How should courts evaluate congressional interventions?

In this chapter, we identify what we term the "antisubjugation" spirit of the Equal Protection of the Laws Clause and recommend how to implement it.

The Antisubjugation Spirit

One way to identify the spirit of the Equal Protection of the Laws Clause would be to identify the narrowest and most "administrable" of possible spirits. This would be similar to what Justice Antonin Scalia did in footnote 6 in his plurality opinion in *Michael H. v. Gerald D.*[5] Joined only by Chief Justice William Rehnquist, he lauded the virtues of "consulting the most specific tradition available" when identifying historically rooted due-process-of-law rights.[6] It is *easier* to determine whether a state has failed to protect former slaves against Klan violence, one might think, than to determine whether a municipality has arbitrarily deployed law-enforcement resources.

But it is clear that the narrowest available end is grossly underinclusive, given both the text of the clause and the constitutional discourse concerning its ratification and enforcement. Why would a clause designed to protect *only* former slaves, *only* against Klan violence, contain race-neutral language at such a high level of generality? Why did Republicans represent that the clause would secure the rights of white Southern Loyalists? Why did they think that travelers who came from "Ethiopia, from Australia, or from Great Britain" were entitled to the protection of the laws? There is too much here that the narrowest of ends cannot explain. So option 1 is out.

The general-equality spirit also seems a poor fit for the available evidence. If the clause was designed to prevent all arbitrary discrimination, why did Republicans choose language that was associated with a particular tradition of "protection" against physical subjugation? How were they able to provide public assurances that voting rights would not follow directly from the ratification of this language? (Keep in mind that any insincerity on this score would not prevent their statements from shaping the public meaning of the clause unless most members of the ratifying public understood them to be lying and ratified it anyway—and we have uncovered no evidence of this.) Based on the widely expressed insistence by Republicans that the clause was limited, combined with how the concept arose in abolitionist constitutionalism, option 4 is out.

But our rejection of option 4 should not be misunderstood. The Equal Protection of the Laws Clause is certainly concerned with equality. But, as we have shown, *all the operative provisions of Section 1 are concerned with equality.* This equality included the equal enjoyment of civil rights and equal access to judicial review of legislative acts that deprive people of life, liberty, or property. The Equal Protection of the Laws Clause *added* to the equality protected by the other clauses, not by adopting an abstract equality principle that would have subsumed them all, but by securing equality of an additional and particular kind: an equality in the protection of civil rights that are adjacent to natural rights. Hence the word "protection."

Republicans did identify particular procedural rights that would be protected by the clause, such as the right to testify. But there is little evidence that the clause was designed to fix a *closed set* of rights in constitutional amber. So we think option 2 is out as well. This leaves us with option 3: protecting all people against subjugation by others, whether state or nonstate actors, to the detriment of their civil rights to life, liberty, and property.

"[T]he equal protection of the laws" was not a legal term of art, the meaning of which had been fixed in antebellum jurisprudence.[7] We have seen that Republicans spoke in general terms of rights to impartial civil and criminal laws, adequate law enforcement, and adequate civil and criminal remedies for rights-violations. Precisely what states were required to do by way of providing reasonable protection was not specified in any detail. This is unsurprising, given that Republicans were confronting extreme and obvious instances of state failure to protect.

Some might consider even the more general spirit of protection—protection against subjugation—provided by option 3 to be underinclusive because it focuses on lack of control over one's natural rights to life, liberty, and property. Robin West argues that natural-rights protection is but one goal—one spirit—that the Equal Protection of the Laws Clause was designed to implement. The other, she contends, was protection against "material deprivation occasioned by isolation from the cooperative economic life of the community, through which individual livelihoods could be fashioned."[8] According to this view, the clause was designed to "protect our natural rights to physical security *and* economic participation."[9]

We do not dispute that *the Fourteenth Amendment* is concerned with economic participation. The Privileges or Immunities Clause, for example, secures to all citizens the contractual rights specified in the Civil Rights Act of 1866. And the Due Process of Law Clause secures to all people the right to obtain judicial review of legislation that implicates life, liberty, or property—including economic legislation. We agree with West that the Fourteenth Amendment was enacted, in part, to authorize civil-rights legislation, which protected economic liberties that were within an entrepreneurial free-labor tradition.[10] Any plausible list of the privileges or immunities of citizenship must include economic-liberty rights—the exercise of which may, of course, be reasonably regulated.

West does not adequately grapple, however, with the natural-rights-focused tradition of protection. Further, we saw in Chapter 11 that only late in the day—post-*Slaughterhouse*—did Republicans converge on the Equal Protection of the Laws Clause as authority for civil-rights legislation that went beyond protection against subjugation with respect to natural rights to life, liberty, and property, such as the Civil Rights Act of 1875. And when Republicans did so, they spoke in terms that strongly suggested that the Privileges or Immunities Clause was the proper source of authority for such legislation.

West correctly criticizes *DeShaney* for effectively denying "the right to the state's protection against the subjugating effects of *private violence*" and neglecting to recognize state *inaction* as an equal protection problem.[11] She fails, however, to produce evidence that the Equal Protection of the Laws Clause was aimed at state inaction in the face of *economic* subjugation. She thus fails to justify her claim that "the state has an obligation to protect citizens from abject subjection to the whims of others occasioned by extreme states of poverty, *no less* than to protect citizens from vulnerability to the threats of physical violence from others."[12] Whether or not the state has such a *moral* obligation, the "no less" proposition is not supported by the duty-to-protect tradition that evidently informed the clause's design. (And a state is free to fulfil any such moral duty with its taxing and spending power.)

That being said, the duty-to-protect tradition delivered normative goods that are not exhausted by natural rights. To equally protect the natural rights of all people was to recognize that, in some fundamental sense, they stood as individuals on an equal moral footing. It thus incorporated all people into a community of moral concern. Although it did not at once obliterate racist, sexist, or classist institutions, it opened up vital economic opportunities and paths to material well-being. These paths were so powerful and promising, they had to be forcibly blocked by private violence and by state coercion in the form of Jim Crow laws.

Like West, we use the term "subjugation," as distinguished from the more familiar "subordination," which is most closely associated with the equal-protection literature of Owen Fiss,[13] Catharine MacKinnon,[14] Derrick Bell,[15] and Kenneth Karst,[16] among others. This requires some explanation. In this literature, subordination connotes "group-disadvantaging" (Fiss),[17] the "maintenance of an underclass" (MacKinnon).[18] As Jack Balkin and Reva Siegel summarize: "Antisubordination theorists contend that guarantees of equal citizenship cannot be realized under conditions of pervasive social stratification and argue that the law should reform institutions and practices that reinforce the secondary social status of historically oppressed groups."[19]

The term "subjugation" is sometimes used as a synonym for "subordination" in antisubordination literature.[20] But we choose subjugation because it is *less* associated with a group-disadvantaging principle that is too narrow to capture the duty-to-protect tradition or Republican discourse surrounding the Equal Protection of the Laws Clause.

To be sure, Republicans were concerned about subordination and the relegation of groups—most especially Blacks—to second-class status. As we emphasized in our discussion of the Privileges or Immunities Clause, there was more to Republican citizenship than the equal enjoyment of natural rights—there was equality in civic life. And certainly Republicans recognized that securing the right to protection to historically oppressed groups would have social consequences.

But the broad language of the clause and of the Republican discourse surrounding it evinces a still more inclusive spirit. Its antisubjugation spirit is directed at *all* state and nonstate conduct that enables some to exercise dominion and control over the life, liberty, and property of others—whether or not these others are part of a group that was historically or recently oppressed, and whether or not they are members of what the Court would later describe as a "discrete and insular" minority.[21]

This spirit includes the protection of an individual child, such as Joshua DeShaney, from being physically subjugated by his own father, regardless of his membership in some such group.

Implementing the Antisubjugation Spirit

How, then, to implement the antisubjugation spirit of the Equal Protection of the Laws Clause? We have seen how the Supreme Court has denied that states are under any general constitutional duty to protect people against physical violence. If our presentation of evidence in Chapter 11 is right, the Court is wrong—as a matter of original meaning. Such a duty is right in the text of the Equal Protection of the Laws Clause. To which one might respond: What ought the Court do differently?

Imagine that the Court were in a future case to revisit *DeShaney*'s reasoning. Suppose it were to acknowledge that, indeed, states have a duty to protect people like Joshua against violence under the Equal Protection of the Laws Clause. Now imagine that the Court were to say that, because the clause does not specify precisely how this duty is to be enforced, the federal judiciary lacks the requisite institutional competence to enforce it. The Court then reaffirms *DeShaney*'s general rule of no state liability on the ground that it is a sensible construction of underdeterminate text. On what ground could we object to this alternative path to the same result, but on the ground of construction rather than interpretation?

One option is to fight the hypothetical. We could insist that the Court lacks the discretion under the letter of Article III to decide to leave constitutional enforcement to other decision-makers just because the justices find the text insufficiently directive, and that instead, they are bound by the text to develop judicially administrable rules of construction that are consistent with the spirit of the text. But we won't do that here.

Instead, we will assume that it is sometimes proper for the Court to "under enforce" the Constitution if the justices have compelling reasons to believe that judicial enforcement will actually result in a net loss in constitutional enforcement efficacy.[22] Under this assumption, should the *DeShaney* rule be preserved? We think not. To appreciate why requires a brief digression.

Ideally, we think the *DeShaney* rule should be replaced with a doctrine that takes into account such well-documented political pathologies as the desire to minimize workload and interest-group capture.[23] With these political pathologies in mind, the doctrine would address the ways that governmental institutions such as administrative agencies and police departments can fail either to regulate adequately or to respond effectively to acknowledged problems. These pathologies are more likely to result in unequal protection than no protection to anyone.

Furthermore, the detrimental effect of these political pathologies has been greatly aggravated by a major change in how social welfare benefits are provided. As David Beito has explained,[24] during "the late nineteenth and early twentieth centuries, millions of Americans received social welfare benefits from their fraternal societies."[25] These organizations usually included "an autonomous system of lodges, a democratic form of internal government, a ritual, and the provision of mutual aid for members and their families."[26]

These organizations were dominated by three types: "secret societies, sick and funeral benefit societies, and life-insurance societies."[27] All three "shared a common emphasis on mutual aid and reciprocity."

More Americans belonged to fraternal societies than any other kind of voluntary association, with the possible exception of churches. A conservative estimate would be that one in three adult males was a member in 1920, including a large segment of the working class. Lodges achieved a formidable presence among blacks and immigrant groups from Eastern and Southern Europe.[28]

Because these societies had close personal knowledge of their members, their mutual aid could effectively be channeled to those truly in need. Along with assistance came informal monitoring and peer pressure. In addition, members were morally inhibited from falsely claiming aid from their brethren.

Above all, organizations such as the Royal Arcanum, the Legion of Honor, and the Knights of Labor lacked the social stigma associated with hierarchical government and private "charity."[29] Fraternal aid "rested on an ethical principle of reciprocity. Donors and recipients often came from the same, or nearly the same, walks of life; today's recipients could be tomorrow's donor, and vice versa."[30] People would more readily accept assistance from those to whom they pledged to assist. Such assistance was considered an entitlement rather than "charity."

With the rise of the welfare state in the twentieth century, these pervasive nonstate voluntary social welfare associations were deliberately crowded out in favor of political institutions. Having reduced the provision of social welfare to political institutions, however, a state's highly imperfect political market may fail to correct itself.[31] Then, when governmental institutions fail people like Joshua, there may be no nongovernmental service-supplier to step into the breach. One way to correct this political market failure is to enforce the Equal Protection of the Laws Clause if it is feasible to do so.

To be sure, the judiciary is itself a governmental institution with pathologies of its own. Yet even the *DeShaney* Court implicitly acknowledged that the judiciary is sometimes competent to respond to pathological behavior within other institutions when it identified two exceptions to the general no-duty rule. These exceptions are the so-called special relationship and state-created danger doctrines.[32] Both have since been elaborated by lower courts.

The theory underlying these exceptions is that, if the state affirmatively *acts*—for example by taking someone into its custody or making someone *more* vulnerable to harm—it assumes corresponding affirmative protective responsibilities that do not ordinarily attach to its inaction. It is not obvious why protective failures falling within these exceptions are any easier for the judiciary to manage. Instead, the state action premise seems to be animating these exceptions—that governmental acts are more constitutionally salient than governmental omissions. As we have seen, however the original public meaning of the "equal protection of the laws" makes this distinction dubious.

Some observers were cautiously optimistic that these exceptions developed by lower courts could be further expanded, if not to swallow the no-duty rule, then to minimize its ill effects.[33] These hopes have been disappointed. As currently devised, the exceptions have instead generated arbitrary result that are not consonant with the spirit of the Equal Protection of the Law Clause.

It has proven difficult to draw a principled distinction between cases that are said to involve "action" and those that are said to involve "inaction."[34] Why wasn't *DeShaney* itself an "action" case, given that Joshua lived with his father because of a court decree? And despite no end of tragic cases resulting from reckless or grossly negligent official conduct, it is extraordinarily difficult for litigants to prevail under either the special-relationship or state-created danger exceptions.[35]

The judicial stumbling block to recognizing a positive right to protection here, however, may be less the Court's principled commitment to its misguided state action doctrine, than its reluctance to turn state governance over to tort lawyers and to juries who will respond to heart-rending stories like that of Joshua DeShaney. Tort liability creates a right to monetary compensation to particular victims. When the tortfeasor is a government agent, unlike suits against private parties, it is the general public who must pay the award, not the bad actor. Those funds come at the expense of other pressing needs of the general public—including protective needs.

Moreover, legislatures make funding tradeoffs; courts do not. There is simply no structural barrier to the aggregate of individual damage claims allotted by individual judicial proceedings—focusing solely on individual harm—overwhelming limited state treasuries. This, we suspect, is the prime motivation for the Court's dogged adherence to the act-omission criterion.

We share this concern. But it goes to the issue of remedy, not the underlying unconstitutionality of a failure to protect that is barred by the original meaning of the Equal Protection of the Laws Clause. Assuming a state's failure of protection is unconstitutional, we see three alternatives to the remedy of tort suits against state agencies for monetary damages, none of which is unproblematic.

First, courts can issue writs of mandamus to compel action by state governments. While avoiding the pecuniary threat posed to state governments by individual actions for monetary damages, this remedy risks enmeshing judges in day-to-day state executive branch functions. Moreover, compelled government action itself often entails the expenditure of funding, and we question whether judges have the power to command state legislatures to raise revenues for judicially mandated expenses.

Second, courts could use the stick of holding states liable in tort for their omissions to induce states to establish state compensation schemes administered outside the courts akin to workers' compensation schemes as an alternative. One of us has suggested this type of mechanism as an alternative to the exclusionary rule for state violations of the Fourth and Fifth Amendments.[36] Or states could enact torts claims acts administered by state courts to compensate executive branch failures to protect individuals. Even if it were in the power of courts to make such a threat, we question whether it would be effective.

Third, Congress could exercise its Section 5 power either to require that states establish some way to compensate victims or to establish its own compensation scheme—not imposing it upon the states but administering a compensation program itself. Compelling states would raise commandeering concerns. And it takes little imagination to foresee the problems inherent in any such federal or state victim compensation program. Workers compensation schemes, after all, are funded primarily by employers, not from general revenue. Again, the fact that the tortfeasor is the government whose assets come from taxpayers creates unique difficulties.

In the absence of a compelling alternative to tort liability, it is unrealistic to expect that the Court will discard *DeShaney* any time in the near future. Its most recent word on failures to protect was *Town of Castle Rock, Colorado v. Gonzales*.[37] There, it overruled an effort made by a state legislature to avoid the strictures of *DeShaney* by requiring police to enforce a restraining order when they have probable cause to believe that it has been violated.[38] It thereby hardened the no-duty rule.

As in *DeShaney*, the Court acknowledged that the facts of *Castle Rock* were "undeniably tragic."[39] The Castle Rock Police Department's decision not to arrest Jessica Gonzales's husband for taking her three children in violation of a restraining order that expressly mandated arrest in case of its violation gave the husband the opportunity to murder Jessica's children.[40] As in *DeShaney*, the Court wrung its hands. But as in *DeShaney*, the Court concluded that its hands were constitutionally tied. It determined that Colorado law did not confer on Jessica a "property" interest in enforcement of the restraining order that implicated the Due Process of Law Clause.[41]

Even more explicitly than *DeShaney*, *Castle Rock* was a Due Process of Law Clause case. Central to the Court's holding was its determination that Jessica was not deprived of any "property."[42] Two justices dissented in *Castle Rock*.[43] But all agreed that "the Federal Constitution itself" did not "grant . . . any individual entitlement to police protection."[44]

As we have shown, this is simply wrong as a matter of original meaning. The current, near-dominant, nonoriginalist reading of the Equal Protection of the Laws Clause as an "equality" clause has not helped matters. That non originalist interpretation has concealed the affirmative duty the clause really does impose on state actors, as well as the corresponding positive right to protection of one's civil rights to life, liberty, and property that really is protected by the clause.

The problem here is not the original meaning of the text but its implementation. It is not about identifying a constitutional right but about deciding what to do about its deprivation. Assuming that the Court will not abandon a no-duty-to-protect rule to which it is clearly attached, other improvements to the doctrine are possible. Ironically, judicial deference, not engagement, holds the key to better enforcing this constitutional right.

As we explained in Chapter 8, Republicans considered Congress to be the federal institution best suited to implement the privileges and immunities of citizenship, and this institutional judgment was embodied in Section 5. We said that this judgment was informed by confidence in Congress's fact-finding capacity and its capacity to enact broad, prospective rules without undue attention to the details of any particular case. Congress is also capable of drawing lines and crafting exceptions, as courts are not.

What should happen when Congress seeks in good faith to do what the judiciary is clearly reluctant to do in the realm of protection? When Congress chooses to step in where states and municipalities have systematically failed? We think that Congress's comparative institutional advantages, combined with the Court's own concerns about the limits of the judicial competence, warrant a measure of judicial deference.

The first step to reform is originalist. The Court should acknowledge that the original public meaning of the Equal Protection of the Laws Clause *does* impose a duty to protect. The second step involves acknowledging the limits of the judicial role and Congress's constitutionally acknowledged comparative institutional advantages. The Court should *allow Congress* to capitalize on its constitutionally acknowledged institutional advantages in this space.

In short, the Court need not repudiate the no-duty rule of *DeShaney*. Instead, it can

1. State explicitly that the Equal Protection of the Laws Clause *does* impose a duty on states to protect people against violence, even if courts are not competent to enforce this duty; and then
2. State explicitly that *Congress* can enforce that duty, so long as its means are appropriately tailored to its protective end—that is, it passes the *McCulloch* test.

Acknowledging the original meaning of the Equal Protection of the Laws Clause in step 1 would allow the congressional enforcement of the constitutional right it protects even where courts fear to tread.

For example, in 2009, Congress enacted a federal "hate crimes" statute that authorizes the federal prosecution of acts of private violence that are motivated by bias related to race, gender, religion, and national origin.[45] Federal courts upheld the statute on Commerce Clause grounds, but as Eric Foner has observed, such decisions "ma[ke] the judiciary look ridiculous."[46] Civil-rights statutes like this one are not designed to ensure the free flow of goods, nor should litigants who seek the benefits of such statutes have to pretend that Congress was so concerned. Affording protection against specific kinds of private violence where state remedies are demonstrably inadequate is permitted by the letter and consistent with the spirit of the Equal Protection of the Laws Clause.

Further, what if the Court starts interpreting the Commerce Clause more faithfully? Consider the Court's resistance to Congress's implementation of the Equal Protection of the Laws Clause in *United States v. Morrison*.[47] In *Morrison*, the Court held unconstitutional the provision in the Violence Against Women Act (VAWA) for a federal remedy for crimes of violence motivated by gender.[48]

Morrison is well known for reaffirming its holding in *United States v. Lopez* that Congress lacks the power to regulate wholly intrastate noneconomic activity. We concur with that holding. But the Court then also refused to uphold VAWA as an exercise of Congress's enumerated power under Section 5 of the Fourteenth Amendment. That was a terrible mistake.

VAWA's federal remedy for gender-motivated crimes avoided many, if not all, of the difficulties we identified with the various alternatives to state tort liability discussed above. It did not undermine federalism by mandating states to do anything. It established a private federal cause of action to be enforced in federal courts. It did not rely on a taxpayer-funded compensation pool. Above all, it did not threaten state treasuries with being drained by juries. Instead, it targeted the private actors whom the states had failed to prevent from violating the rights of women.

In sum, like the Force Bill of 1870, VAWA did what Justice Bradley, in his letter to Judge Woods, said ought to be done: "[A]s it would be unseemly for Congress to interfere directly with state enactments, and as it cannot compel the activity of state officials, the only appropriate legislation it can make is that which will operate directly on offenders and offenses and protect the rights which the amendment secures."[49]

Yet, in *Morrison*, the Court announced and applied a categorical rule against using Section 5 enforcement to regulate private parties. The Court acknowledged that Congress had produced a "voluminous" record indicating that "many participants in state justice systems are perpetuating an array of erroneous stereotypes." It noted that Congress had concluded that "these discriminatory stereotypes often result in insufficient investigation and prosecution of gender-motivated crime, inappropriate focus on the behavior and credibility of the victims of that crime, and unacceptably lenient punishments for those who are actually convicted of gender-motivated violence."[50]

But the Court then held that the record generated by Congress was immaterial because VAWA's civil remedy targeted nonstate actors.[51] Any person who committed a crime of violence motivated by gender could be investigated and prosecuted.[52] So, even if states were unwilling or unable to protect people against gender-motivated violence, Congress was prevented from filling the enforcement gap by regulating particular parties, because the offending parties were not state actors.

Which returns us to the original meaning of the Equal Protection of the Laws Clause. The operative constitutional premise in *Morrison* was "the time honored principle that the Fourteenth Amendment, *by its terms*, prohibits only state action."[53] Thus, no legislation that targeted *non*state action by way of correcting for state *omission* could be appropriate to any proper Section 5 end. We stress "by its terms" because it signaled the Court's reliance on a costly misreading of the text, which we identified in Chapter 12.

As we've seen, "deny[ing]" the equal protection of the laws "includes inaction as well as action."[54] Accordingly, the Court was wrong to assert that the text of the clause barred Congress from implementing its stricture by targeting nonstate actors rather than by regulating state actors. The only question is the *McCulloch* question: Were the means appropriately tailored to the end (here, protection), or were they a mere pretext for achieving a substantive outcome that exceeds the bounds of the Equal Protection of the Laws Clause?

We reject blind deference to legislatures, such as that afforded by "conceivable basis review." But the record on which Congress relied in designing VAWA warranted a presumption of its good faith. VAWA followed several years of congressional hearings, consisting of testimony from victims, law professors, and participants in state justice systems. It received task-force reports on gender bias from twenty-one states, and it found not only that state laws discriminated based on gender but that gender-neutral laws were enforced unequally.[55]

Providing for federal enforcement of rights that states are shown to have been systematically refusing to enforce seems eminently "appropriate." If states are not prosecuting a rights violator criminally, nor providing a victim with an adequate civil remedy, that offender will only face a single private lawsuit by the victim herself. The legal proceedings will just be in a federal rather than in state court. This remedy seems narrowly tailored to the state's unconstitutional omission to act.

If VAWA's civil remedy was to be faulted for anything, it was for the precise right it chose to protect: a right to be free from gender-*motivated* violence.[56] A gender-motivated crime is one committed against a woman (or against a man) because the victim is a woman (or a man). The evidence considered by Congress concerned the unequal enforcement of gender-neutral laws that punish violence against women. A state's discriminatory enforcement of gender-neutral laws when women are the victims is distinct from a state failure to prohibit gender-motivated violence. We are not aware of state laws barring gender-motivated violence that were going unenforced.

Moreover, if the problem is the inadequate state-enforcement of gender-neutral laws barring violence against women, a federal ban on gender-motivated violence is both under- and overinclusive. It is underinclusive insofar as violence against women that is not gender-motivated is going unpunished; it is overinclusive insofar as it bars gender-motivated violence against men. As such the remedy adopted by Congress might not have been congruent and proportional with the states' failure to protect the rights of women.[57]

We express no opinion on whether any of these were genuine problems with VAWA. Our concern is that none of these problems was considered by the Court because the outcome was determined by the state action doctrine which was held to restrict Congress's Section 5 power.[58] Given existing doctrine, it is understandable that Congress was reluctant to appear to be duplicating gender-neutral state laws barring violence against women. But, in the face of a record of discriminatory enforcement of such laws, that is exactly what Congress should be seeking to remedy.

Our criticism of *Morrison's* treatment of Section 5 is two-fold. First, as we have explained, it relied on an erroneous textualist and originalist interpretation of Section 1. The precedents on which it relied misread the original meaning of "the equal protection of the law." Continuing to rely on these erroneous cases because "[e]very Member" of the Court that decided them "had been appointed by President Lincoln, Grant, Hayes, Garfield, or Arthur and that "each of their judicial appointees obviously had intimate knowledge and familiarity with the events surrounding the adoption of the Fourteenth Amendment,"[59] is bad originalism.

Second, the Court took the wrong view of Congress's Section 5 powers. The Court objected that the law was "not aimed at proscribing discrimination by officials which the Fourteenth Amendment might not itself proscribe; it is directed not at any State or state actor, but at individuals who have committed criminal acts motivated by gender bias."[60] Yet this is exactly the type of remedy that avoids the commandeering of state governments—the type of remedy adopted by the Reconstruction Congress and endorsed by Justice Bradley in his letter to Judge Woods.

None of what we have said should be construed as a wholesale rejection of the state-action doctrine. There are two other operative provisions of the Fourteenth Amendment to which the doctrine properly applies. The state action doctrine is consistent with the language and original meaning of the Privileges or Immunities and Due Process of Law Clauses. "*Make or enforce any law*" connotes state activity; so too does the act of *depriving* any person of his or her life, liberty or property without the due process of law.[61]

We also do not adopt the Critical Legal Studies position that the distinction between state action and omission is incoherent and normatively indefensible.[62] One of us strongly utilized that distinction in making the constitutional case against a federal mandate to purchase health insurance. "In the main, persons are responsible for their actions, not for their failure to act."[63] Whatever the merits of the action/omission distinction, however, it has nothing to do with the equal protection of the laws.

The Court should acknowledge its interpretive error and accept the original meaning of the Equal Protection of the Laws Clause. It should then implement that meaning by acknowledging Congress's Section 5 power to fill systematic enforcement gaps, even when the judiciary may be incompetent to do so, so long as the Court is satisfied from a legislative record that Congress has done this in good faith.

Legitimating Current Doctrine

We are often asked: What difference does it make which clause the Court relies on when it applies the Fourteenth Amendment to the states? We would cite the *Morrison* Court's invalidation of Congress's exercise of its Section 5 power as a serious cost of ignoring the original meaning of the Equal

Protection of the Laws Clause. But there is another benefit to be gained as well: legitimizing existing doctrines that have been called into question. In particular, the recognition of a constitutional duty to protect could shore up the Court against criticism of some of its questionable-as-written yet intuitively correct criminal-procedural decisions.

Recall that the original meaning of the duty includes the provision of equal access to the remedial processes of the courts. Yet, it is clear that two sitting justices doubt whether there is any originalist case to be made for *Gideon v. Wainwright*.[64] In *Gideon,* the Court held that states are required by the Fourteenth Amendment to provide with counsel indigent criminal defendants who face possible prison sentences. Dissenting in *Garza v. Idaho*,[65] Justice Clarence Thomas (writing for himself and Justice Neil Gorsuch) stated that "the Sixth Amendment appears to have been understood at the time of ratification as a rejection of the English common-law rule that prohibited counsel, not as a guarantee of government-funded counsel."[66] The dissent did not discuss the text or history of the Fourteenth Amendment.

Justice Thomas's omitting to discuss the Equal Protection of the Laws Clause is not really surprising. Justice Hugo Black's opinion in *Gideon* does not mention the clause—his is a Sixth Amendment opinion. Yet the rule it announced is consonant with Republican concerns about the partial justice doled out by tribunals in formerly Confederate states, which resulted in the unequal protection of the laws.

We express no considered view here on whether *Gideon* has, all things considered, furthered the spirit of the Equal Protection of the Laws Clause. Perhaps *Gideon* has impeded access to justice more than it has helped, as Paul Butler has argued.[67] Our point is more modest: the absence of any recognized right to appointed counsel circa 1868—much less 1791—does not foreclose *Gideon* as a good-faith judicial application of the original meaning of the text.

Finally, there is *Miranda v. Arizona*,[68] which for many originalists is part of the anti-canon of judicial activism. As an interpretation of the Fifth Amendment's guarantee against self-incrimination, *Miranda* seems deeply implausible. But central to the Court's analysis is a concern with physical subjugation—specifically police violence, in the form of the "third degree."[69]

The Court's rule was designed to deter police violence by requiring police to inform *all* people who are interrogated while in custody that they have access to the courts and lawyers, despite their indigence. Here is the key passage in *Miranda* that links the rule to *Gideon* and thereby to access to justice:

The cases before us as well as the vast majority of confession cases with which we have dealt in the past involve those unable to retain counsel. While authorities are not required to relieve the accused of his poverty, they have the obligation not to take advantage of indigence in the administration of justice. Denial of counsel to the indigent at the time of interrogation while allowing an attorney to those who can afford one would be no more supportable by reason or logic than the similar situation at trial and on appeal struck down in *Gideon* v. *Wainwright*, 372 U.S. 335 (1963), and *Douglas* v. *California*, 372 U.S. 353 (1963).[70]

The empirical literature on *Miranda* is voluminous and conflicting.[71] When one of us was a prosecutor who gave *Miranda* warnings to suspects himself, he came to believe that its consciousness-raising effect on the reciting officer was even more important than the effect of the recital on the suspect. Beyond that, we do not opine here on whether *Miranda*'s concrete consequences render it worthy of the high cultural esteem in which it is held. And, given that it is a rule of construction rather than an interpretation of original meaning, Congress could hold hearings and gather evidence on *Miranda*'s costs and benefits and choose to displace its rule with appropriate legislation that better serves the spirit of the Equal Protection of the Laws Clause.[72] But there is more to be said for *Miranda* from an originalist standpoint than has traditionally been thought, thanks not to the original meaning of the Fifth or Sixth Amendments, but to the original meaning of the Equal Protection of the Laws Clause.

There are "unhappy endings" for us here too.[73] Chief Justice Earl Warren's proposition in *Reynolds v. Sims*[74] that "the right of suffrage is a fundamental matter in a free and democratic society"[75] is well supported by our originalist construction of the Privileges or Immunities Clause. We explained how the right of suffrage became a privilege of national citizenship with the passage of the Nineteenth Amendment. But we doubt that either the letter or the spirit of the Equal Protection of the Laws Clause can underwrite "one person, one vote."[76] Republican civil-rights legislation in the wake of the Fourteenth Amendment's ratification surely did protect those exercising their voting rights from violence and intimidation. But the antisubjugation spirit of the Equal Protection of the Laws Clause is simply too attenuated from the issues of vote dilution or effective political representation.

Can "the privileges or immunities of citizens of the United States" save *Reynolds*? This seems doubtful. The Fifteenth and Nineteenth Amendments secure access to the ballot. We concur with the Warren Court's decisions to ensure this access by holding unconstitutional invidious voter qualifications, including poll taxes.[77] We think that the Privileges or Immunities Clause, not the Equal Protection of the Laws Clause, is the proper "hook" for enforcing the right of access once suffrage became a privilege of citizenship.

This properly protected right of ballot access is quite different from a guarantee that one citizen's vote will carry equal weight to that of a citizen in another congressional district, or that one citizen's representative will be subject to the requests and suggestions from the same number of constituents. As the second Justice John Marshall Harlan pointed out in his *Reynolds* dissent, as of 1961, the constitutions of 80 percent of the states recognized bases of apportionment other than geographic spread of population.[78] Simply stated, "one person, one vote" was not deeply rooted in the nation's history and traditions when *Reynolds* was decided, nor was any underlying right to effective voting power that it was designed to secure.

True, today nearly every state measures equalization by the total population of state and local legislative districts.[79] But states have been required to do so since *Reynolds* by *Reynolds*. This development in the positive law has therefore not been the product of state deliberation, experimentation, and gradual convergence. Today, one-person, one-vote enjoys widespread public support. States are free to recognize a right on the part of citizens to have a representative who is subject to the requests and suggestions of the same number of constituents as a citizen of a neighboring jurisdiction.[80] Judicial intervention is largely unnecessary.

But public-opinion polls, or speculations about the outcome of a hypothetical amendment process, should not determine whether states are constitutionally compelled to recognize a right as fundamental. The Court's ruling in *Reynolds* deprived us of the knowledge we need to find that representation based on "one-person one-vote" has become a fundamental right or privilege of national citizenship. Such is the epistemic price for judicial overreaching in advance of a right becoming deeply rooted enough over time to be a privilege of national citizenship.

This allows us to stress a broader point about our fourth category for identifying privileges or immunities of national citizenship. A right cannot be said to be entrenched if its existence is solely a result of the Supreme Court's insistence on its recognition. When the Court does that, it deprives us of the knowledge that is needed to find a right to be deep-rooted in the nation's tradition or history. This remains true regardless of how old that judicially created right may be.

On the other hand, we do not deny that a right can become deeply rooted as a result of a longstanding judicial precedent. The problem is knowing if this has happened. There is one obvious way to discover this. The Supreme Court should reverse its precedent on the ground that it was wrongly decided. If the right it previously protected has subsequently become deeply rooted, we can expect an Article V constitutional amendment to be swiftly enacted to renew it.

We are mindful of the difficulty of obtaining Article V amendments. But when there is truly a national consensus on fundamental matters—such as the rights of eighteen-year-olds to vote—Article V amendments are still possible, even likely. The adoption of the Twenty-Sixth Amendment in 1971 is evidence of this. When that occurs, a right would immediately qualify as a privilege or immunity of national citizenship under our third criterion— namely, enumeration in the federal Constitution after 1868.

Lingering Concerns and Further Implications

We now turn to the objection to our approach that is most likely to be made by fans of the current doctrines applying the Equal Protection of the Laws Clause: What happens to a century's worth of jurisprudence that generally forbids arbitrary discrimination, regardless of whether there are natural life, liberty, or property rights to be protected?[81] An "equal protection" jurisprudence that subjects certain kinds of discrimination to "heightened" scrutiny while relegating others to rational-basis review?[82] An "equal protection" jurisprudence that is expressly concerned with invidious intentions?[83] Does all of this black-letter equal protection law have to go?

No, it does not. A great deal of it may be relocated to other clauses. Adopting the original meaning of the Privileges or Immunities and Due Process of Law Clauses would yield much of the benefit of the Court's current nonoriginalist equal protection doctrine. Recall from Part I that the Privileges or Immunities Clause secures all citizens *equally* against arbitrary discrimination with respect to their civil rights. This includes not only natural rights, but civic-equality rights as well. With respect to citizens, the Privileges or Immunities Clause can easily do most of the work of preventing discrimination that does not implicate natural rights, owing to its concern with civic equality.

As we showed in Part II, the Due Process of Law Clause supplements this work by ensuring that every person has equal access to a judicial tribunal in which legislative acts can be assessed to determine whether they are proper exercises of state police power or are instead arbitrary. Just as the Privileges or Immunities Clause establishes unstratified citizenship with respect to rights of national citizenship, the Due Process of Law and Equal Protection of the Laws Clause establish unstratified personhood with respect to natural rights.

To be sure, the Venn diagram overlap between rights against discrimination that are secured by the Privileges or Immunities Clause and those that are secured by the Equal Protection of the Laws Clause will not be perfect. But while citizenship may have its distinctive privileges, our reading of the Equal Protection of the Laws Clause, together with our reading of the Due Process of Law Clause, will not leave noncitizens at the mercy of citizens' arbitrary preferences.

Furthermore, nothing in the Constitution bars certain privileges from being extended to noncitizens through the democratic process. This last avenue for rights creation is often lost in discussions of judicially enforceable constitutional guarantees. Realistically, it is from such statutes that most of our legal "entitlements" now come.

What about the "tiers of scrutiny" approach of current equal protection doctrine? What if we are right that the Equal Protection of the Laws Clause bars any and all failures by states to protect persons from violations of their rights by state and nonstate actors alike? Does it then follow that the tiers of scrutiny must collapse and that disparate-impact analysis must replace discriminatory-intent analysis? It does not. The inherent limits of the judicial power remains a constraint on what courts may do to enforce the clause.

As we noted in discussing due process of law, the tiers of scrutiny might be justified as heuristics that simplify and improve the overall accuracy of judicial decision-making. With regard to "the equal protection of the laws," tiers of scrutiny might focus attention on those forms of discrimination that are easiest for judges to identify.[84] Likewise, the current focus on intentional discrimination may be justified on the ground that states draw distinctions and allocate resources in "disparate" but justified ways all the time. Those distinctions/resource allocations for which there is evidence of invidious intent are appreciably more likely to be unjustified in respect of proper means-ends fit.

All heuristics are imperfect. And even heuristics that are well adapted to their environment for a time may later become maladaptive. But as revisable constitutional constructions, the tiers of scrutiny and the discriminatory intent requirement should not be rejected out of hand. Not at least until we are confident about whatever might replace them.

We draw the line, however, at the Court claiming that the Equal Protection of the Laws Clause *mandates* tiers of scrutiny or *requires* discriminatory intent. As a matter of original meaning, it does no such thing. Both are merely judicially created, and revisable, constitutional constructions that may or may not be the best way to implement the original meaning of the text. (The theoretical distinction between interpretation and construction makes this easier to appreciate.)

Finally, we earlier explained why the Court was wrong to foreclose Congress from enforcing the clause in ways that the Court believes are outside the competence of the judiciary. Given the outsize role that the courts play in our constitutional culture, we think the Supreme Court should prophylactically affirm that it is "under-enforcing" a provision for institutional reasons.[85] Otherwise, state legislators and members of Congress likely will assume that *they too* cannot enforce the provisions in ways that are within the competence of legislatures. Without judicial endorsement, the public is likely to share in that assumption.

By claiming that states have no constitutional duty to protect people against private violence, the Court abdicated its own duty to give effect to the letter and the spirit of the Equal Protection of the Laws Clause. By attributing an erroneous original meaning to the text, it also undermined the legitimacy of originalism itself. The Court can qualify its more sweeping pronouncements about the Constitution's indifference to civil-rights violations by nonstate actors without compromising its judgment about institutional competence—and it should do so. The Court can do much better by the Equal Protection of the Laws Clause without doing much more than it has already done.

Conclusion

The Fourteenth Amendment in Full

Justice Antonin Scalia's resistance to efforts to revive "the darling of the professoriate"—his derisive term for the Privileges or Immunities Clause— has been attributed to his concern that the clause might be invoked by judges to secure "unenumerated" rights that he deemed illegitimate.[1] We suspect he did have this concern. But we also think something else was going on.

At oral argument in *McDonald v. City of Chicago,* Justice Ruth Bader Ginsburg asked Alan Gura, counsel for the petitioners, what test ought to be used to identify the "privileges or immunities of citizens of the United States." Gura replied that the Privileges or Immunities Clause is "not a free-flowing license, necessarily, for judges to announce unenumerated rights. However, to the extent that we have unenumerated rights which the framers and ratifiers didn't literally understand, they nonetheless left us guideposts that we can. . . ."

At that point, Justice Scalia interjected: "Well, what about rights rooted in the traditions and conscience of our people? Would—would that do the job?" When Gura agreed it would, Scalia responded, "That happens to be the test we have used under substantive due process."[2] This exchange came moments after Scalia had asked Gura why he was "asking us to overrule 150, 140 years of prior law, when—when you can reach your result under substantive due [process]."

The reader who has read this far might wonder whether Justice Scalia's point is applicable to our entire Section 1 project: *So what? So what if the Supreme Court's Fourteenth Amendment doctrine isn't perfect? Don't we have*

373

basically the same level of constitutional protection that the original meaning of the clause provides? (And where we do not, isn't that for the better?) Isn't this project of exclusively academic interest?

We think not, for two fundamental reasons. The first relates to what Richard Fallon calls "sociological legitimacy"—that is, whether a particular legal regime or institution is *perceived* as "deserv[ing] respect or obedience" and people who live under it have "a further disposition to obey the law for reasons besides self-interest."[3] Sociological legitimacy does not depend on an independent moral appraisal of what people *ought* to think—it depends only on what they *do* think.

Tara Leigh Grove has documented that the sociological legitimacy of the federal judiciary cannot be taken for granted. This is so even in a nation where the Supreme Court reliably polls ahead of the other branches of the federal government.[4] At least part of the Court's sociological legitimacy is a function of public perception that it is applying the law rather than something else.

If that is right, then it is risky for the Court to stand by decisions and doctrines about which little if anything positive can be said on the legal merits. The risk might be worth taking in cases of extreme moral urgency.[5] But it is difficult to perceive any moral urgency that could underwrite continued adherence to the *Slaughter-House* or *Civil Rights Cases*. If anything, given the consequences of those decisions for civil rights, the moral imperative would seem to run in the other direction.

The second fundamental reason for the importance of this project relates to what Fallon labels "moral legitimacy." A legal regime is morally legitimate if and only if it provides those who live under it with adequate assurance that its outputs are reasonably just.[6] The assurance that underwrites moral legitimacy is not an on-and-off switch, something you either have or you do not. Moral legitimacy is a matter of degree: exactly *how much* assurance does a constitution provide that its outputs are reasonably just?

Having said this, below a certain—though unquantifiable—threshold, a regime can be said to be morally illegitimate. This occurs when the way a law is made or enforced does not warrant the probabilistic belief that law enforcement is more likely to be just than unjust. A morally legitimate system is one that is above the probabilistic threshold; an illegitimate system is one that is below.

Finally, when it comes to providing assurance that laws restricting liberty are just, moral legitimacy can be greater for some—say, propertied white males—lesser for others—say, white women, free Black people, and Native Americans—and for still others nonexistent—say, Black people held in bondage. As a result, the laws that result from the law-making process provided by the Constitution can bind some in conscience but not others.

We stress that the moral legitimacy of a legal regime is not a function of the intersubjective agreement or perception that dictates the existence of sociological legitimacy. It is a function of moral and institutional reality. A legal regime may be perceived as morally legitimate when it is not actually so, or vice versa. Social movements utilize arguments about moral legitimacy to affect sociological legitimacy—the perception of legitimacy. That is what happened to what was the biggest moral flaw of the Constitution at the Founding.

We have discussed the intra-abolitionist split between William Lloyd Garrison and Wendell Phillips, on the one hand, and Lysander Spooner, William Goodell, and Frederick Douglass, on the other. That debate concerned the moral legitimacy of the antebellum Constitution. Garrison and Phillips's proslavery reading of the Constitution led them to deny that abolitionists could in conscience take an oath to follow the Constitution, a document they set on fire during their rallies. Spooner, Goodell, and Douglass's antislavery reading of the Constitution led them to disagree.

We said that Spooner's interpretive methodology—soon adopted to great effect by Douglass—most closely resembles modern public-meaning originalism. Salmon Chase and the Republicans adopted Spooner's originalist interpretive approach. But their "freedom national, slavery local" interpretation of the constitutional text lay somewhere between the Garrison/Phillips covenant-with-hell reading and Spooner's heroic reading.

The "freedom national" aspect of the Republicans' interpretation enhanced the moral legitimacy of the Constitution. On its originalist interpretation, the federal government had the power to abolish slavery in the District of Columbia, in the territories, and on federal enclaves. On its originalist interpretation, free states had the power to protect their Black citizens from being unjustly seized by slave catchers. Finally, as Sean Wilentz has documented, the text of the Constitution—with its careful use of euphemisms to refer to slavery—studiously refused to endorse the concept of property in man.[7] For those who held to this originalist interpretation, the Supreme Court's ruling in *Dred Scott* was a shock to the system, hastening the rise of the Republican Party.

On the other hand, the "slavery local" aspect of the Republicans' originalist interpretation implicitly conceded that Garrison and Phillips were correct about the antebellum Constitution being deeply morally flawed. The original meaning of the original Constitution not only left states generally free to exercise arbitrary power in the form of slavery within their borders. It also left slavery *better* protected than it was prior to ratification. These features of the Constitution profoundly undermined its moral legitimacy and needed to be changed.

After the Emancipation Proclamation, Republicans were right to think that, for slavery to end as a constitutional matter, the Constitution itself needed to be amended to change its original meaning. In the face of terrorist resistance and the perpetuation of white supremacy through state law by recalcitrant Southerners, John Bingham was also right to perceive a "want" of power in the federal government that needed to be supplied notwithstanding the Thirteenth Amendment. The moral legitimacy of the Constitution thus required a Fourteenth Amendment.

The text of Section 1 of the Fourteenth Amendment, for which Bingham was largely responsible (with an assist from Jacob Howard), can be understood as a series of promises that must reliably be kept, for the sake of the Constitution's moral legitimacy:

- The Citizenship Clause promises full national citizenship to all those who meet its disjunctive criteria of birth or naturalization and who are subject to the jurisdiction of the United States.
- The Privileges or Immunities Clause promises unstratified citizenship for all citizens, with a foundation of fixed civil rights on which subsequent generations can build and expand—but which they cannot destroy.
- The Due Process of Law Clause promises to all persons within our territory that their natural rights to life, liberty, and property, the security of which justifies state power, will not be arbitrarily restricted by states.
- The Equal Protection of the Laws Clause promises these same persons that states will not merely refrain from violating their natural rights but will actively protect them from private actors.

Those promises are expressly backed with the muscle of the federal government: the judiciary, Congress, and the executive (where necessary to enforce the judgments of the former or execute the laws of the latter). Section 1 is enforceable by the federal courts when a proper case or controversy is before them. Section 5 altered our federalism to empower Congress to take action when the states fail to heed these injunctions. Republicans repeatedly used this power to combat both state action and inaction. Our experience both before and after the Civil War showed that federalism's revision—though not obliteration—was necessary to curb the exercise of arbitrary state power.

Our answer to the "so what" questions is this: it is simply not the case that the Court's current Fourteenth Amendment doctrine gives us everything that the original meaning of the Fourteenth Amendment promises. Those promises have been broken time and again over the course of the past century and a half, starting soon after the amendment's adoption. We are happy to concede that some of the moral costs of these broken promises have been mitigated by shifting some of the work of the Privileges or Immunities Clause to the Due Process of Law and Equal Protection of the Laws Clauses. But this shift has been incomplete and has come at the cost of interpretive fidelity, which imposes additional costs beyond depriving us of the Fourteenth Amendment in full.

Enhancing the moral legitimacy of the Constitution has been offered to justify departing from its original meaning. But departing from that meaning to enhance moral legitimacy in some important respects has undermined it in others. As a result, the overall moral legitimacy of the Constitution has suffered a net loss.

Putting the "so what" questions aside, there is another objection that concerns the moral legitimacy of the Constitution as we read it. We have shown that the meaning of "privileges or immunities of citizens of the United States" is not obscured as if by some impenetrable "inkblot."[8] The evidence we have surveyed demonstrates that these rights were not whatever states say they are; they were not all and only those rights that Republican members of the Thirty-Ninth Congress would agree among themselves to include on a list of such rights; nor were they all and only enumerated rights. A privilege or immunity of US citizenship was a civil right of one of two kinds: (1) a positive-law protection or specification of a natural right; or (2) a state-created good that was widespread, entrenched, and deemed central to citizenship.

Yet this positive-law approach to identifying privileges and immunities might seem worrisome to those who share the Reconstruction framers' widespread belief in rights that originate—following the words of the Declaration—in "the laws of Nature and of Nature's God." Could not a stable national consensus be reached around slavery, or torture, or any number of natural-rights-violating practices? Does not our approach hold that whatever the national community says is right for long enough becomes the law—

regardless of its moral merits? Is this not a species of moral relativism? As natural-rights adherents ourselves, we have four responses to these worries.

First, it's critically important to distinguish ontology from both epistemology and political philosophy. Ontology is the study of *what is*. Epistemology is the study of *our knowledge* of what is—how we arrive at justified, true beliefs. And political philosophy is the study of what *form of government* is desirable. The ontology of the rights to life, liberty, and property—what they are—does not dictate how we come to know what forms they ought to take in civil society or how governments ought to secure them. In particular, the fact that natural rights preexist the formation of government and provide criteria by which to evaluate its actions, as we believe, does not foreclose the possibility that the best way to discover these rights is to consult our legal history and deeply rooted traditions.

Second, this is not just our opinion. It is demonstrable that the framers of the Fourteenth Amendment (1) *ontologically* believed that life, liberty, and property rights were natural; (2) *epistemologically* looked to widespread, entrenched practices to determine how best to secure natural rights; and (3) *political-philosophically* considered it necessary to positively entrench those practices via a constitutional amendment that supplied federal power hitherto wanting.

Whatever the merits of deducing privileges and immunities from some set of natural-rights axioms rather than inducing them from what experience had shown to be effective in securing natural rights, Republicans in the Thirty-Ninth Congress overwhelmingly did the latter. Natural-law lawyers may take issue with this. But they cannot enlist Bingham, Howard, or even Charles Sumner as allies.

Third, because the Fourteenth Amendment fixed a floor of natural-rights-securing civil rights, it made it impossible for a future national consensus to constitutionalize slavery, torture, and the like, absent a constitutional amendment. The "absent a constitutional amendment" qualifier might seem unacceptable to some because it apparently concedes that a supermajoritarian consensus could legalize evil. On our natural-rights-informed theory of moral constitutional legitimacy, however, any such amendment would call into question the legitimacy of the entire constitutional regime—as did the slavery provisions of the original Constitution. In any event, whatever one thinks about the ancillary issue of the constitutionality of evil amendments, it has no bearing on anything we have uncovered concerning the letter or spirit of the Fourteenth Amendment.

Fourth and finally, suppose that the framers of the Fourteenth Amendment made epistemic and political-philosophical errors in securing the natural rights retained by the people. Suppose that natural rights would be better identified and better protected if, for example, the Fourteenth Amendment gave federal judges free reign to identify and enforce natural rights as they saw fit. (For the record, we do not believe this would be the case.) We are unaware of any natural-rights devotee who is not also of the belief that public officials who ascend to office under a reasonably just constitution, and who take an oath to uphold it, incur a *defeasible* moral obligation to follow the higher positive law of the Constitution (even as they may disagree about what that law is). And this consensus would include even those who, like Lysander Spooner, question the legitimacy of government itself.

Together with natural-law proponents Jeff Pojanowski and Kevin Walsh, we think that public officials should "adopt a strong, presumptive moral obligation to respect the authority of positive law in a reasonably just legal system."[9] Originalism itself represents such a commitment to the higher positive law of the Constitution. The approach to rights-identification and rights-implementation employed by the framers of the Fourteenth Amendment may or may not have been optimal. But we very much doubt that adhering to it will generate outcomes so morally bad as to release officeholders from their promissory obligation to follow the law.

To return to the importance of our project, the positivist commitment to the higher law of the Constitution is also why we need to get that positive law right. Misunderstanding the meaning of that higher law has undermined, in the minds of some, the legitimacy of enforcing the personal guarantees in the first eight amendments and elsewhere in the Constitution against the states. It has undermined the due process of law's commitment to a judicial process that evaluates the substance of state laws to ensure their fit with a proper legislative end. And this misunderstanding of what is misleadingly called "substantive due process" has also encouraged Supreme Court justices to privilege and enforce their own conception of rights, regardless of whether they are deeply rooted in our nation's tradition and history.

Lest there be any doubt, we adhere to the Founders' and Framers' conception of natural rights.[10] A constitution is morally illegitimate if, when followed, it fails to systemically and adequately protect rights that can be derived from a theory of human nature and the conditions under which human beings can flourish in society with others. The laws authorized by such a constitution do not merit even a prima facie duty of obedience. At most, obedience may be justified as a means of avoiding the consequences of disobedience.[11]

Despite this, we do not believe that the Constitution should be read to protect natural rights when its original meaning does not bear that interpretation. We resist the modern tendency to justify methods of interpretation based solely on whether they produce normatively attractive results. We need to identify an interpretive method that will accurately determine what the law *is* before we can figure out what public officials *ought* to do about it.

"Show us your results and we will tell you whether we 'buy' your method of interpretation" does not accomplish this. Still, we are well aware of this reaction among both academics and the public. For this reason, we have refrained from reciting too many results of our interpretation of the original meaning of the Fourteenth Amendment. But that is not our only reason for such avoidance.

For one thing, originalists can disagree in good faith both over original meaning and over how best to put that meaning into effect. For another, many outcomes are determined by construction, not interpretation. We think greater agreement can be reached on the original meaning of the text if we are not overly distracted by our disagreements over how to apply that text in particular cases.

Besides, in many, if not most, cases, we do not start with normative priors. In such cases, we need an interpretive method in which we are confident to position us to identify the law. To the extent that results matter here, it is in the sense that an interpretive method must equip us to distinguish law from not-law. We think theoretical arguments in favor of originalism such as those we offered in the Introduction, not whether originalism produces outcomes that fit one's normative priors, are the better way to gain this confidence.

Moreover, we might be induced to adjust our normative priors when they are undercut by an interpretive methodology we think is sound. In a pluralistic society, there are normatively compelling reasons to accept reasonably just rules for coordinating social activity that do not require compliance with every feature of *any particular* moral theory. This is an important part of why we value the rule of law.

An interpretive method that gives us less of what we might normatively want than a rival method *in a given case* might appear normatively deficient until we recognize that it is more likely to promote the rule of law in a pluralistic society than its rival. Such rule of law itself can be more normatively valuable to us than any particular result. Whether this is true will depend on the substance of any particular constitution, when accurately interpreted.

Have we practiced what we preach? Has our interpretive methodology led us to conclusions that are at odds with our own expectations? For sure. Our research led us to several significant conclusions about original meaning that conflicted with what we expected to find. For example, we started with a natural rights, not a positive-law conception of privileges or immunities; we began with the working hypothesis that the equal protection of the laws applied solely to their enforcement by state executive branch authorities; and we did not think that Congress's Section 5 powers allowed it to do what the courts could not. But the evidence took us elsewhere.

These and other departures from our previous views, in turn, have led us to favor some results as constitutional that we might previously have thought were not, and vice versa. In other words, our methodology has affected our normative priors. We do not today hold the same set of "right results" we held before embarking on this project.

Nevertheless, we confess that we started this project in the hope that the original Fourteenth Amendment would have something normatively good to offer Americans today—something superior to the Supreme Court's reading. We suspect that no one can embark on such a project without hopes and fears about what one will uncover. Readers can decide for themselves whether we have discovered more "happy endings" than the evidence can bear. And whether they have a method that will systematically outperform ours.[12]

We conclude by expressing our gratitude for the hard work and personal sacrifices that made Section 1 as good as it is, and the Constitution far better than it was at the Founding.

We are grateful to neglected antislavery constitutionalists like Lysander Spooner, Joel Tiffany, and Frederick Douglass for their work in developing the key concepts that comprise Section 1: Republican citizenship, the privileges or immunities adhering to that citizenship, and the due process of law and equal protection of the laws to which all persons are entitled. And we are grateful to them for explaining and refining originalist methodology a century and a half before that label was invented.

We are grateful for the antislavery activism of countless citizens of the United States who are unknown to history but who fought to secure their own republican citizenship—and ours—as a constitutional right in a fight that tragically continued for a century after that citizenship was formally enshrined in the text of the Constitution.

We are grateful to the hundreds of thousands of Americans who gave their lives in a bloody war that ended the scourge of slavery and made possible a new birth of freedom; and to President Abraham Lincoln for leading that fight and doggedly insisting on the Thirteenth Amendment to secure the fruits of victory in our higher law.

We are grateful for the work of the Fourteenth Amendment's framers, such as John Bingham and Jacob Howard, whose names deserve to be as well known as the Framers of the 1788 Constitution; to the congressional Republicans who strove to implement the amendment in the face of massive and often violent resistance with a series of civil-rights acts that help us today to identify its original meaning; and to President Ulysses Grant for his battle to suppress domestic terrorism against American citizens.

We are grateful for the work of lesser-known figures such as Victoria Woodhull and Ida B. Wells, whose powerful arguments on behalf of women anticipated a national consensus around voting rights that they did not live to see. Their efforts succeeded in expanding the privileges of citizenship to include the right of suffrage.

And we are hopeful that the Fourteenth Amendment—"the gem of the Constitution"—will one day shine undiluted.

NOTES

ACKNOWLEDGMENTS

INDEX

NOTES

Preface

1. ERIC FONER, RECONSTRUCTION: AMERICA'S UNFINISHED REVOLUTION, 1863–1877, at 437 (1988).

Introduction

1. Lawrence B. Solum, *The Fixation Thesis: The Role of Historical Fact in Original Meaning,* 91 NOTRE DAME L. REV. 1, 3–4 (2015).
2. RAOUL BERGER, GOVERNMENT BY JUDICIARY: THE TRANSFORMATION OF THE FOURTEENTH AMENDMENT (1977).
3. CINCINNATI COMMERCIAL, August 9, 1866, at 2, col. 3.
4. Paul Brest, *The Misconceived Quest for Original Understanding,* 60 B.U. L. REV. 204 (1980).
5. *Id.* at 205.
6. Prior to Brest, academics distinguished between "interpretivism" and "noninterpretivism." This was a much less clarifying distinction that has completely disappeared from constitutional theory. *See, e.g.,* H. Hamner Hill, *Between Clause-Bound Literalism and Value Imposition: A Positivist Noninterpretivist Theory of Judicial Review, in* PHILOSOPHICAL DIMENSIONS OF THE CONSTITUTION (Diana T. Meyers & Kenneth Kipnis, eds. 1988), p. 96 ("Current debates about the legitimacy of judicial policymaking divide theories into two dominant camps: the interpretivists represented by Raoul Berger, William Rehnquist, and Robert Bork, and the noninterpretivists represented by Thomas Grey, Owen Fiss, William Brennan, and Michael Perry.").
7. Brest, *supra* at 204.
8. *Id.*
9. *Id.* (quoting Home Bldg. & Loan Ass'n v. Blaisdell, 290 U.S. 398, 453 (1934) (Sutherland, J., dissenting)).

10. *Id.* at 222–23 (emphases added).

11. *Id.* at 212–13.

12. The term appears to have been first used in Robert Bennett, *Originalist Theories of Constitutional Interpretation*, 73 Cornell L. Rev. 355, 355 (1988).

13. The first academic defender of "originalism" after Brest took aim at it was Richard Kay. *See* Richard S. Kay, *Adherence to the Original Intentions in Constitutional Adjudication: Three Objections and Responses*, 82 Nw. U. L. Rev. 226, 244 (1988).

14. *See* Edwin Meese III, U.S. Att'y Gen., Address before the American Bar Association (July 9, 1985), *in* The Great Debate: Interpreting Our Written Constitution 1, 9 (Paul G. Cassell ed., 1986).

15. *See* William J. Brennan, Jr., *The Constitution of the United States: Contemporary Ratification*, 27 S. Tex. L. Rev. 433, 435 (1986).

16. *See* Lawrence B. Solum, *Originalism and Constitutional Construction*, 82 Fordham L. Rev. 453, 462–63 (2013) [hereinafter "Solum, *Constitutional Construction*"].

17. Justice Antonin Scalia, Address before the Attorney General's Conference on Economic Liberties in Washington, D.C. (June 14, 1986), *in* Original Meaning Jurisprudence: A Sourcebook 101, 103–04 (U.S. Dep't of Justice ed., 1987).

18. By "nonoriginalism" we mean to refer to all theories of constitutional interpretation that deny one or both of the following: (1) that the linguistic meaning of any given constitutional provision is fixed when it is ratified into law; (2) that the latter original meaning ought to constrain present-day constitutional decision-making. For an elaboration of the Fixation Thesis and Constraint Principle, *see* Lawrence B. Solum, *The Fixation Thesis: The Role of Historical Fact in Original Meaning*, 91 Notre Dame L. Rev. 1, 6–13 (2015). For an overview of nonoriginalisms, including pluralism, moral-reading perfectionism, and pragmatism, *see generally* Mitchell N. Berman, *Constitutional Interpretation: Non-Originalism*, 6 Phil. Compass 408 (2011).

19. Brown v. Board of Education, 345 U.S. 972, 972 (1953).

20. *Id.* (emphases added).

21. 347 U.S. at 486 (emphases added).

22. By "concept," we mean a cognitive unit that is used to categorize things in the world. The criteria governing the application of a concept expressed by a word or phrase are established through discursive practice within interpretive communities. We take the concepts expressed by words and phrases to be shareable, public entities. For an explication of the standard among philosophers and psychologists concerning this "publicity" requirement for any plausible theory of concepts, *see* Jesse J. Prinz, Furnishing the Mind: Concepts and Their Perceptual Basis 14 (2002) ("According to the standard picture, people understand each other's words in virtue of the fact that they understand the same (or quite nearly the same) concepts with those words."). We also regard it as an empirical question whether a concept expressed by a word or phrase holds together things that share no common elements but merely bear a family resemblance to one another, or things that do share common elements. *See* Ludwig Wittgenstein, Philosophical Investigations 32 (P.M.S. Hacker & Joachim Schulte eds., G.E.M. Anscombe et. al trans., rev. 4th ed. 2009) (1953) (arguing that complex concepts share no such criteria).

23. To the extent that there is a dominant theory within originalism of the ontology of linguistic meaning—what meaning consists in—it is intentionalist and grounded in the communicative intentions of the Constitution's Framers. This communicative intentionalism draws on the work of linguist Paul Grice—in particular, on his pathbreaking analysis of the pragmatic features of language. For an overview of

Grice's influence on the philosophy of language, see Stephen Neale, *Paul Grice and the Philosophy of Language*, 15 Linguistics and Philosophy 509 (1992).

How can an intentionalist linguistic ontology be compatible with public-meaning originalism? Larry Solum has elaborated a Gricean account of constitutional communication pursuant to which the framers of constitutional provisions jointly intend that the ratifying public *understand the framers to intend* that the proposed text be read in accordance with ordinary linguistic conventions unless context clearly indicates otherwise. *See* Lawrence B. Solum, *Intellectual History as Constitutional Theory*, 101 Va. L. Rev. 1111, 1136 (2015). This is not, however, the place to defend either Solum's account or a different account of linguistic ontology.

24. Talk of "representative people" or even "most actual people" might be seen as courting what Miranda Fricker has termed "hermeneutical injustice." *See* Miranda Fricker, Epistemic Injustice: Power & the Ethics of Knowing 150–51 (2007). Although the meaning of language is socially determined, Fricker argues, public discourse may not capture the social experiences of all people in a given linguistic community. If a social context is unjust and excludes groups from public discourse, linguistic conventions may reflect and reinforce that exclusion. Fricker offers "sexual harassment" as an example—a phrase that captured a phenomenon that existed before the phrase itself became part of public discourse and that was not part of public discourse because of the ways in which those who experienced it were socially marginalized, *id.* This marginalization gave rise to hermeneutic injustice—"a lacuna where the name of a distinctive social experience should be," *id.*

The more that injustice excludes people from public discourse, the more distinctive social experiences will not be captured in public discourse. The social conditions in which the 1788 Constitution was framed were profoundly unjust in many important respects, and the Constitution's public meaning suffered from it. It is our view, however, that the public meaning of the *amended* Constitution is normatively good enough to bind government officials who promise to follow the Constitution today as a condition of taking office, and that adherence to original public meaning is an important part of that promise's content. We cannot defend these political-philosophical claims at length here—one of us has done so in a separate book. *See generally* Randy E. Barnett, Restoring the Lost Constitution: The Presumption of Liberty (2nd ed. 2013) [hereinafter, "Barnett, Restoring the Lost Constitution"]. For insightful discussions of the normative and interpretive significance of the historical exclusion of marginalized people from constitutional decision-making and discourse, see generally Paul Gowder, *Reconstituting We the People: Frederick Douglass and Jurgen Habermas in Conversation*, 114 Nw. U. L. Rev. 335 (2019); Christina Mulligan, *Diverse Originalism*, 22 U. Pa. J. Const. L. 379 (2018); Annaleigh E. Curtis, *Why Originalism Needs Critical Theory: Democracy, Language, and Social Power*, 38 Harv. Women's L.J. 438 (2015); James E. Fox, *Counterpublic Originalism and the Exclusionary Critique*, 67 Ala. L. Rev. 675 (2015); Jamal Greene, *Originalism's Race Problem*, 517 Denv. U. L. Rev. (2010).

25. For a thorough exploration of the distinctions between determinacy, indeterminacy, and underdeterminacy, *see* Lawrence B. Solum, *On the Indeterminacy Crisis: Critiquing Critical Dogma*, 54 U. Chi. L. Rev. 462 (1987). In brief, a legal question has a single determinate answer "if and only if the set of results that can be squared with the legal materials contains one and only one result," *id.* at 473. A question is *indeterminate* "if and only if the set of results . . . that can be squared with the legal materials is identical with the set of all imaginable results," *id.* A question is *underdeterminate*

"if and only if the set of results . . . that can be squared with the legal materials is a nonidentical subset of the set of all imaginable results," *id.*

26. *See* KEITH E. WHITTINGTON, CONSTITUTIONAL INTERPRETATION: TEXTUAL MEANING, ORIGINAL INTENT, AND JUDICIAL REVIEW (1999); and KEITH E. WHITTINGTON, CONSTITUTIONAL CONSTRUCTION: DIVIDED POWERS AND CONSTITUTIONAL MEANING (1999).

27. For discussions of the origin and development of the distinction, *see* Ralf Poscher, *The Hermeneutic Character of Legal Construction, in* LAW's HERMENEUTICS: OTHER INVESTIGATIONS 207 (Simone Glanert & Fabien Girard eds., 2017); Greg Klass, *Interpretation and Construction 1: Francis Lieber,* NEW PRIVATE LAW: PROJECT ON THE FOUNDATIONS OF PRIVATE LAW BLOG (Nov. 19, 2015), http://blogs.harvard.edu /nplblog/2015/11/19/interpretation-and-construction-1-francis-lieber-greg-klass/ [https://perma.cc/X4AH-MAXD]; Greg Klass, *Interpretation and Construction 2: Samuel Williston,* NEW PRIVATE LAW: PROJECT ON THE FOUNDATIONS OF PRIVATE LAW (Nov. 23, 2015), https://blogs.harvard.edu/nplblog/2015/11/23/interpretation-and -construction-2-samuel-williston-greg-klass/ [https://perma.cc/3CWS-W2Q_5]; Greg Klass, *Interpretation and Construction 3: Arthur Linton Corbin,* NEW PRIVATE LAW: PROJECT ON THE FOUNDATIONS OF PRIVATE LAW BLOG (Nov. 25, 2015), http://blogs.harvard.edu/nplblog/2015/11/25/interpretation-and-construction-3 -arthur-linton-corbin-greg-klass/ [https://perma.cc/AP7C-WZZS].

28. FRANCIS LIEBER, LEGAL AND POLITICAL HERMENEUTICS 44 (Roy M. Mersky & J. Myron Jacobstein eds., 1970) (1839) (emphasis added). How did this distinction become lost and unfamiliar when it was delineated by one of the most eminent nineteenth-century legal scholars and adopted in one of the most influential nineteenth-century constitutional treatises? We can only speculate. One possibility: Lieber assumed that in some nontrivial number of cases there was a "one true meaning" that could be discovered by judges through objective interpretation; *see id.* at 108. This view was subjected to criticism in the early twentieth century by the realists. *See, e.g.,* K.N. Llewellyn, *The Constitution as an Institution,* 34 COLUM. L. REV. 1, 31–40 (1934) (arguing that judges read their own values into the texts they interpret). If that criticism is valid, there is no need to distinguish between interpretation and construction—all judicial decisionmaking takes place within the construction zone. We suspect that the realists found their indeterminacy in the construction zone and then attributed it to interpretation as well, but we have not examined their examples to establish this.

29. THOMAS MACINTYRE COOLEY, A TREATISE ON THE CONSTITUTIONAL LIMITATIONS WHICH REST UPON THE LEGISLATIVE POWER OF THE STATES OF THE AMERICAN UNION (Boston, Little, Brown & Co. 1868).

30. *Id.* at 38 n.1 (quoting LIEBER, at 11).

31. *Id.* (emphasis added).

32. *Id.* at 39 (quoting JOHN BOUVIER, A LAW DICTIONARY, ADAPTED TO THE CONSTITUTION AND LAWS OF THE UNITED STATES OF AMERICA, AND OF THE SEVERAL STATES OF THE AMERICAN UNION (edition unknown)).

33. *Id.* at 38.

34. *Id.*

35. *See* 3 ARTHUR LINTON CORBIN, CORBIN ON CONTRACTS §§ 532–35 (1960 & Supp. 1980); E. Allan Farnsworth, *"Meaning" in the Law of Contracts,* 76 YALE L.J. 939 (1967); Edwin W. Patterson, *The Interpretation and Construction of Contracts,* 64 COLUM. L. REV. 833 (1964).

36. For a discussion of the differences between Lieber's and Corbin's approaches, *see* Lawrence A. Cunningham, *Hermeneutics and Contract Default Rules: An Essay on Lieber and Corbin,* 16 CARDOZO L. REV. 2225 (1995).

37. *See* Keith A. Rowley, *Contract Construction and Interpretation: From the "Four Corners" to Parol Evidence (and Everything in Between),* 69 MISS. L.J. 73 (1999); Lawrence B. Solum, *Originalism and Constitutional Construction,* 82 FORDHAM L. REV. 453, 486–87 (2013) (citing cases deploying the distinction).

38. *See* BARNETT, RESTORING THE LOST CONSTITUTION, the first edition of which was published in 2004.

39. Lawrence B. Solum, *Communicative Content and Legal Content,* 89 NOTRE DAME L. REV. 479, 488 (2013).

40. Solum, *Constitutional Construction,* at 458. Put still another way, whereas giving legal effect to any constitutional text requires constitutional construction, only when giving effect to underdeterminate text need one enter into the construction zone and adopt textually unspecified rules of decision.

41. *See* Jack M. Balkin, *Abortion and Original Meaning,* 24 CONST. COMMENT. 291, 292 (2007) (coining the phrase).

42. Bradwell v. Illinois, 83 U.S. (16 Wall.) 130, 142 (1872); *see* RANDY E. BARNETT, OUR REPUBLICAN CONSTITUTION: SECURING THE LIBERTY AND SOVEREIGNTY OF 'WE THE PEOPLE,' 115–17, 146–49 (2015) (explaining why *Bradwell* was wrongly decided).

43. *E.g.,* PHILIP BOBBITT, CONSTITUTIONAL FATE: THEORY OF THE CONSTITUTION 7–8 (1982); Mitchell N. Berman, *Originalism Is Bunk,* 84 N.Y.U. L. REV. 1, 32 (2009); Michael C. Doff, *Integrating Normative and Descriptive Constitutional Theory: The Case of Original Meaning,* 85 GEO. L.J. 1765, 1794 (1997); Richard H. Fallon, Jr., *A Constructivist Coherence Theory of Constitutional Interpretation,* 100 HARV. L. REV. 1189, 1189–90 (1987); Daniel A. Farber, *The Originalism Debate: A Guide for the Perplexed,* 49 OHIO ST. L.J. 1085, 1086 (1989).

44. PHILIP HAMBURGER, LAW AND JUDICIAL DUTY 54 (2008).

45. 8 Va. (4 Call) 5, 19 (1782).

46. *Id.*

47. *See* Robert G. Natelson, *The Founders' Hermeneutic: The Real Original Understanding of Original Intent,* 68 OHIO ST. L.J. 1239, 1251–53 (2007) (noting that reliance upon the "spirit," "sense," "meaning," or "reason" of an enactment "for purposes of documentary construction—sometimes even at the expense of the literal wording—reflected the norm in Anglo-American jurisprudence").

48. 1 SIR WILLIAM BLACKSTONE, COMMENTARIES ON THE LAWS OF ENGLAND 61 (1765–1769).

49. *See* Solum, *Communicative Content and Legal Content, supra* at 500 (explaining that "the public context may include facts about the general point or purpose of the provision (as opposed to, the 'intention of the author'), and those facts may resolve [textual] ambiguities").

50. RONALD DWORKIN, LAW's EMPIRE 229, 238–50 (1986) (arguing that judges ought to interpret the law in accordance with the "best," most morally acceptable principles that fit existing legal materials and describing this interpretive process.).

51. Brest, *supra* at 231.

52. *Id.* at 205 (emphasis added).

53. *Id.* at 223 (emphasis added).

54. *Id.* (emphasis added).

55. Even if one is unconvinced that collective purposes or intentions really exist in some robust sense, there would remain a compelling normative case for treating them *as if*

they are real in constitutional interpretation no less than in statutory interpretation, where they inform numerous canons of statutory construction. For an as-if argument for intentionalist statutory interpretation that closely resembles public-meaning originalism, *see* Ryan Doerfler, *Who Cares How Congress Really Works*, 66 Duke L.J. 979 (2017). *See also* Daniel Dennett, The Intentional Stance 48–49 (1989) (arguing that human beings attribute beliefs and intentions when doing so helps us explain and predict the behavior of complex systems).

56. Which is not to say that it is uncontroversial. For a summary of ongoing debates between methodological individualists and holists, *see generally* Christian List & Kai Speikermann, *Methodological Individualism and Holism in Political Science: A Reconciliation*, 107 A.M. Pol. Sci. Rev. 629 (2013).

57. *See* Randy E. Barnett, *The Relevance of the Framers' Intent*, 19 Harv. J.L. & Pub. Pol'y 403, 405 (1996).

58. *See, e.g.*, Kyllo v. United States, 533 U.S. 27 (2001) (deciding whether thermal imaging is a "search"); Brown v. Entm't Merchs. Ass'n, 564 U.S. 786 (2011) (deciding whether a California law imposing restrictions on violent video games abridges the "freedom of speech").

59. *See* U.S. Const. Art VI ("The Senators and Representatives before mentioned, and the Members of the several State Legislatures, and all executive and judicial Officers, both of the United States and of the several States, shall be bound by Oath of Affirmation, to support this Constitution.").

60. We do not here enter into a debate over whether the duty of good faith is a *distinctively* fiduciary duty. It is not disputed that fiduciaries are obliged to act in good faith. Further, we do not claim that fiduciary obligations are somehow baked into original meaning or among the "original methods" that the Framers expected to be applied to constitutional interpretation. *See* John O. McGinnis & Michael B. Rappaport, *Original Methods Originalism: A New Theory of Interpretation and the Case Against Construction*, 103 Nw. U. L. Rev. 751, 764 (2009). This is a normative argument—permissible in the context of construction. For further discussion, see Randy E. Barnett & Evan D. Bernick, *The Letter and the Spirit: A Unified Theory of Originalism*, 107 Geo. L.J. 1, 23–32 (2017) [hereinafter, "Barnett & Bernick, *The Letter and the Spirit*"].

61. *See* Richard A. Posner, *Legal Formalism, Legal Realism, and the Interpretation of Statutes and the Constitution*, 37 Case W. Res. L. Rev. 179, 196 (1986) ("A document can manifest a single purpose even though those who drafted and approved it had a variety of private motives and expectations.").

62. Ilan Wurman urges that today's constitutional decision-makers should focus on the "*known* historical problems" that the Constitution's designers were trying to solve. Ilan Wurman, The Second Founding 7 (2020) (emphasis added). We agree, albeit for normative rather than ontological reasons—an artifact may have a purpose that is entirely unknown to anyone but the designer(s), but recourse to obscure purposes would undermine the rule of law, which requires that the law be accessible to those who are required to follow it. We also believe that private explanations of artifactual function can supply probative evidence of known purposes absent contextual reasons to doubt whether those purposes would have been concealed from the public.

63. *See* Barnett, *Framers' Intent*, at 403, 408 (distinguishing "two reasons to consult the Framers. The first views the Framers as wardens; the second as designers or architects").

64. *Id.*

65. *Id.* at 408–09.

66. *Id.* at 409.

67. *See, e.g.,* GERARD N. MAGLIOCCA, AMERICAN FOUNDING SON: JOHN BINGHAM AND THE INVENTION OF THE FOURTEENTH AMENDMENT (2013); Richard L. Aynes, *On Misreading John Bingham and the Fourteenth Amendment,* 103 YALE L.J. 57 (1993); Michael Kent Curtis, *John A. Bingham and the Story of American Liberty: The Lost Cause Meets the "Lost Clause,"* 36 AKRON L. REV. 617, 655–61 (2003); Kurt T. Lash, *The Origins of the Privileges or Immunities Clause, Part II: John Bingham and the Second Draft of the Fourteenth Amendment,* 99 GEO. L.J. 329, 340 (2011) (tracing Bingham's drafting efforts and using his public statements about the text to inform interpretation of the Fourteenth Amendment).

68. Barnett, *Framers' Intent,* at 409.

69. *Id.*

70. John Manning has drawn a similar distinction between the "ulterior" or "background" purposes of a statute and the "implemental" purposes that particular provisions are designed to achieve. *See* John F. Manning, *The New Purposivism,* 2011 SUP. CT. REV. 113, 115 ("[T]he law's 'purpose,' properly understood, embodies not merely a statute's substantive ends (its 'ulterior purposes'), but also Congress's specific choices about the means to carry those ends into effect (its 'implemental purposes').").

71. Thomas B. Colby, *The Sacrifice of the New Originalism,* 99 GEO L.J. 713, 732 (2011).

72. ERIC J. SEGALL, ORIGINALISM AS FAITH 100 (2018)

73. *See* John F. Manning, *Textualism and Legislative Intent,* 91 VA. L. REV. 419, 450 (2005) (arguing that, in the context of statutory interpretation, "efforts to augment or vary the text in the name of serving a genuine but unexpressed legislative intent risks displacing whatever bargain was actually reached").

74. Put another way, we urge textualist originalists to resist the "nirvana fallacy." *See* Harold Demsetz, *Information and Efficiency: Another Viewpoint,* 12 J.L. & ECON. 1, 1 (1969) (criticizing policy analysis grounded in comparisons between imperfect existing institutions and unattainable alternatives).

75. *See* Michael B. Rappaport, *The Original Meaning of the Recess Appointments Clause,* UCLA L. REV. 1487, 1487 (2005).

76. *See* Randy E. Barnett, *The Original Meaning of the Commerce Clause,* 68 U. CHI. L. REV. 101, 101 (2001).

77. *See* John F. Stinneford, *The Original Meaning of "Cruel,"* 105 GEO. L.J. 441, 441 (2017); John F. Stinneford, *The Original Meaning of "Unusual": The Eighth Amendment as a Bar to Cruel Innovation,* 102 Nw. U. L. REV. 1739, 1745–46 (2008).

78. *See* GARY LAWSON, EVIDENCE OF THE LAW: PROVING LEGAL CLAIMS 75 (2017) (arguing that a legal proposition "is deemed correct if it is better, meaning more plausible, than its available alternatives").

79. Jules L. Coleman & Brian Leiter, *Determinacy, Objectivity, and Authority,* 142 U. PA. L. REV. 542, 571 (1993).

80. *See generally* RICHARD H. FALLON, JR., IMPLEMENTING THE CONSTITUTION (2001) (discussing the Court's implementation strategies for enforcing constitutional values).

81. *See* RANDY E. BARNETT, THE STRUCTURE OF LIBERTY: JUSTICE AND THE RULE OF LAW 109–32 (2d ed. 2014) (identifying the evolutionary nature of the common-law decision process as a discovery mechanism). *See generally* A.W.B. SIMPSON, A HISTORY OF THE COMMON LAW OF CONTRACT (1987).

82. *See* James C. Phillips, Daniel M. Ortner & Thomas R. Lee, *Corpus Linguistics & Original Public Meaning: A New Tool to Make Originalism More Empirical*, 126 YALE L.J.F. 21, 21 (2016); Lawrence M. Solan, *Can Corpus Linguistics Help Make Originalism Scientific?*, 126 YALE L.J.F. 57, 57 (2016); Lee J. Strang, *How Big Data Can Increase Originalism's Methodological Rigor: Using Corpus Linguistics to Reveal Original Language Conventions*, 50 U.C. DAVIS L. REV. 1181, 1202 (2017); Lawrence B. Solum, *Triangulating Public Meaning; Corpus Linguistics, Immersion, and the Constitutional Record*, 2017 BYU L. Rev. 1621 (2017).

83. We borrow Dworkin's phrasing of fit and justification here without suggesting a methodological homology. *See* RONALD DWORKIN, LAW'S EMPIRE 239 (1986).

84. *See* Hilary Putnam, *Meaning and Reference*, 70 J. PHILOS. 284 (1973) (imagining a duplicate planet full of English speakers for the purposes of an influential linguistic thought experiment that need not detain us here).

85. *See* Sáenz v. Roe, 526 U.S. 489 (1999).

86. DECLARATION OF INDEPENDENCE (US 1776) (emphasis added).

87. *See* Washington v. Glucksberg, 521 U.S. 702, 721 (1997).

88. We like Akhil Amar's trope of the ballot box, the jury box, and the cartridge box (channeling Frederick Douglass). *See* AKHIL REED AMAR & ALAN HIRSCH, FOR THE PEOPLE: WHAT THE CONSTITUTION REALLY SAYS ABOUT YOUR RIGHTS, at XVII (1998); FREDERICK DOUGLASS, LIFE AND TIMES OF FREDERICK DOUGLASS 386 (Carol Pub. Group ed., 1995) (arguing that "the liberties of the American people were dependent upon the Ballot-box, the Jury-box, and the Cartridge-box, that without these no class of people could live and flourish in this country . . .").

89. *See* PAUL CIMBALA, THE GREAT TASK REMAINING BEFORE US: RECONSTRUCTION AS AMERICA'S CONTINUING CIVIL WAR 66 (2010). This powerful trope was later popularized by Frederick Douglass. *See* FREDERICK DOUGLASS, LIFE AND TIMES OF FREDERICK DOUGLASS 386 (1892) (Carol Pub. Group ed., 1995) (arguing that "the liberties of the American people were dependent upon the Ballot-box, the Jury-box, and the Cartridge-box, that without these no class of people could live and flourish in this country"). The trope was introduced into legal scholarship by Akhil Amar. *See* AKHIL REED AMAR & ALAN HIRSCH, FOR THE PEOPLE: WHAT THE CONSTITUTION REALLY SAYS ABOUT YOUR RIGHTS, at XVII, (1998).

90. Corfield v. Coryell, 6 F. Cas. 546, 551–2 (1823) (emphasis added).

91. *See, e.g.*, 2 WILLIAM W. CROSSKEY, POLITICS AND THE CONSTITUTION IN THE HISTORY OF THE UNITED STATES 1102–08 (1953); LEONARD W. LEVY, ORIGINS OF THE BILL OF RIGHTS 248 (1999); ANDREW C. McLAUGHLIN, A CONSTITUTIONAL HISTORY OF THE UNITED STATES 461 (1935); HUGH E. WILLIS, CONSTITUTIONAL LAW OF THE UNITED STATES 705–06 (1936); Raoul Berger, *"Law of the Land" Reconsidered*, 74 Nw. U. L. REV. 1 (1979); Edward S. Corwin, *The Doctrine of Due Process of Law before the Civil War*, 24 HARV. L. REV. 366, 369–70, 372–73 (1911); Frank H. Easterbrook, *Substance and Due Process*, SUP. CT. REV. 85, 96, 99 (1982); Walton Hamilton, *The Path of Due Process of Law*, in THE CONSTITUTION RECON-SIDERED 167, 168, 176 (Conyers Read ed., 1938); John Harrison, *Substantive Due Process and the Constitutional Text*, 83 VA. L. REV. 493, 502, 517 (1997); Charles M. Hough, *Due Process of Law To-Day*, 32 HARV. L. REV. 218, 221–23 (1919); Andrew T. Hyman, *The Little Word "Due,"* 38 AKRON L. REV. 1, 2 (2005); Keith Jurow, *Untimely Thoughts: A Reconsideration of the Origins of Due Process of Law*, 19 A.M. J. LEGAL HIST. 265 *passim* (1975); Robert P. Reeder, *The Due Process Clauses and "The Substance of Individual Rights,"* 58 U. PA. L. REV. 191, 204, 207, 210 (1910); Charles Warren, *The*

New "Liberty" under the Fourteenth Amendment, 39 HARV. L. REV. 431, 431, 440–42 (1926); Ralph U. Whitten, *The Constitutional Limitations on State-Court Jurisdiction: A Historical-Interpretative Reexamination of the Full Faith and Credit and Due Process Clauses Part 2*, 14 CREIGHTON L. REV. 735 *passim* (1981); Stephen F. Williams, *"Liberty" in the Due Process Clauses of the Fifth and Fourteenth Amendments: The Framers' Intentions*, 53 U. COLO. L. REV. 117, 118, 121, 126 (1981); Christopher Wolfe, *The Original Meaning of the Due Process Clause*, in THE BILL OF RIGHTS: ORIGINAL MEANING AND CURRENT UNDERSTANDING 213, 217, 219 (Eugene W. Hickok Jr. ed., 1991). *See generally* Charles G. Haines, *Judicial Review of Legislation in the United States and the Doctrines of Vested Rights and of Implied Limitations of Legislatures* (pts. 1–3), 2 TEX. L. REV. 257 (1924), 2 TEX. L. REV. 387 (1924), 3 TEX. L. REV. 1 (1924).

92. JOHN HART ELY, DEMOCRACY AND DISTRUST: A THEORY OF JUDICIAL REVIEW 18 (1980).

93. *See, e.g.* JAMAL GREENE, HOW RIGHTS WENT WRONG: WHY OUR OBSESSION WITH RIGHTS IS TEARING AMERICA APART, at XXXV (2021).

94. *See* CLAY S. CONRAD, JURY NULLIFICATION: THE EVOLUTION OF A DOCTRINE (2014).

1. The Early Origins of Privileges or Immunities

1. Transcript of oral argument at 7, McDonald v. City of Chicago, 561 U.S. 742 (2010) (No. 08-1521) (comment of Justice Scalia).

2. *See, e.g.*, Charles Fairman, *Does the Fourteenth Amendment Incorporate the Bill of Rights? The Original Understanding*, 2 STAN. L. REV. 5 (1949); 2 WILLIAM WINSLOW CROSSKEY, POLITICS AND THE CONSTITUTION IN THE HISTORY OF THE UNITED STATES 1083–1175 (1953); William Winslow Crosskey, *Charles Fairman, "Legislative History," and the Constitutional Limitations on State Authority*, 22 U. CHI. L. REV. 1, 2–119 (1954); Alfred Avins, *Incorporation of the Bill of Rights: The Crosskey-Fairman Debates Revisited*, 6 HARV. J. ON LEGIS. 1 (1968); CHARLES FAIRMAN, RECONSTRUCTION AND REUNION, 1864–88, PART One 1388 (1971) (vol. 6 of the OLIVER WENDELL HOLMES DEVISE HISTORY OF THE SUPREME COURT OF THE UNITED STATES); CHARLES FAIRMAN, RECONSTRUCTION AND REUNION, 1864–88, PART Two (1987) (vol. 7 of the HOLMES DEVISE HISTORY); Stanley Morrison, *Does the Fourteenth Amendment Incorporate the Bill of Rights? The Judicial Interpretation*, 2 STAN. L. REV 140 (1949); RAOUL BERGER, GOVERNMENT BY JUDICIARY: THE TRANSFORMATION OF THE FOURTEENTH AMENDMENT (1977); DAVID CURRIE, THE CONSTITUTION IN THE SUPREME COURT: THE FIRST HUNDRED YEARS (1995); MICHAEL KENT CURTIS, NO STATE SHALL ABRIDGE: THE FOURTEENTH AMENDMENT AND THE BILL OF RIGHTS (1986); WILLIAM E. NELSON, THE FOURTEENTH AMENDMENT: FROM POLITICAL PRINCIPLE TO JUDICIAL DOCTRINE (1988); EARL M. MALTZ, CIVIL RIGHTS, THE CONSTITUTION, AND CONGRESS, 1863–1869 (1990); Akhil Reed Amar, *The Bill of Rights and the Fourteenth Amendment*, 101 YALE L.J. 1193 (1992); John Harrison, *Reconstructing the Privileges or Immunities Clause*, 101 YALE L.J. 1385 (1992); Richard L. Aynes, *On Misreading John Bingham and the Fourteenth Amendment*, 103 YALE L.J. 57 (1993); Michael W. McConnell, *Originalism and the Desegregation Decisions*, 81 VA. L. REV. 947 (1995); Douglas G. Smith, *The Privileges and Immunities Clause of Article IV Section 2: Precursor of Section One of the Fourteenth Amendment*, 34 SAN DIEGO L. REV. 809 (1997); Kimberly C. Shankman & Roger Pilon, *Reviving the Privileges or Immunities Clause to Redress the Balance among States, Individuals, and the*

Federal Government, 3 TEX. REV. L. & POL. 1, 21 (1998); Kevin Christopher Newsom, *Setting Incorporationism Straight: A Reinterpretation of the* Slaughter-House Cases, 109 YALE L.J. 643 (2000); James W. Fox, Jr., *Re-Readings and Misreadings:* Slaughter-House, *Privileges or Immunities, and Section Five Enforcement Powers,* 91 KT. L.J. 67 (2002); DAVID SKILLEN BOGEN, PRIVILEGES AND IMMUNITIES 51 (2003); Richard A. Epstein, *Of Citizens and Persons: Reconstructing The Privileges or Immunities Clause of the Fourteenth Amendment,* 1 N.Y.U. J.L. & LIBERTY 334 (2005); REBECCA E. ZIETLOW, ENFORCING EQUALITY: CONGRESS, THE CONSTITUTION, AND THE PROTECTION OF INDIVIDUAL RIGHTS (2006); Bryan H. Wildenthal, *Nationalizing the Bill of Rights: Revisiting the Original Understanding of the Fourteenth Amendment in 1866–67,* 68 OHIO ST. L.J. 1509 (2007); Eric R. Claeys, *Blackstone's Commentaries and the Privileges or Immunities of United States Citizens: A Modest Tribute to Professor Siegan,* 45 SAN DIEGO L. REV. 777 (2008); William J. Rich, *Why Privileges or Immunities? An Explanation of the Framers' Intent,* 42 AKRON L. REV. 1111 (2009); Timothy Sandefur, *Privileges, Immunities, and Substantive Due Process,* 5 N.Y.U. J.L. & LIBERTY 115, 121–32 (2010) Philip Hamburger, *Privileges or Immunities,* 105 Nw. U. L. REV. 61 (2011); KURT T. LASH, THE FOURTEENTH AMENDMENT AND THE PRIVILEGES AND IMMUNITIES OF AMERICAN CITIZENSHIP (2014); CHRISTOPHER R. GREEN, EQUAL CITIZENSHIP, CIVIL RIGHTS, AND THE CONSTITUTION: THE ORIGINAL SENSE OF THE PRIVILEGES OR IMMUNITIES CLAUSE (2015); David R. Upham, *The Meanings of the Privileges and Immunities of Citizenship on the Eve of the Civil War,* 91 NOTRE DAME L. REV. 1117 (2015); Note, *Congress's Power to Define the Privileges and Immunities of Citizenship,* 128 HARV. L. REV. 1206 (2015); ILAN WURMAN, THE SECOND FOUNDING: AN INTRODUCTION TO THE FOURTEENTH AMENDMENT (2020).

3. *See, e.g.,* Akhil Reed Amar, *Substance and Method in the Year 2000,* 28 PEPP. L. REV. 601, 631 n.178 (2001) (observing that "Virtually no serious modern scholar—left, right, and center—thinks that *Slaughterhouse* is a plausible reading of the Fourteenth Amendment"). *But see* LASH, *supra;* Newsom, *supra;* Wildenthal, *supra* at 1622 n.371 challenging the conventional wisdom and arguing that the Court at least left room for incorporation).

4. 92 U.S. 542 (1875).

5. 526 U.S. 489 (1999).

6. The right affirmed in *Saenz*—the right to travel—had already been recognized in previous decisions that did not discuss the clause at all. *See* Edwards v. California, 314 U.S. 160 (1941); United States v. Guest, 383 U.S. 745 (1966).

7. 561 U.S. 742 (2010).

8. 139 S.Ct. 682 (2019).

9. McDonald, 561 U.S. at 758.

10. *See* McDonald v. City of Chicago, oral argument transcript at 7.

11. *See generally* Harrison, *supra;* WURMAN, *supra.*

12. *See* Adamson v. California, 332 U.S. 47, 74–75 (1946) (Black, J., dissenting).

13. *See generally* LASH, *supra.*

14. *See generally* GREEN, *supra.*

15. *See generally* Hamburger, *supra.*

16. CONG. GLOBE, 42nd Cong., 2d Sess. 844 (Sen. John Sherman).

17. *E.g.,* William N. Eskridge, Jr., *Should the Supreme Court Read the Federalist Papers but Not Statutory Legislative History?,* 66 GEO. WASH. L. REV. 1301 (1997); Jack N. Rakove, *Joe the Ploughman Reads the Constitution, or the Poverty of Public Meaning Originalism,* 48 SAN DIEGO L. REV. 475 (2011).

18. *E.g.,* Antonin Scalia & John F. Manning, *A Dialogue on Statutory and Constitutional Interpretation,* 80 Geo. Wash. L. Rev. 1610, 1616 (2012) (denying that he had any objection to "using legislative history as (mildly) informative rather than authoritative: 'the word can mean this because people sometimes use it that way, as the legislative debate shows,' rather than 'the word must mean this because that is what the drafters said it meant.'"); In Re Sinclair, 870 F.2d, 1342 (Easterbrook, J.) ("Legislative history may be invaluable in revealing the setting of the enactment and the assumptions its authors entertained about how their words would be understood.").

19. The literature on collective choice defies comprehensive citation. For a sampling, see Mancur Olson, The Logic of Collective Action (1971); K. Arrow, Social Choice and Individual Values (2d ed. 1963); D. Black, The Theory of Committees and Elections (1958); David A. Skeel, Jr., *Public Choice and the Future of Public-Choice-Influenced Legal Scholarship,* 50 Vand. L. Rev. 647 (1997); D. Mueller, Public Choice III (2003).

20. *See* Neil K. Komesar, *Back to the Future: An Institutional View of Making and Interpreting Constitutions,* 85 Nw. L. Rev. 191, 208 (1987).

21. *See* Michael W. McConnell, *The Originalist Justification for Brown: A Reply to Professor Klarman,* 81 Va. L. Rev. 1937, 1939 (1995).

22. *See* Edward Sapir, Collected Writings of Edward Sapir 320 (David G. Mandelbaum ed., 1968) (coining the term). The term was introduced into originalism by Larry Solum. *See* Lawrence B. Solum, *The Fixation Thesis: The Role of Historical Fact in Original Meaning,* 91 Notre Dame L. Rev. 1, 17 (2015).

23. *See* U.S. Const. Article IV, Section 4 ("The United States shall . . . protect each of [the states] against Invasion; and . . . against domestic Violence.").

24. *See* 3 The Collected Works of James Buchanan, James M. Buchanan & Gordon Tullock, The Calculus of Consent: Logical Foundations of Constitutional Democracy 63 (1962) (Liberty Fund ed., 1999) ("Since no player can anticipate which specific rules might benefit him during a particular play of the game, he can, along with all the other players, attempt to devise a set of rules that will constitute the most interesting game for the average or representative player. It is to the self-interest of each player to do this.").

25. Skidmore v. Swift & Co., 323 U.S. 134, 140 (1944).

26. *See* Green, *supra* at 100

27. Claeys, *supra* at 782.

28. *See* Gordon S. Wood, The Creation of the American Republic, 1776–1787, 264–65 (2d ed., 1998).

29. *See* Michael Kent Curtis, *Historical Linguistics, Inkblots, and Life After Death: The Privileges or Immunities of Citizens of the United States,* 78 N.C. L. Rev. 1071, 1097 (2000).

30. 1 Sir William Blackstone, Commentaries on the Laws of England 123 (1765–1769).

31. *Id.*

32. *Id.* at 125 (emphasis added).

33. *Id.*

34. *Id.*

35. *Id.* (emphasis added).

36. *Id.*

37. Claeys, *supra* at 781.

38. *Id.*

39. *Id.* at 792.
40. *Id.*
41. *Id.*
42. 1 Blackstone's Commentaries at *159.
43. 4 Blackstone's Commentaries at *364.
44. 3 Blackstone's Commentaries at *100.
45. 1 Blackstone's Commentaries at *167.
46. *Id.* at *468.
47. Claeys, *supra* at 788.
48. *See* Eric Foner, The Story of American Freedom 13 (1999) [hereinafter, "Foner, American Freedom"].
49. *See* Aziz Rana, The Two Faces of American Freedom 60 (2011).
50. *Id.* at 78.
51. *Id.* at 79.
52. *Id.*
53. *Id.* at 49.
54. *Id.* at 70.
55. *Id.* at 71.
56. Daniel Dulany, "The Propriety of Imposing Taxes in the British Colonies," *in* 1 Classics of American Political and Constitutional Thought: Origins through the Civil War 181 (Scott J. Hammond et. al, eds., 2007).
57. *Id.*
58. 2 The Works of John Adams app. A. at 525 (Charles F. Adams ed., 1856).
59. *Id.*
60. 1 Resolutions of the Massachusetts House of Representatives, October 29, 1765, *in* The Writings of Samuel Adams, 1764–1769 (Harry Cushing Alonzo, ed., 1904).
61. A.E. Dick Howard, The Road from Runnymede: Magna Carta and Constitutionalism in America 174 (1968).
62. *Id.* at 175.
63. Curtis, *supra* at 1097.
64. The Address to the Inhabitants of Quebec, 1774, 1 Journals of the American Congress: From 1774 to 1788, at 41–43, *reprinted in* 1 The Bill of Rights, A Documentary History 222–33 (Bernard Schwartz ed., 1971).
65. *Id.*
66. *See* Foner, American Freedom, at 15.
67. *Id.* at 16.
68. *Id.*
69. Rana, *supra* at 89; Sean Wilentz, No Property in Man: Slavery and Anti-slavery at the Nation's Founding 5 (2018).
70. Wilentz, *supra* at 5.
71. *See generally* James Q. Whitman, *Why Did the Revolutionary Lawyers Confuse Custom and Reason?*, 58 U. Chi. L. Rev. 1321 (1993).
72. Articles of Confederation art. IV, § 1 (emphasis added).
73. U.S. Const. art. IV, § 2.
74. Robert G. Natelson, *The Original Meaning of the Privileges and Immunities Clause*, 43 Ga. L. Rev. 1117, 1177 (2008)
75. *Id.* at 1179.

76. *See* James Madison, *Notes on the Federal Convention* (August 28, 1787), in 2 THE RECORDS OF THE FEDERAL CONVENTION OF 1787, at 443 (Max Farrand ed., rev. ed. 1937).
77. Somerset v. Stewart 98 ER 499 (1772). The italicized portion of the adopted Fugitive Slave Clause in Article IV makes this intent clear ("No Person held to Service or Labour in one State, *under the Laws thereof. . . .*"), as does the clause's refusal to refer to persons "held to service or labour" as *slaves. See* WILENTZ, *supra* at 112.
78. RANA, *supra* at 87.
79. Mercantilist protectionism by the national government was another matter.
80. Natelson, *supra* at 1182.
81. THE FEDERALIST No. 41 (James Madison) at 220 (Liberty Fund, 2001).
82. *Id.* at 221.
83. THE FEDERALIST No. 80 (Alexander Hamilton), at 413.
84. *Id.*
85. ST. GEORGE TUCKER, BLACKSTONE'S COMMENTARIES: WITH NOTES OF REFERENCE TO THE CONSTITUTION AND THE LAWS, OF THE FEDERAL GOVERNMENT OF THE UNITED STATES, AND THE COMMONWEALTH OF VIRGINIA app. at 365 (1803).
86. 2 JAMES KENT, COMMENTARIES ON AMERICAN LAW 61 (New York: O. Halsted, 1827) (emphasis added).
87. *Id.*
88. Some abolitionists recognized this implication. *E.g.,* WILLIAM JAY, AN INQUIRY INTO THE CHARACTER AND TENDENCY OF THE AMERICAN COLONIZATION AND AMERICAN ANTI-SLAVERY SOCIETIES 41 (New York, Leavitt, Lord & Co., 2nd ed. 1835).
89. WILLIAM RAWLE, A VIEW OF THE CONSTITUTION OF THE UNITED STATES OF AMERICA 85 (Philadelphia, Philip H. Nicklin, Law Bookseller, 1829).
90. *Id.*
91. 3 JOSEPH STORY, COMMENTARIES ON THE CONSTITUTION OF THE UNITED STATES 565 (Boston, Hilliard, Gray, and Co., 1833).
92. *Id.*
93. *See* Arnold T. Guminski, *The Rights, Privileges, and Immunities of the American People: A Disjunctive Theory of Selective Incorporation of the Bill of Rights,* 7 WHITTIER L. REV. 765 (1985); LASH, *supra* at 48.
94. LASH, *supra* at xi.
95. *Id.* at 48.
96. *Id.* at 59.
97. *See generally* Randy E. Barnett & Evan D. Bernick, *The Privileges or Immunities Clause Abridged: A Critique of Kurt Lash on the Fourteenth Amendment,* 95 NOTRE DAME L. REV. 499 (2020).
98. LASH, *supra* at 58.
99. David Morril, Remarks of Mr. Morril in the Senate of the United States on the Missouri Question (January 17, 1820), *in* HILLSBORO TELEGRAPH (AMHERST, N.H.), Mar. 4, 1820, at 1.
100. DANIEL WEBSTER ET AL., A MEMORIAL TO THE CONGRESS OF THE UNITED STATES, ON THE SUBJECT OF RESTRAINING THE INCREASE OF SLAVERY IN NEW STATES TO BE ADMITTED INTO THE UNION 16 (Boston, Sewell Phelps 1819).
101. Barnett & Bernick, *supra* at 540.
102. Upham, *supra* at 1126.
103. Barnett & Bernick, *supra* at 540.
104. *Id.* at 550.

2. The Antislavery Origins of "Privileges or Immunities"

1. *See* Randy E. Barnett & Evan D. Bernick, *The Privileges or Immunities Clause Abridged: A Critique of Kurt Lash on the Fourteenth Amendment,* 95 NOTRE DAME L. REV. 499, 546 (2020).
2. Corfield v. Coryell, 6 F. Cas. 546, 551–52 (C.C.E.D. Pa. 1823) (No. 3230) (emphasis added).
3. Mason's draft differs subtly, but importantly, from the adopted version. *See* PAULINE MAIER, THE DECLARATION OF INDEPENDENCE AND THE CONSTITUTION OF THE UNITED STATES 10–11 (1998) (detailing the changes). It was Mason's draft that was used as a model by other states, *id.* at 16.
4. KURT T. LASH, THE FOURTEENTH AMENDMENT AND THE PRIVILEGES AND IMMUNITIES OF AMERICAN CITIZENSHIP 22 (2014).
5. *Id.*
6. Corfield, 6 F. Cas. at 552.
7. Gerard N. Magliocca, *Rediscovering* Corfield v. Coryell, 95 NOTRE DAME L. REV. 701 (2019).
8. 9 Johns. 507 (N.Y. 1812).
9. *Id.* at 577 (opinion of Kent, C.J.).
10. Quoted in Magliocca, *supra* at 718.
11. 3 H. & McH. 535 (Md. Gen. Ct. 1797).
12. LASH, *supra* at 30.
13. 3 H. & McH., at 554 (emphasis added).
14. Note, Corfield v. Coryell *and the Privileges and Immunities of American Citizenship,* 83 TEX. L. REV. 1483, 1501 (2004).
15. Wm. H. Williams, *The Arrest of Non-Residents for Debt—Constitutionality of the Law,* 2 W.L.J. 265, 266 (1845).
16. *Id.*
17. *Id.*
18. *Id.*
19. Tatem v. Wright, 23 N.J.L. 429, 444 (1852) (Elmer, J., concurring).
20. 51 Ky. (12 B. Mon.) 212, 219 (1851).
21. *See* R. Kent Newmeyer, *Justice Joseph Story on Circuit and a Neglected Phase of American Legal History,* 14 A.M. J. LEGAL. HIST. 112, 125 (1970) ("The circuit justice's decision was law for the people of his jurisdiction (unless and until reversed by the Supreme Court) and their life and property were directly and obviously in his hands.").
22. *See* L.L. RICHARDS, THE SLAVE POWER: THE FREE NORTH AND SOUTHERN DOMINATION, 1780–1860 (2000); ERIC FONER, FREE SOIL, FREE LABOR, FREE MEN: THE IDEOLOGY OF THE REPUBLICAN PARTY BEFORE THE CIVIL WAR 99 (1970) [hereinafter "FONER, IDEOLOGY OF THE REPUBLICAN PARTY"].
23. *See* Randy E. Barnett, *Whence Comes Section One?: The Abolitionist Origins of the Fourteenth Amendment,* 3 J. LEGAL ANALYSIS 165, 179–81 (2011).
24. Barnett & Bernick, *supra* at 534.
25. *Id.* at 533.
26. *Id.* at 534.
27. DANIEL WEBSTER ET AL., A MEMORIAL TO THE CONGRESS OF THE UNITED STATES, ON THE SUBJECT OF RESTRAINING THE INCREASE OF SLAVERY IN NEW STATES TO BE ADMITTED INTO THE UNION 15 (Boston, Sewell Phelps 1819).
28. *Id.* at 16.

29. *Id.* at 11.
30. 34 ANNALS OF CONG. 1232–33 (1819) (statement of Rep. McLane).
31. *Id.* at 1232.
32. Mo. CONST. of 1820, art. III, § 26.
33. *Id.* at 46 (Rep. Mallary).
34. *Id.* at 270 (Rep. Barbour).
35. *See* ROBERT PRICE FORBES, THE MISSOURI COMPROMISE AND ITS AFTERMATH: SLAVERY AND THE MEANING OF AMERICA 110–17 (2007).
36. CONG. GLOBE, 16th Cong., 2d Sess., 454 (1820).
37. *Id.*
38. *Id.*
39. *Id.* at 25.
40. *Id.*
41. *Id.*
42. *See* WILLIAM M. WIECEK, THE SOURCES OF ANTISLAVERY CONSTITUTIONALISM IN AMERICA, 1760–1848, at 124 (1977).
43. *See* EUGENE GENOVESE, ROLL, JORDAN, ROLL: THE WORLD THE SLAVES MADE 562 (1972).
44. *See* DOUGLAS R. EGERTON, HE SHALL GO OUT FREE: THE LIVES OF DENMARK VESEY 200 (1999).
45. *Id.*
46. *See* LEON F. LITWACK, NORTH OF SLAVERY: THE NEGRO IN THE FREE STATES, 1790–1860, at 51 (1961).
47. *Id.*
48. *Id.* at 52.
49. William J. Rich, *Lessons of Charleston Harbor: The Rise, Fall and Revival of Pro-Slavery Federalism,* 36 MCGEORGE L. REV. 569, 582 (2005).
50. *Id.* at 580.
51. *Id.* at 583.
52. *Id.* at 583.
53. *Id.* at 584.
54. *Id.* at 585.
55. *See* STATE DOCUMENTS ON FEDERAL RELATIONS; THE STATES AND THE UNITED STATES 238 (Herman V. Ames ed., 1970).
56. *See* Rich, *supra* at 584–85.
57. Somerset v. Stewart Lofft 1, 98 ER 499 (1772).
58. Derek A. Webb, *The* Somerset *Effect: Parsing Lord Mansfield's Words on Slavery in Nineteenth Century America,* 32 LAW & HIST. REV. 456 (2014).
59. Somerset, 98 ER at 499.
60. Webb, *supra* at 458–59.
61. 35 Mass. 193, 212 (1836).
62. EDLIE L. WONG, NEITHER FUGITIVE NOR FREE: ATLANTIC SLAVERY, FREEDOM SUITS, AND THE LEGAL CULTURE OF TRAVEL 81 (2009).
63. Commonwealth v. Aves, 35 Mass. 193, 225 (1836).
64. *Id.*
65. U.S. CONST., art. IV, § 2.
66. Wong, *supra* at 90.
67. Paul Finkelman, *Prelude to the Fourteenth Amendment: Black Legal Rights in the Antebellum North,* 17 RUTGERS L.J. 444–45 (1985).

68. Several northern states, including New York and Pennsylvania, enacted "sojourners' statutes" that permitted slaveholders to retain slaves for limited periods. WIECEK, *supra* at 194.

69. PAUL FINKELMAN, AN IMPERFECT UNION: SLAVERY, FEDERALISM, AND COMITY 114 (1981).

70. *Id.* at 127.

71. *Id.*

72. *See* MATTHEW KARP, THIS VAST SOUTHERN EMPIRE: SLAVEHOLDERS AT THE HELM OF AMERICAN FOREIGN POLICY 28 (2016).

73. *Id.* at 21.

74. Horatio Gates to Birney, January 24, 1842, *in* 1 LETTERS OF JAMES GILLESPIE BIRNEY 667–69 (Dwight Lowell Dumond ed., 1938).

75. *See generally* KARP, *supra.*

76. *Id.* at 237.

77. 41 U.S. 539 (1842).

78. Paul Finkelman, *The Cost of Compromise and the Covenant with Death,* 38 PEPP. L. REV. 5, 879 (2010) [hereinafter, "Finkelman, *The Cost of Compromise*"].

79. Paul Finkelman, *States' Rights, Southern Hypocrisy, and the Crisis of the Union,* 45 AKRON L. REV. 449, 454 (2011).

80. *See* DAVID L. LIGHTNER, SLAVERY AND THE COMMERCE POWER: HOW THE STRUGGLE AGAINST THE INTERSTATE SLAVE TRADE LED TO THE CIVIL WAR 101 (2006).

81. CONG. GLOBE, 31st Cong., 1st Sess., App. 53 (1850).

82. *Id.* at 244–52.

83. Finkelman, *The Cost of Compromise,* at 862.

84. *Id.* at 863–64.

85. Act of Sept. 9, 1850, ch. 49, 9 Stat. 446 (1850).

86. Fugitive Slave Act of 1850, ch. 60, 9 Stat. 4622 (1850).

87. Finkelman, *The Cost of Compromise,* at 861.

88. *Id.* at 857.

89. *Id.*

90. *See* STEVEN LUBET, FUGITIVE JUSTICE: RUNAWAYS, RESCUERS, AND SLAVERY ON TRIAL 50–51 (2011); James O. Horton & Lois E. Horton, *A Federal Assault: African Americans and the Impact of the Fugitive Slave Law of 1850,* 68 CHI.-KENT. L. REV. 1179, 1194 (1992).

91. 2 THE FREDERICK DOUGLASS PAPERS 380 (John W. Blassingame ed., 1982). *See also* "Is It Right and Wise to Kill a Kidnapper?," *id.,* June 2, 1854 (arguing that violence is justifiable when used to protect oneself, one's family, or community).

92. *See* H. ROBERT BAKER, THE RESCUE OF JOSHUA GLOVER: A FUGITIVE SLAVE, THE CONSTITUTION, AND THE COMING OF THE CIVIL WAR 51–55 (2006).

93. KARP, *supra* at 273.

94. Jones v. Van Zandt, 5 How. 215 (1847). Ohioan John Van Zandt was represented by future–Chief Justice Salmon Chase, who challenged the constitutionality of the Fugitive Slave Act of 1793 in his brief to the Supreme Court. Because the Court deemed that issue to have already been decided in *Prigg v. Pennsylvania,* it denied oral argument in the case. Chase's brief nonetheless was circulated as a pamphlet, spreading his constitutional arguments to a wide audience and burnishing his reputation as the "attorney general for fugitive slaves." *See* Barnett, *Whence Comes Section One?,* at 211–212 (describing the facts of the case); and Randy E. Barnett, *The Remarkable but Forgotten Career of Salmon P. Chase,* 63 CASE W. RSRV. L. REV. 653,

663–67 (2013) (summarizing Chase's constitutional arguments based on the enumerated powers of Congress and on the Due Process of Law Clause of the Fifth Amendment).

95. Strader v. Graham, 10 How. 82 (1851).
96. Ableman v. Booth, 18 How. 479 (1855).
97. 19 How. 383 (1857).
98. *Id.* at 405.
99. *Id.* at 450.
100. *Id.* at 405
101. *Id* at 417.
102. David R. Upham, *The Meanings of the Privileges and Immunities of Citizenship on the Eve of the Civil War*, 91 Notre Dame L. Rev. 1117, 1146 (2015).
103. Lash, *supra* at 41.
104. Dred Scott, 19 How. at 417.
105. *Id.*
106. Southern Slaves in Free State Courts: The Pamphlet Literature 44 (Paul Finkelman ed., 1988).
107. W.A. Larned, "Negro Citizenship," in 15 New Englander 478, 518 (1857); 2 John Codman Hurd, The Law of Freedom and Bondage in the United States 353 (Boston, Little, Brown & Co. 1862).
108. Abraham Lincoln, "A House Divided: Speech at Springfield Illinois," *in* 2 The Collected Works of Abraham Lincoln 461 (Roy P. Basler ed., 1953).
109. Dred Scott, 19 How. at 469 (Nelson, J., concurring).
110. *E.g.,* 1 Thomas R.R. Cobb, An Inquiry into the Law of Negro Slavery in the United States of America 119, 316 (1858); M.T. Wheat, The Progress and Intelligence of Americans 591 (2d ed. 1862).
111. Wash. Globe, December 14, 1835, at 2 (report of Postmaster Kendall to first session of 24th Congress).
112. Cong. Globe, 24th Cong., 1st Sess. 1725 (1836).
113. *Id.* at App'x 74.
114. Wiecek, *supra* at 174–75.
115. *Id.*
116. David Grimsted, American Mobbing, 1828–1861: Towards Civil War 29 (1996).
117. *Id.* at 36.
118. *Id.* at 128.
119. *Id.* at 36.
120. *Id.* at 37.
121. Letter from James Gillespie Birney to Gerrit Smith (August 13, 1835), *in* 1 Letters of James Birney 1831–1857, at 343 (Dwight L. Dumond, ed., 1938).
122. *See* Barnett, *From Antislavery Lawyer to Chief Justice*, at 658–59.
123. Proceedings of the New York Anti-Slavery Convention Held at Utica, October 21, and New York Anti-Slavery State Society Held at Peterboro, October 22, 1835, at 13 (New York, Standard & Democrat Office, 1835).
124. *Id.*
125. *See generally* Foner, Ideology of The Republican Party; J. Mayfield, Rehearsal for Republicanism (1980); K. Stampp, Imperiled Union: Essays on the Background of the Civil War (1980); R. Sewell, Ballots For Freedom (1976); H. Trefousse, The Radical Republicans (1968); E. Foner, Politics and Ideology in the Age of the Civil War (1980).

126. Upham, *supra* at 1151.
127. FONER, IDEOLOGY OF THE REPUBLICAN PARTY, at 261.
128. *Id.* at 61.
129. *E.g.*, RAOUL BERGER, GOVERNMENT BY JUDICIARY: THE TRANSFORMATION OF THE FOURTEENTH AMENDMENT 13 (1977); Michael J. Klarman, Brown, *Originalism, and Constitutional Theory: A Response to Professor McConnell*, 81 VA. L. REV. 1881 (1995).
130. FONER, IDEOLOGY OF THE REPUBLICAN PARTY, at 76. Ironically, just as Reconstruction came to be indelibly associated with "carpet-baggers," and President Ulysses Grant associated with drink and corruption, revisionist historians have successfully identified the committed antislavery activist Chase solely with his political ambitiousness. Few today know him for anything else.
131. *See generally* JOANNE B. FREEMAN, THE FIELD OF BLOOD: VIOLENCE IN CONGRESS AND THE ROAD TO CIVIL WAR (2018).
132. PROCEEDINGS OF THE FIRST THREE REPUBLICAN NATIONAL CONVENTIONS of 1856, 1860, and 1864 (Minneapolis, C.W. Johnson, 1893).
133. Henry H. Simms, *The Controversy Over the Admission of the State of Oregon*, 32 MISS. VALLEY HIST. REV. 355 (1945).
134. *Id.*
135. CONG. GLOBE, 35th Cong., 2d sess. 974 (1859).
136. *Id.*
137. *Id.* at 984.
138. *Id.* (emphasis added).
139. 3 JOSEPH STORY, COMMENTARIES ON THE CONSTITUTION OF THE UNITED STATES 565 (Boston, Hillard, Gray, and Co., 1833).
140. CONG. GLOBE, 35th Cong., 2d. sess. 985 (1859).
141. *Id.* at 1966.
142. *Id.* at 975.
143. *Id.*
144. *Id.*
145. *Id.* at 1967 (Rep. Mason).
146. IRA BERLIN, SLAVES WITHOUT MASTERS: THE FREE NEGRO IN THE ANTEBELLUM SOUTH 173 (1975).
147. *Id.* at 131.
148. *Id.*
149. LEON F. LITWACK, NORTH OF SLAVERY: THE NEGRO IN THE FREE STATES 72 (2009).
150. *See* 1 PROCEEDINGS OF THE BLACK STATE CONVENTIONS, 1840–1865 (Philip S. Foner & George E. Walker eds., 1979); 1 PROCEEDINGS OF THE BLACK NATIONAL AND STATE CONVENTIONS, 1865–1890 (Philip S. Foner & George E. Walker eds., 1986).
151. *E.g.*, Minutes of the State Convention of Colored Citizens of Pennsylvania, December 13–14, 1848, https://omeka.coloredconventions.org/items/show/241("The Almighty having clothed us with the attributes of Human nature, we are placed on an equality with the rest of mankind. The declaration of American Independence, and our own State's Bill of Rights ask no more."); The Minutes of the State Convention of the People of Color of the State of Indiana, August 1, 1851, https://omeka.coloredconventions.org/items/show /269 ("We are deprived of those inherent rights, set forth in the Declaration of Independence, and confirmed by the Constitution of the United States, all of which have been conferred upon foreigners that come into this country.").
152. *E.g.*, Proceedings of the State Convention of Colored People, Albany, New York, July 22–24, 1851, https://omeka.coloredconventions.org/items/show/235 ("The ark of

NOTES TO PAGES 87–89

the covenant was grounded and settled on these indestructible principles, and moreover, in after years, guaranteed by the adoption of the Constitution of the United States, art. 4, sec. 2, clause 1 . . . The colored man's constitutional rights as a citizen have never been questioned until recently"); Indiana Convention of 1851, *supra* ("As Americans we are entitled to all the rights, privileges and immunities of citizenship . . . according to the letter and the spirit of the Constitution of the United States.").

153. *E.g.*, New York Free Suffrage Convention, September 8, 1845, https://omeka .coloredconventions.org/items/show/233 ("Resolved, That the extension of this right [of suffrage] to one portion of the citizens of this State, and the withholding it from the other, however small, is a shameful denial of the fundamental doctrines of genuine Republicanism."); Indiana Convention of 1851, *supra* ("[T]o deny such a right [of suffrage] to one class of Citizens, while it is accorded to another, without good reason for such a discrimination, is manifestly unjust and anti-republican.").

154. *See sources cited supra* at notes 151–53.

3. The Antislavery Origins of Republican Citizenship

1. A note on labels. When discussing antebellum antislavery activism, some scholars reserve the label "abolitionist" for those who, like the Garrisonians, favored the immediate end of slavery everywhere including the original states. Those who advocated for the nonextension of slavery they label as "antislavery." *See, e.g.*, Alexander Tsesis, *Antislavery Constitutionalism*, in 1 ENCYCLOPEDIA OF THE SUPREME COURT OF THE UNITED STATES (David S. Tanenhaus, ed., 2008) ("This political movement sought to prevent the spread of slavery, but it was deferential to the existing order in slave states. Theirs was not a campaign for the immediate end of all slavery, wherever it existed, but against the continued spread of slavery to U.S. territories."). In the constitutional context, however, this semantic distinction is hard to maintain. After all, the Garrisonians are uncontroversially called "abolitionists," yet they too believed that the Constitution did not touch slavery in the slave states (or anywhere else). Activists such as James Birney and Salmon Chase agreed with them about this, and there is no reason to believe that they opposed immediate abolition by the Southern states. In 1900, newspaper publisher Benjamin F. Shaw retrospectively used the term "constitutional abolitionists" to distinguish this group from "radical abolitionists" such as William Lloyd Garrison and Wendell Phillips. *See* Benjamin F. Shaw, *Owen Lovejoy, Constitutional Abolitionism and the Republican Party* in 3 TRANSACTIONS OF THE MCLEAN COUNTY HISTORICAL SOCIETY 59–73 (Ezra Prince ed., Bloomington: Pantagraph Printing, 1900). We adopt Shaw's term, "constitutional abolitionist," but nothing of substance turns on this semantic choice. The label "antislavery constitutionalists" would work just as well.

2. *See generally* MICHAEL KENT CURTIS, NO STATE SHALL ABRIDGE: THE FOURTEENTH AMENDMENT AND THE BILL OF RIGHTS (1986).

3. LEWIS PERRY, RADICAL ABOLITIONISM 188 (1973)

4. RICHARD H. SEWELL, BALLOTS FOR FREEDOM: ANTISLAVERY POLITICS IN THE UNITED STATES 1837–1860, at ix (1976); Randy E. Barnett, *From Antislavery Lawyer to Chief Justice: The Remarkable but Forgotten Career of Salmon P. Chase*, 63 CASE W. RES. L. REV. 653, 654–5 (2013) [hereinafter, "Barnett, *Salmon Chase*."]

5. JOHN FERGUSON HUME, THE ABOLITIONISTS: TOGETHER WITH PERSONAL MEMORIES OF THE STRUGGLE FOR HUMAN RIGHTS 1830–1864, at 11 (1905).

6. Barnett, *Salmon Chase*, at 673.

7. Eric Foner, Free Labor, Free Soil, And Free Men: The Ideology Of The Republican Party 75 (1970) [hereinafter "Foner, Ideology Of The Republican Party"].

8. American Anti-Slavery Society, Declaration of Sentiments (1833), *in* The Radical Reader: A Documentary History Of The American Radical Tradition 125 (Timothy Patrick McCarthy & John Campbell McMillian eds., 2003).

9. *Id.* at 126.

10. *Id.* at 127.

11. *Id.*

12. *See generally* Wendell Phillips, The Constitution: A Pro-Slavery Compact; Or, Excerpts From The Madison Papers, Etc. (New York, American Anti-Slavery Society, 1845). *See* Randy E. Barnett, *Whence Comes Section One?: The Abolitionist Origins of the Fourteenth Amendment*, 3 J. Legal Analysis 165, 203–05 (2011) (discussing the intramural debate between Phillips and Lysander Spooner concerning the Constitution's moral status).

13. William M. Wiecek, The Sources Of Antislavery Constitutionalism In America, 1760–1848, at 240 (1977).

14. *Id.*

15. Wendell Phillips, Can Abolitionists Vote Or Take Office Under The United States Constitution? 14 (New York: American Anti-Slavery Society, 1845).

16. Spooner has also been read as justifying a "language of the law" as distinct from a public meaning approach. John O. McGinnis & Michael B. Rappaport, *Original Methods Originalism: A New Theory of Interpretation and the Case Against Construction*, 103 Nw. U. L. Rev. 751, 764 (2009). This intra-originalist debate is beyond our scope here. Both sides agree that Spooner rejected a "framers' intent" approach, *id.*; Randy E. Barnett, *The Misconceived Assumption about Constitutional Assumptions and Interpretative Conventions*, 70 U. Chi. L. Rev. 615, 643–47 (2003) (describing Spooner's approach); *id.* at 659–60 (briefly critiquing original methods originalism).

17. United States v. Fisher, 2 Cranch 358, 390 (1805). *See* Lysander Spooner, The Unconstitutionality Of Slavery 63 (Boston, Bela Marsh, 1860).

18. Perry, *supra* at 165.

19. Barnett, *Whence Comes Section One?*, at 197.

20. Frederick Douglass, "Change of Opinion Announced, May 23, 1851," *in* The Essential Douglass: Selected Writings And Speeches (Nicholas Buccola ed., 2016).

21. Barnett, *Whence Comes Section One?*, at 174.

22. Report Of The Arguments Of Counsel In The Case Of Prudence Crandall 3 (1834).

23. *Id.* at 34.

24. Donald E. Williams, Jr., Prudence Crandall's Legacy: The Fight For Equality In The 1830s, *Dred Scott*, And *Brown v. Board of Education* 100 (2014).

25. *Id.* at 341.

26. Report, *supra* at 11.

27. *Id.* at 7. Notice the denial that aliens have a right to own land. In Chapter 6, we explain why this common feature of American law is relevant to how the wording of the Civil Rights Act of 1866 was modified after the ratification of the Fourteenth Amendment when Congress broadened it to protect all *persons*, not just citizens.

28. *Id.* at 8 (emphasis added).
29. *Id.* at 13–14 (emphases added)
30. *Id.* at 7.
31. *Id.* at 6.
32. *Id.*
33. *Id.* at 14.
34. *Id.* at 10.
35. *Id.* at 21.
36. Barnett, *Whence Comes Section One?* at 175 n. 25.
37. Howard Jay Graham, Everyman's Constitution: Historical Essays on the Fourteenth Amendment, the "Conspiracy Theory," and American Constitutionalism 184 (1968).
38. Chase's arguments were published in Speech of Salmon P. Chase, In the Case of the Colored Woman, Matilda (1837). Matilda fled from slavery in Missouri to freedom in Cincinnati with the aid of a Black barber and was hired by James Birney. *See* Manisha Sinha, The Slave's Cause: A History of Abolition 388 (2016). The case ended badly; Chase's arguments did not prevail, and Matilda was sold into slavery in New Orleans. *Id.*
39. Graham,. at 198.
40. *Id.* at 200.
41. Charles Olcott, Two Lectures on the Subject of Slavery and Abolition 30 (Massolin: Charles Olcott, 1838).
42. First Annual Report of the New York Young Men's Anti-Slavery Society 7 (New York: Howe & Bates,1834).
43. James Duncan, A Treatise on Slavery 30 (New York: The American Anti-Slavery Society, 1840).
44. Graham, *supra* at 178.
45. *Id.* at 168; Randy E. Barnett, *Was Slavery Unconstitutional before the Thirteenth Amendment? Lysander Spooner's Theory of Interpretation*, 28 Pac. L. J. 977, 979 (1996).
46. Spooner, *supra* at 188.
47. *Id.* at 92.
48. *Id.* at 90.
49. *Id.* at 94.
50. *Id.* at 245.
51. *Id.* at 266.
52. *Id.* at 266.
53. *Id.* at 168
54. *Id.* at 276. Spooner was discussing resident aliens, not their *children,* who were born on US soil. *See* Garrett Epps, *The Citizenship Clause: A "Legislative History,"* 60 A.M. U. L. Rev. 331, 374 (2010) (detailing Spooner and Tiffany's exposition of birthright citizenship).
55. Spooner, *supra* at 8.
56. *Id.* at 90.
57. *Id.* at 91.
58. *Id.* at 101.
59. *Id.* at 132.
60. Joel Tiffany, A Treatise on the Unconstitutionality of American Slavery 88 (Worcester: Thomas Drew, Jr., 1850) [hereinafter "Tiffany, Unconstitutionality of Slavery"].

61. *Id.* at 89.

62. JOEL TIFFANY, A TREATISE ON GOVERNMENT, AND CONSTITUTIONAL LAW 22 (Albany: Weed, Parsons & Co.,1867) [hereinafter, "TIFFANY, TREATISE ON GOVERNMENT"].

63. *Id.* at 23.

64. *Id.*

65. TIFFANY, UNCONSTITUTIONALITY OF SLAVERY, at 87.

66. *Id.* at 98. Although Tiffany used the masculine "he" and "him," as was then common linguistic practice, this was not intended to limit these rights to males; females had all these rights as well. In contrast, as we have and will continue to note, the right of suffrage was different in this respect, and does not appear on Tiffany's list. For a summary of the development of the generic masculine in the eighteenth century and its widespread use in the nineteenth century, see Ann Bodine, "Androcentrism in Prescriptive Grammar: Singular 'They,' Sex-Indefinite 'He,' and 'He' or 'She,'" *in* THE FEMINIST CRITIQUE OF LANGUAGE 124–41 (Deborah Cameron ed., 1990).

67. TIFFANY, UNCONSTITUTIONALITY OF SLAVERY, at 103.

68. *Id.* at 117.

69. *Id.* at 57.

70. *Id.* at 100.

71. *Id.* at 97.

72. *Id.* at 94.

73. *Id.* at 120.

74. *Id.* at 78, 90, 102, 128.

75. *Id.* at 84.

76. TIFFANY, TREATISE ON GOVERNMENT, at 115.

77. Salmon Chase was among them. Indeed, he sought to convince other Liberty party members to disavow the term but was unsuccessful. *See* FONER, THE IDEOLOGY OF THE REPUBLICAN PARTY, at 79–80.

78. *Id.* at 76.

79. See Daniel A. Farber & John E. Muench, *The Ideological Origins of the Fourteenth Amendment*, 1 CONST. COMMENT. 235, 242 (1984); Douglas G. Smith, *Citizenship and the Fourteenth Amendment*, 34 SAN DIEGO L. REV. 681, 695 (1997).

80. Farber & Muench, *supra* at 236.

81. SALMON PORTLAND CHASE, RECLAMATION OF FUGITIVES FROM SERVICE: AN ARGUMENT FOR THE DEFENDANT 93 (Cincinnati: R.P. Donogh & Co., 1847).

82. CONG. GLOBE, 34th Cong., 3d. sess. 189 (1857).

83. 52 JOURNAL OF THE HOUSE OF REPRESENTATIVES OF THE STATE OF OHIO 71 (January 14, 1856).

84. *Id.*

85. *See generally* SEAN WILENTZ, NO PROPERTY IN MAN: SLAVERY AND ANTISLAVERY AT THE NATION'S FOUNDING (2018).

86. FONER, IDEOLOGY OF THE REPUBLICAN PARTY, at 77.

87. CHASE, *supra* at 100, 106. Paul Finkelman argues that Chase adopted this reasoning from an 1836 opinion by New Jersey Supreme Court Chief Joseph C. Hornblower in *State v. The Sheriff of Burlington*. See Paul Finkleman, "Chief Justice Hornblower of New Jersey and the Fugitive Slave Law of 1793," *in* SLAVERY AND THE LAW 114 (Finkelman, ed., 1997) ("Some newspapers, especially the antislavery press, communicated Hornblower's decision. As far west as Ohio the antislavery attorney Salmon P. Chase, a future chief justice of the United States Supreme Court, cited it

for authority in a fugitive slave case. But Chase's citation was probably an exception."). Hornblower's opinion would appear as a pamphlet in 1851 in the wake of the Fugitive Slave Act of 1850.

88. CHASE, *supra* at 102.

89. Argument of Salmon P. Chase, Esq., March 11, 1837, *in* WILLIAM YATES, RIGHTS OF COLORED MEN TO SUFFRAGE, CITIZENSHIP AND TRIAL BY JURY 100 (Philadelphia, Merrihew and Gunn, 1838).

90. WILENTZ, *supra* at 137.

91. FONER, THE IDEOLOGY OF THE REPUBLICAN PARTY, at 84.

92. *Id.* at 85.

93. CONG. GLOBE, 35th Cong., 2d sess. 984 (1859).

94. *Id.* at 99.

95. FONER, IDEOLOGY OF THE REPUBLICAN PARTY, at 149.

96. ALEXANDER KEYSSAR, THE RIGHT TO VOTE: THE CONTESTED HISTORY OF DEMOCRACY IN THE UNITED STATES 26–32 (2000).

97. *See id.* at 50 (describing the emergence of a "presumption in favor of granting the franchise to adult, white men").

98. SOUTHERN SLAVES IN FREE STATE COURTS: THE PAMPHLET LITERATURE 44 (Paul Finkelman ed., 1988).

99. Jan Ellen Lewis, *Rethinking Women's Suffrage in New Jersey, 1776–1807*, 63 RUTGERS L. REV. 1017 (2010).

100. Donald Ratcliffe, *The Right to Vote and the Rise of Democracy, 1787–1828*, 33 JOUR. EARLY REPUBLIC 219, 253 (2013).

101. *Id.*

102. Lewis, *supra.*

103. Corfield v. Coryell, 6 F. Cas. 546, 552 (1823).

104. *E.g.,* Dred Scott v. Sandford, 19 How. 393, 412 (1857).

4. Reconstructing National Citizenship

1. Alexander Tsesis, *A Civil Rights Approach: Achieving Revolutionary Abolitionism Through the Thirteenth Amendment*, 39 U.C. DAVIS L. REV. 1773, 1776 (2005).

2. Ira Berlin, "Emancipation and Its Meaning," *in* UNION & EMANCIPATION: ESSAYS ON POLITICS & RACE IN THE CIVIL WAR ERA 109 (David W. Blight & Brooks D. Simpson eds., 1997).

3. *See* W.E.B. DU BOIS, BLACK RECONSTRUCTION IN AMERICA 149–60 (2007) (1880).

4. See JAMES G. HOLLANDSWORTH, JR., AN ABSOLUTE MASSACRE: THE NEW ORLEANS RACE RIOT OF JULY 30, 1866, at 64–66 (2001) (detailing how a white mob organized by the New Orleans mayor massacred mostly Black marchers outside of a reconvened Louisiana Constitutional Convention); An Act to Provide for the More Efficient Government of the Rebel States, 14 Stat. 428 (1867) ("[N]o legal State governments or adequate protection for life or property now exists in the Rebel States"); CONG. GLOBE, 39th Cong., 2d sess. 82 (Rep. Farnsworth) ("There is no adequate protection now to Union men, to soldiers, or to freedmen . . . I care not what laws you pass here, so long as they remain a dead letter because there is no power to enforce them.").

5. JAMES OAKES, FREEDOM NATIONAL: THE DESTRUCTION OF SLAVERY IN THE UNITED STATES, 1861–65, at 386 (2013).

6. This episode is extensively described in James P. McClure, Leigh Johnsen, Kathleen Norman, & Michael Vanderlan, *Circumventing the Dred Scott Decision: Edward Bates,*

Salmon P. Chase, and the Citizenship of African Americans, 43 CIVIL WAR HISTORY 279 (1997). *See also* KATE MASUR, UNTIL JUSTICE IS DONE: AMERICA'S FIRST CIVIL RIGHTS MOVEMENT, FROM THE REVOLUTION TO RECONSTRUCTION 281–86 (2021).

7. Michael Vorenberg, *Emancipation—Then What?,* NEW YORK TIMES, "DISUNION" BLOG, January 15, 2013, https://opinionator.blogs.nytimes.com/2013/01/15/emancipation-then-what/.

8. McClure et al., *supra* at 280–81, 284 (providing additional background on David M. Selsey); WILLIAM A. BLAIR, WITH MALICE TOWARD SOME: TREASON AND LOYALTY IN THE CIVIL WAR ERA 264–66 (2014) (same).

9. Vorenberg, *supra.*

10. *Id.*

11. *Id.*

12. *Id.*

13. *Id.*

14. MASUR, *supra* at 284.

15. McClure et al., *supra* at 283.

16. *Id.*

17. MASUR, *supra* at 285.

18. Vorenberg, *supra.*

19. *Id.*

20. McClure et al., *supra* at 284.

21. *Id.* at 283.

22. *Id.* at 284.

23. *Id.*

24. United States Department of State, "Opinion of Mr. Attorney-General Bates, Dated November 29, 1862," in FOREIGN RELATIONS OF THE UNITED STATES, PART 2, at 1370 (Washington, DC: US Government Printing Office, 1873), 1370.

25. *Id.* at 1371.

26. *Id.* at 1372.

27. *Id.* at 1370.

28. *Id.*

29. Ordinance of 1787, An Ordinance for the Government of the Territory of the United States Northwest of the Ohio River, art. VI, *reprinted in* THE CONSTITUTIONS OF OHIO 52 (Isaac F. Patterson ed., 1912).

30. Xi Wang, *Black Suffrage & the Redefinition of American Freedom, 1860–1870,* 17 CARDOZO L. REV. 2153, 2177 (1996).

31. Rebecca E. Zietlow, *James Ashley, the Great Strategist of the Thirteenth Amendment,* 15 GEO. J.L. & PUB POL'Y 265, 304 (2017). *See generally,* REBECCA E. ZIETLOW, THE FORGOTTEN EMANCIPATOR: JAMES MITCHELL ASHLEY AND THE IDEOLOGICAL ORIGINS OF RECONSTRUCTION (2017).

32. CONG. GLOBE, 38th Cong., 2d. sess. 155 (1865) (Rep. Davis).

33. CONG. GLOBE, 38th Cong., 2d Sess. 139 (1865).

34. JAMES M. ASHLEY & BENJAMIN W. ARNETT, DUPLICATE COPY OF THE SOUVENIR FROM THE AFRO-AMERICAN LEAGUE OF TENNESSEE TO HON. JAMES M. ASHLEY OF OHIO 334 (1893) [hereinafter, "SOUVENIR"].

35. CONG. GLOBE, 38th Cong., 2d sess. 139 (1865).

36. SOUVENIR, at 340.

37. *Id.*

38. *Id.* at 348.

39. CONG. GLOBE, 38th Cong., 1st sess. 193 (1864).
40. *Id.* at 1202.
41. *Id.*
42. *Id.* Absent from Wilson's list was any reference to what we call the Establishment Clause. Free exercise yes; establishment no.
43. *Id.* at 1203.
44. *Id.* at 2989.
45. *Id.* at 2990.
46. *Id.*
47. *Id.*
48. 7 BREVIER LEGISLATIVE REPORTS: EMBRACING SHORT-HAND SKETCHES OF THE JOURNALS AND DEBATES OF THE GENERAL ASSEMBLY OF THE STATE OF INDIANA 180 (1865).
49. *Id.*
50. *Id.*
51. *Id.* at 221.
52. See *id.* at 222 (Rep. Foulke) (expressing "no fear of the bugbear of negro equality").
53. JOHN HOPE FRANKLIN, RECONSTRUCTION AFTER THE CIVIL WAR 47 (2d ed., 1994).
54. *Id.* at 48.
55. THEODORE BRANTNER WILSON, THE BLACK CODES OF THE SOUTH 30 (1965).
56. DU BOIS, *supra* at 171.
57. DOUGLAS A. BLACKMON, SLAVERY BY ANOTHER NAME: THE RE-ENSLAVEMENT OF BLACK AMERICANS 79 (2008).
58. *Id.* at 130.
59. *See* Dorothy E. Roberts, *Abolition Constitutionalism: The Supreme Court 2018 Term: Foreword*, 133 HARV. L. REV. 1, 70 (2019).
60. *Id.*
61. *See* Bailey v. Alabama, 219 U.S. 219 (1911). This "Lochner-era" decision was decided 7–2, with Justice Oliver Wendell Holmes, Jr., in a dissent that deserves to be more infamous. *See Bailey*, 219 U.S. at 246 (Holmes, J., dissenting) ("Neither public document nor evidence discloses a law which by its administration is made something different from what it appears on its face, and therefore the fact that in Alabama it mainly concerns the blacks does not matter.") As Aziz Huq writes, statutes that criminalized breach of contract were designed to "criminalize[] blacks' refusal to labor" and thereby "ensur[e] a constant pool of readily-available and cheap labor." *See Peonage and Contractual Liberty*, 101 COL. L. REV. 351, 362 (2001).
62. FONER, RECONSTRUCTION: AMERICA'S UNFINISHED REVOLUTION 208 (2014) (1988) [hereinafter "FONER, RECONSTRUCTION"].
63. *Id.*
64. FONER, RECONSTRUCTION, at 69.
65. Act of Mar. 3, 1865, ch. 90, 13 Stat. 507. 508.
66. CONG. GLOBE, 39th Cong., 1st sess. 209 (1866).
67. Act of July 16, 1866, ch. 200, § 14, 14 Stat. 176.
68. See CONG. GLOBE, 39th Cong., 1st sess. 474 (1866) (statement of Sen. Trumbull) (characterizing the act as an effort to "destroy all the [] discriminations" in the Codes and listing examples).
69. Civil Rights Act of 1866, ch. 31, § 1, 14 Stat. 27, 27.
70. *Id.* (emphasis added).
71. CONG. GLOBE, 39th Cong., 1st sess. 476 (1866).

72. *Id.* at 599.
73. *Id.* at 595 (Sen. Davis).
74. *Id.*
75. *Id.* at 600 (Sen. Trumbull).
76. *Id.*
77. *Id.* at 606.
78. *Id.* at 474.
79. *Id.* at 475.
80. *Id.*
81. *Id.*
82. *Id.* at 764.
83. *Id.* at 1117.
84. *Id.*
85. *Id.*
86. *Id.*
87. *Id.* at 1118.
88. *Id.*
89. *Id.*
90. *Id.*
91. *Id.*
92. *Id.*
93. *Id.*
94. *Id.* (emphasis added).
95. *Id.* at 1119.
96. 6 Pet. 539, 615 (1842).
97. Cong Globe, 39th Cong., 1st. sess. 1291 (1866) (emphasis added).
98. *Id.*
99. *Id.*
100. *Id.* at 1292.
101. *Id.*
102. *Id.*
103. 7 Pet. 243 (1833).
104. Cong. Globe, 39th Cong., 1st sess. at 1089.
105. *Compare* Kurt T. Lash, The Fourteenth Amendment and the Privileges and Immunities of American Citizenship 94–96 (2014) with Randy E. Barnett & Evan D. Bernick, *The Privileges or Immunities Clause Abridged: A Critique of Kurt Lash on the Fourteenth Amendment,* 95 Notre Dame L. Rev. 499, 515, 544–45 (2020).
106. *See* Civil Rights Act of 1866, ch. 31, § 1, 14 Stat. 27, 27.
107. Cong. Globe, 39th Cong., 1st sess. at 1367 (1866).
108. *Id.* at 1809.
109. Cong. Globe, 39th Cong., 1st sess. 1119 (1866).
110. *Id.* at 1835.
111. *Id.*
112. *Id.* (emphasis added).
113. *Id.* at 1836.
114. *Id.* at 1680.
115. *Id.* at 1757.
116. *Id.*
117. *Id.*

118. *Id.*
119. *Id.*
120. *Id.*
121. *Id.* at 1759.
122. *Id.* at 1415.

5. The Letter

1. Cong. Globe, 39th Cong., 1st sess. app. 1 (1866).
2. *Id.*
3. Cong. Globe, 39th Cong., 1st sess. 14 (1865).
4. Cong. Globe, 39th Cong., 1st sess. 157 (1866).
5. *Id.*
6. Id. at 158.
7. *Id.* To avoid any possible confusion, we note that the parenthetical comment was Bingham's not ours.
8. Raoul Berger, Government by Judiciary: The Transformation of the Fourteenth Amendment 145 (1977); Charles Fairman, *Does the Fourteenth Amendment Incorporate the Bill of Rights? The Original Understanding*, 2 Stan. L. Rev. 5, 25–26 (1949).
9. Wm. H. Williams, *The Arrest of Non-Residents for Debt—Constitutionality of the Law*, 2 W.L.J. 265, 266 (1845).
10. *Id.* (emphasis added).
11. *Id.*
12. *Id.*
13. Cong. Globe, 39th Cong., 1st sess. 14 (1865).
14. *Id.* at 158.
15. *Id.* at 157.
16. *Id.* (emphasis added).
17. Benjamin Kendrick, The Journal of the Joint Committee of Fifteen on Reconstruction 61 (1914).
18. This proposed amendment was introduced to the Joint Committee on Reconstruction on January 16, 1866. Kendrick, *supra* at 49, 51.
19. *Id.* at 61.
20. *See* Gerard N. Magliocca, The Heart of the Constitution: How the Bill of Rights Became the Bill of Rights (2018); Michael Douma, *How the First Ten Amendments Became the Bill of Rights*, 15 Geo. J.L. & Pub. Pol'y 593 (2017); Pauline Maier, *The Strange History of the Bill of Rights*, 15 Geo. J.L. & Pub Pol'y 497 (2017).
21. Webster's Complete Dictionary of the English Language 133 (1880). We thank Gerard Magliocca for this example.
22. *See* Kurt T. Lash, *The Enumerated-Rights Reading of the Privileges or Immunities Clause: A Response to Barnett and Bernick*, 95 Notre Dame L. Rev. 591, 621–30 (2019) [*hereinafter, "Lash, Response to Barnett and Bernick"*]. Lash has yet to reconcile this claim with his broader all-and-only-enumerated rights theory of the Privileges or Immunities Clause. Lash's theory holds that enumerated rights include those specified elsewhere in the Constitution—such as the right to habeas corpus and the right to vote for federal representatives. *See* Kurt T. Lash, The Fourteenth Amendment and the Privileges and Immunities of American Citizenship 148, 300 (2014). As Lash recognizes, Bingham stated that the Fourteenth Amendment

would provide *only* for the enforcement of the Bill of Rights. *See* 39th Cong. Globe, 1st Sess. 1088 (1866) (Rep. Bingham) (stating that Section 1 was designed "to arm the Congress of the United States . . . with the power to enforce the bill of rights as it stands in the Constitution today. It 'hath that extent—no more.'"). So if Lash is right about the meaning of "bill of rights," either Bingham or Lash is wrong about the Fourteenth Amendment's "extent"—it covers some but not all enumerated rights.

23. *See, e.g.,* 6 Charles Fairman, History of the Supreme Court of the United States: Reconstruction and Reunion, 1864–1888, Part I, 1288 (1971) (describing Bingham as "confused" and opining that he held "peculiar conceptions").

24. Cong. Globe, 39th Cong., 1st sess. 1089 (1866).

25. *Id.* (emphases added).

26. *Id.* at 1064.

27. *Id.* ("What are these amendments to the Constitution, numbered one to ten, one of which is the fifth article in question? . . . They constitute *the bill of rights, a bill of rights* for the protection of the citizen, and defining and limiting the power of Federal *and State* legislation." (emphases added)). After Bingham called Hale's attention to Article IV, Section 2, Hale replied, "I omit the consideration of that section for the reason that my argument is directed exclusively to the consideration of the final clause of the amendment proposes, which is founded on the fifth article of the amendment. . . . The last-named section is therefore outside the range of my remarks on this occasion," *id.*

28. *Id.* at 1089.

29. Maier, *supra,* Douma, *supra,* and Magliocca, *supra,* do not claim that no one *ever* referred to the first eight or ten amendments as "a bill of rights" or even "the bill of rights." Their claim is that the phrase "the Bill of Rights" lacked today's standard meaning of the first ten amendments. Hence, providing examples of the term being used by others to refer to the first eight or ten amendments, as Hale did, does not refute their thesis.

30. Cong. Globe, 39th Cong., 1st Sess. 1089 (1866).

31. *Id.* at 1095.

32. *Id.* at 1095.

33. *Id.* at 1095.

34. *Id.*

35. *Id.* at 1088.

36. *Id.*

37. *Id.*

38. *Id.*

39. *Id.*

40. *Id.* at 1063.

41. *Id.*

42. *Id.*

43. *Id.* at 1066.

44. *Id.*

45. Kendrick, *supra* at 296.

46. *Id.* at 82, 85.

47. See Earl M. Maltz, *The Fourteenth Amendment as Political Compromise—Section One in the Joint Committee on Reconstruction,* 45 Ohio St. L.J. 933, 959 (1985).

48. Kendrick, *supra* at 87.

49. Maltz, *supra* at 947.

50. Cong Globe, 39th Cong., 1st sess. 2542 (1866).
51. *Id.*
52. *Id.*
53. *Id.*
54. *Id.*
55. *Id.*
56. *Id.* at 2542.
57. *Id.* at 2459.
58. *Id.* at 2133.
59. *Id.*
60. *Id.*
61. Cong. Globe, 39th Cong., 1st sess. 2766 (1866).
62. *Id.* at 2765. The Privileges and Immunities Clause appears at U.S. Const. art. IV, §2, cl. 1.
63. 6 F. Cas. 546 (C.C.Pa. 1823).
64. Cong. Globe, 39th Cong., 1st sess. 2765 (1866) (emphasis added).
65. *Id.* Among other rights, Howard omitted the rights of criminal defendants to indictment by grand jury, to confront witnesses, to have compulsory processes for obtaining witnesses in their favor, and to have the assistance of counsel for their defense, *id. See* U.S. Const. amend. 5; Donald A. Dripps, *The Fourteenth Amendment, the Bill of Rights, and the (First) Criminal Procedure Revolution*, 18 J. Contemp. Legal Is 469, 477 (2009). Howard's list also did not refer to what we call the Establishment Clause as any kind of right. Kurt Lash has claimed that, though originally a federalism provision, by 1868, the Establishment Clause was thought to protect an individual right, but Howard's seemingly intentional omission undermines this claim. *See* Kurt T. Lash, *The Second Adoption of the Establishment Clause: The Rise of the Nonestablishment Principle*, 27 Ariz. St. L.J. 1085, 1154 (1995) (concluding that "[b]y 1868, the (Non)Establishment Clause was understood to be a liberty as fully capable of incorporation as any other provision in the first eight amendments to the Constitution.").
66. Cong. Globe, 39th Cong., 1st sess. 2765 (1866) (emphasis added).
67. *Id.* at 2766.
68. *Id.* at 2766.
69. Notes of Jacob Howard on the Fourteenth Amendment's Privileges or Immunities Clause (1866), http://www.tifs.org/sources/Howard.pdf at 3. *See* Christopher R. Green, *Incorporation, Total Incorporation, and Nothing But Incorporation?*, 24 Wm. & Mary Bill Rts. J. 93, 109 (2015) (discussing Howard's notes).
70. The Boston Daily Advertiser told its readers that
    The Senate having taken up the amendment, Mr. Howard explained it, section by section. The first clause of the first section was intended to secure to the citizens of all the States *the privileges which are in their nature fundamental, and which belong of right to all persons in a free government*. There was now no power in the Constitution to enforce its guarantees of those rights. They stood simply as declarations, and the States were not restricted from violating them, except by their own local constitutions and laws. The great object of the first section, fortified by the fifth, was to compel the States to observe these guarantees, and to throw the same shield over the black man as over the white, over the humble as over the powerful.
    Dixon, *Reconstruction: The Debate in the Senate*, Bos. Daily Advertiser, May 24, 1866, at 1 (emphasis added). Moreover, this was decidedly not a comity-only reading of either Howard's speech or the amendment itself.

71. Cong. Globe, 39th Cong., 1st sess. 2766.
72. *Id.*
73. *Id.*
74. *Id.*
75. *Id.*
76. *Id.*
77. *Id.*
78. *Id.* at 2765.
79. *Id.*
80. *See* Cong. Globe, 42d Cong., 1st sess. app. at 84 (1871).
81. U.S. Const. amend. XIV, § 3.
82. Christopher R. Green, Equal Citizenship, Civil Rights, and the Constitution: The Original Sense of the Privileges or Immunities Clause 52 (2015).
83. U.S. Const. amend. XIV, § 2. *See* Green, *supra* at 136 (discussing these claims).
84. E.g., Representative Thaddeus Stevens, "Speech of the Honorable Thaddeus Stevens Delivered at Bedford Penn," September 4, 1866, *in* Cincinnati Commercial, Speeches of the Campaign of 1866: In the States of Ohio, Indiana, and Kentucky 27 (1866) [hereinafter, "Speeches of the Campaign of 1866."]
85. *See* Cong. Globe, 39th Cong., 1st sess., at 2459 (Rep. Stevens); *id.* at 2462 (Rep. Garfield); *id.* at 2511 (Rep. Eliot); *id.* at 2788–89 (Sen. Stewart).
86. *E.g.*, The Wheeling Intelligencer, August 7, 1866 (Gov. Morton).
87. *See* David W. Blight, Frederick Douglass 483 (2018); Frederick Douglass, "Reconstruction," Atlantic Monthly, December 1866, at 761, 765 (identifying the right to vote as a privilege of citizenship and criticizing the Fourteenth Amendment for providing an "emasculated citizenship").
88. Majority and Minority Reports on the Proposed Fourteenth Amendment before the Legislative Committee on Federal Relations, H.R. 149, Gen. Ct., Reg. Sess. (Mass. 1867).
89. *Id.*
90. *E.g.*, Cong. Globe, 39th Cong., 1st sess. 599–600 (1866) (Sen. Trumbull); *id.* at 1117 (Rep. Wilson); *id.* at 2459 (Rep. Stevens); *id.* at 2883 (Rep. Latham).
91. *E.g.*, John Harrison, *Reconstructing the Privileges or Immunities Clause*, 101 Yale L.J. 1385, 1416 (1992). Earl M. Maltz, Civil Rights, the Constitution, and Congress, 1863–1869, at 66–67 (1990).
92. *E.g.*, Cong. Globe, 39th Cong., 1st sess. 1757 (Sen. Trumbull);
93. Civil Rights Act of 1866, ch. 31, § 1, 14 Stat. 27, 27.
94. Cong. Globe, 39th Cong., 1st sess. app. 157 (1866) (emphasis added).
95. *Id.*
96. *Id.* at 1413.
97. *See* James W. Fox, Jr., *Re-Readings and Misreadings:* Slaughter-House, *Privileges or Immunities, and Section Five Enforcement Powers*, 91 Ky. L.J. 67, 98 n.113 (2002).
98. *See* Harrison, *supra* at 1403 n. 59 (quoting *id.* at 1293 (Rep. Shellabarger)).
99. Harrison, at 1403.
100. Cong. Globe, 39th Cong., 1st sess. 1293 (1866).
101. *Id.* at 1270.
102. The Wheeling Intelligencer, July 23, 1868, at 2.
103. *Id.*
104. The Daily Standard, October 6, 1866, at 2.

105. *E.g.*, The Wheeling Daily Intelligencer, June 20, 1866, at 2 (Section 2 "clearly recognizes the principle, and when ratified will establish it beyond all question, that suffrage is not one of the 'privileges and immunities of citizens'"); Richmond Weekly Palladium, August 2, 1866, at 1 (stating that "[i]f the right of suffrage is a privilege or immunity of citizens of the United States as such, then it has always been so" and denying the conditional); The Daily Standard, October 6, 1866, at 4 (question of suffrage "left entirely to the States, as it has ever been").

106. *E.g.*, Schuyler Colfax, "Speech in Indianapolis, Ind., Aug. 7, 1988," *in* Speeches of the Campaign of 1866, at 14; the Civil Rights Act of 1866 specifies "what the rights of a citizen of the United States are"); Senator Lyman Trumbull, "Senator Lyman Trumbull in Chicago, Aug. 2, 1866," *id.* at 6; "Great Speech of General Logan: At Chicago, Tuesday Evening, Aug. 14," Am. Citizen, September 5, 1866, at 1.

107. *E.g.*, Cong. Globe, 39th Cong., 1st sess. 2766 (1866) (Sen. Howard); Majority and Minority Reports on the Proposed Fourteenth Amendment before the Legislative Committee on Federal Relations, H.R. 149, Gen. Ct., Reg. Sess. (Mass. 1867); George Paschal, "Letter to the Editor, The Fourteenth Article," N.Y. Trib., August 6, 1868, at 2.

108. *E.g.*, Chicago Tribune, October 10, 1866, at 2 (proposed amendment "mak[es] citizenship uniform" by placing "beyond all question the legal or civil status of the whole people upon a common equality"; among the rights of citizenship are "right to purchase and hold real estate, to sell and lease the same, and, when dying, to devise it"); The Hanford Democrat, August 23, 1866, at 1 (reprint from the Chicago Republican) (Privileges or Immunities Clause secures "all the civil rights secured . . . either by constitution, statute, or the common law of the land" and the question of which precise rights are secured is "left to be determined by the decisions of the courts, under the Constitution, the common law and the usages, customs and practice of the civilized nations of the earth"); The New York Times, November 3, 1866, at 1 (rights "common to the people of all the States"); The Leavenworth Bulletin, April 4, 1866, at 1 (secures "all the immunities and privileges of equal citizenship" derived "from one common law").

109. Chicago Tribune, October 10, 1866, at 2.

110. *Id.*

111. *See, e.g.*, Lash, *supra*; Kevin Christopher Newsom, *Setting Incorporationism Straight: A Reinterpretation of the* Slaughter-House Cases, 109 Yale L.J. 643 (2000).

112. *See* Ludwig Wittgenstein, Philosophical Investigations 35–38 (P.M.S. Hacker & Joachim Schulte eds., G.E.M. Anscombe et. al trans., rev. 4th ed., 2009) (1953).

6. Enforcing Citizenship

1. *See* Michael McConnell, *Originalism and the Desegregation Decisions*, 81 Va. L. Rev. 953, 1105 (1995) (identifying post-ratification deliberations over civil-rights legislation as the best evidence of whether the original meaning of the Fourteenth Amendment prohibited segregated schools).

2. *E.g.*, Cong. Globe, 40th Cong., 3d sess. at 1000 (1869) (Sen. Edmunds); *id.* at 1003 (Sen. Sumner); *id.* at 558 (Sen. Boutwell); *id.* at 1004 (Sen. Yates).

3. Cong. Globe, 40th Cong., 3d sess. at 1003 (1869) (Sen. Howard).

4. *Id.*

5. *Id.*

6. *Id.* at 1004.
7. *Id.*
8. *Id.*
9. *Id.*
10. *Id.*
11. *See* WYN CRAIG WADE, THE FIERY CROSS: THE KU KLUX KLAN IN AMERICA 40 (1987).
12. *Id.* at 79.
13. CONG. GLOBE, 42d Cong., 1st sess., 236, 244 (1871); Robert J. Kaczorowski, *Federal Enforcement of Civil Rights during the First Reconstruction*, 23 FORDHAM URB. L.J. 155, 158 (1995).
14. Enforcement Act of 1870, §§ 16, 18, 16 Stat. at 144.
15. *Id.* at § 6.
16. *Id.* at § 16.
17. CONG. GLOBE, 41st Cong., 2d sess. 3 (1869).
18. *Id.*
19. Polly J. Price, *Alien Land Restrictions in the American Common Law: Exploring the Relative Autonomy Paradigm*, 43 A.M. J. LEGAL. HIST. 152, 157 (1999).
20. *Id.* at 156–57.
21. S. Misc. Doc. No. 41–16 (1870).
22. A.G. Riddle, "Speech in Support of the Woodhull Memorial, Before the Judiciary Committee of the House of Representatives," *in* 2 HISTORY OF WOMAN SUFFRAGE 448, 453 (Elizabeth Cady Stanton et al. eds, (Rochester, NY, Susan B. Anthony, 1881).
23. *Id.* (emphasis added).
24. H.R. Rep. No. 41–22, at 1 (1871).
25. *Id.*
26. *Id.*
27. VICTORIA C. WOODHULL, A LECTURE ON CONSTITUTIONAL EQUALITY, DELIVERED AT LINCOLN HALL, WASHINGTON, D.C., FEBRUARY 16, 1871 (New York, Journeymen Printers' Cooperative Association, 1871).
28. *Id.*
29. *Id.*
30. *Id.*
31. *Id.*
32. *Id.*
33. *Id.*
34. *Id.*
35. *Id.* at 468.
36. *Id.* at 468–69.
37. *Id.* at 471.
38. *Id.* at 472.
39. *Id.* at 470.
40. *Id.* at 475 (emphasis added).
41. *Id.* (emphases added).
42. *Id.*
43. *Id.* at 476.
44. *See* KURT LASH, THE FOURTEENTH AMENDMENT AND THE PRIVILEGES AND IMMUNITIES OF CITIZENSHIP 114 (2014).

45. See Randy E. Barnett & Evan D. Bernick, *The Privileges or Immunities Clause Abridged: A Critique of Kurt Lash on the Fourteenth Amendment*, 95 NOTRE DAME L. REV. 499, 540 (2020) [hereinafter, "Barnett & Bernick, *Privileges or Immunities Abridged*"].

46. Civil Rights Act of April 20, 1871, ch. 22, 17 Stat. 13 (1871).

47. CONG. GLOBE, 42d Cong., 1st sess. app. 69 (1871).

48. *Id.* at 73.

49. CONG. GLOBE, 42d Cong., 1st sess. 310 (1871).

50. H.R. REP. NO. 41–22, at 1 (1871).

51. CONG. GLOBE, 42d Cong., 1st sess. app. at 84 (1871).

52. *Id.*

53. Barnett & Bernick, *Privileges or Immunities Abridged*, at 576.

54. CONG. GLOBE, 42d Cong., 1st sess. app. at 86 (1871).

55. *Id.*

56. *Id.*

57. *Id.*

58. In an 1851 speech uncovered by Gerard Magliocca, Bingham made clear the source of this precise language—John Milton. GERARD N. MAGLIOCCA, AMERICAN FOUNDING SON: JOHN BINGHAM AND THE INVENTION OF THE FOURTEENTH AMENDMENT 35 (2013) (quoting Bingham as referring to "the liberty whereof John Milton spake" and mentioning "the freedom of the press, the freedom of speech and of conscience"). As Magliocca observes, "[a] typical Bingham speech was filled with citations and scholarly allusions that few members of Congress could match," *id.* at 49.

59. CONG. GLOBE, 42d Cong., 1st sess., at 188 (1871).

60. *Id.*

61. *Id.*

62. *Id.*

63. *Id.*

64. *Id.* at 228.

65. *Id.*

66. *Id.* at 696.

67. *Id.* at 693.

68. *Id.*

69. *Id.* at 693.

70. Christopher R. Green, *The Original Sense of the (Equal) Protection Clause: Pre-Enacting History*, 19 GEO. MASON U. C.R. L.J. 1 (2008).

71. 21 Ohio St. 198 (1871).

72. *Id.* at 209.

73. 26 F. Cas. 79 (C.C.S.D. Ala. 1871).

74. *Id.* at 81.

75. Joseph Bradley to William Woods, March 12, 1871, Joseph Bradley Papers, The New Jersey Historical Society (emphasis added).

76. 15 F. Cas. 649.

77. *Id.* at 651.

78. *Id.*

79. *Id.*

80. CONG. GLOBE, 42d Cong., 1st sess. 500 (1871).

81. THOMAS MACINTYRE COOLEY, A TREATISE ON THE CONSTITUTIONAL LIMITATIONS WHICH REST UPON THE LEGISLATIVE POWER OF THE STATES OF THE AMERICAN UNION (Boston, Little, Brown, and Company, 2nd ed. 1871).

82. *Id.* at 294.
83. *Id.* at 397.
84. John Norton Pomeroy, An Introduction to the Constitutional Law of the United States 178 (Cambridge, The Riverside Press, 9th ed. 1886).
85. Timothy Farrar, A Manual of the Constitution of the United States of America 199, 200, 402 (Cambridge, John Wilson and Son, 1867).
86. *Id.* at 199.
87. George W. Paschal, The Constitution of the United States Defined and Carefully Annotated 290 (Washington, DC, W. H. & O.H. Morrison, Law Booksellers, 1868).
88. Randy E. Barnett, *The Three Narratives of the* Slaughter-House Cases, 41 J. Sup. Ct. Hist. 295, 298 (2016).
89. *Id.* at 299.
90. Live-Stock Dealers, 15 F. Cas. at 651.
91. *See* Bryan Wildenthal, *How I Learned to Stop Worrying and Love the* Slaughter-House Cases: *An Essay in Constitutional-Historical Revisionism,* 23 T. Jefferson L. Rev. 241 (2000) ("All the scholarly greats, it seems—yea, the verdict of history itself—have condemned it for so narrowly construing the Privileges and Immunities Clause as to render that provision a nullity, a dead letter, a piece of constitutional roadkill.").
92. Slaughter-House, 16 Wall. at 71.
93. *Id.* at 78.
94. *Id.*
95. *Id.* at 79–80.
96. *Id.* at 98.
97. See, e.g., Saenz v. Roe, 119 S. Ct. 1518, 1538 (1999) (Thomas, J., dissenting) ("The Slaughter-House Cases sapped the [Privileges or Immunities] Clause of any meaning."); Akhil Reed Amar, *The Bill of Rights and the Fourteenth Amendment,* 101 Yale L.J. 1193, 1229 (1992) ("Miller's argument . . . seemed to resist, if not reject, total incorporation of the first eight amendments."); Robert Bork, The Tempting of America: The Political Seduction of the Law 180 (1990) ("[T]he privileges and immunities clause[] has remained the cadaver that it was left by the Slaughter-House Cases."); The Constitution of the United States of America: Analysis and Interpretation 965 (Edward S. Corwin ed., 1953) ("[T]he privileges and immunities clause [was] . . . rendered a 'practical nullity' by a single decision of the Supreme Court rendered within five years after its ratification."); Michael Kent Curtis, No State Shall Abridge: The Fourteenth Amendment and the Bill of Rights 175 (1986) ("[By its construction of the Fourteenth Amendment [in *Slaughter-House,*] the Court effectively nullified the intent to apply the Bill of Rights to the states."); 2 Walter L. Fleming, Documentary History of Reconstruction 423 (1907) (placing the discussion of the *Slaughter-House Cases* within a chapter entitled "The Undoing of Reconstruction"); Joseph B. James, The Ratification of the Fourteenth Amendment 205 (1984) (commenting that Justice Miller's "opinion in the Slaughter House Cases of 1873 . . . set the pattern of narrow interpretation of the Fourteenth Amendment for a long time"); Erwin Chemerinsky, *The Supreme Court and the Fourteenth Amendment: The Unfulfilled Promise,* 25 Loy. L.A. L. Rev. 1143, 1144 (1992) ("Through judicial interpretation the Court has rendered the Privileges or Immunities Clause a nullity."); Curtis, *supra* at 76 ("[Slaughter-House] left protections of Bill of Rights liberties to the tender mercies of the very states that had so recently made mincemeat of them."); Charles Fairman, "What Makes a Great

Justice? Mr. Justice Bradley and the Supreme Court, 1870–1892," *in* THE BACON LECTURES ON THE CONSTITUTION OF THE UNITED STATES: 1940–1950, at 425, 458 (Arthur N. Holcombe, ed., 1953) ("Justice Miller. for a bare majority of the Court, construed the Amendment narrowly . . . The privileges and immunities clause was virtually scratched from the Constitution."); Morton J. Horwitz, *The Supreme Court, 1992 Term-Foreword: The Constitution of Change: Legal Fundamentality Without Fundamentalism,* 107 HARV. L. REV. 30, 84 (1993) ("Justice Miller's opinion . . . virtually emptied the Privileges and Immunities Clause of content . . ."). Even those who challenge the conventional wisdom acknowledge its "almost crushing weight," Kevin Christopher Newsom, *Setting Incorporationism Straight: A Reinterpretation of the* Slaughter-House Cases, 109 YALE L.J. 643, 648 (2000).
98. Slaughter-House, 16 Wall. at 118 (Bradley, J., dissenting).
99. *Id.* at 119–20.
100. *Id.* at 120.
101. *Id.*
102. *Id.*
103. *Id.*
104. *Id.* at 123.
105. *Id.* at 118.
106. *See generally* William E. Forbath, *The Ambiguities of Free Labor: Labor and the Law in the Gilded Age,* 1985 WIS. L. REV. 767 (1985); ADAM M. CARRINGTON, JUSTICE STEPHEN FIELD'S COOPERATIVE CONSTITUTION OF LIBERTY (2018).
107. Slaughter-House, 16 Wall. at 84.
108. *Id.* at 87 (emphasis added).
109. *Id.* at 95.
110. *Id.* at 96.
111. *Id.* at 125.
112. *Id.* at 98.
113. *Id.* at 102.
114. Bradwell v. Illinois, 16 Wall. 130, 139 (1873).
115. *Id.* at 141.
116. *Id.*
117. Bradley allowed that there might be "exceptional cases" but stated that "the rules of civil society must be adapted to the general constitution of things," *id.* at 141–42.
118. *Id.* at 142 (emphasis added).
119. 92 U.S. 542 (1876).
120. Eric FONER, RECONSTRUCTION: AMERICA'S UNFINISHED REVOLUTION, 1863–1877, at 437 (1988).
121. LeeAnna KEITH, THE COLFAX MASSACRE: THE UNTOLD STORY OF BLACK POWER, WHITE TERROR, AND THE DEATH OF RECONSTRUCTION 80 (2008).
122. *Id.* at 87.
123. *Id.*
124. NICHOLAS LEMANN, REDEMPTION: THE LAST BATTLE OF THE CIVIL WAR 12 (2007).
125. *Id.*
126. *Id.*
127. KEITH, *supra* at 89.
128. *Id.* at 149.
129. *Id.* at 98.

130. LEMANN, *supra* at 22–23.
131. United States v. Cruikshank, 92 U.S. 543, 552–57 (1873).
132. *Id.* at 551–53.
133. *Id.* at 553.
134. *Id.* at 551.
135. *Id.* at 552.
136. *Id.* at 553.
137. *Id.* at 549.
138. *Id.* at 552.
139. CONG. GLOBE, 42d Cong., 1st sess. 500 (1871) (Sen. Frelinghuysen); *id.* at 334 (Rep. Hoar).
140. *E.g.*, 3 CONG. REC. 1792 (1875) (Sen. Boutwell).
141. *E.g.*, 3 CONG. REC. 943 (1875) (Rep. Lynch).
142. *E.g.*, 2 CONG. REC. 384–85 (1874) (Rep. Mills); *id.* at 405–06 (Rep. Durham); *id.* at 415 (Rep. Bright); *id.* at 419 (Rep. Herndon).
143. *E.g.*, 4 CONG. REC., 44th Cong., 1st sess. at 2067 (1876) (Sen. Bayard); *id.* at 2067 (Sen. Merrimon); 9 CONG. REC., 46th Cong., 1st sess.at 258 (1879) (Rep. McLane); *id.* at 600 (Sen. Maxey).
144. 4 CONG. REC., 44th Cong., 1st sess. at 2067 (1876).
145. Richard Aynes, *Constricting the Law of Freedom: Justice Miller, The Fourteenth Amendment, and The* Slaughter-House Cases, 70 CHI.-KENT L. REV. 627, 681 (1994).
146. Richard L. Aynes, *On Misreading John Bingham and the Fourteenth Amendment*, 103 YALE L.J. 57, 87 (1993).
147. 2 CONG. REC., 43d Cong., 1st sess. 3451 (1874) (Sen. Frelinghuysen).
148. *Id.* at 4087 (Sen. Morton).
149. 3 CONG. REC., 43d Cong., 2d sess. 1792 (1874).
150. 2 CONG. REC., 43d Cong., 1st sess. 4088 (Sen. Edmunds).
151. *Id.* at 4148 (Sen. Howe).
152. CONG. GLOBE, 41st Cong., 2d sess. 3434 (1870).
153. *Id.*
154. *See* McConnell, *supra* at 978–80, 1052–87.
155. Alexander Tsesis, *Freedom to Integrate: A Desegregationist Perspective on the Thirteenth Amendment*, 38 U. TOL. L. REV. 791, 803 (2007).
156. 109 U.S. 3 (1883).
157. Alfred Avins, *The Civil Rights Act of 1875 and the Civil Rights Cases Revisited: State Action, the Fourteenth Amendment, and Housing*, 14 UCLA L. REV. 4, 22 (1966).
158. *Id.*
159. *Id.* at 12, 15.
160. CONG. GLOBE, 42d Cong., 2d sess. 383 (1872).
161. We use this term in the classical sense, as distinct from the conception of "Republican citizenship," which we claim informs the Fourteenth Amendment.
162. *Id.* at 383–84.
163. *Id.*
164. McConnell, *supra* at 1081.
165. *Id.* at 1043–44.
166. *E.g.*, CONG. GLOBE, 42d Cong., 2d sess. 3190 (Sen. Ferry); *id.* at 3192 (Sen. Trumbull); *id.* at app. 5 (Sen. Morrill).
167. *Id.* at 762.
168. *Id.* (quoting Cummings v. Missouri, 4 Wall. 277, 321–2 (1867)).
169. Cummings, 4 Wall. at 321–22.

170. McConnell, *supra* at 1005.
171. CONG. GLOBE, 42d Cong., 2d sess. at 827–8 (1872).
172. 2 CONG. RECORD 3451–55 (1874)
173. *Id.* at 4088.
174. *Id.* at 409.
175. CONG. GLOBE, 42d Cong., 2d sess. 3191 (1872).
176. *Id.* at app. 4.
177. James W. Fox, Jr., *Re-Readings and Misreadings:* Slaughter-House, *Privileges or Immunities, and Section Five Enforcement Powers,* 91 KY. L.J. 67, 154 (2002).
178. Green, *supra* at 98–99.
179. CONG. GLOBE, 39th Cong. 1st sess. 1117 (1866).
180. *Id.*
181. CONG. GLOBE, 42d Cong., 2d sess. 381 (emphasis added).
182. Fox, *supra* at 138.
183. *E.g.,* CONG. GLOBE, 42d Cong., 2d sess. 844 (Sen. Sherman); *id.* at 3191 (Rep. Morton).
184. *Id.* at 3191.
185. *Id.*
186. *Id.* at 3090.
187. *Id.* at 3191.
188. *Id.*
189. *Id.*
190. *Id.*
191. *Id.*
192. *Id.*
193. *Id.* at 844.
194. 100 U.S. 303, 309 (1880).
195. Furthermore, *Strauder* concerned the constitutionality of Congress using its Section 5 power to create a right of removal to federal court from a state that restricted jury composition by race. We return to this issue in Part III.
196. *Id.* at 383.
197. Barnett & Bernick, *Privileges or Immunities Abridged,* at 575.
198. Corfield, 6 F. Cas. at 552 (emphasis added).
199. Committee Draft of the Virginia Declaration of Rights and Edited by the Virginia Convention (May 27, 1776), ConSource, https://www.consource.org/document/committee-draft-of-the-virginia-declaration-of-rights-and-edited-by-the-virginia-convention-1776-5-27/.
200. James Madison, "Speech in Congress Proposing Constitutional Amendments (June 8, 1789)," in JAMES MADISON, WRITINGS 437, 449–49 (Jake N. Rakove, ed., 1999). Madison's entire "first" proposal that he said "may be called a bill of rights" was:
First, That there be prefixed to the constitution a declaration, that all power is originally rested in, and consequently derived from, the people.
That Government is instituted and ought to be exercised for the benefit of the people; which consists in the enjoyment of life and liberty, with the right of acquiring and using property, and generally of pursuing and obtaining happiness and safety.
That the people have an indubitable, unalienable, and indefeasible right to reform or change their Government, whenever it be found adverse or inadequate to the purposes of its institution.
1 *Annals of Cong.* 433–34 (1789).

201. 1 ANNALS OF CONG. at 454 (1789).
202. CONG. GLOBE, 42d Cong., 2d sess. 843 (1872). See Green, *supra* at 106-06.
203. 1 ANNALS OF CONG. at 454.
204. *See* Jack M. Balkin, *The Reconstruction Power*, 85 N.Y.U. L. REV. 1801 (2010); Ryan C. Williams, *Originalism and the Other Desegregation Decision*, 99 VA. L. REV. 493 (2013).
205. *See* JAMES OAKES, FREEDOM NATIONAL: THE DESTRUCTION OF SLAVERY IN THE UNITED STATES, 1861–1865, at xx (2012) (describing how Republicans "produced a remarkable string of unanimous or near-unanimous votes . . . designed to undermine slavery, beginning in July of 1861").
206. *See* Randy E. Barnett, *Whence Comes Section One? The Abolitionist Origins of the Fourteenth Amendment*, 3 J. LEGAL ANALYSIS 165, 174–76 (2011).
207. Williams, *supra* at 580.
208. *Id.* CONG. GLOBE, 39th Cong., 1st sess. 2896.
209. *See, e.g.*, Adarand Constructors, Inc. v. Pena, 515 U.S. 200, 215 (1995) (applying *Bolling* to federal practice of giving primary contractors a financial incentive to hire subcontractors on the basis of race); Metro Broadcasting, Inc. v. FCC, 697 U.S. 547, 604–06 (1990) (O'Connor, J., dissenting) (stating that *Bolling* requires strict scrutiny for all federal racial classifications, including "benign" race conscious measures); Ricci v. DeStefano, 557 U.S. 557, 594 (2009) (Scalia, J., concurring) (arguing that *Bolling* casts constitutional doubt on Title VII's disparate-impact provisions).

7. Competing Originalist Interpretations

1. *E.g.*, Bryan H. Wildenthal, *Nationalizing the Bill of Rights: Scholarship and Commentary on the Fourteenth Amendment in 1867–1873*, 18 J. CONTEMP. LEGAL ISSUES 153, 305 (2009); Kevin Christopher Newsom, *Setting Incorporationism Straight: A Reinterpretation of the* Slaughter-House Cases, 109 YALE L.J. 643, 648 (2000); KURT T. LASH, THE FOURTEENTH AMENDMENT AND THE PRIVILEGES AND IMMUNITIES OF AMERICAN CITIZENSHIP 253 (2014).
2. Adamson v. California, 332 U.S. 46, 50–51 (1947)
3. *Id.* at 51.
4. *Id.* at 51–52.
5. Adamson, 332 U.S. at 68 (Black. J., dissenting).
6. *Id.* at 89.
7. *See, e.g.*, Chicago, Burlington & Quincy Railroad Co. v. City of Chicago, 166 U.S. 226 (1897) ("A judgment of a state court, even if authorized by statute, whereby private property is taken for public use, without compensation made or secured to the owner, is, upon principle and authority, wanting in the due process of law required by the Fourteenth Amendment of the Constitution of the United States."); Gitlow v. New York, 268 U.S. 652, 666 (1925) ("For present purposes, we may and do assume that freedom of speech and of the press which are protected by the First Amendment from abridgment by Congress are among the fundamental personal rights and 'liberties' protected by the due process clause of the Fourteenth Amendment from impairment by the States.").
8. Adamson, 332 U.S. at 70.
9. *See generally* William Winslow Crosskey, *Charles Fairman, "Legislative History," and the Constitutional Limitations on State Authority*, 22 U. CHI. L. REV. 1, 2–119 (1954); Alfred Avins, *Incorporation of the Bill of Rights: The Crosskey-Fairman Debates*

Revisited, 6 Harv. J. On Legis. 1 (1968); Michael Kent Curtis, No State Shall Abridge: The Fourteenth Amendment and the Bill of Rights (1986); Richard L. Aynes, *On Misreading John Bingham and the Fourteenth Amendment*, 103 Yale L.J. 57 (1993); Wildenthal, *supra;* Newsom, *supra.*

10. Cong. Globe, 39th Cong., 2d sess. 811 (1867).
11. Wildenthal, *supra* at 305.
12. We disagree. In our view, it was always an individual or personal guarantee. *See* Randy E. Barnett, *Was the Right to Keep and Bear Arms Conditioned on Service in an Organized Militia*, 83 Tex. L. Rev. 237 (2004) (reviewing H. Richard Uviller & William G. Merkel, The Militia and the Right to Arms, or, How the Second Amendment Fell Silent (2002)).
13. Akhil Reed Amar, The Bill of Rights: Creation and Reconstruction 254–55 (1998).
14. Kurt T. Lash, *The Second Adoption of the Establishment Clause: The Rise of the Non-Establishment Principle*, 27 Ariz. St. L. J. 1085, 1154 (1995).
15. *Id.*
16. *Id.* at 1143.
17. Thomas MacIntyre Cooley, A Treatise on the Constitutional Limitations Which Rest upon the Legislative Power of the States of the American Union 469–70 (2d ed. Boston, Little, Brown & Co., 2nd ed., 1871).
18. Steven G. Calabresi & Sarah E. Agudo, *Individual Rights under State Constitutions When the Fourteenth Amendment Was Ratified in 1868: What Rights Are Deeply Rooted in American History and Tradition*, 87 Tex. L. Rev. 7, 31 (2008).
19. *Id.* at 32.
20. Cong. Globe, 39th Cong., 1st sess. 2765 (1866) (emphasis added).
21. Cong. Globe, 38th Cong., 1st sess. 1202 (1864).
22. Lash, *supra* at 300.
23. *See generally* Barnett & Bernick, *Privileges or Immunities Abridged.*
24. *Id.* at 524–25.
25. *Id.* at 554.
26. *See, e.g.,* Cong. Globe, 40th Cong., 3d sess. at 1003 (1869) (Sen. Howard), which is quoted in Chapter 6.
27. Civil Rights Act of 1866, ch. 31, § 1, 14 Stat. 27 (1866).
28. Enforcement Act of 1870, ch. 114, 16 Stat. 140, 140–146 (1870).
29. *See* Lash, *supra* at 114 (questioning the conventional wisdom that "the Fourteenth Amendment represented a consensus attempt to constitutionalize the Civil Rights Act" and highlighting Bingham's opposition to it).
30. *See* Randy E. Barnett & Evan D. Bernick, *The Privileges or Immunities Clause Abridged: A Critique of Kurt Lash on the Fourteenth Amendment*, 95 Notre Dame L. Rev. 499, 555–59 (2020) [hereinafter, "Barnett & Bernick, *Privileges or Immunities Abridged*"] (identifying Lash's four theories).
31. *Compare id.*, with Kurt T. Lash, *The Enumerated-Rights Reading of the Privileges or Immunities Clause: A Response to Barnett and Bernick*, 95 Notre Dame L. Rev. 591 (2019).
32. Act of April 9, 1866, ch. 31, 14 Stat. 27, § 1 (reenacted by Enforcement Act of 1870, ch. 114, § 18, 16 Stat. 140, 144 (1870) (codified at amended at 42 U.S.C. §§ 1981–82 (1987)) (emphases added).
33. *See* Michael Kent Curtis, *Further Adventures of the Nine-Lived Cat: A Response to Mr. Berger on Incorporation of the Bill of Rights*, 43 Ohio St. L.J. 89, 111 (1982);

Wildenthal, *supra* at 1543 (describing Berger's omissions to consider highly probative evidence).

34. Wildenthal, *supra* at 1581.
35. John Harrison, *Reconstructing the Privileges or Immunities Clause*, 101 YALE L.J. 1385, 1469 (1992).
36. *Id.* at 1456.
37. *Id.*
38. *Id.* at 1456.
39. ILAN WURMAN, THE SECOND FOUNDING: AN INTRODUCTION TO THE FOURTEENTH AMENDMENT 6 (2020).
40. Lawrence B. Solum, *Originalism and the Natural Born Citizen Clause*, 107 MICH. L. REV. FIRST IMPRESSIONS 22, 25 (2008).
41. Barnett & Bernick, *Privileges or Immunities Abridged*, at 509.
42. CONG. GLOBE, 39th Cong., 1st Sess. 2765–6 (1866).
43. WURMAN, *supra* at 111.
44. *Id.* at 5.
45. *Id.* at 110.
46. Hamburger, *supra* at 63.
47. *Id.* at 119.
48. *Id.* at 115.
49. LASH, *supra* at 283.
50. *Id.* at 68.
51. Hamburger, *supra* at 105.
52. LASH, *supra* at 197.
53. Hamburger, *supra* at 71.
54. *Id.* at 109–10.
55. WM. COOPER NELL, THE COLORED PATRIOTS OF THE AMERICAN REVOLUTION 109 (Boston, Robert F. Walcutt 1855).
56. *Id.* at 123.
57. Green, *Pre-Enactment History*.
58. MALTZ, *supra* at 109.
59. *Id.* at 117.
60. *Id.* at 118.
61. Douglas G. Smith, *Citizenship and the Fourteenth Amendment*, 34 SAN. DIEGO L. REV. 681, 806 (1997).
62. *Id.* at 686.
63. *Id.* at 805.
64. *E.g.*, Cong. Globe, 42d Cong., 2d Sess. 342 (1872) (Sen. Sumner).
65. Christopher R. Green, *The Original Sense of the (Equal) Protection Clause: Pre-Enacting History*, 19 GEO. MASON U. C.R. L.J. 1, 93 (2008).
66. *Id.*
67. *Id.*
68. *Id.* at 114.
69. *Id.* at 115.
70. *Id.* at 134.
71. *Id.*
72. *See generally* NADINE STROSSEN, HATE: WHY WE SHOULD RESIST IT WITH FREE SPEECH, NOT CENSORSHIP (2018).

8. The Spirit

1. See Randy E. Barnett & Evan D. Bernick, *The Letter and the Spirit: A Unified Theory of Originalism*, 107 GEO. L.J. 1, 23–32 (2017) [hereinafter, "Barnett & Bernick, *The Letter and the Spirit*"]; Randy E. Barnett & Evan D. Bernick, *No Arbitrary Power: An Originalist Theory of the Due Process of Law*, 60 WILLIAM & MARY L. REV. 1599 (2019).

2. Barnett & Bernick, *The Letter and the Spirit*, at 29.

3. *See* JACOBUS TENBROEK, EQUAL UNDER LAW 95–115 (1965).

4. *See* Trisha Olson, *The Natural Law Foundation of the Privileges or Immunities Clause of the Fourteenth Amendment*, 48 ARK. L. REV. 347, 393–96 (1995) (tracing developing belief in paramount national citizenship within the Liberty, Free Soil, and Republican Parties).

5. JOEL TIFFANY, A TREATISE ON THE UNCONSTITUTIONALITY OF AMERICAN SLAVERY 94 (Worcester, Thomas Drew, Jr., 1850); LYSANDER SPOONER, THE UNCONSTITUTIONALITY OF SLAVERY 119 (Boston, Bela Marsh, 1845).

6. TIFFANY, *supra* at 56, 97; SPOONER, *supra* at 247.

7. TIFFANY, *supra* at 57–8; SPOONER, *supra* at 247.

8. TIFFANY, *supra* at 54; SPOONER, *supra* at 89.

9. TIFFANY, *supra* at 87.

10. *Id.* at 97–99.

11. *Id.* at 120–23. For an overview of the constitutional arguments advanced by other abolitionist supporters of paramount national citizenship, *see generally* Randy E. Barnett, *Whence Comes Section One?: The Abolitionist Origins of the Fourteenth Amendment*, 3 J. LEGAL ANALYSIS 165 (2011).

12. Daniel A. Farber & John E. Muench, *Ideological Origins of the Fourteenth Amendment*, 1 CONST. COMMENT. 235, 241 (1984).

13. MICHAEL KENT CURTIS, NO STATE SHALL ABRIDGE: THE FOURTEENTH AMENDMENT AND THE BILL OF RIGHTS 54 (1986)

14. *See generally* JOHN G.A. POCOCK, THE MACHIAVELLIAN MOMENT: FLORENTINE POLITICAL THOUGHT AND THE ATLANTIC REPUBLICAN TRADITION (1975). The literature on classical republicanism and its influence on the founders is immense, and we do not undertake to compare this idea with the conception of Republican citizenship we describe here.

15. *See, e.g.,* CONG. GLOBE, 39th Cong., 1st sess. 1118 (1866) (Rep. Wilson) (no "express delegation" of federal power in Constitution necessary to "protect a citizen of the United States against a violation of his rights by the law of a single state").

16. *See* 1 WILLIAM BLACKSTONE, COMMENTARIES ON THE LAWS OF ENGLAND 49 (1865). *See* Arthur Bestor, *The American Constitutional War as a Constitutional Crisis*, 69 A.M. HIST. REV. 327, 333 (1964) ("The word 'sovereignty' was constantly on the lips of southern politicians. The concept they were invoking was one that Blackstone had defined. . . . 'State sovereignty' was, in essence, the slaveholder's authority writ large.").

17. *See* JOHN QUINCY ADAMS, AN ORATION ADDRESSED TO THE CITIZENS OF THE TOWN OF QUINCY ON THE FOURTH OF JULY, 1831, THE FIFTY-FIFTH ANNIVERSARY OF THE INDEPENDENCE OF THE UNITED STATES OF AMERICA 22 (Boston, Richardson, Lord and Holbrook, 1831) (arguing that state sovereignty theory would enable "uncontrolled, despotic sovereignties" to "trample with impunity, through a long career of after ages, at interminable or exterminating war with one another, upon the

indefeasible and unalienable rights of man"). On Adams's influence on antislavery politicians and lawyers, *see* Timothy Sandefur, *Privileges, Immunities, and Substantive Due Process,* 5 N.Y.U. J.L. & LIBERTY 115, 128–31 (2010).

18. Farber & Muench, *supra* at 241–42, 249.

19. *See* john a. powell & Stephen Menendian, *Beyond Public/Private: Understanding Excessive Corporate Prerogative,* 100 KY. L.J. 43, 48 (2011).

20. Alfred Avins, *The Civil Rights Act of 1875: Some Reflected Light on the Fourteenth Amendment and Public Accommodations,* 66 Colum. L. Rev. 873, 888 (1966).

21. Civil Rights Cases, 109 U.S. at 26 (Harlan, J., dissenting) (emphasis added).

22. *Id.* at 47.

23. *Id.* at 41.

24. *Id.* at 40.

25. "This Decision Has Humbled the Nation," October 22, 1883, *in* THE SPEECHES OF FREDERICK DOUGLASS: A CRITICAL EDITION (John R. McKivigan et al., eds. 2018).

26. See CONG. GLOBE, 42d Cong., 2d sess. 383 (Sen. Sumner) (distinguishing inns and boarding-houses on the ground that the latter lack an obligation to serve all travelers).

27. 394 US 557, 565 (1969) ("Whatever may be the justifications for other statutes regulating obscenity, we do not think they reach into the privacy of one's own home. If the First Amendment means anything, it means that a State has no business telling a man, sitting alone in his own house, what books he may read or what films he may watch. Our whole constitutional heritage rebels at the thought of giving government the power to control men's minds.").

28. *See* Roberts v. United States Jaycees, 468 U.S. 609, 617–18 (1984) ("the Court has concluded that choices to enter into and maintain certain intimate human relationships must be secured against undue intrusion by the State because of the role of such relationships in safeguarding the individual freedom that is central to our constitutional scheme.").

29. For a valuable discussion of the distinction between "positive laws that secure natural rights, especially rights that connect directly to the moral rights of life, liberty, and property" for the benefit of all people, and "rights-securing legal protections that may properly be reserved for the special enjoyment of citizens," *see* Eric R. Claeys, *Blackstone's Commentaries and the Privileges or Immunities of United States Citizens: A Modest Tribute to Professor Siegan,* 45 SAN DIEGO L. REV. 777 (2008).

30. *See* Obergefell v. Hodges, 576 U.S. 644, 661, (2015) (Thomas, J., dissenting) (denying that substantive due process is "defensible" on originalist grounds).

31. The Due Process of Law Clause also provides protections to noncitizen "persons," but our aim at this juncture is to identify the work done by this clause in evaluating the substance of laws in relation to the work done by the Privileges or Immunities Clause in identifying substantive rights.

32. 520 U.S. 702 (1997).

33. Glucksberg, 521 U.S. at 721 (quoting Snyder v. Massachusetts, 291 U.S. 97, 105 (1934)).

34. *Id.* (internal citations omitted).

35. *See* Randy E. Barnett, *Scrutiny Land,* 106 MICH. L. REV. 1479 (2007) [hereinafter "Barnett, *Scrutiny Land.*"].

36. 491 U.S. 110, 127 n. 6.

37. See Kenji Yoshino, *A New Birth of Freedom?: Obergefell v. Hodges,* 129 HARV L. REV. 147, 154–59 (2015) (tracing Justice Rehnquist's majority opinion in *Glucksberg* to Justice Scalia's plurality opinion in *Michael H.*).

38. 491 U.S. 110 (1989).
39. Laurence H. Tribe & Michael C. Dorf, *Levels of Generality in the Definition of Rights*, 57 U. Chi. L. Rev. 1057, 1088 (1990).
40. *Id.* at 1087.
41. *Id.* at 1088.
42. *Id.* at 1088–89.
43. *Id.* at 1089.
44. Barnett, *Scrutiny Land*, at 1490.
45. Raich v. Gonzales, 500 F. 3d 850, 865 (9th Cir. 2007).
46. *See* Sheldon Gelman, *Life and Liberty: Their Original Meaning, Historical Antecedents, and Current Significance in the Debate over Abortion Rights*, 78 Minn. L. Rev. 585 (1993) (tracing right to bodily integrity back to Magna Carta).
47. *See* James S. Witherspoon, *Reexamining* Roe: *Nineteenth-Century Abortion Statutes and the Fourteenth Amendment*, 17 St. Mary's' L.J. 29, 44 (1985) (finding that twenty-seven of thirty states that restricted access to abortion prohibited abortion attempts before quickening).
48. 6 F. Cas. 546,551–52 (1823).
49. *See* Troxel v. Granville, 530 U.S. 57, 91 (2000) (Scalia, J. dissenting) (declaring that "a right of parents to direct the upbringing of their children is among the 'unalienable Rights' with which the Declaration of Independence proclaims 'all men . . . are endowed by their Creator.'").
50. Speech of James Madison, June 8, 1789, *in* Creating the Bill of Rights: The Documentary Record from the First Congress 81 (Helen E. Veit et al. eds., 1991) [hereinafter "Creating the Bill of Rights"].
51. *Id.*
52. 14 Stat. 27.
53. Creating the Bill of Rights, at 81.
54. 17 Wheat. 159, 207 (1819).
55. Marbury, 1 Cranch at 177.
56. H.R.J. Res. 264, 91st Cong., 1st Sess. (1969).
57. Michael W. McConnell, *The Right to Die and the Jurisprudence of Tradition*, 1997 Utah L. Rev. 665, 695 (1997) [hereinafter "McConnell, *The Right to Die*"].
58. *See, e.g.,* Timbs v. Indiana, 139 S. Ct. 682, 687 (2018) ("A Bill of Rights protection is incorporated, we have explained, if it is 'fundamental to our scheme of ordered liberty,' or 'deeply rooted in this Nation's history and tradition.'").
59. 530 U.S. 57 (2000).
60. U.S. Const. Amend IX (emphasis added). *See* Randy E. Barnett, *The Ninth Amendment: It Means What It Says*, 85 Tex. L. Rev 1–82 (2006) (showing that the original meaning of "rights . . . retained by the people" was a reference to natural rights.).
61. 1 Annals of Cong. 732 (Joseph Gales ed., 1789).
62. McConnell, *The Right to Die*, at 683.
63. U.S. Const. amend. XIV, § 5.
64. *See, e.g.,* Michael W. McConnell, *Institutions and Interpretation: A Critique of* City of Boerne v. Flores, 111 Harv. L. Rev. 153, 178 n.153 (1997) [hereinafter, "McConnell, *Institutions and Interpretation*"]; Akhil Reed Amar, *Intratextualism*, 112 Harv. L. Rev. 747, 822–27 (1999); Robert J. Kaczorowski, *Congress's Power to Enforce Fourteenth Amendment Rights: Lessons from Federal Remedies the Framers Enacted*, 42 Harv. J. On Legis 187, 200–03 (2005); Jack M. Balkin, *The Reconstruction Power*, 85 N.Y.U. L. Rev. 1801, 1810 (2010).

65. 17 U.S. 159, 203 (1819) ("Let the end be legitimate, let it be within the scope of the constitution, and all means which are appropriate, which are plainly adapted to that end, which are not prohibited, but consist with the letter and spirit of the constitution, are constitutional.").
66. CONG. GLOBE, 39th Cong., 1st sess. 1118 (1866).
67. *Id.* at 1836.
68. 494 U.S. 872 (1990).
69. See 42 U.S.C. § 2000bb(b) (stating that the act is designed "to restore the compelling interest test").
70. 521 U.S. 507, 532 (1997).
71. *Id.* at 533.
72. CONG. GLOBE, 42d Cong., 2d sess. 525 (1872).
73. *See* Chevron U.S.A., Inc. v. Nat. Res. Def. Council, Inc., 467 U.S. 837, 844 (1984).
74. *See* PHILIP HAMBURGER, IS ADMINISTRATIVE LAW UNLAWFUL? 315 (2014).
75. *See* Michael Herz, Chevron *is Dead; Long Live* Chevron, 115 COLUM. L. REV. 1867, 1893 (2015).
76. McConnell, *Institutions and Interpretations,* at 184; J. Balkin, *supra* at 1827.
77. See Rebecca E. Zietlow, *To Secure these Rights: Congress, Courts and the 1964 Civil Rights Act,* 52 RUTGERS L. REV. 945, 976 (2005).
78. *Id.* at 977.
79. JOHN G. STEWART, THE CIVIL RIGHTS ACT OF 1964: TACTICS II, IN THE CIVIL RIGHTS ACT OF 1964: THE PASSAGE OF THE LAW THAT ENDED RACIAL SEGREGATION 312 (Robert D. Loevy ed., 1997).
80. ROBERT D. LOEVY, TO END ALL SEGREGATION: THE POLITICS OF THE PASSAGE OF THE CIVIL RIGHTS ACT OF 1964 51 (1990).
81. CONG. Q. WKLY. REP. 1131 (July 12, 1963).
82. REBECCA E. ZIETLOW, ENFORCING EQUALITY: CONGRESS, THE CONSTITUTION, AND THE PROTECTION OF INDIVIDUAL RIGHTS, at 52 (2006).
83. GERALD N. ROSENBERG, THE HOLLOW HOPE: CAN COURTS BRING ABOUT SOCIAL CHANGE? 52–53 (1991).
84. 378 U.S. 241, 280 (1964) (Douglas, J., concurring).
85. *See* Randy E. Barnett, *The Original Meaning of the Commerce Clause,* 68 U. CHI. L. REV. 101 (2001).
86. Smith, 494 U.S. at 890.
87. Testimony of Robert Bork, WALL ST. J., October 5, 1987, at 22, col. 1.
88. See Russell L. Caplan, *The History and Meaning of the Ninth Amendment,* 69 VA. L. REV. 223 (1983).
89. ROBERT H. BORK, THE TEMPTING OF AMERICA: THE POLITICAL SEDUCTION OF THE LAW 184–85 (1990).
90. McDonald v. City of Chicago, 561 U.S. 742, 855 (Thomas, J., concurring).

9. The Letter

1. See, *e.g.,* 2 WILLIAM WINSLOW CROSSKEY, POLITICS AND THE CONSTITUTION IN THE HISTORY OF THE UNITED STATES 1102–08 (1953); LEONARD W. LEVY, ORIGINS OF THE BILL OF RIGHTS 248 (1999); ANDREW C. MCLAUGHLIN, A CONSTITUTIONAL HISTORY OF THE UNITED STATES 461 (1935); HUGH EVANDER WILLIS, CONSTITUTIONAL LAW OF THE UNITED STATES 705–06 (1936); Raoul Berger, *"Law of the Land" Reconsidered,* 74 NW. U. L. REV. 1, 27–29 (1979); Edward S. Corwin, *The Doctrine of*

Due Process of Law before the Civil War, 24 Harv. L. Rev. 366, 369–70, 372–73 (1911); Frank H. Easterbrook, *Substance and Due Process*, 1982 Sup. Ct. Rev. 85, 96, 99; Walton H. Hamilton, "The Path of Due Process of Law," in The Constitution Reconsidered 167, 168, 176 (Conyers Read ed., 1938); John Harrison, *Substantive Due Process and the Constitutional Text*, 83 Va. L. Rev. 493, 502, 517 (1997); Charles M. Hough, *Due Process of Law-To-Day*, 32 Harv. L. Rev. 218, 221–23 (1919); Andrew T. Hyman, *The Little Word "Due,"* 38 Akron L. Rev. 1, 2 (2005); Keith Jurow, *Untimely Thoughts: A Reconsideration of the Origins of Due Process of Law*, 19 A.M. J. Legal Hist. 265 passim (1975); Robert P. Reeder, *The Due Process Clauses and "The Substance of Individual Rights,"* 58 U. Pa. L. Rev. 191, 204, 207, 210 (1910); Charles Warren, *The New "Liberty" under the Fourteenth Amendment*, 39 Harv. L. Rev. 431, 431, 440–42 (1926); Ralph U. Whitten, *The Constitutional Limitations on State-Court Jurisdiction: A Historical-Interpretative Reexamination of the Full Faith and Credit and Due Process Clauses Part 2*, 14 Creighton L. Rev. 735 passim (1981); Stephen F. Williams, *"Liberty" in the Due Process Clauses of the Fifth and Fourteenth Amendments: The Framers' Intentions*, 53 U. Colo. L. Rev. 117, 118, 121, 126 (1981); Christopher Wolfe, *The Original Meaning of the Due Process Clause*, in The Bill of Rights: Original Meaning and Current Understanding 213, 217, 219 (Eugene W. Hickok, Jr., ed., 1991). *See generally* Charles Grove Haines, *Judicial Review of Legislation in the United States and the Doctrines of Vested Rights and of Implied Limitations of Legislatures* (pts. 1–3), 2 Tex. L. Rev. 257 (1924), 2 Tex L. Rev. 387 (1924), 3 Tex. L. Rev. 1 (1924).

2. Frederick Mark Gedicks, *An Originalist Defense of Substantive Due Process: Magna Carta, Higher-Law Constitutionalism, and the Fifth Amendment*, 58 Emory L.J. 585, 588 (2009).

3. John Hart Ely, Democracy and Distrust: A Theory of Judicial Review 18 (1980).

4. Gedicks, *supra* at 595–96.

5. Ryan C. Williams, *The One and Only Substantive Due Process Clause*, 120 Yale L.J. 408, 505–06 (2010).

6. Timothy Sandefur, *In Defense of Substantive Due Process, or the Promise of Lawful Rule*, 35 Harv. J.L. & Pub. Pol'y 283, 292 (2012).

7. Nathan S. Chapman & Michael W. McConnell, *Due Process as Separation of Powers*, 121 Yale L.J. 1672, 1677–79 (2012).

8. Other notable defenses of substantive due process include Bernard H. Siegan, Economic Liberties and the Constitution (1980); James W. Ely, Jr., *The Oxymoron Reconsidered: Myth and Reality in the Origins of Substantive Due Process*, 16 Const. Comment. 315 (1999); Robert E. Riggs, *Substantive Due Process in 1791*, 1990 Wis. L. Rev. 941.

9. U.S. Const. amend. V., XIV § 1.

10. The Federalist No. 80, at 400 (Alexander Hamilton) (Ian Shapiro ed., 2009).

11. Randy E. Barnett & Evan D. Bernick, *The Letter and the Spirit: A Unified Theory of Originalism*, 107 Geo. L.J. 1, 43–44 (2017).

12. *Id.* at 41. The same is true for regulations issued by state administrative agencies operating under statutory grants of authority as well as ordinances and by-laws issues by municipal corporations that are acting as agents of the state.

13. *See* Jamal Greene, How Rights Went Wrong.

14. *See, e.g.,* Berger, *supra* at 1; Ely, Jr., *supra* at 320.

15. Magna Carta, ch. 39 (1215), *reprinted in* Ralph V. Turner, Magna Carta through the Ages app. at 231 (2003) (emphasis added).

16. *See* J. C. HOLT, MAGNA CARTA 276 (George Garnett & John Hudson eds., 3d ed. 2015) (concluding that Article 39 was "aimed" primarily against "arbitrary disseisin at the will of the king," against "summary process," and against "arrest and imprisonment on an administrative order").

17. *Id.* at 39–40.

18. Liberty of Subject Act 1354, 28 Edw. 3 c. 3 (emphasis added); *see also* HOLT, *supra* at 40 (emphasis added) ("[Due process of law] . . . was construed . . . to exclude procedure before the Council or by special commissions and to limit intrusions into the sphere of action of the common-law courts").

19. TURNER, *supra* at 123–24 (emphasis added) (quoting 42 Edw. 3 c. 3).

20. 5 W. S. HOLDSWORTH, A HISTORY OF ENGLISH LAW 428 n.5 (1924).

21. *See* Paul Raffield, *Contract, Classicism, and the Common-Weal: Coke's Reports and the Foundations of the Modern English Constitution*, 17 L. & LITERATURE 69, 77 (2005).

22. Prohibitions Del Roy (1607) 77 Eng. Rep. 1342, 1342; 12 Co. Rep. 64, 64.

23. 5 HOLDSWORTH, *supra* at 440.

24. *See* PHILIP HAMBURGER, LAW AND JUDICIAL DUTY 179–217 (2008) [hereinafter "HAMBURGER, DUTY"] (describing how this came to be understood as "an ordinary part of their duty").

25. *Id.* at 194.

26. *Id.* at 237–39.

27. *Id.* at 239.

28. *Id.* at 238.

29. Dr. Bonham's Case (1610) 77 Eng. Rep. 646; 8 Co. Rep. 113 b.

30. *See* Chapman & McConnell, *supra* at 1689–92 (summarizing the debate over the meaning of Coke's words).

31. Dr. Bonham's Case, 77 Eng. Rep. at 646.

32. *Id.*

33. *Id.*

34. *Id.* at 652.

35. *See* HAMBURGER, DUTY at 54.

36. *Id.* at 274.

37. An account of the imprisonment of the Kentish petitioners and the ensuing dispute appears in Philip A. Hamburger, *Revolution and Judicial Review: Chief Justice Holt's Opinion in* City of London v. Wood, 94 COLUM. L. REV. 2091, 2097–2111 (1994).

38. *Id.* at 2100.

39. City of London v. Wood (1701) 88 Eng. Rep. 1592; 12 Mod. 669.

40. *Id.* at 1602.

41. *Id.*

42. JOHN LOCKE, THE SECOND TREATISE OF CIVIL GOVERNMENT 62 (J. W. Gough ed., 1948) (1690).

43. City of London, 88 Eng. Rep. at 1602.

44. Hamburger, *supra* at 2100.

45. LOCKE, *supra* at 84; *see* HAMBURGER, DUTY at 215.

46. *See* HAMBURGER, DUTY at 209–10.

47. *Id.* at 398.

48. Riggs, *supra* at 974–75.

49. 1 N.C. (Mart.) 42 (1787).

50. *See* HAMBURGER, DUTY at 449–50.

51. Bayard, 1 N.C. (Mart.) at 42–43.

52. *See* Hamburger, Duty, at 4, 51–52 (quoting act of December 29, 1785, *reprinted in* The Laws of the State of North-Carolina, Passed at Newbern, December 1785, at 12–13 (Newbern, Arnett & Hodge 1786)).

53. *Id.* at 452 n.150 (quoting Protest, December 28, 1785, *in* The Journals of the General Assembly of the State of North-Carolina 51, 51 (2d pagination series, Newbern, Arnett & Hodge 1786)).

54. *See* Bayard, 1 N.C. (Mart.) at 45.

55. Hamburger, Duty at 453 (quoting Correspondence (New Bern, June 7, 1786), Pa. Packet, July 1, 1786).

56. Bayard, 1 N.C. (Mart.) at 45.

57. *Id.*

58. *Id.*

59. 3 The Papers of Alexander Hamilton 483 n.1 (Harold C. Syrett & Jacob E. Cooke eds., 1962) ("[Hamilton's] first *Letter from Phocion* was a public indictment of the majority in the state legislature and the inhabitants of New York City who in violation of the fifth and sixth articles of the treaty of peace not only refused to restore confiscated Loyalist property, but ignored the prohibition against further confiscation or prosecution.").

60. Letter from Phocion to the Considerate Citizens of New-York, on the Politics of the Day (N.Y., Samuel Loudon 1784), *reprinted in* 3 The Papers of Alexander Hamilton, at 483, 484–85.

61. N.Y. Const. art. XIII (Apr. 20, 1777), *reprinted in* 1 Laws of the State of New-York 1, 9 (New York, Thomas Greenleaf ed., 1792).

62. Letter from Phocion, *supra* at 485.

63. *Id.*

64. *Id.* at 485–6.

65. Alexander Hamilton, *Remarks on an Act for Regulating Elections*, Daily Advertiser, February 8, 1787, *reprinted in* 4 The Papers of Alexander Hamilton 34, 34 n.1, 35 (Harold C. Syrett & Jacob E. Cooke eds., 1962) (quoting 1787 N.Y. Laws 383) [hereinafter "Hamilton Papers."]

66. *Id.* at 35 (emphasis added and omitted). Hamilton's statement has been interpreted to mean that the law-of-the-land clause did not constrain the legislature. *See* Raoul Berger, Government by Judiciary 221–22 (2d ed. 1997) (1977). Given that Hamilton was arguing that a proposed legislative amendment violated the law-of-the-land clause, this interpretation is implausible.

67. 4 Hamilton Papers, *supra*, at 36.

68. *Id.* at 35–36 (emphasis omitted).

69. *Id.*

70. 1 St. George Tucker, Blackstone's Commentaries app. at 203 (Philadelphia, W.Y. Birch & A. Small 1803).

71. 2 James Kent, Commentaries on American Law 13 (N.Y., W. Kent 6th ed. 1848) (1826).

72. 3 Joseph Story, Commentaries on the Constitution of the United States § 1783 (Boston, Hilliard, Gray & Co. 1833).

73. *See* 2 Kent, at 13; 3 Story, § 1783; 1 St. George Tucker, app. at 203.

74. *See* Act of May 6, 1776, ch. 1, § 8, 1776 Va. Laws, in A Collection of All Such Public Acts of the General Assembly and Ordinances of the Conventions of Virginia 33, 33 (Richmond, Thomas Nicolson & William Prentis 1785) ("[T]hat no man be deprived of his liberty except by the law of the land, or the judgement of his peers.").

75. U.S. CONST. art. VI, cl. 2; *see* Chapman & McConnell 8, *supra* at 1724.

76. S*ee* Chapman & McConnell, *supra* at 1724.

77. 1 ANNALS OF CONG. 434 (1789) (Joseph Gales ed., 1834).

78. U.S. CONST. art I, § 9, cl. 3.

79. Chapman and McConnell attribute similar significance to this initial placement. *See* Chapman & McConnell, *supra* at 1722.

80. 1 ANNALS OF CONG., at 436; Chapman & McConnell, *supra* at 1723.

81. 1 ANNALS OF CONG., at 436.

82. Chapman & McConnell, *supra* at 1722–23; *see also* PHILIP HAMBURGER, IS ADMINISTRATIVE LAW UNLAWFUL? 255–56 (2014) [hereinafter, "HAMBURGER, UNLAWFUL"] ("[T]he Constitution recites its due process and other procedural rights at its conclusion rather than merely in Article II, and it states them in the passive voice . . . mak[ing] clear that these rights limit all parts of government.").

83. *See, e.g.,* Butler v. Craig, 2 H. & McH. 214, 215, 226–27, 235–36 (Md. 1787); Zylstra v. Corp. of Charleston, 1 S.C.L. (1 Bay) 382, 387–88 (Ct. Com. Pl. 1794) (opinion of Burke, J.); JAMES M. VARNUM, THE CASE, TREVETT AGAINST WEEDEN, 1–36 (Providence, John Carter 1786), *as reprinted in* 1 THE BILL OF RIGHTS: A DOCUMENTARY HISTORY 417, 417–29 (Bernard Schwartz ed., 1971)

84. *See, e.g.,* Allen's Adm'r v. Peden, 4 N.C. (Car. L. Rep.) 442, 442 (1816); Bayard v. Singleton, 1 N.C. (Mart.) 42, 45, 47 (1787); Merrill v. Sherburne, 1 N.H. 199 passim (1818); Dash v. Van Kleeck, 7 Johns. 477, 480, 482–84 (N.Y. Sup. Ct. 1811) (opinion of Yates, J.); Vanhorne's Lessee v. Dorrance, 2 U.S. (2 Dall.) 304, 306–07, 310–11 (C.C.D. Pa. 1795).

85. *See* CLAY S. CONRAD, JURY NULLIFICATION: THE EVOLUTION OF A DOCTRINE 47–48 (2014).

86. *See id.*

87. *See, e.g.,* Allen's Adm'r, 4 N.C. (Car. L. Rep.) at 442; Bayard, 1 N.C. (Mart.) at 45, 47; Merrill, 1 N.H. 199 *passim;* Dash, 7 Johns. at 480, 482–84; Vanhorne's Lessee, 2 U.S. (2 Dall.) at 306–07, 310–11.

88. Thomas Jefferson, *Kentucky Resolutions of 1798 and 1799, reprinted in* 4 THE DEBATES IN THE SEVERAL STATE CONVENTIONS ON THE ADOPTION OF THE FEDERAL CONSTITUTION 566, 567–68 (Jonathan Elliot ed., 2d ed., D.C., Jonathan Elliot 1836) (emphasis added).

89. 5 U.S. (1 Cranch) 137, 176–77 (1803) (emphasis added).

90. 17 U.S. (4 Wheat.) 316, 406 (1819) (emphasis added).

91. *See id.*

92. 5 N.C. (1 Mur.) 58, 88 (1805) (emphasis added).

93. Ex'rs of Cruden v. Neale, 2 N.C. (1 Hayw.) 338, 341 (1796) (per curium) (emphasis added); *see also* Tr. of Dartmouth Coll. v. Woodward, 1 N.H. 111, 130 (1817) (explaining that to be "law of the land," statutes must be "not repugnant to any other clauses in the constitution").

94. 3 U.S. (3 Dall.) 386, 386–87 (1798) (opinion of Chase, J.).

95. *Id.* at 398 (opinion of Iredell, J.).

96. *Id.* at 392–93 (opinion of Chase, J.).

97. *Id.* at 390–91, 395.

98. *Id.* at 392–93.

99. *Id.* at 388 (emphasis omitted).

100. *Id.*(emphasis added).

101. *Id.*

102. *Id.* (emphasis omitted).
103. *See id.* at 398 (opinion of Iredell, J.).
104. *Id.* (emphasis added).
105. *Id.* at 398–99.
106. *See* ROBERT H. BORK, THE TEMPTING OF AMERICA: THE POLITICAL SEDUCTION OF THE LAW 44–45 (1990) ("The better view of state legislative power is that, as Justice Iredell said . . . it encompasses the power to make any enactment whatsoever that is not forbidden by a provision of a constitution.").
107. Gedicks, *supra* at 651–54 (documenting how Iredell's view was "largely rejected by state constitutional decisions of the period").
108. 2 U.S. (2 Dal.) 304, 310 (C.C.D. Pa. 1795) (emphasis added).
109. 10 U.S. (6 Cranch) 87, 136 (1810) (emphases added).
110. 1 S.C.L. (1 Bay) 252, 253–54 (Ct. Com. Pl. 1792).
111. *Id.* at 254.
112. *Id.* at 254–55.
113. In an article appearing shortly before this book went to press, Max Crema and Larry Solum articulated perhaps the sparest account of the original meaning of "due process of law" in the Fifth Amendment. *See* Max Crema & Lawrence B. Solum, *The Original Meaning of the Fifth Amendment Due Process of Law Clause*, 107 VA. L. REV. (forthcoming 2022). They adduce evidence that the phrase—contrary to longstanding conventional wisdom—was not synonymous with "law of the land" or "due course of law" in 1791. Whereas "law of the land" meant "the common law, statute law, or custom[s] of England"—essentially, the British Constitution—and "due course of law" meant a traditional legal proceeding, due process of law meant only the process of issuing a valid writ stating a cause of action triable by a court. So long as such a writ was issued, anything that followed was consistent with due process of law.

    At points, Crema and Solum seem to suggest that writs were no more and no less than orders from courts. If so, and if due process of law in the Fifth Amendment means only a guarantee of service of a writ or some legally valid alternative prior to the deprivation of life, liberty, or property, it seems to follow that due process of law has here no substantive component. Due process of law would not require that a person in fact engage in conduct that confirmed to a recognized cause of action or that a statute in fact be authorized by the Constitution.

    We cannot parse here the voluminous body of evidence that Crema and Solum have presented in support of their challenge to the conventional scholarly wisdom. But we have concerns. For example, even if they are right that due process of law did not require more than a valid writ, due process of law would have a substantive component. As one of us has written elsewhere, writs described the substance of a good cause of action—they defined a cause of action and its available remedies. A person could not be held liable absent a demonstration that they engaged in conduct that satisfied some writ. The available writs, then, defined and constrained the substance of the law that could be used to deprive people of their life, liberty, or property through a civil suit or a criminal prosecution. *See* RANDY E. BARNETT, OXFORD INTRODUCTION TO U.S. LAW: CONTRACTS 1–4 (2010) (describing the writs of debt, detinue, and covenant, which provided the substance of the law governing the making of contracts). There is an analogy here to the right to a jury trial, which during the Founding era guaranteed a jury's review of the substance of the law. *See* CONRAD, *supra.* (Crema and Solum also reject the close association we have seen in post-Founding, antebellum sources of due process of law with a jury trial.)

Crema and Solum are careful to emphasize, however, that "due process of law" *became* conflated with "due course of law" and "law of the land" during the antebellum period, thanks largely to the influence of Joseph Story. Accordingly, they do not make any claims about the original meaning of the Due Process of Law Clause of the Fourteenth Amendment—the principal focus of our study. Indeed, they find that a new generation of jurists began to read a rich substantive meaning of "law of the land" into the Fifth Amendment and state law-of-the-land provisions—including in cases that we highlight in this book. In this way, their findings *strengthen* our case for a substantive understanding of "due process of law" in the Fourteenth Amendment.

114. 17 U.S. (4 Wheat.) 518, 581–82 (1819) (argument of Daniel Webster) (emphasis added).

115. Chapman & McConnell, *supra* at 1765–66; *see also* Regents of the Univ. of Md. v. Williams, 9 G. & J. 365, 412 (Md. 1838) ("An act which only affects and exhausts itself upon a particular person, or his rights and privileges, and has no relation to the community in general, is rather a sentence than a law." (citation omitted)).

116. *See* Wally's Heirs v. Kennedy, 10 Tenn. (2 Yerg.) 554, 555 (1831); Vanzant v. Waddell, 10 Tenn. (2 Yerg.) 260, 269–70 (1829) (opinion of Catron, J.).

117. *See* Bank v. Cooper, 10 Tenn. (2 Yerg.) 599, 607–08 (1831) (emphasis added); Bagg's Appeal, 43 Pa. St. 512, 414 (1862) ("Any form of direct government action on private rights, which, if unusual, is dictated by no imperious public necessity, or which makes a special law for a particular person, or gives directions for the regulation and control of a particular case after it has arisen, is always arbitrary and dangerous in principle, and almost always unconstitutional."); *see also* Sears v. Cottrell, 5 Mich. 251, 254 (1858) ("By 'the law of the land' we understand laws that are general in their operation, and that affect the rights of all alike; and not a special act of the legislature, passed to affect the rights of an individual against his will, and in a way which the same rights of other persons are not affected by existing laws."); Jordan v. Overseers of Dayton, 4 Ohio 294, 309–10 (1831) (denying that a state may "pass a law for the purpose of destroying a right created by the constitution" and affirming that judges have a "duty" to "hold [such laws] void"); Dunn v. City Council of Charleston, 16 S.C.L. (Harp.) 189, 200 (Const. Ct. 1824) ("Any act of partial legislation, which operates oppressively upon one individual, in which the community has no interest, is not the law of the land.").

118. *See* CONG. GLOBE, 39th Cong., 1st sess. 1089 (1866).

119. *Id.*

120. 27 U.S. (2 Pet.) 627 (1829).

121. 18 U.S. (9 Cranch) 43 (1815).

122. 13 Wend. 325 (N.Y. Sup. Ct. 1835).

123. 4 Hill 140 (N.Y. 1843).

124. CONG. GLOBE, 39th Cong., 1st sess. 1833 (1866).

125. *Id.*

126. Wilkinson, 27 U.S. (2 Pet.) 627, 657 (1829).

127. 27 U.S. (2 Pet.) at 657.

128. 18 U.S. (9 Cranch) at 50.

129. *Id.* at 52.

130. 13 Wend. at 328.

131. 4 Hill 140, 145–57 (N.Y. Sup. Ct. 1843).

132. *Id.* at 145.

133. *Id.*

134. *Id.*

135. *Id.* at 147 (emphasis omitted).

136. *Id.*

137. *Id.* at 145–46.

138. *Id.* at 147.

139. *Id.*

140. *See also* Regents of the Univ. of Md. v. Williams, 9 G. & J. 365, 408 (Md. 1838) ("[T]here is a fundamental principle of right and justice, inherent in the nature and spirit of the social compact, the character and genius of our government, the causes from which they sprang, and the purposes for which they were established, that rises above and restrains and sets bounds to the power of legislation, which the legislature cannot pass without exceeding its rightful authority"); White v. White, 4 How. Pr. 102, 111 (N.Y. Sup. Ct. 1849) ("[The security of the citizen against . . . arbitrary legislation rests upon the broader and more solid ground of natural rights, and is not wholly dependent upon [textual] negatives. The exercise of such a power is incompatible with the nature and objects of all governments, and is destructive to the great end and aim for which government is instituted, and is subversive of the fundamental principles upon which all free governments are organized."); Currie's Adm'rs v. Mut. Assur. Soc'y, 14 Va. (4 Hen. & M.) 315, 438–39 (1809) ("[L]egislature[s] [are limited] . . . by the principles and provisions of the constitution and bill of rights, and by those great rights and principles, for the preservation of which all just governments are founded.").

141. *Cf.* Taylor v. Porter & Ford, 4 Hill 140, 145–47 (N.Y. Sup. Ct. 1843); Williams 6, at 464.

142. *Cf.* Taylor, 4 Hill at 145–47.

143. *See, e.g.,* Locke v. Davey, 540 U.S. 712, 715 (2004) (explaining that a state's refusal to give aid to a postsecondary student who was pursuing a degree in theology did not violate the Free Exercise Clause of the First Amendment without ever referencing the Due Process of Law Clause).

144. *Id.*

145. *See, e.g.,* Cantwell v. Connecticut, 310 U.S. 296, 303 (1940).

146. *See* David E. Bernstein, Rehabilitating Lochner: Defending Individual Rights against Progressive Reform 109–10 (2011) (observing that "enforcing the First Amendment right of freedom of speech against the states via the Due Process Clause is literally an exercise in protecting a substantive right through that clause," as is the incorporation of any other enumerated right through the same means).

147. *See* Heart of Atlanta Motel, Inc. v. United States, 379 U.S. 241, 243–44, 258 (1964) (stating that Congress did not violate the Commerce Clause, nor the Fifth Amendment, with the enactment of the Civil Rights Act of 1964).

148. *See* Gedicks, *supra* at 668.

149. *See* Taylor v. Porter & Ford, 4 Hill 140, 145–47 (N.Y. Sup. Ct. 1843).

150. McCulloch v. Maryland, 17 U.S. (4 Wheat.) 316, 423 (1819) (emphases added).

151. *See* U.S. Const. amend. V.

152. *See* U.S. Const. amend. XIV, § 1.

153. *E.g.,* Kerry v. Din, 576 U.S. 86, 92 (2015) (Scalia, J.) (plurality opinion); Obergefell v. Hodges, 576 U.S. 644, 665 (2015) (Thomas, J., dissenting).

154. Chapman & McConnell, *supra* at 1722–73.

155. *Id.* at 1722.

156. Scott v. Sandford, 60 U.S. (19 How.) 393, 450 (1857) (emphasis added).

157. 2 Parker Cim. Rep. 421, 468, 488–89 (N.Y. 1856).

158. *Id.* at 461.

159. Chapman & McConnell, *supra* at 1772.

160. *Id.*

161. *Id.* at 1769–70.

162. *See id.* at 1772.

163. R. Williams, *supra* at 467.

164. Scott v. Sandford, 60 U.S. (19 How.) 393, 624 (1857) (Curtis, J., dissenting).

165. 98 Eng. Rep. 499, 510; Lofft 1, 19.

166. Scott, 60 U.S. (19 How.) at 593 (Curtis, J., dissenting).

167. R. Williams, *supra* at 468–69.

168. *See, e.g., id.* at 469 n.281.

169. *See, e.g.,* Fisher v. McGirr, 67 Mass. (1 Gray) 1 (1854); People v. Gallagher, 4 Mich. 244 (1856); Lincoln v. Smith, 27 Vt. 328 (1855).

170. *See* Chapman & McConnell, *supra* at 1678 ("None of [the antebellum decisions] invalidated a general and prospective statute on the ground that it interfered with unenumerated but inalienable rights, was unreasonable, or exceeded the police power.").

171. *Id.* at 1769.

172. 123 U.S. 623, 666 (1887) (quoting Patterson v. Kentucky, 97 U.S. 501, 506 (1879)).

173. *Id.* at 669 (emphasis added).

174. McCulloch v. Maryland, 17 U.S. (4 Wheat.) 316, 423 (1819).

175. Chapman & McConnell, *supra* at 1772.

176. R. Williams, *supra* at 462–63 (observing that by 1860 fourteen states had accepted the vested-rights interpretation).

177. *See* Ilan Wurman, *The Origins of Substantive Due Process*, 87 U. CHI. L. REV. 815 (2020).

178. *Id.* at 819.

179. *Id.*

180. *Id.* at 865.

181. ILAN WURMAN, THE SECOND FOUNDING: AN INTRODUCTION TO THE FOURTEENTH AMENDMENT 6 (2020).

182. *See* Chapman & McConnell, *supra* at 1677.

183. *See* R. Williams, *supra* at 511.

184. R. Williams, *supra* at 425.

185. *Id.* at 426.

186. *Id.*

187. Mugler v. Kansas, 123 U.S. 623, 669 (1887).

188. Commonwealth v. Tewksbury, 52 Mass. (11 Met.) 55 (1846).

189. Cooper v. Schultz, 32 How. Pr. 107 (N.Y. Sup. Ct. 1866).

190. Coates v. City of New York, 7 Cow. 585 (N.Y. Sup. Ct. 1827).

191. *See* Lowell J. Howe, *The Meaning of "Due Process of Law" Prior to the Adoption of the Fourteenth Amendment*, 18 CALIF. L. REV. 583, 609 (1930).

192. Austin v. Murray, 33 Mass. (16 Pick.) 121, 126 (1834).

193. *Id.*

194. *Id.*

195. *See* Harrison, *supra* at 542–44, 546–48, 551.

196. *Id.* at 546.

197. *Id.* at 546–47

198. *See* McCulloch v. Maryland, 17 U.S. (2 Wheat.) 316, 406 (1819).

199. *See* THE FEDERALIST No. 33, at 161 (Alexander Hamilton).
200. *Id.*
201. *Id.*
202. *Id.* at 548.
203. *See* Chapman & McConnell, *supra* at 1721.
204. *See id.* at 1718.
205. Christopher R. Green, *Duly Convicted: The Thirteenth Amendment as Procedural Due Process*, 15 GEO. J.L. & PUB. POL'Y 73, 75–78, 90–92, 113 (2017).
206. *Id.* at 113.
207. *Id.*
208. *See id.* at 111.
209. *See id.* at 91–92.
210. *Id.* at 90 (quoting ARK. CONST. of 1864, art. V).
211. Letter from Abraham Lincoln to Frederick Steele (January 20, 1864), *in* 7 THE COLLECTED WORKS OF ABRAHAM LINCOLN 141 (Roy P. Basler ed., 1953).
212. *See* Green, *supra* at 91.
213. 1 JOHN W. BURGESS, POLITICAL SCIENCE AND COMPARATIVE CONSTITUTIONAL LAW: SOVEREIGNTY AND LIBERTY 185, 207 (Boston, Ginn & Co. 1893).
214. CONG. GLOBE, 38th Cong., 1st sess. 1712 (1864).
215. *See* Green, *supra* at 85–86, 91 (quoting CONG. GLOBE, 38th Cong., 1st sess. 1712 (1864)).

10. The Spirit

1. *See* Prohibitions del Roy (1607) 77 Eng. Rep. 1342, 1342–43; 12 Co. Rep. 64, 64–65.
2. *See, e.g.,* PHILIP Hamburger, LAW AND JUDICIAL DUTY 194–95, 197–99, 202 (2009).
3. *See* Bank of Columbia v. Okely, 17 U.S. (4 Wheat.) 235, 244 (1819) ("As to the words from Magna Charta . . . after volumes spoken and written with a view to their exposition, the good sense of mankind has at length settled down to this: that they were intended to secure the individual from the arbitrary exercise of the powers of government, unrestrained by the established principles of private rights and distributive justice.").
4. *See* CLAY S. CONRAD, JURY NULLIFICATION: THE EVOLUTION OF A DOCTRINE 19, 131 (2014); John Harrison, *Substantive Due Process and the Constitutional Text*, 83 VA. L. REV. 493, 529 (1997).
5. JOHN LOCKE, THE SECOND TREATISE OF CIVIL GOVERNMENT 67 (J. W. Gough ed., 1948) (1690) (emphasis added).
6. *See* Harrison, *supra* at 529.
7. R. George Wright, *Arbitrariness: Why the Most Important Idea in Administrative Law Can't Be Defined, and What This Means for the Law in General*, 44 U. RICH. L. REV. 839, 842 (2010).
8. *Id.* at 842–43.
9. *Id.* at 843.
10. *See id.* at 843, 849–50, 859.
11. *See* RANDY E. BARNETT, RESTORING THE LOST CONSTITUTION: THE PRESUMPTION OF LIBERTY 11–12, 45–46, 48–49, 51–52 (2004) (describing and confronting the problem of constitutional legitimacy).
12. THE FEDERALIST No. 80, at 400 (Alexander Hamilton). *See also* DECLARATION OF INDEPENDENCE (US 1776) ("deriving their *just powers* from the consent of the governed.") (emphasis added).

13. *See* McCulloch v. Maryland, 17 U.S. (4 Wheat.) 316,411–13 (1819). Note, however, that the Constitution also expressly recognizes "other[]" unenumerated "rights . . . retained by the people." U.S. CONST. amend. IX.

14. *See* McCulloch, 17 U.S. at 429–30, 436; Trs. of the Univ. of N.C. v. Foy, 5 N.C. (1 Mur.) 56, 63 (1805).

15. *See* Jordan v. Overseers of Dayton, 4 Ohio 294, 309–10 (1831).

16. U.S. CONST. amend. XIV, § 1.

17. ROBERT H. Bork, THE TEMPTING OF AMERICA: THE POLITICAL SEDUCTION OF THE LAW at 166 (1990)(opining that "[n]o judge is entitled to interpret an ink blot," and asserting, without citing authority, that "[the Privileges or Immunities] clause has been a mystery since its adoption"). *But see* Bruce Ackerman, *Robert Bork's Grand Inquisition*, 99 YALE L.J. 1419, 1430 (1990) (book review) (observing that Bork "does not mention, let alone grapple with, important books" that might have aided him in dissolving the ink blot).

18. *See, e.g.,* Harrison, *supra* at 547.

19. *See, e.g.,* Whole Woman's Health v. Hellerstedt, 136 S. Ct. 2292, 2300 (2016).

20. *See* United States v. Carolene Prods. Co., 304 U.S. 144, 152 n.4 (1938).

21. *See* Whole Woman's Health, 136 S. Ct. at 2300, 2309 (holding unconstitutional state restrictions on the unenumerated fundamental right to terminate a pregnancy after applying the undue burden test, and rebuking the lower court for "equat[ing] the judicial review applicable to the regulation of a constitutionally protected personal liberty with the less strict review applicable where, for example, economic legislation is at issue").

22. Carolene Prods. Co., 304 U.S. at 152 n.4.

23. *See generally* JOHN HART ELY, DEMOCRACY AND DISTRUST: A THEORY OF JUDICIAL REVIEW 75–77 (1980).

24. Our favorite rendition of it is Jack M. Balkin, *The Footnote*, 83 Nw. L. REV. 275 (1988), which takes the form of a forty-seven-page footnote. For an account stressing the role that Oliver Wendell Holmes, Jr. and his acolyte Felix Frankfurter played in this development, *see* JAMAL GREENE, How RIGHTS WENT WRONG: WHY OUR OBSESSION WITH RIGHTS IS TEARING AMERICA APART 58–67 (2021) (describing Frankfurter as an "inveterate sycophant and social climber," who "devoted much of his professional life to ensuring" that "Holmes's 'conception of the Constitution'" became "'part of the political habits of the country.'" [quoting Frankfurter]).

25. *See* BARNETT, *supra* at 253, 255.

26. Neil K Komesar, *A Job for the Judges: The Judiciary and the Constitution in a Massive and Complex Society*, 86 MICH. L. REV. 657, 691–93 (1988).

27. *See id.* at 691.

28. *See id.*

29. The claim that the legislative process is less likely to generate arbitrary products in the context of economic regulation than it is in other contexts has been forcefully challenged. *See* William H. Riker & Barry R. Weingast, *Constitutional Regulation of Legislative Choice: The Political Consequences of Judicial Deference to Legislatures*, 74 VA. L. REV. 373, 398–99 (1988) (drawing on public choice theory to advance the argument that the majoritarian legislatures cannot be counted on to respect citizens' rights in any respect). But even if legislators are equally likely to enact arbitrary economic regulations as to enact arbitrary speech regulations, it does not follow that judges are equally likely to identify the first set of regulations correctly as they are the second set; they may well be better at identifying the second set. We stress that we are

assuming institutional facts that might justify some form of tiered scrutiny in order to critique the current form of tiered scrutiny, not making a normative argument for a particular form of tiered scrutiny. We argue here only that the rationality review articulated in *Carolene Products* is well-calculated to implement the spirit of the due process of law.

30. Jamal Greene misses this as well, misattributing modern conceivable basis review to *Carolene Products* rather than to *Williamson*. *See* GREENE, *supra* at 66. But he is not wrong about where we eventually ended up.

31. O'Gorman & Young, Inc. v. Hartford Fire Ins. Co., 282 U.S. 251, 257–58 (1931).

32. *See* Williamson v. Lee Optical of Okla., Inc., 348 U.S. 483, 487–88 (1955) ("[T]he law need not be in every respect logically consistent with its aims to be constitutional. It is enough that there is an evil at hand for correction, and that it might be thought that the particular legislative measure was a rational way to correct it.").

33. *See* United States v. Carolene Prods. Co., 304 U.S. 144, 153–54 (1938) (clarifying that the judiciary may explore whether facts exist to support "a rational basis for legislation whose constitutionality is attacked"). Komesar disagrees and considers our compromise unstable. *See* Neil K. Komesar, *Leaving the Land of Easy Answers: Regulatory Takings,* Rucho, *and the Nature of Constitutional Analysis*, 2020 WIS. L. REV. 363, 378–380 (2020) (praising our historical research but criticizing our comparative institutional analysis).

34. *Id.* at 152.

35. *See id.* at 153.

36. *Id.* at 152–4 (emphasis added).

37. *Id.* at 152 (emphasis added).

38. *Id.* at 153–54

39. *Id.* at 152.

40. *Id.*

41. *See* Geoffrey P. Miller, *The True Story of Carolene Products*, SUP. CT. REV. 397, 417 (1987) (explaining that although "[the case against filled milk] had the appearance of scientific rigor," it was "utterly unproved").

42. Act of June 18, 1910, ch. 309, § 17, 36 Stat. 539, 557 (1910) (repealed 1976).

43. Act of August 12, 1976, Pub. L. No. 94–381, §§ 1–2, 90 Stat. 1119, 1119 (1976).

44. *See* Comment, *The Three-Judge Court Act of 1910: Purpose, Procedure and Alternatives*, 62 J. CRIM. L. CRIMINOLOGY & POLICE SCI. 205, 205 (1971) (describing the origins, benefits and procedural burdens of the three judge panel act).

45. Michael T. Morley, *Nationwide Injunctions, Rule 23(b)(2), and the Remedial Powers of the Lower Courts*, 97 B.U. L. REV. 615, 631 (2017); *see also* Michael E. Solimine, *Congress, Ex parte Young, and the Fate of the Three-Judge District Court*, 70 U. PITT. L. REV. 101, 11318 (2008); Michael E. Solimine, *Ex Parte Young: An Interbranch Perspective*, 40 U. TOL. L. REV. 999, 1002–03 (2009).

46. Lee Optical of Okla., Inc. v. Williamson, 120 F. Supp. 128, 132 (W.D. Okla. 1954).

47. OKLA. STAT. tit. 59, §§ 941–942 (1953).

48. Lee Optical, 120 F. Supp. at 135.

49. *Id.* at 136–7.

50. *Id.* at 138 (citing Louis K Liggett Co. v. Baldridge, 278 U.S. 105, 111 (1928)).

51. *Id.* at 137 n.20.

52. *Id.* at 143.

53. Williamson v. Lee Optical of Okla., Inc., 348 U.S. 483, 491 (1955).

54. *Id.* at 487–88.

55. *Id.* at 487.

56. 508 U.S. 307, 313–16 (1993).

57. *Id.*

58. *Id.* at 323 n.3 (Stevens, J., concurring).

59. *See* United States v. Carolene Prods. Co., 304 U.S. 144, 152–54 (1938).

60. *See* Lee Optical, 348 U.S. at 487–88.

61. *See* McCulloch v. Maryland, 17 U.S. (4 Wheat.) 316, 423 (1819).

62. *Id.* (emphases added).

63. *See* U.S. Const. art. I, § 8, cl. 18

64. Alexander Hamilton, *Opinion of Alexander Hamilton on the Constitutionality of a National Bank* (Feb. 23, 1791), *in* Legislative and Documentary History of the Bank of the United States: Including the Original Bank of North America 98 (photo. reprint 1967) (Washington, DC, Gales and Seaton, M. St. Clair Clarke & D. A. Hall eds., 1832).

65. *See* Sikes v. Teleline, Inc., 281 F.3d 1350, 1362 (11th Cir. 2002) (explaining that "[a] presumption is generally employed to benefit a party who does not have control of the evidence on an issue," and that it would therefore be "unjust to employ a presumption to relieve a party of its burden of production when that party has all the evidence regarding that element of the claim").

66. *See id.* (explaining that when a party has a burden of production, they "must present evidence 'to rebut or meet the presumption.'" (quoting Fed. R. Evid. 301)).

67. *See* Randy E. Barnett & Evan D. Bernick, *The Letter and the Spirit: A Unified Theory of Originalism*, 107 Geo. L.J. 1, 23–26 (2017).

68. *See* Mary Siegel, *The Illusion of Enhanced Review of Board Actions*, 15 U. Pa. J. Bus. L. 599, 603–04 (2013) (providing rationale for Delaware courts' use of the business judgement rule, which gives fiduciaries significant room for error).

69. *Id.*

70. *See* Barnett & Bernick, *supra* at 29–32.

71. *Id.*

72. *See id.*, at 35–51.

11. The Proper Ends of Legislative Power

1. *See* McCulloch v. Maryland, 17 U.S. (4 Wheat.) 316, 411–12 (1819) (emphasis omitted).

2. The Federalist No. 45 12, at 206 (James Madison).

3. U.S. Const. art. I, § 1 (emphasis added).

4. *See id.* art. I, § 8; *id.* art. IV §§ 1, 3.

5. *See, e.g., id.* amends. XII, § 2, XIV, § 5, XV, § 2, XVI, XVIII, XIX, XXIV, § 2, XXVI, § 2. We take no position here on whether the Constitution authorizes Congress to pursue still other ends—including those listed in the Preamble—by exercising implied powers that are *not* incidental to enumerated ones. For an argument that it does, see John Mikhail, *The Constitution and the Philosophy of Language: Entailment, Implicature, and Implied Powers*, 101 Va. L. Rev. 1063 (2015). But we would contest a claim that Congress's powers are limitless or that there is no such thing as a constitutionally illegitimate congressional end. This is not Mikhail's position.

6. *Id.* amend. X.

7. *See* Letter to George Washington from Edmund Randolph (February 12, 1791), Nat'l Archives: Founders Online, http://founders.archives.gov/documents

/Washington/05-07-020200-0001 [https//perma.cc/3PAT-KL9T]; Letter to George Washington from Thomas Jefferson (February 15, 1791), NAT'L ARCHIVES: FOUNDERS ONLINE, http://founders.archives.gov/documents/Washington/05-07-02 0207 [https://perma.ccIK9LN-UBC8]; Letter to George Washington from Alexander Hamilton (December 13, 1790), NAT'L ARCHIVES: FOUNDERS ONLINE, http://founders.archives.gov/documents/Washington/05-07-02-0035 [https://perma.cc /G7WV7NPS].

8. 1 ANNALS OF CONG. 1944 (1791) (Joseph Gales ed., 1834).

9. *Id.* at 1896.

10. *Id.* at 1898.

11. *Id.*

12. 4 THE DEBATES IN THE SEVERAL STATE CONVENTIONS ON THE ADOPTION OF THE FEDERAL CONSTITUTION 423 (Jonathan Elliot ed., Washington, DC, Jonathan Elliot, 2nd ed. 1836) (statement of James Madison).

13. Alexander Hamilton, *Opinion of Alexander Hamilton on the Constitutionality of a National Bank* (February 23, 1791), *in* LEGISLATIVE AND DOCUMENTARY HISTORY OF THE BANK OF THE UNITED STATES: INCLUDING THE ORIGINAL BANK OF AMERICA 98 (photo. reprint 1967) (Washington, Gales and Seaton, M. St. Clair Clark & D.A. Hall eds., 1832) [hereinafter "Hamilton"].

14. *Id.* (emphases added).

15. (4 Wheat. 316, 421 (1819).

16. *Id.* at 422.

17. *See* Hamilton, *supra.*

18. McCulloch, 4 Wheat. at 423.

19. Marshall would subsequently rely on the limiting principle of the "pretext" passage to avoid the charge that the opinion of the Court was too latitudinarian. *See* John Marshall, *A Friend of the Constitution III,* ALEXANDRIA GAZETTE, July 2, 1819, *reprinted in* JOHN MARSHALL'S DEFENSE OF McCULLOCH V. MARYLAND 173 (Gerald Gunther, ed., 1969) ("Congress certainly may not, under the pretext of collecting taxes, or of guaranteeing to each state a republican form of government, alter the laws of descents; . . . the means [must] have a plain relation to the end.").

20. Hamilton, *supra* at 98. The Supreme Court's decision in *U.S. v. Darby,* 312 U.S. 100 (1941), rejected *sub silentio* this limitation of congressional power identified by Marshall. *See* Randy E. Barnett & Evan D. Bernick, *The Letter and the Spirit: A Unified Theory of Originalism,* 107 GEO. L.J. 1, 43–44 (2017).

21. *See, e.g., id.;* VA. CONST. art IV, § 14.

22. 3 U.S. (3 Dall.) 386, 388 (1798) (opinion of Chase, J.).

23. U.S. CONST. art. I, § 8.

24. 188 U.S. 321, 357 (1903) (Harlan., J).

25. *Id.* at 362–63 (emphasis added).

26. *Id.* at 365 (Fuller, J. dissenting).

27. THE FEDERALIST No. 45 12, at 208 (James Madison)

28. U.S. CONST. amend X.

29. *See infra* Part III.B.2.

30. 22 U.S. (9 Wheat.) 1, 203 (1824).

31. *Id.*

32. For a comprehensive history of the police power across continents and centuries, *see generally* MARKUS DIRK DUBBER, THE POLICE POWER: PATRIARCHY AND THE FOUNDATIONS OF AMERICAN GOVERNMENT (2005). For an overview of the police

power as both a source of and limitation on state police power in America, *see generally* Daniel B. Rodriguez, *The Inscrutable (Yet Irrepressible) State Police Power*, 9 N.Y.U. J.L. & LIBERTY 662 (2015).

33. *See* DUBBER, *supra* at 3.
34. *Id.* at 120 ("Virtually every definition of the police power was accompanied by the remark that it cannot be, and has not been, defined . . . [it] 'has remained without authoritative or generally accepted definition.'" (quoting ERNST FREUND, THE POLICE POWER, PUBLIC POLICY, AND CONSTITUTIONAL RIGHTS iii (1904))).
35. *Id.* at 120–21.
36. *See, e.g.,* State v. Buzzard, 4 Ark. 18, 41 (1842); State v. Glen, 52 N.C. 321, 327 (1859); Shaw v. Kennedy, 1 N.C. (Taylor) 158, 160, 163 (1817); Thorpe v. Rutland, 27 Vt. 140, 149 (1855).
37. *See* Commonwealth v. Alger, 61 Mass. 53, 64 (1843).
38. *Id.* at 84–85.
39. *See* Caleb Nelson, *Judicial Review of Legislative Purpose*, 83 N.Y.U. L. REV. 1784, 1790 (2008).
40. *See* 15 N.C. 1, 29–30 (1833); *see also* Jordan v. Overseers of Dayton, 4 Ohio 294, 309–10 (1831) ("If the state should pass a law for the purpose of destroying a right created by the constitution, this court will do its duty [and hold it void]; but an attempt by the legislature, in good faith, to regulate the conduct of a portion of its citizens, in a matter strictly pertaining to its internal economy, we can not but regard as a legitimate exercise of power.").
41. *See* Hoke v. Henderson, 15 N.C. 1, 26 (1833).
42. *Id.* at 27.
43. *See, e.g.,* Sunbury & Erie R.R. v. Cooper, 33 Pa. 278, 286 (1859) ("[T]he judicial authority of the state is instituted to judge of the fulfilment of the duties of private relations, and not to decide whether legislators have faithfully fulfilled theirs.").
44. Hamilton, *supra* at 98 (emphasis omitted).
45. *See* Lowell J. Howe, *The Meaning of "Due Process of Law" Prior to the Adoption of the Fourteenth Amendment*, 18 CALIF. L. REV. 583, 589 (1930) (examining police power cases and concluding that they are unified by the Lockean premise that "government cannot take from any person life, liberty or property except when such a taking is necessary to secure life, liberty and property to the individuals generally who compose society"). For an argument that the attribution of the police power to American governments was a negative development, despite such efforts to "limit the damage," see HAMBURGER, *supra* 98, at 466 n.a (contending that it has "undermined the specialized and enumerated powers established by American constitutions").
46. THE DECLARATION OF INDEPENDENCE para. 2 (U.S. 1776) (emphasis added).
47. *Id.*
48. *See Thomas M. Cooley*, MICH. L. (2009), https://www.law.umich.edulhistory andtraditions/faculty/FacultyLists/Alpha-Faculty/Pages/CooleyThomasM.aspx [https://perma.cc/PH7Q-GQ6R].
49. *See* THOMAS MACINTYRE COOLEY, A TREATISE ON THE CONSTITUTIONAL LIMITATIONS WHICH REST UPON THE LEGISLATIVE POWER OF THE STATES OF THE AMERICAN UNION, 572 (Boston, Little, Brown, and Company, 2nd ed. 1871) (emphasis added).
50. *Id.*
51. *See id.* at 746.
52. Hurtado v. California, 110 U.S. 516, 535 (1884).

53. *Cf. id.* at 535–37.
54. *See* RANDY E. BARNETT, RESTORING THE LOST CONSTITUTION: THE PRESUMPTION OF LIBERTY 337 (2004).
55. *See id.* at 331–33.
56. *See, e.g.,* Morris R. Cohen, *Legal Theories and Social Science,* 25 INT'L J. ETHICS 469, 480 (1915); Edward S. Corwin, *Social Insurance and Constitutional Limitations,* 26 YALE L.J. 431, 431–32 (1917); Robert L. Hale, *Value and Vested Rights,* 27 COLUM. L. REV. 523, 529 (1927).
57. *See* Corwin, *supra* at 431–32.
58. *See id.* (explaining how courts elastically construed the "police power" to allow the state to promote the "general welfare" by legislation "reasonably adapted" to that end).
59. JOHN W. COMPTON, THE EVANGELICAL ORIGINS OF THE LIVING CONSTITUTION 8 (2014).
60. *See id.*
61. *See id.* at 110–11.
62. *See id.* at 89–90.
63. 123 U.S. 623, 653, 657 (1887).
64. *Id.* at 661.
65. *Id.* at 662.
66. J.I. Clark Hare, Lecture XXXIV, *in* 2 AMERICAN CONSTITUTIONAL LAW 746, 772 (Boston, Little, Brown & Co. 1889).
67. *See id.* at 772–73.
68. 163 U.S. 537, 552 (1896).
69. *Id.* at 550.
70. *Id.*
71. 118 U.S. 356, 374 (1886) (holding unconstitutional a facially neutral San Francisco ordinance that required everyone who operated a wooden laundry to secure a permit after determining that it was designed to discriminate against immigrants from China).
72. Plessy, 163 U.S. at 550.
73. James B. Thayer, *The Origin and Scope of the American Doctrine of Constitutional Law,* 7 HARV. L. REV. 129 (1893). Thayer, *id.* at 140, argued that legislation should "not . . . be declared void unless the violation of the constitution is so manifest as to leave no room for reasonable doubt" (quoting Commonwealth v. Smith, 4 Binn. 117 (1811)).
74. Plessy, 163 U.S. at 557 (Harlan, J., dissenting).
75. *Id.* at 550 (majority opinion).
76. *Id.* at 562 (Harlan, J., dissenting).
77. *Id.* at 559.
78. *Id.*
79. *See id.*
80. *See id.* at 552–64.
81. *See id.* at 545 (majority opinion).
82. *Compare* Yick Wo v. Hopkins, 118 U.S. 356 (1886), *with* Barbier v. Connolly, 113 U.S. 27 (1885) (refusing to inquire into ends of facially neutral ordinance prohibiting night work only in laundries, despite allegation that the purpose was to force Chinese-owned laundries out of business).
83. *See, e.g.,* Rodriguez, *supra* at 664–65.
84. *See id.* at 676.

85. *See id.*
86. *See* Howe, *supra* at 609.
87. *See* BARNETT, *supra* at 331 (arguing that such laws fall within the "Lockean construction of the police power of the states").
88. That is, it did not include what Cass Sunstein has termed "naked preferences." Cass R. Sunstein, *Naked Preferences and the Constitution,* 84 COLUM. L. REV. 1689, 1689 (1984) (arguing that numerous constitutional provisions, including the Due Process of Law Clauses, forbid "the distribution of resources or opportunities to one group rather than another solely on the ground that those favored have exercised the raw political power to obtain what they want.").
89. *See* Rodriguez, *supra* at 677.
90. *See* Rodriguez, *supra* at 677.
91. *See* Howe, *supra* at 609.
92. *See* Brief of the Institute for Justice as *Amicus Curiae* in Support of Petitioners, at 1617, Lawrence v. Texas, 123 S. Ct. 2472 (2003) (No. 02-102).
93. *See id.* at 3 (arguing at length that states have no such power).
94. That is to say, an "incompletely theorized agreement" can be reached about the constitutional propriety of protecting public health, safety, and public morals. Cass R. Sunstein, *Incompletely Theorized Agreements,* 108 HARV. L. REV. 1733, 1735 (1995); *see* CASS R. SUNSTEIN, LEGAL REASONING AND POLITICAL CONFLICT 35–61 (1996) (defining and describing incompletely theorized agreements).

    The "rights-conflict" formulation might be seen as question-begging. If one recognizes a "right" to be free from the justified belief that immoral conduct is taking place in private, suddenly a private-morals power can be defended as a means of reducing rights conflicts. We answer the question by distinguishing between scarce and nonscarce rights in a manner suggested by the phrase, "Your liberty to swing your fist ends where my nose begins." One important reason why one's liberty ends where another's face begins is that any further "liberty" would eliminate options from another's choice set. There is a physical incompatibility between one person's fist-swinging, on the one hand, and another person's freedom of movement in the direction of the fist, on the other. Whatever may be said of the effects of knowing that someone else is participating in private sexual activity with another consenting adult, it does not prevent the knower from doing anything. In contrast, recognizing a right of the knower to suppress the private activity of another person would have exactly that affect. For a valuable discussion of "moral externalities" and the distinction between scarce and nonscarce rights, see Aristides N. Hatzis, *Moral Externalities: An Economic Approach to the Legal Enforcement of Morality, in* LAW AND ECONOMICS: PHILOSOPHICAL ISSUES AND FUNDAMENTAL QUESTIONS 236–37 (Aristides N. Hatzis & Nicholas Mercuro eds., 2015). As with the much-maligned public–private distinction, one can grant that what is and what is not a rights conflict is contingent on positive law without denying the normative desirability of distinguishing between the immoral and the rights-violating. Indeed, without more, this contingency tells us nothing about the value of the distinction. *See* Brian Leiter, *Rethinking Legal Realism: Towards a Naturalized Jurisprudence,* 76 TEX. L. REV. 267, 273 (1997) (arguing that "[f]rom the fact that a 'private' realm is a creature of government regulation it does not follow that government action in that realm is normatively indistinguishable from government action in the public realm[]" because "the key issue is the normative justification for the baseline itself[.]").

95. *See* Ryan C. Williams, *The One and Only Substantive Due Process Clause*, 120 YALE L.J. 408, 494 (2010).

96. *See* Brief of the Institute for Justice 459, *supra* at 14.

97. *See id.* at 15.

98. *See* Barnett & Bernick, *supra* at 3.

99. *See id.* at 14.

100. *See* Howe, *supra* at 598.

101. *See* Williams, *supra* at 505.

102. *See* Dan M. Kahan, *The Cognitively Illiberal State*, 110 STAN. L. REV. 101, 103–4 (2006) (describing how and why "disputes over the morally sectarian visions to be expressed by the law" have been replaced in modern liberal societies by "contestation over the means to be employed to attain society's secular ends"); Thomas B. Nachbar, *The Rationality of Rational Basis Review*, 102 VA. L. REV. 1627, 1661, 1682 (2016) (tracing and criticizing the Court's privileging of "consequentialist, utilitarian" ends over "[c]onstitutive [e]nds" related to the expression of the social meaning of behavior).

103. *See id.* at 1672.

104. See THOMAS G. WEST, THE POLITICAL THEORY OF THE AMERICAN FOUNDING 230 (2017) (arguing that this contrast "characterized all [the Founders'] sex and marriage policies").

105. LAWRENCE M. FRIEDMAN, CRIME AND PUNISHMENT IN AMERICAN HISTORY 138 (1993).

106. *See generally* COMPTON, *supra*; THOMAS C. LEONARD, ILLIBERAL REFORMERS: RACE, EUGENICS & AMERICAN ECONOMICS IN THE PROGRESSIVE ERA (2016).

107. *See* Bowers v. Hardwick, 478 U.S. 186, 192–93 (1986) (declining to recognize "a fundamental right to homosexuals to engage in acts of consensual sodomy" because "[s]odomy was a criminal offense at common law and was forbidden by the laws of the original 13 States when they ratified the Bill of Rights," and "when the Fourteenth Amendment was ratified, all but 5 of the 37 States in the Union had criminal sodomy laws").

108. *See* WEST, *supra* at 219.

109. *Id.* at 232 ("[T]he founders believed that discouraging sex outside of marriage (both heterosexual and homosexual) promotes the integrity of marriage, which they regarded as a fundamental condition of the social compact required by natural rights theory.").

110. *See* WEST, *supra* at 228.

111. *See* Brief of the Institute for Justice, *supra* at 16.

112. *See id.*

113. *See id.*

114. See Rodriguez, *supra* at 677.

115. *See id.* at 679.

116. *See* Sunstein, at 1718.

117. See *id.* at 590.

118. CASS R. SUNSTEIN, A CONSTITUTION OF MANY MINDS: WHY THE FOUNDING DOCUMENT DOESN'T MEAN WHAT IT MEANT BEFORE 8 (2009).

119. *See* Jack M. Balkin, *Which Republican Constitution?*, 32 CONST. COMMENT. 31, 46–49 (2017).

120. *Id.*

121. *Id.* at 44. For helpful overviews of this scholarship, see Daniel T. Rodgers, *Republicanism: The Career of a Concept*, 79 J. AM. HIST. 11, 17 (1992); Robert E. Shalhope,

Toward a Republican Synthesis: The Emergence of an Understanding of Republicanism in American Historiography, 29 WM. & MARY Q. 49, 57–58 (1972); Suzanna Sherry, *Responsible Republicanism: Educating for Citizenship,* 62 U. CHI. L. REV. 131, 135 (1995).

122. GEORGE H. SMITH, THE SYSTEM OF LIBERTY: THEMES IN THE HISTORY OF CLASSICAL LIBERALISM 27 (2013).

123. *See id.* at 26–48.

124. *See id.* at 28. Smith notes that Madison recommended that a declaration be affixed to the Constitution that read, in part, "[t]hat government is instituted, and ought to be exercised for the benefit of the people; which consists in the enjoyment of life and liberty, with the right of acquiring and using property, and generally of pursuing and obtaining happiness and safety," *id.* at 29 (quoting James Madison, Speech in Congress Proposing Constitutional Amendments, *reprinted in* JAMES MADISON: WRITINGS 441 (Jack N. Rakove ed., 1999)).

125. James Wilson, *Of the Natural Rights of Individuals,* in 2 THE COLLECTED WORKS OF JAMES WILSON 1053, 1061 (Kermit L. Hall & Mark David Hall eds., 2007).

126. O. W. HOLMES, JR., THE COMMON LAW 1 (Boston, Little, Brown, & Co. 1881).

127. *See* Daniel A. Farber & John E. Muench, *Ideological Origins of the Fourteenth Amendment,* 1 CONST. COMMENT. 235, 241 (1994).

128. *See id.*

129. *See id.*

130. *See* Rodgers, *supra* at 25.

131. *See* Farber & Muench, *supra* at 241.

132. *See id.* at 242–43.

133. *See id.* at 246.

134. *See, e.g.,* MICHAEL KENT CURTIS, NO STATE SHALL ABRIDGE: THE FOURTEENTH AMENDMENT AND THE BILL OF RIGHTS 236 (1986); JACOBUS TENBROEK, EQUAL UNDER LAW 117–19 (1965); JACOBUS TENBROEK, THE ANTISLAVERY ORIGINS OF THE FOURTEENTH AMENDMENT 115–18 (1951); WILLIAM M. WIECEK, THE SOURCES OF ANTISLAVERY CONSTITUTIONALISM IN AMERICA, 1760–1848, at 202–03 (1977); Randy E. Barnett, *Whence Comes Section One?: The Abolitionist Origins of the Fourteenth Amendment,* 3 J. LEGAL ANALYSIS 165 (2011); Farber & Muench, *supra* at 235–36; Timothy Sandefur, *Privileges, Immunities, and Substantive Due Process,* 5 N.Y.U. J. L. & LIBERTY 115, 135 (2010).

135. CURTIS, *supra* at 215.

136. *Id.* at 41.

137. CONG. GLOBE, 34th Cong., 3d sess., app. 139 (1857).

138. Lochner v. New York, 198 U.S. 45, 75 (1905) (Holmes, J., dissenting).

139. *See* Sandefur, *supra* at 172.

12. The Letter

1. *See* United States v. Morrison, 529 U.S. 598. 621 (2000).

2. *See, e.g.,* Alfred Avins, *The Equal Protection of the Laws: The Original Understanding,* 12 N.Y.L.F. 385 (1966); DAVID CURRIE, THE CONSTITUTION IN THE SUPREME COURT: THE FIRST HUNDRED YEARS, 1789–1888, at 349 (1985); Earl Maltz, *The Concept of Equal Protection of the Laws—A Historical Inquiry,* 22 SAN DIEGO L. REV. 499 (1985); John Harrison, *Reconstructing the Privileges or Immunities Clause,* 101 YALE L.J. 1385, (1992); Christopher R. Green, *The Original Sense of the (Equal) Protection*

Clause: Pre-Enacting History, 19 GEO. MASON U. C.R.L.J. 1, 93 (2008) [hereinafter "Green, *Pre-Enacting History*"]; Christopher R. Green, *The Original Sense of the (Equal) Protection Clause: Subsequent History and Interpretation*, 19 U.C.R.L.J. 219 (2008) [hereinafter, "Green, *Subsequent History*"]; WILLIAM J. STUNTZ, THE COLLAPSE OF AMERICAN CRIMINAL JUSTICE 104–05 (2011).

3. *See, e.g.*, Robin West, *Toward an Abolitionist Interpretation of the Fourteenth Amendment*, 94 W. VA. L. REV. 111, 129 (1991); Steven J. Heyman, *The First Duty of Government: Protection, Liberty, and the Fourteenth Amendment*, 41 DUKE L.J. 507 (1991).

4. *See* Green, *Pre-Enacting History*, at 34–40.

5. *Id.* at 39; Heyman, *supra* at 547.

6. 77 Eng. Rep. 377, 383 (1608).

7. *Id.*

8. *Id.* at 384.

9. G.S. Rowe & Alexander W. Knott, *Power, Justice, and Foreign Relations in the Confederation Period: The Marbois-Longchamps Affair, 1784–1786*, 104 PA. MAG. HIST. & BIOGRAPHY 275 (1980).

10. *Id.* at 293.

11. *Id.* at 304.

12. DECLARATION OF INDEPENDENCE (1776) (emphasis added).

13. Green, *Pre-Enacting History*, at 35. *See, e.g.*, N.C. Const. of 1776, pmbl, ("[A]llegiance and protection are, in their nature, reciprocal, and the one should of right be refused when the other is withdrawn."); N.J. Const. of 1776, pmbl. ("[A]llegiance and protection are, in the nature of things, reciprocal ties, each equally depending on the other, and liable to be dissolved by the others being refused or withdrawn."); Pa. Const. of 1776, pmbl "[T]he inhabitants of this commonwealth have in consideration of protection only, heretofore acknowledged allegiance to the king of Great Britain; and the said king has . . . withdrawn that protection. . . .").

14. 2 JAMES KENT, COMMENTARIES ON AMERICAN LAW 15 (1826).

15. *Id.* at 333–34.

16. *Id.* at 331–32.

17. Remarks by Henry Stanton before the Massachusetts House of Representatives (February 23 & 24, 1837), *in* E. BORMANN, FORERUNNERS OF BLACK POWER: THE RHETORIC OF ABOLITION 63–64 (1971).

18. ANTI-SLAVERY BUGLE, October 27, 1855, at 1.

19. Ohio State Convention of Colored Men, 1858, https://omeka.coloredconventions.org/items/show/254.

20. BORMANN, *supra* at 63–64.

21. Proceedings of the Second Annual Convention of the Colored Citizens of the State of California (1856), https://omeka.coloredconventions.org/items/show/268.

22. Proceedings of the State Convention of Colored Citizens of the State of Illinois (1856), https://omeka.coloredconventions.org/items/show/262.

23. Proceedings of the Convention of the Colored People of Virginia (1865), https://omeka.coloredconventions.org/items/show/272.

24. Proceedings of the State Convention of Colored Citizens of the State of Illinois (1856)(emphases added), https://omeka.coloredconventions.org/items/show/262.

25. Proceedings of the State Convention of the Colored Men of the State of Ohio (1857), https://omeka.coloredconventions.org/items/show/253.

26. Proceedings of the California State Convention of the Colored Citizens (1865), https://omeka.coloredconventions.org/items/show/268.

27. *Id.*
28. *See, e.g.,* Proceedings of the Colored National Convention Held in Rochester (1853); Address of the Colored Convention to the People of Alabama (1867); Proceedings of the Iowa State Colored Convention (1868), https://omeka.coloredconventions.org /items/show/567.
29. *See* GERARD N. MAGLIOCCA, THE HEART OF THE CONSTITUTION: HOW THE BILL OF RIGHTS BECAME THE BILL OF RIGHTS 6 (2017).
30. CONG. GLOBE, 39th Cong., 1st sess. 1088 (1866) (emphasis added).
31. B.B. KENDRICK, THE JOURNAL OF THE JOINT COMMITTEE OF FIFTEEN ON RECONSTRUCTION 83–85 (1914).
32. *Id.* at 35
33. Maltz, *supra* at 504 n.22.
34. CONG. GLOBE, 39th Cong., 1st sess., 2542 (1866) (emphases added).
35. *Id.*
36. *Id.*
37. *Id.*
38. CONG. GLOBE, 39th Cong., 1st sess., at 2542 (emphasis added).
39. *Id.*
40. *Id.* at 2766.
41. *Id.*
42. *Id.*
43. *Id.* at 2890.
44. *Id.*
45. THE WHEELING DAILY INTELLIGENCER, September 5, 1866, at 2.
46. *Id.*
47. *Id.*
48. *Id.*
49. *Id.*
50. THE COURIER-JOURNAL, July 19, 1866, at 2.
51. *Id.*
52. *Id.*
53. THE WEEKLY REPUBLICAN, September 27, 1866, at 2.
54. *Quoted in* JAMES EDWARD BOND, NO EASY WALK TO FREEDOM: RECONSTRUCTION AND THE RATIFICATION OF THE FOURTEENTH AMENDMENT 60 (1943).
55. *Id.*
56. Appendix to the Pennsylvania Legislative Record XCIX (1867), *quoted in* James E. Bond, *The Original Understanding of the Fourteenth Amendment in Illinois, Ohio, and Pennsylvania,* 18 AKRON L. REV. 435, 463 (1984).
57. *See* WYN CRAIG WADE, THE FIERY CROSS: THE KU KLUX KLAN IN AMERICA 40 (1987).
58. *See Report on Memphis Riots and Massacres,* H.R. Rep. No. 101, 39th Cong., 1st sess. 30.
59. CONG. GLOBE, 42d Cong., 1st sess., 236, 244 (1871); Robert J. Kaczorowski, *Federal Enforcement of Civil Rights during the First Reconstruction,* 23 FORDHAM URB. L. J. 155, 158 (1995).
60. 17 Stat. 13 (1871)
61. *Id.* at § 3.
62. CONG. GLOBE, 42d Cong., 1st sess. App. 608 (1871) (emphasis added).
63. *Id.* at 153 (emphasis added).
64. *Id.* at 80 (emphasis added).

65. *Id.* at 300 (emphasis added).
66. *Id.* at 428 (emphasis added).
67. *Id.* at 85 (emphasis added).
68. *Id.* at 697.
69. *Id.*
70. *Id.* at 608.
71. *See id.* at 83 (Rep. Bingham).
72. *Id.* at 315.
73. *Id.*
74. *Id.* (emphases added).
75. *Id.* at 482
76. *Id.*
77. *Id.*
78. CONG. GLOBE, 41st Cong., 3d. sess. 203 (1870).
79. *Id.*
80. *Id.*
81. CONG. GLOBE, 42d. Cong., 1st sess., Appendix, 83 (1871).
82. *Id.*
83. CONG. GLOBE, 41st. Cong., 2d. sess., 3871 (1870).
84. *Id.*
85. *Id.*
86. CONG. GLOBE, 42d Cong., 1st sess., 506 (1870).
87. *Id.* (emphases added).
88. *Id.*
89. NEW ERA, June 16, 1870, at 2.
90. *Id.*
91. CONG. GLOBE, 41st Cong., 2d sess.1329 (1870).
92. *Id.* (emphasis added).
93. CONG. GLOBE, 42d Cong., 2d sess. 847 (1873).
94. *Id.*
95. CONG. GLOBE, 43d Cong., 2d sess., 1795 (1875).
96. *Id.* at 1796.
97. *See* Green, *Pre-Enacting History,* at 275–77 (discussing State ex rel. Garnes v. McCann, 21 Ohio St. 198 (1872), State ex rel. Stoutmeyer v. Duffy, 7 Nev. 342, 1872 WL 3049 (1872), People ex rel. Dietz v. Easton, 13 Abb. Pr. 159 (N.Y. Sup. Ct. 1872)).
98. People v. Brady, 40 Cal. 198 (1870).
99. *Id.* at 203.
100. *Id.* at 213.
101. Bradwell v. State of Illinois, 16 Wall. 130 (1873) was decided the same day as the Slaughter-House Cases. The Court made plain that *The Slaughter-House Case*'s holding doomed Bradwell's cause. *See* Bradwell, 83 Wall. at 139 ("The opinion just delivered in the Slaughter-House Cases renders elaborate argument in the present case unnecessary").
102. Green, *Subsequent Interpretation,* at 273–74.
103. Bradwell, 83 U.S. at 136 (argument of counsel).
104. *Id.* at 272.
105. 2 JOSEPH STORY, COMMENTARIES ON THE CONSTITUTION OF THE UNITED STATES 676 (Thomas Cooley, ed., Boston, Little, Brown, and Company, 1873).
106. Roberts v. Boston, 59 Mass. 198 (1849).
107. *Id.* at 206.

108. *Id.*
109. 2 STORY, *supra* at 677.
110. *Id.* n.2 (referring readers to "the learned argument of Mr. Sumner").
111. *See* Michael W. McConnell, *Originalism and the Desegregation Decisions*, 81 VA. L. REV. 947, 1003 (1995); Green, *Subsequent Interpretation*, at 255.
112. 2 CONG. REC. 412 (1874).
113. *Id.* (emphases added).
114. *Id.* at 3455.
115. *Id.* (emphasis added).
116. *Id.* at 409.
117. Melissa Saunders, *Equal Protection, Class Legislation, and Colorblindness*, 96 MICH. L. REV. 245, 288–89 (1997).
118. *See* McConnell, *supra.*
119. 2 CONG. REC. 10 (1874) (emphasis added).
120. 18 Stat. 335 (1875) (emphasis added).
121. 103 U.S. 303, 308 (1880).
122. *Id.* (emphasis added).
123. *Id.* at 309.
124. 100 U.S. 339 (1880).
125. *Id.* at 345 (emphasis added).
126. *Id.*
127. *Id.* at 368 (Field, J., dissenting).
128. 109 U.S. 3 (1883).
129. *Id.* at 23.
130. 25 F. Cas. 707 (1874).
131. *Id.* at 713,
132. Joseph P. Bradley, Letter to William B. Woods, March 12, 1871, Joseph Bradley Papers, New Jersey Historical Society.
133. *See* PAMELA BRANDWEIN, RETHINKING THE JUDICIAL SETTLEMENT OF RECONSTRUCTION (2011).
134. *Id.* at 98.
135. *Id.* at 163.
136. Specifically, she traces the Court's abandonment to a series of decisions including Plessy v. Ferguson, 163 U.S. 537 (1896), Giles v. Harris, 189 U.S. 475 (1903), James v. Bowman, 190 U.S. 127 (1903), and Hodges v. United States, 203 U.S. 1 (1906). BRANDWEIN, *supra* at 186.
137. *Id.* at 120.
138. *Id.* at 161.
139. *See* Michael Kent Curtis, *Rethinking the Judicial Settlement of Reconstruction by Pamela Brandwein*, 1 A.M. POL. THOUGHT 161 (2012).
140. *Id.* at 163.
141. Bradley to Woods, *supra.*
142. 491 U.S. 189 (1989).
143. 812 F.2d 298, 301 (7th Cir. 1987).

13. The Spirit

1. See DeShaney, 489 U.S., at 191–93.
2. *Id.* at 193.

3. 812 F.32d 298, 199 (1987).
4. DeShaney, 489 U.S. at 189.
5. 491 U.S. 110 (1989).
6. *Id.* at 128 n. 6.
7. Christopher R. Green, *The Original Sense of the (Equal) Protection Clause: Pre-Enacting History,* 19 Geo. Mason U. C.R.L.J. 1, 45 (2008).
8. Robin West, Progressive Constitutionalism: Reconstructing the Fourteenth Amendment 31–32 (1993).
9. *Id.* at 36.
10. *See generally* Eric Foner, Free Labor, Free Soil, And Free Men: The Ideology of The Republican Party (1970).
11. West, *supra* at 33 (emphases added).
12. *Id.* at 35 (emphasis added).
13. *See, e.g.,* Owen W. Fiss, *Groups and the Equal Protection Clause,* 5 Phil. & Pub. Aff. 107 (1976) (proposing the "group-disadvantaging principle").
14. *See, e.g.,* Catharine MacKinnon, Sexual Harassment of Working Women 119 (1979) (contending that courts should determine "whether [a] policy or practice integrally contributes to the maintenance of an underclass or a deprived position").
15. *See, e.g.,* Derrick A. Bell, *Who's Afraid of Critical Race Theory?,* 1995 U. Ill. L. Rev. 893, 900–01 (1995) (describing critical race theory as being committed to "antisubordination," specifically, "wide-scale resistance" to "standards and institutions created by and fortifying white power").
16. *See, e.g.,* Kenneth L. Karst, *The Liberties of Equal Citizens: Groups and the Due Process Clause,* 55 UCLA Law Rev. 99, 102 (2007) (contending that "equal citizenship's antisubordination values" have contributed to the development of substantive due process).
17. Fiss, *supra* at 107.
18. MacKinnon, *supra* at 119.
19. Jack M. Balkin & Reva B. Siegel, *The American Civil Rights Tradition: Anticlassification or Antisubordination?,* 58 U. Miami L. Rev. 9 (2003).
20. *E.g.* West, *supra.*
21. *See* United States v. Carolene Products Co., 304 U.S. 144, 153 n. 4 (1938).
22. *See* Lawrence Gene Sager, *Fair Measure: The Legal Status of Underenforced Constitutional Norms,* 9 Harv. L. Rev. 1212 (1978).
23. See Jack M. Beermann, *Administrative Failure and Local Democracy: The Politics of DeShaney,* 1990 Duke L.J. 1078, 1101–04 (1990).
24. See David T. Beito, From Mutual Aid to the Welfare State: Fraternal Societies and Social Services, 1890–1967 (2000).
25. *Id.* at 1.
26. *Id.*
27. *Id.* at 1–2.
28. *Id.* at 2.
29. *Id.* at 3.
30. *Id.*
31. *Id.* at 3.
32. *See, e.g.,* Erwin Chemerinsky, *Government Duty to Protect: Post-DeShaney Developments,* 19 Touro L. Rev. 679 (2002); Karen M. Blum, DeShaney: *Custody, Creation of Danger, and Culpability,* 27 Loy. L. A. L. Rev. 435 (1993); Laura Oren, *Some Thoughts on the State-Created Danger Doctrine:* DeShaney *Is Still Wrong and* Castle Rock *Is More of the Same,* 16 Temp. Pol. Pol'y & Civ. Rts. L. Rev. 47, 47–48 (2006).

33. *See, e.g.,* Thomas A. Eaton & Michael Wells, *Government Action as a Constitutional Tort:* DeShaney *and Its Aftermath,* 66 Wash. L. Rev. 107, 166 (1991) (contending that *DeShaney* should not be read "as a blanket prohibition on constitutional tort liability for government inaction").

34. David A. Strauss, *Due Process, Government Action, and Private Wrongs,* 1989 Sup. Ct. Rev. 53, 64 (1989).

35. Oren, *supra* at 48.

36. *See* Randy E. Barnett, *Resolving the Dilemma of the Exclusionary Rule: An Application of Restitutive Principles of Justice,* 32 Emory L.J. 937 (1983).

37. 545 U.S. 748 (2005).

38. *Id.* at 768.

39. *Id.* at 755.

40. *Id.* at 752–54.

41. *Id.* at 764.

42. *Id.*

43. Namely, Justice John Paul Stevens and Justice Ruth Bader Ginsburg.

44. Castle Rock, 545 U.S. at 773 (Stevens, J., dissenting).

45. 123 Stat. 2835 (2009), codified in relevant part at 18 U.S.C. § 249.

46. Eric Foner, The Second Founding: How the Civil War and Reconstruction Made the Constitution 172 (2019).

47. 529 U.S. 598 (2000).

48. See 42 U.S.C. § 13981.

49. Joseph P. Bradley, Letter to William B. Woods, March 12, 1871, Joseph Bradley Papers, New Jersey Historical Society.

50. Morrison, 529 U.S. at 620.

51. *Id.* at 626.

52. *Id.*

53. *Id.* at 621 (emphasis added).

54. Bradley to Woods, *supra.*

55. Kermit Roosevelt III, *Bait and Switch: Why* United States v. Morrison *Is Wrong about Section 5,* 100 Cornell L. Rev. 603, 621 (2015).

56. We also express no view of VAWA's other provisions—for instance, its myriad funding provisions that incentivize state and local police departments to aggressively pursue domestic violence claims. These aspects of VAWA have been criticized by intersectional feminists as having the unintended consequence of contributing to subjugation, particularly of people of color. For an overview of the debate between carceral and intersectional feminists over VAWA's empowerment of police, prosecutors, and other state agents, *see* Nancy Whittier, *Carceral and Intersectional Feminism in Congress: The Violence Against Women Act, Discourse, and Policy,* 30 Gender & Soc'y 791 (2016). For a history of carceral feminism that includes a discussion of VAWA, *see* Aya Gruber, The Feminist War on Crime: The Unexpected Role of Women's Liberation in Mass Incarceration 148–49 (2020).

57. *See* Florida Prepaid Postsecondary Ed. Expense Bd. v. College Savings Bank, 527 U. S. 627, 639 (1999) (prophylactic legislation under § 5 must have a "congruence and proportionality between the injury to be prevented or remedied and the means adopted to that end.").

58. As a fallback from its reliance on the state action doctrine, the Court does note that the remedy might have been inadequately tailored to the constitutional violation. Morrison, 529 U.S. at 626–27 ("Congress' findings indicate that the problem of

discrimination against the victims of gender-motivated crimes does not exist in all States, or even most States. . . . [T]he remedy was [not] directed only to those States in which Congress found that there had been discrimination").

59. *Id.* at 622.

60. *Id.* at 626.

61. Christopher R. Green, *The Original Sense of the (Equal) Protection Clause: Subsequent History and Interpretation*, 19 U.C.R. L.J. 219, 231 (2008).

62. *E.g.*, Robert Hale, *Coercion and Distribution in a Supposedly Non-Coercive State*, 38 Pol. Sci. Q. 470 (1923); Louis Michael Seidman & Mark V. Tushnet, Remnants of Belief: Contemporary Constitutional Issues 49–71 (1997); Cass. R. Sunstein, *State Action Is Always Present*, 3 Chi. J. Int'l L. 465 (2002); Gary Peller & Mark Tushnet, *State Action and a New Birth of Freedom*, 92 Geo. L.J. 779 (2004). For a defense of the state-action principle, see Lillian BeVier & John Harrison, *The State Action Principle and Its Critics*, 96 Va. L. Rev. 1767 (2010).

63. *See* Randy E. Barnett, *Commandeering the People: Why the Individual Health Insurance Mandate is Unconstitutional*, 5 N.Y.U. J.L. & Liberty 581, 606 (2010)

64. 372 U.S. 335 (1963).

65. 139 S. Ct. 738 (2019).

66. *Id.* at 757 (Thomas, J., dissenting).

67. See Paul D. Butler, *Poor People Lose: Gideon and the Critique of Rights*, 122 Yale. L.J. 2176 (2013).

68. 384 U.S. 436 (1966).

69. *Id.* at 445–46.

70. *Id.* at 472–73.

71. *Compare, e.g.*, Paul G. Cassell, Miranda's *Social Cost: An Empirical Reassessment*, 90 N.W. U. L. Rev. 387 (1996); Stephen J. Schulhofer, Miranda's *Practical Effect: Substantial Benefits and Vanishingly Small Social Costs*, 90 Nw. U. L. Rev. 500 (1996).

72. In a quick response to *Miranda*, Congress enacted 18 U.S.C. § 3501, which provided that a confession shall be admissible in a federal criminal prosecution if voluntary and that "[t]he trial judge in determining the issue of voluntariness shall take into consideration all the circumstances surrounding the giving of the confession." For a discussion of the legislative history of this attempt to displace *Miranda*, see Yale Kamisar, *Can (Did) Congress "Overrule"* Miranda?, 85 Cornell L. Rev. 883, 887–906 (2000). We agree with Kamisar that "the much-vaunted superior fact-finding capacity of Congress was little in evidence" and thus did not warrant deference, *id.* at 906. But we think the Court in *Dickerson v. United States* went too far in holding that Congress lacked the power to supersede *Miranda* by legislation. 530 U.S. 428, 327 (2000).

73. On constitutional "happy endings," see William N. Eskridge, Jr. & Sanford V. Levinson, *Antigone and Creon, in* Constitutional Stupidities, Constitutional Tragedies 248, 248 (William N. Eskridge & Sanford Levinson eds., 1998).

74. 377 U.S. 533 (1964).

75. *Id.* at 562.

76. *Id.* at 558 (quoting Gray v. Sanders, 372 U.S. 363, 381 (1963)).

77. *See* Harper v. Virginia Bd. of Elections 383 U.S. 662 (1966); Kramer v. Union Free School Dist. No. 15, 395 U.S. 621 (1969).

78. *Id.* at 611.

79. Evenwel v. Abbott, 136 S. Ct. 1122, 1124 (2016).

80. *See* Pamela S. Karlan, *The Fire Next Time: Reapportionment after the 2000 Census*, 50 Stan. L. Rev. 731, 741 (1998) (observing that "one person, one vote has occasioned no

backlash and seems wildly popular across the political spectrum"); Robert B. McKay, *Reapportionment: Success Story of the Warren Court*, 67 MICH. L. REV. 223, 224–25 (1968) (finding that the decisions faced little resistance, unlike other Warren Court decisions).

81. *See* Adarand Constructors, Inc. v. Pena, 515 U.S. 200 (1995) (applying Equal Protection of the Laws Clause to racial preferences for subcontracting on federal projects).

82. *See* United States v. Carolene Products Co., 304 U.S. 144, 153 n. 4 (1938).

83. *See* Arlington Heights v. Metropolitan Housing Development Corp., 429 U.S. 252 (1977).

84. See Robin West, *Equality Theory, Marital Rape, and the Promise of the Fourteenth Amendment*, 42 FLA. L. REV. 45, 72–74 (1990); Neil K. Komesar, *A Job for the Judges: The Judiciary and the Constitution in a Massive and Complex Society*, 86 MICH. L. REV. 657, 709–10 (1988).

85. *See* Lawrence Sager, *Fair Measure: The Legal Status of Underenforced Constitutional Norms*, 91 HARV. L. REV. 1212 (1978).

Conclusion

1. Neil Siegel, *Prudentialism in* McDonald v. City of Chicago, 6 DUKE J. CONST. L. & PUB. POL'Y 16, 20 (2011); RICHARD L. HASEN, JUSTICE OF CONTRADICTIONS: ANTONIN SCALIA AND THE POLITICS OF DISRUPTION 52 (2018).

2. McDonald v. City of Chicago, oral argument transcript at 10–11.

3. RICHARD H. FALLON, JR., LAW AND LEGITIMACY IN THE SUPREME COURT 23 (2018).

4. *See* Tara Leigh Grove, *The Origins (and Fragility) of Judicial Independence*, 71 VAND. L. REV. 465 (2018).

5. *See* FALLON, *supra* at 37 (suggesting that *Bolling v. Sharpe* might be morally justified even if legally incorrect).

6. For a detailed account of this theory of constitutional legitimacy, *see* RANDY E. BARNETT, RESTORING THE LOST CONSTITUTION: THE PRESUMPTION OF LIBERTY 11–86 (2004) (defending a theory of constitutional legitimacy that is based on individual natural rights rather than on individual consent).

7. SEAN WILENTZ, NO PROPERTY IN MAN: SLAVERY AND ANTISLAVERY AT THE NATION'S FOUNDING 8 (2018).

8. ROBERT H. BORK, THE TEMPTING OF AMERICA: THE POLITICAL SEDUCTION OF THE LAW 166 (1990).

9. *See* Jeffrey A. Pojanowski & Kevin C. Walsh, *Enduring Originalism*, 105 GEO. L.J. 97, 100 (2016).

10. Which is not to say we endorse every conclusion they reached on the basis of natural-rights reasoning.

11. *See* RANDY E. BARNETT, THE STRUCTURE OF LIBERTY: JUSTICE AND THE RULE OF LAW 109–32 (2d ed. 2014) (presenting a theory of natural rights and the rule of law).

12. See William N. Eskridge, Jr., & Sanford V. Levinson, *Antigone and Creon*, in CONSTITUTIONAL STUPIDITIES, CONSTITUTIONAL TRAGEDIES 248, 248 (William N. Eskridge & Sanford Levinson, eds., 1998) (discussing constitutional "happy endings").

ACKNOWLEDGMENTS

The day we met was the day we began collaborating. On Thursday morning, June 16, 2016, Randy gave a talk to the Judicial Engagement Fellows of the Institute for Justice, at a seminar held at the Virginia Tech Research Center in Alexandria, Virginia. In his talk, he described six key distinctions in constitutional theory. The first was the interpretation-construction distinction.[1] He then offered a tentative theory of good faith constitutional construction based on the spirit as opposed to the letter of the text.

Evan was in attendance as the assistant director of IJ's Center for Judicial Engagement. During a break he approached Randy in the hallway and asked if his idea was like the one being developed by Gary Lawson, Guy Seidman, and Rob Natelson. Randy replied that it was. Impressed that Evan knew about this scholarship and immediately got the connection, Randy asked if Evan wanted to develop this theory together. Evan agreed. Soon afterward, he left the Institute for Justice and became a fellow of the Georgetown Center for the Constitution. The result of this collaboration

---

1. The other five were:
   - Constitutional meaning vs. judicial role
   - Democratic or collective popular sovereignty vs. republican or individual popular sovereignty
   - Judicial activism / restraint vs. judicial engagement
   - Judicial power vs. judicial duty
   - Judicial restraint vs. judicial constraint

was an article in the *Georgetown Law Journal,* on which the Introduction of this book is based.[2]

The plan was to write a series of three articles, one on each branch of government, which would culminate in a book on good faith constitutionalism. The *Georgetown Law Journal* article concerned good faith judging in the construction zone. A second coauthored piece in the *William & Mary Law Review,* concerning the good faith exercise of the legislative power, focused on the due process of law.[3] A third piece, solo-authored by Evan—also in the *Georgetown Law Journal*—concerned good faith enforcement by the executive branch and focused on the equal protection of the laws.[4] The contemplated book never materialized because another project interceded.

In September 2018, Randy asked Evan if he was up for taking a fresh look at Kurt Lash's many writings on the Privileges or Immunities Clause. Evan agreed, and over the course of the next couple of months, he drafted a lengthy critique of Lash's enumerated-rights-theory, which became the basis of our coauthored article in the *Notre Dame Law Review.* Our intention was then, in another article, to articulate a competing theory of the Privileges or Immunities Clause. But after reviewing Evan's voluminous research, it became clear to Randy that a project on the Privileges or Immunities Clause was too complex for an article, and the idea of this book was born. The first references to this "book" in the electronic record appear in September 2019.

As it happened, our previously published work had already given us a fresh take on the original meaning of the Due Process of Law and Equal Protection of the Laws Clauses. By combining that research with the Privileges or Immunities Clause we became increasingly confident that we had something new to say about the original meaning of the most frequently litigated parts of the Fourteenth Amendment. And we became convinced that we could not say it, or sufficiently engage with the dozens

2. Portions of the Introduction were first published as Barnett and Bernick, "The Letter and the Spirit: A Unified Theory of Originalism," *Georgetown Law Journal* 107:1 (2018).

3. Chapter 8 builds on ideas first discussed in, and much of the text of Chapters 10 and 11 was first published in, Barnett and Bernick, "No Arbitrary Power: An Originalist Theory of the Due Process of Law," *William & Mary Law Review,* 60:5 (2019), pp. 1599–1683.

4. Portions of Chapters 12 and 13 were first published in Bernick, "Antisubjugation and the Equal Protection of the Laws," *Georgetown Law Journal,* 110:1 (2021).

of plausible competing accounts of these provisions, within the confines of the law journals.

Although some of the work in this book has been published before,[5] every chapter is informed by evidence that was uncovered, or incorporates conversations that took place, or scholarship that went to print, after our initial publications. As we describe in the Conclusion, in light of all this evidence, our prior views of each of these clauses has had to be revised in ways that surprised us. We were learning up until the moment that we submitted the final manuscript to Harvard University Press, and we expect to continue to learn from the conversations that this book will start.

We are indebted to a great many people who provided encouragement, constructive criticism, and advice as our project took its ultimate shape. They include Larry Alexander, Jack Balkin, Stephanie Barclay, Will Baude, David Bernstein, Sam Bray, Jud Campbell, Adam Carrington, Laurence Claus, Richard Fallon, Kim Forde-Mazrui, Nicole Garnett, Rick Garnett, Christopher Green, JoAnn Koob, Kurt Lash, Sandy Levinson, Nelson Lund, Joyce Malcolm, Michael McConnell, John McGinnis, John Mikhail, Paul Moreno, Christina Mulligan, James Oakes, Jeff Pojanowski, Sai Prakash, Mike Ramsey, Mike Rappaport, Fred Schauer, Larry Solum, William Treanor, David Upham, Kevin Walsh, Robin West, Sean Wilentz, and Ilan Wurman. We received invaluable feedback on our manuscript during faculty workshops at the Antonin Scalia Law School, the University of Virginia School of Law, Notre Dame Law School, the University of San Diego School of Law, and Hillsdale College, as well as from Georgetown students in Randy's "Recent Books on the Constitution" seminar. And we received critical support from the Georgetown Center for the Constitution's program managers—first from Fran Djoukeng, then from her successor, Elana Quint. Betsy Kuhn provided her usual exemplary proofreading of the page proofs.

A comprehensive list of acknowledgments is impossible. One of the most important lessons that we gleaned from the history canvassed in this book is that the Fourteenth Amendment did not emerge fully formed from the minds of a few "great men." It was hewn into the Constitution by a mass antislavery political movement composed of a multitude of persons whose names have been lost to history. That movement's abiding faith in the possibility of

---

5. Chapter 4 touches on concepts presented in Barnett's book *Our Republican Constitution: Securing the Liberty and Sovereignty of We the People* (New York: Broadside Books, 2016), pp. 98–101.

Republican citizenship and in the due process of law and the equal protection of the laws for all people was essential to making the supreme law of the land far better than it was in 1788 or in 1791. Indeed, the coalition that brought the Republican Party to power ultimately made the Constitution as good as the most radical proponent of abolitionist constitutionalism—those who believed with Frederick Douglass that the Constitution was a "glorious liberty document"—insisted that it was, in the face of Supreme Court decisions to the contrary.

Justice to both the dead and the living demands that we honor their sacrifices through word and deed—not only by telling of their accomplishments but by making the law on the ground consistent with the letter and spirit of their handiwork. Our fondest hope is that this book will provide resources, not only for judges and legislators, but for all Americans who are committed to our ongoing constitutional project—resources they can use to deliver on the Fourteenth Amendment's promises.

Those who still believe in the American experiment with its written constitution need a better narrative. We believe this book provides one. Our narrative is largely one of tragedy rather than of triumph. But it is most assuredly a narrative of progress. Thanks to those who enshrined the Fourteenth Amendment into its text—together with other amendments like the Fifteenth and Nineteenth—our Constitution is far better today than it was in 1788. Today, it is this amended Constitution that needs to be defended from strident and ill-informed attacks on it. But to defend the Constitution as amended first requires that one accurately interpret its letter and identify its spirit. That is the mission of this book.

INDEX

Morrison, U.S. v. (2000), 362–365
Morton, Oliver P., 184, 187, 252, 332–333, 342, 346
Mugler v. Kansas (1887), 282–284, 308

natural rights: in abolitionist constitutionalism, 99, 101–103; and civil rights, 22–23, 25, 27, 43; constitutional legitimacy and, 376–381; Due Process of Law Clause and, 313–315; Equal Protection of the Laws Clause and, 321–324, 353–354, 369; and privileges and immunities, 49–51, 53–54; in Republican constitutionalism, 117, 121, 153, 155, 169, 191–193, 197–201, 214, 219, 230, 241, 249
"Negro Seamen Acts," 69–71
Nell, William Cooper, 218
Nineteenth Amendment, 244–245, 367–368
Ninth Amendment, 249, 256, 292
Northwest Ordinance, 113, 287

Olcott, Charles, 97
Oregon, admission of, 84–86
originalism: and the Fourteenth Amendment, 19–21; history of, 2–6; and the interpretation–construction distinction, 6–8; and original public meaning, 5–6; theories of construction within, 10–12

Paschal, George, 173–174, 209
Phillips, Wendell, 91–92, 375
Plessy v. Ferguson (1896), 308–309
police powers, 282, 302–304, 306–309, 313, 315
political rights: and abolitionists, 87, 98–99; and the Privileges or Immunities Clause, 106, 125, 145, 158–159, 220, 245; and Republicans, 83, 220; and voting rights, 83, 87, 88–89, 157–160, 163–166, 244–245, 367
Pomeroy, John Norton, 173, 209
positive-law rights, 22–25, 49–50, 149, 200, 242, 377, 381. See also civil rights
positive rights, 350, 359, 361

Posner, Richard, 350, 352
Prigg v. Pennsylvania (1842): abolitionist resistance to, 75; influence on Republican conceptions of congressional power, 123, 130, 141
Privileges and Immunities Clause: and admission of Missouri, 66–69; and admission of Oregon, 84–86; comity-only legal meaning of, 63–65; emergent fundamental-rights public meaning of, 65–88
Privileges or Immunities Clause: antidiscrimination theories of, 213–219; civil rights protected by, 22–28, 49, 99–102, 126, 196, 201; congressional enforcement of, 250–256; enumerated-rights theories of, 206–213; fundamental-rights theories of, 219–223; judicial enforcement of, 233–250; original "spirit"/function of, 223–233
proslavery: antebellum federal hegemony of, 65; imperialist ambitions of, 74; and Privileges and Immunities Clause, 80
Pufendorf, Samuel, 102, 219, 230

rational-basis review: vs. conceivable-basis review, 293, 296–297; and economic liberty, 292, 294–298; origins of, 293
Rehnquist, William, 235, 352
Republican Party: abolitionism and, 89–90, 96–97; ideology of, 82–84; and U.S. citizenship, 102–108
Reynolds v. Sims (1964), 367
Roberts, Dorothy, 118

Saunders, Melissa, 346
Scalia, Antonin: and original public meaning, 4, 255; and Privileges or Immunities Clause, 373; and unenumerated rights, 248, 257, 279
schooling rights: and abolitionist activism, 93–96; in Brown v. Board of Education, 4, 30; as common-law rights, 185–186; as privileges of U.S. citizenship, 24–26, 30; Republican debate over, 189–191, 193